Honda CBF1000/A and CB1000R/RA
Service and Repair Manual

by Matthew Coombs

Models covered

CBF1000. 998cc. 2006 to 2010
CBF1000A. 998cc. 2006 to 2010
CB1000R. 998cc. 2008 to 2011
CB1000RA. 998cc. 2008 to 2011

(4927-336)

ABCDE
FGHIJ
KLMNO
PQRST

© Haynes Publishing 2012

A book in the Haynes Service and Repair Manual Series

All rights reserved. No part of this book may be reproduced or transmitted in any form or by any means, electronic or mechanical, including photocopying, recording or by any information storage or retrieval system, without permission in writing from the copyright holder.

ISBN: **978 1 84425 927 4**

Printed in the USA

Haynes Publishing
Sparkford, Yeovil, Somerset BA22 7JJ, England

Haynes North America, Inc
861 Lawrence Drive, Newbury Park, California 91320, USA

Haynes Publishing Nordiska AB
Box 1504, 751 45 Uppsala, Sweden

Contents

LIVING WITH YOUR HONDA

Introduction
The Birth of a Dream	Page	0•4
Acknowledgements	Page	0•8
About this manual	Page	0•8
Identification numbers	Page	0•9
Buying spare parts	Page	0•9
Safety first!	Page	0•10

Pre-ride checks
Coolant level	Page	0•11
Suspension, steering and final drive	Page	0•11
Brake fluid levels	Page	0•12
Engine oil level	Page	0•14
Clutch fluid level	Page	0•14
Tyres	Page	0•16
Legal and safety checks	Page	0•16

Model development
	Page	0•17
Bike spec	Page	0•18

MAINTENANCE

Routine maintenance and servicing
Specifications	Page	1•2
Lubricants and fluids	Page	1•2
Maintenance schedule	Page	1•3
Component locations	Page	1•4
Maintenance procedures	Page	1•8

Contents

REPAIRS AND OVERHAUL

Engine, transmission and associated systems

Engine, clutch and transmission	Page	2•1
Cooling system	Page	3•1
Engine management system	Page	4•1

Chassis components

Frame and suspension	Page	5•1
Brakes, wheels and final drive	Page	6•1
Fairing and bodywork	Page	7•1

Electrical system

	Page	8•1

Wiring diagrams

	Page	8•34

REFERENCE

Tools and Workshop Tips	Page	REF•2
Security	Page	REF•20
Lubricants and fluids	Page	REF•23
Conversion factors	Page	REF•26
MOT Test Checks	Page	REF•27
Storage	Page	REF•32
Fault Finding	Page	REF•35
Technical Terms Explained	Page	REF•44

Index

	Page	REF•48

Introduction

The Birth of a Dream

by Julian Ryder

There is no better example of the Japanese post-war industrial miracle than Honda. Like other companies which have become household names, it started with one man's vision. In this case the man was the 40-year old Soichiro Honda who had sold his piston-ring manufacturing business to Toyota in 1945 and was happily spending the proceeds on prolonged parties for his friends. However, the difficulties of getting around in the chaos of post-war Japan irked Honda, so when he came across a job lot of generator engines he realised that here was a way of getting people mobile again at low cost.

A 12 by 18-foot shack in Hamamatsu became his first bike factory, fitting the generator motors into pushbikes. Before long he'd used up all 500 generator motors and started manufacturing his own engine, known as the 'chimney', either because of the elongated cylinder head or the smoky exhaust or perhaps both. The chimney made all of half a horsepower from its 50 cc engine but it was a major success and became the Honda A-type.

Less than two years after he'd set up in Hamamatsu, Soichiro Honda founded the Honda Motor Company in September 1948. By then, the A-type had been developed into the 90 cc B-type engine, which Mr Honda decided deserved its own chassis not a bicycle frame. Honda was about to become Japan's first post-war manufacturer of complete motorcycles. In August 1949 the first prototype was ready. With an output of three horsepower, the 98 cc D-type was still a simple two-stroke but it had a two-speed transmission and most importantly a pressed steel frame with telescopic forks and hard tail rear end. The frame was almost triangular in profile with the top rail going in a straight line from the massively braced steering head to the rear axle. Legend has it that after the D-type's first tests the entire workforce went for a drink to celebrate and try and think of a name for the bike. One man broke one of those silences you get when people are thinking, exclaiming 'This is like a dream!' 'That's it!' shouted Honda, and so the Honda Dream was christened.

Honda C70 and C90 OHV-engined models

'This is like a dream!' 'That's it' shouted Honda

Mr Honda was a brilliant, intuitive engineer and designer but he did not bother himself with the marketing side of his business. With hindsight, it is possible to see that employing Takeo Fujisawa who would both sort out the home market and plan the eventual expansion into overseas markets was a masterstroke. He arrived in October 1949 and in 1950 was made Sales Director. Another vital new name was Kiyoshi Kawashima, who along with Honda himself, designed the company's first four-stroke after Kawashima had told them that the four-stroke opposition to Honda's two-strokes sounded nicer and therefore sold better. The result of that statement was the overhead-valve 148 cc E-type which first ran in July 1951 just two months after the first drawings were made. Kawashima was made a director of the Honda Company at 34 years old.

The E-type was a massive success, over 32,000 were made in 1953 alone, a feat of mass-production that was astounding by the

Introduction 0•5

standards of the day given the relative complexity of the machine. But Honda's lifelong pursuit of technical innovation sometimes distracted him from commercial reality. Fujisawa pointed out that they were in danger of ignoring their core business, the motorised bicycles that still formed Japan's main means of transport. In May 1952 the F-type Cub appeared, another two-stroke despite the top men's reservations. You could buy a complete machine or just the motor to attach to your own bicycle. The result was certainly distinctive, a white fuel tank with a circular profile went just below and behind the saddle on the left of the bike, and the motor with its horizontal cylinder and bright red cover just below the rear axle on the same side of the bike. This was the machine that turned Honda into the biggest bike maker in Japan with 70% of the market for bolt-on bicycle motors, the F-type was also the first Honda to be exported. Next came the machine that would turn Honda into the biggest motorcycle manufacturer in the world.

The C100 Super Cub was a typically audacious piece of Honda engineering and marketing. For the first time, but not the last, Honda invented a completely new type of motorcycle, although the term 'scooterette' was coined to describe the new bike which had many of the characteristics of a scooter but the large wheels, and therefore stability, of a motorcycle. The first one was sold in August 1958, fifteen years later over nine-million of them were on the roads of the world. If ever a machine can be said to have brought mobility to the masses it is the Super Cub. If you add in the electric starter that was added for the C102 model of 1961, the design of the Super Cub has remained substantially unchanged ever since, testament to how right Honda got it first time. The Super Cub made Honda the world's biggest manufacturer after just two years of production.

The CB250N Super Dream became a favorite with UK learner riders of the late seventies and early eighties

Honda's export drive started in earnest in 1957 when Britain and Holland got their first bikes, America got just two bikes the next year. By 1962 Honda had half the American market with 65,000 sales. But Soichiro Honda had already travelled abroad to Europe and the USA, making a special

The GL1000 introduced in 1975, was the first in Honda's line of GoldWings

0•6 Introduction

Carl Fogarty in action at the Suzuka 8 Hour on the RC45

An early CB750 Four

point of going to the Isle of Man TT, then the most important race in the GP calendar. He realised that no matter how advanced his products were, only racing success would convince overseas markets for whom 'Made in Japan' still meant cheap and nasty. It took five years from Soichiro Honda's first visit to the Island before his bikes were ready for the TT. In 1959 the factory entered five riders in the 125 class. They did not have a massive impact on the event being benevolently regarded as a curiosity, but sixth, seventh and eighth were good enough for the team prize. The bikes were off the pace but they were well engineered and very reliable.

The TT was the only time the West saw the Hondas in '59, but they came back for more the following year with the first of a generation of bikes which shaped the future of motorcycling – the double-overhead-cam four-cylinder 250. It was fast and reliable – it revved to 14,000 rpm – but didn't handle anywhere near as well as the opposition. However, Honda had now signed up non-Japanese riders to lead their challenge. The first win didn't come until 1962 (Aussie Tom Phillis in the Spanish 125 GP) and was followed up with a world-shaking performance at the TT. Twenty-one year old Mike Hailwood won both 125 and 250 cc TTs and Hondas filled the top five positions in both races. Soichiro Honda's master plan was starting to come to fruition, Hailwood and Honda won the 1961 250 cc World Championship. Next year Honda won three titles. The other Japanese factories fought back and inspired Honda to produce some of the most fascinating racers ever seen: the awesome six-cylinder 250, the five-cylinder 125, and the 500 four with which the immortal Hailwood battled Agostini and the MV Agusta.

When Honda pulled out of racing in '67 they had won sixteen rider's titles, eighteen manufacturer's titles, and 137 GPs, including 18 TTs, and introduced the concept of the modern works team to motorcycle racing. Sales success followed racing victory as Soichiro Honda had predicted, but only because the products advanced as rapidly as the racing machinery. The Hondas that came to Britain in the early '60s were incredibly sophisticated. They had overhead cams where the British bikes had pushrods, they had electric starters when the Brits relied on the kickstart, they had 12V electrics when even the biggest British bike used a 6V system. There seemed no end to the technical wizardry. It wasn't that the technology itself was so amazing but just like that first E-type, it was the fact that Honda could mass-produce it more reliably than the lower-tech competition that was so astonishing.

When in 1968 the first four-cylinder CB750 road bike arrived the world of motorcycling changed for ever, they even had to invent a new word for it, 'Superbike'. Honda raced again with the CB750 at Daytona and won the

Introduction

World Endurance title with a prototype DOHC version that became the CB900 roadster. There was the six-cylinder CBX, the CX500T – the world's first turbocharged production bike, they invented the full-dress tourer with the GoldWing, and came back to GPs with the revolutionary oval-pistoned NR500 four-stroke, a much-misunderstood bike that was more a rolling experimental laboratory than a racer. Just to show their versatility Honda also came up with the weird CX500 shaft-drive V-twin, a rugged workhorse that powered a new industry, the courier companies that oiled the wheels of commerce in London and other big cities.

It was true, though, that Mr Honda was not keen on two-strokes – early motocross engines had to be explained away to him as lawnmower motors! However, in 1982 Honda raced the NS500, an agile three-cylinder lightweight against the big four-cylinder opposition in 500 GPs. The bike won in its first year and in '83 took the world title for Freddie Spencer. In four-stroke racing the V4 layout took over from the straight four, dominating TT, F1 and Endurance championships with the RVF750, the nearest thing ever built to a Formula 1 car on wheels. And when Superbike arrived Honda were ready with the RC30. On the roads the VFR V4 became an instant classic while the CBR600 invented another new class of bike on its way to becoming a best-seller. The V4 road bikes had problems to start with but the VFR750 sold world-wide over its lifetime while the VFR400 became a massive commercial success and cult bike in Japan. The original RC30 won the first two World Superbike Championships is 1988 and '89, but Honda had to wait until 1997 to win it again with the RC45, the last of the V4 roadsters. In Grands Prix, the NSR500 V4 two-stroke superseded the NS triple and became the benchmark racing machine of the '90s. Mick Doohan secured his place in history by winning five World Championships in consecutive years on it.

In yet another example of Honda inventing a new class of motorcycle, they came up with the astounding CBR900RR FireBlade, a bike with the punch of a 1000 cc motor in a package the size and weight of a 750. It became a cult bike as well as a best seller, and with judicious redesigns continues to give much more recent designs a run for their money.

When it became apparent that the high-tech V4 motor of the RC45 was too expensive to produce, Honda looked to a V-twin engine to power its flagship for the first time. Typically, the VTR1000 FireStorm was a much more rideable machine than its opposition and once accepted by the market formed the basis of the next generation of Superbike racer, the VTR-SP-1.

One of Mr Honda's mottos was that technology would solve the customers' problems, and no company has embraced cutting-edge technology more firmly than Honda. In fact Honda often developed new technology, especially in the fields of materials science and metallurgy. The embodiment of that was the NR750, a bike that was misunderstood nearly as much as the original NR500 racer. This limited-edition technological tour-de-force embodied many of Soichiro Honda's ideals. It used the latest techniques and materials in every component, from the oval piston, 32-valve V4 motor to the titanium coating on the windscreen, it was – as Mr Honda would have wanted – the best it could possibly be. A fitting memorial to the man who has shaped the motorcycle industry and motorcycles as we know them today.

Fit For Purpose

To be fair, it was Suzuki who started it. Take a slightly out of date superbike engine, retune it for more torque (don't say de-tuned, they won't like it) and surround it with budget cycle parts. Sell 'em cheap and no-one will care about the steel frame, as opposed to aluminium, and the conventional, skinny forks. Well if you get it right, as Suzuki did with the first Bandits back in 1995, you don't hear any complaints about the thing

The CX500 – Honda's first V-Twin and a favorite choice of dispatch riders

The VFR400R was a cult bike in Japan and a popular grey import in the UK

0•8 Introduction

The 2009 CBF1000

The 2008 CB1000R

being built down to a price, you sit back and count the money.

Suzuki's success did not go unnoticed. Honda's Hornet was their first response, using first a retuned CBR600 motor and then introducing a bigger version, the 900, using a similarly treated FireBlade engine. Both were introduced as sports-orientated machines with an upright riding position. The CBF range arrived with a subtly different label. And again the first models were middleweights, a CBR-engined 600 and a 500 twin. They were designed specifically for less-experienced riders, a lot of attention was paid to reducing seat height, with the bonus that they still had enough performance to satisfy more experienced riders who weren't bothered about being on the cutting edge of motorcycle fashion.

The 1000ccc CBF arrived in 2006, an extension of what Honda were now calling the Just Fit programme. The 1000 would not be aimed at newly qualified riders, as the first two models were, but the emphasis on ensuring the bike was physically manageable was retained as well as an emphasis on useable power. Market research showed that the over-30 year olds who were the target audience were interested in roll-on power for midrange acceleration rather than ultimate performance. Nevertheless, instead of using an old version of the flagship 'Blade's engine, the current edition was used. However, the way it makes power was radically altered: peak power was reduced from around 170hp to just over 95. The telling number though, is the torque figure. The FireBlade makes 114Nm at 10,000rpm whereas the CBF makes only slightly less, 93Nm, but at much lower revs – just 6500rpm. The 'Blade is Honda's Superbike homologation machine and therefore has to make as much power as possible; revs aren't really an issue. They are for the rider who Honda think is in the market for an easy to ride all-rounder. He or she gets very strong roll-on acceleration in any gear in a package fitted around a CBR600 spine frame.

If there was a criticism of the CBF, and this is a matter of personal taste, it is that its styling was bland. Honda deliberately went for a middle of the road look, reasoning that the Hornet was the sporty option for those who didn't want a full-blown superbike. However, when the carbureted motor of the Hornet became marginal with respect to emissions legislation, the CBF's fuel-injected motor was used in the new CB1000R which, in 2008, appeared with a look about as far removed from the CBF as possible.

The new bike was still billed as a naked sportster but the new bike had a real hard edge. The motor got a chunk more top-end power than the CBF but still well down on the donor 'Blade at 92hp indicating the emphasis was still very much on the midrange roll-on. The cycle parts were also beefed up. The chassis, still a spine, was all aluminium and it got upside-down forks and wider wheels. But the styling was unashamedly aggressive – very streetfighter. The hunched-forward look, abbreviated tail, single-sided swinging arm holding a new four-spoke design wheel, and very trick angular cross-section exhaust move the R about as far from the sensible look of the CBF as it's possible to get.

The trend for this look was set by the mightily successful Triumph Speed and Street Triples, bikes which convinced riders old and new that a full-on super-sports 1000 isn't necessarily the most fun you can have on the roads. Honda, typically, offer you that brand of fun in two completely different suits of clothes: the sensible, practical CBF with optional fitted luggage, or the extrovert option. The choice is yours!

Acknowledgements

Our thanks are due to Bransons Motorcycles of Yeovil who supplied the machines featured in the illustrations throughout this manual. We would also like to thank NGK Spark Plugs (UK) Ltd for supplying the colour spark plug condition photographs, the Avon Rubber Company for supplying information on tyre fitting and Draper Tools Ltd for some of the workshop tools shown.

Thanks are also due to Julian Ryder who wrote the introduction 'The Birth of a Dream' and to Honda (UK) Ltd. who supplied model photographs.

About this Manual

The aim of this manual is to help you get the best value from your motorcycle. It can do so in several ways. It can help you decide what work must be done, even if you choose to have it done by a dealer; it provides information and procedures for routine maintenance and servicing; and it offers diagnostic and repair procedures to follow when trouble occurs.

We hope you use the manual to tackle the work yourself. For many simpler jobs, doing it yourself may be quicker than arranging an appointment to get the motorcycle into a dealer and making the trips to leave it and pick it up. More importantly, a lot of money can be saved by avoiding the expense the shop must pass on to you to cover its labour and overhead costs. An added benefit is the sense of satisfaction and accomplishment that you feel after doing the job yourself.

References to the left or right side of the motorcycle assume you are sitting on the seat, facing forward.

We take great pride in the accuracy of information given in this manual, but motorcycle manufacturers make alterations and design changes during the production run of a particular motorcycle of which they do not inform us. No liability can be accepted by the authors or publishers for loss, damage or injury caused by any errors in, or omissions from, the information given.

Illegal copying

It is the policy of Haynes Publishing to actively protect its Copyrights and Trade Marks. Legal action will be taken against anyone who unlawfully copies the cover or contents of this Manual. This includes all forms of unauthorised copying including digital, mechanical, and electronic in any form. Authorisation from Haynes Publishing will only be provided expressly and in writing. Illegal copying will also be reported to the appropriate statutory authorities.

Identification numbers 0•9

Frame and engine numbers

The frame serial number is stamped into the right-hand side of the steering head. The engine number is stamped into the back of the lower crankcase on CBF1000/A models and into the right-hand side of the upper crankcase on CB1000R/RA models. Both of these numbers should be recorded and kept in a safe place so they can be given to law enforcement officials in the event of a theft. The VIN plate is on the left-hand side of the frame. There is a colour code label on the frame under the seat. The throttle bodies also have an ID number stamped into them.

The frame serial number, engine serial number, and colour code should also be kept in a handy place (such as with your driver's licence) so they are always available when purchasing or ordering parts for your machine.

Models are identified using the model name, i.e. CBF1000 or CB1000R for standard models, CBF1000A and CB1000RA for models with ABS, or CBF1000/A and CB1000R/RA to cover both standard and ABS types.

Model	Year
CBF1000-6/A-6	2006
CBF1000-7/A-7	2007
CBF1000-8/A-8	2008
CBF1000-9/A-9	2009
CBF1000-A/A-A	2010
CB1000R-9/RA-9	2008-09
CB1000R-A/RA-A	2010
CB1000R-B/RA-B	2011

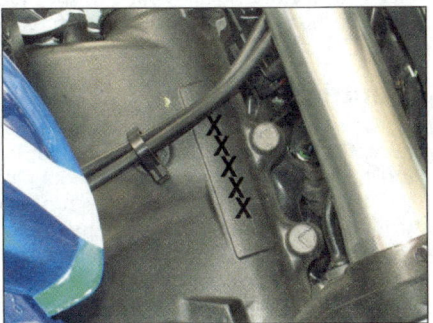

The frame number is stamped into the right-hand side of the steering head

The engine number is stamped into the rear of the lower crankcase on CBF1000/A models . . .

. . . and into the right-hand side of the upper crankcase on CB1000R/RA models

The VIN plate (arrowed) is riveted to the left-hand side of the frame

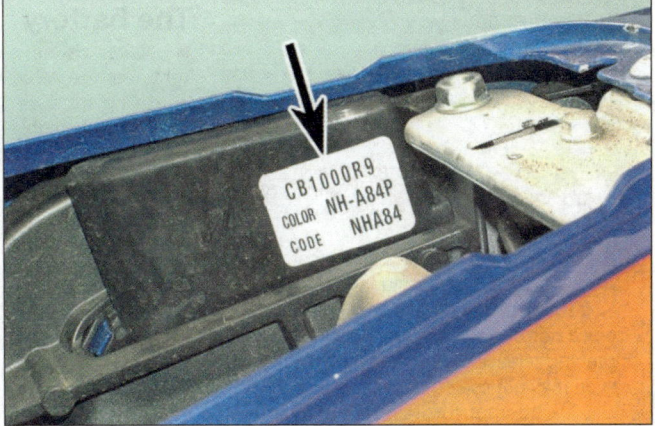

The colour code label is on the rear sub-frame

Buying spare parts

Once you have found all the identification numbers, record them for reference when buying parts. Since the manufacturers change specifications, parts and vendors (companies that manufacture various components on the machine), providing the ID numbers is the only way to be reasonably sure that you are buying the correct parts for your model.

Whenever possible, take the worn part to the dealer so direct comparison with the new component can be made. Along the trail from the manufacturer to the parts shelf, there are numerous places that the part can end up with the wrong number or be listed incorrectly.

The two places to purchase new parts for your motorcycle – the franchised or main dealer and the parts/accessories store – differ in the type of parts they carry. While dealers can obtain every single genuine part for your motorcycle, the accessory store is usually limited to normal high wear items such as chains and sprockets, brake pads, spark plugs and cables, and to tune-up parts and various engine gaskets, etc. Rarely will an accessory outlet have major suspension components, camshafts, transmission gears, or engine cases.

Used parts can be obtained from breakers for roughly half the price of new ones, but you can't always be sure of what you're getting. Once again, take your worn part to the breaker for direct comparison, or when ordering by mail order make sure that you can return it if you are not happy.

Whether buying new, used or rebuilt parts, the best course is to deal directly with someone who specialises in your particular make.

Safety First!

Professional mechanics are trained in safe working procedures. However enthusiastic you may be about getting on with the job at hand, take the time to ensure that your safety is not put at risk. A moment's lack of attention can result in an accident, as can failure to observe simple precautions.

There will always be new ways of having accidents, and the following is not a comprehensive list of all dangers; it is intended rather to make you aware of the risks and to encourage a safe approach to all work you carry out on your bike.

Asbestos

● Certain friction, insulating, sealing and other products - such as brake pads, clutch linings, gaskets, etc. - contain asbestos. Extreme care must be taken to avoid inhalation of dust from such products since it is hazardous to health. If in doubt, assume that they do contain asbestos.

Fire

● Remember at all times that petrol is highly flammable. Never smoke or have any kind of naked flame around, when working on the vehicle. But the risk does not end there - a spark caused by an electrical short-circuit, by two metal surfaces contacting each other, by careless use of tools, or even by static electricity built up in your body under certain conditions, can ignite petrol vapour, which in a confined space is highly explosive. Never use petrol as a cleaning solvent. Use an approved safety solvent.

● Always disconnect the battery earth terminal before working on any part of the fuel or electrical system, and never risk spilling fuel on to a hot engine or exhaust.

● It is recommended that a fire extinguisher of a type suitable for fuel and electrical fires is kept handy in the garage or workplace at all times. Never try to extinguish a fuel or electrical fire with water.

Fumes

● Certain fumes are highly toxic and can quickly cause unconsciousness and even death if inhaled to any extent. Petrol vapour comes into this category, as do the vapours from certain solvents such as trichloroethylene. Any draining or pouring of such volatile fluids should be done in a well ventilated area.

● When using cleaning fluids and solvents, read the instructions carefully. Never use materials from unmarked containers - they may give off poisonous vapours.

● Never run the engine of a motor vehicle in an enclosed space such as a garage. Exhaust fumes contain carbon monoxide which is extremely poisonous; if you need to run the engine, always do so in the open air or at least have the rear of the vehicle outside the workplace.

The battery

● Never cause a spark, or allow a naked light near the vehicle's battery. It will normally be giving off a certain amount of hydrogen gas, which is highly explosive.

● Always disconnect the battery ground (earth) terminal before working on the fuel or electrical systems (except where noted).

● If possible, loosen the filler plugs or cover when charging the battery from an external source. Do not charge at an excessive rate or the battery may burst.

● Take care when topping up, cleaning or carrying the battery. The acid electrolyte, evenwhen diluted, is very corrosive and should not be allowed to contact the eyes or skin. Always wear rubber gloves and goggles or a face shield. If you ever need to prepare electrolyte yourself, always add the acid slowly to the water; never add the water to the acid.

Electricity

● When using an electric power tool, inspection light etc., always ensure that the appliance is correctly connected to its plug and that, where necessary, it is properly grounded (earthed). Do not use such appliances in damp conditions and, again, beware of creating a spark or applying excessive heat in the vicinity of fuel or fuel vapour. Also ensure that the appliances meet national safety standards.

● A severe electric shock can result from touching certain parts of the electrical system, such as the spark plug wires (HT leads), when the engine is running or being cranked, particularly if components are damp or the insulation is defective. Where an electronic ignition system is used, the secondary (HT) voltage is much higher and could prove fatal.

Remember...

✗ **Don't** start the engine without first ascertaining that the transmission is in neutral.

✗ **Don't** suddenly remove the pressure cap from a hot cooling system - cover it with a cloth and release the pressure gradually first, or you may get scalded by escaping coolant.

✗ **Don't** attempt to drain oil until you are sure it has cooled sufficiently to avoid scalding you.

✗ **Don't** grasp any part of the engine or exhaust system without first ascertaining that it is cool enough not to burn you.

✗ **Don't** allow brake fluid or antifreeze to contact the machine's paintwork or plastic components.

✗ **Don't** siphon toxic liquids such as fuel, hydraulic fluid or antifreeze by mouth, or allow them to remain on your skin.

✗ **Don't** inhale dust - it may be injurious to health (see Asbestos heading).

✗ **Don't** allow any spilled oil or grease to remain on the floor - wipe it up right away, before someone slips on it.

✗ **Don't** use ill-fitting spanners or other tools which may slip and cause injury.

✗ **Don't** lift a heavy component which may be beyond your capability - get assistance.

✗ **Don't** rush to finish a job or take unverified short cuts.

✗ **Don't** allow children or animals in or around an unattended vehicle.

✗ **Don't** inflate a tyre above the recommended pressure. Apart from overstressing the carcass, in extreme cases the tyre may blow off forcibly.

✔ **Do** ensure that the machine is supported securely at all times. This is especially important when the machine is blocked up to aid wheel or fork removal.

✔ **Do** take care when attempting to loosen a stubborn nut or bolt. It is generally better to pull on a spanner, rather than push, so that if you slip, you fall away from the machine rather than onto it.

✔ **Do** wear eye protection when using power tools such as drill, sander, bench grinder etc.

✔ **Do** use a barrier cream on your hands prior to undertaking dirty jobs - it will protect your skin from infection as well as making the dirt easier to remove afterwards; but make sure your hands aren't left slippery. Note that long-term contact with used engine oil can be a health hazard.

✔ **Do** keep loose clothing (cuffs, ties etc. and long hair) well out of the way of moving mechanical parts.

✔ **Do** remove rings, wristwatch etc., before working on the vehicle - especially the electrical system.

✔ **Do** keep your work area tidy - it is only too easy to fall over articles left lying around.

✔ **Do** exercise caution when compressing springs for removal or installation. Ensure that the tension is applied and released in a controlled manner, using suitable tools which preclude the possibility of the spring escaping violently.

✔ **Do** ensure that any lifting tackle used has a safe working load rating adequate for the job.

✔ **Do** get someone to check periodically that all is well, when working alone on the vehicle.

✔ **Do** carry out work in a logical sequence and check that everything is correctly assembled and tightened afterwards.

✔ **Do** remember that your vehicle's safety affects that of yourself and others. If in doubt on any point, get professional advice.

● If in spite of following these precautions, you are unfortunate enough to injure yourself, seek medical attention as soon as possible.

Pre-ride checks

Coolant level

> **Warning: DO NOT remove the radiator pressure cap to add coolant. Topping up is done via the coolant reservoir tank filler. DO NOT leave open containers of coolant about, as it is poisonous.**

Before you start:
✔ Make sure you have a supply of coolant available (a mixture of 50% distilled water and 50% corrosion inhibited ethylene glycol anti-freeze is needed).

✔ Check the coolant level when the engine is at normal working temperature. Take the motorcycle on a short run to allow it to reach normal temperature.
Caution: Do not run the engine in an enclosed space such as a garage or workshop.
✔ Stop the engine. Support the motorcycle on the centrestand (where fitted) or otherwise using an auxiliary stand, making sure it is upright and on level ground.
✔ On CBF1000/A models the coolant reservoir is located under the rider's seat.
✔ On CB1000R/RA models the coolant reservoir is located under the front of the fuel tank on the left-hand side.

Bike care:
● Use only the specified coolant mixture. It is important that the correct proportion of anti-freeze is used in the system all year round, and not just in the winter. Do not top the system up using only water, as the system will become too diluted.
● Do not overfill the reservoir tank. If the coolant is significantly above the UPPER level line at any time, the surplus should be siphoned or drained off to prevent the possibility of it being expelled out of the overflow hose.
● If the coolant level falls steadily check the system for leaks (see Chapter 1). If no leaks are found and the level continues to fall, it is recommended that the machine is taken to a Honda dealer for a pressure test.

CBF1000/A models

1 The coolant level should lie between the upper and lower level lines (arrowed) that are marked on the reservoir.

2 If the coolant level is on or below the LOWER line, remove the rider's seat and the left-hand side cover (see Chapter 7). Remove the reservoir filler cap.

3 Top the reservoir up with the recommended coolant mixture to the UPPER level line, using a suitable funnel if required. Fit the cap. Install the side cover and seat (see Chapter 7).

CB1000R/RA models

1 The coolant level should lie between the upper and lower level lines (arrowed) that are marked on the reservoir.

2 If the coolant level is on or below the LOWER line, remove the protection grille (see Chapter 7). Remove the reservoir filler cap.

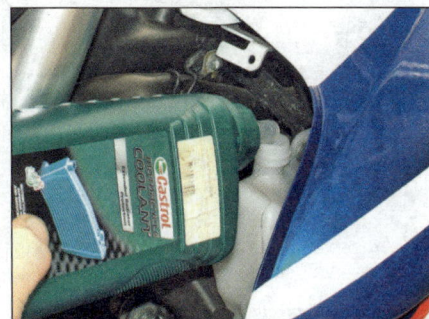

3 Top the reservoir up with the recommended coolant mixture to the UPPER level line, using a suitable funnel if required. Fit the cap. Install the protection grille (see Chapter 7).

Suspension, steering and final drive

Suspension and Steering:
● Check that the front and rear suspension operates smoothly without binding (see Chapter 1).
● Check that the suspension is adjusted as required (see Chapter 5).
● Check that the steering moves smoothly from lock-to-lock.

Drive chain:
● Check that the chain isn't too loose or too tight, and adjust it if necessary (see Chapter 1).
● If the chain looks dry, lubricate it (see Chapter 1).

Pre-ride checks

Brake fluid levels

 Warning: Brake hydraulic fluid can harm your eyes and damage painted surfaces, so use extreme caution when handling and pouring it and cover surrounding surfaces with rag. Do not use fluid that has been standing open for some time, as it is hygroscopic (absorbs moisture from the air) which can cause a dangerous loss of braking effectiveness.

Before you start:

✔ The front brake fluid reservoir is on the right-hand handlebar. The rear brake fluid reservoir is located on the right-hand side at the rear.
✔ Make sure you have the correct hydraulic fluid – DOT 4.
✔ Wrap a rag around the reservoir being worked on to ensure that any spillage does not come into contact with painted surfaces.
✔ Support the bike on the upright on level ground. When checking the fluid in the front reservoir, turn the handlebars to the left so the reservoir is level.

Bike care:

● The fluid in the front and rear brake master cylinder reservoirs will drop as the brake pads wear down. If the fluid level is low check the brake pads for wear (see Chapter 1), and replace them with new ones if necessary (see Chapter 6).
● If either fluid reservoir requires repeated topping-up there is a leak somewhere in the system, which must be investigated immediately (see Chapter 1).
● Check for signs of fluid leakage from the hydraulic hoses and/or brake system components – if found, rectify immediately (see Chapter 6).
● Check the operation of both brakes before taking the machine on the road; if there is evidence of air in the system (spongy feel to lever or pedal), it must be bled (see Chapter 6).

REAR BRAKE (ALL MODELS)

1 The rear brake fluid level is visible through the reservoir body – it must be between the UPPER and LOWER level lines (arrowed).

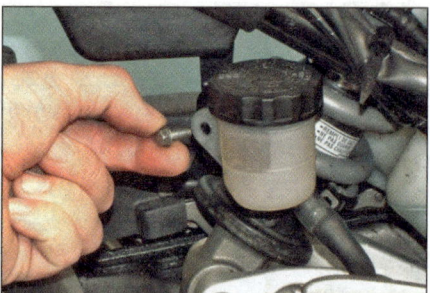

2 If the level is on or below the LOWER line on CBF1000/A models, unscrew the reservoir mounting bolt and displace the reservoir so the cap is clear.

3 If the level is on or below the LOWER line on CB1000R/RA models, unscrew the reservoir mounting bolt and displace the reservoir so the cap is clear . . .

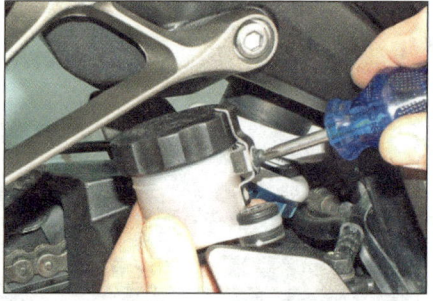

4 . . . then unscrew the reservoir cap clamp screw and displace the clamp.

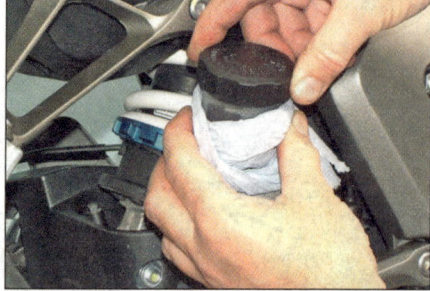

5 Unscrew the reservoir cap, then remove the diaphragm plate and diaphragm.

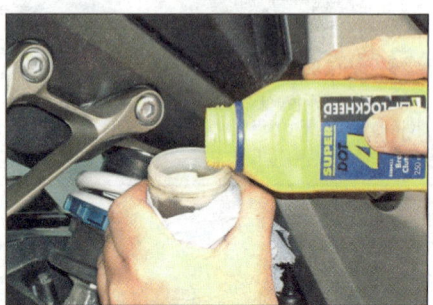

6 Top up with new clean DOT 4 hydraulic fluid, until the level is up to the UPPER line. Do not overfill and take care to avoid spills (see **Warning** above).

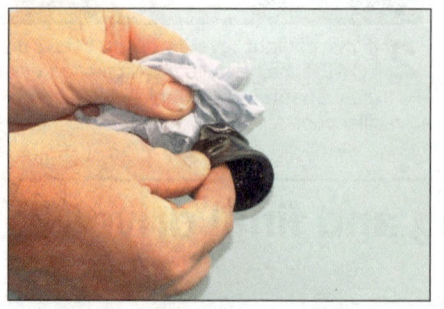

7 Wipe any moisture off the diaphragm with a tissue.

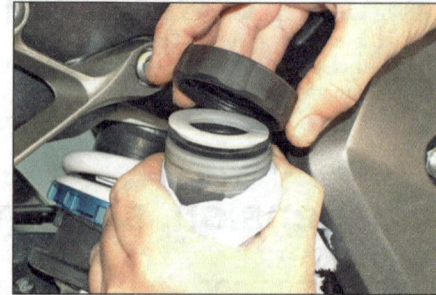

8 Ensure that the diaphragm is correctly seated before installing the plate and cap, then fit the cap clamp and/or remount the reservoir, according to model.

Pre-ride checks 0•13

FRONT BRAKE
CBF1000/A MODELS

1 The front brake fluid level is visible through the window in the reservoir body – it must be above the LOWER level line (arrowed).

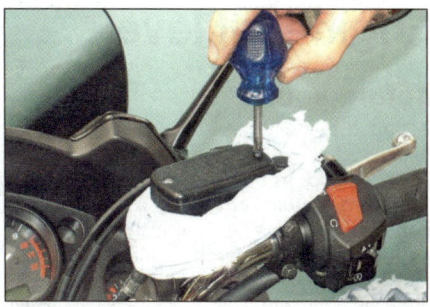

2 If the level is on or below the LOWER line, undo the reservoir cover screws and remove the cover, diaphragm plate and diaphragm.

3 Top up with new clean DOT 4 hydraulic fluid, until the level is up to the upper level line cast inside the reservoir. Do not overfill and take care to avoid spills (see **Warning** on page 0•12).

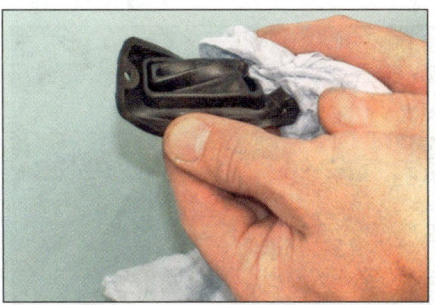

4 Wipe any moisture off the diaphragm with a tissue.

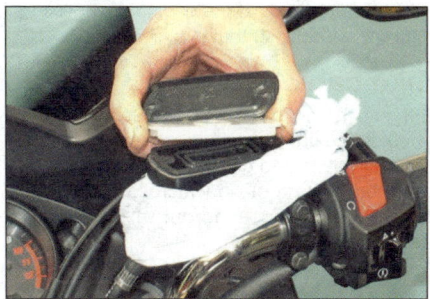

5 Ensure that the diaphragm is correctly seated before installing the plate and cover. Secure the reservoir cover with its screws.

FRONT BRAKE
CB1000R/RA MODELS

1 The front brake fluid level is visible through the window in the reservoir body – it must be between the UPPER and LOWER level lines (arrowed).

2 If the level is on or below the LOWER line, unscrew the reservoir cap clamp screw and displace the clamp, then unscrew the cap and remove the diaphragm plate and diaphragm.

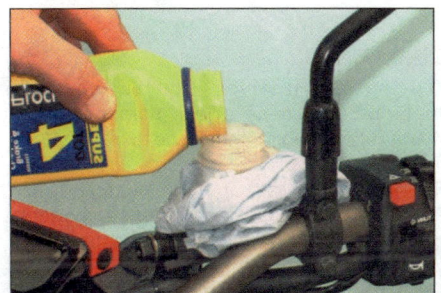

3 Top up with new clean DOT 4 hydraulic fluid, until the level is up to the UPPER line. Do not overfill and take care to avoid spills (see **Warning** on page 0•12).

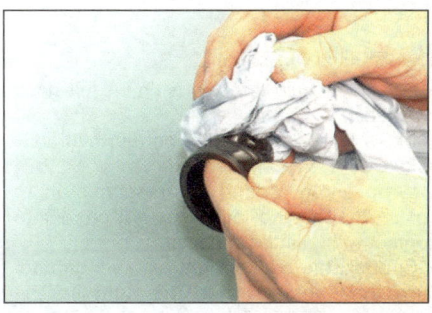

4 Wipe any moisture off the diaphragm with a tissue.

5 Ensure that the diaphragm is correctly seated before installing the plate and cap and fitting the clamp.

0•14 Pre-ride checks

Engine oil level

Before you start:
✔ Start the engine and let it idle for 3 to 5 minutes.
Caution: Do not run the engine in an enclosed space such as a garage or workshop.
✔ Stop the engine. Support the motorcycle on the centrestand (where fitted) or otherwise using an auxiliary stand, making sure it is upright and on level ground. Allow it to stand undisturbed for 2 to 3 minutes for the oil level to stabilise.
✔ The oil level inspection window is located on the right-hand side of the engine. If necessary wipe the window so that it is clean.

Bike care:
● If you have to add oil frequently, check whether you have any oil leaks from the engine joints, oil seals and gaskets. If not, the engine could be burning oil, in which case there will be white smoke coming out of the exhaust (see *Fault Finding*).

The correct oil:
● Modern, high-revving engines place great demands on their oil. It is very important that the correct oil is used.
● Always use a good quality motorcycle oil of the specified type and viscosity and do not overfill the engine. Do not use oils designed for car engines.
Caution: Do not use chemical additives or oils labelled "ENERGY CONSERVING". Such additives or oils could cause clutch slip.

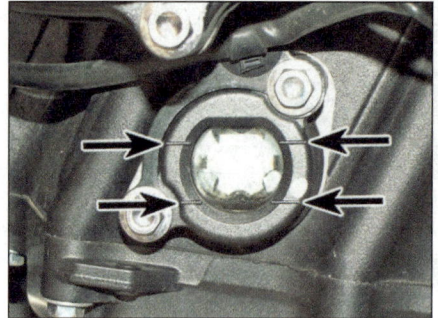

1 With the motorcycle vertical, the oil level should lie between the upper and lower level lines (arrowed).

2 If the level is on or below the lower line unscrew the oil filler cap (arrowed).

3 Top up the engine with the recommended grade and type of oil to bring the level almost up to the upper line on the inspection window. Do not overfill.

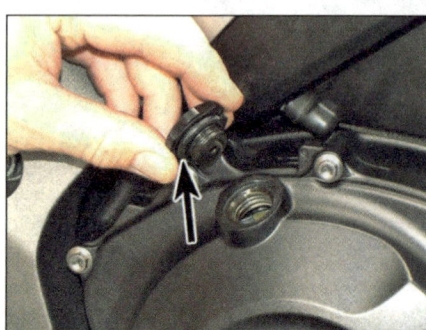

4 Make sure the filler cap O-ring (arrowed) is in good condition and correctly seated before fitting the cap.

Oil type	API grade SG or higher, JASO MA, motorcycle oil
Oil viscosity	SAE 10W30

Clutch fluid level

⚠ **Warning: Clutch hydraulic fluid can harm your eyes and damage painted surfaces, so use extreme caution when handling and pouring it and cover surrounding surfaces with rag. Do not use fluid from an opened container as it is hygroscopic (absorbs moisture from the air) which can cause a loss of clutch effectiveness.**

Before you start:
✔ The clutch fluid reservoir is on the left-hand handlebar.
✔ Make sure you have the correct hydraulic fluid. DOT 4 is recommended.
✔ Wrap a rag around the reservoir on to ensure that any spillage does not come into contact with painted surfaces.
✔ Support the bike upright on level ground. Turn the handlebars to the right so the reservoir is level.

Bike care:
● If the fluid reservoir requires repeated topping-up there is a leak somewhere in the system, which must be investigated immediately.
● Check for signs of fluid leakage from the hydraulic hose and release system components – if found, rectify immediately (see Chapter 2).
● Check the operation of the clutch before taking the machine on the road; if there is evidence of air in the system (spongy feel to lever, difficulty selecting gears and clutch drag), it must be bled (see Chapter 2).

Pre-ride checks

CLUTCH FLUID CBF1000/A MODELS

1 The clutch fluid level is visible through the window in the reservoir body – it must be above the LOWER level line (arrowed).

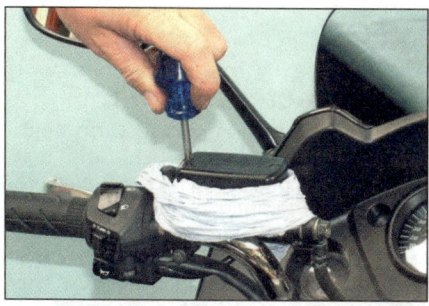

2 If the level is on or below the LOWER line, undo the reservoir cover screws and remove the cover, diaphragm plate and diaphragm.

3 Top up with new clean DOT 4 hydraulic fluid, until the level is up to the upper level line inside the reservoir. Do not overfill and take care to avoid spills (see **Warning** on page 0•14).

4 Wipe any moisture off the diaphragm with a tissue.

5 Ensure that the diaphragm is correctly seated before installing the plate and cover. Secure the reservoir cover with its screws.

CLUTCH FLUID CB1000R/RA MODELS

1 The clutch fluid level is visible through the window in the reservoir body – it must be between the UPPER and LOWER level lines (arrowed).

2 If the level is on or below the LOWER line, unscrew the reservoir cap clamp screw and displace the clamp, then unscrew the cap and remove the diaphragm plate and diaphragm.

3 Top up with new clean DOT 4 hydraulic fluid, until the level is up to the UPPER line. Do not overfill and take care to avoid spills (see **Warning** on page 0•14).

4 Wipe any moisture off the diaphragm with a tissue.

5 Ensure that the diaphragm is correctly seated before installing the plate and cap and fitting the clamp.

Pre-ride checks

Tyres

The correct pressures:
- The tyres must be checked when **cold**, not immediately after riding. Note that tyre pressure is affected by both ambient temperature and atmospheric pressure and so can change daily.
- Incorrect tyre pressures will cause abnormal tread wear and unsafe handling. Low tyre pressures may cause the tyre to slip on the rim or come off.
- Use an accurate pressure gauge. Many forecourt gauges are wildly inaccurate. If you buy your own, spend as much as you can justify on a quality gauge.
- Proper air pressure will increase tyre life and provide maximum stability and ride comfort.

Front	Rear
36 psi (2.5 Bar)	42 psi (2.9 Bar)

Tyre care:
- Check the tyres carefully for cuts, tears, embedded nails or other sharp objects and excessive wear. Operation of the motorcycle with excessively worn tyres is extremely hazardous, as traction and handling are directly affected.
- Pick out any stones or nails which may have become embedded in the tyre tread. If left, they will eventually penetrate through the casing and cause a puncture.
- Ensure the dust cap is in place. If air escapes when the cap is removed the valve could be loose in its core – a simple tool that is cheaply available and sometimes incorporated in the cap is needed to tighten the valve. Check the condition of the valve.
- If tyre damage is apparent, or unexplained loss of pressure is experienced, seek the advice of a tyre fitting specialist without delay.

Tyre tread depth:
- At the time of writing UK law requires that tread depth must be at least 1 mm over 3/4 of the tread breadth all the way around the tyre, with no bald patches. Many riders, however, consider 2 mm tread depth minimum to be a safer limit. Honda recommend a minimum of 1.5 mm on the front and 2 mm on the rear, but note that German law requires a minimum of 1.6 mm for each tyre.
- Many tyres now incorporate wear indicators in the tread. Identify the location marking on the tyre sidewall to locate the indicator bar and replace the tyre if the tread has worn down to the bar.

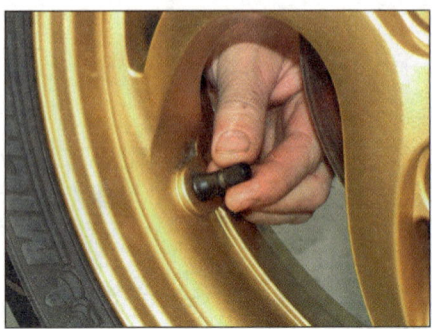

1 Remove the dust cap from the valve. Do not forget to fit the cap after checking the pressure.

2 Check the tyre pressures when cold.

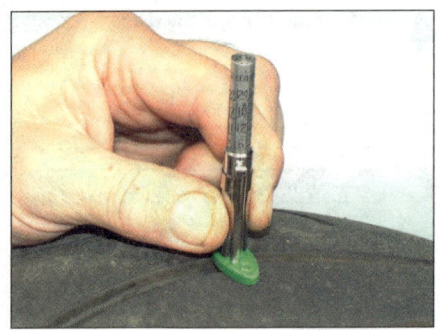

3 Measure tread depth at the centre of the tyre using a depth gauge.

4 Tyre tread wear indicators (A) and its location marking (B) on the edge or sidewall (according to manufacturer).

Legal and safety

Lighting and signalling:
- Take a minute to check that the headlights, tail and brake lights, licence plate light, instrument lights and turn signals all work correctly.
- Check that the horn sounds when the button is pressed.
- A working speedometer, graduated in mph, is a statutory requirement in the UK.

Safety:
- Check that the throttle grip rotates smoothly when opened and snaps shut when released, in all steering positions. Also check for the correct amount of freeplay (see Chapter 1).
- Check that the brake lever and pedal, clutch lever and gearchange lever operate smoothly. Lubricate them at the specified intervals or when necessary (see Chapter 1).
- Check that the engine shuts off when the kill switch is operated. Check the starter interlock circuit (see Chapter 1).
- Check that sidestand return springs hold the stand up securely when retracted.

Fuel:
- This may seem obvious, but check that you have enough fuel to complete your journey. If you smell petrol or notice signs of fuel leakage, rectify the cause immediately.
- Ensure you use the correct grade fuel – see Chapter 4 Specifications.

Model development and bike spec 0•17

CBF1000/A

The CBF1000/A was launched in 2006. It was designed as an all-rounder to complement the existing range of more specifically focused litre-plus bikes and to complete the range represented in smaller capacity by the CBF500 and CBF600.

The CBF uses the in-line four cylinder liquid-cooled engine from the CBR1000RR-4 to RR-7 Fireblade, but re-tuned to provide greater torque output and therefore more flexible drive in the low and mid-ranges. Drive to the double overhead camshafts which actuate the four valves per cylinder is by chain from the right-hand end of the crankshaft. The clutch is a conventional wet multi-plate unit actuated hydraulically, and the gearbox is the cassette-type, meaning it can be easily removed with the engine still in the frame. Drive to the rear wheel from the six-speed box is by chain and sprockets.

Honda's PGM-FI fuel injection system supplies fuel and air to the engine via 36mm throttle bodies and two inlet valves per cylinder, with exhaust gases exiting via another two valves per cylinder into a four-into-two exhaust system with closed-loop catalytic converter. An electronic engine management system controls both the injection system and the ignition system. All European models feature Honda's immobiliser system (HISS).

The engine sits in a frame developed from the CBF600, comprising a steel mono-backbone with hangers holding the engine at the front and cast aluminium plates bolted on to hold the engine at the back, and using the engine as a stressed member.

Front suspension is by oil-damped 41 mm forks with cartridge dampers. Rear suspension is by a single shock absorber with adjustable spring pre-load, and a box-section steel swingarm with Honda's Pro-Link.

The hydraulic braking system on the standard model has two twin piston sliding calipers acting on 296 mm discs at the front, and one single piston sliding caliper acting on a 240 mm disc at the rear. The hydraulic braking system on the A model has a combined anti-lock (CBS/ABS) braking system, with two triple piston sliding calipers acting on 296 mm discs at the front, and one triple piston sliding caliper acting on a 240 mm disc at the rear. The CBS links the rear brake to part of the front, actuating the centre piston in the right-hand caliper via a proportional control valve, whenever the pedal is depressed.

All models feature an adjustable seat that can be raised and lowered through three positions, and an adjustable windshield that has two positions.

Available in silver, black, blue, green and orange in 2006, silver, black, blue and red in 2007, silver, black, red and yellow in 2008, silver, black, red and white in 2009 and 2010.

CB1000R/RA

The CB1000R/RA was launched in 2008. It was designed as a replacement for the ageing 900 Hornet, with the design focused on street-style naked performance.

The CB-R uses the engine unit fitted to the CBF1000.

Honda's PGM-FI fuel injection system supplies fuel and air to the engine via 36mm throttle bodies and two inlet valves per cylinder, with exhaust gases exiting via another two valves per cylinder into a four-into-one exhaust system with closed-loop catalytic converter. An electronic engine management system controls both the injection system and the ignition system. All European models feature Honda's immobiliser system (HISS).

The engine sits in an aluminium mono-backbone frame with hangers holding the engine at the front and plates to hold the engine at the back, and using the engine as a stressed member.

Front suspension is by oil-damped 43 mm upside-down forks with cartridge dampers adjustable for spring pre-load and both rebound and compression damping. Rear suspension is by a single shock absorber with adjustable spring pre-load and rebound damping, and a single-sided aluminium swingarm.

The hydraulic braking system on the standard model has two radial calipers with four opposed pistons acting on 310 mm discs at the front, and a twin piston sliding caliper acting on a 256 mm disc at the rear.

The hydraulic braking system on the A model has a combined anti-lock braking system (CBS/ABS or C-ABS), with two triple piston sliding calipers acting on 310 mm discs at the front, and a twin piston sliding caliper acting on a 256 mm disc at the rear. The CBS links the rear brake to part of the front, actuating the centre piston in the right-hand caliper via a proportional control valve, whenever the pedal is depressed.

The 2011 models features thicker aluminium handlebars and an LED position light.

Available in green, black, white and silver in 2008 and 2009, red/black, black, beige and white in 2010, and black, white and a new HRC Tricolour version in 2011.

Dimensions and weights

CBF1000/A models
Overall length . . . . 2156 mm
Overall width. 782 mm
Overall height . . . . 1238 mm
Wheelbase . . . . 1483 mm
Seat height . . . . 800 ± 15 mm
Ground clearance. . . . . 130 mm
Kerb weight
    Standard models . . . . 244 kg
    ABS models . . . . 251 kg
Maximum weight capacity . . . . 195 kg

CB1000R/RA models
Overall length . . . . 2105 mm
Overall width. 785 mm
Overall height . . . . 1095 mm
Wheelbase . . . . 1445 mm
Seat height . . . . 825 mm
Ground clearance. . . . . 130 mm
Kerb weight
    Standard models . . . . 217 kg
    ABS models . . . . 222 kg
Maximum weight capacity . . . . 188 kg

Bike spec

Engine
Type	Four-stroke in-line four
Capacity	998 cc
Bore	75.0 mm
Stroke	56.5 mm
Compression ratio	
CBF1000 models	11.0 to 1
CB1000R models	11.2 to 1
Cooling system	Liquid cooled
Clutch	Wet multi-plate
Transmission	Six-speed constant mesh
Final drive	Chain and sprockets
Camshafts	DOHC, chain-driven
Fuel system	PGM-FI fuel injection
Ignition system	Computer-controlled digital transistorised with electronic advance

Chassis – CBF models
Frame type	Mono backbone
Rake and trail	26°, 111 mm
Fuel tank	
Capacity (including reserve)	19.3 litres
Reserve volume	approx. 4.0 litres
Front suspension	
Type	41 mm oil-damped cartridge-type telescopic forks
Travel	108 mm
Adjustment	none
Rear suspension	
Type	Single shock absorber, rising rate linkage, steel swingarm
Travel (at axle)	120 mm
Adjustment	Spring pre-load
Wheels	17 inch 6-spoke alloy
Tyres	
Front	120/70-ZR17M/C (58W)
Rear	160/60-ZR17M/C (69W)
Front brake	
Standard models	Twin 296 mm floating discs with twin piston sliding calipers
ABS models	Twin 296 mm floating discs with triple piston sliding calipers
Rear brake	
Standard models	Single 240 mm disc with single piston sliding caliper
ABS models	Single 240 mm disc with triple piston sliding caliper

Chassis – CB-R models
Frame type	Mono backbone
Rake and trail	25°, 99 mm
Fuel tank	
Capacity (including reserve)	17.0 litres
Reserve volume	approx. 4.0 litres
Front suspension	
Type	43 mm oil-damped upside down cartridge-type telescopic forks
Travel	109 mm
Adjustment	Spring pre-load, rebound and compression damping
Rear suspension	
Type	Single shock absorber, single-sided aluminium swingarm
Travel (at axle)	128 mm
Adjustment	Spring pre-load, rebound damping
Wheels	
Front	17 inch 4-spoke alloy
Rear	17 inch 5-spoke alloy
Tyres	
Front	120/70-ZR17M/C (58W)
Rear	180/55-ZR17M/C (73W)
Front brake	
Standard models	Twin 310 mm floating discs with four opposed-piston calipers
ABS models	Twin 310 mm floating discs with triple piston sliding calipers
Rear brake	Single 265 mm disc with twin piston sliding caliper

Chapter 1
Routine maintenance and servicing

Contents

	Section number
Air filter	18
Battery	20
Brake fluid level check	see *Pre-ride checks*
Brake system	3
Clutch	4
Clutch fluid level check	see *Pre-ride checks*
Coolant level check	see *Pre-ride checks*
Cooling system	9
Crankcase breather	2
Drive chain and sprockets	1
Engine oil and filter	8
Engine oil level check	see *Pre-ride checks*
Engine wear assessment	see Chapter 2

	Section number
Fuel system	5
Headlight aim	11
Idle speed control system	see Chapter 4
Nuts and bolts	17
PAIR (pulse secondary air) system	10
Spark plugs	7
Sidestand, centrestand and starter interlock circuit	12
Stand, lever pivot and cable lubrication	16
Steering head bearings	14
Suspension	13
Throttle cables	6
Valve clearances	19
Wheels, tyres and wheel bearings	15

Degrees of difficulty

| **Easy,** suitable for novice with little experience | **Fairly easy,** suitable for beginner with some experience | **Fairly difficult,** suitable for competent DIY mechanic | **Difficult,** suitable for experienced DIY mechanic | **Very difficult,** suitable for expert DIY or professional |

Maintenance specifications

Engine
Cylinder numbering	1 to 4 from left to right
Spark plug type	
CBF1000/A models	NGK CR8EH-9 or Nippondenso U24FER9
CB1000R/RA models	NGK IMR9E-9HES or Nippondenso VUH27ES
Spark plug electrode gap	0.8 to 0.9 mm
Engine idle speed	1200 ± 100 rpm
Valve clearances (COLD engine)	
Intake valves	0.16 ± 0.03 mm
Exhaust valves	0.32 ± 0.03 mm

Cycle parts
Drive chain slack	
CBF1000/A models	20 to 30 mm
CB1000R/RA models	25 to 35 mm
Throttle cable freeplay	2 to 6 mm
Tyre pressures (cold)	see *Pre-ride checks*
Steering head bearing pre-load (see text)	
CBF1000/A models	9.8 to 13.7 N (1.0 to 1.4 kgf; 2.2 to 3.1 lbf)
CB1000R/RA models	9.8 to 12.5 N (1.0 to 1.3 kgf; 2.2 to 2.9 lbf)

Lubricants and fluids
Engine oil type	SAE 10W30, API grade SG or higher, JASO MA, motorcycle oil
Engine oil capacity	
Oil change	2.7 litres
Oil and filter change	
CBF1000/A models	approx. 3.0 litres
CB1000R/RA models	approx. 3.5 litres
Coolant type	50% distilled water, 50% corrosion inhibited ethylene glycol anti-freeze

Coolant capacity	**Radiator and engine**	**Reservoir**
CBF1000/A models	2.71 litres	0.30 litres
CB1000R/RA models	3.0 litres	0.35 litres

Brake/clutch fluid	DOT 4
Drive chain	SAE 80 or 90 gear oil or chain lubricant suitable for O-ring chains
Steering head bearings	Urea based multi-purpose grease with EP2 rating
Steering head bearing adjuster nut threads	Engine oil
Stand pivots	Multi-purpose grease
Wheel bearing seal lips	Multi-purpose grease
Gearchange lever/rear brake pedal/footrest pivots	Multi-purpose grease
Gearchange linkage rod ball joints	Multi-purpose grease
Swingarm pivot bearings and seals	
CBF1000/A models	Lithium based multi-purpose grease with EP2 rating grease
CB1000R/RA models	Molybdenum disulfide grease
Shock absorber pivot bearings and seals	
CBF1000/A models	Lithium based multi-purpose grease with EP2 rating grease
CB1000R/RA models	Repsol MP2 grease
Shock absorber pre-load adjuster ring	Molybdenum paste
Throttle cables	Cable lubricant
Throttle cable ends	Multi-purpose grease
Front brake lever pivot and pushrod	Silicone grease
Clutch lever pivot and pushrod	Silicone grease
Brake caliper slider pins and boots	Silicone grease
Rear master cylinder pushrod and boot	Silicone grease

Torque settings
Cooling system drain bolt	12 Nm
Engine oil drain plug	30 Nm
Engine oil filter	26 Nm
Fork clamp bolts (top yoke)	22 Nm
Rear axle nut – CBF1000/A models	98 Nm
Rear wheel bearing holder clamp bolt – CB1000R/RA models	74 Nm
Spark plugs	16 Nm
Steering head bearing adjuster nut	
CBF1000/A models	25 Nm
CB1000R/RA models	26 Nm
Steering stem nut	103 Nm
Timing inspection cap	18 Nm

Maintenance schedule 1•3

Note: The Pre-ride checks outlined in the owner's manual cover those items which should be inspected before every ride. Also perform the pre-ride inspection at every maintenance interval (in addition to the procedures listed). The intervals listed below are the intervals recommended by the manufacturer for the models covered in this manual.

Pre-ride
- [ ] See 'Pre-ride checks' at the beginning of this manual

After the initial 600 miles (1000 km)
Note: This check is performed by a Honda dealer after the first 600 miles (1000 km) from new. Thereafter, maintenance is carried out according to the following intervals of the schedule.

Every 600 miles (1000 km)
- [ ] Check, adjust, clean and lubricate the drive chain (Section 1)

Every 4000 miles (6000 km) or 6 months
- [ ] Clean the crankcase breather (Section 2)
- [ ] Check the brake pads for wear (Section 3)

Every 8000 miles (12,000 km) or 12 months
Carry out the items under the 4000 mile (6000 km) check, plus the following:
- [ ] Check the brake system and brake light switch operation (Section 3)
- [ ] Check the clutch (Section 4)
- [ ] Check the fuel system and hoses (Section 5)
- [ ] Check the throttle cables and adjust if necessary (Section 6)
- [ ] Check the spark plugs – CBF1000/A models (Section 7)
- [ ] Change the engine oil and fit a new filter (Section 8)
- [ ] Check the cooling system (Section 9)
- [ ] Check the PAIR (pulse secondary air) system (Section 10)
- [ ] Check the headlight beam aim (Section 11)
- [ ] Check the stand(s) and starter interlock circuit (Section 12)
- [ ] Check the front and rear suspension (Section 13)
- [ ] Check the steering head bearings and adjust if necessary (Section 14)
- [ ] Check the condition of the wheels, wheel bearings and tyres (Section 15)
- [ ] Lubricate the clutch, gearchange and brake levers, brake pedal, stand pivots, and the throttle cables (Section 16)
- [ ] Check the tightness of all nuts, bolts and fasteners (Section 17)

Every 12,000 miles (18,000 km) or 18 months
Carry out all the items under the 4000 mile (6000 km) check, plus the following:
- [ ] Clean and check air filter element (Section 18)

Every 12,000 miles (18,000 km) or two years
Carry out all the items under the 4000 mile (6000 km) check, plus the following:
- [ ] Change the brake fluid and clutch fluid (Sections 3 and 4)

Every 16,000 miles (24,000 km) or two years
Carry out all the items under the 8000 mile (12,000 km) check, plus the following:
- [ ] Fit new spark plugs – CBF1000/A models (Section 7)
- [ ] Check the spark plugs – CB1000R/RA models (Section 7)
- [ ] Check the valve clearances and adjust if necessary (Section 19)

Every 24,000 miles (36,000 km) or two years
Carry out all the items under the 12,000 mile (18,000 km) and 8000 mile (12,000 km) checks, plus the following:
- [ ] Change the coolant (Section 9)

Every 32,000 miles (48,000 km)
Carry out all the items under the 16,000 mile (24,000 km) checks, plus the following:
- [ ] Fit new spark plugs – CB1000R/RA models (Section 7)

Non-scheduled maintenance
- [ ] Check the battery (Section 20)
- [ ] Change the front fork oil (Section 13)
- [ ] Re-grease the swingarm and shock absorber bearings (Section 13)
- [ ] Re-grease the steering head bearings (Section 14)

1•4 Routine maintenance and servicing

CBF1000/A component locations on right side

1 Rear brake fluid reservoir
2 Battery
3 Coolant pressure cap
4 Front brake fluid reservoir
5 Throttle cable upper adjuster
6 Oil filter
7 Timing inspection cap
8 Oil level window
9 Oil filler cap
10 Rear brake light switch
11 Rear brake pedal height adjuster
12 Drive chain adjuster

Routine maintenance and servicing 1•5

CBF1000/A component locations on left side

1 Clutch fluid reservoir
2 Steering head bearing adjuster
3 Crankcase breather hose
4 Crankcase breather drain
5 Air filter
6 Coolant reservoir
7 Drive chain adjuster
8 Drive chain slider
9 Clutch release cylinder
10 Coolant drain bolt
11 Oil drain bolt

1•6 Routine maintenance and servicing

CB1000R/RA component locations on right side

1 Rear brake fluid reservoir
2 Coolant pressure cap
3 Throttle cable upper adjuster
4 Front brake fluid reservoir
5 Oil filter
6 Timing inspection cap
7 Oil level window
8 Oil filler cap
9 Rear brake light switch
10 Rear brake pedal height adjuster

Routine maintenance and servicing 1•7

CB1000R/RA component locations on left side

1 Clutch fluid reservoir
2 Steering head bearing adjuster
3 Crankcase breather hose
4 Crankcase breather drain
5 Air filter
6 Battery
7 Drive chain adjuster clamp
8 Drive chain slider
9 Clutch release cylinder
10 Coolant drain bolt
11 Oil drain bolt
12 Coolant reservoir

1•8 Routine maintenance and servicing

1 This Chapter is designed to help the home mechanic maintain his/her motorcycle for safety, economy, long life and peak performance.

2 Deciding where to start or plug into the routine maintenance schedule depends on several factors. If your motorcycle has been maintained according to the warranty standards and has just come out of warranty, start routine maintenance as it coincides with the next mileage or calendar interval. If you have owned the machine for some time but have never performed any maintenance on it, start at the nearest interval and include some additional procedures to ensure that nothing important is overlooked. If you have just had a major engine overhaul, then start the maintenance routine from the beginning. If you have a used machine and have no knowledge of its history or maintenance record, combine all the checks into one large service initially and then settle into the specified maintenance schedule.

3 Before beginning any maintenance or repair, clean the machine thoroughly, especially around the oil filter, oil drain plug, body panels, drive chain, suspension, wheels, etc. Cleaning will help ensure that dirt does not contaminate the engine and will allow you to detect wear and damage that could otherwise easily go unnoticed. If you use a pressure washer make sure you do not direct the jet at wheel bearing and suspension seals and at the steering head, or at any electrical/ignition components and connectors.

4 Certain maintenance information is sometimes printed on labels attached to the motorcycle. If the information on the labels differs from that included here, use the information on the label.

1 Drive chain and sprockets

Check

1 A neglected drive chain won't last long and will quickly damage the sprockets. Routine chain adjustment and lubrication isn't difficult and will ensure maximum chain and sprocket life.

2 To check the chain, place the bike on its sidestand and shift the transmission into neutral. Make sure the ignition switch is OFF.

3 Push up on the bottom run of the chain and measure the slack midway between the two sprockets, then compare your measurement to that listed for your model in this Chapter's Specifications (see illustration). As the chain stretches with wear, adjustment will periodically be necessary (see below). Since the chain will rarely wear evenly, roll the bike forward so that another section of chain can be checked (having an assistant to do this makes the task a lot easier); do this several times to check the entire length of chain, and mark the tightest spot.

Caution: Riding the bike with a chain that is too tight or too loose could lead to damage.

4 In some cases where lubrication has been neglected, corrosion and dirt may cause the links to bind and kink, which effectively shortens the chain's length and makes it tight (see illustration). Thoroughly clean and work free any such links, then highlight them with a marker pen or paint. Take the bike for a ride.

5 After the bike has been ridden, repeat the measurement for slack in the highlighted area. If the chain has kinked again and is still tight, replace it with a new one (see Chapter 6). A rusty, kinked or worn chain will damage the sprockets and a tight chain can damage transmission bearings. If in any doubt as to the condition of a chain, it is far better to install a new one than risk damage to other components and possibly yourself.

6 Check the entire length of the chain for damaged rollers, loose links and pins, and missing O-rings and replace it with a new one if necessary. *Note: Never install a new chain on old sprockets, and never use the old chain if you install new sprockets – replace the chain and sprockets as a set.*

Adjustment

CBF1000/A models

7 Move the bike so that the tightest point of the chain is at the centre of its bottom run, then put it on the sidestand.

8 Slacken the rear axle nut (see illustration).

9 Slacken the locknut on the adjuster on each side of the swingarm (see illustration). Turn

1.3 Push up on the chain and measure the slack

1.4 Neglect has caused the links in this chain to kink

1.8 Slacken the axle nut (arrowed)

1.9a Slacken the locknut (A) on each side, then turn each adjuster nut (B) as required

Routine maintenance and servicing 1•9

1.9b Make sure the index lines are in the same position each side relative to the slot in the swingarm. When the arrow aligns with the red zone, fit a new chain

1.13 Slacken the clamp bolt (arrowed)

each adjuster nut evenly until the amount of freeplay specified at the beginning of the Chapter is obtained at the centre of the bottom run of the chain – if the chain was slack turn the nuts clockwise; if the chain was tight turn them anti-clockwise, then move the wheel forwards in the swingarm to take up the gap. Following adjustment, check that the index lines on each adjustment marker are in the same position in relation to the rear edge of the slot in the swingarm (see illustration). It is important the position is the same on each side otherwise the rear wheel will be out of alignment with the front. Always make sure that the each adjuster nut is butted against the end of the swingarm. If there is a difference in the positions, adjust one side so that its position is exactly the same as the other. Check the chain freeplay again and readjust if necessary.

10 Also check the alignment of the wear decal on the left-hand side with the index arrow on the marker (see illustration 1.9b). When the index arrow meets the red REPLACE CHAIN zone, the drive chain has stretched excessively and must be replaced with a new one (see Chapter 6).

11 When adjustment is complete, counter-hold the adjuster nuts and tighten the locknuts (see illustration 1.9a). Now tighten the axle nut to the torque setting specified at the beginning of the Chapter (see illustration 1.8). Recheck the adjustment as above, then place the machine on its centrestand or an auxiliary stand and spin the wheel to make sure it runs freely.

CB1000R/RA models

12 Move the bike so that the tightest point of the chain is at the centre of its bottom run, then put it on the sidestand.

13 Slacken the rear wheel bearing holder clamp bolt on the swingarm (see illustration).

14 Using a suitable C-spanner, such as the one supplied in the bike's tool kit, rotate the bearing holder clockwise or anti-clockwise as required until the correct chain tension is obtained at the centre of the bottom run of the chain (see illustration).

15 Check the alignment of the wear decal on the caliper bracket with the index mark on the lug on the swingarm (see illustration). When the red REPLACE CHAIN zone aligns with the index mark, the drive chain has stretched excessively and must be replaced with a new one (see Chapter 6).

16 When the chain has the correct amount of slack, tighten the bearing holder clamp bolt to the torque setting specified at the beginning of the Chapter (see illustration 1.13).

Cleaning and lubrication

17 If required, wash the chain using a dedicated aerosol cleaner, or in paraffin (kerosene) or a suitable non-flammable or high flash-point solvent that will not damage the O-rings, using a soft brush to work any

1.14 Turn the bearing holder as required using the tool provided

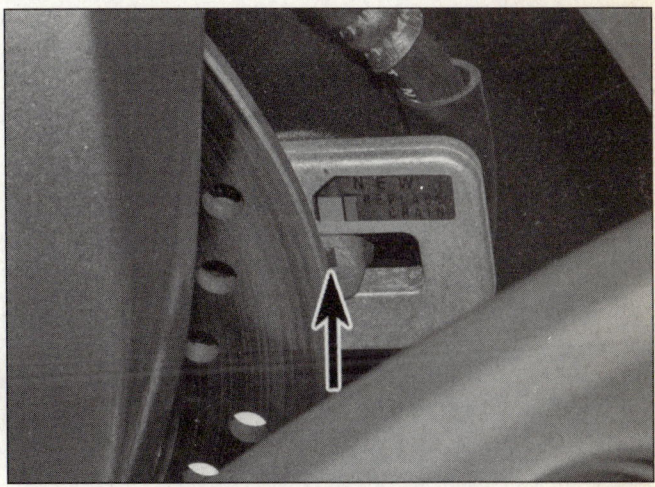

1.15 Check the alignment of the red zone on the decal with the index mark (arrowed) on the lug

1•10 Routine maintenance and servicing

1.17 Using a chain cleaning brush

1.18 Apply the lubricant to the overlapping sections of the sideplates

1.19a Check the sprocket teeth . . .

1.19b . . . in the areas indicated

dirt out if necessary **(see illustration)**. Wipe the cleaner off the chain and allow it to dry. If the chain is excessively dirty remove it from the machine and allow it to soak in the paraffin or solvent (see Chapter 6).
Caution: Don't use petrol (gasoline), an unsuitable solvent or other cleaning fluids which might damage the internal sealing properties of the chain. Don't use high-pressure water to clean the chain. The entire process shouldn't take longer than ten minutes, otherwise the O-rings could be damaged.

18 The best time to lubricate the chain is after the motorcycle has been ridden. When the chain is warm, the lubricant will penetrate the joints between the side plates better than when cold. **Note:** *Honda specifies SAE 80 to SAE 90 gear oil or an aerosol chain lube that it is suitable for O-ring chains; do not use any other chain lubricants – the solvents could damage the O-rings.* Apply the lubricant to the area where the sideplates overlap – not the middle of the rollers **(see illustration)**.

 Apply the lubricant to the top of the lower chain run, so centrifugal force will work the oil into the chain when the bike is moving. After applying the lubricant, let it soak in a few minutes before wiping off any excess.

1.20 Check the amount of wear on the slider (arrowed) – wear limit markers are provided top and bottom

⚠ **Warning: Take care not to get any lubricant on the tyres or brake system components. If any of the lubricant inadvertently contacts them, clean it off thoroughly using a suitable solvent or dedicated brake cleaner before riding the machine.**

Sprocket check

19 Remove the front sprocket cover (see Chapter 6). Check the teeth on the front and rear sprockets for wear **(see illustrations)**. If the teeth are worn excessively, replace the chain and both sprockets with a new set.
20 With the sprocket cover removed check the amount of wear on the chain slider around the front of the swingarm **(see illustration)** – if the rubbing surfaces of the slider have worn to the markers remove the swingarm and replace the slider with a new one (see Chapter 5). On CB1000R/RA models also check the chain guide in the middle of the swingarm.

Routine maintenance and servicing 1•11

2.1 Undo the screws and remove the cover

2.2 Release the clamp (arrowed)

2 Crankcase breather

Note: *The crankcase breather should be checked more frequently if the bike is constantly ridden in wet conditions or at full throttle, or if it has fallen over, or whenever deposits are seen in the drain collector.*

1 Remove the left-hand side cover (see Chapter 7). On CB1000R/RA models remove the air duct cover **(see illustration)**.
2 Release the clamp and remove the drain collector and allow any deposits to drain into a rag **(see illustration)**.
3 Clean the collector and check its condition – replace it with a new one if there are any cracks or splits. Fit the collector and secure it with the clamp.
4 Check the condition of the crankcase breather hose that runs between the left-hand end of the valve cover and the right-hand side of the air filter housing **(see illustration)**. Check for cracks and splits and replace it with a new one if any are evident. Make sure the hose is not kinked or trapped, and is securely connected at each end.
5 Install the cover(s).

3 Brake system

2.4 Crankcase breather hose (arrowed)

Brake pad wear check

1 Each brake pad has wear indicators in the form of grooves in the face of the friction material, or cut-outs in the side of the material **(see illustrations)**. The wear indicators should be plainly visible by looking from below each front caliper, and from behind the rear caliper, but note that an accumulation of road dirt and brake dust could make them difficult to see.
2 If the pads are worn to the bottom of the grooves or to the beginning of the cut-outs, they must be replaced with new ones. **Note:** *Some after-market pads may use different indicators to those on the original equipment.*
3 If the indicators aren't visible, then the amount of friction material remaining should be, and it will be obvious when the pads need

3.1a Brake pad wear indicator grooves (arrowed) – front caliper, CB1000R

3.1b Brake pad wear indicator cut-out (arrowed) – all calipers, CBF1000A

1•12 Routine maintenance and servicing

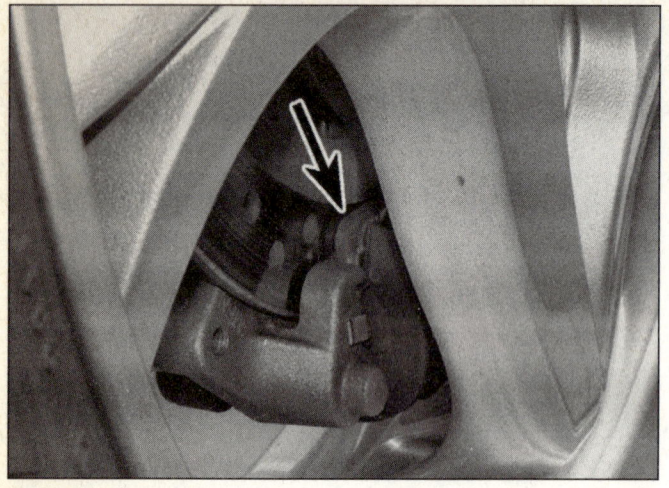

3.3 Brake pad friction material (arrowed) – rear caliper, CB1000R

3.10 Check all hoses, pipes and unions for cracks and leaks

replacing **(see illustration)**. Honda do not specify a minimum thickness for the friction material, but anything less than 1 mm should be considered excessively worn.

4 Also, with the exception of the single piston caliper fitted to the rear on standard CBF models, check for uneven wear in the brake pads, which is indicative of a sticking or seized piston. If found, the calipers must be overhauled (see Chapter 6).

5 If the pads are dirty or if you are in doubt as to the amount of friction material remaining, remove them for inspection (see Chapter 6). If the pads are excessively worn, also check the brake discs (see Chapter 6).

6 Refer to Chapter 6 for details of pad removal and installation.

Brake system check

7 A routine general check of the brake system will ensure that any problems are discovered and remedied before the rider's safety is jeopardised.

8 Check the brake pads for wear (see above) and make sure the fluid level in the reservoirs is correct (see *Pre-ride checks*).

9 Check the brake lever and pedal pivots for sloppy or rough action, excessive play, bends, and other damage. Replace any damaged parts with new ones (see Chapter 5). Clean and lubricate the lever and pedal pivots if their action is stiff or rough (see Section 16). If the lever or pedal is spongy, bleed the brakes (see Chapter 6).

10 Look for leaks at the hose and pipe connections and check for cracks in the hoses, pipes and unions **(see illustration)**. If leakage or cracked or damaged hoses are found, renew the hoses as described in Chapter 6. Make sure all brake hose and pipe fasteners are tight. Similarly check for any signs of fluid leakage from the caliper and master cylinder – overhaul and seal renewal will be necessary if found (see Chapter 6).

11 Make sure the brake light operates when the front brake lever is pulled in. The front brake light switch, mounted on the underside of the master cylinder, is not adjustable. If it fails to operate properly, check it (see Chapter 8).

12 Make sure the brake light is activated just before the rear brake takes effect. The rear brake light switch is mounted behind the right-hand footrest bracket. If adjustment is necessary, hold the switch body and turn the adjuster ring until the brake light is activated when required – do not turn the switch itself **(see illustrations)**. If the brake light comes on too late or not at all, turn the ring clockwise so the switch is drawn up out of its bracket. If the brake light comes on too soon or is permanently on, turn the ring anti-clockwise so the switch is drawn down into the bracket. If the switch doesn't operate the brake light, check it (see Chapter 8).

13 On CBF1000A and CB1000RA models raise the front wheel off the ground; do this on CBF1000A models by placing the bike on its centrestand and having an assistant press down on the rear, and on CB1000RA models

3.12a Rear brake light switch adjuster ring (arrowed) – CBF/A models

3.12b Rear brake light switch adjuster ring (arrowed) – CB-R/RA models

Routine maintenance and servicing 1•13

3.14a On CBF/A models push the lever away and turn the adjuster as required . . .

3.14b . . . aligning the notch with the index mark

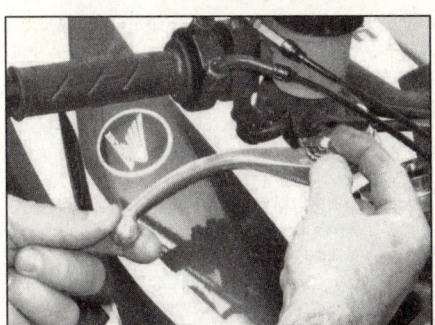

3.14c On CB-R/A models push the lever away and turn the adjuster . . .

by using a front paddock stand. Press the rear brake pedal down and check that the front wheel is locked by the brake. If the wheel can be turned, the linked braking system (CBS) is faulty and must be checked (see Chapter 6).

14 The front brake lever has a span adjuster which alters the distance of the lever from the handlebar. On CBF1000/A models each setting is identified by a notch in the adjuster ring aligning with the arrow on the lever – push the lever away from the handlebar and turn the adjuster ring to alter the span, making sure that the notch specific to the desired setting is aligned with the arrow on the lever **(see illustrations)**. On CB1000R/RA models each setting is identified by a number on the adjuster aligning with the triangular index mark on the lever – push the lever away from the handlebar and turn the adjuster ring until the setting which best suits the rider is obtained, then release the lever **(see illustration)**. Do not set the adjuster between the defined settings.

15 The height of the rear brake pedal can be adjusted to suit the rider's preference if required. Slacken the locknut securing the clevis on the master cylinder pushrod, then turn the pushrod using a spanner on the hex at the top of the rod until the pedal is at the desired height **(see illustration)**. On completion tighten the locknut. Note that at a low setting the bottom of the pushrod must clear the clevis by 1 mm and at a high setting must still be visible under the top of the clevis. Adjust the rear brake light switch after adjusting the pedal height (see Step 11).

Brake fluid change

16 The brake fluid should be changed at the prescribed interval. Refer to Chapter 6 for details. Ensure that all the old fluid is pumped from the hydraulic system and that the level in the fluid reservoir is checked and the brakes tested before riding the motorcycle.

4 Clutch

Clutch check

1 All models are fitted with an hydraulic clutch. Make sure the fluid level in the reservoir is correct (see *Pre-ride checks*).

3.14d . . . aligning the required setting with the index mark

3.15 Slacken the locknut (A) and turn the pushrod using the hex (B) to adjust pedal height

1•14 Routine maintenance and servicing

4.4 Check the clutch hose and unions for cracks and leaks

5.2 Check all fuel tank and throttle body hoses, and the fuel rail and injector joints – throttle bodies shown removed

2 Check the clutch lever pivot and pushrod for sloppy or rough action, excessive play, bends, and other damage. Replace any damaged parts with new ones (see Chapter 5). Clean and lubricate the lever pivot and pushrod components if lever action is stiff or rough (see Section 16).

3 Check the operation of the clutch. If there is evidence of air in the system (spongy feel to the lever, difficulty in engaging gear, drag when in gear), bleed the clutch (see Chapter 2). If the lever feels stiff or sticky, overhaul the release mechanism (see Chapter 2).

4 Look for leaks at the hose connections and check for cracks in the hose (see illustration). If leakage or a cracked or damaged hose is found, renew the hose as described in Chapter 2. Similarly check for any signs of fluid leakage from the release cylinder and master cylinder – overhaul and seal renewal will be necessary if found (see Chapter 2).

5 The clutch lever has a span adjuster which alters the distance of the lever from the handlebar in exactly the same way as the front brake lever – refer to Section 3, Step 14 for details.

Clutch fluid change

6 The clutch fluid should be changed at the prescribed interval. Refer to Chapter 2 for details. Ensure that all the old fluid is pumped from the system and that the level in the fluid reservoir is checked and the clutch tested before riding the motorcycle.

5 Fuel system

Warning: *Petrol (gasoline) is extremely flammable, so take extra precautions when you work on any part of the fuel system. Don't smoke or allow open flames or bare light bulbs near the work area, and don't work in a garage where a natural gas-type appliance is present. If you spill any fuel on your skin, rinse it off immediately with soap and water. When you perform any kind of work on the fuel system, wear safety glasses and have a fire extinguisher suitable for a Class B type fire (flammable liquids) on hand.*

1 Remove the fuel tank (see Chapter 4).

2 Check the fuel tank, the fuel supply hose, the tank drain and breather hoses, the throttle body vacuum hoses and idle system hoses for signs of leaks, cracks, deterioration or damage (see illustration). In particular check that there are no leaks from the fuel hose or hose unions. Replace hoses with new ones as required, referring to the relevant section in Chapter 4.

3 Check the joint between the fuel pump mounting plate and the tank, and on CB1000R/RA models between the fuel level sensor and the tank. If there is evidence of fuel leakage, check the mounting nuts are tight (see Chapter 4 Specifications for the pump plate nut torque setting). If the leak persists, remove the pump or level sensor as required and fit a new seal (see Chapter 4).

4 Inspect the joints between the fuel rails, the injectors and the throttle bodies (see illustration 5.2). If there are any leaks, remove the fuel rails and fit new seals and O-rings to the injectors and/or rails as required (see Chapter 4).

6 Throttle cables

1 Make sure the throttle grip rotates smoothly and freely from fully closed to fully open with the front wheel turned at various angles. The grip should return automatically from fully open to fully closed when released.

2 If the throttle sticks, this is probably due to a cable fault. Remove the cables (see Chapter 4) and lubricate them (see Section 16). Check that the inner cables slide freely and easily in the outer cables. If not, replace the cables with new ones.

3 With the cables removed, make sure the throttle twistgrip rotates freely on the handlebar – dirt combined with a lack of lubrication can cause the action to be stiff. If necessary, undo the handlebar end-weight screw and remove the end-weight, then slide the twistgrip off the handlebar (see illustration). Clean any old grease from the bar and the inside of the tube. Smear some multi-purpose grease onto the bar, then refit the twistgrip. When fitting the end-weight, align the boss with the cut-out on the inner weight inside the handlebar. Clean the threads of the screw, then apply a suitable non-permanent thread locking compound, hold the weight and tighten the screw. Install the cables, making sure they are correctly routed (see Chapter 4). If this fails to improve the operation of the throttle, the cables must be replaced with new ones. Note that in very rare cases the fault could lie in the throttle bodies. Remove the air filter housing (see Chapter 4) and check the action of the throttle pulley and linkage.

4 With the throttle operating smoothly, check for a small amount of freeplay in the cables, measured in terms of the amount of twistgrip rotation before the throttle opens,

6.3 Undo the screw to free the end-weight and twistgrip

Routine maintenance and servicing 1•15

6.4 Throttle cable freeplay is measured in terms of twistgrip rotation

6.5 Slacken the adjuster locknut (A) and turn the adjuster (B) as required

and compare the amount to that listed in this Chapter's Specifications **(see illustration)**. If it's incorrect, adjust the cables to correct it as follows.

5 Initially adjust freeplay using the adjuster in the throttle opening cable where it leaves the throttle pulley housing on the handlebar. Loosen the locknut and turn the adjuster in or out as required until the specified amount of freeplay is obtained (see this Chapter's Specifications), then retighten the locknut **(see illustration)**.

6 If the adjuster has reached its limit of adjustment, reset it to its start point by turning it fully in, so that freeplay is at a maximum, then raise or remove the fuel tank (see Chapter 4) to access the adjuster at the throttle body end.

7 The adjuster is on the rear cable in the bracket. Slacken the adjuster locknut, then screw the adjuster in or out as required, making sure the captive nut remains held in the bracket, thereby threading itself along the adjuster as you turn it, until the specified amount of freeplay is obtained, then tighten the locknut **(see illustration)**. Subsequent adjustments can be made at the throttle twistgrip end when required. If the cable cannot be adjusted as specified, replace it with a new one (see Chapter 4). Check that the throttle twistgrip operates smoothly and snaps shut quickly when released.

⚠ *Warning: Turn the handlebars all the way through their travel with the engine idling. Idle speed should not change. If it does, the cables may be routed incorrectly. Correct this condition before riding the bike.*

7 Spark plugs

Check

1 Make sure your spark plug socket is the correct size before attempting to remove the plugs – a suitable one is supplied in the motorcycle's tool kit which is stored under the passenger seat.

CBF1000/A models

Special tool: A wire gauge or feeler gauge set is necessary for measuring the spark plug gap (see illustration 7.10a).

2 Remove the fuel tank (see Chapter 4). Displace the Nos. 1 and 4 cylinder ignition coil to improve access to the Nos. 1 and 2 spark plug caps on the left-hand side (see Chapter 4). To further improve access to the No. 3 cap disconnect the crankcase breather hose and unscrew the thermostat housing bolt to allow some movement **(see illustration)**.

3 Clean the area around each spark plug cap to prevent any dirt falling into the spark plug channels.

4 Work on one spark plug at a time. Pull the cap off the plug **(see illustration 7.16)**.

5 Using either the plug removing tool supplied in the bike's toolkit or a deep spark plug socket and extension, unscrew and remove the plug **(see illustrations 7.17a and b)**.

6.7 Throttle cable adjuster locknut (A) and adjuster (B)

7.2 Detach the hose (A), then unscrew the bolt (B)

1•16 Routine maintenance and servicing

7.10a Using a feeler blade to measure the spark plug electrode gap

7.10b Adjusting the electrode gap

As the plugs are quite recessed, slip a short length of hose over the end of the plug to use as a tool to thread it into place. The hose will grip the plug well enough to turn it, but will start to slip if the plug begins to cross-thread in the hole – this will prevent damaged threads.

Stripped plug threads in the cylinder head can be repaired with a thread insert – see 'Tools and Workshop Tips' in the Reference section.

6 Before cleaning the plug refer to the colour spark plug chart at the end of this manual and compare the firing end of each plug to those shown, identifying any abnormal condition and assessing its cause if necessary.
7 Clean the electrodes using a wire brush – if any deposits do not come off replace the plugs with new ones. Cleaning spark plugs by sandblasting is fine as long as you clean the plugs with a high flash-point solvent afterwards. Also clean any deposits off the white ceramic body of the plug.
8 Check the condition of the cleaned electrodes. Both the centre and side electrodes should have square edges and the side electrodes should be of uniform thickness. Check for evidence of a cracked or chipped insulator around the centre electrode. Check the plug threads, the washer and the ceramic insulator body for cracks and other damage.
9 If in doubt concerning the condition of the plugs, replace them with new ones, as the expense is minimal.
10 If the plugs can be re-used check the gap between the electrodes with a wire type gauge or feeler gauge **(see illustration)**. The gap should be as given in the Specifications at the beginning of this chapter. If the electrodes have worn and the gap is wider than it should be, or for some reason the gap is narrower than it should be (if the plug has been dropped for instance) carefully bend the outer electrode as required to restore the correct gap **(see illustration)**.
11 Fit the plug into the end of the tool, then use the tool to insert the plug **(see illustration 7.17b)**. Alternatively there are dedicated plug insertion tools, or you can use some hose (see **Haynes Hint**). Thread the plugs as far as possible into the head turning the tool or hose by hand, making sure they do not cross-thread. Once the plugs are finger-tight, tighten them using a spanner on the tool supplied or a socket drive **(see illustration 7.17a)**. If a torque wrench can be applied, tighten the spark plugs to the torque setting specified at the beginning of the Chapter. Otherwise, if new plugs are being used tighten them by 1/2 a turn after the washer has seated, and if the old plugs are being reused tighten them by 1/8 to 1/4 turn after they have seated, according to feel. Do not over-tighten them.
12 Fit the cap onto the plug and push it down so it is fully seated **(see illustration 7.16)**.
13 Install all displaced and removed components (see Step 2).

CB1000R/RA models

Special tool: *A wire gauge is necessary for this job – do not use a blade type gauge* **(see illustration 7.10b)**.
14 Remove the fuel tank (see Chapter 4). Displace and support the coolant reservoir **(see illustration)**. Displace the ignition coils as required on either side to improve access (see Chapter 4).
15 Clean the area around each combined ignition coil/spark plug cap to prevent any dirt falling into the spark plug channels.
16 Work on one spark plug at a time. Pull the cap off the plug **(see illustration)**.
17 Using either the plug removing tool

7.14 Unscrew the bolts (arrowed) then displace and support the reservoir

7.16 Pull the cap off the plug

Routine maintenance and servicing 1•17

7.17a Unscrew the plug . . .

7.17b . . . and lift it out with the tool - the rubber insert should grip around the plug top

supplied in the bike's toolkit or a deep spark plug socket, unscrew and remove the plug **(see illustrations)**.

18 Check the condition of the electrodes, referring to the spark plug reading chart at the end of this manual if signs of contamination are evident. Note that contaminated iridium plugs should not be cleaned – discard them and install new ones.

19 Examine the pointed iridium-tipped centre electrode; if the tip has rounded off, the plug is worn **(see illustration)**. Measure the gap between the two electrodes with a wire type gauge only **(see illustration)** – do not use blade type feeler gauges because the iridium tip might be damaged. The gap should be as given in the Specifications at the beginning of this chapter; if the electrodes have worn and the gap is 1 mm or more, or for some reason the gap is narrower than it should be (if the plug has been dropped for instance) a new plug must be installed. Do not bend the outer electrode to adjust the gap.

20 Check the threads, the washer and the ceramic insulator body for cracks and other damage.

21 Note that Honda advise that the specified iridium plugs only must be fitted – do not substitute with conventional plugs.

22 Fit the plug into the end of the tool, then use the tool to insert the plug **(see illustration 7.17b)**. Since the cylinder head is made of aluminium, which is soft and easily damaged,

thread the plugs as far as possible into the head turning the tool by hand. Once the plugs are finger-tight, the job can be finished with a spanner on the tool supplied or a socket drive **(see illustration 7.17a)**. If a torque wrench can be applied, tighten the spark plugs to the torque setting specified at the beginning of the Chapter. Otherwise, if new plugs are being used tighten them by 1/2 a turn after the washer has seated, and if the old plugs are being reused tighten them by 1/8 to 1/4 turn after they have seated. Do not over-tighten them.

23 Fit the cap onto the plug and push it down so it is fully seated **(see illustration 7.16)**.

24 Install all displaced and removed components (see Step 2).

Renewal

25 At the prescribed interval, whatever the condition of the existing spark plugs, remove the plugs as described above and install new ones.

8 Engine oil and filter

Special tool: *A filter removing tool is necessary for this job. You can purchase one as a Honda spare part (as a kit along with the oil filter or separately) or alternatively there are several after-market options (see Step 6).*

 Warning: *Be careful when draining the oil, as the exhaust, the engine, and the oil itself can cause severe burns.*

1 Consistent routine oil and filter changes are the single most important maintenance procedure you can perform. The oil not only lubricates the internal parts of the engine, transmission and clutch, but it also acts as a coolant, a cleaner, a sealant, and a protector. Because of these demands, the oil takes a terrific amount of abuse and should be replaced often with new oil of the recommended grade and type. The oil filter should be changed with every oil change.

> **HAYNES HINT** *Saving a little money on the difference in cost between a good oil and a cheap oil won't pay off if the engine is damaged.*

2 Before changing the oil, warm up the engine so the oil will drain easily. On CBF1000A models place the bike on its centrestand on level ground. On all other models support the bike upright using an auxiliary stand. The oil drain plug is in the front of the sump on the left-hand side, and the filter is on the left-hand side of the engine at the front.

3 Unscrew the oil filter cover bolts and remove the cover **(see illustration)**.

7.19a Check the iridium tip of the electrode for wear and damage

7.19b Use a wire gauge to check for wear of the electrode

8.3 Unscrew the bolts (arrowed) and remove the cover

1•18 Routine maintenance and servicing

8.4 Unscrew the oil filler cap to act as a vent

8.5a Unscrew the oil drain plug . . .

8.5b . . . and allow the oil to completely drain

8.5c Depending on the type, the sealing washer may need to be cut off

4 Unscrew the oil filler cap from the clutch cover to vent the crankcase and to act as a reminder that there is no oil in the engine **(see illustration)**.
5 Position a large clean drain tray below the engine, so it is under the drain plug and the filter. Unscrew the oil drain plug and allow the oil to flow into the tray **(see illustrations)**. Discard the sealing washer and replace it with a new one **(see illustration)**.
6 Unscrew the filter using a filter socket (one can be obtained with the new filter from Honda dealers under part No. 07HAA-PJ70101, or otherwise there are commercially available equivalents available), filter pliers, or a filter removing strap or a chain-wrench, and tip any residual oil into the drain tray **(see illustrations)**. The filter socket is preferable

8.6a Unscrew the filter using a filter removing socket or strap . . .

8.6b . . . and allow the oil to drain

Routine maintenance and servicing 1•19

8.7a Fit the drain plug using a new sealing washer...

8.7b ...and tighten it to the specified torque

8.8 Measure the length of exposed thread

8.9a Smear clean oil onto the seal...

8.9b ...then fit the filter and tighten it as described

because it provides a means of tightening the new filter to the correct torque.

7 When the oil has completely drained, fit the new sealing washer onto the plug, then fit the plug into the sump and tighten it to the torque setting specified at the beginning of the Chapter **(see illustrations)**. Do not overtighten it as the threads in the sump are easily damaged.

8 Before fitting the filter measure the length of exposed thread on the oil filter boss to check that it didn't unscrew when removing the filter – there should be 14.4 to 15.4 mm of thread exposed **(see illustration)**.

9 Smear clean engine oil onto the threads and rubber seal on the new filter, then thread the filter onto the engine **(see illustrations)**. Tighten it to the specified torque setting using the filter socket if available, or tighten the filter as tight as possible by hand, or by the number of turns specified on the filter itself or its packaging. **Note:** *Do not use a strap or chain-type filter removing tool to tighten the filter as you will damage it.*

10 Refill the engine to the proper level using the recommended type and amount of oil (see Specifications) **(see illustration)**. With the motorcycle vertical, the oil level should lie between the upper and lower level lines on the inspection window **(see illustration)**. Check

8.10a Add the specified type and amount of oil...

8.10b ...so the level is between the level lines (arrowed)

1•20 Routine maintenance and servicing

the condition of the O-ring on the filler cap and replace it with a new one if it is damaged or worn **(see illustration 8.4)**. Fit the filler cap.

11 Start the engine and let it run for two or three minutes (make sure that the oil pressure light extinguishes after a few seconds). Shut it off, wait a few minutes, then check the oil level again. If necessary, add more oil to bring the level close to the upper line, but do not go above it.

12 Check around the drain plug and the filter for leaks. If leaks are evident, and the plug and filter are correctly tightened using a new washer and a lubricated seal, there is another cause which must be investigated before riding the bike.

13 Fit the oil filter cover.

14 The old oil drained from the engine cannot be re-used and should be disposed of properly. Check with your local refuse disposal company, disposal facility or environmental agency to see whether they will accept the used oil for recycling. Don't pour used oil into drains or onto the ground.

> **HAYNES HiNT**
>
> *Check the old oil carefully – if it is very metallic coloured, then the engine is experiencing wear from break-in (new engine) or from insufficient lubrication. If there are flakes or chips of metal in the oil, then something is drastically wrong internally and the engine will have to be disassembled for inspection and repair. If there are pieces of fibre-like material in the oil, the clutch is experiencing excessive wear and should be checked.*

9 Cooling system

Check

⚠️ **Warning: The engine must be cool before beginning this procedure.**

1 Check the coolant level in the reservoir (see *Pre-ride checks*).

2 On CBF1000/A models remove the fairing side panels (see Chapter 7). On CB1000R/RA models remove the radiator shroud (see Chapter 7). On all models remove the fuel tank (see Chapter 4).

3 Check the entire cooling system for evidence of leaks. Examine each rubber coolant hose along its entire length. Look for cracks, abrasions and other damage. Squeeze each hose at various points to see whether they are dried out or hard **(see illustration)**. They should feel firm, yet pliable, and return to their original shape when released. If necessary, replace them with new ones (see Chapter 3).

4 Check for evidence of leaks at each cooling system hose connection, and around the pump on the left-hand side of the engine, at the inlet union on the left-hand end of the cylinder block and the outlet union on the back of the cylinder head, at the thermostat housing, and around the oil cooler on the front of the engine. Tighten the hose clips carefully to prevent future leaks. If the pump is leaking around the cover, check that the bolts are tight. If they are, remove the cover and replace the cover and cover plate O-rings with new ones (see Chapter 3).

5 To prevent leakage of coolant from the cooling system to the lubrication system and vice versa, two seals are fitted on the pump shaft. The coolant seal on the water pump side is of the mechanical type which bears on the rear face of the impeller. The oil seal, which is mounted behind the mechanical seal is of the normal feathered lip type. On the underside of the pump housing there is a drain hole **(see illustration)**. If either seal fails, the drain allows the coolant or oil to escape. If on inspection the drain shows signs of continuous leakage, particularly with the engine running, remove the pump and replace it with a new one (see Chapter 3) – it comes as an assembly and the seals are not available separately. Note that a small amount of coolant weeping is normal – if in doubt seek the advice of your dealer.

6 Check the radiator on the front of the engine for leaks and other damage **(see illustration)**. Leaks in the radiator leave tell-tale scale deposits or coolant stains on the outside of the core below the leak. If leaks are noted, remove the radiator (see Chapter 3) and have it repaired or replace it with a new one – do not use a liquid leak stopping compound to try to repair leaks.

7 Check the radiator fins for mud, dirt and insects, which may impede the flow of air through it. If the fins are dirty, remove the radiator (see Chapter 3) and clean it using water or low pressure compressed air directed through the fins from the inner side of the radiator. If the fins are bent or distorted, straighten them carefully with a screwdriver. If the air flow is restricted by bent or damaged fins over more than 20% of the radiator's surface area, replace the radiator with a new one.

⚠️ **Warning: Do not remove the pressure cap when the engine is hot. It is good practice to cover the cap with a heavy cloth and turn the cap slowly anti-clockwise. If you hear a hissing sound (indicating that there is still pressure in the system), wait until it stops, then continue turning the cap until it can be removed.**

8 Remove the pressure cap from the filler neck by turning it anti-clockwise until it reaches the stop. If you hear a hissing sound (indicating there is still pressure in the system), wait until it stops. Now press down on the cap and continue turning it until it can be removed **(see illustration)**.

9 Check the condition of the coolant in the system. If it is rust-coloured or if accumulations of scale are visible, drain, flush and refill the system with new coolant (see below). Check the antifreeze content of the coolant with an antifreeze hydrometer – a 50% content

9.3 Check all the coolant hoses as described

9.5 Check the pump drain hole (arrowed) for signs of leakage

9.6 Check the radiator and fins as described

9.8 Remove the pressure cap as described

Routine maintenance and servicing 1•21

9.12 Check the oil cooler (arrowed) and its hoses for leaks and damage

9.15a Unscrew the bolt (arrowed) . . .

9.15b . . . and allow the coolant to drain

should give a reading of 1.084 at 5°C to 1.074 at 25°C, varying accordingly in between. The system must have the correct coolant mixture (see Specifications) – if the coolant is too weak (too little anti-freeze) there will not be adequate protection against freezing and corrosion, and if it is too strong the ability to cool the engine is reduced. If the hydrometer indicates an incorrect mixture, drain, flush and refill the system (see below).

10 The function of the pressure cap is crucial to the correct running of the cooling system. Check the cap seal for cracks and other damage. If the coolant level consistently drops and/or the bike overheats, and no evidence of leaks can be found, have the cap pressure checked by a Honda dealer, or just fit a new one – the expense is minimal. If a new cap does not cure the problem have the entire system pressure checked by a dealer.

11 Fit the cap by turning it clockwise until it reaches the first stop then push down on it and continue turning until it can turn no further. Start the engine and let it reach normal operating temperature, then check for leaks again. As the coolant temperature increases, the electric fan (mounted on the back of the radiator) should come on automatically and the temperature should begin to drop. If not, refer to Chapter 3 and check the fan and fan circuit.

12 Check the oil cooler on the front of the engine for any signs of oil leakage between it and the engine **(see illustration)**. If there is leakage check the cooler bolts are tight. If the leakage persists you will have to fit a new O-ring between the cooler and the engine (see Chapter 2). Check that the coolant hoses are secure on the unions, and that there is no evidence of coolant leakage from the body of the cooler. If there is, the cooler is damaged and must be replaced with a new one.

Change the coolant

⚠️ **Warning:** *Allow the engine to cool completely before performing this maintenance operation. Also, don't allow anti-freeze to come into contact with your skin or the painted surfaces of the motorcycle. Rinse off spills immediately with plenty of water. Anti-freeze is highly toxic if ingested. Never leave anti-freeze lying around in an open container or in puddles on the floor; children and pets are attracted by its sweet smell and may drink it. Check with local authorities (councils) about disposing of anti-freeze. Many communities have collection centres which will see that anti-freeze is disposed of safely. Anti-freeze is also combustible, so don't store it near open flames.*

Draining

13 Remove the fuel tank (see Chapter 4). On CBF1000/A models remove the battery (see Chapter 8).

14 Remove the pressure cap from the filler neck on the thermostat cover by turning it anti-clockwise until it reaches a stop **(see illustration 9.8)**. If you hear a hissing sound (indicating there is still pressure in the system), wait until it stops. Now press down on the cap and continue turning the cap until it can be removed. Also remove the coolant reservoir cap.

15 Position a suitable container beneath the water pump on the left-hand side of the engine. Unscrew the drain bolt and allow the coolant to completely drain **(see illustrations)**. A new sealing washer is needed, but keep the old one for use during flushing if required.

16 On CBF1000/A models trace the radiator overflow hose from the filler neck to the joint in the back of the battery housing, then release the clamp, disconnect the hose at the hose joint and drain the reservoir into the container. On CB1000R/RA models disconnect the radiator overflow hose from the bottom of the reservoir and allow the reservoir to drain into the container **(see illustrations)**.

Flushing

17 Flush the system with clean tap water by inserting a hose in the filler neck. Allow the water to run through the system until it is clear and flows out cleanly. If the radiator is extremely corroded, remove it (see Chapter 3) and have it cleaned by a specialist. Also flush the reservoir, then reconnect the hose.

18 Clean the drain hole then fit the drain bolt using the old sealing washer.

19 Fill the cooling system via the filler neck with clean water mixed with a flushing compound **(see illustration 9.25)**. Make sure the flushing compound is compatible with aluminium components, and follow the manufacturer's instructions carefully. Fit the pressure cap.

20 Start the engine and allow it to reach normal operating temperature. Let it run for about ten minutes.

21 Stop the engine. Let it cool for a while, then cover the pressure cap with a heavy rag and turn it anti-clockwise to the first stop, releasing any pressure that may be present in the system. Once the hissing stops, push down on the cap and remove it completely.

22 Drain the system once again.

23 Fill the system with clean water and repeat Steps 20 to 22.

Refilling

24 Fit the drain bolt using a new sealing washer and tighten it to the torque setting specified at

9.16a Detach the hose . . .

9.16b . . . and allow the reservoir to drain

1•22 Routine maintenance and servicing

9.24 Fit the drain bolt using a new sealing washer

9.25 Fill the system as described

the beginning of the Chapter. Reconnect the reservoir hose **(see illustration)**.

25 Fill the system to the base of the radiator filler neck with the proper coolant mixture (see this Chapter's Specifications) **(see illustration)**. *Note: Pour the coolant in slowly to minimise the amount of air entering the system, and when full carefully waggle the bike from side to side to dislodge any trapped air.* Fill the reservoir to the UPPER level line (see *Pre-ride checks*).

26 Start the engine and allow it to idle for 2 to 3 minutes. Flick the throttle twistgrip part open 3 or 4 times, so that the engine speed rises to approximately 4000 to 5000 rpm, then stop the engine. Any air trapped in the system should bleed back to the radiator filler neck.

27 If necessary, top up the coolant level to the base of the radiator filler neck, then fit the pressure cap. Also top up the coolant reservoir to the UPPER level line and fit the cap.

28 Start the engine and allow it to reach normal operating temperature, then shut it off. Let the engine cool then remove the pressure cap as described in Step 21. Check that the coolant level is still up to the base of the upper radiator filler neck. If it's low, add the specified mixture until it reaches the base of the filler neck. Refit the cap.

29 Check the coolant level in the reservoir and top up if necessary.

30 Check the system for leaks. Install the fuel tank (see Chapter 4). On CBF1000/A models install the battery (see Chapter 8).

31 Do not dispose of the old coolant by pouring it down the drain. Instead pour it into a heavy plastic container, cap it tightly and take it into an authorised disposal site or service station – see *Warning* at the beginning of this Section.

Hose renewal

32 The hoses will deteriorate with age and should be replaced with new ones regardless of their apparent condition (see Chapter 3).

10 PAIR (Pulse secondary air supply) system

1 To reduce the amount of unburned hydrocarbons released in the exhaust gases, a pulse secondary air supply (PAIR) system is fitted. The system consists of the control valve (mounted above the valve cover on the top of the engine), the reed valves (fitted in the valve cover) and the hoses between the air filter housing, the control valve and the reed valves. The control valve is actuated electronically by the ECM.

2 Under normal operating conditions, the valve allows filtered air to be drawn through the reed valves and cylinder head passages and into the exhaust ports. The air mixes with the exhaust gases, causing any unburned particles of the fuel in the mixture to be burnt in the exhaust port/pipes. This process changes a considerable amount of hydrocarbons and carbon monoxide into relatively harmless carbon dioxide and water. The reed valves in the valve cover are fitted to prevent the flow of exhaust gases back up the cylinder head passages and into the air filter housing.

3 The system is not adjustable and requires little maintenance. Raise the fuel tank (see Chapter 4). Check that the hoses are not kinked or pinched, are in good condition and are securely connected at each end **(see illustration)**. Replace any hoses that are cracked, split or generally deteriorated with new ones.

4 Refer to Chapter 4 for further information on the system and for checks if it is believed to be faulty.

11 Headlight aim

Note: An improperly adjusted headlight may cause problems for oncoming traffic or provide poor, unsafe illumination of the road ahead. Before adjusting the headlight aim, be sure to consult with local traffic laws and regulations – for UK models refer to MOT Test Checks in the Reference section.

1 The headlight beam can adjusted both horizontally and vertically. Before making any adjustment, check that the tyre pressures are correct and the suspension is adjusted as required. Make any adjustments to the headlight aim with the machine off its stand and on level ground, with the fuel tank half full and with an assistant sitting on the seat. If the bike is usually ridden with a passenger on the back, have a second assistant to do this.

CBF1000/A models

2 Remove the fairing side panels (see Chapter 7). Vertical adjustment is made by turning the adjuster knob on the top of the relevant beam unit **(see illustration)**. Turn it clockwise to move the beam up, and anti-clockwise to move it down.

3 Horizontal adjustment is made by turning the adjuster knob on the bottom of the

10.3 Check the PAIR system hoses (A) as described. PAIR control valve (B)

11.2 Vertical adjusters (A), horizontal adjusters (B) – CBF

Routine maintenance and servicing 1•23

11.4 Vertical adjuster (A), horizontal adjuster (B) – CB-R

12.1a Check the sidestand springs (arrowed) . . .

relevant beam unit **(see illustration 11.2)**. When adjusting the left-hand beam turn the adjuster clockwise to move the beam to the right, and anti-clockwise to move it to the left. When adjusting the right-hand beam turn the adjuster clockwise to move the beam to the left, and anti-clockwise to move it to the right.

CB1000R/RA models

4 Vertical adjustment is made by turning the adjuster knob on the top of the beam unit **(see illustration)**. Turn it clockwise to move the beam up, and anti-clockwise to move it down.

5 Horizontal adjustment is made by turning the adjuster knob on the bottom of the beam unit **(see illustration 11.4)**. Turn the adjuster clockwise to move the beam to the right, and anti-clockwise to move it to the left.

12 Sidestand, centrestand and starter interlock circuit

1 Check the stand springs for damage and distortion **(see illustrations)**. The springs must be capable of retracting the stand fully and holding it retracted when the motorcycle is in use. If a spring is sagged or broken it must be replaced with a new one.

2 Lubricate the stand pivots regularly (see Section 16).

3 Check the stand and its mount(s) for bends and cracks. Stands can often be repaired by welding.

4 Check the operation of the starter interlock circuit as follows:

- Make sure the transmission is in neutral, then retract the stand and start the engine. Pull in the clutch lever and select a gear. Keeping the clutch lever pulled in, extend the sidestand. The engine should stop as the sidestand is extended.
- Make sure the engine is in neutral and the sidestand is down, then start the engine. Pull the clutch lever in and select a gear. The engine should cut out.
- Check that when the sidestand is down the engine can only be started if the transmission is in neutral, and when the sidestand is up and the transmission is in gear the engine can only be started if the clutch lever is pulled in.

5 If the circuit does not operate as described, check the sidestand switch, neutral switch, clutch switch and diodes, and the circuit between them (see Chapter 8).

13 Suspension

1 The suspension components must be maintained in top operating condition to ensure rider safety. Loose, worn or damaged suspension parts decrease the motorcycle's stability and control.

Front suspension check

2 While standing alongside the motorcycle, apply the front brake and push on the handlebars to compress the forks several times. See if they move up-and-down smoothly without binding **(see illustration)**. If binding is felt, the forks should be disassembled and inspected (see Chapter 5).

3 Inspect each fork inner tube for scratches, corrosion and pitting in the area of travel

12.1b . . . and on CBF1000A the centrestand springs (arrowed) as described

13.2 Compress the forks to check their action. Check the inner tube (A) for pitting and signs of oil leakage

1•24 Routine maintenance and servicing

13.4 Check for leakage above the dust seal (arrowed), then lever it up and check for corrosion below

13.7 Compress the rear suspension to check its action

through the seals, which will cause seal failure **(see illustration 13.2)** – if the damage is excessive, new inner tubes should be fitted (see Chapter 5), or the fitted ones must be re-chromed using hard chrome.

4 Also check the inner tubes for signs of oil leakage. Carefully lever the dust seal out using a flat-bladed screwdriver and inspect the area around the oil seal **(see illustration)**. If leakage is evident, the seals must be replaced with new ones (see Chapter 5). If there is evidence of corrosion between the oil seal retaining ring and its groove in the fork tube, spray the area with a penetrative lubricant, otherwise the ring will be difficult to remove if needed. Press the dust seal back into the outer tube on completion.

5 Check the tightness of all suspension nuts and bolts to be sure none have worked loose, referring to the torque settings specified at the beginning of Chapter 5.

Rear suspension check

6 Inspect the rear shock absorber for fluid leakage. If leakage is found, the shock must be replaced with a new one (see Chapter 5).

7 With the aid of an assistant to support the bike, compress the rear suspension several times **(see illustration)**. It should move up-and-down freely without binding. If any binding is felt, the worn or faulty component must be identified and checked. The problem could be due to either the shock absorber or its bush or bearing, the swingarm bearings, or on CBF models the suspension linkage bearings.

8 On CBF1000A models place the motorcycle on its centrestand so that the rear wheel is off the ground. On all other models support the bike using an auxiliary stand that does not take the weight of the bike through any part of the rear suspension, or lift it using a hoist. Grab the swingarm and rock it from side-to-side **(see illustration)** – there should be no discernible movement at the rear.

9 Next, grasp the top of the rear wheel and pull it upwards **(see illustration)** – there should be no discernible freeplay before the shock absorber begins to compress.

10 If there's a little movement or a slight clicking can be heard, check the tightness of the swingarm pivot bolt nut, referring to the procedure in Chapter 5, and re-check for movement. Also check the shock absorber mounting bolts/nuts, and on CBF models the suspension linkage mounting bolts/nuts. If there is still some noise or freeplay after everything has been correctly tightened then there is either a worn bush or bearing in the shock absorber mountings, or worn swingarm bearings, or on CBF models worn linkage bearings. The worn components must be identified and replaced with new ones (see Chapter 5).

11 You can make a more accurate assessment by isolating the swingarm from the shock absorber or linkage, according to model – remove the rear wheel (see Chapter 6) and the bolt securing the shock absorber or linkage to the swingarm (see Chapter 5).

13.8 Checking for play in the swingarm bearings

13.9 Checking for play in the rear shock, and on CBF models the suspension linkage, mountings

Routine maintenance and servicing 1•25

12 Grasp the rear of the swingarm with one hand and place your other hand at the junction of the swingarm and the frame. Try to move the rear of the swingarm from side-to-side. Any wear (play) in the bearings should be felt as movement between the swingarm and the frame at the front. If there is any play, the swingarm will be felt to move forward and backward at the front (not from side-to-side). Next, move the swingarm up and down through its full travel. It should move freely, without any binding or rough spots. If there is any play in the swingarm or if it does not move freely, remove the bearings for inspection (see Chapter 5).

13 With the shock absorber or linkage detached check the bearings and bush in each component for corrosion and wear and failure of the seals, referring to Chapter 5 for details according to model, and clean and re-grease or replace components as required.

Front fork oil change

14 Although there is no set interval for changing the fork oil, the oil will degrade over a period of time and lose its damping qualities. Refer to Chapter 5, Sections 6 and 7 for details of front fork removal, oil draining and refilling. The forks do not need to be completely disassembled to change the oil.

Rear suspension bearing lubrication

15 Although there is no set interval for re-greasing the suspension bearings, over a considerable mileage, and if the bike is often ridden in wet conditions (or through incorrect use of jet washers) the seals may fail and allow dirt and water to get in, in which case the grease in the bearings will be washed out or will harden.

16 The shock absorber and swingarm, and on CBF models the linkage, should be removed periodically and the bearings cleaned and re-greased as necessary (see Chapter 5, Sections 11, 12 and 13).

14 Steering head bearings

Freeplay check and adjustment

1 Steering head bearings can become dented, rough or loose during normal use of the machine. In extreme cases, worn or loose steering head bearings can cause steering wobble – a condition that is potentially dangerous.

Check

2 On CBF1000A models place the motorcycle on its centrestand on level ground, and raise the front wheel off the ground, either by having an assistant press down on the rear, or by placing a jack under the engine (use a piece of wood between the jack head and the engine to spread the weight). On all other models raise the front wheel off the ground using an auxiliary stand or stands that do not interfere with movement of the steering. Always make sure that the bike is properly supported and secure.

3 Point the front wheel straight-ahead and slowly move the handlebars from lock to lock. Any dents, tightness or roughness in the bearing races will be felt – if the bearings are too tight the bars will not move smoothly and freely. Again point the wheel straight-ahead, and tap the front of the wheel to one side. The wheel should 'fall' under its own weight to the limit of its lock, indicating that the bearings are not too tight (take into account the restriction that cables, hoses and wiring may have). Check for similar movement to the other side.

4 If a spring balance (see Specifications for range required) is available, attach one end to the fork tube between the top and bottom yokes and hold it out at right angles to the yoke (see illustration). With the steering straight-ahead, pull on the balance and check the reading at which the handlebars start to turn. If the reading is below the minimum value specified in the pre-load range given in the Specifications at the beginning of the Chapter, the steering head is too loose, if the reading is above the maximum value specified the steering head is too tight. If the steering doesn't perform as described, and it's not due to the resistance of cables or hoses, then the bearings should be adjusted as described below.

5 Next, grasp the bottom of the forks and gently pull and push them forward and backward (see illustration). Any looseness or freeplay in the steering head bearings will be felt as front-to-rear movement of the forks. If play is felt, adjust the bearings as described below.

HAYNES HiNT *Make sure you are not mistaking any movement between the bike and stand, or between the stand and the ground, for freeplay in the bearings. Do not pull and push the forks too hard – a gentle movement is all that is needed. Freeplay between the fork tubes due to worn bushes can also be misinterpreted as steering head bearing play – do not confuse the two.*

Adjustment

Special tool: *Either the Honda special tool (part No. 07916-3710101), equivalent peg spanner, or a suitably sized C-spanner is necessary for this procedure – see Step 11.*

6 As a precaution, on CBF1000/A models remove the fairing (see Chapter 7), and on all models remove the fuel tank (see Chapter 4). Though not actually essential, this will prevent the possibility of damage should a tool slip. On CB1000R/RA models remove the headlight assembly (see Chapter 8).

7 Displace the handlebars from the top yoke and rest them on some rag, tying or supporting them so they are secure (see Chapter 5). On CB1000R/RA models remove the cap from the steering stem nut (see illustration).

14.4 Checking steering head bearing pre-load using a spring balance

14.5 Feeling for play in the steering head bearings

14.7 Remove the cap from the nut

1•26 Routine maintenance and servicing

14.8a Slacken the fork clamp bolt (arrowed) on each side

14.8b Unscrew the steering stem nut . . .

14.9 . . . then gently ease the handlebar/yoke assembly up off the forks and support it securely

14.10a Bend down the tabs securing the locknut . . .

14.10b . . . then unscrew the locknut . . .

14.10c . . . and remove the lockwasher

Routine maintenance and servicing 1•27

8 Slacken the fork clamp bolts in the top yoke **(see illustration)**. Unscrew the steering stem nut **(see illustration)**. If desired, you can now fit the handlebars back onto the yoke and secure them using a couple of the bolts, tightening them enough to prevent the bars rotating.

9 Gently ease the top yoke and handlebar assembly up off the fork tubes, on CB1000R/A models noting how it locates on the headlight stay, and support it clear, using rag to protect other components **(see illustration)**.

10 Bend the lockwasher tabs out of the notches in the locknut **(see illustration)**. Unscrew the locknut using your fingers **(see illustration)** – it shouldn't be tight. If it is tight use a C-spanner or a suitable drift located in one of the notches **(see illustration 14.11a or b)**. Remove the lockwasher **(see illustration)**. Inspect the tabs for cracks or signs of fatigue. If there is any sign of damage, discard the lockwasher and use a new one; otherwise the old one can be re-used, but note that Honda recommend using a new one as a matter of course.

11 To turn the adjuster nut you need either a C-spanner, a suitable drift to locate in one of the notches, or the Honda service tool (part No. 07916-3710101) or a suitable peg spanner (which can be made by cutting castellations into an old socket) **(see illustrations)**. Slacken the adjuster nut slightly until pressure is just released using. If the Honda tool or a peg spanner is available, tighten the adjuster nut to the torque setting specified at the beginning of the Chapter, then turn the steering from lock-to-lock five times, then reapply the specified torque setting to the nut. If the tool is not available, tighten the adjuster nut using a C-spanner or drift until all freeplay is removed, yet the steering is able to move freely. The object is to set the adjuster nut so that the bearings are under a very light loading, just enough to remove any freeplay, but not so much that the steering is prevented from moving freely from side-to-side. If the torque setting is applied check the physical feel as described as well. If you have the spring balance (see Step 4), set the adjuster nut so that the steering starts to move at around the mid-point of the pre-load range given in the Specifications at the beginning of the Chapter. ***Caution: Take great care not to apply excessive pressure because this will cause premature failure of the bearings.***

12 If the bearings cannot be correctly adjusted, disassemble the steering head and check the bearings and races (see Chapter 5).

13 With the bearings correctly adjusted, fit the lockwasher, using a new one if the tabs are weakened or cracked, onto the adjuster nut and fit the two short tabs into the notches in the adjuster nut **(see illustration 14.10c)**.

14 Fit the locknut and tighten it finger-tight **(see illustration 14.10b)**. Tighten the locknut further (but no more than 90°) until its notches align with the remaining lockwasher tabs, making sure the adjuster nut does not turn as well (though that is unlikely). Secure the locknut in position by bending up the long lockwasher tabs into its notches **(see illustration)**.

14.11a Adjust the bearings as described using either a C-spanner . . .

14.11b . . . or a drift

14.11c Use a home-made tool as shown or the Honda tool to apply the correct torque settings as described

14.14 Bend the tabs up into the notches in the locknut

Routine maintenance and servicing

15 Fit the top yoke onto the steering stem, on CB1000R/RA models making sure it locates onto the headlight stay grommets **(see illustration 14.9)**. Displace the handlebars from the yoke if refitted. Fit the steering stem nut and tighten it to the torque setting specified at the beginning of the Chapter **(see illustration)**. On CB1000R/RA models fit the cap into the nut **(see illustration 14.7)**.
16 Tighten the fork clamp bolts to the specified torque **(see illustration 14.8a)**.
17 Install the handlebars (see Chapter 5).
18 Check the bearing adjustment as described above and re-adjust if necessary.
19 Install the fuel tank (Chapter 4) and fairing (Chapter 7) as required.

Lubrication

20 Over a considerable time the grease in the bearings will be dispersed or will harden allowing the ingress of dirt and water.
21 The steering head should be disassembled periodically and the bearings cleaned and re-greased (see Chapter 5, Sections 9 and 10).

15 Wheels, tyres and wheel bearings

Wheels

1 Cast wheels are virtually maintenance free, but they should be kept clean and checked periodically for cracks and other damage. Also check the wheel runout and alignment (see Chapter 6). Never attempt to repair damaged cast wheels; they must be replaced with new ones if damaged. Check that the wheel balance weights are fixed firmly to the wheel rim. If you suspect that a weight has fallen off, have the wheel rebalanced by a motorcycle tyre specialist.

14.15 Tighten the stem nut to the specified torque

Tyres

2 Check the tyre condition and tread depth thoroughly – see *Pre-ride checks*. Check the valve rubber for signs of damage or deterioration and have it replaced with a new one if necessary by a tyre fitting specialist. Also, make sure the valve stem cap is in place and tight **(see illustration)**.

Wheel bearings

3 Wheel bearings will wear over a considerable mileage and should be checked periodically to avoid handling problems.
4 On CBF1000A models place the motorcycle on its centrestand. When checking the front wheel raise the wheel off the ground, either by having an assistant press down on the rear, or by placing a jack under the engine (use a piece of wood between the jack head and the engine to spread the weight). On all other models support the motorcycle upright using an auxiliary stand so that the wheel being examined is off the ground.
5 Check for any play in the bearings by pushing and pulling the wheel against the hub **(see illustration)**. When checking the front wheel turn the handlebars to full lock on one side and hold the wheel against the lock. Also rotate the wheel and check that it turns smoothly and without any grating noises (bearing in mind that the brakes and final drive make some noise – do not confuse them).
6 If any play is detected in the hub, or if the wheel does not rotate smoothly (and this is not due to brake or transmission drag), the wheel should be removed and the bearings inspected for wear or damage (see Chapter 6).

16 Stand, lever pivots and throttle cable lubrication

Pivot points

1 Since the controls, cables and various other components of a motorcycle are exposed to the elements, they should be checked and lubricated periodically to ensure safe and trouble-free operation.
2 The footrest pivots, clutch and brake lever pivots, brake pedal and gearchange lever pivots and linkage, and stand pivots should be lubricated frequently. In order for the lubricant to be applied where it will do the most good, the component should be disassembled and cleaned (see Chapter 5). The lubricant recommended by Honda for each application is listed at the beginning of the Chapter. If an aerosol lubricant is being used, it can be applied to the pivot joint gaps and will usually work its way into the areas where friction occurs, so less disassembly of the component is needed (however it is always better to do so and clean off all corrosion, dirt and old lubricant first). If motor oil or light grease is being used, apply it sparingly as it may attract dirt (which could cause the controls to bind or wear at an accelerated rate). **Note:** *An alternative lubricant for the control lever pivots is a dry-film lubricant (available from many sources by different names).*

15.2 Check each valve as described and make sure a cap is fitted

15.5 Checking for play in the wheel bearings

Routine maintenance and servicing 1•29

16.3a Fit the cable into the adapter ...

16.3b ... and tighten the screw to seal it in ...

Throttle cables

Special tool: *A cable lubricating adapter is necessary for this procedure* **(see illustration 16.3c)**.

3 To lubricate the cables, disconnect the relevant cable at its upper end, then lubricate it with a pressure adapter and aerosol cable lubricant **(see illustrations)**. See Chapter 4 for throttle cable removal procedures.

17 Nuts and bolts

1 Since vibration of the machine tends to loosen fasteners, all nuts, bolts, screws, etc. should be periodically checked for proper tightness.
2 Pay particular attention to the following, referring to the relevant Chapter:
 Spark plugs
 Engine oil drain plug
 Lever and pedal bolts
 Footrest and stand bolts
 Engine mounting bolts/nuts
 Shock absorber, suspension linkage (CBF models), and swingarm pivot bolts/nuts
 Handlebar bolts
 Front fork clamp bolts (top and bottom yoke) and fork top bolts
 Steering stem nut
 Front wheel axle bolt and axle clamp bolt
 Rear wheel axle nut
 Front sprocket bolt and rear sprocket nuts
 Brake caliper and master cylinder mounting bolts
 Brake hose banjo bolts and caliper bleed valves
 Brake disc bolts
 Exhaust system bolts/nuts
3 If a torque wrench is available, use it along with the torque settings given at the beginning of this and other Chapters.

18 Air filter

Caution: *If the machine is continually ridden in wet or dusty conditions, the filter should be replaced more frequently.*
1 Remove the left-hand side cover (see Chapter 7).
2 On CB1000R/RA models undo the air intake duct cover screws and remove the cover **(see illustration 2.1)**.
3 Undo the air intake duct screws and displace the duct **(see illustration)** – there is no need to disconnect the vacuum hose from the diaphragm valve (you can just rest the duct on the footpeg) unless you prefer to do so, or if you are removing the air filter housing/throttle body assembly **(see illustration)**.

16.3c ... then apply the lubricant using the nozzle provided inserted in the hole in the adapter

18.3a Undo the screws and displace the duct ...

18.3b ... and if required disconnect the vacuum hose (arrowed)

1•30 Routine maintenance and servicing

18.4 Withdraw the filter element

18.5 Direct the air in the opposite direction of normal flow

4 Withdraw the filter element from the housing **(see illustration)**.
5 Clean the filter by tapping it on a hard surface to dislodge any dirt, then use compressed air to blow through it, directing the air in the opposite way to normal flow, i.e. from the outside **(see illustration)**. Do not use any solvents or cleaning agents on the element. If the element is excessively dirty or is damaged replace it with a new one.
6 Fit the filter element into the housing, making sure it seats properly **(see illustration 18.4)**.
7 Make sure the air duct O-ring is in good condition and seated in its groove – fit a new O-ring if necessary. If disconnected, connect the vacuum hose to the diaphragm valve **(see illustration 18.3b)**. Fit the air duct and tighten the screws **(see illustration 18.3a)**. On CB1000R/RA models fit the air duct cover **(see illustration 2.1)**.
8 Install the side cover (see Chapter 7).

19 Valve clearances

Special tool: *A set of feeler gauges is necessary for this job (see illustration 19.7).*
1 The engine must be completely cool for this maintenance procedure, so let the bike stand overnight before beginning.
2 Remove the spark plugs (see Section 7). Remove the valve cover (see Chapter 2). Refer to Chapter 2, Section 8 and retract the cam chain tensioner plunger as described.
3 Make a chart or sketch of all valve positions so that a note of each clearance can be made against the relevant valve. The cylinders are numbered 1 to 4 from left to right. The intake valves are on the back of the cylinder head and the exhaust valves are on the front.
4 Unscrew the timing inspection cap from the clutch cover **(see illustration)**. Check the condition of its O-ring and obtain a new one if necessary.
5 To check the valve clearances the engine must be turned so that the valve being checked is closed. The engine can be turned using a socket on the timing rotor bolt and turning it in a clockwise direction only **(see illustration 19.6a)**.
6 Turn the engine clockwise until the line next to the T mark on the timing rotor aligns with the static timing mark, which is a notch or pointer in the inspection hole rim, and the IN and EX marks on the intake and exhaust camshaft sprockets respectively are facing away from each other and are flush with the cylinder head top surface **(see illustrations)**. If the sprocket marks are facing towards each other, rotate the engine clockwise one full turn (360°) until the line next to the T mark again aligns with the static timing mark. The sprocket marks will now be facing away.
7 With the engine in this position, check the clearances on the Nos. 1 and 3 cylinder intake

19.4 Unscrew the timing inspection cap (arrowed)

19.6a Turn the engine clockwise using the bolt . . .

Routine maintenance and servicing 1•31

19.6b ... until the line next to the T mark aligns with the notch (arrowed) ...

19.6c ... and the camshaft sprocket marks are as shown

19.7 Insert the feeler gauge between the base of the cam lobe and the top of the follower as shown

19.8 Turn the engine 180° so the marks are aligned as shown

valves, remembering there are two valves per cylinder. Insert a feeler gauge of the same thickness as the correct valve clearance (see Specifications) between the camshaft lobe and the follower of each valve and check that it is a firm sliding fit – you should feel a slight drag when the you pull the gauge out **(see illustration)**. If not, use the feeler gauges to obtain the exact clearance. Record the measured clearance on the chart.

8 Now rotate the engine 180° clockwise until the line next to the T mark on the timing rotor is diametrically opposite the static timing mark – the scribed line on the rotor will now be in the 12 o'clock position **(see illustration)**. With the engine in this position, check the clearances on the Nos. 2 and 4 cylinder exhaust valves using the method described in Step 7.

9 Now rotate the engine 180° clockwise until the line next to the T mark aligns with the static timing mark again **(see illustration 19.6b)**. With the engine in this position, check the clearances on the Nos. 2 and 4 cylinder intake valves using the method described in Step 7.

10 Now rotate the engine 180° clockwise until the line next to the T mark on the timing rotor is once again diametrically opposite the static timing mark and the scribed line is at the 12 o'clock position **(see illustration 19.8)**. With the engine in this position, check the clearances on the Nos. 1 and 3 cylinder exhaust valves using the method described in Step 7.

11 When all clearances have been measured and charted, identify whether the clearance on any valve falls outside the specified range. If any do, the shim must be replaced with one of a thickness which will restore the correct clearance.

12 Shim replacement requires removal of the camshafts (see Chapter 2). Place rags over the spark plug holes and the cam chain tunnel to prevent a shim from dropping into the engine on removal. Work on one valve at a time to prevent the possibility of mixing up the followers, which must be returned to their original location. If you want to remove more than one shim and follower at a time, store them in a marked container or bag, denoting which cylinder and which valve the shim and follower are from, so that they do not get mixed up.

13 With the camshaft removed, remove the cam follower of the valve in question using a magnet or the suction created by a valve lapping tool, or long nosed pliers can be used with care **(see illustration)**. Retrieve the shim either from the

19.13a Carefully lift out the follower using grips, a lapping tool or a magnet ...

1•32 Routine maintenance and servicing

19.13b . . . and retrieve the shim (arrowed) from inside it . . .

19.13c . . . or from the top of the valve

19.14a The shim size is marked on one face . . .

inside of the follower or pick it out of the top of the valve spring retainer using either a magnet, a screwdriver with a dab of grease on it (the shim will stick to the grease), or a very small screwdriver and a pair of pliers **(see illustrations)**. Do not allow the shim to fall into the engine.

14 Measure and record the thickness of the shim using a micrometer **(see illustrations)**.

15 Calculate the required replacement shim by using the formula a = (b − c) + d, where a is the required replacement shim size, b is the measured valve clearance, c is the specified valve clearance, and d is the existing shim thickness. For example:

The measured clearance of an intake valve is 0.22 mm, so b = 0.22

The specified clearance range for an intake valve is 0.13 to 0.19 mm, the mid-point being 0.16 mm, so c = 0.16
The thickness of the existing shim is 2.00 mm, so d = 2.0
Therefore, the required replacement shim a = 0.22 − 0.16 + 2.0 (a = 2.06 mm). The nearest available size to this 2.05 mm (Step 16).

Note: *If the required replacement shim is greater than 2.900 mm (the largest available), the valve is probably not seating correctly due to a build-up of carbon deposits and should be checked and cleaned or resurfaced as required (see Chapter 2).*

16 Shims are available in 0.025 mm increments from 1.200 mm to 2.900 mm. A size mark should be stamped on one face of the shim – a shim marked 175 is 1.75 mm thick. Obtain the replacement shim, then lubricate it with molybdenum disulphide oil (a 50/50 mixture of molybdenum disulphide grease and engine oil) and fit it into the recess in the top of the valve spring retainer with the size mark facing up **(see illustration 19.13c)**.

17 Check that the shim is correctly seated, then lubricate the follower with molybdenum disulphide oil and fit it onto the valve, making sure it fits squarely in its bore **(see illustration)**. Repeat the process for any other valves until the clearances are correct, then install the camshafts (see Chapter 2).

18 Rotate the crankshaft clockwise several turns to seat the new shim(s), then check the clearances again.

19 Reset the cam chain tensioner and install the valve cover (see Chapter 2). Install the spark plugs (see Section 7).

20 Install all disturbed components in a reverse of the removal sequence. Install the timing inspection cap using a new O-ring if required, and smear the O-ring and the cap threads with grease. Tighten the cap to the torque setting specified at the beginning of the Chapter.

20 Battery

1 All models covered in this manual are fitted with a sealed MF (maintenance free) battery. **Note:** *Do not attempt to remove the battery caps to check the electrolyte level or battery specific gravity. Removal will damage the caps, resulting in electrolyte leakage and battery damage.* All that should be done is to check that the terminals are clean and tight and that the casing is not damaged or leaking. See Chapter 8 for further details.

2 If the machine is not in regular use, disconnect the battery and give it a refresher charge every month to six weeks (see Chapter 8).

19.14b . . . but check the thickness of the shim using a micrometer

19.17 Fit the follower onto the valve

Chapter 2
Engine, clutch and transmission

Contents

	Section number
Alternator	see Chapter 8
Balancer shaft	30
Cam chain tensioner	8
Camshafts and followers	9
Cam chain, tensioner blade and front guide	10
Clutch check	see Chapter 1
Clutch	14
Clutch release mechanism	15
Component access	2
Connecting rod and main bearing information	25
Connecting rods and bearings	27
Crankcases and cylinder bores	24
Crankcase separation and reassembly	23
Crankshaft and main bearings	26
Crankshaft position sensor	see Chapter 4
Cylinder head removal and installation	11
Cylinder head and valve overhaul	12
Engine wear assessment	3
Engine removal and installation	4
Engine disassembly and reassembly general information	5
Gearchange mechanism	16
General information	1

	Section number
Neutral switch	see Chapter 8
Oil and filter change	see Chapter 1
Oil cooler	6
Oil level check	see *Pre-ride checks*
Oil pressure switch	see Chapter 8
Oil pump	22
Oil sump, oil strainer and pressure relief valve	21
Pistons	28
Piston rings	29
Running-in procedure	31
Selector drum and forks	20
Spark plugs	see Chapter 1
Starter clutch and gears	13
Starter motor	see Chapter 8
Thermostat and housing	see Chapter 3
Transmission shaft overhaul	19
Transmission cassette removal and installation	17
Transmission shaft and bearing removal and installation	18
Valve clearance check and adjustment	see Chapter 1
Valve cover	7
Water pump	see Chapter 3

Degrees of difficulty

Easy, suitable for novice with little experience	**Fairly easy,** suitable for beginner with some experience	**Fairly difficult,** suitable for competent DIY mechanic	**Difficult,** suitable for experienced DIY mechanic	**Very difficult,** suitable for expert DIY or professional

Specifications

General
Type	Four-stroke in-line four
Capacity	998 cc
Cylinder numbering	1 to 4 from left to right
Firing order	1-2-4-3
Bore	75.0 mm
Stroke	56.5 mm
Compression ratio	
CBF1000/A models	11.0 to 1
CB1000R/RA models	11.2 to 1
Cooling system	Liquid cooled
Lubrication	Wet sump, trochoid pump
Clutch	Wet multi-plate
Transmission	Six-speed constant mesh, cassette loading
Final drive	Chain and sprockets

Camshafts and followers

Intake lobe height
  CBF1000/A models
    Standard.. 34.62 to 34.70 mm
    Service limit (min)... 34.60 mm
  CB1000R/RA models
    Standard.. 36.02 to 36.10 mm
    Service limit (min)... 36.00 mm
Exhaust lobe height
  CBF1000/A models
    Standard.. 34.58 to 34.66 mm
    Service limit (min)... 34.56 mm
  CB1000R/RA models
    Standard.. 36.08 to 36.16 mm
    Service limit (min)... 36.06 mm
Oil clearance
  Standard... 0.020 to 0.062 mm
  Service limit (max).. 0.10 mm
Runout (max)... 0.05 mm
Camshaft follower diameter
  Standard... 25.978 to 25.993 mm
  Service limit (min).. 25.97 mm
Camshaft follower bore diameter
  Standard... 26.010 to 26.026 mm
  Service limit (min).. 26.04 mm

Cylinder head

Warpage (max).. 0.10 mm

Valves, guides and springs

Valve clearances... see Chapter 1
Stem diameter
  Intake valve
    Standard.. 4.475 to 4.490 mm
    Service limit (min)... 4.465 mm
  Exhaust valve
    Standard.. 4.465 to 4.480 mm
    Service limit (min)... 4.455 mm
Guide bore diameter
  Standard... 4.500 to 4.512 mm
  Service limit (max).. 4.540 mm
Stem-to-guide clearance
  Intake valve
    Standard.. 0.010 to 0.037 mm
    Service limit... 0.075 mm
  Exhaust valve
    Standard.. 0.020 to 0.047 mm
    Service limit... 0.085 mm
Seat width
  Standard... 0.90 to 1.10 mm
  Service limit (max).. 1.50 mm
Valve guide height above cylinder head.......................... 16.0 to 16.3 mm
Valve spring free length
  Standard... 39.5 mm
  Service limit (min).. 38.7 mm

Starter clutch

Starter driven gear hub OD
  Standard... 45.657 to 45.673 mm
  Service limit (min).. 45.642 mm
Starter idle gear ID
  Standard... 10.013 to 10.035 mm
  Service limit (max).. 10.05 mm
Starter idle gear shaft OD
  Standard... 9.991 to 10.000 mm
  Service limit (min).. 9.98 mm

Clutch

Friction plates	8
Plain plates	7
Friction plate thickness	
Type A (innermost and outermost plates)	
Standard	3.72 to 3.88 mm
Service limit (min)	3.4 mm
Type B	
Standard	3.22 to 3.38 mm
Service limit (min)	2.9 mm
Plain plate warpage (max)	0.3 mm
Spring free length	
Standard	56.8 mm
Service limit (min)	55.7 mm
Clutch guide OD	
Type A, no marking	
Standard	35.004 to 35.012 mm
Service limit (min)	34.994 mm
Type B, with marking	
Standard	34.996 to 35.004 mm
Service limit (min)	34.986 mm
Clutch guide ID (both types)	
Standard	27.993 to 28.003 mm
Service limit (max)	28.012 mm
Primary driven gear ID	
Type A	
Standard	41.008 to 41.016 mm
Service limit (min)	41.026 mm
Type B	
Standard	41.000 to 41.008 mm
Service limit (min)	41.018 mm
Input shaft OD at clutch guide	
Standard	27.980 to 27.990 mm
Service limit (max)	27.960 mm

Clutch release mechanism

Clutch fluid	DOT 4
Master cylinder bore ID	
Standard	12.700 to 12.743 mm
Service limit (max)	12.755 mm
Piston OD	
Standard	12.657 to 12.684 mm
Service limit (max)	12.645 mm

Oil pump

Oil pressure (at oil pressure switch, with engine warm)	74 psi (5.2 Bar) @ 6000 rpm, oil @ 80°C
Inner rotor tip-to-outer rotor clearance	
Standard	0.15 mm
Service limit (max)	0.20 mm
Outer rotor-to-body clearance	
Standard	0.15 to 0.21 mm
Service limit (max)	0.35 mm
Rotor end-float	
Standard	0.04 to 0.09 mm
Service limit (max)	0.17 mm
Oil pump drive sprocket ID	
Standard	35.025 to 35.145 mm
Service limit	35.155 mm
Oil pump drive sprocket guide OD	
Standard	34.975 to 34.991 mm
Service limit	34.965 mm
Oil pump drive sprocket guide ID	
Standard	28.000 to 28.021 mm
Service limit	28.030 mm
Input shaft OD at sprocket guide	
Standard	27.980 to 27.990 mm
Service limit (max)	27.960 mm

Selector drum and forks

Selector fork end thickness
    Standard... 5.93 to 6.00 mm
    Service limit (min)... 5.90 mm
Selector fork bore ID
    Standard... 12.000 to 12.018 mm
    Service limit (max).. 12.03 mm
Selector fork shaft OD
    Standard... 11.957 to 11.968 mm
    Service limit (min)... 11.95 mm

Cylinder bores

Cylinder compression
    CBF1000/A models... 159 psi (11.0 Bar) @ 350 rpm
    CB1000R/RA models....................................... 218 psi (15.3 Bar) @ 300 rpm
Bore
    Standard... 75.000 to 75.015 mm
    Service limit (max).. 75.100 mm
Warpage (max).. 0.10 mm
Ovality (out-of-round) (max).................................. 0.10 mm
Taper (max)... 0.10 mm

Crankshaft and bearings

Main bearing oil clearance
    Standard... 0.019 to 0.037 mm
    Service limit (max).. 0.05 mm
Crankshaft runout (max)....................................... 0.05 mm

Connecting rods

Small-end internal diameter
    Standard... 17.030 to 17.042 mm
    Service limit (max).. 17.048 mm
Small-end-to-piston pin clearance
    Standard... 0.030 to 0.046 mm
    Service limit.. 0.070 mm
Big-end side clearance
    Standard... 0.05 to 0.20 mm
    Service limit (max).. 0.25 mm
Big-end oil clearance
    Standard... 0.030 to 0.052 mm
    Service limit (max).. 0.06 mm

Pistons

Piston diameter (measured 9 mm up from skirt, at 90° to piston pin axis)
    Standard... 74.960 to 74.980 mm
    Service limit (min)... 74.895 mm
Piston-to-bore clearance
    Standard... 0.020 to 0.055 mm
    Service limit (min)... 0.10 mm*
    + 0.25 oversize pistons.................................... 0.015 to 0.050 mm
Piston pin diameter
    Standard... 16.994 to 17.000 mm
    Service limit (min)... 16.980 mm
Piston pin bore diameter in piston
    Standard... 17.002 to 17.008 mm
    Service limit (max).. 17.030 mm
Piston pin-to-piston pin bore clearance
    Standard... 0.002 to 0.014 mm
    Service limit.. 0.04 mm

If the piston-to-bore clearance exceeds the service limit, the cylinders can be rebored – Honda supply +0.25 oversize pistons and rings. The piston-to-bore clearance must be as specified for oversize pistons

Piston rings
Ring end gap (installed)
  Top ring
    CBF1000/A models
      Standard.. 0.22 to 0.32 mm
      Service limit (max)...................................... 0.52 mm
    CB1000R/RA models
      Standard.. 0.17 to 0.27 mm
      Service limit (max)...................................... 0.52 mm
  Second ring
    Standard.. 0.48 to 0.63 mm
    Service limit (max)...................................... 0.82 mm
  Oil ring side-rail
    Standard.. 0.20 to 0.70 mm
    Service limit (max)...................................... 1.0 mm
Ring-to-groove clearance
  Top ring
    Standard.. 0.050 to 0.085 mm
    Service limit (max)...................................... 0.125 mm
  Second ring
    CBF1000/A models
      Standard.. 0.015 to 0.050 mm
      Service limit (max)...................................... 0.075 mm
    CB1000R/RA models
      Standard.. 0.015 to 0.045 mm
      Service limit (max)...................................... 0.070 mm

Transmission

	CBF1000/A models	**CB1000R/RA models**
Gear ratios (no. of teeth)		
Primary reduction	1.604 to 1 (77/48)	1.604 to 1 (77/48)
Final reduction	2.687 to 1 (43/16)	2.750 to 1 (44/16)
1st gear	2.714 to 1 (38/13)	2.538 to 1 (33/13)
2nd gear	1.941 to 1 (33/17)	1.941 to 1 (33/17)
3rd gear	1.578 to 1 (30/19)	1.578 to 1 (30/19)
4th gear	1.363 to 1 (30/22)	1.363 to 1 (30/22)
5th gear	1.217 to 1 (28/23)	1.217 to 1 (28/23)
6th gear	1.115 to 1 (29/26)	1.115 to 1 (29/26)

Input shaft 5th and 6th gears ID
  Standard.. 31.000 to 31.025 mm
  Service limit (max)...................................... 31.04 mm
Input shaft 5th and 6th gears bush OD
  Standard.. 30.955 to 30.980 mm
  Service limit (min)...................................... 30.935 mm
Input shaft 5th and 6th gears gear-to-bush clearance
  Standard.. 0.020 to 0.070 mm
  Service limit (max)...................................... 0.10 mm
Input shaft 5th gear bush ID
  Standard.. 27.985 to 28.006 mm
  Service limit (max)...................................... 28.016 mm
Input shaft OD at 5th gear bush point
  Standard.. 27.967 to 27.980 mm
  Service limit (min)...................................... 27.957 mm
Input shaft-to-bush clearance at 5th gear bush point
  Standard.. 0.005 to 0.039 mm
  Service limit (max)...................................... 0.06 mm
Output shaft 1st gear ID
  Standard.. 28.000 to 28.021 mm
  Service limit (max)...................................... 28.04 mm
Output shaft 2nd, 3rd and 4th gears ID
  Standard.. 33.000 to 33.025 mm
  Service limit (max)...................................... 33.04 mm
Output shaft 2nd gear bush OD
  Standard.. 32.955 to 32.980 mm
  Service limit (min)...................................... 32.935 mm
Output shaft 3rd and 4th gears bush OD
  Standard.. 32.950 to 32.975 mm
  Service limit (min)...................................... 32.93 mm

Transmission (continued)

Output shaft 2nd gear gear-to-bush clearance
    Standard .... 0.020 to 0.070 mm
    Service limit (max) .... 0.10 mm
Output shaft 3rd and 4th gears gear-to-bush clearance
    Standard .... 0.025 to 0.075 mm
    Service limit (max) .... 0.11 mm
Output shaft 2nd gear bush ID
    Standard .... 29.985 to 30.006 mm
    Service limit (max) .... 30.021 mm
Output shaft OD at 2nd gear bush point
    Standard .... 29.967 to 29.980 mm
    Service limit (min) .... 29.96 mm
Output shaft-to-bush clearance at 2nd gear bush point
    Standard .... 0.005 to 0.039 mm
    Service limit (max) .... 0.06 mm

Torque settings

Cam chain front guide blade pivot bolt .... 12 Nm
Cam chain tensioner blade pivot bolt .... 10 Nm
Camshaft holder bolts .... 12 Nm
Camshaft sprocket bolts .... 20 Nm
Clutch hose banjo bolt .... 34 Nm
Clutch master cylinder clamp bolts .... 12 Nm
Clutch nut .... 128 Nm
Clutch spring bolts .... 12 Nm
Connecting rod bolts
    Torque setting – new bolts .... 20 Nm
    Torque setting – oil clearance check (old bolts) ... 14 Nm
    Angle setting .... + 90°
Crankcase bolts
    Crankshaft journal 9 mm bolts
        Torque setting .... 20 Nm
        Angle setting .... + 150°
    Crankcase 8 mm bolts .... 24 Nm
    Crankcase 7 mm bolts .... 18 Nm
Cylinder head 9 mm bolts .... 51 Nm
Engine mountings
    CBF1000/A models
        Front mounting bolts .... 60 Nm
        Upper and lower rear mounting bolt nuts .... 60 Nm
        Swingarm pivot bolt nut .... 98 Nm
        Swingarm pivot bracket bolt nuts .... 69 Nm
    CB1000R/RA models
        Front mounting bracket-to-frame bolt nuts ..... 49 Nm
        Front mounting bolts .... 59 Nm
        Upper and lower rear bracket-to-frame bolt nuts .. 49 Nm
        Upper and lower rear mounting bolt nuts .... 59 Nm
        Swingarm pivot bolt nut .... 98 Nm
        Swingarm pivot bracket bolt nuts .... 69 Nm
Footrest bracket bolts
    CBF1000/A models .... 27 Nm
    CB1000R/RA models .... 37 Nm
Oil pressure switch .... 12 Nm
Oil pump cover bolts .... 8 Nm
Oil pump driven sprocket bolt .... 15 Nm
Selector drum bearing retainer bolts .... 12 Nm
Selector drum cam bolt .... 12 Nm
Starter clutch bolt .... 83 Nm
Stopper arm bolt .... 12 Nm
Timing inspection cap .... 18 Nm
Transmission cassette plate bolts .... 29 Nm
Transmission shaft bearing retainer bolts .... 12 Nm
Valve cover bolts .... 10 Nm

Engine, clutch and transmission 2•7

1 General information

The engine/transmission unit is a liquid-cooled in-line four cylinder. The sixteen valves are operated by double overhead camshafts which are chain driven off the right-hand end of the crankshaft. The engine/transmission is a unit assembly constructed from aluminium alloy. The crankcase divides horizontally.

The crankcase incorporates a wet sump, pressure-fed lubrication system which uses a dual rotor trochoidal oil pump that is chain-driven off the back of the clutch. The system has an oil strainer in the pick-up, a pressure relief valve in the feed from the pump to the filter, an oil filter, an oil cooler, and an oil pressure switch in the main gallery.

The alternator is on the left-hand end of the crankshaft. The water pump is on the left-hand side of the engine, and its drive shaft is keyed to the oil pump drive shaft. The ignition timing triggers are on the outside of the starter clutch body which is on the right-hand end of the crankshaft. The crankshaft position sensor is mounted in the clutch cover.

Power from the crankshaft is routed to the transmission via the clutch. The clutch is of the wet, multi-plate type and is gear-driven off the crankshaft. The clutch is operated hydraulically. The transmission is a six-speed constant-mesh unit of the cassette type which allows removal and installation with the engine in the frame. Final drive to the rear wheel is by chain and sprockets.

2 Component access

Operations possible with the engine in the frame

The components and assemblies listed below can be removed without having to remove the engine/transmission assembly from the frame. If however, a number of areas require attention at the same time, removal of the engine is recommended.

Valve cover
Cam chain tensioner and blades
Camshafts and cam chain
Clutch
Gearchange mechanism
Alternator
Oil filter and oil cooler
Oil sump, oil pump, oil strainer and oil pressure relief valve
Starter motor
Starter clutch/timing rotor
Water pump
Selector drum and forks
Transmission shafts

Operations requiring engine removal

It is necessary to remove the engine/transmission assembly from the frame to gain access to the following components.
Cylinder head
Crankshaft and bearings
Balancer shaft and bearings
Connecting rods and bearings
Pistons, piston rings and cylinder bores

3 Engine wear assessment

Cylinder compression check

Special tool: *A compression gauge is needed, with a threaded adaptor (10 mm) to fit the spark plug holes (use either the Honda gauge and adapter (pt. No. 07RMJ-MY50100) or an aftermarket version) to ensure a perfect seal. Depending on the outcome of the initial test, a squirt-type oil can may also be needed.*

1 Poor engine performance may be caused by leaking valves, incorrect valve clearances, a leaking head gasket, or worn pistons, piston rings or cylinder walls. A cylinder compression check will highlight these conditions and can also indicate the presence of excessive carbon deposits in the cylinder head, and a leakdown test (for which special equipment is needed – consult a Honda dealer) will pinpoint the actual cause(s) of the problem.

2 Start by making sure the valve clearances are correctly set (see Chapter 1). Also make sure the battery is well charged.

3 Run the engine until it is at normal operating temperature. Remove the spark plugs (see Chapter 1).

4 Fit the threaded adapter and gauge into the No. 1 cylinder spark plug hole.

5 With the ignition switch ON, the kill switch set to RUN, and the throttle held fully open, turn the engine over on the starter motor until the gauge reading has built up and stabilised **(see illustration)**.

6 Compare the reading on the gauge to the cylinder compression figure specified at the beginning of the Chapter. Repeat for the remaining cylinders.

7 If a reading is low, it could be due to a worn cylinder bore, piston or rings, failure of the head gasket, or worn valve seats. To determine which is the cause, pour a small quantity of engine oil into the spark plug hole to seal the rings, then repeat the compression test. If the figures are noticeably higher the cause is worn cylinder, piston or rings. If there is no change the cause is a leaking head gasket or worn valve seats.

8 If the reading is high there could be a build-up of carbon deposits in the combustion chamber. Remove the cylinder head and scrape all deposits off the piston and the cylinder head (see Chapter 2).

Engine oil pressure check

Special tool: *An oil pressure gauge is required to perform this test.*

9 The oil pressure warning light should come on when the ignition switch is turned ON and extinguish a few seconds after the engine is started. If the oil pressure light comes on whilst the engine is running, low oil pressure is indicated – stop the engine immediately and carry out an oil level check *(see Pre-ride checks).*

10 An oil pressure check must be carried out if the warning light comes on when the engine is running yet the oil level is good. A pressure check can also provide useful information about the condition of the engine's lubrication system.

11 To check the oil pressure, a suitable gauge and adapter (which screws into the main oil gallery in place of the oil pressure switch) will be needed. Honda can provide a gauge and adapter (pt. Nos. 07506-3000001 and 07406-0030000) for this purpose, or one can be obtained commercially. You will also need some rags to catch and mop up any residual oil that gets lost in between removing the oil pressure switch and installing the gauge – place the bike on its sidestand so that the oil gathers at the other end of the gallery to reduce spillage.

12 Check the oil level (see *Pre-ride checks*). Warm the engine up to normal operating temperature then stop it.

13 Remove the oil pressure switch (see Chapter 8). Screw the gauge adapter in its place. Connect the oil pressure gauge to the adapter.

14 Start the engine and briefly increase the engine speed to 6000 rpm whilst watching the gauge reading. The oil pressure should be similar to that given in the Specifications at the start of this Chapter.

15 If the pressure is significantly lower than the standard, either the pressure relief valve is stuck open, the oil pump or its drive mechanism is faulty, the oil strainer or filter is blocked, or there is other engine damage. Also make sure the correct grade oil is being used. Begin diagnosis by checking the oil filter, strainer and relief valve, then the oil pump (see

3.5 Testing cylinder compression – make sure the throttle is held fully open while turning the engine over

2•8 Engine, clutch and transmission

Sections 21 and 22). If those items check out okay, chances are the bearing oil clearances are excessive and the engine needs to be overhauled.

16 If the pressure is too high, either an oil passage is clogged, the relief valve is stuck closed or the wrong grade of oil is being used.
17 Stop the engine and unscrew the gauge and adapter from the crankcase.

⚠ **Warning: Be careful when removing the pressure gauge adapter as the exhaust pipes, the engine and the oil itself can cause severe burns.**

18 Install the oil pressure switch (sere Chapter 8). Check the oil level (see *Pre-ride checks*). Connect the wiring and secure it with the screw, then fit the boot over the switch.

4 Engine removal and installation

Caution: *The engine is very heavy. Engine removal and installation should be carried out with the aid of at least one assistant; personal injury or damage could occur if the engine falls or is dropped.*

Note: *As each mounting bolt is removed store it along with any related washer, nut and spacer to avoid parts getting mixed up, making installation easier.*

Removal

1 On CBF1000A models support the bike on its centrestand. On all other models support the bike upright using an auxiliary stand or stands that will not interfere with engine removal. Make sure the bike is on level ground, and block the front wheel or tie the front brake on. Note that the engine removal procedure requires that the swingarm pivot brackets be displaced on CBF1000/A models and removed, along with the swingarm pivot bolt, on CB1000R/RA models, so the bike must not be supported through the rear suspension or under the pivot brackets. A hoist can be used to lift the rear of the bike off the ground if available. In the accompanying photos blocks of wood and axle stands placed under the bottom of the frame were used after removing the exhaust system **(see illustration)**. Also place a block of wood under the rear wheel to take its weight, but not so the suspension is compressed. Work can be made easier by raising the machine to a suitable working height on an hydraulic ramp or a suitable platform. Make sure the motorcycle is secure and will not topple over (also see *Tools and Workshop Tips* in the Reference section).
2 On CBF1000/A models remove the fairing side panels and the left-hand seat cowl (see Chapter 7).
3 If the engine is dirty, particularly around its mountings, wash it thoroughly. This will make work much easier and rule out the possibility of caked on lumps of dirt falling into some vital component.
4 Drain the engine oil and the cooling system (see Chapter 1). If required remove the oil filter (see Chapter 1).
5 Disconnect the negative (–) lead from the battery (see Chapter 8).

6 Remove the fuel tank along with the drain and breather hoses, noting their routing (see Chapter 4). Remove the air filter housing and the throttle bodies (see Chapter 4). Plug the engine intake manifolds with clean rag.
7 Remove the radiator and the thermostat housing along with their hoses, noting their routing (see Chapter 3). Detach and remove any coolant hoses not already removed as required depending on what work is to be carried out, noting their positions and routing.
8 Remove the exhaust system (see Chapter 4).
9 Remove the front sprocket (see Chapter 6). Slip the drive chain off the end of the output shaft and let it rest against the front of the swingarm.
10 Remove the ignition coils (see Chapter 4).
11 Detach the PAIR system hoses and the crankcase breather hose from the valve cover, and remove the breather hose **(see illustrations)**.
12 If required, remove the starter motor (see Chapter 8). If you wish to leave the starter motor in situ, pull back the rubber cover on its terminal, then unscrew the nut and disconnect the lead **(see illustration)**. Also unscrew the mounting bolt securing the earth lead and detach the lead **(see illustration)**.
13 On CBF1000/A models disconnect the grey 8-pin wiring connector for the engine sub-loom supplying the neutral switch, oil pressure switch, speed sensor and intake air temperature (IAT) sensor – it is located at the back of the valve cover. Disconnect the alternator (white 3-pin) wiring connector **(see illustration)**.

4.1 Bike supported by blocks of wood and axle stands, backed up by a jack

4.11a Detach the PAIR hose (arrowed) on each side . . .

4.11b . . . and the crankcase breather hose (arrowed)

4.12a Unscrew the nut (arrowed) and detach the power lead . . .

4.12b . . . then unscrew the bolt (arrowed) and detach the earth lead

4.13 The alternator connector is inside the boot (arrowed)

Engine, clutch and transmission 2•9

4.14a Disconnect the engine sub-loom connector (arrowed) . . .

4.14b . . . and the alternator connector (arrowed)

14 On CB1000R/RA models disconnect the black 6-pin wiring connector for the engine sub-loom supplying the neutral switch, oil pressure switch and speed sensor **(see illustration)**. Disconnect the alternator (black 3-pin) wiring connector from the regulator/rectifier **(see illustration)**. Remove the horn (see Chapter 8).
15 Disconnect the crankshaft position (CKP) sensor (red 2-pin) wiring connector **(see illustrations)**.
16 Note the routing of all engine-related wiring and free it from any guides on the frame. Make sure the loom-side connectors and wiring are free from any guides or ties on the engine. Disconnect and move aside any other wiring as required. Note that on CBF1000/A models the IAT sensor wiring will come away with the engine as it is part of the engine sub-loom.
17 At this point, position an hydraulic or mechanical jack under the engine with a block of wood between the jack head and sump. Make sure the jack is centrally positioned so the engine will not topple in any direction when the last mounting bolt is removed. Raise the jack to take the weight of the engine, but make sure it is not lifting the bike and taking the weight of that as well. The idea is to support the engine so that there is no pressure on any of the mounting bolts once they have been slackened, so they can be easily withdrawn.

Note that it may be necessary to alter the position of the jack as some of the bolts are removed to relieve the stress transferred to the other bolts.

CBF1000/A models

18 Unscrew the front mounting bolt on each side, noting the washers, and remove the spacers, noting which fits where **(see illustration)**.
19 Slacken the nuts on the right-hand ends of the upper and lower rear mounting bolts counter-holding the bolt heads if necessary **(see illustrations)**.
20 Unscrew the swingarm pivot bolt nut and remove the washer **(see illustration)**.

4.15a CKP sensor wiring connector (arrowed) – CBF1000/A

4.15b CKP sensor wiring connector (arrowed) – CB1000R/RA

4.18 Unscrew the bolt (A) and remove the spacer (B) on each side

4.19a Slacken the nuts (arrowed) on the upper rear bolt . . .

4.19b . . . and the lower rear bolt

4.20 Unscrew the swingarm pivot bolt nut (A), then the pivot bracket bolt nuts (B)

2•10 Engine, clutch and transmission

4.25 Unscrew the bolts (arrowed) and displace the bracket

4.26 Unscrew the swingarm pivot bolt nut (A) and the pivot bracket bolt nuts (B)

4.27a Withdraw the pivot bracket bolts . . .

4.27b . . . withdraw the swingarm bolt and remove the bracket, then refit the swingarm bolt to support the swingarm

21 Unscrew the nuts on the right-hand ends of the swingarm pivot bracket bolts, counter-holding the bolt heads if necessary **(see illustration 4.20)**. Withdraw the bolts from the left, then draw the left-hand pivot bracket out just enough until it can be turned slightly anti-clockwise, pivoting on the swingarm bolt.
22 Unscrew the nut and remove the washer from the lower rear mounting bolt **(see illustration 4.19b)**. Check that the engine is properly supported by the jack, then withdraw the bolt. Remove the spacer from between the engine and frame on the right-hand side.
23 Unscrew the nut and remove the washer from the upper rear mounting bolt **(see illustration 4.19a)**. Support the engine and withdraw the bolt. Remove the spacer from the right-hand side.
24 The engine can now be removed from the frame (see **Caution** above). Check that all wiring, cables and hoses are free and clear, then carefully lower the jack slightly and manoeuvre the engine forward until it clears the frame. Fully lower the jack, then with the aid of an assistant remove the jack from under the engine and remove the engine.

CB1000R/RA models

25 Unscrew the rider's right-hand footrest bracket bolts and displace the bracket, supporting it clear **(see illustration)**.
26 Unscrew the nut and remove the washer from the right-hand ends of the swingarm pivot bolt and pivot bracket bolts, counter-holding the bolt heads if necessary **(see illustration)**. Displace the right-hand pivot bracket and support it clear, using rag for protection. Place a support under the swingarm.
27 Withdraw the pivot bracket bolts, noting the washers, then remove the swingarm pivot bolt and bracket assembly **(see illustrations)**. Reinsert the swingarm pivot bolt.
28 Unscrew the front mounting bolt on each side and remove the spacer **(see illustrations)**.
29 Unscrew the nuts and remove the washers from the front mounting bracket-to-frame

4.28a Unscrew the bolt (arrowed) . . .

4.28b . . . and remove the spacer (arrowed) on each side

Engine, clutch and transmission 2•11

4.29 Unscrew the nuts (arrowed), then withdraw the bolts and remove the bracket

4.30a Unscrew the nuts (arrowed) and remove the bracket and spacer . . .

4.30b . . . then withdraw the bolts (arrowed) and remove the bracket, noting the dowels

bolts, then withdraw the bolts and remove the bracket **(see illustration)**.
30 Unscrew the nuts on the right-hand ends of the lower rear mounting bolt and engine bracket bolts, counter-holding the bolt heads if necessary **(see illustration)**. Remove the bracket and the spacer on the mounting bolt. Check that the engine is properly supported by the jack, then withdraw the lower rear mounting bolt and bracket bolts from the left-hand side, noting which fits where, and remove the bracket and its dowels **(see illustration)** – fit each bolt back into its correct location in the bracket as a guide for installation as each bolt is a different length.
31 Unscrew the nuts on the right-hand ends of the upper rear mounting bolt and engine bracket bolts, counter-holding the bolt heads if necessary **(see illustration)**. Remove the bracket and the spacer on the mounting bolt **(see illustration)**. Support the engine, then withdraw the upper rear mounting bolt and bracket bolts from the left-hand side, noting which fits where, and remove the bracket **(see illustration)** – again fit each bolt back into its correct location in the bracket as a guide for installation as each bolt is a different length.
32 The engine can now be removed from the frame (see **Caution** above). Check that all wiring, cables and hoses are free and clear, then carefully lower the jack slightly and manoeuvre the engine forward until it clears the frame. Fully lower the jack, then with the aid of an assistant remove the jack from under the engine and remove the engine.

Installation

Note: *To prevent corrosion which could lead to bolts being seized, smear copper grease onto the bolt shafts, not the threads, to prevent the possibility of them seizing in the collars or the engine or frame.*

CBF1000/A models

33 Manoeuvre the engine into position under the frame and lift it onto the jack. Raise the engine to align all the mounting bolt holes, making sure that all cables and wiring are correctly routed and do not get trapped. Note that it may be necessary to adjust the jack as some of the bolts are installed and tightened to realign the other bolt holes.
34 Install the upper and lower rear mounting bolts (the upper bolt is shorter than the lower) from the left-hand side, fitting the spacers between the engine and frame on the right-hand side. Fit the washers and secure the nuts finger-tight **(see illustrations 4.19a and b)**.
35 Install the front mounting bolt on each side with its washer and spacer – the longer spacer goes with the longer bolt in the left-hand side **(see illustration 4.18)**. Tighten the bolts finger-tight.
36 Tighten the front bolts to the torque setting specified at the beginning of the Chapter. Now tighten the nut on the upper rear bolt to the specified torque, then tighten the nut on the lower bolt to the specified torque – counter-hold the bolt heads if required.
37 Realign and position the left-hand swingarm pivot bracket, then insert the bracket bolts from the left. On the right-hand side fit the swingarm pivot bolt washer and nut and tighten the nut to the specified torque **(see illustration 4.20)**. Fit the bracket bolt nuts and tighten them to the specified torque.

CB1000R/RA models

38 Manoeuvre the engine into position under the frame and lift it onto the jack. Raise the engine to align all the mounting bolt holes, making sure that all cables and wiring are correctly routed and do not get trapped. Note that it may be necessary to adjust the jack as some of the bolts are installed and tightened to realign the other bolt holes.
39 Install the upper rear bracket, bracket bolts and engine mounting bolt from the left-hand side **(see illustration 4.31c)**. On the right-hand side fit the spacer over the mounting bolt, then fit the bracket and secure the nuts finger-tight **(see illustrations 4.31b and a)**.
40 Install the lower rear bracket on the left-hand side, making sure the dowels are in place and locate correctly, then fit the bracket bolts and engine mounting bolt **(see illustration 4.30b)**. On the right-hand side fit the spacer over the mounting bolt, then fit the bracket and secure the nuts finger-tight **(see illustration 4.30a)**.
41 Install the front mounting bracket, bolts, washers and nuts and finger-tighten the nuts **(see illustration 4.29)**. Install the front mounting bolt on each side with its spacer **(see illustrations 4.28b and a)**. Tighten the bolts finger-tight.

4.31a Unscrew the nuts (arrowed) and remove the bracket . . .

4.31b . . . and spacer . . .

4.31c . . . then withdraw the bolts (arrowed) and remove the bracket

2•12 Engine, clutch and transmission

42 Tighten the nuts on the lower rear engine bracket-to-frame bolts to the torque setting specified at the beginning of the Chapter – counter-hold the bolt heads if required. Now tighten the nuts on the upper bracket-to-frame bolts to the specified torque. Now tighten the nuts on the front bracket-to-frame bolts to the specified torque.

43 Tighten the nut on the lower rear engine mounting bolt to the specified torque, then tighten the nut on the upper bolt to the specified torque – counter-hold the bolt heads if required.

44 Tighten the front mounting bolts to the specified torque.

45 Withdraw the swingarm pivot bolt. Position the left-hand swingarm pivot bracket, then insert the swingarm pivot bolt, followed by the bracket bolts with their washers, longer one in the bottom, from the left **(see illustrations 4.27b and a)**. On the right-hand side fit the pivot bracket onto the bolts, then fit the swingarm pivot bolt washer and nut and tighten the nut to the specified torque **(see illustration 4.26)**. Fit the bracket bolt washers and nuts and tighten them to the specified torque.

46 Fit the footrest bracket and tighten the bolts to the specified torque **(see illustration 4.25)**.

All models

47 The remainder of the installation procedure is the reverse of removal, referring to the relevant Chapters where directed, and noting the following points:

- Use new gaskets on the exhaust pipe connections.
- Make sure all wires, throttle cables and all hoses are correctly routed and connected, and secured by any clips or ties.
- Refill the engine with oil and coolant (see Chapter 1).
- Adjust the throttle cable freeplay.
- Adjust the drive chain (see Chapter 1).
- Start the engine and check that there are no oil or coolant leaks.

5 Engine disassembly and reassembly general information

1 Before beginning the engine overhaul, read through the related procedures to familiarise yourself with the scope and requirements of the job. Overhauling an engine is not all that difficult, but it is time consuming. Check on the availability of parts and make sure that any necessary special tools are obtained in advance.

2 Most work can be done with a decent set of typical workshop hand tools, although a number of precision measuring tools are required for inspecting parts to determine if they are worn.

3 To ensure maximum life and minimum trouble from a rebuilt engine, everything must be assembled with care in a spotlessly clean environment.

6.3 Slacken the clamps (arrowed) and detach the hoses

6.4a Unscrew the bolts (arrowed) . . .

6.4b . . . and remove the cooler

6.6 Fit a new O-ring into the groove

Disassembly

4 Before disassembling the engine, thoroughly clean and degrease its external surfaces. This will prevent contamination of the engine internals, and will also make the job a lot easier and cleaner. A high flash-point solvent, such as paraffin (kerosene) can be used, or better still, a proprietary engine degreaser. Use old paintbrushes and toothbrushes to work the solvent into the various recesses of the casings. Take care to exclude solvent or water from the electrical components and intake and exhaust ports.

⚠ *Warning: The use of petrol (gasoline) as a cleaning agent should be avoided because of the risk of fire.*

5 When clean and dry, position the engine on the workbench, leaving suitable clear area for working. Gather a selection of small containers, plastic bags and some labels so that parts can be grouped together in an easily identifiable manner. Also get some paper and a pen so that notes can be taken. You will also need a supply of clean rag, which should be as absorbent as possible.

6 Before commencing work, read through the appropriate section so that some idea of the necessary procedure can be gained. When removing components note that great force is seldom required, unless specified (checking the specified torque setting of the particular bolt being removed will indicate how tight it is, and therefore how much force should be needed). In many cases, a component's reluctance to be removed is indicative of an incorrect approach or removal method – if in any doubt, re-check with the text.

7 When disassembling the engine, keep 'mated' parts together (including gears, cylinder bores, pistons, connecting rods, valves, etc, that have been in contact with each other during engine operation). These 'mated' parts must be reused or replaced as an assembly.

8 A complete engine/transmission disassembly should be done in the following general order with reference to the appropriate Sections.

 Remove the valve cover
 Remove the camshafts
 Remove the cylinder head
 Remove the starter motor (see Chapter 8)
 Remove the starter clutch
 Remove the cam chain and blades
 Remove the clutch
 Remove the gearchange mechanism
 Remove the transmission shafts/selector drum and forks
 Remove the alternator (see Chapter 8)
 Remove the oil sump
 Remove the oil pump
 Separate the crankcase halves
 Remove the crankshaft
 Remove the connecting rods and pistons
 Remove the balancer shaft

Reassembly

9 Reassembly is accomplished by reversing the general disassembly sequence.

Engine, clutch and transmission 2•13

6 Oil cooler

Note: *The oil cooler can be removed with the engine in the frame. If the engine has been removed, ignore the steps which do not apply.*

Removal

1 The cooler is located on the front of the engine.
2 Drain the engine oil (see Chapter 1). Drain the coolant (see Chapter 1).
3 Slacken the clamp securing each hose to the cooler and detach the hoses **(see illustration)**.
4 Unscrew the three bolts and remove the cooler **(see illustrations)**. Discard the O-ring as a new one must be used.
5 Check the cooler body for cracks and dents and any evidence of coolant leakage and replace it with a new one if necessary. Also check the hoses for splits, cracks, hardening and deterioration and fit new ones if required.

Installation

6 Installation is the reverse of removal, noting the following:
- Ensure the mating surfaces of the crankcase and the cooler are clean and dry.
- Use a new O-ring on the cooler body and smear it with clean engine oil. Make sure it seats in its groove **(see illustration)**.
- Make sure the coolant hoses are pressed fully onto their unions and are secured by the clamps.
- Fill the engine with oil to the correct level (see Chapter 1).
- Refill the cooling system (see Chapter 1).

7 Valve cover

Note: *The valve cover can be removed with the engine in the frame. If the engine has been removed, ignore the steps which do not apply.*

Removal

1 Remove the fuel tank (see Chapter 4).
2 On CBF1000/A models remove the No. 1 and 4 cylinder ignition coil and its bracket (see Chapter 4). On CB1000R/RA models, remove the coolant reservoir (see Chapter 3), then remove both ignition coils and their brackets (see Chapter 4).
3 Remove the PAIR system control valve along with its hoses (see Chapter 4). Remove the crankcase breather hose, disconnecting it from both the valve cover on the left side and from the air filter housing on the right **(see illustration 4.11b)**.
4 Unscrew the four valve cover bolts and lift the cover off the cylinder head – if the engine is in the frame take care when removing it as it is quite a tight fit and the cover is easily scratched **(see illustrations)**. If the cover is stuck, do not try to lever it off with a screwdriver. Tap it gently around the sides with a rubber hammer or block of wood to dislodge it. Note the rubber washers for the bolts and remove them if they are loose **(see illustration 7.11)**.
5 The rubber gasket is normally glued into the groove in the cover, and is best left there if it is reusable. If the gasket is in any way damaged, deformed or deteriorated, remove it.
6 Note the four dowels that link the PAIR system air passages between the valve cover and cylinder head and remove them for safekeeping if they are loose (which is unlikely), taking care not to drop them if they are not in the valve cover **(see illustration)**.
7 If required, remove the PAIR system reed valves (see Chapter 4).

Installation

8 If removed, install the PAIR system reed valves (see Chapter 4).
9 If removed, fit the PAIR system dowels into the valve cover **(see illustration 7.6)**.
10 Examine the valve cover gasket for signs of damage or deterioration and fit a new one if necessary. If a new one is used, clean all traces of the old glue from the groove in the cover and clean it and the cylinder head mating surface with solvent. Fit the new gasket into the groove and over the PAIR dowels, using a suitable glue, sealant or grease to hold it in place **(see illustration)**. Also apply a suitable sealant to the cut-outs in the cylinder head **(see illustration)**.
11 Position the valve cover on the cylinder head, making sure the gasket stays in place

7.4a Unscrew the bolts (arrowed) on the left . . .

7.4b . . . and on the right . . .

7.4c . . . and carefully remove the cover

7.6 PAIR system air passage dowels (arrowed)

7.10a Make sure the gasket locates correctly and stays there

7.10b Apply a sealant to the cutouts (arrowed) in the cylinder head

2•14 Engine, clutch and transmission

7.11 Make sure the UP mark on each washer (arrowed) faces up

8.1 Unscrew the cap bolt and remove the washer

(see illustration 7.4c). If removed, fit the rubber washers into the cover, using new ones if required, and making sure they are installed with the UP mark facing up **(see illustration)**. Install the cover bolts and tighten them to the specified torque setting **(see illustrations 7.4a and b)**.

12 Install the remaining components in the reverse order of removal.

8 Cam chain tensioner

Note: *The cam chain tensioner can be removed with the engine in the frame. If the engine has been removed, ignore the steps which do not apply.*

Removal

1 Unscrew the tensioner cap bolt and remove the sealing washer **(see illustration)**.
2 If the Honda tensioner holding tool (pt. no. 07ZMG-MCAA400 for CBF models, or 070MG-0010100 for CB-R models) is available, fit it onto the end of the tensioner and turn it clockwise until the plunger is fully retracted and held. Unscrew the tensioner mounting bolts, then withdraw the tensioner from the engine **(see illustration 8.3a)**.
3 If a holding tool is not available, first slacken the tensioner mounting bolts slightly **(see illustration)**. Insert a small flat-bladed screwdriver in the end of the tensioner so that it engages the slotted plunger **(see illustration)**. Turn the screwdriver clockwise until the plunger is fully retracted and hold it in this position while unscrewing the tensioner mounting bolts. Remove the bolts, then withdraw the tensioner from the engine and release the screwdriver – the plunger will spring back out once the screwdriver is removed, but can be easily reset on installation.
4 Discard the gasket and sealing washers as new ones must be used on installation. Do not attempt to dismantle the tensioner.

Installation

5 Check that the plunger moves smoothly when wound into the tensioner and springs back out freely when released **(see illustration 8.7a)**. Ensure the tensioner and cylinder block surfaces are clean and dry.
6 If the Honda holding tool is being used and has been removed, fit it onto the end of the tensioner and turn it clockwise until the plunger is fully retracted and held. Fit new sealing washers onto the tensioner mounting bolts. Fit a new gasket onto the tensioner body with the tab positioned so it will face to the middle of the engine, then fit the tensioner with its mounting bolts and washers, and tighten them **(see illustration 8.7b)**. Remove the tool, then fit the tensioner cap bolt with a new sealing washer and tighten it **(see illustration 8.1)**.
7 If the tool is not available, first fit new sealing washers onto the tensioner mounting bolts. Insert a small flat-bladed screwdriver in the end of the tensioner so that it engages the slotted plunger **(see illustration)**. Turn the screwdriver clockwise until the plunger is fully retracted and hold it in this position whilst the tensioner is installed. Fit a new gasket onto the tensioner body with the tab positioned so it will face to the middle of the engine, then fit the tensioner with its mounting bolts and washers, and tighten them **(see illustration)**. Release and remove the screwdriver, then fit the tensioner cap bolt with a new sealing washer and tighten it **(see illustration 8.1)**.

8.3a Slacken the mounting bolts (arrowed) slightly . . .

8.3b . . . then insert the screwdriver and retract the plunger

8.7a Insert the screwdriver and retract the plunger . . .

8.7b . . . then fit a new gasket and install the tensioner

Engine, clutch and transmission 2•15

9.2 Remove the timing inspection cap

9.3a Turn the engine clockwise using the bolt . . .

9.3b . . . until the line next to the T mark aligns with the notch (arrowed) . . .

9 Camshafts and followers

Note: *The camshafts can be removed with the engine in the frame. Place clean rags over the spark plug holes and the cam chain tunnel to prevent any component from dropping into the engine.*

Removal

1 Remove the spark plugs (see Chapter 1). Remove the valve cover (see Section 7).
2 Unscrew the timing inspection cap from the clutch cover **(see illustration)**. Check the condition of its O-ring and obtain a new one if necessary.
3 The engine must be turned so that the No. 1 piston is at TDC (top dead centre) on its compression stroke. Turn the engine using a suitable socket on the timing rotor bolt and turning it in a clockwise direction only until the line next to the T mark on the timing rotor aligns with the static timing mark, which is a notch or pointer in the inspection hole rim, and the IN and EX marks on the intake and exhaust camshaft sprockets respectively are facing away from each other and are flush with the cylinder head top surface **(see illustrations)**. If the marks are facing towards each other, rotate the engine clockwise one full turn (360°) until the line next to the T mark again aligns with the static timing mark. The sprocket marks will now be facing away.
4 Either remove the cam chain tensioner (see Section 8), or if you prefer, using the tensioner holding tool as described in Section 8, Step 2, retract and lock the tensioner plunger. Unscrew the bolts securing the top cam chain guide and remove it **(see illustration)**.
5 There are three camshaft holders, each bridging both camshafts **(see illustration)**. Of the two larger holders, the one on the right-hand side is marked R and the one on the left-hand side L, and these letters are at the front **(see illustration)**. Note the numbers

9.3c . . . and the camshaft sprocket marks are as shown

9.4 Unscrew the bolts and remove the guide

9.5a Camshaft holders (arrowed)

9.5b Note the ID letter and the bolt numbers on each holder

2•16 Engine, clutch and transmission

9.6a Unscrew the bolts as described and remove the holders

9.6b Remove the sealing rings and discard them

9.7 Camshaft identity mark

marked on the holders, adjacent to each bolt. These numbers denote the **tightening** sequence for the holder bolts.

6 Unscrew the camshaft holder bolts, slackening them evenly and a very little at a time in a **reverse** of the tightening sequence marked on the holders. Remove the bolts, noting which fits where as some are different, and lift off the holders, noting how they fit **(see illustration)**. Note the sealing washers fitted with the eight bolts around the spark plug bores **(see illustration 9.28d)**. Remove the sealing rings from their grooves around the spark plug holes on the underside of the holders, noting how they also locate around the PAIR system air passage dowels **(see illustration)**. Discard them as new ones must be used. Do not remove the locating dowels or air passage dowels unless they are loose and liable to drop out.

Caution: Make sure the holders lift up squarely and evenly and do not stick on a dowel or distort from some of the bolts being slackened more than the others as they or a camshaft could easily break.

7 The camshafts are marked for identification – the intake camshaft is marked IN and the exhaust camshaft is marked EX **(see illustration)**. If the marks aren't clear make your own as the camshafts must be installed in their original location.

8 Remove the intake camshaft first, then the exhaust. Carefully lift each camshaft in turn off the head and disengage the sprocket from the chain **(see illustrations 9.27a and 9.26a)**. Wire the chain to another component or secure it using a rod of some sort to prevent it from dropping. While the camshafts are out do not rotate the crankshaft. Place rags over the spark plug holes and the cam chain tunnel to prevent anything from dropping into the engine on removal.

9 If the followers and shims are being removed from the cylinder head, obtain a container which is divided into sixteen compartments, and label each compartment with the location of a valve, i.e. intake or exhaust camshaft, left or right valve. If a container is not available, use labelled plastic bags (egg cartons also do very well!). Remove the cam follower of the valve in question using a magnet or the suction created by a valve lapping tool, or long nosed pliers can be used with care **(see illustration)**. Retrieve the shim either from the inside of the follower or pick it out of the top of the valve spring retainer using either a magnet, a screwdriver with a dab of grease on it (the shim will stick to the grease), or a very small screwdriver and a pair of pliers **(see illustrations)**. Do not allow the shim to fall into the engine.

10 If required unscrew the sprocket bolts and take the sprockets off the camshafts **(see illustration)**. Both sprockets are identical and are therefore interchangeable, but mark them according to their camshaft so they can be installed in their original position. Also make alignment marks between the sprocket and the camshaft so that the sprocket can be installed the correct way round to avoid confusion when setting up the timing.

Inspection

11 Inspect the bearing surfaces of the camshaft holders and cylinder head and the corresponding journals on the camshafts. Look for score marks, deep scratches and evidence of spalling (a pitted appearance). Check the oil passages for clogging.

12 Check the camshaft lobes for heat discoloration (blue appearance), score marks, chipped areas, flat spots and spalling. Measure the height of each lobe with a

9.9a Carefully lift out the follower using a lapping tool, grips or a magnet . . .

9.9b . . . and retrieve the shim (arrowed) from inside it . . .

9.9c . . . or from the top of the valve

9.10 Camshaft sprocket bolts (arrowed)

Engine, clutch and transmission 2•17

9.12 Measure the height of the camshaft lobes with a micrometer

9.21a Measure the external diameter of each follower . . .

9.21b . . . and the internal diameter of each bore

micrometer **(see illustration)** and compare the results to the minimum height listed in this Chapter's Specifications. If damage is noted or wear is excessive, the camshaft must be replaced with a new one.

13 Check the amount of camshaft runout by supporting each end on V-blocks, and measuring any runout using a dial gauge. If the runout exceeds the specified limit the camshaft must be replaced with a new one.

> **HAYNES HiNT** *Refer to Tools and Workshop Tips in the Reference section for details of how to read a micrometer and dial gauge.*

14 Next, check the camshaft journal oil clearances. In order to negate the probability of the camshafts rotating (due to the fact that some of the lobes will be depressing their valves) as the holder bolts are tightened down, which will disturb the Plastigauge and lead to a false measurement, the valves should be removed from the cylinder head (if the cylinder head is being fully checked and overhauled due to wear you will be doing this anyway). To do this the head must be removed from the engine, which means removing the engine from the frame (see Sections 4, 11 and 12). Clean the camshafts and the bearing surfaces in the cylinder head and camshaft holder with a clean lint-free cloth, then lay each camshaft in its correct location in the cylinder head (see Step 7).

15 Cut some strips of Plastigauge and lay one piece on each journal, parallel with the camshaft centreline. Make sure the camshaft holder dowels are installed **(see illustration 9.28a)**. If the valves are installed, install the holders and tighten the bolts as described in Step 28. If the valves have been removed, install the holders as described in Step 28, noting that if preferred you can do each holder separately rather than all three at the same time, and tighten the bolts evenly and a little at a time in a criss-cross sequence to the specified torque setting, making sure the holders are pulled down squarely onto the dowels. While doing this, don't let the camshafts rotate, or the Plastigauge will be disturbed and you will have to start again.

16 Now unscrew the camshaft holder bolts as described in Step 6 (valves installed) or evenly and a little at a time in a criss-cross sequence (valves removed), and lift off the holder.

17 To determine the oil clearance, compare the crushed Plastigauge (at its widest point) on each journal to the scale printed on the Plastigauge container. Compare the results to this Chapter's Specifications. If the oil clearance is greater than specified, replace the camshaft with a new one and recheck the clearance. If the clearance is still too great, also replace the cylinder head and holder with new ones.

> **HAYNES HiNT** *Before replacing the camshafts, cylinder head or holders because of damage, check with motorcycle cylinder head specialists to see whether worn components can be renewed. Due to the cost of new components it is recommended that all options be explored before condemning them as trash!*

18 Except in cases of oil starvation, the cam chain should wear very little. If the chain has stretched excessively, which makes it difficult to maintain proper tension, or if it is stiff or the links are binding or kinking, replace it with a new one. Refer to Section 10 for replacement.

19 Check the sprockets for wear, cracks and other damage, and replace them with new ones if necessary (see Steps 10 and 22). If the sprockets are worn, the cam chain is also worn, and so probably is the sprocket on the crankshaft. If severe wear is apparent, the entire engine should be disassembled for inspection.

20 Inspect the cam chain guides and tensioner blade (see Section 10).

21 Inspect the outer surface of each cam follower for evidence of scoring or other damage. If a follower is in poor condition, it is probable that the bore in the cylinder head in which it works is also damaged. Check for clearance between each follower and its bore. Measure the outer diameter of each follower and the inner diameter of its bore and compare the results to the Specifications **(see illustrations)**. If any follower is worn beyond its service limit replace it with a new one. If any bore is worn beyond its limit, is seriously out-of-round or tapered, replace the cylinder head with a new one.

Installation

22 If removed, fit the sprockets onto the camshafts. Make sure they are the correct way round and in their original location as identified by the marks made on removal (Step 10) **(see illustration and 9.10)**. Clean the threads of the bolts and apply a suitable non-permanent thread locking compound, and tighten them to the torque setting specified at the beginning of the Chapter.

9.22 Camshaft and sprocket alignment

2•18 Engine, clutch and transmission

9.23 Fit each shim into its recess, then fit the follower onto the valve

9.26a Install the exhaust camshaft as described . . .

9.26b . . . so the EX mark is positioned as shown

9.27a Install the intake camshaft as described . . .

9.27b . . . so the IN mark is as shown

23 If removed, lubricate each shim and its follower with molybdenum disulphide oil (a 50/50 mixture of molybdenum disulphide grease and engine oil). Fit each shim into its recess in the top of the valve spring retainer with the size mark facing up, making sure it is correctly seated **(see illustration 9.9c)**. **Note:** *It is most important that the shims and followers are returned to their original valves otherwise the valve clearances will be inaccurate.* Fit each follower, making sure it fits squarely in its bore **(see illustration)**.

24 Make sure the bearing surfaces on the camshafts and in the cylinder head are clean, then apply molybdenum disulphide oil (a 50/50 mixture of molybdenum disulphide grease and engine oil) to each of them. Also apply it to the camshaft journals and lobes. Make sure that none gets on the mating surfaces between the holder and the head, or in the bolt holes.

25 Check that the line next to the T mark on the timing rotor aligns with the notch or pointer in the inspection hole rim **(see illustration 9.3b)**.

26 Lay the exhaust camshaft (marked EX) onto the head with the EX mark on the sprocket facing forward and level with the cylinder head top mating surface **(see illustrations and 9.22)**. Fit the cam chain around the sprocket as you install the camshaft, pulling up on the chain to remove all slack in the front run between the crankshaft and the camshaft.

27 Lay the intake camshaft (marked IN) onto the head with the IN mark on the sprocket facing back and level with the cylinder head top mating surface **(see illustrations and 9.22)**. Fit the cam chain around the sprocket as you install the camshaft, pulling on it to remove all slack from between the two camshaft sprockets. Any slack in the chain must lie in the rear run of the chain between the intake camshaft and the crankshaft so that it is later taken up by the tensioner.

28 Make sure the bearing surfaces in the camshaft holders are clean. Make sure the camshaft holder bolt dowels and PAIR system air passage dowels are installed **(see illustration)**. Fit new sealing rings smeared with oil into the grooves around the spark plug holes on the underside of the main holders, making sure they also locate around the PAIR system air passage dowels. Apply molybdenum disulphide oil (a 50/50 mixture of molybdenum disulphide grease and engine oil) to the bearing surfaces. Lay the holders in the head making sure they are correctly positioned (see Step 5) **(see illustrations)**. Apply clean engine oil to the threads and under the heads of all the camshaft holder bolts. Install the bolts, not forgetting new sealing washers with the eight bolts around the spark plug bores, and fitting the six longer bolts into the front and rearmost right-hand holes, and tighten

9.28a Camshaft holder dowels (arrowed). Fit new sealing rings over the air passage dowels and into the grooves around the plug holes

9.28b Install the holders . . .

9.28c . . . making sure they are correctly positioned

Engine, clutch and transmission 2•19

9.28d Do not forget the sealing washers with the spark plug bore bolts ...

9.28e ... and fit the longer bolts as shown (arrowed)

them finger-tight **(see illustrations)**. First gradually and evenly tighten the centre bolts Nos. 1-2-7-8 in that order until the dowels in the holder enter their bores in the head. Now tighten all the bolts evenly and a little at a time in the correct sequence (i.e. 1 to 20), again making sure the holder is being pulled down squarely.

Caution: Whilst tightening the bolts, make sure the holders are being pulled evenly and squarely down and are not binding on the dowels or tilting to one side – if they do, adjust the relevant bolts until the holders are again square to the head. A holder or camshaft is likely to break if they are not tightened down evenly and squarely.

29 If the tensioner tool was used to retract and hold the tensioner plunger, remove it to release the plunger. If the tensioner was removed, use a piece of wooden dowel to press on the back of the cam chain tensioner blade via the tensioner bore in the cylinder block to ensure that any slack in the cam chain is taken up and transferred to the rear run of the chain (where it will later be taken up by the tensioner). At this point check that all the timing marks are still in **exact** alignment as described in Step 3 **(see illustrations 9.3b and c and 9.26b and 9.27b)**. Note that it is easy to be slightly out (one tooth on the sprocket) without the marks appearing drastically out of alignment. If the marks are out, verify which sprocket is misaligned, then either reinstall the tensioner locking tool and retract the plunger, or remove the wooden dowel. Unscrew the sprocket's bolts and slide it off the camshaft, then disengage it from the chain. Move the camshaft round as required, then fit the sprocket back into the chain and onto the camshaft, and check the marks again. With everything correctly aligned, clean the sprocket bolts and apply a suitable non-permanent thread locking compound, and tighten them to the torque setting specified at the beginning of the Chapter.

Caution: If the marks are not aligned exactly as described, the valve timing will be incorrect and the valves may strike the pistons, causing extensive damage to the engine.

30 Install the cam chain top guide and tighten its bolts **(see illustration 9.4)**. Install the cam chain tensioner (see Section 8), if removed.

31 Turn the engine clockwise through two full turns and check again that all the timing marks still align (see Step 3) **(see illustrations 9.3b and c and 9.26b and 9.27b)**. Check the valve clearances and adjust them if necessary (see Chapter 1).

32 Install the timing inspection cap using a new O-ring if required, and smear the O-ring and the cap threads with grease **(see illustration 9.2)**. Tighten the cap to the torque setting specified at the beginning of the Chapter.

33 Install the valve cover (see Section 7). Install the spark plugs (see Chapter 1).

10 Cam chain, tensioner blade and front guide

Note: *The cam chain and its blades can be removed with the engine in the frame. If the engine has been removed, ignore the steps which do not apply.*

Removal

1 Remove the camshafts – this procedure involves removing the top guide blade (see Section 9).
2 Remove the starter clutch (see Section 13).
3 Unscrew the tensioner blade pivot bolt and draw the blade out of the engine, noting the washer that fits behind it **(see illustrations)**.
4 Draw the cam chain off the crankshaft sprocket and out of the engine **(see illustration)**. Slide the sprocket off the end of the crankshaft, noting the offset wide splines

10.3a Tensioner blade (A), front guide blade (B)

10.3b Unscrew the pivot bolt, noting the washer behind the blade

10.4 Remove the cam chain and slide the sprocket off the shaft

2•20 Engine, clutch and transmission

10.5a Unscrew the pivot bolt . . .

10.5b . . . and draw the guide blade out of the engine

10.5c Note the collar in the pivot

that mean it can only be installed in one position.

5 Unscrew the front guide blade pivot bolt and draw the blade out of the engine **(see illustrations)**. Note the washer with the bolt and the collar that fits from the inside **(see illustration)**.

Inspection

Cam chain and sprockets

6 Check the chain for binding, kinks and any obvious damage and replace it with a new one if necessary. Check the camshaft and crankshaft sprocket teeth for wear and replace if necessary.

11.4a Cylinder head 6 mm bolts (arrowed)

Tensioner and guide blades

7 Check the sliding surface and edges of the blades for excessive wear, deep grooves, cracking and other obvious damage, and replace them with new ones if necessary.

Installation

8 Installation of the sprocket, chain and blades is the reverse of removal. Do not omit the washer that fits behind the tensioner blade **(see illustration 10.3b)**, or the collar in the guide blade **(see illustration 10.5c)**. Clean the threads of the bolts and apply a suitable non-permanent thread locking compound, and tighten them to the torque settings specified at the beginning of the Chapter.

11 Cylinder head removal and installation

Note: *To remove the cylinder head the engine must be removed from the frame.*

Removal

1 Remove the engine (see Section 4). Tilt the engine back and to the left to drain any residual coolant from the inlet and outlet unions. If required remove the outlet union (see Chapter 3).

2 Remove the valve cover (see Section 7).

3 Remove the camshafts, followers and shims (see Section 9). If required and not already done (i.e. if the holding tool was used when removing the camshafts) remove the cam chain tensioner (see Section 8).

4 The cylinder head is secured by two 6 mm bolts and ten 9 mm bolts with fitted washers (i.e. they can't be separated from the bolts) **(see illustrations)**. First unscrew and remove the 6 mm bolts. Now unscrew and remove the 9 mm bolts, slackening them evenly and a little at a time in a criss-cross pattern working from the outside to the middle until they are all loose.

5 Hold the cam chain up and pull the cylinder head up off the block, and pass the cam chain down through the tunnel **(see illustration)**. Do not let the chain fall into the crankcase – secure it with a piece of wire or metal bar to prevent it from doing so. If the head is stuck, tap around the joint faces with a soft-faced mallet. Do not attempt to free the head by inserting a screwdriver between the head and block mating surfaces – you'll damage them.

6 Remove the cylinder head gasket and discard it as a new one must be used. If they are loose, remove the dowels from the cylinder

11.4b Cylinder head 9 mm bolts (arrowed)

11.5 Carefully lift the head up off the block

Engine, clutch and transmission 2•21

11.10 Install the dowels (arrowed) then lay the new gasket on the block

11.12 Lubricate and install the bolts and tighten them as described to the specified torque setting

block or the underside of the cylinder head (see illustration 11.10).
7 Check the cylinder head gasket and the mating surfaces on the cylinder head and crankcase for signs of leakage, which could indicate warpage. Refer to Section 12 and check the cylinder head gasket surface for warpage.
8 Clean all traces of old gasket material from the cylinder head and crankcase. If a scraper is used, take care not to scratch or gouge the soft aluminium. Be careful not to let any of the gasket material fall into the crankcase, the cylinder bore or the oil and coolant passages.

Installation

9 Lubricate the cylinder bores with engine oil. If removed, fit the dowels into the block (see illustration 11.10).
10 Ensure both cylinder head and crankcase mating surfaces are clean. Lay the new head gasket over the cam chain and blades and onto the crankcase, locating it over the dowels and making sure all the holes are correctly aligned (see illustration). Never re-use the old gasket.
11 Carefully fit the cylinder head onto the block, making sure it locates correctly onto the dowels (see illustration 11.5). Feed the cam chain up through the tunnel as you install the head, then secure it in place with a piece of wire to prevent it from falling back down.
12 Apply some molybdenum disulphide oil (a 50/50 mixture of molybdenum disulphide grease and engine oil) to the threads and the seating surfaces of the heads and washers of all the bolts. Note that if new bolts are being installed, first remove any anti-rust coating by cleaning them with solvent. Install the bolts and tighten them all finger-tight (see illustration). Tighten the 9 mm bolts evenly and a little at a time in a criss-cross pattern working from the middle to the outside to the torque setting specified at the beginning of the Chapter. Now tighten the 6 mm bolts (see illustration 11.4a).
13 Install the remaining components in a reverse of their removal sequence, referring to the relevant Sections or Chapters (see Steps 3 to 1).

12 Cylinder head and valve overhaul

1 Because of the complex nature of this job and the special tools and equipment required, most owners leave servicing of the valves, valve seats and valve guides to a professional. However, you can make an initial assessment of whether the valves are seating correctly, and therefore sealing, by pouring a small amount of solvent into each of the valve ports. If the solvent leaks past any valve into the combustion chamber area the valve is not seating correctly and sealing.
2 With the correct tools (a valve spring compressor is essential – make sure it is suitable for motorcycle work), you can also remove the valves and associated components from the cylinder head, clean them and check them for wear to assess the extent of the work needed, and, unless seat cutting or guide replacement is required, grind in the valves and reassemble them in the head.
3 A dealer service department or specialist can replace the guides and re-cut the valve seats.
4 After the valve service has been performed, be sure to clean it very thoroughly before installation on the engine to remove any metal particles or abrasive grit that may still be

12.6a Compressing the valve spring(s) using a valve spring compressor

12.5 Valve components
1 Collets
2 Spring retainer
3 Valve spring
4 Spring seat
5 Valve stem oil seal
6 Valve

present from the valve service operations. Use compressed air, if available, to blow out all the holes and passages.

Disassembly

5 Before proceeding, arrange to label and store the valves along with their related components in such a way that they can be returned to their original locations without getting mixed up (see illustration). Either use the same container as the cam followers and shims are stored in (see Section 9), or obtain a separate container and label each compartment accordingly. Alternatively, labelled plastic bags will do just as well.
6 Compress the valve spring on the first valve with a spring compressor, making sure it is correctly located onto each end of the valve assembly (see illustration). On the top of the valve the adaptor needs to be about the same size as the spring retainer – if it is too big it will contact the follower bore and mark it, and if it is too small it will be difficult to remove and install the collets (see illustration). On the underside of the head make sure the plate on the compressor only contacts the

12.6b Make sure the compressor locates correctly both on the top of the spring retainer . . .

2•22 Engine, clutch and transmission

TOOL TIP

Protect the follower bore in the cylinder head from scratches by the valve spring compressor using either the Honda tool (Part No. 07HMG-MR70002) or by fabricating a shield from an old 35 mm film canister. Cut the canister to the dimensions shown.

12.6c ... and on the bottom of the valve

12.7a Remove the collets ...

valve and not the soft aluminium of the head **(see illustration)** – if the plate is too big for the valve, use a spacer between them. Do not compress the spring any more than is absolutely necessary.

Caution: Take great care not to mark the cam follower bore with the spring compressor.

7 Remove the collets, using a magnet or a screwdriver with a dab of grease on it **(see illustration)**. Carefully release the valve spring compressor and remove the spring retainer, noting which way up it fits, the spring and the valve **(see illustrations)**. If the valve binds in the guide and won't pull through, push it back into the head and deburr the area around the collet groove with a very fine file or whetstone **(see illustration)**.

8 Pull the valve stem seal off the top of the valve guide with pliers and discard it (the old seals should never be reused) **(see illustration)**. Remove the spring seat, noting which way up, it fits – using a magnet is the easiest way to remove it **(see illustration)**.

9 Repeat the procedure for the remaining valves. Remember to keep the parts for each valve together so they can be reinstalled in the same location.

10 Clean the cylinder head with solvent and dry it thoroughly. Compressed air will speed the drying process and ensure that all holes and recessed areas are clean. **Note:** *Do not use a wire brush mounted in a drill motor to clean the combustion chambers as the head material is soft and may be scratched or eroded away by the wire brush.*

11 Clean all of the valve springs, collets, retainers and spring seats with solvent and dry them thoroughly. Do the parts from one valve at a time so that no mixing of parts between valves occurs.

12 Scrape off any deposits that may have formed on the valve, then use a motorised wire brush to remove deposits from the valve heads and stems. Again, make sure the valves do not get mixed up.

Inspection

13 Inspect the head very carefully for cracks and other damage. If cracks are found, a new head is required. Check the camshaft bearing surfaces for wear and evidence of seizure.

12.7b ... the spring retainer ...

12.7c ... the spring ...

12.7d ... and the valve

12.7e If the valve stem (2) won't pull through the guide, deburr the area (1) above the collet groove

12.8a Pull the seal off the valve stem ...

12.8b ... then remove the spring seat

Engine, clutch and transmission 2•23

12.15 Measure the valve seat width

12.16a Measure the valve stem diameter with a micrometer

12.16b Measure the valve guide with a small bore gauge, then measure the bore gauge with a micrometer

Check the camshafts and holders for wear as well (see Section 9).

14 Using a precision straight-edge and a feeler gauge set to the warpage limit listed in the specifications at the beginning of the Chapter, check the head gasket mating surface for warpage. Refer to *Tools and Workshop Tips* in the Reference section for details of how to use the straight-edge. If the head is warped beyond the limit specified at the beginning of this Chapter, consult a Honda dealer or take it to a specialist repair shop for an opinion, though be prepared to have to buy a new one.

15 Examine the valve seats in the combustion chamber. If they are pitted, cracked or burned, the head will require work beyond the scope of the home mechanic. Measure the valve seat width and compare it to this Chapter's Specifications **(see illustration)**. If it exceeds the service limit, or if it varies around its circumference, overhaul is required.

16 Working on one valve and guide at a time, measure the valve stem diameter **(see illustration)**. Clean the valve's guide using a guide reamer and cutting oil to remove any carbon build-up – insert the reamer from the underside of the head and turn it clockwise only. Now measure the inside diameter of the guide (at both ends and in the centre of the guide) with a small bore gauge, then measure the gauge with a micrometer **(see illustration)**. Measure the guide at the ends and at the centre to determine if they are worn in a bell-mouth pattern (more wear at the ends). Subtract the stem diameter from the valve guide diameter to obtain the valve stem-to-guide clearance. If the stem-to-guide clearance is greater than listed in this Chapter's Specifications, replace whichever component is beyond its specification limits with a new one. If the valve guide is within specifications, but is worn unevenly, it should be replaced with a new one. Repeat for the other valves.

17 Carefully inspect each valve face, stem and collet groove area for cracks, pits and burned spots.

18 Rotate the valve and check for any obvious indication that it is bent, in which case it must be replaced with a new one. Check the end of the stem for pitting and excessive wear. The presence of any of the above conditions indicates the need for valve servicing.

19 Check the end of each valve spring for wear and pitting. Measure the spring free length and compare it to the specifications **(see illustration)**. If a spring is shorter than specified it has sagged and must be replaced with a new one. Also place the spring upright on a flat surface and check it for bend by placing a ruler against it, or alternatively lay it against a set square **(see illustration)**. If the bend in any spring is excessive, it must be replaced with a new one.

20 Check the spring seats, retainers and collets for obvious wear and cracks. Any questionable parts should not be re-used, as extensive damage will occur in the event of failure during engine operation.

21 If the inspection indicates that no overhaul work is required, the valve components can be reinstalled in the head.

Reassembly

22 Unless a valve service has been performed, before installing the valves in the head they should be ground in (lapped) to ensure a positive seal between the valves and seats. This procedure requires coarse and fine valve grinding compound and a valve grinding tool (either hand-held or drill driven – note that some drill-driven tools specify using only a fine grinding compound). If a grinding tool is not available, a piece of rubber or plastic hose can be slipped over the valve stem (after the valve has been installed in the guide) and used to turn the valve.

23 Apply a small amount of coarse grinding compound to the valve face **(see illustration)**. Smear some molybdenum disulphide oil (a 50/50 mixture of molybdenum disulphide grease and engine oil) to the valve stem, then slip the valve into the guide **(see illustration 12.29)**. **Note:** *Make sure each valve is installed in its correct guide and be careful not to get any grinding compound on the valve stem.*

24 Attach the grinding tool to the valve and rotate the tool between the palms of your hands. Use a back-and-forth motion (as though rubbing your hands together) rather than a circular motion (i.e. so that the valve rotates alternately clockwise and anti-clockwise rather than in one direction only)

12.19a Measure the free length of each valve spring . . .

12.19b . . . and check it for bend

12.23 Apply dabs of paste round the valve face

2•24 Engine, clutch and transmission

12.24 Rotate the valve grinding tool back and forth between the palms of your hands

12.27 Fit the spring seat using a rod to guide it if necessary

12.28 Fit a new valve stem seal and press it squarely into place

(see illustration). If a motorised tool is being used, take note of the correct drive speed for it – if your drill runs too fast and is not variable, use a hand tool instead. Lift the valve off the seat and turn it at regular intervals to distribute the grinding compound properly. Continue the grinding procedure until the valve face and seat contact area is of uniform width, and unbroken around the entire circumference.

25 Carefully remove the valve and wipe off all traces of grinding compound, making sure none gets in the guide. Use solvent to clean the valve and wipe the seat area thoroughly with a solvent soaked cloth.

26 Repeat the procedure with fine valve grinding compound, then use solvent to clean the valve and flush the guide, and wipe the seat area thoroughly with a solvent soaked cloth. Repeat the entire procedure for the remaining valves. On completion thoroughly clean the entire head again, then blow through all passages with compressed air. Make sure all traces of the grinding compound have been removed before assembling the head.

27 Working on one valve at a time, lay the spring seat in place in the cylinder head with its shouldered side facing up (see illustration). As it is easy to cock the seat on the top of the valve guide, and then tricky to get it to sit properly, install it using a rod as a guide for it to slide down.

28 Fit a new valve stem seal onto the guide – note that the seals for the intake valves are marked around their upper rim and those for the exhaust valves are plain. Fit them using finger pressure, a stem seal fitting tool or an appropriate size deep socket, pushing the seal squarely onto the end of the valve guide until it is felt to clip into place (see illustration). Make sure the seal does not get cocked sideways as it could be damaged.

29 Coat the valve stem with molybdenum disulphide oil (a 50/50 mixture of molybdenum disulphide grease and engine oil), then slide it into its guide, rotating it slowly to avoid damaging the seal (see illustration). Check that the valve moves up-and-down freely in the guide.

30 Next, fit the spring, with the closer-wound coils facing down into the cylinder head (see illustration 12.7c). Fit the spring retainer, with its shouldered side facing down so that it fits into the top of the spring (see illustration).

31 Apply a small amount of grease to the collets to help hold them in place. Compress the valve spring with a spring compressor, making sure it is correctly located onto each end of the valve assembly (see Step 6) (see illustrations 12.6a, 12.6b and 12.6c). Do not compress the spring any more than is necessary to slip the collets into place. Locate each collet in turn into the groove in the valve stem using a screwdriver with a dab of grease on it (see illustration). Carefully release the compressor, making sure the collets seat and lock in the retaining groove.

32 Repeat the procedure for the remaining valves. Remember to keep the parts for each valve together and separate from the other valves so they can be reinstalled in the same location.

33 Support the cylinder head on blocks so the valves can't contact the work surface, then tap the end of each valve stem lightly to seat the collets in their grooves (see illustration).

12.29 Lubricate the stem and slide the valve into its correct location

12.30 Fit the valve spring then fit the spring retainer

12.31 Locate each collet in its groove in the top of the valve stem

12.33 Seat the collets as described

> **HAYNES HINT** *Check for proper sealing of the valves by pouring a small amount of solvent into each of the valve ports. If the solvent leaks past any valve into the combustion chamber the valve grinding operation on that valve should be repeated.*

34 After the cylinder head and camshafts have been installed, check the valve clearances and adjust as required (see Chapter 1).

Engine, clutch and transmission 2•25

13.2 Remove the idle gear and shaft

13.3 Wedge some rag between the gears (arrowed) to jam them while unscrewing the bolt

13.4a Unscrew the bolt...

13 Starter clutch and gears

Note: *The starter clutch can be removed with the engine in the frame. If the engine has been removed, ignore the steps which do not apply.*

Check

1 The operation of the starter clutch can be checked while it is in situ. Remove the starter motor (see Chapter 8). Check that the reduction gear is able to rotate freely clockwise as you look at it via the starter motor aperture, but locks when rotated clockwise. If not, the starter clutch is faulty and should be removed for inspection.

Removal

2 Remove the clutch cover (see Section 14, Steps 1 to 3). Withdraw the idle gear shaft and remove the gear **(see illustration)**.

3 To prevent the crankshaft from turning while unscrewing the starter clutch bolt, either engage 6th gear and have an assistant hold the rear brake on hard with the rear tyre in firm contact with the ground, or alternatively wedge a thick piece of rag material or a piece of aluminium (DO NOT use steel) between the primary drive and driven gears at the top as shown **(see illustration)**.

4 Unscrew the bolt and remove the washer **(see illustration)**. Slide the starter clutch off the shaft, noting the offset wide splines that mean it can only be installed in one position **(see illustration)**. Remove the thrust washer **(see illustration)**.

5 If you need to remove the reduction gear first remove the clutch (see Section 14). Remove the reduction gear **(see illustration)**.

Inspection

6 With the starter clutch face down on a workbench, check that the starter driven gear rotates freely clockwise and locks against the rotor anti-clockwise **(see illustration)**. If it doesn't, the starter clutch should be dismantled for further investigation.

7 Withdraw the starter driven gear from the starter clutch **(see illustration)**. If the gear appears stuck, rotate it clockwise as you withdraw it to free it from the starter clutch. Remove the needle bearing.

8 Check the condition of the sprags inside the clutch body – if they are damaged, marked or flattened at any point, the sprag assembly must be replaced with a new one **(see illustration)**. To remove the sprag assembly release the circlip that holds it in its housing and note which way round it fits. Install the new assembly in a reverse sequence, with the

13.4b ...then slide the starter clutch off...

13.4c ...and remove the thrust washer

13.5 Remove the reduction gear

13.6 Check the operation of the clutch as described

13.7 Withdraw the driven gear and remove the bearing

13.8 Check the sprags (A). The sprag assembly is held by the circlip (B)

2•26 Engine, clutch and transmission

13.11 Fit the bearing between the hub and the boss

13.14a Fit the lubricated bolt with its washer

13.14b Wedge the rag between the gears at the bottom (arrowed) . . .

13.14c . . . to prevent rotation while tightening the bolt

13.15 Engage the idle gear with the reduction gear and driven gear

white paint mark facing out of the housing. Secure the sprag assembly with the circlip. Apply clean engine oil to the sprags.

9 Check the external surface on the driven gear hub **(see illustration 13.7)**. Measure the outside diameter of the hub and check that it has not worn beyond the service limit specified. Check the needle roller bearing and the bearing surfaces on the starter driven gear hub and the starter clutch housing boss. If the bearing surfaces show signs of excessive wear or the bearing itself is worn or damaged, they should be replaced with new ones.

10 Check the teeth of the reduction and idle gears and the corresponding teeth of the starter driven gear and starter motor drive shaft. Replace the gears and/or starter motor if worn or chipped teeth are discovered on related gears. Also check the idle gear shaft for damage, and check that the gear is not a loose fit on it. Measure the external diameter of the shaft and the diameter of its bore in the idle gear replace them with new ones if worn beyond the service limits specified at the beginning of the Chapter. Check the reduction gear shaft ends and the bores they run in for wear.

Installation

11 Lubricate the outside of the starter driven gear hub with clean engine oil, then fit the gear into the clutch, rotating it clockwise as you do so to spread the sprags and allow the hub to enter **(see illustration 13.7)**. Lubricate the needle roller bearing with clean engine oil and fit it over the starter clutch boss **(see illustration)**.

12 If removed, lubricate the reduction gear shaft ends with clean engine oil then locate the inner end of the shaft in its bore in the crankcase, engaging it with the starter motor shaft teeth if installed **(see illustration 13.5)**. Install the clutch (see Section 14).

13 Slide the thrust washer onto the crankshaft and against the cam chain sprocket **(see illustration 13.4c)**. Align the wide splines on the starter clutch with those on the crankshaft and slide the starter clutch on with the driven gear on the inside **(see illustration 13.4b)**.

14 Apply clean oil to the threads and under the head of the starter clutch bolt. Install the bolt with its washer and tighten it to the torque setting specified at the beginning of the Chapter, noting that if using rag or a piece of aluminium to prevent crankshaft rotation it must now be wedged between the primary drive and driven gears at the bottom as shown **(see illustrations)** – if using a piece of aluminium block the hole to the sump with rag in case you drop it.

15 Lubricate the idle gear shaft with clean engine oil and fit it into the gear. Locate the idle gear, shouldered side inwards **(see illustration 13.2)**, between the reduction gear and the driven gear and slide the shaft into its bore in the crankcase **(see illustration)**.

16 Install the clutch cover (see Section 14, Steps 30 to 32).

14 Clutch

Note 1: *The clutch can be removed with the engine in the frame. If the engine has been removed, ignore the steps which don't apply.*
Note 2: *The clutch nut must be discarded and a new one used on installation – it is best to obtain the new nut in advance.*

Clutch removal

1 Drain the engine oil (see Chapter 1).
2 Trace the crankshaft position (CKP) sensor wiring from the top of the clutch cover and disconnect it at the red 2-pin wiring connector **(see illustration 4.15a or b)**. Feed the connector down to the cover, noting its routing.

Engine, clutch and transmission 2•27

14.3a Unscrew the bolts (arrowed) and remove the cover

14.3b Remove the thrust washer and the wave washer (arrowed) from the shaft

3 Working evenly in a criss-cross pattern, unscrew the clutch cover bolts **(see illustration)**. Remove the cover. Note that there is a thrust washer and a wave washer on the end of the idle gear shaft which may come away with the cover and could therefore drop from it – if they stay on the end of the shaft remove them for safekeeping **(see illustration)**. Be prepared to catch any residual oil. Remove the two dowels from either the cover or the crankcase if they are loose.

4 Withdraw the idle gear shaft and remove the gear **(see illustration 13.2)**.

5 Working in a criss-cross pattern, gradually slacken the clutch spring bolts until pressure is released **(see illustration)**. To prevent the assembly from turning, cover it with a rag and hold it securely – the bolts are not very tight. If available, have an assistant to hold the clutch while you unscrew the bolts. Remove the bolts and springs, then remove the pressure plate **(see illustration)**. Remove the lifter from either the back of the pressure plate or the end of the shaft **(see illustration 14.28a)**. If required withdraw the pushrod from the shaft **(see illustration)**.

6 Remove the clutch friction and plain plates, hooking them out when necessary, noting how they fit and keeping them in order **(see illustrations 14.27c, b and a)**. Note how the tabs on the outer friction plate locate in the shallow slots in the housing, while the rest sit in the deep slots. The outer and inner friction plates are different to the rest – they have a larger internal diameter. The inner plain plate differs to the rest in that it has a different surface coating. Remove the anti-judder spring and spring seat, noting which way round they fit **(see illustrations 14.26b and a)**.

7 The clutch nut rim is staked against the input shaft. Unstake the nut using a hammer and punch – take care not to damage the threads on the end of the shaft **(see illustration)**. To remove the clutch nut, the input shaft must be locked. This can be done in several ways. If the engine is in the frame, engage 6th gear and have an assistant hold the rear brake on hard with the rear tyre in firm contact with the ground. Alternatively, the Honda service tool (Pt. No. 07724-0050002), or a similar commercially available can be used to stop the clutch centre from turning whilst the nut is slackened **(see illustration)**. Unscrew the nut and remove the spring washer and the thrust washer **(see illustrations 14.25b and a)**. Discard the nut as a new one must be used on installation.

8 Remove the clutch centre and the thrust washer from the shaft **(see illustrations 14.24b and a)**.

14.5a Unscrew the bolts (arrowed) and remove the springs . . .

14.5b . . . then remove the pressure plate

14.5c Withdraw the pushrod if required

14.7a Unstake the nut . . .

14.7b . . . then unscrew it as described and remove the washers

2•28 Engine, clutch and transmission

14.9 Ease the bearing and guide out from the middle of the housing then remove the housing

14.10 Ease the guide out from the middle of the sprocket then remove the sprocket and chain

14.11 Measuring clutch friction plate thickness

9 Ease out the clutch guide and needle bearing from between the clutch housing and the input shaft – this can be done using a magnet and by sliding the housing on the shaft to help push them along **(see illustration)**. Remove the clutch housing. Note how the holes in the back of the housing engage with the pins on the oil pump drive sprocket.

10 If required, draw the oil pump drive sprocket guide out to create slack in the chain, then remove the sprocket and chain **(see illustration)**.

Inspection

11 After an extended period of service the clutch friction plates will wear and promote clutch slip. Measure the thickness of each friction plate using a Vernier caliper or micrometer **(see illustration)**. If any plate has worn to or beyond the service limits given in the Specifications at the beginning of the Chapter, or if any of the plates smell burnt or are glazed, the friction plates must be replaced with a new set.

12 The plain plates should not show any signs of excess heating (bluing). Check for warpage using a flat surface and feeler gauges **(see illustration)**. If any plate exceeds the maximum permissible amount of warpage, or shows signs of bluing, all plain plates must be replaced with a new set.

13 Measure the free length of each clutch spring **(see illustration)**. Place each spring upright on a flat surface and check it for bend by placing a ruler against it, or alternatively lay it against a set square. If any spring is below the minimum free length specified or if the bend in any spring is excessive, replace all the springs as a set. Also check the anti-judder spring and spring seat for damage or distortion and replace them with new ones if necessary.

14 Inspect the friction plates and the clutch housing for burrs and indentations on the edges of the protruding tabs on the plates and/or the slots in the housing **(see illustration)**. Similarly check for wear between the inner teeth of the plain plates and the slots in the clutch centre **(see illustration)**. Wear of this nature will cause clutch drag and slow disengagement during gear changes as the plates will snag when the pressure plate is lifted. With care a small amount of wear can be corrected by dressing with a fine file, but if this is excessive the worn components should be replaced with new ones.

15 Inspect the needle roller bearing and the bearing surfaces on the clutch guide and in the clutch housing **(see illustrations)**. If there are any signs of wear, pitting or other damage the affected parts must be replaced with

14.12 Check the plain plates for warpage

14.13 Measure the free length of the clutch springs and check them for bend

14.14a Check the friction plate tabs and housing slots . . .

14.14b . . . and the plain plate teeth and centre slots as described

14.15a Check the bearing and the bearing surfaces on the guide . . .

14.15b . . . and in the housing (arrowed)

Engine, clutch and transmission 2•29

14.19 Primary drive gear (arrowed)

14.22a Slide the drive sprocket onto the guide ...

14.22b ... and fit the chain over the driven sprocket

new ones. A new bearing must be selected according to marks on the primary driven gear and clutch guide – the primary driven gear will be marked A or B, and the guide will either have a 2 mm hole or not on its outer (grooved) rim. Refer to the table below for your model to select the correct bearing.

	Guide with marking	Guide without marking
Primary driven gear marked A	Bearing B	Bearing A
Primary driven gear marked B	Bearing C	Bearing B

16 Using a Vernier caliper, measure the internal and external diameter of the clutch guide, the internal diameter of the clutch housing and the external diameter of the input shaft where the guide sits **(see illustrations 14.15a and b)**. Make sure you refer to the correct specifications for the guide on your model – on models with a marked guide the marking is on the outer (grooved) rim. Compare the measurements to the specifications at the beginning of the Chapter and replace any part that is worn beyond its service limit with a new one. Similarly measure the internal and external diameter of the oil pump drive sprocket guide, the internal diameter of the sprocket and the external diameter of the input shaft where the guide sits.

17 Check the pressure plate and its bearing for signs of wear or damage and roughness **(see illustration 14.28a)**. Check that the bearing outer race is a good fit in the centre, and that the inner race rotates freely without any rough spots.

18 Check the pushrod is not bent by rolling it on a flat surface. Check the lifter for signs of wear or damage. Replace any parts necessary with new ones. The hydraulic release mechanism is covered in Section 15.

19 Check the teeth of the primary driven gear on the back of the clutch housing and the corresponding teeth of the primary drive gear on the crankshaft **(see illustration)**. Replace the clutch housing and/or crankshaft with a new one if worn or chipped teeth are discovered.

Installation

20 Remove all traces of old sealant from the crankcase and clutch cover surfaces. Note that if removed the starter reduction gear must be installed now as it cannot be fitted once the clutch is in place – see Section 13, Step 12.

21 Smear the inside and outside of the oil pump drive sprocket guide and the inside of the sprocket with molybdenum disulphide oil (a 50/50 mixture of molybdenum disulphide grease and engine oil). Slip the chain around the sprocket.

22 Slide the sprocket onto the shaft, making sure the pins face out, and engage the lower end of the chain with the driven sprocket **(see illustrations)**. Slide the guide onto the input shaft with the grooved end outwards and into the drive sprocket **(see illustration 14.10)**.

23 Smear the inside and outside of the clutch guide, the inside of the clutch housing and the needle bearing with molybdenum disulphide oil (a 50/50 mixture of molybdenum disulphide grease and engine oil). Position the clutch housing on the shaft and hold it then slide the clutch guide and needle bearing onto the shaft and into the centre of the housing **(see illustrations)**. Make sure that the primary drive and driven gear teeth engage and the pins on the oil pump drive sprocket locate in the holes in the rear of the housing – turn the driven sprocket with your finger while pressing on the housing until the pins are felt to locate and the housing moves in a bit further, then double-check by making sure the sprocket can't turn independently of the housing.

24 Slide the thrust washer onto the shaft **(see illustration)**. Slide the clutch centre onto the shaft splines **(see illustration)**.

14.23a Position the housing over the shaft, engaging the gears and locating it on the sprocket pins ...

14.23b ... then slide the guide and bearing in

14.24a Fit the thrust washer ...

14.24b ... and the clutch centre

2•30 Engine, clutch and transmission

14.25a Fit the thrust washer and the spring washer, with the OUT mark facing out

14.25b Fit a new clutch nut . . .

14.25c . . . and tighten it to the specified torque

14.25d Stake the nut against the detent in the shaft end

14.26a Fit the anti-judder spring seat . . .

14.26b . . . and spring . . .

14.26c . . . so the spring's outer edge is raised off the seat

14.27a Identify the friction plate with the larger internal diameter and fit that first, locating it over the anti-judder assembly . . .

14.27b . . . then fit a plain plate

14.27c Locate the tabs on the outer friction plate into the shallow slots in the housing

25 Fit the thrust washer and the spring washer with its OUT mark facing out **(see illustration)**. Smear the new clutch nut threads and seat with oil, then thread it onto the input shaft and, using the method employed on removal to lock the shaft (see Step 7), tighten the nut to the torque setting specified at the beginning of the Chapter **(see illustrations)**. Stake the rim of the nut into the indent on the end of the shaft, taking care not to damage the threads **(see illustration)**.

26 Fit the anti-judder spring seat into the clutch centre, then fit the spring so that its outer edge is raised off the seat and facing outwards **(see illustrations)**.

27 Coat each clutch plate with engine oil prior to installation, then build up the plates as follows. Fit a friction plate with the larger internal diameter over the spring and spring seat **(see illustration)**, then fit the plain plate with the different surface coating, then alternate standard friction plates and plain plates until all except the other friction plate with the larger internal diameter are installed, then fit that with its tabs fitting into the shallow slots in the housing **(see illustrations)**.

28 Lubricate the bearing in the pressure plate, the lifter and the pushrod with oil. Fit the

Engine, clutch and transmission 2•31

14.28a Fit the lifter into the bearing

14.28b Fit the pressure plate, making sure it locates in the slots . . .

14.28c . . . then install the springs and bolts and tighten them as described

lifter into the bearing **(see illustration)**. Slide the pushrod into the shaft if removed **(see illustration 14.5c)**. Fit the pressure plate onto the clutch, engaging the protrusions on its inner rim in the slots in the clutch centre **(see illustration)**. Fit the springs and the bolts then counter-hold the clutch housing and tighten them evenly in a criss-cross sequence to the specified torque setting **(see illustration)**.

29 Lubricate the idle gear shaft with clean engine oil and fit it into the gear. Locate the idle gear, shouldered side inwards **(see illustration 13.2)**, between the reduction gear and the driven gear and slide the shaft into its bore in the crankcase **(see illustration 13.15)**.

30 Fit the wave washer and the thrust washer onto the end of the starter idle gear shaft **(see illustration 14.3b)**. Lubricate the reduction and idle gear shaft outer ends with oil.

31 Apply a smear of a suitable sealant (such as Three Bond 1207B or equivalent RTV sealant – ask your dealer) to the entire mating surface on the clutch cover **(see illustration)**. Fit the two dowels into the crankcase if removed **(see illustration)**. Fit the cover onto the dowels. Fit all the bolts finger tight, then tighten them evenly and a little at a time in a criss-cross pattern **(see illustration 14.3a)**.

32 Reconnect the CKP sensor connector, making sure the wiring is correctly routed. Fill the engine with oil to the correct level (see Chapter 1).

14.31a Apply the sealant as described

14.31b Make sure the dowels (arrowed) are fitted

15 Clutch release mechanism

Master cylinder

Note: If the master cylinder is being overhauled read through the entire procedure first and make sure that you have obtained all the new parts required, including some new DOT 4 brake/clutch fluid – a rebuild kit is available that includes the boot, circlip, piston assembly (incorporating seal and cup) and spring, but note that on CB1000R/RA models the reservoir O-rings must be obtained separately.

Removal

Caution: If the master cylinder is in need of an overhaul all old fluid should be flushed from the system (see Step 44). Overhaul of the cylinder must be done in a spotlessly clean work area to avoid contamination and possible failure of the hydraulic system components. Do not, under any circumstances, use petroleum-based solvents to clean the parts. Use clean DOT 4 hydraulic fluid, or denatured alcohol only, as described. To prevent damage from spilled fluid, always cover paintwork when working on the system.

1 Disconnect the wiring connectors from the clutch switch **(see illustration)**. On CB1000R/RA models remove the mirror (see Chapter 7).

2 If the master cylinder is just being displaced, follow this Step only: unscrew the master cylinder clamp bolts and remove the back of the clamp, noting how it fits, then position the master cylinder assembly clear of the handlebar **(see illustration)**. Ensure no strain is placed on the hydraulic hose. Keep the reservoir upright to prevent air entering the system.

3 If the master cylinder is being overhauled, follow Steps 4 to 8. Also remove the clutch lever (see Chapter 5).

4 If the system has not been drained, on CBF1000/A models slacken the reservoir cover screws, and on CB1000R/RA models undo the reservoir cap clamp screw then

15.1 Pull the connectors (arrowed) off the switch terminals

15.2 Master cylinder clamp bolts (arrowed)

2•32 Engine, clutch and transmission

15.4a On CBF models slacken the cover screws

15.4b On CB-R models free the clamp and slacken the cap

15.5 Clutch hose banjo bolt (arrowed)

slacken the reservoir cap **(see illustrations)**.

5 Unscrew the clutch hose banjo bolt and detach the banjo union, noting its alignment with the master cylinder **(see illustration)**. Wrap clingfilm around the banjo union and secure the hose in an upright position to minimise fluid loss. Discard the sealing washers as new ones must be fitted on reassembly.

6 Unscrew the master cylinder clamp bolts and remove the back of the clamp, noting how it fits, then lift the master cylinder and reservoir away from the handlebar **(see illustration 15.2)**.

7 Remove the reservoir cover or cap, diaphragm plate and diaphragm. Drain the brake fluid from the master cylinder and reservoir into a suitable container. Wipe any remaining fluid out of the reservoir with a clean rag.

8 If required, undo the screw securing the clutch switch and remove the switch.

Overhaul

9 On CB1000R/RA models, if required undo the screw inside the reservoir and remove the reservoir and its O-rings **(see illustration 15.10)**. Discard the O-rings as new ones must be used.

10 Carefully remove the pushrod and rubber boot from the master cylinder **(see illustration)**. Depress the piston and use circlip pliers to remove the circlip, then slide out the piston assembly and the spring, noting how they fit. If they are difficult to remove, apply low pressure compressed air to the fluid outlet. Lay the parts out in the proper order to prevent confusion during reassembly.

11 Clean all parts with clean brake/clutch fluid. If compressed air is available, blow it through the fluid galleries to ensure they are clear (make sure the air is filtered and unlubricated).

Caution: Do not, under any circumstances, use a petroleum-based solvent to clean brake parts.

12 Check the master cylinder bore for corrosion, scratches, nicks and score marks. If the necessary measuring equipment is available, compare the dimensions of the piston and bore to those given in the Specifications at the beginning of this Chapter. If damage or wear is evident, the master cylinder must be replaced with a new one. If the master cylinder is in poor condition, then the release cylinder should be checked as well.

13 The pushrod, dust boot, circlip, piston components and spring are all included in the master cylinder rebuild kit. Use all of the new parts, regardless of the apparent condition of the old ones.

1 Reservoir cap
2 Diaphragm plate
3 Diaphragm
4 Reservoir
5 O-rings
6 Master cylinder
7 Brake light switch and screw
8 Spring
9 Piston (incorporating seal and cup)
10 Circlip
11 Rubber boot
12 Pushrod

15.10 Clutch master cylinder assembly

Engine, clutch and transmission 2•33

15.26 Clutch hose banjo bolt (arrowed)

15.27a Release cylinder bolts (arrowed)

15.27b Withdraw the pushrod if required

15.27c Secure the piston with a cable-tie if the cylinder is not being overhauled

14 Smear the cup and seal with DOT 4 fluid. Fit them into their grooves in the piston so their flared ends will fit into the master cylinder first.
15 Lubricate the master cylinder bore with DOT 4 fluid. Fit the spring wide end first into the master cylinder.
16 Lubricate the piston with clean brake fluid and slide it into the master cylinder and up against the spring. Make sure the lips on the cup and seal do not turn inside out. Push the piston in to compress the spring and install the new circlip. Smear the pushrod and rubber boot with silicone grease. Fit the pushrod into the rubber boot so the lips locate in the groove and press the boot into place in the end of the cylinder.
17 On CB1000R/RA models, if removed fit new reservoir O-rings smeared with DOT 4 fluid onto the master cylinder then locate the reservoir. Clean the threads of the screw and apply a thread locking compound, and tighten it lightly.

Installation

18 If removed, fit the clutch switch onto the master cylinder.
19 Attach the master cylinder to the handlebar, aligning the inner side of the clamp joint with the punch mark on the top of the handlebar on CBF1000/A models, and the outer side on CB1000R/RA models, then fit the back of the clamp with its UP mark facing up (see illustration 15.2). Tighten the upper bolt to the torque setting specified at the beginning of this Chapter, followed by the lower bolt.
20 Connect the clutch hose to the master cylinder, using new sealing washers on each side of the banjo fitting. Align the hose as noted on removal (see illustration 15.5). Tighten the banjo bolt to the torque setting specified at the beginning of this Chapter.
21 Install the clutch lever (see Chapter 5).

22 Connect the clutch switch wiring (see illustration 15.1).
23 Fill the fluid reservoir with new DOT 4 brake/clutch fluid (see Pre-ride checks). Refer to Step 44 and bleed the air from the system. Inspect the reservoir diaphragm and fit a new one it if it is damaged or deteriorated.
24 Check the operation of the clutch before riding the motorcycle.

Release cylinder

Note: *If the release cylinder is being overhauled read through the entire procedure first and make sure that you have obtained all the new parts required, including some new DOT 4 brake/clutch fluid.*

Removal

Caution: *If the release cylinder is in need of an overhaul all old fluid should be flushed from the system (see Step 44). Overhaul must be done in a spotlessly clean work area to avoid contamination and possible failure of the hydraulic system components. Do not, under any circumstances, use petroleum-based solvents to clean the parts. Use clean DOT 4 hydraulic fluid, or denatured alcohol only, as described. To prevent damage from spilled fluid, always cover paintwork when working on the system.*

25 To prevent the possibility of damage from spilled fluid cover surrounding painted components with rag.
26 If required unscrew the clutch hose banjo bolt and detach the banjo union, noting its alignment with the release cylinder (see illustration). Wrap clingfilm around the banjo union and secure the hose in an upright position to minimise fluid loss. Discard the sealing washers as new ones must be fitted on reassembly.
27 Unscrew the release cylinder bolts and remove the cylinder from the sprocket cover (see illustration). Remove the dowels if they are loose (see illustration 15.39). Remove the gasket and discard it as a new one must be used. If required withdraw the pushrod (see illustration). Fit a cable-tie around the release cylinder as shown to prevent the piston creeping out if required (see illustration).

Overhaul

28 Clean the exterior of the cylinder with denatured alcohol or brake system cleaner.
29 Withdraw the piston from cylinder (see

2•34 Engine, clutch and transmission

15.29 Release cylinder assembly

1. Oil seal
2. O-rings
3. Piston
4. Spring
5. Release cylinder
6. Bleed valve

illustration). If the piston cannot be withdrawn by hand, it can be pushed out by applying compressed air to the clutch hose union hole. Only low pressure should be required, such as is generated by a foot pump. Wrap the release cylinder in a wad of rag to prevent the piston being forcibly expelled.

30 Remove the spring, noting how it fits.

31 Carefully remove the fluid seals and pushrod seal from the piston, noting which way round the pushrod seal fits. Discard the fluid seals as new ones must be used. Replace the pushrod seal with a new one if necessary.

32 Clean the piston and cylinder with DOT4 fluid or denatured alcohol. If compressed air is available, use it to dry the parts thoroughly (make sure it's filtered and unlubricated).

Caution: Do not, under any circumstances, use a petroleum-based solvent to clean master cylinder parts.

33 Inspect the cylinder bore and piston for signs of corrosion, nicks and burrs and loss of plating. If surface defects are present, the cylinder assembly must be replaced with a new one. If it is in bad shape the master cylinder should also be checked. No specifications are given to check piston and bore wear.

34 Lubricate the new piston fluid seals with the grease provided in the rebuild kit. Fit the seals into the grooves.

35 Fit the new pushrod seal to the piston and smear it with brake fluid.

36 Fit the narrow end of the spring over the boss on the inner end of the piston.

37 Lubricate the cylinder with clean brake fluid and fit the spring and piston into the bore. Make sure the spring remains correctly positioned and take great care to ensure the fluid seals are not dislodged or damaged as they enter the bore. Using your thumbs, push the piston all the way in, making sure it enters the bore squarely.

Installation

38 Remove all traces of gasket from the cylinder and cover sealing surfaces.

39 Ensure the locating dowels are fitted and fit a new gasket onto the sprocket cover **(see illustration)**. If removed make sure the pushrod is straight and clean and smear it with oil, then slide it into place **(see illustration 15.27b)**.

40 Apply a smear of silicone grease to the pushrod end and the seal lips **(see illustration)**. Fit the release cylinder, aligning it with the pushrod and locating dowels **(see illustration)**. Install the bolts and tighten them.

41 Position a new sealing washer on each side of the clutch hose end fitting then connect the hose to the cylinder. Ensure it is correctly positioned against its stop then tighten the banjo bolt to the specified torque **(see illustration 15.26)**.

42 Fill the master cylinder with new DOT4 hydraulic fluid (see *Pre-ride checks*) and bleed the hydraulic system (see Step 44).

43 Check for leaks and thoroughly test the operation of the clutch before riding the motorcycle.

Clutch release mechanism bleeding

44 The procedure for bleeding the clutch and for changing the fluid or draining the

15.39 Fit a new gasket onto the dowels (arrowed)

15.40a Smear some silicone grease onto the pushrod and its seal lips (arrowed) . . .

15.40b . . . then fit the release cylinder

Engine, clutch and transmission 2•35

system is the same as for the brake system – refer to Chapter 6, Section 11. The bleed valve is on the top of the release cylinder **(see illustration)**.

16 Gearchange mechanism

Note: *The gearchange mechanism can be removed with the engine in the frame. If the engine has been removed, ignore the steps which don't apply.*

Removal

1 Remove the left-hand side cover (see Chapter 7).
2 On CBF1000/A models undo the air intake duct screws and displace the duct **(see illustration)**, then disconnect the vacuum hose from the diaphragm valve.
3 On CB1000R/RA models remove the air filter housing/throttle body assembly (see Chapter 4).

15.44 Clutch release cylinder bleed valve (arrowed)

4 Make sure the transmission is in neutral. Remove the front sprocket (see Chapter 6).
5 Unscrew the gearchange mechanism cover bolts and remove the cover **(see illustration)**. Remove the dowels if they are loose. Discard the gasket as a new one must be used.
6 Note how the gearchange shaft centralising spring ends fit on each side of the locating pin in the casing, and how the pawls on the selector arm locate onto the pins on the end of the selector drum cam. Note the washer on the gearchange shaft and remove it if required – there is also one on the inner end of the shaft.
7 Grasp the end of the shaft and withdraw the shaft/arm assembly **(see illustration)**. Retrieve the inner washer from the crankcase if it didn't come with the shaft.
8 To access and remove the gearchange mechanism stopper arm, which is on the right-hand end of the selector drum, remove the clutch (see Section 14) – there is no need to remove the oil pump drive sprocket and chain. Block the holes into the sump with clean rag to prevent anything falling in. Note how the stopper arm spring ends locate and how the roller on the arm locates in the neutral detent on the selector drum cam, then unscrew the stopper arm bolt and remove the arm, the washer and the spring, noting how they fit **(see illustration)**.

Inspection

9 Check the selector arm for cracks, distortion and wear of its pawls, and check

16.2 Undo the screws (arrowed) and remove the duct

16.5 Unscrew the bolts (arrowed) and remove the cover

16.7 Withdraw the shaft/arm assembly, noting how it fits

16.8 Note how the spring ends locate, and how the roller sits in the neutral detent, then unscrew the bolt (arrowed) and remove the arm

2•36 Engine, clutch and transmission

16.9a Check the selector arm pawls (arrowed) . . .

16.9b . . . and the pins on the end of the drum

16.9c Centralising spring (A), inner washer (B), circlip (C)

16.9d Make sure the locating pin (arrowed) is tight

for any corresponding wear on the pins on the selector drum end **(see illustrations)**. Inspect the shaft centralising spring for fatigue, wear or damage **(see illustration)**. If any is found, they must be replaced with new ones. To replace the shaft spring, slide the inner washer off the shaft, then remove the circlip and slide the spring off the shaft, noting how its ends locate. Fit the new spring, locating the ends on each side of the tab, and secure it with the circlip, making sure the chamfered side faces the spring and it locates in its groove. Slide the washer against the circlip. Also check that the centralising spring locating pin in the crankcase is securely tightened **(see illustration)**. If it is loose, remove it, clean the threads and apply a non-permanent thread locking compound to its threads, then tighten it.

10 Check the stopper arm roller and the detents in the selector drum cam for any wear or damage, and make sure the roller turns freely. Inspect the stopper arm return spring for fatigue, wear or damage **(see illustration 16.8)**. Replace any components that are worn or damaged with new ones. If required, remove the selector drum cam by counter-holding it and unscrewing the bolt in its centre – take care how you hold it as its rim must not be marked **(see illustration 20.5)**. Note the locating pins in the end of the drum and remove them for safekeeping if required **(see illustration 20.14a)**. Remove the collar if required **(see illustration 20.6a)**. On installation fit the collar with its shouldered end innermost. Fit the cam locating pins into their holes then locate the cam on the end of the drum with the OUT mark facing out – it can only fit one way **(see illustrations 20.14a and b)**. Clean the threads of the cam bolt and apply a suitable non-permanent thread locking compound, and tighten it to the torque setting specified at the beginning of the Chapter, counter-holding the drum as before **(see illustration 20.14c)**.

11 Check the gearchange shaft is straight and look for damage to the splines. If the shaft is bent you can attempt to straighten it, but if the splines are damaged the shaft must be replaced with a new one. Also check the condition of the shaft oil seal in the cover. If it is damaged, deteriorated or shows signs of leakage it must be replaced with a new one – lever out the old seal with a seal hook or screwdriver **(see illustration)**. With the seal removed, check the condition of the needle bearing, and replace that with a new one as well if necessary **(see illustration)**. Fit the new bearing and press or drive the new seal squarely into place using your fingers, a seal driver or suitable socket **(see illustration)**.

16.11a Lever out the seal

16.11b Check the bearing (arrowed)

16.11c Press the new seal into its housing

Engine, clutch and transmission 2•37

16.12a Fit the spring onto its post

16.12b Fit the bolt through the arm and fit the washer onto the bolt – note that the arm is installed with the roller on the inside

16.13a Make sure the spring ends (A) and washers (B) are correctly fitted

16.13b Make sure everything is correctly positioned

16.14a Fit a new gasket onto the dowels (arrowed) . . .

16.14b . . . and apply some sealant to the crankcase joints . . .

Installation

12 If removed, locate the stopper arm return spring onto its post, then fit the bolt through the stopper arm and fit the washer **(see illustrations)**. Clean the threads of the bolt and apply a suitable non-permanent thread locking compound. Fit the arm, locating the roller onto the neutral detent on the selector drum and making sure the spring ends are positioned correctly. Tighten the bolt to the torque setting specified at the beginning of the Chapter. Check that the arm and spring ends are correctly positioned **(see illustration 16.8)**. Install the clutch (see Section 14).

13 Check that the shaft centralising spring is properly positioned and slide the washers onto each end of the shaft if removed **(see illustration)**. Slide the shaft into place **(see illustration 16.7)**, locating the selector arm pawls onto the pins on the selector drum and the centralising spring ends onto each side of the locating pin in the crankcase **(see illustration)**.

14 Remove the rag that was blocking the sump. Apply some grease to the lips of the gearchange shaft oil seal in the cover, and wrap a single layer of insulating tape around the splines on the shaft to protect the seal. Fit the dowels and a new gasket onto the cover **(see illustration)**. Fit the cover over the shaft **(see illustrations)**. Clean the threads of the bottom cover bolt and apply a thread locking compound **(see illustration)**. Install and tighten the bolts. Remove the insulating tape from around the gearchange shaft splines.

15 Install the front sprocket (see Chapter 6).

16 On CBF1000/A models make sure the air duct seal is seated in its groove. Fit the air duct and tighten the screws. On CB1000R/RA models install the air filter housing/throttle body assembly (see Chapter 4).

17 Install the side cover (see Chapter 7).

17 Transmission cassette removal and installation

Note: The transmission cassette can be removed with the engine in the frame.

Removal

1 Remove the clutch and the oil pump drive sprocket and chain (see Section 14). Remove the gearchange mechanism (see Section 16).

2 Stuff some rag into the opening to the sump. Unscrew the cassette plate bolts **(see illustration)**. Grasp the transmission input shaft and pull the cassette out of the

16.14c . . . then install the cover

16.14d Apply a thread lock to the bottom bolt

17.2a Unscrew the bolts (arrowed) . . .

2•38 Engine, clutch and transmission

17.2b ... and draw the cassette out of the crankcase

17.2c Remove the oil jet

crankcase, pushing or tapping the output shaft with a soft hammer to help ease it out if necessary (see illustration). Note that there is an oil jet in the crankcase which may come away with the cover and drop off (hence the rag) – if not, retrieve the jet from its bore (see illustration). Remove the three dowels from either the cassette plate or the crankcase if they are loose (see illustration 17.6).

3 Support the plate on blocks of wood with the transmission shafts pointing up. If required remove the selector forks, the transmission shafts and the selector drum (see Sections 18 and 20). The transmission shaft and selector drum bearings are covered in those Sections. Note that the transmission output shaft oil seal should be replaced with a new one if the cassette is removed, and the bearing must be removed first as the seal is shouldered on its inner side – see Section 18.

Installation

4 Support the plate on blocks of wood with the transmission shafts pointing up. Make sure both transmission shafts are correctly seated and their related pinions and the selector forks are all correctly engaged.
5 Position the gears in the neutral position and check the shafts are free to rotate easily and independently (i.e. the input shaft can turn whilst the output shaft is held stationary).
6 Clean the oil jet in solvent and blow it through with compressed air if available, then fit it into its bore in the crankcase with its smaller diameter end facing in (see illustration 17.2c). Fit the three dowels into the cassette plate if removed (see illustration).
7 Lubricate the transmission shafts, gears, selector drum tracks, selector forks and shafts with oil. Smear some grease on the new output shaft oil seal lips.
8 Fit the transmission assembly into the crankcase, making sure the inner ends of the shafts and drum locate correctly in their bores or bearings (see illustration 17.2b). Push the cassette plate fully against the crankcase making sure it locates onto the dowels (see illustration).
9 Fit the bolts and tighten them evenly and a little at a time in the sequence shown to the torque setting specified at the beginning of the Chapter (see illustration 17.2a).
10 Install the gearchange mechanism (see Section 16). Install the oil pump drive sprocket and chain and the clutch (see Section 14).

18 Transmission shaft and bearing removal and installation

Shaft removal

1 Remove the transmission cassette (see Section 17).
2 Support the plate on blocks of wood with the transmission shafts pointing up.
3 Remove the selector forks and shafts (Section 20, Step 3).
4 Grasp both transmission shafts together, in particular holding the 1st gear pinion on the plate end of the output shaft as it can drop off, and lift them out of the plate. Note that there is a thrust washer on the end of the output shaft that may drop off, although you will not be able to get hold of it until the shaft is part way out of the plate (see illustration).
5 If necessary, the transmission shafts can be disassembled and inspected for wear or damage (see Section 19).

Bearing removal and installation

6 After removing the shafts, refer to *Tools and Workshop Tips* (Section 5) in the Reference Section and check the transmission shaft bearings in the crankcase and plate. Replace the bearings with new ones if necessary.
7 To remove the input shaft bearing in the plate unscrew the three bolts and remove the

17.6 Make sure the dowels (arrowed) are fitted

17.8 Make sure the shaft ends and dowels all locate correctly

18.4 Grasp both shafts, and holding the bottom gear and thrust washer on the end of the output shaft, lift them out of the plate

Engine, clutch and transmission 2•39

18.7a Input shaft bearing retainer bolts (A); selector drum bearing retainer bolts (B); output shaft bearing retainer bolt (C) . . .

18.7b . . . and bearing retainer (D)

retainer **(see illustration)**. The output shaft bearing is held on the inside of the plate by a retainer secured by a bolt on the outside **(see illustration)**. The output shaft bearing in the crankcase is held by a retainer secured by a bolt on the inside **(see illustration)**. The input shaft bearing in the crankcase can only be removed after the crankcase has been split into halves as it has a pin locating in a hole which means it can't be driven out **(see illustration 23.11c)**.

8 Remove the bearings using a puller, or by driving them out with a socket, using heat to free them if necessary – note that you can drive the output shaft bearing and oil seal out at the same time using a socket on the seal **(see illustration)**. Alternatively the output shaft oil seal can be driven out from the crankcase after removing the bearing. Fit the new seal from the inside and make sure its shoulder seats correctly in the housing **(see illustration)**. Fit the output shaft crankcase bearing with its lipped rim on the inside so that its retainer seats on the lip **(see illustration)**. Fit the output shaft cassette plate bearing with its lipped rim on the inside of the plate so that its retainer seats on the lip.

9 Clean the threads of the retainer bolts and apply thread lock, and tighten them to the torque setting specified at the beginning of the chapter, fitting the input shaft retainer with the marked side facing out, and the output shaft retainers with the shaped end fitting onto the lipped bearing outer race.

Shaft installation

10 Position both transmission shafts together so their related pinions engage.

11 Make sure the thrust washer is on the right-hand end of the output shaft, and use some oil or grease to help keep it in place **(see illustration 19.36c)**. Grasp the shafts as shown, using your finger to keep the thrust washer and 1st gear pinion in place, and locate them in the cassette plate, making sure they seat correctly **(see illustration)**.

18.7c Output shaft crankcase bearing retainer (arrowed)

18.8a Drive the seal and bearing out at the same time

18.8b Make sure the seal and bearing . . .

18.8c . . . are fitted the correct way round

18.8d The application of heat to the bearing housing makes them easier to remove and install

18.11 Slide the shafts into the cassette making sure the washer stays on the end of the output shaft

2•40 Engine, clutch and transmission

12 Make sure both transmission shafts are correctly seated and their related pinions are correctly engaged.
13 Install the selector forks and shafts (see Section 20, Steps 17 and 18).
14 Install the transmission cassette (see Section 17).

19 Transmission shaft overhaul

1 Remove the transmission shafts (see Sections 17 and 18). Always disassemble the transmission shafts separately to avoid mixing up the components.

HAYNES HINT: When disassembling the transmission shafts, place the parts on a long rod or thread a wire through them to keep them in order and facing the proper direction.

Input shaft
Disassembly

2 The thrust washer on the left-hand end of the shaft has a slightly out-of round section on its inner rim that locates in a groove in the shaft (see illustration) – this prevents the washer and 2nd gear pinion sliding off the end of the shaft when removing and installing the transmission cassette. To remove the washer slip one or two flat-bladed screwdrivers behind it at the out-of-round section and lever it out of the groove and towards the end of the shaft (see illustration). Use a heat gun on the washer to expand it if required – we found it helped. If the washer becomes distorted to the extent it cannot be re-used discard it and obtain a new one.
3 Slide the 2nd gear pinion off the shaft, noting which way round it fits (see illustration 19.19).
4 Slide the tabbed lockwasher off the shaft, then turn the slotted splined washer to offset the splines and slide it off the shaft, noting how they fit together (see illustrations 19.18c, b and a). Slide the 6th gear pinion and its splined bush off the shaft, followed by the splined washer (see illustrations 19.17c, b and a).
5 Remove the circlip, then slide the 3rd/4th gear pinion off the shaft (see illustrations 19.16b and a).
6 Remove the circlip, then slide the splined washer, the 5th gear pinion and its bush, and the thrust washer off the shaft (see illustrations 19.15e, d, c, b and a). The 1st gear pinion is integral with the shaft (see illustration).

Inspection

7 Wash all of the components in clean solvent and dry them off.
8 Check the gear teeth for cracking, chipping, pitting and other obvious wear or damage. Any pinion that is damaged as such must be replaced with a new one.
9 Inspect the dogs and the dog holes in the gears for cracks, chips, and excessive wear especially in the form of rounded edges. Make sure mating gears engage properly. Replace the paired gears as a set if necessary.
10 Check for signs of scoring or bluing on the pinions, bushes and shaft. This could be caused by overheating due to inadequate lubrication. Check that all the oil holes and passages are clear. Replace any damaged pinions or bushes.
11 Check that each pinion moves freely on the shaft or its bush but without undue freeplay. Check that each bush moves freely on the shaft but without undue freeplay. If the necessary equipment is available the individual components for which dimensions are given in the Specifications at the beginning of this Chapter can be measured to assess the extent of wear.
12 The shaft is unlikely to sustain damage unless the engine has seized, placing an unusually high loading on the transmission, or the machine has covered a very high mileage. Check the surface of the shaft, especially where a pinion turns on it, and replace the shaft if it has scored or picked up, or if there are any cracks. Damage of any kind can only be cured by replacement.
13 Check the washers and circlips and replace any that are bent or appear weakened or worn. Use new ones if in any doubt. Note that it is good practice to renew all circlips when overhauling gearshafts.

Reassembly

14 During reassembly, apply molybdenum disulphide oil (a 50/50 mixture of molybdenum disulphide grease and clean engine oil) to the mating surfaces of the shaft, pinions and bushes. Fit the stamped circlips and washers so that their chamfered side faces the pinion that thrusts against it so the sharp side takes the thrust. When installing the circlips, do not expand their ends any further than is necessary, and locate the ends so the gap between then aligns with a spline groove as shown.
15 Slide the thrust washer onto the left-hand end of the shaft, followed by the 5th gear pinion bush (see illustrations). Fit the 5th gear pinion onto the bush with its dogs

19.2a The washer has an out-of-round section (arrowed) on its inner rim that locates in the groove

19.2b Carefully lever the washer out of the groove, using some heat if necessary

19.6 1st gear pinion (arrowed) is part of the shaft

19.15a Slide the thrust washer . . .

19.15b . . . the 5th gear pinion bush . . .

Engine, clutch and transmission 2•41

19.15c . . . the 5th gear pinion . . .

19.15d . . . and the splined washer onto the shaft . . .

19.15e . . . and secure them with the circlip . . .

facing away from the integral 1st gear **(see illustration)**. Slide the splined washer onto the shaft, then fit the circlip, making sure that it locates correctly in the groove in the shaft **(see illustrations)**.

16 Slide the combined 3rd/4th gear pinion onto the shaft with the larger 4th gear pinion facing the 5th gear pinion **(see illustration)**. Fit the circlip, making sure it is locates correctly in its groove in the shaft **(see illustrations)**.

17 Slide the splined washer onto the shaft, followed by the 6th gear pinion splined bush, aligning the oil hole in the bush with the hole in the shaft. Slide the 6th gear pinion onto the bush, making sure its dogs face the 3rd/4th gear pinion **(see illustrations)**.

19.15f . . . making sure it locates properly in its groove

19.16a Slide the combined 3rd/4th gear pinion onto the shaft . . .

19.16b . . . and secure it with the circlip . . .

19.16c . . . making sure it locates properly in its groove

19.17a Slide the splined washer . . .

19.17b . . . the 6th gear pinion splined bush . . .

19.17c . . . and the 6th gear pinion onto the shaft

2•42 Engine, clutch and transmission

19.18a Slide on the slotted splined washer . . .

19.18b . . . and locate it as shown . . .

19.18c . . . then slide on the tabbed lockwasher and locate its tabs in the slots

18 Slide the slotted splined washer onto the shaft and locate it in its groove, then turn it in the groove so that the splines on the washer align with the splines on the shaft and secure the washer in the groove **(see illustrations)**. Slide the tabbed lockwasher onto the shaft and locate the tabs in the slots in the outer rim of the splined washer **(see illustration)**.

19 Slide the 2nd gear pinion onto the end of the shaft with the chamfered side of the teeth facing the 6th gear pinion **(see illustration)**.

20 Fit the special thrust washer onto the end of the shaft and drive it down to the groove using a suitable socket until the out-of-round section on its inner rim locates in the groove **(see illustrations and 19.2a)**.

21 Check that all components have been correctly installed **(see illustration)**.

Output shaft

Disassembly

22 Slide the thrust washer off the shaft, followed by the 1st gear pinion and its needle roller bearing, the thrust washer and the 5th gear pinion **(see illustrations 19.36c, b and a, and 19.35b and a)**.

23 Remove the circlip, then slide the splined washer, the 4th gear pinion and its splined bush off the shaft **(see illustrations 19.34d, c, b and a)**.

24 Slide the tabbed lockwasher off the shaft, then turn the slotted splined washer to offset the splines and slide it off the shaft, noting how they fit together **(see illustrations 19.33c, b and a)**.

25 Slide the 3rd gear pinion and its splined bush, followed by the splined washer, off the shaft **(see illustrations 19.32c, b and a)**.

26 Remove the circlip, then slide the 6th gear pinion off the shaft **(see illustrations 19.31b and a)**.

27 Remove the circlip, then slide the splined washer, the 2nd gear pinion and its bush off the shaft **(see illustrations 19.30d, c, b and a)**.

Inspection

28 Refer to Steps 7 to 13 above.

Reassembly

29 During reassembly, apply molybdenum disulphide oil (a 50/50 mixture of molybdenum disulphide grease and clean engine oil) to the mating surfaces of the shaft, pinions and bushes. Fit the stamped circlips and washers so that their chamfered side faces the pinion that thrusts against it so the sharp side takes the thrust. When installing the circlips, do not expand their ends any further than is

19.19 Slide the 2nd gear pinion onto the shaft

19.20a Fit the washer onto the shaft . . .

19.20b . . . and drive it down so its rim locates in the groove

19.21 The complete assembly should be as shown

Engine, clutch and transmission 2•43

19.30a Slide the 2nd gear pinion bush . . .

19.30b . . . the 2nd gear pinion . . .

19.30c . . . and the splined washer onto the shaft . . .

necessary, and locate the ends so the gap between then aligns with a spline groove as shown.

30 Slide the 2nd gear pinion bush onto the shaft, then slide the 2nd gear pinion onto the bush with its dog holes facing away from the collar, followed by the splined washer **(see illustrations)**. Fit the circlip, making sure it is locates correctly in its groove in the shaft **(see illustrations)**.

31 Slide the 6th gear pinion onto shaft with its selector fork groove facing away from the 2nd gear pinion, then fit the circlip, making sure it is locates correctly in its groove in the shaft **(see illustrations)**.

32 Slide the splined washer and the 3rd gear pinion splined bush onto the shaft, making sure the oil hole in the bush aligns with the hole in the shaft, then slide the 3rd gear pinion

19.30d . . . and secure them with the circlip . . .

19.30e . . . making sure it locates in the groove

onto its bush with its dog holes facing the 6th gear pinion **(see illustrations)**.

33 Slide the slotted splined washer onto the

shaft and locate it in its groove, then turn it in the groove so that the splines on the washer align with the splines on the shaft and secure

19.31a Slide the 6th gear pinion onto the shaft . . .

19.31b . . . and secure it with the circlip . . .

19.31c . . . making sure it locates in the groove

19.32a Slide the splined washer . . .

19.32b . . . the 3rd gear pinion splined bush . . .

19.32c . . . and the 3rd gear pinion onto the shaft

2•44 Engine, clutch and transmission

19.33a Slide the slotted splined washer onto the shaft . . .

19.33b . . . and locate it as shown

19.33c Slide the lockwasher onto the shaft and engage it with the slotted washer

19.34a Slide the 4th gear pinion splined bush . . .

the washer in the groove (**see illustrations**). Slide the tabbed lockwasher onto the shaft and locate the tabs in the slots in the outer rim of the splined washer (**see illustration**).

34 Slide the 4th gear pinion splined bush onto the shaft, making sure the oil hole in the bush aligns with the hole in the shaft (**see illustration**). Slide the 4th gear pinion onto its bush with its dog holes face away from the 3rd gear pinion (**see illustration**). Slide the splined washer on, then fit the circlip, making sure it is locates correctly in its groove in the shaft (**see illustrations**).

35 Slide the 5th gear pinion onto the shaft with its selector fork groove facing the 4th gear pinion, followed by the thrust washer (**see illustrations**).

19.34b . . . the 4th gear pinion . . .

19.34c . . . and the splined washer onto the shaft . . .

19.34d . . . and secure them with the circlip . . .

19.34e . . . making sure it locates in the groove

19.35a Slide the 5th gear pinion . . .

19.35b . . . and the thrust washer onto the shaft

Engine, clutch and transmission 2•45

19.36a Slide the needle bearing . . .

19.36b . . . the 1st gear pinion . . .

19.36c . . . and the thrust washer onto the shaft

19.37 The assembled shaft should be as shown

20.3 Keep the forks and shafts mated and the forks the correct way up. Note the identification markings on the forks

20.5 Counter-hold the drum and unscrew the cam bolt

36 Slide the 1st gear pinion needle roller bearing onto the shaft, then slide the 1st gear pinion onto the bearing with its dog holes facing the 5th gear pinion **(see illustrations)**. Fit the thrust washer **(see illustration)**.

37 Check that all components have been correctly installed **(see illustration)**.

20 Selector drum and forks

Removal

1 Remove the transmission cassette (see Section 17).

2 If not already done support the plate on blocks of wood with the transmission shafts pointing up.

3 Before removing the selector forks, note that the forks for the output shaft are marked RL, and the fork for the input shaft is marked C. If no letters are visible, mark them yourself using a felt pen. Withdraw the shaft from the input shaft fork and remove the fork, noting how it locates **(see illustrations 20.18b and a)**. Withdraw the shaft from the output shaft forks and remove the forks, noting how they locate **(see illustrations 20.17e, d, c, b and a)**. Once removed, slide the forks back onto the shafts to keep them mated **(see illustration)**.

4 Refer to Section 18, Step 4 and remove the transmission shafts.

5 If not already done, refer to Section 16, Step 8 and remove the stopper arm. Counter-hold the selector drum using a rod passed through its middle and unscrew the selector cam bolt **(see illustration)**. Note the locating pins in the end of the drum and remove them for safekeeping **(see illustration 20.14a)**.

6 Remove the collar, then withdraw the selector drum from the plate **(see illustrations)**.

Inspection

7 Inspect the selector forks for any signs of wear or damage, especially around the fork ends where they engage with the groove in the pinion. Check that each fork fits correctly in its pinion groove. Check closely to see if the forks are bent. If the forks are in any way damaged they must be replaced with new ones.

8 Measure the thickness of the fork ends and compare the readings to the specifications **(see illustration)**. Replace the forks with new ones if they are worn beyond their specifications.

20.6a Remove the collar . . .

20.6b . . . and then the drum

20.8 Measure the fork end thickness

2•46 Engine, clutch and transmission

20.9a Check the fit of each fork on the shaft . . .

20.9b . . . then measure the fork bore ID and the fork shaft OD

20.11 Check the guide pins and their grooves in the drum

9 Check that the forks fit correctly on their shaft **(see illustration)**. They should move freely with a light fit but no appreciable freeplay. Measure the internal diameter of the fork bores and the corresponding diameter of the fork shaft **(see illustration)**. Replace the forks and/or shafts with new ones if they are worn beyond their specifications. Check that the shaft holes in the plate and crankcase are neither worn nor damaged.

10 Check each selector fork shaft is straight by rolling it along a flat surface. A bent rod will cause difficulty in selecting gears and make the gearchange action heavy. Replace the shaft with a new one if it is bent.

11 Inspect the selector drum grooves and selector fork guide pins for signs of wear or damage **(see illustration)**. If either component shows signs of wear or damage the fork(s) and drum must be replaced with new ones.

12 Check that the bearing on the selector drum rotates freely and has no sign of freeplay between it and the casing **(see illustration)**. To fit a new bearing, remove the selector drum pin boss by unscrewing the bolt in its centre – pass a rod through the drum to counter-hold it **(see illustration)**. Note the locating pin in the end of the drum and remove it for safekeeping if required. Remove the old bearing and fit a new one (see *Tools and Workshop Tips* in the Reference Section if necessary). Install the pin boss, seating it on the locating pin. Clean the threads of the bolt and apply a suitable non-permanent thread locking compound, and tighten it, counter-holding the drum as before.

13 Also check the bearing in the cassette plate **(see illustration 18.7a)**. To remove the bearing unscrew the two retainer bolts. If the bearing is tight remove it using a puller,

or by driving it out with a socket, using heat to free it if necessary. On installation clean the retainer bolt threads and apply thread lock, and tighten them to the torque setting specified at the beginning of the chapter.

Installation

14 Slide the selector drum into its bearing in the plate and fit the collar with its shouldered end innermost **(see illustrations 20.6b and a)**. Fit the cam locating pins into their holes then locate the cam on the end of the drum with the OUT mark facing out – it can only fit one way **(see illustrations)**. Clean the threads of the cam bolt and apply a suitable non-permanent thread locking compound, and tighten it to the torque setting specified at the beginning of the Chapter, counter-holding the drum as before **(see illustration and 20.5)**. Turn the selector drum so the neutral detent in the cam is correctly positioned for the stopper arm.

15 Refer to Section 16, Step 12 and install the stopper arm.

16 Install the transmission shafts (see Section 18, Step 11).

17 Lubricate the selector fork ends and bores and the shafts with clean engine oil as you fit them. Fit the fork for the 5th gear pinion on the output shaft into its groove with the RL mark facing the cassette plate, then locate the fork's guide pin in its groove in the selector drum, lifting the gear slightly to align

20.12a Check the bearing

20.12b Unscrew the bolt (arrowed) and remove the pin boss to release the bearing

20.14a Fit the locating pins . . .

20.14b . . . then locate the cam, with the OUT mark facing out, onto the pins

20.14c Apply thread lock to the bolt

Engine, clutch and transmission 2•47

20.17a Locate the 5th gear RL fork in its pinion . . .

20.17b . . . and pivot it so the guide pin locates in its groove

20.17c Locate the 6th gear RL fork in its pinion . . .

20.17d . . . and pivot it so the guide pin locates in its groove

20.17e Slide the shaft through the forks and into its bore in the plate

20.18a Locate the C fork in its pinion . . .

it if required **(see illustrations)**. Fit the fork for the 6th gear pinion on the output shaft into its groove with the RL mark facing away from the cassette plate, then locate the fork's guide pin in its groove in the selector drum **(see illustrations)**. Slide the shaft through each fork and into its bore in the plate **(see illustration)**.

18 Now fit the fork for the 3rd/4th gear pinion on the input shaft into its groove with the C mark facing away from the cassette plate **(see illustration)**. Locate the fork's guide pin in its groove in the selector drum, lifting the gear slightly to align them if required, then slide the shaft through the fork and into its bore in the plate **(see illustration)**.

19 Install the transmission cassette (see Section 17).

21 Oil sump, oil strainer and pressure relief valve

Note: *The oil sump, oil strainer and pressure relief valve can be removed with the engine in the frame. If the engine has been removed, ignore the steps which don't apply.*

Removal

1 Drain the engine oil (see Chapter 1).
2 Remove the exhaust system (see Chapter 4).
3 Unscrew the sump bolts, slackening them evenly in a criss-cross sequence to prevent distortion, and remove the sump **(see illustration)**.

20.18b . . . then pivot it so the guide pin locates in its groove and slide the shaft through

21.3 Unscrew the bolts (arrowed) and remove the sump

2•48 Engine, clutch and transmission

21.4a Remove the strainer, noting how the tab locates in the groove . . .

21.4b . . . and remove the rubber seal

21.5 Pull the relief valve out of its socket

4 Pull the strainer out of the oil pump, noting how it locates (see illustration). Remove the rubber seal and discard it as a new one must be used (see illustration).
5 Pull the pressure relief valve out of its socket (see illustration). Discard the O-ring as a new one must be used.

Inspection

6 Remove all traces of sealant from the sump and crankcase mating surfaces, and clean the inside of the sump with solvent. Blow the sump dry with compressed air if available.
7 Clean the oil strainer in solvent and remove any debris caught in the mesh. If the strainer gauze is damaged, replace the strainer with a new one.
8 Push the relief valve plunger into the valve body and check that it moves smoothly and freely against spring pressure (see illustration). If not, remove the circlip, noting that it is under spring pressure, then remove the washer, spring and plunger. Clean all components in solvent, then check the plunger and the valve body for evidence of scoring, wear and any other damage. If any is found, replace the relief valve with a new one – individual components are not available. Otherwise, coat the plunger with oil and fit it closed end first back into the valve and recheck the movement. If it is good, install the spring and washer and secure them with the circlip.

Installation

9 Fit a new O-ring onto the relief valve and smear it with clean oil, then push the valve into its socket (see illustration and 21.5).
10 Fit a new rubber seal smeared with clean oil into the strainer socket in the pump (see illustration). Do not fit it onto the strainer as it will distort when the strainer is fitted. Fit the strainer, locating the tab in the cut-out (see illustration).
11 Clean the mating surfaces of the sump and crankcase with solvent. Apply a suitable sealant (such as Three Bond 1207B or equivalent RTV sealant – ask your dealer) to the sump mating surface (see illustration). Position the sump onto the crankcase and fit the bolts finger-tight (see illustration). Tighten the bolts evenly and a little at a time in a criss-cross pattern (see illustration 21.3).
12 Install the exhaust system (see Chapter 4).
13 Fill the engine with the correct type and quantity of oil as described in Chapter 1.
14 Start the engine and check that there are no leaks around the sump.

21.8 Push the plunger into the body and check that it moves smoothly

21.9 Fit a new O-ring onto the relief valve body

21.10a Lubricate the rubber seal and fit it into the crankcase

21.10b Locate the tab in the slot (arrowed)

21.11a Apply the sealant . . .

21.11b . . . then install the sump

Engine, clutch and transmission 2•49

22.3a Unscrew the bolts (arrowed) and remove the pump

22.3b Remove the O-ring and collar, and the dowels (arrowed) if loose

22.5a Driven sprocket bolt (A); oil pump cover bolts (B)

22 Oil pump

Note: *The oil pump can be removed with the engine in the frame. If the engine has been removed, ignore the steps which don't apply.*

Removal

1 Remove the clutch and the oil pump drive sprocket and chain (see Section 14).
2 Remove the sump and the oil strainer (see Section 21).
3 Unscrew the three bolts securing the pump to the crankcase, then remove the pump, noting how it fits **(see illustration)**. Remove the dowels from either the crankcase or the pump if they are loose **(see illustration)**. Remove the oil passage collar and O-ring and discard the O-ring – a new one must be used.

Inspection

4 If required lock the oil pump driven sprocket to prevent it from turning and unscrew the bolt **(see illustration 22.5a)**. Remove the driven sprocket.
5 Unscrew the bolts securing the cover to the pump body, then remove the cover **(see illustrations)**.
6 Remove the drive pin and thrust washer then withdraw the shaft from the cover **(see illustration)**. Remove the inner and outer rotors from the body, noting which way round they fit.
7 Clean all the components in solvent.
8 Inspect the pump body, shaft and rotors for scoring and wear. If any damage, scoring or uneven or excessive wear is evident, replace the pump with a new one (individual components are not available).
9 Fit the inner and outer rotors into the pump body, then slide the shaft through the inner rotor. Align the rotors as shown and measure the clearance between the inner rotor tip and the outer rotor with a feeler gauge and compare it to the service limit listed in the specifications at the beginning of the Chapter **(see illustration)**. If the clearance measured is greater than the maximum listed, replace the pump with a new one.
10 Measure the clearance between the outer rotor and the pump body with a feeler gauge and compare it to the maximum clearance listed in the specifications at the beginning of the Chapter **(see illustration)**. If the clearance measured is greater than the maximum listed, replace the pump with a new one.
11 Lay a straight-edge across the rotors and the pump body and, using a feeler gauge, measure the rotor end-float (the gap between the rotors and the straight-edge **(see illustration)**. If the clearance measured is greater than the maximum listed, replace the pump with a new one.
12 Check the pump drive chain and drive and driven sprockets for wear or damage, and replace them with a new set if necessary.
13 If the pump is good, make sure all the components are clean, then lubricate them with new engine oil.
14 Fit the outer rotor into the pump body. Fit the inner rotor into the outer rotor with the cut-outs in the inner rotor facing out.
15 Fit the dowels into the cover if removed. Slide the drive shaft through the cover, making

22.5b Draw the pump body off the shaft

22.6 Remove the drive pin (B) and the washer (A) then withdraw the shaft

22.9 Measure the inner rotor tip-to-outer rotor clearance as shown (shaft shown removed for clarity)

22.10 Measure the outer rotor-to-body clearance as shown

22.11 Measure rotor end-float as shown

2•50 Engine, clutch and transmission

22.15 Align the drive pin ends (A) with the cut-outs (B)

22.19a Fit the pump onto its dowels and collar

22.19b Make sure the shafts engage correctly

sure the end with the driven sprocket bolt hole is on the outer side so the tabbed end fits through the pump body. Slide the thrust washer onto the shaft then fit the drive pin into its hole in the shaft **(see illustration 22.6)**. Turn the shaft to align the drive pin ends with the cut-outs in the inner rotor **(see illustration)**. Fit the cover onto the pump, locating the drive pin ends into the cut-outs **(see illustration 22.5b)**. Fit the bolts and tighten them to the torque setting specified at the beginning of the Chapter **(see illustration 22.5a)**.

16 Rotate the pump shaft by hand and check it turns the rotors smoothly and freely.

17 If removed, clean the threads of the sprocket bolt threads. Locate the sprocket on the shaft with the OUT mark facing out, then apply a suitable non-permanent thread locking compound to the bolt and tighten it to the torque setting specified at the beginning of the chapter, counter-holding the sprocket as before **(see illustration 22.5a)**.

Installation

18 Fit the pump locating dowels if removed **(see illustration 22.3b)**. Fit the oil passage collar then fit a new O-ring smeared with clean oil around the collar.

19 Install the pump, rotating the drive shaft to align the tab on its end with the slot in the water pump shaft, and making sure it locates correctly on the dowels and collar **(see illustrations)**. Fit the mounting bolts and tighten them, noting that the longer bolt fits into the hole near the sprocket.

20 Install the oil pump drive sprocket and chain and clutch (see Section 14). Pour some clean engine oil into the pump via the strainer socket and rotate the shaft to prime it **(see illustration)**. Install the oil strainer and the sump (see Section 21).

23 Crankcase separation and reassembly

Note: *To separate the crankcase halves, the engine must be removed from the frame.*
Note: *The 9 mm main journal crankcase bolts are of the stretch type, which can only be used in a running engine once, though they can be used when performing the oil clearance check detailed in Section 26 to prevent having to buy two sets of new bolts. The new bolts come pre-coated with an oil additive which must not be cleaned off.*

Separation

1 To access the pistons, connecting rods, crankshaft, balancer shaft and the main and big-end bearings, the crankcase must be split into its two halves.

2 Before the crankcases can be separated the following components must be removed:
  Valve cover (Section 7)
  Camshafts (Section 9) – see Note
  Cylinder head (Section 11) – see Note
  Alternator (Chapter 8)
  Starter clutch (Section 13)
  Cam chain and blades (Section 10) – see Note
  Gearchange mechanism (Section 16)
  Clutch, oil pump drive chain and sprocket (Section 14)
  Transmission cassette (Section 17)
  Water pump (Chapter 3)
  Oil cooler (Section 6)
  Starter motor (Chapter 8)
  Oil sump, strainer and pressure relief valve (Section 21)
  Oil pump (Section 22)
  Speed sensor (Chapter 8)

Note: *If the crankcases are being separated to inspect the crankshaft without removing it, the camshafts and cylinder head can remain in situ. To remove the crankshaft without removing the connecting rods and pistons, the camshafts must be removed but the head can stay. However, if removal of the connecting rod assemblies is intended, full disassembly of the top-end is necessary. If required the cam chain can remain loose on the crankshaft after the camshafts have been removed, and can be taken off after the crankshaft has been removed.*

3 Release the oil pressure switch wire from the clamp. Pull the rubber boot off the switch, then undo the terminal screw and detach the wiring **(see illustration)**. Pull the rubber

22.20 Prime the pump with oil before fitting the sump

23.3a Disconnect the wiring from the oil pressure switch . . .

Engine, clutch and transmission 2•51

23.3b ... and the neutral switch

23.4 Unscrew the bolts and remove the window, noting the wiring clamp

boot off the neutral switch, then undo the terminal nut and detach the wiring **(see illustration)**.

4 Unscrew the oil level inspection window bolts and remove the window **(see illustration)**. Discard the O-ring as a new one must be used. Note the wiring clamp secured by the upper bolt.

5 Unscrew the six 7 mm upper crankcase bolts evenly, a little at a time and in a criss-cross sequence until they are finger-tight, then remove them, noting the one at the front fitted with a sealing washer **(see illustrations)**. **Note:** *As each bolt is removed, store it in its relative position in a cardboard template of the crankcase halves. This will ensure all bolts and washers are installed in the correct location on reassembly.* Note that new sealing washers should be used on assembly where fitted, though it is wise to keep the old ones with the bolts for the time being as a pattern for the new ones.

6 Unscrew the five 8 mm upper crankcase bolts evenly, a little at a time and in a criss-cross sequence until they are finger-tight, then remove them.

7 Turn the engine upside down.

8 Unscrew the six 7 mm and one 8 mm lower crankcase bolts evenly, a little at a time and in a criss-cross sequence until they are finger-tight, then remove them **(see illustrations)**. **Note:** *As each bolt is removed, store it in its relative position in a cardboard template of the crankcase halves. This will ensure all bolts are installed in the correct location on reassembly.*

9 Now unscrew the ten 9 mm crankshaft journal bolts evenly, a little at a time and in a **reverse** of the tightening sequence (see

23.5a Upper crankcase 7 mm bolts (A) ...

23.5b ... and 8 mm bolts (B)

23.8a Lower crankcase 7 mm bolts (arrowed) ...

23.8b ... and 8 mm bolt (arrowed)

2•52 Engine, clutch and transmission

23.9 9 mm crankshaft journal bolts (arrowed)

23.10 Carefully separate the crankcase halves

illustration 23.22b), i.e. starting from the outside and working to the centre, until they are finger-tight, then remove them **(see illustration)**.
10 Carefully lift the lower crankcase half off the upper half, using a soft-faced hammer to tap around the joint to initially separate the halves if necessary **(see illustration)**. **Note:** *If the halves do not separate easily, make sure all fasteners have been removed. Do not try and separate the halves by levering against the crankcase mating surfaces as they are easily scored and will leak oil in the future if damaged.* The lower crankcase half will come away with the balancer shaft, leaving the crankshaft in the upper crankcase half.
11 Remove the three locating dowels from the crankcase if they are loose (they could be in either crankcase half), and the two oil orifices, noting how they fit **(see illustrations)**. Remove the transmission input shaft bearing, noting how the pin locates in the hole **(see illustration)**. Remove the clutch pushrod oil seal and discard it – a new one must be used **(see illustration)**. Check the condition of the input shaft bearing and replace it with a new one if necessary (see Section 18, Step 7).
12 Refer to Sections 24 to 30 for the removal, inspection and installation of the components housed within the crankcases.

Reassembly

Special tool: *A degree disc is required for tightening the crankshaft journal bolts* **(see illustration 23.22c)**.
13 Remove all traces of sealant from the crankcase mating surfaces.
14 Make sure the crankshaft, connecting rods and pistons and the balancer shaft and their bearings are in place in the upper and lower crankcase halves. Fit a new clutch pushrod oil seal, locating its lip in the groove as shown **(see illustration 23.11d)**. Fit the transmission input shaft bearing, locating its pin in the hole **(see illustration 23.11c)**.
15 Generously lubricate the crankshaft and balancer shaft, particularly around the bearings, with clean engine oil, then use a rag soaked in high flash-point solvent to wipe over the mating surfaces of both crankcase halves to remove all traces of oil.
16 If removed, fit the three locating dowels and the two oil orifices in the upper crankcase half **(see illustrations 23.11a and b)**. Make sure the orifices are installed the correct way up and so their flat sides locate correctly in the bores **(see illustration)**.
17 To enable easy engagement of the balancer

23.11a Remove the dowels (arrowed) if they are loose . . .

23.11b . . . and the oil orifices (arrowed)

23.11c Remove the bearing, noting how the pin locates in the hole (arrowed), . . .

23.11d . . . and the clutch pushrod oil seal (arrowed)

23.16 Install the oil orifices with the flats locating against the corresponding flats in their bores

Engine, clutch and transmission 2•53

23.17 Make an alignment mark, then slacken the pinch bolt (arrowed) and turn the shaft so the punch mark is at the bottom

23.18a Unscrew the bolt...

23.18b ...then obtain a suitable replacement as described...

23.18c ...to locate in the hole (arrowed) in the shaft

23.18d Make sure the crankshaft is correctly aligned as shown

shaft driven gear with its drive gear on the crankshaft the backlash adjustment must be set to a maximum (more information on backlash and its importance is given in Section 30). If not already done (if the balancer shaft was removed from the crankcase – see Section 30), first make an alignment mark on the balancer shaft holder with the punch mark on the end of the balancer shaft – this will give a good indication as to the starting point for resetting the backlash adjustment after the crankcases have been assembled **(see illustration)**. Slacken the balancer shaft holder pinch bolt, then turn the shaft until the punch mark on its end is facing down (the shaft provides an eccentric adjustment which alters the backlash).

18 Now both the balancer shaft and the crankshaft must be correctly positioned. Unscrew and remove the bolt below the balancer **(see illustration)**. Discard its sealing washer. Obtain either the Honda special tool (pt. no. 90004-MM5-000, which is a 6 x 18 mm bolt with a coned end), or its equivalent from your stash of old bolts (make sure the thread pitch is identical to the bolt removed), ground at the end so it is coned instead of flat **(see illustration)**. Identify the hole in the balancer shaft into which the bolt end must locate, then turn the shaft until the hole aligns with the bolt hole in the crankcase, then thread the special bolt into the crankcase until its shaped end locates in the hole in the balancer, thereby locking it to prevent it turning **(see illustration)**. Set the crankshaft so that the No. 1 (left-hand) piston is at top dead centre in its bore, then turn it slightly clockwise until the centre of the 5th spline anti-clockwise from the wide spline on the right-hand (starter clutch) end aligns with the lower triangular mark on the crankcase as shown **(see illustration)**.

19 Apply a small amount of suitable sealant (Three-Bond 1207B or equivalent RTV sealant – ask your dealer) to the outer mating surface of the lower crankcase half as shown **(see illustration)**.

Caution: Apply the sealant only to the shaded areas. Do not apply an excessive amount as it will ooze out when the case halves are assembled and may obstruct oil passages. Do not apply the sealant close to any of the bearing shells or surfaces, or oil passages.

20 Check again that all components are in position, and that the bearing shells are still correctly located in the lower crankcase half. Carefully fit the lower crankcase half down onto the upper crankcase half, making sure the dowels and oil orifices locate correctly **(see illustration 23.10)**. As the balancer shaft and crankshaft gears engage, the paint marks on their teeth should match as shown; note that the crankshaft may turn slightly as the teeth mate **(see illustration)**. Check that the lower crankcase half is correctly seated.

23.19 Apply the sealant to the shaded area shown

23.20 Make sure the painted teeth mesh together

2•54 Engine, clutch and transmission

23.22a Use new bolts for the crankshaft journals and fit the longer ones at the outer ends

23.22b Tighten the bolts as described in the sequence shown to the specified torque . . .

21 To double check alignment, or if the paint marks have come off or are not visible, temporarily fit the starter clutch and timing rotor assembly onto the end of the crankshaft aligning the wide splines (see Section 13), and check that the line next to the 'T' mark on the timing rotor aligns with the higher triangle mark on the crankcase. If the marks do not align, or if you are not sure, remove the lower crankcase and start again, noting that you may have to clean and re-seal the mating surfaces. When you are happy everything is correctly aligned and fitted remove the special bolt locking the balancer shaft and replace it with the original, but using a new sealing washer (see illustration 23.18a). Tighten the bolt.
Caution: The crankcase halves should fit together without being forced. If the casings are not correctly seated, remove the lower crankcase half and investigate the problem. Do not attempt to pull them together using the crankcase bolts as the casing will crack and be ruined.
22 Install the ten NEW 9 mm crankshaft journal bolts, fitting the four longer bolts into the outer ends (see illustration and 23.9). Clean the threads of the six 7 mm and one 8 mm lower crankcase bolts and insert them in their original locations (see illustrations 23.8a and b). Secure all bolts finger-tight.

Now tighten the 9 mm crankshaft journal bolts evenly and a little at a time in the numerical sequence shown to the torque setting specified at the beginning of the Chapter (see illustration). Now, using a degree disc, tighten each bolt in turn and in one go by a further 150°, again following the numerical sequence (see illustration).
23 Next tighten the 8 mm bolt to the specified torque. Now tighten the 7 mm bolts evenly and a little at a time in a criss-cross sequence starting in the middle and working outwards to the specified torque setting.
24 Turn the engine over. Clean the threads of the six 7 mm bolts and the five 8 mm bolts and insert them in their original locations (see illustrations 23.5a and b) – do not forget to fit a new sealing washer with the 7 mm bolt at the front (see illustration). Secure the bolts finger-tight at first, then tighten the 8 mm bolts evenly and a little at a time in a criss-cross sequence starting in the middle and working outwards to the specified torque setting, followed by the 7 mm bolts.
25 With all crankcase fasteners tightened, check that the crankshaft and balancer shaft rotate smoothly and easily, but at this stage do not worry about any noise from the gear teeth. Refer to Section 30 and adjust the backlash following the static adjustment procedure.

26 Fit a new O-ring smeared with oil into the groove on the inside of the oil level inspection window (see illustration). Fit the window, not forgetting the wiring clamp, and tighten the bolts (see illustration 23.4). Reconnect the engine sub-loom wiring to the neutral switch and oil pressure switch (see illustrations 23.3b and a). Install all other removed assemblies in a reverse of the sequence given in Step 2.

24 Crankcases and cylinder bores

Crankcases

1 After the crankcases have been separated, remove the crankshaft and its bearing shells, connecting rods and pistons, balancer shaft, speed sensor, neutral switch and oil pressure switch, referring to the relevant Sections of this Chapter, and to Chapter 8 for the speed sensor and oil pressure and neutral switches. If there are any other components or assemblies that have not been removed as part of your stripdown procedure, for example the starter motor or the coolant inlet union, remove these as well, referring to the relevant Chapter.

23.22c . . . and then through the specified angle using a degree disc

23.24 Use a new sealing washer on this bolt

23.26 Fit a new O-ring onto the oil level window

Engine, clutch and transmission 2•55

24.2a Piston oil jet bolts (arrowed)

24.2b Note the letter on each jet which matches the letter on the cylinder rim (arrowed)

24.8a Fit the holders into the jets

2 On CB1000R/RA models unscrew the bolt securing each piston oil jet and remove the jets with their holders (see illustration) – note that each jet is marked with the letter A or B according to its location (see illustration). Separate the jets from the holders (see illustration 24.8a).

3 Clean the crankcases thoroughly with new solvent and dry them with compressed air. Blow out all oil passages with compressed air. Clean the inside of the oil level inspection window. Clean and blow through the piston oil jets and holders.

4 Remove all traces of old gasket sealant from the mating surfaces. Clean up minor damage to the surfaces with a fine sharpening stone or grindstone.

Caution: Be very careful not to nick or gouge the crankcase mating surfaces or oil leaks will result. Check both crankcase halves very carefully for cracks and other damage.

5 Small cracks or holes in aluminium castings can be repaired with an epoxy resin adhesive as a temporary measure. Permanent repairs can only be done by argon-arc welding, and only a specialist in this process is in a position to advise on the economy or practical aspect of such a repair. If any damage is found that can't be repaired, replace the crankcase halves as a set.

6 Damaged threads can be economically reclaimed using a diamond section wire insert, for example of the Heli-Coil type (though there are other makes), which are easily fitted after drilling and re-tapping the affected thread.

7 Sheared studs or screws can usually be removed with extractors, which consist of a tapered, left-hand thread screw of very hard steel. These are inserted into a pre-drilled hole in the stud, and usually succeed in dislodging the most stubborn stud or screw. If a stud has sheared above its bore line, it can be removed using a conventional stud extractor which avoids the need for drilling.

> **HAYNES HiNT** *Refer to Tools and Workshop Tips for details of installing a thread insert and using screw extractors.*

8 On CB1000R/RA models fit the holders into the piston oil jets (see illustration). Fit the jets, making sure the ones marked A are fitted into the Nos. 2 and 3 cylinders and the ones marked B are fitted into the Nos. 1 and 4 cylinders (see illustration 24.2b). Clean the threads of the bolts and apply a suitable non-permanent thread locking compound, and tighten them (see illustration).

9 Install all components and assemblies, referring to the relevant Sections of this and the other Chapters, before reassembling the crankcase halves.

Cylinder bores

Note: Do not attempt to separate the cylinder liners from the cylinder block. The liners are made of an aluminium/ceramic powdered metal composite and so great care must be taken not to scratch or gouge them.

10 Check the cylinder walls carefully for scratches and score marks.

11 Using a precision straight-edge and a feeler gauge set to the warpage limit listed in the specifications at the beginning of the Chapter, check the block gasket mating surface for warpage. Refer to *Tools and Workshop Tips* in the Reference section for details of how to use the straight-edge. If warpage is excessive the crankcases must be replaced with new ones.

12 Using telescoping gauges and a micrometer (see *Tools and Workshop Tips*), check the dimensions of each cylinder to assess the amount of wear, taper and ovality. Measure near the top (but below the level of the top piston ring at TDC), centre and bottom (but above the level of the oil ring at BDC) of the bore, both parallel to and across the crankshaft axis (see illustrations). Compare the results to the specifications at the beginning of the Chapter. If the cylinders are worn, oval or tapered beyond the service limit they can be re-bored – an oversize (+ 0.25) set of pistons and rings is available. Note that the person carrying out the re-bore must be aware of the piston-to-bore clearance for the oversize pistons and rings (see Specifications).

13 If the precision measuring tools are not available, take the upper crankcase to a Honda dealer or specialist motorcycle repair shop for assessment and advice.

24.8b Apply a thread lock to the bolts

24.12a Measure the cylinder bore in the directions shown . . .

24.12b . . . using a telescoping gauge, then measure the gauge with a micrometer

2•56 Engine, clutch and transmission

25 Connecting rod and main bearing information

1 Even though new main and connecting rod bearings are generally fitted during engine overhaul, the old bearings should be retained for close examination as they may reveal valuable information about the condition of the engine.
2 Bearing failure occurs mainly because of lack of lubrication, the presence of dirt or other foreign particles, overloading the engine and/or corrosion. Regardless of the cause of bearing failure, it must be corrected before the engine is reassembled to prevent it from happening again.
3 When examining the bearings, lay them out on a clean surface in the same general position as their location on the crankshaft journals. This will enable you to match any noted bearing problems with the corresponding crankshaft journal.
4 Dirt and other foreign particles get into the engine in a variety of ways. They may be left in the engine during assembly or they may pass through filters or breathers, then get into the oil and from there into the bearings. Metal chips from machining operations and normal engine wear are often present. Abrasives are sometimes left in engine components after reconditioning operations, especially when parts are not thoroughly cleaned using the proper cleaning methods. Whatever the source, foreign objects often end up imbedded in the soft bearing material and are easily recognised. Large particles will not imbed in the bearing and will score or gouge the bearing and journal. The best prevention for this cause of bearing failure is to clean all parts thoroughly and keep everything spotlessly clean during engine reassembly. Regular oil and filter changes are also recommended.
5 Lack of lubrication or lubrication breakdown has a number of interrelated causes. Excessive heat (which thins the oil), overloading (which squeezes the oil from the bearing face) and oil leakage or throw off (from excessive bearing clearances, worn oil pump or high engine speeds) all contribute to lubrication breakdown. Blocked oil passages will starve a bearing of lubrication and destroy it. When lack of lubrication is the cause of bearing failure, the bearing material is wiped or extruded from the steel backing of the bearing. Temperatures may increase to the point where the steel backing and the journal turn blue from overheating.

HAYNES HINT *Refer to Tools and Workshop Tips for bearing fault finding.*

6 Riding habits can have a definite effect on bearing life. Full throttle low speed operation, or labouring the engine, puts very high loads on bearings, which tend to squeeze out the oil film. These loads cause the bearings to flex, which produces fine cracks in the bearing face (fatigue failure). Eventually the bearing material will loosen in pieces and tear away from the steel backing. Short trip riding leads to corrosion of bearings, as insufficient engine heat is produced to drive off the condensed water and corrosive gases produced. These products collect in the engine oil, forming acid and sludge. As the oil is carried to the engine bearings, the acid attacks and corrodes the bearing material.
7 Incorrect bearing installation during engine assembly will lead to bearing failure as well. Tight fitting bearings which leave insufficient bearing oil clearances result in oil starvation. Dirt or foreign particles trapped behind a bearing insert result in high spots on the bearing which lead to failure.
8 To avoid bearing problems, clean all parts thoroughly before reassembly, double check all bearing clearance measurements and lubricate the new bearings with clean engine oil during installation.

26 Crankshaft and main bearings

Note: *To remove the crankshaft the engine must be removed from the frame and the crankcase halves separated.*
Note: *The crankshaft journal bolts are of the stretch type and can only be used in a running engine once, though they can be used when performing the oil clearance check to prevent having to buy two sets of new bolts.*
Special tool: *A degree disc is required for tightening the crankshaft journal bolts if performing an oil clearance check (see illustration 23.22c).*

Removal

1 Remove the engine from the frame (see Section 4) and separate the crankcase halves (see Section 23).
2 Refer to Section 27 and detach the connecting rods from the crankpins. Push the rods and pistons up to the tops of the bores so that the bottom ends are clear of the crankshaft, taking care to keep the rods clear of the cylinder liners – it is best to protect the liners with some rag **(see illustration 27.4c)**.
Note: *If no work is to be carried out on the piston/connecting rod assemblies there is no need to remove them from the bores. If you do need to remove them, continue to refer to Section 27.*
3 Lift the crankshaft out of the upper crankcase half, bringing the cam chain with it if it hasn't been removed, and taking care not to dislodge the main bearing shells **(see illustration)**. Wrap some rag around each connecting rod to protect the cylinder walls.
4 If necessary remove the main bearing shells from the crankcase halves using a small screwdriver inserted in the notch to lift them out, but make sure you keep them in order **(see illustration)**. If they are being re-used they must be returned to their original locations.

Inspection

5 Clean the crankshaft with solvent, squirting it under pressure through all the oil passages. If available, blow the crank dry with compressed air, and also blow through the oil passages. Check the primary drive gear and the balancer drive gear for wear or damage. If any of the gear teeth are excessively worn, chipped or broken, the crankshaft must be replaced with a new one. If wear or damage is found, also inspect the primary driven gear on the back of the clutch housing (see Section 14), and the balancer shaft driven gear (see Section 30).
6 Refer to Section 25 and examine the main bearing shells. If they are scored, badly scuffed or appear to have been seized, new bearings must be installed. Always replace the main bearings as a set selected as described in Steps 21 and 22. If they are badly damaged, check the corresponding crankshaft journals. Evidence of extreme heat, such as discoloration, indicates that lubrication failure has occurred. Thoroughly check the oil pump and pressure relief valve as well as all oil holes and passages before reassembling the engine.
7 Give the crankshaft journals a close visual examination, paying particular attention where damaged bearings have been discovered. If the journals are scored or pitted in any way

26.3 Lift the crankshaft out of the crankcase

26.4 Remove the shells from their housings

Engine, clutch and transmission 2•57

26.13 Place a strip of Plastigauge on each bearing journal

26.16 Measure the crushed Plastigauge using the scale on the pack

26.19 Measure the diameter of the main journal as shown

a new crankshaft will be required. Note that undersizes are not available, precluding the option of regrinding the crankshaft.

8 Place the crankshaft on V-blocks and check the runout at the main bearing journals using a dial gauge. Compare the reading to the maximum specified at the beginning of the Chapter. If the runout exceeds the limit, the crankshaft must be replaced with a new one.

Oil clearance check

9 Whether new bearing shells are being fitted or the original ones are being reused, the main bearing oil clearance should be checked before the engine is reassembled. Main bearing oil clearance is measured with a product known as Plastigauge. It is best to remove the balancer shaft from the lower crankcase before making the check as engagement of the balancer drive and driven gears when assembling the crankcases causes the crankshaft to turn slightly, and this could disturb the Plastigauge, leading to a false reading – see Section 30.

10 Remove the shells if not already done **(see illustration 26.4)**. Clean the backs of the shells and the bearing housings in both crankcase halves.

11 Press the bearing shells into their cut-outs, ensuring that the tab on each shell engages in the notch in the crankcase **(see illustration 26.24)**. Make sure the bearings are fitted in the correct locations and take care not to touch any shell's bearing surface with your fingers.

12 Ensure the shells and crankshaft are clean and dry. Lay the crankshaft in position in the upper crankcase **(see illustration 26.3)**. Fit the three crankcase dowels if removed **(see illustration 23.11a)**.

13 Cut five lengths of the appropriate size Plastigauge (they should be slightly shorter than the width of the crankshaft journals). Place a strand of Plastigauge on each (cleaned) journal, avoiding the oil hole **(see illustration)**. During the procedure make sure the crankshaft is not rotated at all as this will disturb the Plastigauge and give false readings, in which case you must start again.

14 Carefully fit the lower crankcase half onto the upper half **(see illustration 23.10)**. Check that the lower half is correctly seated. **Note:** *Do not install and tighten the crankcase bolts if the casing is not correctly seated.* Install the ten 9 mm crankshaft journal bolts, fitting the four longer bolts into the outer ends **(see illustrations 23.9 and 23.22a)**. Secure all bolts finger-tight at first, then tighten them evenly and a little at a time in the numerical sequence shown to the torque setting specified at the beginning of the Chapter **(see illustration 23.22b)**. Now, using a degree disc, tighten each bolt in turn by a further 150°, again following the numerical sequence **(see illustration 23.22c)**.

15 Slacken each bolt evenly and a little at a time in a reverse of the tightening sequence, i.e. starting from the outside and working to the centre, until they are all finger-tight, then remove the bolts. Carefully lift off the lower crankcase half, making sure the Plastigauge is not disturbed.

16 Compare the width of the crushed Plastigauge on each crankshaft journal to the scale printed on the Plastigauge envelope to obtain the main bearing oil clearance **(see illustration)**. Compare the reading to the specifications at the beginning of the Chapter.

17 On completion carefully scrape away all traces of the Plastigauge material from the crankshaft journal and bearing shells; use a fingernail or other object which is unlikely to score them.

18 If the oil clearance is within the range listed in this Chapter's Specifications and the bearings are in perfect condition, they can be re-used.

19 If the oil clearance on any journal is beyond the service limit, measure the journal and compare the result to the appropriate size range in the table below to see if it has worn **(see illustration)**. If it has refer to Steps 21 and 22 and use the specifications given in the bearing selection table to determine whether different shells that correspond with the actual journal diameter (as opposed to its given size code) can be used. If the journal is the correct diameter for its given size code, replace the bearing shells with new ones according to the size codes. Check the oil clearance once again. Always replace all of the shells at the same time.

20 If the crankshaft has worn beyond the narrowest diameter given it must be replaced with a new one, and new shells selected according to that crankshaft.

Main bearing shell selection

21 Replacement bearing shells for the main bearings are supplied on a selected fit basis. Code numbers and letters stamped on the crankshaft and crankcase, or the actual measured size of the crankshaft journal, are used to identify the correct replacement bearings. The crankshaft main bearing journal size numbers are stamped on the outside of the left-hand crankshaft web and will be either a 1, 2 or 3 **(see illustration)**. The first number, after the L, is for the left-hand journal, and the numbers correspond consecutively for each journal. The corresponding main bearing housing size letters are stamped into the left-hand side of the upper crankcase half and will be either an A, B or C **(see illustration)**. The left-hand letter corresponds to the left-hand journal, and the letters correspond consecutively from left to right.

26.21a Main bearing journal size numbers

26.21b Main bearing housing size letters

2•58 Engine, clutch and transmission

22 A range of bearing shells is available. To select the correct bearing for a particular journal, use the table below and cross-refer the main bearing journal size number (stamped on the crank web) or measured size with the main bearing housing size letter (stamped on the crankcase) to determine the colour code of the bearing required. For example, if the journal code is 3, and the housing code is A, then the bearing required is yellow. The colour is marked on the side of the shell **(see illustration 27.22)**.

Main bearing journal code	Main bearing housing code		
	A	B	C
1 (34.000 to 34.006 mm)	Red	Pink	Yellow
2 (33.994 to 34.000 mm)	Pink	Yellow	Green
3 (33.988 to 33.994 mm)	Yellow	Green	Brown

Installation

23 Clean the backs of the bearing shells and the bearing cut-outs in both crankcase halves. If new shells are being fitted, ensure that all traces of the protective grease are cleaned off using paraffin (kerosene). Wipe the shells and crankcase halves dry with a lint-free cloth. Make sure all the oil passages and holes are clear, and blow them through with compressed air if it is available.
24 Press the bearing shells into their locations. Make sure the tab on each shell engages in the notch in the casing **(see illustration)**. Make sure the bearings are fitted in the correct locations and take care not to touch any shell's bearing surface with your fingers. Lubricate each shell with molybdenum disulphide oil (a 50/50 mixture of molybdenum disulphide grease and clean engine oil).
25 Lower the crankshaft into position in the upper crankcase, making sure all bearings remain in place **(see illustration 26.3)**.
26 Refer to Section 27 and fit the connecting rods and caps onto the crankshaft.
27 Reassemble the crankcase halves (see Section 23).

27 Connecting rods and bearings

Note 1: *To remove the connecting rods the engine must be removed from the frame and the crankcases separated.*
Note 2: *The connecting rod bolts can only be used in a running engine once, though they can be used when performing the oil clearance check to prevent having to buy two sets of new bolts.*
Special tools: *A piston ring compressor is necessary for the installation procedure **(see illustration 27.25a)**. A degree disc is also required for tightening the bolts to the correct torque.*

Removal

1 Remove the engine from the frame (see Section 4) and separate the crankcase halves (see Section 23).
2 Before detaching the rods from the crankshaft, measure the side clearance (the gap between the connecting rod big-end and the crankshaft web) with a feeler gauge **(see illustration)**. If the clearance is greater than the service limit listed in this Chapter's Specifications, replace the rod with a new one, then check the clearance again. If the clearance is still excessive, replace the crankshaft with a new one.
3 Using paint or a felt marker pen, mark the relevant cylinder identity on each connecting rod and cap **(see illustration 27.2)**. Mark across the cap-to-connecting rod join that faces the front of the engine to ensure that everything is fitted the correct way around and onto the correct rod on reassembly. Note that the number already across the rod and cap indicates rod size grade **(see illustration 27.21b)**.
4 Unscrew the connecting rod cap bolts **(see illustration)**. Separate the caps from the crankpin, noting the locating pins **(see illustration)**. Push the rods and pistons up to the tops of the bores so that the bottom ends are clear of the crankshaft, taking care to keep the rods clear of the cylinder liners – it is best to protect the liners with some rag **(see illustration)**. Remove the crankshaft (see Section 26). Wrap some rag around each connecting rod to protect the cylinder walls.
5 Turn the crankcase on its side. Push each piston/connecting rod assembly up its bore and remove it from the top making sure the connecting rod does not mark the cylinder walls **(see illustration)**. The piston crown is

26.24 Fit the shells, locating the tabs in the notches (arrowed)

27.2 Measure the gap (arrowed) between the big-end and the web using a feeler gauge

27.4a Unscrew the bolts (arrowed) . . .

27.4b . . . and remove the connecting rod caps

27.4c Push the rods off the crankpins and up the bores

27.5 Carefully lift the piston and rod assembly out of the bore. Note the IN mark location (arrowed)

Engine, clutch and transmission 2•59

27.9a Check for freeplay between the rod and pin

27.9b Measure the external diameter of the pin and the internal diameter of the rod small-end

27.10 Remove the shells as shown

marked IN, and that faces the intake side of the cylinder, the same way as the oil hole in the top of the big-end of the connecting rod on CBF models, and as the tab for the bearing shell on CB-R models.

HAYNES HiNT *To ease removal of the pistons, very carefully remove any ridge of carbon built up on the top of each cylinder bore using a scraper, stanley blade or scouring cloth. If there is a pronounced wear ridge, remove it using a ridge reamer.*

Caution: *Do not try to remove the piston/ connecting rod from the bottom of the cylinder bore. The piston will not pass the crankcase main bearing webs. If the piston is pulled right to the bottom of the bore the oil control ring will expand and lock the piston in position. If this happens it is likely the ring will break.*

6 Keep the rod, cap, bolts (if they are to be used for an oil clearance check), and the bearing shells (if they are to be reused) together in their correct positions to ensure correct installation – fit the caps back onto the rods and finger-tighten the bolts to make sure.

7 Remove the pistons from the connecting rods if required (see Section 28), but note that if you are doing a big-end oil clearance check they are best left installed as they will prevent the rod rotating on the crankpin and disturbing the Plastigauge.

Inspection

8 Check the connecting rods for cracks and other obvious damage.
9 Apply clean engine oil to the piston pin, insert it into the connecting rod small-end and check for any freeplay between the two **(see illustration)**. Measure the pin external diameter at its centre, and the small-end bore diameter, then calculate the difference to obtain the small-end-to-piston pin clearance **(see illustration)**. Compare the result to the specifications at the beginning of the Chapter. If the clearance is greater than specified,

replace the components that are worn beyond their specified limits with new ones.
10 Refer to Section 25 and examine the connecting rod bearing shells. If they are scored, badly scuffed, corroded, or appear to have seized, new shells must be installed. Remove the shells from the rods and caps using a small screwdriver inserted in the notch to lift them out **(see illustration)**. Always replace the shells in the connecting rods as a set. If they are badly damaged, check the corresponding crankpin. Evidence of extreme heat, such as discoloration, indicates that lubrication failure has occurred. Be sure to thoroughly check the oil pump and pressure relief valve as well as all oil holes and passages before reassembling the engine.
11 Have the rods checked for twist and bend by a Honda dealer if you are in doubt about their straightness.

Oil clearance check

12 Whether new bearing shells are being fitted or the original ones are being reused, the connecting rod bearing oil clearance should be checked prior to reassembly. Check the clearance on two rods at a time, doing Nos. 1 and 4 together and Nos. 2 and 3 together, turning the crankshaft as required so their crankpins are positioned to give best access.
13 Remove the shells from the rods and caps **(see illustration 27.10)**. Clean the backs of the bearing shells and the bearing housings in both the connecting rod and cap.
14 Press the bearing shells into their housings, making sure the tab on each shell engages the notch in the connecting rod/ cap **(see illustration 27.24)**. Make sure the bearings are fitted in the correct location and take care not to touch any shell's bearing surface with your fingers. Refer to Step 25 and fit the rods and pistons into their bores. Turn the crankcase over and lay the crankshaft in the upper crankcase half (makes sure the main bearing shells are installed), and position it so the crankpins being checked are central and uppermost. Pull the connecting rods onto the crankpins, making sure they are the correct way round so previously made markings align (Step 3) **(see illustration 27.4c)**.
15 Cut a length of the appropriate size

Plastigauge (it should be slightly shorter than the width of the crankpin). Place a strand of Plastigauge on each crankpin journal being checked, making sure it is not over the oil hole. Fit the caps onto the rods **(see illustrations 27.4b)**. Make sure each cap is fitted the correct way around so the previously made markings align **(see illustration 27.2)**. Apply some clean oil to the threads and under the heads of the connecting rod bolts **(see illustration 27.28a)**. Install the bolts and tighten them evenly and a little at a time to the oil clearance (old bolt) torque setting specified at the beginning of the Chapter all the time ensuring that the crankshaft does not rotate. Now, using a degree disc, tighten each bolt in turn by a further 90° **(see illustration 27.28b)**. It is highly advisable to have an assistant to hold the crankshaft down in the crankcase while tightening the bolts as it could lift.
16 Slacken the bolts and remove the connecting rod caps. Compare the width of the crushed Plastigauge on the crankpin to the scale printed on the Plastigauge envelope to obtain the connecting rod bearing oil clearance. Compare the reading to the specifications at the beginning of the Chapter.
17 On completion carefully scrape away all traces of the Plastigauge material from the crankpin and bearing shells using a fingernail or other object which is unlikely to score the shells. Repeat the procedure for the other two rods.
18 If the clearance is within the range listed in this Chapter's Specifications and the bearings are in perfect condition, they can be re-used.
19 If the clearance is beyond the service limit, measure the crankpin in several places to see if it has worn, and if it has (and is not out-of-round) refer to Steps 21 and 22 and use the specifications given in the bearing selection table to determine whether different shells that correspond with the actual crankpin diameter (as opposed to its given size code) can be used. If the crankpin is the correct diameter for its given size code, replace the bearing shells with new ones according to the size codes. Check the oil clearance once again. Always replace all of the shells at the same time.
20 If the crankshaft has worn beyond the

2•60 Engine, clutch and transmission

27.21a Crankpin journal size letters

27.21b Connecting rod size number

27.22 The colour is on the side of the shell

narrowest diameter given it must be replaced with a new one, and new shells selected according to that crankshaft.

Bearing shell selection

21 Replacement bearing shells for the big-end bearings are supplied on a selected fit basis. Code letters and numbers stamped on the crankshaft and connecting rod, or the actual measured size of the crankpin journal, are used to identify the correct replacement bearings. The crankpin journal size letters are stamped on the outside of the left-hand crankshaft web, and will be either an A, B or C **(see illustration)**. The first letter after the L is for the No. 1 cylinder connecting rod (left-hand journal), and the letters correspond consecutively for each cylinder. The connecting rod size code number is marked across the flat face of the connecting rod and cap and will be either a 1, 2 or 3 **(see illustration)**.

22 A range of bearing shells is available. To select the correct bearing shell colour code for a particular big-end, use the table below and cross-refer the crankpin journal size letter (stamped on the web) or measured size with the connecting rod size number (stamped on the rod). For example, if the crankpin size is B, and the connecting rod size is 1, then the bearing required is green. The colour is marked on the side of the shell **(see illustration)**.

Crankpin journal code	Connecting rod code 1	2	3
A (36.497 to 36.503 mm)	Yellow	Green	Brown
B (36.491 to 36.497 mm)	Green	Brown	Black
C (36.485 to 36.491 mm)	Brown	Black	Blue

Installation

23 Fit the pistons onto the connecting rods (see Section 28).
24 Clean the backs of the bearing shells and the bearing housings in both cap and rod. If new shells are being fitted, ensure that all traces of any protective grease are cleaned off using paraffin (kerosene). Wipe the shells, cap and rod dry with a clean lint free cloth. Install the bearing shells in the connecting rods and caps, making sure the tab on each shell engages the notch in the connecting rod/cap **(see illustration)**. Lubricate the shells with molybdenum disulphide oil (a 50/50 mixture of molybdenum disulphide grease and clean engine oil).
25 Position the crankcase the correct way up. Lubricate the pistons, rings and cylinder bores with clean engine oil. Wrap some rag round the bottom of each connecting rod. Fit a piston ring compressor around the first piston being installed and tighten it to compress the rings – a compressor is required because

there is very little lead-in for the rings to be easily fed in by hand **(see illustration)**. Locate the piston/connecting assembly on the top of the bore with the IN mark on the piston crown on the intake side **(see illustration 27.5)** and tap the top of the piston using a wooden or plastic tool (such as the handle end of a hammer) until the piston is completely in the bore **(see illustration)**. If resistance is felt a ring may be catching on the rim – do not try to force it in as rings are easily broken. Tighten the compressor a bit more to squash the ring. Install the other pistons/rods in the same way.
26 Carefully turn the crankcase upside down. Install the crankshaft (see Section 26), and position it so two of the crankpins (i.e. either for Nos. 1 and 4 cylinders, or for Nos. 2 and 3) are central and uppermost.
27 Lubricate those crankpins with molybdenum disulphide oil (a 50/50 mixture of molybdenum disulphide grease and clean engine oil). Remove the rag and carefully pull the corresponding connecting rods onto the crankpins, taking care not to mark the cylinders **(see illustration 27.4c)**. Fit the caps onto the rods, locating the pins in the holes **(see illustration 27.4b)**. Make sure the previously made markings align, and that the rods are facing the right way (see Step 3).
28 Apply some clean oil to the threads and under the heads of the NEW connecting rod bolts, then fit them and tighten them

27.24 Fit the shells, locating the tabs in the notches (arrowed)

27.25a Fit the compressor over the piston and rings and compress the rings by tightening the bands on the compressor using an Allen key

27.25b Fit the rod into the bore and rest the compressor on the crankcase then tap the top of the piston with a soft tool so that it enters

Engine, clutch and transmission 2•61

27.28a Install the lubricated bolts and tighten them as described first to the specified torque . . .

27.28b . . . and then through the specified angle

28.2 Note the IN mark on the piston (arrowed) faces the intake side, as does the oil hole or bearing notch (according to model) in the big-end

finger-tight **(see illustration)**. First tighten them evenly and a little at a time to the new bolt torque setting specified at the beginning of the Chapter. Now, using a degree disc, tighten each bolt in turn and in one go by a further 90° **(see illustration)**. It is highly advisable to have an assistant to hold the crankshaft down in the crankcase while tightening the bolts as it could lift.

29 Check that the crankshaft is free to rotate easily, then position it with the remaining crankpins easily accessible and install the other connecting rods in the same way. Check to make sure that all components have been returned to their original locations using the marks made on disassembly.

30 Check that the rods rotate smoothly and freely on the crankpins. If there are any signs of roughness or tightness, remove the rods and recheck the bearing clearance. Sometimes tapping the bottom of the connecting rod cap will relieve tightness, but if in doubt, recheck the clearances.

31 Reassemble the crankcase halves (see Section 23).

28 Pistons

Note: *To remove the pistons the engine must be removed from the frame and the crankcase halves separated.*

Removal

1 Remove the connecting rods (see Section 27).
2 Before removing the piston from the connecting rod, use a sharp scriber or felt marker pen to write the cylinder identity on the crown of each piston (or on the inside of the skirt if the piston is dirty and going to be cleaned). Each piston crown should already be marked IN (though it may be invisible until the piston is cleaned) and this mark faces the intake side of the cylinder, the same way as the oil hole in the top of the big-end of the connecting rod on CBF models, and as the tab for the bearing shell on CB-R models **(see illustration)**.

3 Carefully prise out the circlip on one side of the piston using needle-nose pliers or a small flat-bladed screwdriver inserted into the notch **(see illustration)**. Push the piston pin out from the other side to free the piston from the connecting rod **(see illustration)**. Remove the other circlip and discard them as new ones must be used. When the piston has been removed, slide its pin back into its bore so that related parts do not get mixed up.

> **HAYNES HiNT**
> *If a piston pin is a tight fit in the piston bosses, use a heat gun to heat the piston – this will expand the alloy piston sufficiently to release its grip on the pin. If the piston pin is particularly stubborn, extract it using a drawbolt tool, but be careful to protect the piston's working surfaces.*

4 Using your thumbs or a piston ring removal and installation tool, carefully remove the rings from the pistons **(see illustrations 29.10, 29.9a and b, 29.7c, b and a)**. Do not nick or gouge the pistons in the process. Carefully note which way up each ring fits and in which groove as they must be installed in their original positions if being reused. The upper surface of the top ring should be marked with the letter R at one end, and the second (middle) ring marked RN **(see illustration 29.9a)**. The top and middle rings can also be identified by their cross-section profiles.

5 Scrape all traces of carbon from the tops of the pistons. A hand-held wire brush or a piece of fine emery cloth can be used once most of the deposits have been scraped away. Do not, under any circumstances, use a wire brush mounted in a drill motor to remove deposits from the pistons; the piston material is soft and will be eroded away by the wire brush.

6 Use a piston ring groove cleaning tool to remove any carbon deposits from the ring grooves. If a tool is not available, a piece broken off an old ring will do the job. Be very careful to remove only the carbon deposits. Do not remove any metal and do not nick or gouge the sides of the ring grooves.

7 Once the deposits have been removed, clean the pistons with solvent and dry them thoroughly. If the identification mark previously made on the piston is cleaned off, be sure to re-mark it with the correct identity. Make sure the oil return holes below the oil ring groove are clear.

Inspection

8 Carefully inspect each piston for cracks around the skirt, at the pin bosses and at the ring lands. Normal piston wear appears as even, vertical wear on the thrust surfaces of the piston. If the skirt is scored or scuffed, the engine may have been suffering from overheating and/or abnormal combustion, which causes excessively high operating temperatures. Also check that the circlip grooves are not damaged.

9 A hole in the top of the piston, in one

28.3a Prise out the circlip using a suitable tool in the notch . . .

28.3b . . . then push out the pin and separate the piston from the rod

2•62 Engine, clutch and transmission

28.10 Measure the piston ring-to-groove clearance with a feeler gauge

28.11 Measure the piston diameter with a micrometer at the specified distance from the bottom of the skirt

28.12 Measure the external diameter of the pin near each end and the internal diameter of the bore in the piston

extreme, or burned areas around the edge of the piston crown, indicate that pre-ignition or knocking under load have occurred. If you find evidence of any problems the cause must be corrected or the damage will occur again (see *Fault Finding* in the *Reference* section).

10 Measure the piston ring-to-groove clearance by laying each piston ring in its groove and slipping a feeler gauge in beside it **(see illustration)**. Make sure you have the correct ring for the groove (see Step 4). Check the clearance at three or four locations around the groove. If the clearance is greater than specified, replace both the piston and rings as a set. If new rings are being used, measure the clearance using the new rings. If the clearance is greater than that specified, the piston is worn and must be replaced with a new one.

11 Check the piston-to-bore clearance by measuring the bore (see Section 24), then measure the piston the correct distance up from the bottom of the skirt and at 90° to the piston pin axis **(see illustration)**. Make sure each piston is matched to its correct cylinder. Refer to the Specifications at the beginning of the Chapter and subtract the piston diameter from the bore diameter to obtain the clearance. If it is greater than the specified figure, the piston must be replaced with a new one (assuming the bore itself is within limits).

12 Apply clean engine oil to the piston pin, insert it into the piston and check for any freeplay between the two. Measure the pin external diameter near each end, and the pin bores in the piston **(see illustration)**. Calculate the difference to obtain the piston pin-to-piston pin bore clearance. Compare the result to the specifications at the beginning of the Chapter. If the clearance is greater than specified, replace the components that are worn beyond their specified limits. If not already done (see Section 27), repeat the measurements between the pin and the connecting rod small-end.

Installation

13 Inspect and install the piston rings (see Section 29).
14 Lubricate the piston pin, the piston pin bore and the connecting rod small-end bore with molybdenum disulphide oil (a 50/50 mixture of molybdenum disulphide grease and clean engine oil).
15 When fitting the pistons onto the connecting rods make sure the IN mark on the piston crown faces the same way as the oil hole in the top of the big-end of the connecting rod on CBF models, and as the tab for the bearing shell on C-R models **(see illustration 28.2)**.
16 Fit a *new* circlip into one side of the piston (do not re-use old circlips). Line up the piston on its correct connecting rod, and insert the piston pin from the other side **(see illustration)**. Secure the pin with the other *new* circlip **(see illustration)**. When fitting the circlips, compress them only just enough to fit them in the piston, and make sure they are properly seated in their grooves with the open end away from the removal notch.
17 Install the connecting rods (see Section 27) and reassemble the crankcase halves (see Section 23).

29 Piston rings

Note: *It is good practice to replace the piston rings with new ones when an engine is being overhauled.*

Removal

1 See Section 28, Step 4.

Inspection

2 Whether re-using the old rings or fitting new ones, check the installed end gaps with the rings installed in the bore, as follows. Lay out each piston with its ring set and keep them together so the rings will be matched with the same piston and bore during the measurement procedure and engine assembly.
3 Insert the top ring into the top of the bore and square it up with the bore walls by pushing it in with the top of the piston **(see illustration)**. The ring should be at least 20 mm below the top edge of the bore, so it is within its area of travel in the bore. Slip a feeler gauge between the ends of the ring and compare

28.16a Slide the pin through the piston and rod . . .

28.16b . . . and secure it with new circlips

29.3a Fit the ring in its bore . . .

Engine, clutch and transmission 2•63

29.3b ... and square it up using the piston ...

29.3c ... then measure the end gap using a feeler gauge

29.7a Fit the oil ring expander in its groove ...

29.7b ... then fit the lower side rail ...

29.7c ... and the upper side rail on each side of it

29.9a Note the marking on each ring and make sure it faces up

the measurement to the specifications at the beginning of the Chapter (see illustration).

4 If the gap is larger or smaller than specified, double check to make sure that you have the correct rings before proceeding; excess end gap is not critical unless it exceeds the service limit.

5 If the service limit is exceeded with new rings, check the bore for wear (see Section 24). If the gap is too small, the ring ends may come in contact with each other during engine operation, which can cause serious damage.

6 Repeat the procedure for the middle ring and the oil control ring side-rails, but not the expander ring. Remember to keep the rings, pistons and bores matched up.

Installation

7 Fit the oil control ring (lowest on the piston) first. It is composed of three separate components, namely the expander and the upper and lower side-rails. Slip the expander into the groove, making sure the ends don't overlap (see illustration). Next fit the lower side-rail (see illustrations). Do not use a piston ring installation tool on the side-rails as they may be damaged. Instead, place one end of the side-rail into the groove between the expander and the ring land. Hold it firmly in place and slide a finger around the piston while pushing the rail into the groove. Next, fit the upper side-rail in the same manner (see illustration). Check that the ends of the expander have not overlapped.

8 After the three oil ring components have been installed, check to make sure that both the upper and lower side-rails can be turned smoothly in the ring groove.

9 Fit the second (middle) ring next – it should be marked with the letters RN at one end, and it can also be identified by its cross-section profile (see illustration). Make sure that the ring is installed with the identification letter facing up. Fit the ring into the middle groove in the piston (see illustration). Do not expand the ring any more than is necessary to slide it into place. To avoid breaking the ring, use a piston ring installation tool.

10 Finally, fit the top ring, marked with the letter R, in the same manner into the top groove in the piston (see illustration). Make sure the identification letter near the end gap is facing up.

11 Once the rings are correctly installed, check they move freely without snagging and stagger their end gaps as shown (see illustration).

29.9b Install the middle ring ...

29.10 ... and the top ring as described

29.11 Piston ring installation details – stagger the ring end gaps as shown

2•64 Engine, clutch and transmission

30.2a Make an alignment mark between the shaft and the holder, then slacken the pinch bolt (arrowed) . . .

30.2b . . . unscrew the mounting bolt and slide the holder off

30 Balancer shaft

Note: *To remove the balancer shaft the engine must be removed from the frame and the crankcase halves separated.*

Removal

1 Separate the crankcase halves (see Section 23) – the balancer shaft is in the lower half.
2 Make an alignment mark on the balancer shaft holder with the punch mark on the end of the balancer shaft – this will give a good indication as to the starting point for resetting the backlash adjustment when the crankcases are reassembled **(see illustration)**. Slacken the balancer shaft holder pinch bolt, then unscrew the holder mounting bolt and slide the holder off the shaft **(see illustration)**.
3 Support the balancer gear/weight assembly, then withdraw the shaft and remove the gear/weight **(see illustration)**. Discard the shaft O-ring as a new one must be used.

Inspection

4 Inspect the teeth on the gear for signs of wear or damage, and replace it with a new one if necessary. If damage is found, check the teeth on the drive gear on the crankshaft. The gear/weight can be disassembled if required – all components are available individually.
5 Remove the washer from each end of the gear/weight, noting which fits where **(see illustrations 30.9d and e)**. Slide the shaft back into the gear/weight and check that it runs freely and smoothly in the bearings. If there is any evidence of wear on the shaft, or it is a sloppy fit in the bearings, and the bearings are good, replace the shaft with a new one. If the bearings do not run smoothly and freely, or if there is any wear or damage evident, replace them with new ones. Note that all components are matched by size and should be replaced either as a set, or by matching them using the coded markings (see Steps 7 and 8). Withdraw the shaft and the bearings **(see illustration 30.9c)**. Clean them with solvent.
6 Separate the weight from the gear **(see illustration 30.9b)**. Check the condition of the rubber dampers in the gear for damage, deformation and deterioration, and replace them with new ones if necessary **(see illustration 30.9a)**.

Bearing selection

7 Replacement bearings for the balancer are supplied on a selected fit basis according to the internal diameter (ID) of the end it runs in. Code letters stamped on the weight web are used to identify the correct replacement bearings, which are colour coded. The balancer gear/weight size code letters (the right-hand one for the gear end and the left-hand one for the weight end) will be either an A, a B or a C **(see illustration)**.
8 Measure the internal diameter of each end of the balancer and check it according to its letter against the specifications given in the table below to check the weight bearing surface has

30.3 Withdraw the shaft and lift the balancer out

30.7 Balancer gear and weight size code letters

Engine, clutch and transmission 2•65

30.9a Fit the dampers onto the gear . . .

30.9b . . . then fit the gear onto the balancer, aligning the marks

30.9c Fit the bearings into the bore . . .

30.9d . . . then fit the shouldered washer . . .

30.9e . . . and the dished washer

not worn. If it has worn beyond its specification replace the balancer with a new one and select new bearings according to the numbers on the new one. If the balancer has not worn select new bearings according to the letters. For example, if the gear end size is B, then the bearing required for the gear end of the shaft is white. The colour is marked on the bearing.

Balancer gear/ weight ID codes	Bearing colour
A – 26.996 to 27.000 mm	Blue
B – 26.991 to 26.996 mm	White
C – 26.987 to 26.991 mm	Green

Installation

9 Smear the dampers with grease, then fit them onto the gear **(see illustration)**. Fit the gear onto the balancer, aligning the mark on the inner rim with the line on the balancer, and making sure the dampers locate correctly **(see illustration)**. Lubricate the bearings with clean oil and slide them into the balancer, making sure they are correctly located according to the codes (see Steps 7 and 8) **(see illustration)**. Fit the shouldered washer onto the gear end and the dished washer onto the weight end **(see illustrations)**.
10 Fit a new O-ring onto the balancer shaft and smear it with clean oil **(see illustration)**. Position the balancer gear/weight assembly in the crankcase, then slide the shaft in with the O-ring on the outer end **(see illustration 30.3)**.
11 Turn the shaft using a screwdriver until the punch mark faces down **(see illustration)**. Fit the holder onto the end of the shaft and tighten its mounting bolt **(see illustration 30.2b)**. Temporarily tighten the shaft pinch bolt.
12 Reassemble the crankcase halves (see Section 23).
13 Carry out the static backlash adjustment procedure (see below).
14 Turn the engine clockwise through 360° (one full turn) and check that the crankshaft and balancer marks still align (see Section 23). Finish rebuilding the engine and install it (see Section 4).
15 Carry out the dynamic backlash adjustment procedure (see below).

Backlash adjustment

Note: *A backlash adjustment is provided so that the gears mesh at their optimum point for quiet running with minimal wear. If the amount of backlash is too great, the shafts will clatter. If the gears are running tight, they will whine, and wear very quickly. At the optimum point the gears will run very quietly – it is easy to tell the difference with the engine running. Adjustment is possible due to the offset which allows eccentric movement of the balancer gear in relation to its drive gear when the shaft is turned. The static adjustment procedure allows the backlash to be set up in roughly the optimum position, but the dynamic procedure should always be carried out as well to fine tune the setting.*

Static adjustment

Note: *This procedure must be carried out when the engine is cold.*

16 Slacken the balancer shaft holder pinch bolt **(see illustration 30.2a)**.
17 Turn the shaft slightly anti-clockwise using a screwdriver in the slotted end, then turn it clockwise until resistance is felt – at this point backlash between the gears has been eliminated **(see illustration)**.

30.10 Fit a new O-ring into the outer groove

30.11 Turn the shaft so the punch mark is at the bottom

30.17 Turn the shaft using a screwdriver

2•66 Engine, clutch and transmission

Now turn the shaft anti-clockwise so the slot moves one graduation as marked on the holder, then temporarily tighten the pinch bolt.

18 Now carry out the dynamic adjustment procedure (see below).

Dynamic adjustment

Note: *This procedure must be carried out when the engine is warm.*

19 Start the engine and allow it to warm up, then let it idle.

20 Slacken the balancer shaft holder pinch bolt **(see illustration 30.2a)**.

21 Turn the shaft slightly one way then the other to find the point at which the gears run at their quietest. Too far one way and the gears will whine (no backlash), too far the other and they will clatter (excessive backlash). Rev the engine and check that there is no unwanted noise at varying speeds.

22 On completion, tighten the pinch bolt.

31 Running-in procedure

1 Make sure the engine oil and coolant levels are correct (see *Pre-ride checks*). Make sure there is fuel in the tank.

2 Turn the engine kill switch to the ON position and shift the gearbox into neutral. Turn the ignition ON.

3 Start the engine and allow it to run at a moderately fast idle until it reaches operating temperature.

⚠ **Warning: If the oil pressure warning light doesn't go off, or it comes on while the engine is running, stop the engine immediately.**

4 If a lubrication failure is suspected, stop the engine immediately and try to find the cause. If an engine is run without oil, even for a short period of time, severe damage will occur.

5 Check carefully for oil and coolant leaks and make sure the transmission and controls, especially the brakes, function properly before road testing the machine.

6 Treat the machine gently for the first few miles to make sure oil has circulated throughout the engine and any new parts installed have started to seat.

7 Even greater care is necessary if new pistons/rings have been fitted or a re-bore carried out, and the bike will have to be run in as when new. This means greater use of the transmission and a restraining hand on the throttle until at least 300 miles (500 km) have been covered. There's no point in keeping to any set speed limit – the main idea is to keep from labouring the engine and to gradually increase performance up to the 300 miles (500 km) mark. Experience is the best guide, since it's easy to tell when an engine is running freely.

8 Upon completion of the road test, and after the engine has cooled down completely, recheck the valve clearances (see Chapter 1) and check the engine oil and coolant levels (see *Pre-ride checks*).

… 3•1

Chapter 3
Cooling system

Contents

	Section number		Section number
Coolant change	see Chapter 1	General information	1
Coolant hoses, pipes and unions	8	Oil cooler	see Chapter 2
Coolant level check	see Pre-ride checks	Radiator	5
Coolant reservoir	7	Temperature display and ECT sensor	3
Cooling fan and fan relay	2	Thermostat and housing	4
Cooling system checks	see Chapter 1	Water pump	6

Degrees of difficulty

Easy, suitable for novice with little experience	Fairly easy, suitable for beginner with some experience	Fairly difficult, suitable for competent DIY mechanic	Difficult, suitable for experienced DIY mechanic	Very difficult, suitable for expert DIY or professional

Specifications

Coolant
Mixture type and capacity .... see Chapter 1

ECT sensor
Resistance @ 80°C .... 2.1 to 2.6 K-ohms
Resistance @ 120°C .... 650 to 730 ohms

Thermostat
Opening temperature .... 80 to 84°C
Fully open .... 90 to 95°C
Valve lift .... 8 mm (min)

Radiator
Cap valve opening pressure .... 16 to 20 psi (1.1 to 1.4 Bar)

Torque settings
Cooling fan assembly – CBF1000/A models
   Fan blade nut .... 2.7 Nm
   Fan bracket bolts .... 8.5 Nm
   Fan motor nuts .... 5 Nm
Cooling fan assembly – CB1000R/RA models
   Fan blade nut .... 2.7 Nm
   Fan shroud bolts .... 4.5 Nm
   Fan motor bolts .... 5 Nm
ECT sensor .... 23 Nm
Water pump bolts .... 12 Nm

3•2 Cooling system

1 General information

The cooling system uses a water/anti-freeze coolant to carry away excess heat from the engine and maintain as constant a temperature as possible. The cylinders are surrounded by a water jacket from which the heated coolant is circulated by thermo-syphonic action in conjunction with a water pump, which is driven by the oil pump. The hot coolant passes upwards to the thermostat and through to the radiator. The coolant then flows across the core of the radiator, then to the water pump and back to the engine. Coolant is also circulated around the oil cooler.

A thermostat is fitted in the system to prevent the coolant flowing through the radiator when the engine is cold, therefore accelerating the speed at which the engine reaches normal operating temperature. An engine coolant temperature (ECT) sensor mounted in the thermostat housing provides information for the temperature display (CB-R models) on the instrument panel, and to the ECM (electronic control module). A cooling fan fitted to the back of the radiator aids cooling in extreme conditions by drawing extra air through. The fan motor is controlled by a relay which receives a signal from the ECM which in turn receives information from the ECT sensor.

The complete cooling system is partially sealed and pressurised, the pressure being controlled by a valve contained in the spring-loaded radiator cap. By pressurising the coolant the boiling point is raised, preventing premature boiling in adverse conditions. The overflow pipe from the system is connected to a reservoir into which excess coolant is expelled under pressure. The discharged coolant automatically returns to the radiator by the vacuum created when the engine cools.

⚠ **Warning:** *Do not remove the pressure cap from the radiator when the engine is hot. Scalding hot coolant and steam may be blown out under pressure, which could cause serious injury. When the engine has cooled, place a thick rag, like a towel, over the pressure cap; slowly rotate the cap anti-clockwise to the first stop. This procedure allows any residual pressure to escape. When the steam has stopped escaping, press down on the cap while turning it anti-clockwise and remove it.*
Caution: *Do not allow anti-freeze to come in contact with your skin or painted surfaces of the motorcycle. Rinse off any spills immediately with plenty of water. Anti-freeze is highly toxic if ingested. Never leave anti-freeze lying around in an open container or in puddles on the floor; children and pets are attracted by its sweet smell and may drink it. Check with the local authorities about disposing of used anti-freeze. Many communities will have collection centres which will see that anti-freeze is disposed of safely.*

2.2a Cooling fan wiring connector (arrowed) – CBF models

2.2b Cooling fan wiring connector (arrowed) – CB-R models

Caution: *At all times use the specified type of anti-freeze, and always mix it with distilled water in the correct proportion. The anti-freeze contains corrosion inhibitors which are essential to avoid damage to the cooling system. A lack of these inhibitors could lead to a build-up of corrosion which would block the coolant passages, resulting in overheating and severe engine damage. Distilled water must be used as opposed to tap water to avoid a build-up of scale which would also block the passages.*

2 Cooling fan and fan relay

Cooling fan

Check

1 The cooling fan is on the back of the radiator. If the engine is overheating and the cooling fan does not come on, check the cooling fan fuse (see Chapter 8). If the fuse is good, check the relay (see below).

2 To test the cooling fan motor, remove the fuel tank (see Chapter 4). Disconnect the fan wiring connector (2-pin black on CBF1000/A models, 2-pin natural on CB1000R/RA models) **(see illustrations)**. Using a 12 volt battery and two jumper wires with suitable connectors, connect the battery positive (+) lead to the black/blue wire terminal on the fan side of the wiring connector, and the battery negative (–) lead to the black wire terminal on the connector. Once connected the fan should operate. If it does not, and the connector and wiring between it and the motor is good, then the fan motor is faulty. Individual components are available for the fan assembly.

Removal and installation – CBF1000/A models

⚠ **Warning:** *The engine must be completely cool before carrying out this procedure.*

3 Remove the radiator (see Section 5).
4 Remove the rubber shroud, noting how it fits. Unscrew the bolts and remove the fan **(see illustration)**.
5 If required unscrew the fan blade nut and

1 Rubber shroud
2 Fan bracket
3 Fan motor
4 Fan blade

2.4 Fan assembly components – CBF1000/A

Cooling system 3•3

2.9 Unscrew the bolts (arrowed) and remove the shroud

2.10a Fan blade nut (arrowed)

remove the blade. Free the wiring from the clamp. Undo the three nuts on the front of the fan motor and separate the motor from its bracket.

6 Installation is the reverse of removal. Tighten the fan motor nuts to the torque setting specified at the beginning of the Chapter. Clean the threads of the motor shaft. Align the flats on the motor shaft with those in the bore in the fan blade. Apply a suitable non-permanent thread locking compound to the fan blade nut and tighten it to the specified torque. Tighten the bracket bolts to the specified torque.

7 Install the radiator (see Section 5).

Removal and installation – CB1000R/RA models

8 Remove the radiator (see Section 5).
9 Unscrew the fan shroud bolts, noting the washers, and remove the fan assembly **(see illustration)**.
10 If required unscrew the fan blade nut and remove the blade **(see illustration)**. Free the wiring from the guide. Undo the three bolts on the front of the fan motor and separate the motor from the shroud **(see illustration)**.
11 Installation is the reverse of removal. Tighten the fan motor bolts to the torque setting specified at the beginning of the Chapter. Clean the threads of the motor shaft. Align the flats on the shaft with those in the bore in the fan blade. Apply a suitable non-permanent thread locking compound to the fan blade nut and tighten it to the specified torque. Tighten the shroud bolts to the specified torque.
12 Install the radiator (see Section 5).

Cooling fan relay

Check

13 If the engine is overheating and the cooling fan does not come on, first check the cooling fan fuse (see Chapter 8).
14 If the fuse is good, remove the relay (see Step 19 or 20).
15 Set a multimeter to the ohms x 1 scale and connect it across the relay's A and B terminals **(see illustration)**. There should be no continuity (infinite resistance). Using a fully-charged 12 volt battery and two insulated jumper wires, connect the positive (+) terminal of the battery to the C terminal on the relay, and the negative (–) terminal to the D terminal on the relay. At this point the relay should be heard to click and the multimeter read 0 ohms (continuity). If this is the case the relay is proved good. If the relay does not click when battery voltage is applied and still indicates no continuity (infinite resistance) across its terminals, it is faulty and must be replaced with a new one.

16 If the relay is good, check for battery voltage at the red/green (CBF1000/A models) or blue/orange (CB1000R/RA models) wire in the wiring connector with the ignition switch ON. If there is no voltage, check the wiring between the relay and the fusebox for continuity, referring to the relevant wiring diagram at the end of Chapter 8. Next check for voltage in the black/white wire, and if there is none check the wire to the engine stop relay for continuity, then check the engine stop

2.10b Free the wiring (A), then unscrew the bolts (B)

2.15 Fan relay test set-up

3•4 Cooling system

2.19a Displace the turn signal relay...

2.19b ...then displace the relay box

2.19c Release the brown connector...

2.19d ...then pull the relay off it

2.20a Release the clip (arrowed) and open the lid...

2.20b ...then pull the relay out

relay (see Chapter 4, Section 7). If voltage is present, check that there is continuity to earth in the black/blue wire with the ignition switch OFF. If there is no continuity, check the wiring between the relay, the fan wiring connector, the fan, then back to the connector and then in the green wire to earth. If all is good check the green/blue wire between the relay and the ECM (electronic control module). There should be continuity in all wires.

17 If the fan is on the whole time, refer to Step 19 or 20 according to model and remove the relay – the fan should stop. If it does, the relay is defective and must be replaced with a new one.

18 If the fan works but is suspected of cutting in at the wrong temperature, check the ECT sensor (see Section 3).

3.3 Temperature sensor wiring connector (arrowed)

Removal and installation

19 On CBF1000/A models, remove the right-hand seat cowl (see Chapter 7). Displace the turn signal relay, then displace the relay box **(see illustrations)**. Release the retainers for the brown wiring connector and draw the connector out, then disconnect the relay from the connector **(see illustrations)**.

20 On CB1000R/RA models, remove the rider's seat (see Chapter 7). Open the fuse box lid, then pull the relay out **(see illustrations)**.

21 Installation is the reverse of removal.

3 Temperature display and ECT sensor

Temperature display

1 On CBF1000/A models the circuit consists of the ECT sensor mounted in the thermostat housing and the warning light in the instrument cluster.

2 On CB1000R/RA models the circuit consists of the ECT sensor mounted in the thermostat housing and the digital display and warning light in the instrument cluster. When the ignition is first switched on all the segments in the LCD display should come on temporarily – this serves as an indication that the display is functioning correctly (if not, refer to Chapter 8). Under normal operating conditions, when the coolant temperature is below 34°C the display will show '- -'. When the temperature is between 35°C and 132°C the display will show the actual temperature. Once the temperature reaches 122°C the display will start to flash, and the temperature warning symbol will come on. If this occurs stop the engine and check the coolant level in the reservoir (see *Pre-ride checks*). If the temperature goes above 132°C the display will continue to show 132°C.

3 If the temperature warning light does not come on, raise the fuel tank (see Chapter 4). Disconnect the ECT sensor wiring connector **(see illustration)**. Using a jump wire connect the green/blue wire terminal in the connector to earth. Turn the ignition ON – the warning light should come on. If it does, replace the sensor with a new one. If it doesn't, on CBF1000/A models remove the fairing (see Chapter 7), and on CB1000R/RA models remove the instrument cowl (see Chapter 7). Disconnect the instrument cluster wiring connector **(see illustration 3.4a and b or 3.4c)**. Check the green/blue wire for continuity between the ECT sensor and instrument cluster wiring connectors. If there is no continuity repair the wiring. If there is continuity the instrument cluster could be faulty – refer to Chapter 8.

4 If the light is on the whole time, raise the fuel tank (see Chapter 4). Disconnect the ECT sensor wiring connector **(see illustration 3.3)**. Turn the ignition ON – if the light is off the sensor is faulty. If the light is still on, on CBF1000/A models remove the fairing (see Chapter 7), then displace the rubber shroud and disconnect the instrument cluster wiring

Cooling system 3•5

3.4a Displace the rubber shroud ...

3.4b ... then disconnect the instrument wiring connector

3.4c Disconnect the instrument wiring connector

connector **(see illustrations)**. On CB1000R/RA models remove the instrument cowl (see Chapter 7), then disconnect the instrument cluster wiring connector **(see illustration)**. Check the green/blue wire for continuity to earth – if there is continuity, locate the fault and repair it. If not the instrument cluster could be faulty (see Chapter 8).

ECT sensor

Check

5 The resistance of the sensor changes with changes in temperature – see the Specifications at the beginning of the chapter. While in theory it is possible to bench-test the sensor at those temperatures, in practice the test is difficult to set up and perform.

6 However you can test the resistance of the sensor in the bike with the engine cold, warm and hot. Raise the fuel tank (see Chapter 4). Disconnect the ECT sensor wiring connector **(see illustration 3.3)**. Connect the positive probe of a multimeter set to read resistance to the green/blue wire terminal on the switch and the negative probe to the body of the switch and compare the readings to those specified, taking into account any variation. If the sensor fails it is most likely to give a zero, constant value, or infinite resistance reading at all temperatures.

Removal and installation

⚠ **Warning: The engine must be completely cool before carrying out this procedure.**

7 Drain the cooling system (see Chapter 1). Raise the fuel tank (see Chapter 4). The sensor is mounted in the thermostat housing **(see illustration 3.3)**.

8 Disconnect the ECT sensor wiring connector.

9 Unscrew and remove the sensor, and discard the sealing washer.

10 Fit a new sealing washer onto the sensor. Fit the sensor and tighten it to the torque setting specified at the beginning of the Chapter. Connect the wiring.

11 Refill the cooling system (see Chapter 1).

4 Thermostat and housing

1 The thermostat is automatic in operation and should give many years service without requiring attention. In the event of a failure, the valve will probably jam open, in which case the engine will take much longer than normal to warm up. Conversely, if the valve jams shut, the coolant will be unable to circulate and the engine will overheat. Neither condition is acceptable – the fault must be investigated promptly.

Thermostat

Removal

⚠ **Warning: The engine must be completely cool before carrying out this procedure.**

2 Drain the cooling system (see Chapter 1).

3 Slacken the clamp and detach the hose from the thermostat cover **(see illustration)**.

4 Unscrew the cover bolts and detach it from the housing, noting the earth wire terminal on CB1000R/RA models **(see illustration)**.

5 Withdraw the thermostat, noting how it fits **(see illustration)**.

Check

6 Examine the thermostat visually before carrying out the test. If it remains in the open position at room temperature, it should be replaced with a new one. Also check the condition of the seal.

7 Suspend the thermostat by a piece of wire in a container of cold water. Place a thermometer capable of reading temperatures up to 110°C in the water so that the bulb is close to the thermostat **(see illustration)**.

4.3 Slacken the clamp (arrowed) and detach the hose

4.4 Unscrew the bolts (arrowed) and detach the cover ...

4.5 ... then withdraw the thermostat from the housing

4.7 Thermostat testing set-up

3•6 Cooling system

4.9 Fit a new seal if necessary

4.14a Detach the crankcase breather hose

4.14b Detach the overflow hose (A), then slacken the clamps (B) and detach the hoses, and unscrew the mounting bolt (C)

Heat the water, noting the temperature when the thermostat opens, and compare the result with the specifications given at the beginning of the Chapter. Also check the amount the valve opens after it has been heated for a few minutes and compare the measurement to the specifications. If the readings obtained differ from those given, the thermostat is faulty and must be replaced with a new one.

8 In the event of thermostat failure, if the thermostat is permanently closed, as an emergency measure only it can be removed and the machine used without it (this is better than leaving it in as the engine will overheat). If it is permanently open you are better to leave it in. In both cases take care when starting the engine from cold as it will take much longer than usual to warm up. Ensure that a new unit is installed as soon as possible.

Installation

9 Check the seal for signs of damage or deterioration and fit a new one if necessary **(see illustration)**. Fit the thermostat into the housing with the bleed hole at the top **(see illustration 4.5)**.
10 Fit the cover and tighten the bolts, not forgetting the earth wire terminal on CB1000R/RA models **(see illustration 4.4)**.
11 Reconnect the hose **(see illustration 4.3)**. Fill the cooling system (see Chapter 1).

Thermostat housing
Removal

⚠ **Warning: The engine must be completely cool before carrying out this procedure.**

12 Drain the cooling system (see Chapter 1).
13 Disconnect the ECT sensor wiring connector **(see illustration 3.3)**. On CB1000R/RA models unscrew the outer cover bolt and detach the earth wire **(see illustration 4.4)**.
14 Disconnect the crankcase breather hose from the air filter housing **(see illustration)**. Detach the radiator overflow hose from the filler neck **(see illustration)**. Slacken the clamps securing the hoses to the housing and detach them, noting which fits where.
15 Unscrew the thermostat housing bolt and remove the housing.

Installation

16 Remount the housing and connect the hoses **(see illustrations 4.14b and a)**.
17 Connect the ECT sensor wiring, and on CB1000R/RA models the earth wire **(see illustrations 3.3 and 4.4)**.
18 Fill the cooling system (see Chapter 1).

5 Radiator

Note: *If the radiator is being removed as part of the engine removal procedure, detach the hoses from their unions on the engine rather than on the radiator and remove the radiator complete with its hoses. Note the routing of the hoses.*

Removal

⚠ **Warning: The engine must be completely cool before carrying out this procedure.**

1 Drain the cooling system (see Chapter 1).
2 Disconnect the fan wiring connector (2-pin black on CBF1000/A models, 2-pin natural on CB1000R/RA models) **(see illustration 2.2a or b)**.
3 On CB1000R/RA models remove the coolant reservoir (see Section 7).
4 Slacken the clamps securing the hoses to the radiator and detach them **(see illustrations)**.
5 On CBF1000/A models release the rubber shield and unscrew the mounting bolt on each side at the top, noting the washers **(see illustration)**. Displace the radiator from its lower mounting pegs on the frame and remove it, taking care not to catch the fins on anything **(see illustration)**.

5.4a Detach the hose (arrowed) from the right-hand side of the radiator . . .

5.4b . . . and from the left-hand side – CB-R shown, CBF has two hoses on the left

5.5a Release the rubber shroud and unscrew the bolt (arrowed) on each side . . .

5.5b . . . then release the radiator from the peg (arrowed) on each side

Cooling system 3•7

5.6a Unscrew the lower mounting bolt (A), then the upper bolt (B) on each side . . .

5.6b . . . then displace the radiator and free the wiring (arrowed)

5.7 Note the collars and check the condition of the grommets

6 On CB1000R/RA models unscrew the lower mounting bolt, noting the washer (see illustration). Unscrew the radiator upper mounting bolts, noting the washers, then displace the radiator and release the horn wiring from the right-hand side of the fan shroud (see illustration). Remove the radiator taking care not to catch the fins on anything.

7 Note the arrangement of the collars and rubber grommets in the radiator mounts (see illustration). Replace the grommets with new ones if they are damaged, deformed or deteriorated.

8 Check the radiator for signs of damage and clear any dirt or debris that might obstruct air flow and inhibit cooling. If the radiator fins are badly damaged or broken the radiator must be replaced with a new one. To enable full examination and cleaning, remove the cooling fan (see Section 2).

Installation

9 Installation is the reverse of removal, noting the following.
- Ensure the coolant hoses are in good condition (see Chapter 1), and are securely retained by their clamps, using new ones if necessary.
- Make sure the rubber grommets are in place.
- Make sure the collars are correctly fitted in the grommets (see illustration 5.7).
- Make sure that the fan wiring is correctly connected.
- On completion refill the cooling system as described in Chapter 1.

Pressure cap check

10 If problems such as overheating or loss of coolant occur, check the entire system as described in Chapter 1. If there are no obvious problems and leaks the radiator cap opening pressure should be checked by a Honda dealer with the special tester required to do the job. If the cap is defective, replace it with a new one.

6 Water pump

Check

1 Refer to Chapter 1, Section 9.

Removal

2 Drain the coolant (see Chapter 1).

6.3a Slacken the clamps (arrowed) and detach the hoses

3 Slacken the clamps securing the coolant hoses to the pump and detach the hoses, noting which fits where (see illustration). Unscrew the top and bottom bolts, then draw the pump from the crankcase, noting how it fits (see illustrations). It may be necessary to lever it out to overcome the O-ring on the pump body. Remove the O-ring from the rear of the body and discard it as a new one must be used (see illustration 6.7).

4 To remove the cover, unscrew the remaining bolts – if the cover is stuck use a screwdriver in the cut-outs provided to lever it off (see illustration). Remove the separator plate and the O-rings from the cover and pump (see illustrations 6.6c, b and a). Discard the O-rings as new ones must be used. Remove the dowels if they are loose.

5 Wiggle the water pump impeller back-and-forth and in-and-out (see illustration). If there is excessive movement, replace the pump

6.3b Unscrew the bolts . . .

6.3c . . . and withdraw the pump

6.4 Unscrew the bolts and remove the cover

6.5 Check the pump impeller as described

3•8 Cooling system

6.6a Fit the dowels (arrowed), and the new O-ring into its groove . . .

6.6b . . . then fit the separator

6.6c Fit the new O-ring into the groove

with a new one. Also check for corrosion or a build-up of scale in the pump body and clean or replace the pump as necessary.

Installation

6 Fit the dowels into the cover if removed. Smear one new O-ring with grease and fit it into the groove in the cover **(see illustration)**. Fit the separator plate onto the cover **(see illustration)**. Lubricate the other O-ring and fit it onto the groove in the housing **(see illustration)**. Fit the cover onto the housing **(see illustration 6.4)**. Install the three bolts, using a new sealing washer on the drain bolt, and tighten them to the torque setting specified at the beginning of the Chapter **(see illustration)**.

7 Apply a smear of engine oil to the new pump body O-ring and fit it into the groove in the body **(see illustration)**. Slide the pump into the crankcase, turning the shaft as required to align the slot in its end with the tab on the oil pump shaft **(see illustration 6.3c)**. Make sure the bolt holes are aligned. Install the mounting bolts and tighten them to the torque setting specified at the beginning of the Chapter **(see illustration 6.3b)**.

8 Fit the coolant hoses onto the pump cover and secure them with their clamps **(see illustration 6.3a)**.

9 Refill the cooling system (see Chapter 1).

6.6d Use a new sealing washer on the bolt

6.7 Fit a new O-ring onto the body

7 Coolant reservoir

Removal

CBF1000/A models

1 The coolant reservoir is located in front of the rear shock absorber. Remove the shock absorber (see Chapter 5), and the battery (see Chapter 8). Get a suitable container to drain the coolant into.

2 Trace the radiator overflow hose from the filler neck to the joint in the back of the battery housing, then release the clamp, disconnect the hose at the hose joint and drain the coolant into the container.

3 Detach the breather hose from the top of the reservoir **(see illustration)**. Unscrew the bolts and remove the reservoir.

CB1000R/RA models

4 The coolant reservoir is located behind the shroud on the left-hand end of the radiator. Remove the shroud (see Chapter 7), and raise the fuel tank (see Chapter 4). Get a suitable container to drain the coolant into.

5 Detach the radiator overflow hose from the bottom of the reservoir and drain the coolant into the container **(see illustrations)**.

6 Detach the breather hose from the top of

7.3 Detach the breather hose (A), then unscrew the bolts (B)

7.5a Detach the overflow hose . . .

7.5b . . . and drain the reservoir

Cooling system 3•9

7.6 Detach the breather hose (A), then unscrew the bolts (B)

8.4 Inlet pipe bolt (A) and union bolts (B)

the reservoir **(see illustration)**. Unscrew the bolts and remove the reservoir, then remove the cap and tip out any remaining coolant into the container.

Installation

7 Installation is the reverse of removal. Refill the reservoir to the UPPER level line with the specified coolant mixture (see *Pre-ride checks*).

8 Coolant hoses, pipes and unions

Removal

1 Before removing a hose, drain the coolant (see Chapter 1).
2 Use a screwdriver to slacken the larger-bore hose clamps, then slide them back along the hose and clear of the union spigot. The smaller-bore hoses are secured by spring clamps which can be expanded by squeezing their ears together with pliers.
Caution: The radiator unions are fragile. Do not use excessive force when attempting to remove the hoses.

3 If a hose proves stubborn, release it by rotating it on its union before working it off. If all else fails, cut the hose with a sharp knife. Whilst this means replacing the hose with a new one – it is preferable to buying a new radiator.
4 The inlet pipe (CB1000R/RA models only) and union to the engine are on the left-hand end of the cylinder block – the pipe is secured in the union by a single bolt, and the union is secured by two bolts **(see illustration)**. If the pipe is removed, the seal must be replaced with a new one, and if the union is removed, the O-ring must be replaced with a new one.
5 The outlet pipe from the engine is on the back of the cylinder head and can be removed by unscrewing its bolt **(see illustration)** – note the wiring guide fitted with it on CB1000R/RA models. If the pipe is removed, the seal must be replaced with a new one.

Installation

6 Slide the clamps onto the hose and then work the hose on to its union as far as the spigot where present.
7 Rotate the hose on its unions to settle it in position before sliding the clamps into place and tightening them securely.

8.5 Outlet pipe bolt (arrowed)

> **HAYNES HINT**
> *If the hose is difficult to push on its union, soften it by soaking it in very hot water, or alternatively a little soapy water on the union can be used as a lubricant.*

8 If the inlet or outlet unions have been removed, fit them using a new O-ring, using a dab of grease to hold it in place if necessary.
9 Refill the cooling system (see Chapter 1).

Chapter 4
Engine management system

Contents

	Section number		Section number
Air filter	see Chapter 1	Fuel tank	2
Air filter housing and throttle bodies	3	General information and precautions	1
Air intake system	8	Idle speed control system	9
Catalytic converter(s)	16	Ignition coils	18
Clutch switch	see Chapter 8	Ignition switch	see Chapter 8
Exhaust system	14	Ignition system check	17
Fuel gauge and level sensor	12	Ignition timing	19
Fuel injection system components	7	Immobiliser system	20
Fuel injection system description	5	Neutral switch	see Chapter 8
Fuel injection system fault diagnosis	6	Pulse secondary air (PAIR) system	15
Fuel pressure check	10	Sidestand switch	see Chapter 8
Fuel pump	11	Spark plugs	see Chapter 1
Fuel rails and injectors	4	Throttle cable check and adjustment	see Chapter 1
Fuel system check	see Chapter 1	Throttle cables	13

Degrees of difficulty

Easy, suitable for novice with little experience | **Fairly easy,** suitable for beginner with some experience | **Fairly difficult,** suitable for competent DIY mechanic | **Difficult,** suitable for experienced DIY mechanic | **Very difficult,** suitable for expert DIY or professional

Specifications

General information
Cylinder numbering .... 1 to 4 from left to right
Firing order 1-2-4-3
Spark plugs .... see Chapter 1

Fuel
Grade .... Unleaded. Minimum 91 RON (Research Octane Number) for Europe
Fuel tank
  CBF1000/A models
    Capacity (including reserve) .... 19.3 litres
    Reserve volume .... approx. 4.0 litres
  CB1000R/RA models
    Capacity (including reserve) .... 17.0 litres
    Reserve volume .... approx. 4.0 litres

Fuel injection system
Idle speed	1200 ± 100 rpm
Fuel pressure at specified idle speed	50 psi (3.5 Bar)
Minimum fuel flow rate	189 cc every 10 seconds

Fuel injection system test data
Crankshaft position (CKP) sensor	
Resistance	approx. 450 to 500 ohms at 20°C (68°F)
Minimum peak voltage output	0.7 volt
Engine coolant temperature (ECT) sensor resistance	2.3 to 2.6 K-ohms at 20°C (68°F)
Fuel injector resistance	11.1 to 12.3 ohms at 20°C (68°F)
Intake air temperature (IAT) sensor resistance	1 to 4 K-ohms between 20 to 30°C (68 to 86°F)
Oxygen sensor heater resistance	10 to 40 ohms at 20°C (68°F)

Air intake system
Air intake control valve resistance	28 to 32 ohms @ 20°C

Idle speed control system
Idle speed control valve resistance	120 to 140 ohms @ 20°C

Fuel level sensor
Resistance
  CBF1000/A models

Full position	4 to 10 ohms
Empty position	90 to 100 ohms

  CB1000R/RA models

Full position	8 to 12 ohms
Empty position	182 to 188 ohms

PAIR system
PAIR system control valve solenoid resistance	23 to 27 ohms @ 20°C

Ignition coils
Note: *All values given are only accurate at 20°C (68°F)*

Primary winding resistance	approximately 2.8 ohms
Secondary winding resistance	
With plug caps	approximately 32 K-ohms
Without plug caps	approximately 22 K-ohms
Plug cap resistance	approximately 5 K-ohms
Initial voltage (see text)	Battery voltage (approximately 12 volts)
Minimum peak voltage (see text)	100 volts
Ignition timing (F mark)	5° BTDC at idle

Torque settings
Exhaust system
  CBF1000/A models

Downpipe flange nuts	20 Nm

  CB1000R/RA models

Downpipe flange nuts	12 Nm
Chamber mounting bolt	22 Nm
Silencer mounting bolts/nut	22 Nm
Shield screws	12 Nm
Clamp bolts	22 Nm
Footrest bracket bolts (CB1000R/RA models)	37 Nm
Fuel pump assembly mounting plate nuts	12 Nm
Fuel rail bolts	5 Nm
Fuel hose banjo bolt (CBF1000/A models)	22 Nm
Fuel tank pivot bolt nut	12 Nm
Oxygen sensor	
CBF1000/A models	44 Nm
CB1000R/RA models	25 Nm
PAIR system reed valve cover bolts	12 Nm
Swingarm pivot bolt nut (CB1000R/RA models)	98 Nm
Swingarm pivot bracket bolt nuts (CB1000R/RA models)	69 Nm
Timing inspection cap	18 Nm

Engine management system 4•3

1 General information and precautions

General information

Fuel system

The fuel supply system consists of the fuel tank with internal fuel pump assembly incorporating the pressure regulator, filter, strainer, and on CBF1000/A models the level sensor, the fuel hose, the fuel rails, the fuel injectors, the throttle bodies, and the throttle cables. CB1000R/RA models have a separate fuel level sensor. The fuel pump is switched on and off via a relay. The engine management system, known as PGM-FI, supplies fuel and air to the engine via 36 mm throttle bodies. The injectors are operated by the Engine Control Module (ECM) using the information obtained from the various sensors it monitors (refer to Section 5 for more information on the operation of the fuel injection system).

Both models have a fuel gauge incorporated in the instrument cluster, actuated by the level sensor inside the fuel tank.

Ignition system

The transistorised electronic ignition system is combined with the fuel injection system, both being controlled by the ECM (engine control module). The ignition system comprises a timing rotor, crankshaft position sensor (CKP sensor), the engine control module (ECM), the ignition coils and the spark plugs. There are two conventional coils, one firing cylinders 1 and 4, the other firing cylinders 2 and 3, operating on the 'wasted spark' principal.

The triggers on the timing rotor, which are incorporated in the starter clutch housing on the right-hand end of the crankshaft, generate a signal in the CKP sensor as the crankshaft rotates. The CKP sensor sends that signal to the ECM which, in conjunction with information received from the throttle position sensor and engine coolant temperature sensor, calculates the ignition timing and supplies the ignition coils with the power necessary to produce a spark at the plugs. There is no provision for adjusting the ignition timing.

The system incorporates a safety interlock circuit which will cut the ignition if the sidestand is extended whilst the engine is running and in gear, or if a gear is selected whilst the engine is running and the sidestand is down. It also prevents the engine from being started if the sidestand is down and the engine is in gear. The engine can be started with the sidestand up when it is in gear as long as the clutch lever is pulled in.

All UK models are fitted with an immobiliser system (HISS – Honda Ignition Security System) as standard. The system will not allow the engine to be started unless the correct key is used. The immobiliser system has its own fault diagnosis function.

Note: *Individual engine management system components can be checked but not repaired. If system troubles occur, and the faulty component can be isolated, the only cure for the problem in most cases is to replace the part with a new one. Keep in mind that most electronic parts, once purchased, cannot be returned. To avoid unnecessary expense, make very sure the faulty component has been positively identified before buying a new part.*

Precautions

⚠ **Warning:** *Petrol (gasoline) is extremely flammable, so take extra precautions when you work on any part of the fuel system. Always remove the battery (see Chapter 8). Don't smoke or allow open flames or bare light bulbs near the work area, and don't work in a garage where a natural gas-type appliance is present. If you spill any fuel on your skin, rinse it off immediately with soap and water. When you perform any kind of work on the fuel system, wear safety glasses and have a fire extinguisher suitable for a class B type fire (flammable liquids) on hand.*

With the fuel injection system, some residual pressure will remain in the fuel feed hoses and fuel rail assemblies after the motorcycle has been used. Before disconnecting any fuel hose, release fuel system pressure as described in Section 2. It is vital that no dirt or debris is allowed to enter the fuel tank or the fuel rail assembly whilst the fuel hoses are disconnected. Any foreign matter in the fuel system components could result in injector damage or malfunction. Ensure the ignition is switched OFF before disconnecting or reconnecting any fuel injection system wiring connector. If a connector is disconnected or reconnected with the ignition switched ON, the engine control module (ECM) may be damaged.

Always perform service procedures in a well-ventilated area to prevent a build-up of fumes.

Never work in a building containing a gas appliance with a pilot light, or any other form of naked flame. Ensure that there are no naked light bulbs or any sources of flame or sparks nearby.

Do not smoke (or allow anyone else to smoke) while in the vicinity of petrol (gasoline) or of components containing it. Remember the possible presence of vapour from these sources and move well clear before smoking.

Check all electrical equipment belonging to the house, garage or workshop where work is being undertaken (see the Safety first! section of this manual). Remember that certain electrical appliances such as drills, cutters etc, create sparks in the normal course of operation and must not be used near petrol (gasoline) or any component containing it. Again, remember the possible presence of fumes before using electrical equipment.

Always mop up any spilt fuel and safely dispose of the rag used.

Any stored fuel that is drained off during servicing work must be kept in sealed containers that are suitable for holding petrol (gasoline), and clearly marked as such; the containers themselves should be kept in a safe place. Note that this last point applies equally to the fuel tank if it is removed from the machine; also remember to keep its filler cap closed at all times.

Read the *Safety first!* section of this manual carefully before starting work.

2 Fuel tank

⚠ *Warning: Refer to the precautions given in Section 1 before starting work.*

Raise

1 Make sure the fuel cap is secure.
2 On CBF1000/A models remove the seats, the side covers and the fairing side panels (see Chapter 7). Disconnect the battery negative (–) lead (see Chapter 8).
3 On CB1000R/RA models remove the seats, the side covers and the radiator shroud (see Chapter 7).
4 Unscrew the front mounting bolts, noting the washers on CB1000R/RA models **(see illustration)**. Prepare a suitable support to fit between the front tank bracket and the frame. On CBF1000/A models you can use the C-spanner fitted into the handle, both from the bike's toolkit, locating the handle over the lug on the side of the frame and the spanner in the left-hand bolt hole in the tank

2.4a Unscrew the tank front mounting bolts

4•4 Engine management system

2.4b CBF models have a lug to take the handle...

2.4c ...and the C-spanner locates as shown

2.4d A piece of wood can be used to support the tank

(see illustrations). On CB1000R/RA models you can thread one of the tank bolts back into its hole in the frame, then locate the socket from the toolkit over it, fit the handle from the toolkit into the socket, locate the handle under the slit in the front bracket of the tank, then fit the screwdriver into the handle from the top so it can't slip out. Alternatively prepare your own support such as a piece of wood **(see illustration)**. Raise the front of the tank and locate the support – make sure the support is secure.

Removal

Note: *Removing the tank involves a certain amount of unavoidable fuel spillage, which is obviously dangerous. Refer to the precautions given in Section 1 before starting work, and have plenty of rag to hand. Once the tank has been removed, rest it on some soft rag to prevent damaging the paintwork or hose unions. Try to time the removal procedure with a near empty tank, which makes it much easier to lift.*

5 Raise the tank as described above.
6 Disconnect the fuel pump wiring connector **(see illustrations)**. On CB1000R/RA models also disconnect the fuel level sensor wiring connector **(see illustration)**.
7 To eliminate any residual pressure in the fuel system start the engine and let it idle until it stops.
8 Disconnect the battery negative (–) lead (see Chapter 8).
9 Clean any dirt from the quick-release connector on the fuel hose – on CBF1000/A models disconnect the hose from its union on the throttle body fuel rail, and on CB1000R/RA models disconnect the hose from its union on the fuel pump. Place a wad of rag for catching any residual fuel in the hose under the connector. Pull the rubber restrictor out of the connector retainer, noting how it seats **(see illustration)**. Press the retainer tabs in and pull the connector off the pipe union **(see illustration)**. Remove the retainer – note that Honda specify to replace it with a new one whenever the fuel hose is disconnected. Also check the condition of the restrictor and replace it with a new one if necessary. Seal the union and the connector with a plastic bag or the finger from a latex glove to prevent dirt getting in.
10 Disconnect the fuel tank drain and breather hoses **(see illustration)**.
11 On CBF1000/A models unscrew the

2.6a Fuel pump/level sensor wiring connector – CBF models

2.6b Fuel pump wiring connector – CB-R models

2.6c Fuel level sensor wiring connector – CB-R models

2.9a Pull the rubber restrictor out of the retainer...

2.9b ...then press the retainer tabs in and pull the connector off

2.10 Detach the hoses (arrowed)

Engine management system 4•5

2.11 Unscrew the bolt (arrowed)

2.12a Unscrew the nut . . .

2.12b . . . withdraw the bolt . . .

tank retaining strap bolt on the frame **(see illustration)**.

12 Remove the support from the front of the tank and lower the tank. Unscrew the nut on the left-hand end of the tank pivot bolt on CBF1000/A models and from the right-hand end on CB1000R/RA models, then withdraw the bolt **(see illustrations)**. Carefully lift the tank off the frame and remove it **(see illustration)**. Remove the collars from the front mounting grommets if required – on CBF1000/A models they fit from the top, and on CB1000R/RA models from the underside **(see illustration 2.14)**.

13 Check all the tank rubbers and hoses for signs of damage or deterioration and replace them with new ones if necessary **(see illustration)**.

Installation

14 Fit the mounting rubbers into their mounts if removed, and fit the collars into the front mounts, from the top on CBF1000/A models and on CB1000R/RA models from the underside **(see illustration)**.

15 Depending on how the tank has been stood and how full it is there is the possibility of fuel having made its way into the breather pipe which could spurt out of the hose on the base when it is moved – be prepared with some rag for this. Once the tank is upright the pipe will fill itself with air.

16 Position the tank on the frame and insert the pivot bolt, from the right on CBF1000/A models **(see illustration 2.12b)** and from the left on CB1000R/RA models. Fit the nut and tighten it to the torque setting specified at the beginning of the Chapter. Raise and support the tank as before.

17 On CBF1000/A models fit the tank retaining strap onto the frame **(see illustration 2.11)**.

18 Connect the fuel tank drain and breather hoses **(see illustration 2.10)**.

19 If removed fit the rubber restrictor onto the pipe union between the two ribs. Fit a new retainer into the connector, aligning the tabs with the holes **(see illustration)**. Fit the connector onto the pipe and push it until both retainer tabs click into place, then try to pull the connector off to make sure it has locked **(see illustration)**. Fit the rubber restrictor into the retainer, so the tabs cannot be pushed in.

20 Connect the fuel pump wiring connector **(see illustration 2.6a or b)**. On CB1000R/RA models connect the fuel level sensor wiring connector **(see illustration 2.6c)**. Make sure all the hoses and wiring are securely connected.

21 Turn the ignition ON to allow the fuel pump to pressurise the system. Check for leaks at the hose connector.

22 Remove the prop and pivot the tank down onto the frame, making sure the fuel supply and breather/overflow hoses do not get squashed or kinked. Fit and tighten the front mounting bolts, on CB1000R/RA models with their washers **(see illustration 2.4a)**.

Repair

23 All repairs to the fuel tank should be carried out by a professional who has experience in this critical and potentially dangerous work. Even after cleaning and flushing of the fuel system, explosive fumes can remain and ignite during repair of the tank.

2.12c . . . and remove the tank

2.13 Check all tank mounting rubbers

2.14 Make sure the collars are fitted as described for your model

2.19a Fit a new retainer into the connector . . .

2.19b . . . then push the connector onto the union

4•6 Engine management system

3.4 Disconnect the wiring connector (A) and detach the hose (B)

3.5 Disconnect the hose (A) and unscrew the bolt (B)

24 If the fuel tank is removed from the bike, it should not be placed in an area where sparks or open flames could ignite the fumes coming out of the tank. Be especially careful inside garages where a natural gas-type appliance is located, because the pilot light could cause an explosion.

3 Air filter housing and throttle bodies

⚠ **Warning: Refer to the precautions given in Section 1 before starting work.**

1 The air filter housing and throttle bodies are removed as an assembly, and can be separated after removal if required.

Removal

CBF1000/A models

2 Remove the fuel tank (see Section 2).
3 Remove the air filter (see Chapter 1).
4 Disconnect the IAT sensor wiring connector and the PAIR system supply hose **(see illustration)**.
5 Disconnect the crankcase breather hose **(see illustration)**. Unscrew the thermostat housing mounting bolt.
6 Disconnect the throttle body sub-loom wiring connector **(see illustration)**. Undo the connector bracket screw and displace the bracket **(see illustration)**.
7 Disconnect the idle speed control valve wiring connector **(see illustration)**.
8 Detach the throttle cables from the twistgrip on the handlebar (see Section 13). Draw the cables out from under the top yoke, releasing them from their guide(s) and noting their routing.
9 Release the alternator wiring from its clamp **(see illustration)**.
10 Fully slacken the clamps on the cylinder head side of the intake rubbers **(see illustration)**.
11 Unscrew the air filter housing mounting bolt **(see illustration)**.

3.6a Disconnect the wiring connector (arrowed) . . .

3.6b . . . and undo the bracket screw

3.7 Disconnect the wiring connector (arrowed)

3.9 Release the wiring from the clamp (arrowed)

3.10 Slacken the clamp screws (arrowed)

3.11 Unscrew the bolt (arrowed)

Engine management system 4•7

3.16 Undo the screw and lift the chamber off the housing

3.17 Disconnect the wiring connector (arrowed)

3.18 Disconnect the wiring connectors (arrowed) from the coil on each side

12 Draw the housing/throttle body assembly back and manoeuvre it out, bringing the throttle cables with it, noting their routing. Cover or plug the intake ducts on the cylinder head.

CB1000R/RA models

13 Remove the fuel tank (see Section 2).
14 Remove the air filter (see Chapter 1).
15 Detach the throttle cables from the twistgrip on the handlebar (see Section 13). Draw the cables out from under the top yoke, releasing them from their guide(s) and noting their routing.
16 Remove the resonator chamber from the right-hand side of the housing **(see illustration)**.
17 Disconnect the PAIR system control valve wiring connector **(see illustration)**.
18 Disconnect the wiring connectors from the ignition coils **(see illustration)**.
19 Disconnect the PAIR system supply hose and crankcase breather hose **(see illustrations)**.
20 Disconnect the ECT sensor wiring connector **(see illustration)**.
21 Disconnect the air intake system vacuum hose from the right-hand side of the throttle bodies **(see illustration)**.
22 Disconnect the sidestand switch wiring connector **(see illustration)**.
23 Unscrew the air filter housing mounting bolt **(see illustration)**.
24 Release the hoses and wiring from the guide on the left-hand side **(see illustration)**.

3.19a Disconnect the PAIR hose (arrowed) . . .

3.19b . . . and the crankcase breather hose

3.20 Disconnect the wiring connector

3.21 Pull the vacuum hose off

3.22 Disconnect the wiring connector

3.23 Unscrew the bolt (arrowed)

3.24 Release the hoses and wiring from the guide (arrowed)

4•8 Engine management system

3.25 Disconnect the hose (arrowed)

3.27 Unscrew the bolts (arrowed) and displace the bracket

3.29a Unscrew the nuts (arrowed) and displace the bracket . . .

25 Disconnect the hose from the air intake system control valve **(see illustration)**.
26 Remove the exhaust system silencer (see Section 14).
27 Unscrew the rider's right-hand footrest bracket bolts and displace the assembly **(see illustration)**.
28 Disconnect the oxygen sensor wiring connector **(see illustration 7.22b)** – if required undo the vacuum chamber bracket bolt to improve clearance.
29 Unscrew the nuts and remove the washers from the right-hand ends of the swingarm pivot bracket bolts and swingarm pivot bolt, counter-holding the bolt heads if necessary **(see illustration)**. Displace the pivot bracket and release the oxygen sensor wiring and air intake system hoses from their guides on the inside **(see illustration)**.
30 Release the wiring sub-loom from the guide on the air intake duct on the right-hand side **(see illustration)**. Undo the screws and remove the duct.
31 Disconnect the throttle body sub-loom wiring connectors and the CKP sensor wiring connector **(see illustration)**. Free the connectors from the bracket.
32 Undo the ECM bracket screws and remove the bracket **(see illustration)**. If required remove the ECM (see Section 7), but it can stay on the housing if preferred.
33 Fully slacken the clamps on the cylinder head side of the intake rubbers **(see illustration)**. Draw the housing/throttle body assembly back and manoeuvre it out to the left, bringing the throttle cables with it, noting their routing **(see illustration)**. Cover or plug the intake ducts on the cylinder head.

Caution: Tape over or stuff clean rag into each cylinder head intake after removing the throttle body assembly to prevent anything getting in.

Caution: Do not snap the throttle cam/valves from fully open to fully closed once the cables have been disconnected because this can lead to engine idle speed problems.

Installation

34 Installation is the reverse of removal, noting the following:
● Do not forget to remove the covers or plugs from the intake ducts on the cylinder head.
● Check the condition of the intake rubbers and replace them with new ones if necessary (see Step 56).
● Check the condition of all hoses and replace them with new ones if they are in any way damaged or deteriorated.
● Make sure the intake rubber clamps are correctly orientated with the hole in each

3.29b . . . and release the wiring and hoses from the guides (arrowed)

3.30 Release the wiring from the guide (A), then undo the screws (B) and remove the duct

3.31 Disconnect the wiring connectors (arrowed) and release them from the bracket

3.32 Undo the screws (arrowed) and remove the bracket

3.33a Slacken the clamp screws (arrowed) . . .

3.33b . . . then remove the assembly

Engine management system 4•9

clamp over the peg on the rubber **(see illustration 3.34a)**.
● Tighten the intake rubber clamps so that the gap between the ends is 9 to 11 mm. Lubricate the inside of the rubbers with a light smear of engine oil to aid installation.
● On CB1000R/RA models the air filter housing bolt threads into a rubber wellnut fitted in a hole in the frame, rather than threading directly into the frame itself. The wellnut is held in its hole only by a rubber rim, and when fitting the bolt it is easy to push on the nut, at which point the rim gives way and the nut disappears inside the frame. If you are lucky it may drop down the back and fall out of the hole in the bottom of the frame, or lodge somewhere close to it so you can retrieve it. If it lodges high up you may be able to dislodge it using some wire. To prevent this happening make sure the mount in the housing is perfectly aligned with the nut before inserting the bolt, and push the mount against the rubber rim to help keep it in place; insert the bolt carefully, making sure the threads have engaged before using a tool.
● Make sure all wiring connectors are securely connected.
● Make sure all cables, hoses and wiring are correctly routed.
● On CB1000R/RA models tighten the swingarm pivot bracket bolt nuts, swingarm pivot bolt nut and footrest bracket bolts to the torque settings specified at the beginning of the Chapter.
● On CB1000R/RA models make sure the right-hand air duct O-ring is in good condition and seated in its groove **(see illustration 3.34b)** – fit a new O-ring if necessary.
● Check throttle cable freeplay at the twistgrip and adjust if necessary (see Chapter 1).

Disassembly (throttle body removal)

CBF1000/A models

35 Remove the air intake system control valve, vacuum chamber and hoses, including the one-way valve (see Section 8).
36 Disconnect the MAP sensor wiring

3.34a Make sure the hole in each clamp is seated over its peg on the intake rubber

3.34b Make sure the O-ring is in good condition and correctly seated

3.43 Disconnect the IAT sensor wiring connector

3.44 Disconnect the TP sensor wiring connector

connector and pull the vacuum hose off **(see illustration 3.45)**.
37 Make a note of which connector fits onto which injector. Disconnect the wiring connectors from the injectors and throttle position sensor and displace the sub-loom, releasing it from the clamps and noting its routing **(see illustrations 3.46 and 3.44)**.
38 Undo the screws securing the upper section of the filter housing and remove it **(see illustrations 3.49a and b)**. Note the rubber seals and remove them if required **(see illustration 3.49c)**.
39 Undo the air funnel/throttle body mounting screws, then remove the funnels and detach the throttle body assembly from the lower section of the filter housing **(see illustrations 3.50a and b)**. Remove the throttle body seals **(see illustration 3.50c)** – new ones must be used.
40 If required detach the throttle cables (see Section 13).

41 If required remove the fuel rail and injectors (see Section 4).
42 If required remove the idle speed control valve (see Section 9).

CB1000R/RA models

43 Disconnect the IAT sensor wiring connector **(see illustration)**.
44 Disconnect the throttle position sensor wiring connector **(see illustration)**.
45 Disconnect the MAP sensor wiring connector and pull the vacuum hose off **(see illustration)**.
46 Make a note of which connector fits onto which injector. Disconnect the wiring connectors from the injectors **(see illustration)**.
47 Disconnect the wiring connector from the idle speed control valve **(see illustration)**.
48 Release the wiring sub-loom from the guides, noting its routing, and move it aside.

3.45 Disconnect the MAP sensor wiring connector and detach the hose

3.46 Disconnect the injector wiring connectors

3.47 Disconnect the idle control valve wiring connector

4•10 Engine management system

3.49a Undo the screws (arrowed) . . .

3.49b . . . and remove the upper section

3.49c Check the seals and fit new ones if necessary, making sure they seat correctly

49 Undo the screws securing the upper section of the filter housing and remove it **(see illustrations)**. Note the rubber seals and remove them if required **(see illustration)**.
50 Undo the air funnel/throttle body mounting screws, then remove the funnels and detach the throttle body assembly from the lower section of the filter housing **(see illustrations)**. Remove the throttle body seals **(see illustration)** – new ones must be used.
51 If required clean any dirt from the quick-release connector on the fuel hose. Place a wad of rag for catching any residual fuel in the hose under the connector. Pull the rubber restrictor from the connector retainer,

noting how it seats **(see illustration)**. Press the retainer tabs in and pull the connector off the fuel rail union and remove the hose **(see illustration)**. Remove the retainer **(see illustration)** – note that Honda specify to replace it with a new one whenever the fuel hose is disconnected. Also check the condition of the restrictor and replace it with a new one if necessary. Seal the union and the connector with a plastic bag or the finger from a latex glove to prevent dirt getting in.
52 If required detach the throttle cables (see Section 13).
53 If required remove the fuel rail and injectors (see Section 4).

3.50a Undo the screws (arrowed) and remove the funnels . . .

3.50b . . . and detach the throttle bodies

3.50c Remove the seals and fit new ones on reassembly

3.51a Pull the rubber restrictor out of the retainer . . .

3.51b . . . then press the retainer tabs in and pull the connector off

3.51c Remove the retainer from the union

Engine management system 4•11

3.55 Check all hoses for cracks, splits, kinks and any other signs of damage or deterioration

3.57a Fit the new retainer into the connector . . .

54 If required remove the idle speed control valve (see Section 9).

Inspection

55 Check the throttle body hoses for signs of damage or deterioration and replace any suspect hoses with new ones **(see illustration)**. Make sure all hoses are securely connected.

56 Check the intake rubbers for signs of damage or deterioration. If required slacken the clamp screws and remove the rubbers from the throttle bodies, noting their orientation and the position of the clamps **(see illustration 3.34a)**. Also note that the rubber for the No. 1 (left-hand) throttle body is different. When refitting the rubbers locate the ribs on each side of the lug on the throttle body, and seat the hole in each clamp over the peg on the rubber. Tighten the clamps so that the gap between the ends is 11 to 13 mm.

Caution: The throttle body assembly must be treated as a sealed unit. NEVER loosen any of the white-painted nuts/bolts/screws on the assembly as these are pre-set at the factory to ensure correct synchronisation of the throttle valves.

Caution: NEVER use a solvent-based cleaner to clean the throttle body components. The throttle bores are covered with a molybdenum coating which could be removed by the cleaner.

Reassembly

57 Reassembly is the reverse of removal, noting the following:
- New throttle body seals must be used **(see illustration 3.50c)**. Check the condition of the housing and air duct seals and replace them with new ones if they are damaged or deformed or have deteriorated **(see illustration 3.49c)**. Make sure the seals seat properly in the grooves.
- Check the condition of all hoses and replace them with new ones if they are in any way damaged or deteriorated **(see illustration 3.55)**.
- The centre screw in the recessed hole in the upper section of the air filter housing is shorter than the perimeter screws **(see illustration 3.49a)**.
- Make sure all wiring connectors are securely connected.
- Make sure all cables, hoses and wiring are correctly routed.
- On CB1000R/RA models, when fitting the fuel hose, if removed fit the rubber restrictor onto the pipe union. Fit a new retainer into the connector, aligning the tabs with the holes **(see illustration 3.57a)**. Fit the connector onto the pipe and push it until both retainer tabs click into place, then try to pull the connector off to make sure it has locked **(see illustration 3.57b)**. Fit the rubber restrictor into the retainer.
- On CB1000R/RA models the air funnels must be fitted so the taller ones are in the centre – there is an R marked on the right-hand funnel pair that aligns with an R marked on the housing **(see illustration 3.57c)**.

4 Fuel rails and injectors

⚠️ **Warning: Refer to the precautions given in Section 1 before starting work.**

Check

1 If the engine runs, start it and allow it to idle. Check the operation of each injector using sounding rod held against it; an injector will emit a 'clicking' noise when functioning. If any injector is silent, either the injector or its wiring harness is faulty.

2 If the engine does not run, remove the fuel tank (see Section 2). Disconnect the wiring connector from the injector **(see illustration 3.46)**.

3 Connect an ohmmeter between the injector terminals and measure the resistance **(see illustration)**. Compare the reading for the

3.57b . . . and push the connector on so it clicks into place

3.57c Make sure the funnels are fitted as described

4.3 Check the resistance of the injector

4•12 Engine management system

4.7a Unscrew the bolts (arrowed) . . .

4.7b . . . and lift the fuel rail and injector assembly off

4.7c Remove the seals from the nozzles . . .

4.7d . . . or the injector seats

4.8a Pull each injector out . . .

4.8b . . . and remove its O-ring

injector to that given in the Specifications. If the resistance differs greatly replace the injector with a new one.

4 Check that there is no continuity to earth on the black/white wire terminal on the injector. If there is, replace the injector with a new one.

5 Check for battery voltage at the black/white wire terminal in the wiring connector with the ignition ON and the kill switch set to RUN. If there is no voltage, check the wiring between the injector and the engine stop relay, then check the relay. Check for continuity in the other wire to the ECM connector.

Removal

6 Remove the air filter housing and throttle body assembly, then separate them (see Section 3).

7 Unscrew the fuel rail bolts **(see illustration)**. Carefully lift off the fuel rail assembly and injectors **(see illustration)**. Remove the seals from the injector nozzles, or from the injector seat if they stayed in the throttle body **(see illustrations)**. Discard them as new ones must be used.

8 If required pull the injectors out of the fuel rail **(see illustration)**. Remove the O-rings and discard them **(see illustration)** – new ones must be used.

9 If required pull each fuel rail off the centre joint piece **(see illustration)**. Remove the O-rings and discard them – new ones must be used **(see illustration)**.

Installation

10 If the fuel rails have been separated from the joint piece, fit a new O-ring lubricated with clean engine oil into the groove in the end of each rail **(see illustration 4.9b)**. Push each rail onto the joint, making sure the O-ring stays in place **(see illustration 4.9a)** – on CBF1000/A models the fuel hose union on the joint piece must face to the left-hand fuel rail.

11 If the injectors have been removed from their rail, fit a new O-ring lubricated with clean engine oil into the groove in the top of each injector **(see illustration 4.8b)**.

12 Align the injector connector with the raised tab on the rail and ease it into place, taking care not to dislodge the O-ring **(see illustration 4.8a)**.

13 Fit a new seal lubricated with clean engine oil onto each injector nozzle **(see illustration 4.7c)**.

14 Fit the fuel rail assembly, making sure each injector enters its seat and the seals stay in place and locate correctly **(see illustration)**. Fit the fuel rail bolts and tighten them to the torque setting specified at the beginning of the Chapter.

4.9a Separate the rails and joint piece if required . . .

4.9b . . . then remove the O-rings

4.14 Make sure each injector and seal seat correctly

Engine management system 4•13

15 Install the throttle bodies and air filter housing (see Section 3). Run the engine and check that the fuel system is working correctly before taking the machine out on the road.

5 Fuel injection system description

1 All models are equipped with Honda's programmed fuel injection (PGM-FI) system. It is controlled by a management system with an engine control module (ECM) that operates both the injection and ignition systems.
2 The engine control module (ECM) monitors signals from the following sensors.
- Throttle position (TP) sensor – informs the ECM of the throttle position, and the rate of throttle opening or closing.
- Engine coolant temperature (ECT) sensor – informs the ECM of engine temperature. It also actuates the temperature display or warning light (see Chapter 3).
- Manifold absolute pressure (MAP) sensor – informs the ECM of the engine load by monitoring the pressure in the throttle body intake tracts.
- Intake air temperature (IAT) sensor – informs the ECM of the temperature of the air entering the throttle body.
- Crankshaft position (CKP) sensor – informs the ECM of engine speed and crankshaft position.
- Speed sensor – informs the ECM of the motorcycle's road speed (see Chapter 8).
- Oxygen sensor – informs the ECM of the oxygen content of the exhaust gases.
- Lean angle sensor – cuts the ignition and fuel pump if the bike falls over.

3 All the information from the sensors is analysed by the ECM, and from that it determines the appropriate ignition and fuelling requirements of the engine. The ECM controls each fuel injector by varying its pulse width – the length of time the injector is held open – to provide more or less fuel, as appropriate for cold starting, warm up, idle, cruising, and acceleration. The injection system is fully sequential, with each injector receiving its own signal from the ECM. The injectors are mounted in the throttle bodies on the engine side of the throttle valve.
4 Cold starting, warm up and idle speeds are controlled by an automatic idle control system, which basically takes the place of a manual choke lever. A control valve, actuated by the ECM, allows additional air to bypass the throttle valves when the throttle is closed, and this increases the engine idle speed.
5 If there is an abnormality in any of the readings obtained from any sensor, the ECM enters its back-up mode. In this event, the ECM ignores the abnormal sensor signal, and assumes a pre-programmed value which will allow the engine to continue running (albeit at reduced efficiency). If the ECM enters this back-up mode, or when any faults occur, the fuel injection system (FI) warning light in the instrument cluster will come on or flash (depending on circumstances), and the relevant fault code will be stored in the ECM memory. The fault can be identified using the fault codes which can be accessed using the self-diagnosis function (see Section 6). However if there are certain faults detected in the injectors or the crankshaft position sensor, the back-up mode becomes ineffective and the ECM will not allow the engine to run at all.
6 All UK models have an immobiliser system (HISS – Honda Ignition Security System) which will not allow the engine to be started unless the correct key is used. A fault in this system should not be confused with a fuel injection system fault. The immobiliser system has its own warning light and fault diagnosis function (see Section 20).

6 Fuel injection system fault diagnosis

1 If the fuel injection system (FI) warning light on the instrument cluster illuminates when the motorcycle is running, a fault has occurred in the fuel injection/ignition system. The engine control module (ECM) will store the relevant fault code in its memory and this code can be read as follows using the self-diagnostic mode of the ECM. While the engine is running above 5000 rpm and the motorcycle is being ridden, the light will come on and stay on. When the motorcycle is on its sidestand and the engine is idling, the light will flash, the pattern of the flashes indicating the code for the fault the ECM has identified.
2 If the engine can be started, place the motorcycle on its sidestand then start the engine and allow it to idle. Whilst the engine is idling, observe the FI warning light on the instrument cluster.
3 If the engine cannot be started, place the motorcycle on its sidestand. With the kill switch in the run position turn the engine over on the starter motor for more than ten seconds and observe the FI warning light on the instrument cluster.
4 Alternatively, and to check for any stored fault codes even though the warning light has not illuminated, on CBF1000/A models remove the passenger seat, and on CB1000R/RA models remove the right-hand side cover (see Chapter 7) to gain access to the fuel injection system data link connector (DLC), which is a 4-pin connector coming out of the wiring loom **(see illustrations)**. Ensure the ignition is switched OFF. Using either the Honda SCS service connector (pt. no. 070PZ-ZY30100), or a short jumper wire, connect between the brown and green wire terminals in the connector. With the terminals connected,

6.4a Data link connector (arrowed) – CBF1000/A

6.4b Data link connector (arrowed) – CB1000R/RA

4•14 Engine management system

Fault code (No. of flashes)	Symptoms	Possible causes
0 – no code; warning light off	Engine does not start	Blown fuse (PGM-FI 30A fuse or starter/ignition 10A fuse)
		Faulty power supply to or from electronic control module (ECM)
		Faulty engine stop relay or wiring
		Faulty engine stop switch or wiring
		Faulty ignition switch
		Faulty lean angle sensor or wiring
		Faulty electronic control module (ECM)
0 – no code; warning light off	Engine runs normally	Open or short circuit in FI warning light wiring
		Faulty electronic control module (ECM)
0 – no code; warning light constantly on	Engine runs normally	Short circuit in data link connector or wiring
		Faulty electronic control module (ECM)
1	Engine runs normally	Faulty manifold absolute pressure (MAP) sensor or wiring
2	Engine runs normally	Manifold absolute pressure (MAP) sensor vacuum hose disconnected/broken
7	Engine difficult to start at low temperatures	Faulty engine coolant temperature (ECT) sensor or wiring
8	Poor throttle response	Faulty throttle position (TP) sensor or wiring
9	Engine runs normally	Faulty intake air temperature (IAT) sensor or wiring
11	Engine operates normally	Faulty speed sensor or wiring
12	Engine does not start	Faulty No. 1 injector or wiring
13	Engine does not start	Faulty No. 2 injector or wiring
14	Engine does not start	Faulty No. 3 injector or wiring
15	Engine does not start	Faulty No. 4 injector or wiring
21	Engine operates normally	Faulty oxygen sensor or wiring
23	Engine operates normally	Faulty oxygen sensor heating element
29	Engine stalls, hard to start, rough idle	Faulty idle speed control valve

make sure the kill switch is in the RUN position then turn the ignition ON and observe the FI warning light. If there are stored fault codes, the light will flash.

5 The warning light emits long (1.3 second) and short (0.5 second) flashes to give out the fault code. A long flash is used to indicate the first digit of a double digit fault code (i.e. 10 and above). If a single digit fault code is being displayed (i.e. 0 – 9), there will be a number of short flashes equivalent to the code being displayed. For example, two long (1.3 sec) flashes followed by five short (0.5 sec) flashes indicates the fault code number 25. If there is more than one fault code, there will be a gap before the other codes are revealed (the codes will be revealed in order, starting with the lowest and finishing with the highest). Once all codes have been revealed, the ECM will continuously run through the code(s) stored in its memory, revealing each one in turn with a short gap between them. The fault codes are shown in the table above. Once all the codes have been revealed, switch off the ignition and (where necessary) remove the auxiliary wire or SCS connector from the data link connector. Identify the fault using the table above, then refer below for checking procedures.

6 Once the fault has been identified and corrected, it will be necessary to reset the system by removing the fault code from the ECM memory. To do this, ensure the ignition is switched OFF, then bridge the brown and green wire terminals of the data link connector (DLC) (see Step 4). Make sure the kill switch is in the RUN position, then turn the ignition switch ON. Disconnect the auxiliary wire or tool from the DLC. When the wire is disconnected the warning light should come on for about five seconds, during which time the auxiliary wire must be reconnected. The light should start to flash when it is reconnected, indicating that all fault codes have been erased. Turn off the ignition then remove the auxiliary wire. Check the FI warning light (in some cases it may be necessary to repeat the erasing procedure more than once).

7 If a fault appears, use the diagnostic function and fault code system described above to work out which component is faulty. First ensure that the relevant system wiring connectors are securely connected and free of corrosion – poor connections are the cause of the majority of problems. Also check the wiring itself for any obvious faults or breaks, and use a continuity tester to check the wiring between the component, its connectors and the ECM, referring to the wiring diagrams at the end of Chapter 8. Next refer to Section 7 to see if there are any other specific checks that can be made on that particular component using home equipment. If this fails to reveal the cause of the problem, the motorcycle should be taken to a Honda dealer for testing. They will have the special tools which should locate the fault quickly and simply.

8 Also ensure that the fault is not due to poor maintenance – i.e. check that the air filter element is clean, that the spark plugs are in good condition, that the valve clearances are correctly adjusted, the cylinder compression pressures are correct, and the ignition timing is correct (refer to Chapters 1 and 2, and to Section 19). It is also worth removing the sensor(s) in question (see Section 7) and checking that the sensing tip or head is clean and not obstructed by anything. Where there is a vacuum hose to a sensor, make sure it is securely connected at both ends and has no cracks or splits.

7 Fuel injection components

Caution: Ensure the ignition is switched OFF before disconnecting/reconnecting any fuel injection system wiring connector. If a connector is disturbed with the ignition switched ON the engine control module (ECM) could be damaged.

Special tool: *Honda specify a peak voltage adapter (Honda pt. no. 07HGJ-0020100) plus an aftermarket digital multimeter having an impedance of 10 M-ohm/DCV minimum for the crankshaft position sensor test (see Step 40).*

Manifold absolute pressure (MAP) sensor

Check

1 The MAP sensor is mounted on the air

Engine management system 4•15

7.1a MAP sensor wiring connector (A), vacuum hose (B) and mounting screw (C) – CBF1000/A

7.1b MAP sensor wiring connector (A), vacuum hose (B) and mounting screw (C) – CB1000R/RA

filter housing **(see illustrations)**. Remove the fuel tank (see Section 2). Make sure that the vacuum hoses to it are securely fixed at both ends, and have no cracks or splits.

2 To check the input circuit connect the positive (+) lead of a voltmeter to the yellow/red terminal of the sensor wiring connector, then connect the negative (–) lead to a good earth. Turn the ignition switch ON and set the kill switch to RUN and check that a voltage of 4.75 to 5.25 volts is present. If it isn't, check for continuity in the yellow/red wire to the ECM. If there is no continuity locate the break and repair it. If the wiring is good, the ECM could be faulty. If the voltage was good, check for continuity in the light green/yellow wire to earth. If there is continuity locate the short circuit and repair it. If the wiring is good, the MAP sensor is faulty.

3 To check the output circuit check for the same voltage between the light green/yellow and green/orange wire terminals of the connector. If there is voltage, the MAP sensor is faulty. If there is no voltage, check for continuity to the ECM in the each of the wires. If there is none, trace the fault in the wire and repair it. If all the wiring is good the ECM could be faulty.

Removal and installation

4 Remove the fuel tank (see Section 2).
5 Disconnect the wiring connector and detach the vacuum hose from the sensor **(see illustration 7.1a or b)**. Undo the screw and remove the sensor – access is restricted, so an angled screwdriver is required. If access is too restricted for the tools available, remove the air filter housing and throttle body assembly (see Section 3).
6 Installation is the reverse of removal.

Engine coolant temperature (ECT) sensor

Note: *The sensor also operates the coolant temperature display – refer to Chapter 3 to check this aspect of its function.*

Check

7 The ECT sensor is mounted in the thermostat housing **(see illustration)**. Raise the fuel tank to access it (see Section 2).
8 Disconnect the wiring connector from the sensor. With the engine cold, connect an ohmmeter between the pink/white and green/orange wire terminals on the sensor and measure its resistance. Compare the reading obtained to that given in the Specifications, noting that the specified value is valid at 20°C (68°F); the sensor resistance will increase at lower temperatures and decrease at higher temperatures. If the resistance reading differs greatly from that specified, the sensor is probably faulty.
9 If the sensor resistance is good, check its power supply. Connect the positive (+) lead of a voltmeter to the pink/white wire terminal in the sensor wiring connector, then connect the negative (–) lead to a good earth. Turn the ignition switch ON and check that a voltage of 4.75 to 5.25 volts is present. If it isn't, check for continuity in the pink/white wire to the ECM. If there is no continuity locate the break and repair it. If the wiring is good, the ECM could be faulty. If voltage was present, now connect the negative lead to the green/orange terminal of the connector and check that the same voltage is present. If it isn't, there is a fault in the green/orange wire or the ECM. If there is voltage, the ECM is probably faulty.

Removal and installation

⚠ **Warning: The engine must be completely cool before carrying out this procedure.**

10 see Chapter 3, Section 3.

Throttle position (TP) sensor

Check

11 The sensor is on the left-hand end of the throttle body assembly. Disconnect the wiring connector from the sensor **(see illustration)**. Connect the positive (+) lead of a voltmeter to the yellow/red terminal of the sensor wiring connector, then connect the negative (–) lead to a good earth. Turn the ignition switch ON and check that a voltage of 4.75 to 5.25 volts is present. If it isn't, there is a break in the yellow/red wire or a fault in the ECM. If voltage was present, now connect the negative lead to the green/orange wire terminal of the connector and check that the same voltage is present. If it isn't, there is a break in the green/orange wire or a fault the ECM. If there is voltage, check for continuity to the ECM in the red/yellow wire. If all the wiring is good have the sensor output voltage checked by a Honda dealer. If that is good, then the ECM is faulty.

7.7 ECT sensor (arrowed)

7.11 TP sensor (arrowed)

7.13a IAT sensor (arrowed) – CBF1000/A

7.13b IAT sensor (arrowed) – CB1000R/RA

Removal and installation

12 The throttle sensor is an integral part of the throttle body assembly and is not available separately **(see illustration 7.11)**. If the sensor is faulty, a complete new throttle body assembly will have to be installed, though it is worth checking with your Honda dealer or parts specialist whether anything can be done to avoid this.

Intake air temperature (IAT) sensor

Check

13 On CBF1000/A models the sensor is mounted in the top of the air filter housing **(see illustration)** – remove the fuel tank to access it (see Section 2). On CB1000R/RA models the sensor is mounted in the left-hand side of the air filter housing **(see illustration)** – remove the left-hand side cover to access it (see Chapter 7). Disconnect the wiring connector from the sensor.

14 With the sensor cold, connect an ohmmeter across the sensor terminals and measure its resistance. Compare the reading obtained to that given in the Specifications noting that the specified value is valid between 20 to 30°C (68 to 86°F); the sensor resistance will increase at lower temperatures and decrease at higher temperatures. If the resistance reading differs greatly from that specified, the sensor is probably faulty.

15 If the sensor appears to be functioning correctly, check its power supply. Connect the positive (+) lead of a voltmeter to the grey/blue terminal of the sensor wiring connector, then connect the negative (–) lead to a good earth. Turn the ignition switch ON and check that a voltage of 4.75 to 5.25 volts is present. If it isn't, there is a break in the grey/blue wire or a fault in the ECM. If voltage was present, now connect the negative lead to the green/orange terminal of the connector and check that the same voltage is present. If it isn't, there is a break in the green/orange wire or a fault in the ECM. If all the wiring is good have the sensor output voltage checked by a Honda dealer. If that is good, then the ECM is faulty.

Removal and installation

16 On CBF1000/A models the sensor is mounted in the top of the air filter housing **(see illustration 7.13a)** – remove the fuel tank to access it (see Section 2). On CB1000R/RA models the sensor is mounted in the left-hand side of the air filter housing **(see illustration 7.13b)** – remove the left-hand side cover to access it (see Chapter 7).

17 Disconnect the wiring connector from the sensor.

18 Undo the screws and remove the sensor.

19 Installation is the reverse of removal – where fitted replace the O-ring with a new one.

Vehicle speed sensor

20 See Chapter 8, Section 16.

Fuel injectors

21 See Section 4.

Oxygen sensor

Check

22 On CBF1000/A models the sensor is located in the rear of the exhaust downpipe assembly – remove the right-hand seat cowl to access the wiring connector (see Chapter 7) **(see illustration)**. On CB1000R/RA models the sensor is in the centre chamber of the exhaust system – remove the exhaust silencer (see Section 14) to access the wiring connector, then if required undo the vacuum chamber bracket bolt to improve clearance **(see illustration)**.

23 Apart from the wiring and connector checks which are outlined in Section 6, the operation of the oxygen sensor itself cannot be checked – if the sensor circuit is good (have this checked by a dealer for confirmation) and the sensor is thought to be faulty, replace it with a new one.

24 To check the sensor heater, disconnect the wiring connector. Connect an ohmmeter between the white wire terminals on the sensor side of the connector and check that the resistance is between 10 and 40 ohms. Also check that there is no continuity to earth (ground) in each white wire. If the resistance is not as specified or if there is continuity to earth, replace the sensor with a new one.

25 Check for battery voltage between the black/white (+) wire terminal and earth with the ignition ON. If there is no voltage, check the black/white wire for continuity to the engine stop relay, then check the relay. If there is voltage check for continuity to the ECM in the black/green wire.

7.22a Oxygen sensor wiring connector is inside the boot (arrowed) behind the ECM – CBF1000/A

7.22b Unscrew the bolt (A) and displace the chamber to improve access to the connector (B)

Engine management system 4•17

7.27 Oxygen sensor (arrowed)

7.28 Using a purpose made oxygen sensor socket means the wiring does not interfere so a torque wrench can be applied on installation

Removal and installation

Note: *The oxygen sensor is delicate and will not work if dropped or knocked, or if any cleaning materials are used on it. Ensure the exhaust system is cold before proceeding. To tighten the sensor to the correct torque setting either a special socket to accommodate the sensor wiring (you can get one from Honda or source a commercially available equivalent), or a crows foot socket, is required* **(see illustration 7.28)**.

26 Remove the exhaust system (see Section 14).

27 Unscrew the oxygen sensor and remove it from the exhaust system **(see illustration)**.

28 Installation is the reverse of removal. Tighten the sensor to the torque setting specified at the beginning of the Chapter **(see illustration)**.

Idle speed control valve

29 See Section 9.

Lean angle sensor

Check

30 On CBF1000/A models remove the fairing (see Chapter 7) – the sensor is mounted between the yokes **(see illustration)**. On CB1000R/RA models remove the rider's seat (see Chapter 7) – the sensor is behind the battery on the left **(see illustration)**.

31 With the ignition switch ON and the kill switch set to run, connect the positive (+) lead of a voltmeter to the white/black wire terminal of the lean angle sensor connector and the negative (-) lead to the green wire terminal and check that battery voltage (approximately 12 volts) is present. If not check the lean angle sensor fuse (see Chapter 8). If that is good check the white/black wire from the fuse to the connector for continuity, then check the green wire for continuity to earth.

32 If the voltage and wiring are good, undo the screws, noting the washers, and displace the sensor. Hold the sensor horizontal and switch the ignition ON; the engine stop relay (behind the right-hand seat cowl on CBF1000/A models and in the fuse/relay box to the rear of the battery on CB1000R/RA models **(see illustration 7.50d or 7.51b)** should click, indicating the power supply is closed (on). Slowly tilt the sensor to the left whilst listening to the engine stop relay; once the sensor reaches an angle of approximately 60° the relay should be heard to click, indicating the power supply is open (off). Switch the ignition OFF and return the sensor to the horizontal, then switch the ignition back ON again (engine stop relay should click again) and tilt the sensor to the right. The engine stop relay should be heard to click again once the sensor reaches an angle of around 60°.

33 If the relay does not click, first check the red/blue wire between the sensor and the relay, and if that is good check the relay. If all is good, it is likely the sensor is faulty.

7.30a Lean angle sensor (A) and its wiring connector (B) and mounting screws (C) – CBF1000/A

7.30b Lean angle sensor (A) and its wiring connector (B) and mounting screws (C) – CB1000R/RA

4•18 Engine management system

7.38a CKP sensor wiring connector (arrowed) – CBF1000/A

7.38b CKP sensor wiring connector (arrowed) – CB1000R/RA

7.39 Checking CKP sensor resistance

Removal and installation

34 On CBF1000/A models remove the fairing (see Chapter 7) – the sensor is mounted between the yokes **(see illustration 7.30a)**. On CB1000R/RA models remove the rider's seat (see Chapter 7) – the sensor is behind the battery on the left **(see illustration 7.30b)**.
35 Disconnect the sensor wiring connector. Undo the screws, noting the washers, and remove the sensor.
36 Installation is the reverse of removal. Make sure the sensor is fitted with its UP mark facing upwards and with the wiring facing forwards.

Crankshaft position (CKP) sensor

Check

37 On CBF1000/A models remove the right-hand fairing side panel (see Chapter 7). On CB1000R/RA models remove the right-hand side cover (see Chapter 7).
38 The sensor is in the clutch cover on the right-hand side of the engine. Trace the wiring from the sensor and disconnect it at the red wiring connector **(see illustrations)**. Perform the following check(s).
39 Using an ohmmeter check for continuity between each wire terminal in the sensor side of the connector and earth (ground). If there is continuity in either wire the sensor is faulty. Measure the resistance of the sensor by connecting the meter, set to the ohms x 100 scale, to the terminals and compare the reading to that specified at the beginning of the chapter **(see illustration)**. If the value obtained differs greatly or is zero or infinity the sensor is faulty.
40 Connect the positive (+) lead of a voltmeter and peak voltage adapter arrangement to the yellow wire terminal on the sensor and the negative (–) lead to the white/yellow wire terminal. Turn the engine over on the starter motor and note the voltage reading obtained. If this reading is below the specified minimum, the sensor is faulty.
41 If the sensor functions correctly check both wires to the ECM for continuity. If the wiring is good the ECM could be faulty.

Removal and installation

42 Remove the clutch cover (see Chapter 2, Section 14, Steps 1 to 3). The sensor is mounted inside it.
43 Undo the sensor mounting bolts and wiring guide bolt, then free the wiring grommet from the cover and remove the sensor **(see illustration)**.
44 Remove all traces of sealant from the sensor wiring grommet and clutch cover and apply a smear of fresh sealant to the grommet.
45 Locate the grommet and sensor correctly in the cover and tighten the sensor bolts and wiring guide bolt **(see illustration 7.43)**. Clean the sensor tip.
46 Install the clutch cover (see Chapter 2, Section 14, Steps 30 to 32).

Engine stop relay

Check

47 Remove the relay (see below).
48 Set a multimeter to the ohms x 1 scale and connect it across the relay's A and B terminals **(see illustration)**. There should be no continuity (infinite resistance). Using a fully-charged 12 volt battery and two insulated jumper wires, connect the positive (+) terminal of the battery to the C terminal on the relay, and the negative (–) terminal to the D terminal on the relay. At this point the relay should be heard to click and the multimeter read 0 ohms (continuity). If this is the case the relay is proved good. If the relay does not click when battery voltage is applied and still indicates no continuity (infinite resistance) across its terminals, it is faulty and must be replaced with a new one.

7.43 Unscrew the sensor bolts (A) and the wiring guide bolt (B), then free the wiring grommet (C)

7.48 Relay test set-up

Engine management system 4•19

7.50a Displace the turn signal relay . . .

7.50b . . . then displace the relay box

7.50c Release the blue connector . . .

7.50d . . . then pull the relay off

7.51a Release the clip (arrowed) and open the lid . . .

7.51b . . . then pull the relay out

49 If the relay is good refer to the wiring diagrams at the end of Chapter 8 and check the wiring and connectors in the circuit to and from the relay.

Removal and installation

50 On CBF1000/A models, remove the right-hand seat cowl (see Chapter 7). Displace the turn signal relay, then displace the relay box **(see illustrations)**. Release the retainers for the blue wiring connector and draw the connector out, then disconnect the relay from the connector **(see illustrations)**.
51 On CB1000R/RA models, remove the rider's seat (see Chapter 7). Open the fuse box lid, then pull the relay out **(see illustrations)**.
52 Installation is the reverse of removal.

Fuel cut-off relay

Check

53 Remove the relay (see below).

54 Set a multimeter to the ohms x 1 scale and connect it across the relay's A and B terminals **(see illustration 7.48)**. There should be no continuity (infinite resistance). Using a fully-charged 12 volt battery and two insulated jumper wires, connect the positive (+) terminal of the battery to the C terminal on the relay, and the negative (–) terminal to the D terminal on the relay. At this point the relay should be heard to click and the multimeter read 0 ohms (continuity). If this is the case the relay is proved good. If the relay does not click when battery voltage is applied and still indicates no continuity (infinite resistance) across its terminals, it is faulty and must be replaced with a new one.
55 If the relay is good refer to the wiring diagrams at the end of Chapter 8 and check the wiring and connectors in the circuit to and from the relay.

Removal and installation

56 On CBF1000/A models, remove the right-hand seat cowl (see Chapter 7). Displace the turn signal relay, then displace the relay box **(see illustrations 7.50a and b)**. Release the retainers for the brown wiring connector and draw the connector out, then disconnect the fuel cut-off relay from the connector **(see illustration)**.
57 On CB1000R/RA models, remove the rider's seat (see Chapter 7). Open the fuse box lid **(see illustration 7.51a)**, then pull the relay out **(see illustration)**.
58 Installation is the reverse of removal.

Engine control module (ECM)

Check

59 The engine control module (ECM) itself cannot be checked, but a process of elimination of other possible faulty components can point to it being faulty. First check the FI system fuse (see Chapter 8). Next disconnect

7.56a Release the brown connector . . .

7.56b . . . then pull the relay off it

7.57 Pull the relay out

4•20 Engine management system

7.61 ECM (arrowed) – CBF1000/A

7.62 Draw the ECM out to access the wiring connectors – where fitted remove the security bracket (arrowed) first

the ECM wiring connectors (see Steps 60-on) and check for loose or broken terminal pins in the connectors or ECM sockets, then check for continuity in each wire to/from the ECM and to its related component or connector, or to earth (ground) as appropriate, according to the wiring diagram for your model at the end of Chapter 8, and referring to the electrical system fault finding at the beginning of Chapter 8 – start with the wires to/from the engine stop relay, fuel cut-off relay and lean angle sensor, and the green, green/pink, green/black, and green/orange wires to earth (ground). If any wire does not show continuity check the connectors and terminals in the circuit before assuming there is a break in the wire. Alternatively take the bike to a Honda dealer who will plug in their diagnostic tester.

Removal and installation

60 Make sure the ignition is OFF.

61 On CBF1000/A models remove the right-hand seat cowl (see Chapter 7). Release the rubber strap **(see illustration)**. Lift the ECM and disconnect the wiring connectors. The model photographed was fitted with an anti-tamper cover secured by one-way bolts that can be done up but not undone – where fitted, drive the screw heads round using a suitable punch or cold chisel to remove them.

62 On CB1000R/RA models remove the right-hand side cover (see Chapter 7). Displace the ECM, and where fitted remove the protection bracket **(see illustration)**. Disconnect the wiring connectors and remove the ECM.

63 Installation is the reverse of removal. Refer to Section 20 to register the new ECM with the HISS system.

8 Air intake system

Air intake diaphragm valve

Removal

1 Remove the left-hand side cover (see Chapter 7).
2 On CB1000R/RA models undo the air intake duct cover screws and remove the cover **(see illustration)**.
3 Undo the air intake duct screws and displace the duct, then disconnect the vacuum hose from the diaphragm valve **(see illustrations)**.
4 Turn the diaphragm valve anti-clockwise, then unhook the rod from the flap in the duct and remove the valve **(see illustration)**.

Inspection

5 Make sure the vacuum hoses between the diaphragm valve, the control valve, the vacuum chamber, the one-way valve and the throttle bodies are all in good condition, are securely connected at each end, and are not kinked, split or cracked **(see illustrations 8.3b, 8.9, 8.10 and 8.16)**. If a hose has a split the system will not work as it relies on vacuum. Replace the hoses with new ones if necessary.
6 Make sure the flap opens and closes – if not repair it, or replace the duct with a new one **(see illustration)**. Check that the rod moves in and out of the diaphragm valve – if not replace the valve with a new one.
7 The diaphragm valve can be checked by applying a vacuum of 250 mm Hg to its union using a vacuum tool to see whether the rod moves. If the rod does not move the diaphragm may be split.

Installation

8 Installation is the reverse of removal. Make sure the vacuum hose is securely connected at each end. Make sure the air duct rubber seal is in good condition and seated in its groove – fit a new seal if necessary.

8.2 Undo the screws (arrowed) and remove the cover

8.3a Undo the screws (arrowed) . . .

8.3b . . . then displace the duct and disconnect the hose (arrowed) and remove the duct

8.4 Release the valve and unhook the rod

8.6 Check the action of the flap in the duct

Engine management system 4•21

8.9 Air intake control valve (A) and vacuum chamber (B)

8.10 Air intake control valve (arrowed)

Air intake control valve
Removal
9 On CBF1000/A models remove the fuel tank (see Section 2). Disconnect the wiring connector then detach the vacuum hoses, noting which fits where **(see illustration)**. Undo the screw and remove the valve.
10 On CB1000R/RA models remove the left-hand side cover (see Chapter 7). Undo the screw and displace the valve, then detach the vacuum hoses, noting which fits where, and disconnect the wiring connector **(see illustration)**.

Inspection
11 Refer to Step 5 and check the air intake system vacuum hoses.
12 Check the operation of the control valve by blowing through the union A; no air should flow through the valve and out of unions B **(see illustration)**. Now connect a 12 volt battery, positive (+) to the black/white wire terminal, negative (-) to the yellow/black terminal, and repeat the check; air should now flow freely through the valve.
13 Check the resistance of the control valve windings by connecting an ohmmeter between its connector terminals and compare the reading obtained to that given in the Specifications **(see illustration)**. Replace the valve with a new one if faulty.

Installation
14 Installation is the reverse of removal. Make sure the vacuum hoses and wiring connector are securely connected.

Air intake one-way valve and vacuum chamber
Removal
15 On CBF1000/A models remove the fuel tank (see Section 2). To remove the vacuum chamber first remove the control valve (see Step 9) – the screw that secure it also secures the chamber **(see illustration 8.9)**. Detach the vacuum hoses, noting which fits where, then remove the chamber, noting how it locates on the air filter housing. The one-way valve is connected in the vacuum hose above the throttle bodies – note which way round it fits,

8.12 Test the control valve as described

then detach the hoses and remove the valve.
16 On CB1000R/RA models the vacuum chamber has the one-way valve incorporated in it. Remove the exhaust silencer (see Section 14). Detach the vacuum hoses, noting which fits where, then unscrew the bracket bolt and remove the assembly, noting how the bracket locates **(see illustration)**. If required detach the chamber from the bracket.

8.13 Checking the control valve resistance

8.16 Vacuum chamber (A) and its bracket bolt (B)

4•22 Engine management system

8.18 Test the valve as described – CBF1000/A

8.19 Test the valve as described – CB1000R/RA

Inspection

17 Refer to Step 5 and check the air intake system vacuum hoses.
18 On CBF1000/A models check the operation of the one-way valve by blowing through the union A – air should flow through the valve and out of unions B and C **(see illustration)**. Now blow through union B; no air should flow through the valve and out of unions A and C.
19 On CB1000R/RA models check the operation of the one-way valve by blowing through the union A; no air should flow through the valve and out of union B **(see illustration)**. Now blow through union B; air should flow freely through the valve and out of union A.
20 Check the vacuum chamber for signs of damage and replace it with a new one if necessary.

Installation
21 Installation is the reverse of removal. Make sure the vacuum hoses are securely connected at each end.

9 Idle speed control system

Warning: Refer to the precautions given in Section 1 before starting work.

Check

1 Idle speed is controlled automatically by a valve that adjusts a flow of air which by-passes the throttle valves in the throttle bodies. The valve is actuated by the ECM and adjusts according to information received from sensors on engine and air temperature and throttle position. When the ignition is switched ON the valve self-checks by turning through its range of movement, and should emit a beep. If there is a fault a fault code should be indicated by the FI warning light in the instrument cluster (see Section 6).
2 If the engine idle speed is not as specified at the beginning of the Chapter, and there is no fault indicated, check the throttle cable freeplay, spark plugs, air filter and the valve clearances (see Chapter 1). Also inspect the intake ducts and rubbers for anything loose or cracked that could cause an air leak, causing a weak mixture.
3 Remove the fuel tank (see Section 2). Disconnect the control valve wiring connector **(see illustration 3.7)**. Check the connector wires and terminals are secure and clean. Check the resistance of the control valve windings by connecting an ohmmeter first between the black/yellow and black/orange wire terminals on the valve, and then between the black/blue and black/red wire terminals. The resistance in each case should be as specified at the beginning of the chapter. If not, replace the valve with a new one.
4 If the valve is good check each wire between the connector and the ECM for continuity (see Section 6). If all is good the ECM could be faulty.
5 Make sure air distribution hoses are in good condition and are securely connected at each end **(see illustration)**. The air hose unions have an O-ring, which if deteriorated could cause an air leak – if necessary remove the air filter housing and throttle body assembly, then separate the throttle bodies from the housing (see Section 3). Remove the unions and replace the O-rings with new ones **(see illustrations)**.

9.5a Make sure the hoses are in good condition and securely connected

9.5b Undo the screw (arrowed) . . .

9.5c . . . remove the plate . . .

9.5d . . . and each union . . .

9.5e . . . and fit new O-rings

Engine management system 4•23

9.8a Undo the screws (arrowed) and remove the plate . . .

9.8b . . . then draw the valve out. Remove and discard the O-ring (arrowed)

9.8c Make sure the valve turns

Removal

6 Remove the air filter housing and throttle body assembly, then separate the throttle bodies from the housing (see Section 3).

7 Clean the area around the valve to prevent any dirt entering the air passages.

8 Undo the control valve screws and remove the plate, then draw the valve out **(see illustrations)**. Discard the O-ring – a new one must be used **(see illustration)**. Check the action of the valve by turning it.

Installation

9 Fit a new O-ring onto the valve and smear it with clean oil **(see illustration)**. Align the groove in the valve with the pin in its housing – turn the valve if required, then insert the valve **(see illustration)**. Fit the plate, seating the cut-out over the lug, and tighten the screws **(see illustration)**.

10 Install the throttle bodies and air filter housing (see Section 3).

10 Fuel pressure check

> **Warning:** Refer to the precautions given in Section 1 before starting work.

Note: *A pressure gauge along with some adapters and hoses that are compatible with the quick-release fittings of the bike's fuel hose are required for this check. Honda can supply the various parts required, but it may be cheaper to get a dealer to perform the check, especially as hopefully you will not need the equipment more than once.*

1 Disconnect the battery negative (–) terminal (see Chapter 8).

2 Raise the fuel tank and disconnect the fuel hose (see Section 2, Steps 1 to 4 and 9).

3 Connect the fuel gauge assembly between the fuel tank and the throttle bodies.

4 Connect the battery negative (–) lead. Start the engine and allow it to idle at the specified speed. Note the pressure present in the fuel system by reading the gauge, then turn the engine off. Compare the reading obtained to that given in the Specifications.

5 If the fuel pressure is higher than specified, the pressure regulator in the fuel pump or the pump itself is faulty and must be replaced with a new one (see Section 11).

6 If the fuel pressure is lower than specified, first check for a leak, which should be obvious from the smell of fuel. If there are no leaks check for a pinched or blocked tank breather hose or fuel hose. Next remove the pump (see Section 11), and check the strainer for a blockage (though this is unlikely). Otherwise the fuel filter or pressure regulator, both of which are integral components of the pump assembly, or the pump itself, are faulty, and so the pump must be replaced with a new one.

7 On completion, disconnect the battery negative (–) lead again. Remove the fuel gauge assembly, being prepared to catch any residual fuel, then reconnect the bike's fuel hose and lower the tank, referring to Section 2, Step 19.

8 Reconnect the battery. Start the engine and check that there is no sign of fuel leakage.

11 Fuel pump

> **Warning:** Refer to the precautions given in Section 1 before starting work.

Check

1 The fuel pump is located inside the fuel tank. The fuel pump should run for a few seconds when the ignition is switched ON to pressurise the fuel system, and then cut out until the engine is started. If the pump is thought to be faulty, first check the main fuse and the FI fuse (see Chapter 8) then proceed as follows.

2 Raise the fuel tank (see Section 2).

3 Make sure the ignition is switched OFF then disconnect the fuel pump wiring connector **(see illustration 2.6a or 6b)**. Connect the positive (+) lead of a voltmeter to the brown wire terminal on the loom side of the connector and the negative (–) lead to the green wire terminal. Switch the ignition ON whilst noting the reading obtained on the meter.

4 If battery voltage is present for a few seconds, the fuel pump circuit is operating correctly and the fuel pump itself is faulty and must be replaced with a new one.

5 If no reading is obtained, check the fuel pump circuit wiring for continuity and make

9.9a Fit a new O-ring . . .

9.9b . . . then align and insert the valve . . .

9.9c . . . and fit the plate and screws

4•24 Engine management system

11.7a Fuel hose banjo bolt (A), fuel pump mounting plate nuts (arrowed) – note the wiring clamp (B)

11.7b Carefully draw the pump out . . .

11.7c . . . and remove the seal

11.8a Fuel pump mounting plate nuts (arrowed)

11.8b Carefully draw the pump out . . .

sure all the connectors are free from corrosion and are securely connected. Repair/replace the wiring as necessary and clean the connectors using electrical contact cleaner. If this fails to reveal the fault, check the following components.
- Engine stop switch (see Chapter 8, Section 19).
- Fuel cut-off relay (see Section 7).
- Engine stop relay (see Section 7).
- Lean angle sensor (see Section 7).
- Engine control module (ECM) (see Section 7).

Removal

6 Remove the fuel tank (see Section 2). Drain or siphon as much fuel as possible from the tank. Make sure the fuel cap is secure, then place the tank upside down on plenty of rag.

7 On CBF1000/A models, if required, unscrew the fuel supply hose banjo bolt and remove the upper sealing washer, detach the banjo union and remove the lower sealing washer catching any remaining fuel **(see illustration)**. Unscrew the fuel pump mounting plate nuts. Carefully lift the pump assembly from the tank along with the mounting plate seal **(see illustration)**. Remove the seal, noting how it fits, and discard it **(see illustration)** – a new one must be used on installation.

8 On CB1000R/RA models unscrew the fuel pump mounting plate nuts **(see illustration)**. Carefully lift the pump assembly from the tank along with the mounting plate seal **(see illustration)**. Remove the seal, noting how it fits, and discard it **(see illustration)** – a new one must be used on installation.

9 On CB1000R/RA models remove the rubber cover from the fuel strainer, noting how it locates **(see illustration)**. On all models check the strainer for signs of dirt and clean it if necessary – note that the strainer is part of the fuel pump and is not available separately **(see illustration)**. On CB1000R/RA models refit the rubber cover, hooking the peg into the hole.

11.8c . . . and remove the seal

11.9a Displace the rubber cover to reveal the strainer (arrowed) – CB1000R/RA

11.9b Fuel strainer (arrowed) – CBF1000/A

Engine management system 4•25

Installation

10 Make sure the wiring terminal screws, nuts and connectors are tight, both on the pump and the base.

11 Ensure the mounting plate and tank surfaces are clean and dry. Fit the new seal onto the plate – carefully pull the rubber locating legs through so the ribs are past the holes in the plate **(see illustrations)**.

12 Carefully manoeuvre the pump assembly into the tank, making sure it is correctly positioned as shown, and seat the seal and plate over the studs **(see illustrations 11.7b and a or 11.8b and a)**.

13 Fit the nuts and tighten them finger-tight. Now tighten them evenly and a little at a time in the numerical sequence shown for your model to the torque setting specified at the beginning of the Chapter **(see illustrations)**.

14 On CBF1000/A models connect the fuel supply hose using new sealing washers, one on each side of the banjo union, and tighten the bolt to the torque setting specified at the beginning of the Chapter.

15 Install the fuel tank (see Section 2).

12 Fuel gauge and level sensor

11.11a Fit a new seal . . .

11.11b . . . and pull the legs through

11.13a Fuel pump nut tightening sequence – CBF1000/A models

11.13b Fuel pump nut tightening sequence – CB1000R/RA models

Check

CBF1000/A models

1 The circuit consists of the level sensor in the fuel tank and the fuel gauge, which is part of the instrument cluster. Under normal circumstances with the tank full the needle should point to F, and when the needle enters the red zone there are only about 4 litres left.

2 If the gauge does not work, check the amount of fuel in the tank, then raise the fuel tank (see Section 2), and disconnect the fuel pump wiring connector **(see illustration 2.6a)**. Connect an ohmmeter or multimeter set to the ohms scale to the red/black and black/white wire terminals in the pump side of the wiring connector and measure the resistance. Compare the reading obtained to those given for a full and empty tank at the beginning of the Chapter, adjusting for the amount of fuel you estimate is there.

3 To accurately check the sensor remove the pump assembly (see Section 11). Check the float arm for damage and look for fuel inside the float, also check that it moves up and down smoothly and freely and check the wiring. Connect the meter to the pump connector as above, then manually move the float up and down to simulate movement between the full and empty positions, and compare the resistance readings given **(see illustrations)**. If not as specified replace the pump assembly with a new one.

4 If the level sensor appears to be functioning correctly, check for continuity in the grey/black wire between the pump connector and the instrument cluster connector, and in the green wire to earth, referring to Chapter 8. If the wiring is good the gauge could be faulty – see Chapter 8.

CB1000R/RA models

5 The circuit consists of the level sensor in the fuel tank and the fuel gauge, which is

12.3a Check the resistance with the float arm in the full position . . .

12.3b . . . and the empty position – CBF1000/A models

4•26 Engine management system

12.8a Check the resistance with the float arm in the full position...

12.8b ... and the empty position – CB1000R/RA models

part of the instrument cluster LCD display. Under normal circumstances with the tank full all segments of the gauge will show, and when there are only about 4 litres left the final segment will flash. The system performs its own self diagnosis when the ignition is turned ON, and if a fault is detected in the wiring circuit the display will operate as follows – this starts with the centre segment coming on, then the adjacent segments, followed by the outer segments, then the centre section will go out, followed by the adjacent segments, then the outer segments, and this pattern will repeat until the fault is repaired.

6 If a fault is indicated, raise the fuel tank (see Section 2), and disconnect the level sensor wiring connector (see illustration 2.6c). Connect a jumper wire between the terminals in the loom side of the connector then turn the ignition ON – if the segments are still performing their routine check for continuity in the grey/black wire between the pump connector and the instrument cluster connector, and in the green wire to earth, referring to Chapter 8. If the wiring is good the instrument PCB is faulty (see Chapter 8).

7 If all the segments come on, connect an ohmmeter or multimeter set to the ohms scale to the red/black and black/white wire terminals in the pump side of the wiring connector and measure the resistance. Compare the reading obtained to those given for a full and empty tank at the beginning of the Chapter, adjusting for the amount of fuel you estimate is there.

8 To accurately check the sensor, remove it from the tank (see below). Check the float arm for damage and look for fuel inside the float, and check that it moves up and down smoothly and freely, and check the wiring. Connect the meter to the sensor connector as above, then manually move the float up and down to simulate movement between the full and empty positions, and compare the resistance readings given (see illustrations). If not as specified replace the sensor with a new one.

Removal and installation

9 If the gauge is faulty replace the instrument cluster PCB with a new one (see Chapter 8).

10 If the sensor is faulty on CBF1000/A models replace the pump assembly with a new one (see Section 11).

11 If the sensor is faulty on CB1000R/RA models remove the fuel tank (see Section 2). Drain or siphon as much fuel as possible from the tank. Make sure the fuel cap is secure, then place the tank upside down on plenty of rag. Unscrew the nuts and carefully lift the sensor out of the tank, taking care not to snag the float (see illustrations). Remove the O-ring and discard it – a new one must be used.

12 Fit a new O-ring into the groove in the tank (see illustration). Manoeuvre the sensor float into the tank and seat the plate over the studs with the wiring pointing to the right-hand side of the tank. Fit the nuts and tighten them evenly and a little at a time in a criss-cross sequence. Install the tank and check for leakage around the sensor plate.

13 Throttle cables

Warning: Refer to the precautions given in Section 1 before proceeding.

Removal

1 On CBF1000/A models remove the fairing (see Chapter 7). Trace the wiring from the right-hand switch housing on the handlebar and disconnect it at the connectors (see illustration). Feed the wiring back to the switch, freeing it from any clips and ties and noting its routing.

2 Slacken the cable adjuster locknut, then thread the adjuster fully in to get maximum

12.11a Unscrew the nuts (arrowed) and remove the guides ...

12.11b ... then draw the sensor out

12.12 Fit a new O-ring into the groove

Engine management system 4•27

13.1 Trace the wiring from the switch and disconnect it at the connectors

13.2a Slacken the locknut (A) and turn the adjuster (B) in

freeplay in the cable **(see illustration)**. Slacken the locknut holding the rear cable in the bracket on the throttle bodies, then unscrew the adjuster and slip the cable out of the bracket **(see illustrations)**.

3 Unscrew the cable elbow nuts at the throttle pulley housing **(see illustration)**. Remove the housing screws and separate the halves **(see illustrations)**. Detach the cable nipples from the pulley, then withdraw the throttle closing cable from the housing **(see illustrations)**. Thread the housing off the throttle opening cable then draw the cable elbow out of the housing **(see illustration)**. Mark each cable to ensure it is connected correctly on installation.

13.2b Slacken the locknut (A) and turn the adjuster (B) out . . .

13.2c . . . to free the cable from the bracket

13.3a Unscrew the nuts (arrowed)

13.3b Housing screws (arrowed) – CBF1000/A

13.3c Housing screws (arrowed) – CB1000R/RA

13.3d Detach the cables from the pulley . . .

13.3e . . . then withdraw the closing cable . . .

13.3f . . . and thread the housing off the opening cable

4•28 Engine management system

13.5a Unscrew the hex (arrowed) to free the cable from the bracket . . .

13.5b . . . and detach the cable ends from the cam

13.8 Locate the pin (A) in the hole (B)

4 Remove the air filter housing and throttle body assembly (see Section 3). Mark each cable according to its location.
5 Unscrew the hex on the closing (front) cable enough to free the captive nut, then release the cable from the bracket and detach the cable end from the cam **(see illustrations)**. Detach the opening (rear) cable end from the cam.

Installation

6 Fit the opening cable end into the rear socket in the throttle body cam. Fit the closing cable end into the front of the throttle cam then fit the cable into the bracket and fully tighten the hex **(see illustrations 13.5b and a)**.
7 Install the throttle body and air filter housing assembly (see Section 3).
8 Fit the throttle opening cable elbow into the upper socket of the throttle pulley housing and thread the housing on without it becoming tight on the bottom of the threads **(see illustration 13.3f)** – the elbow must stay loose so that it aligns itself. Fit the closing cable into the lower socket **(see illustration 13.3e)**. Lubricate the cable nipples with multi-purpose grease and fit them into the throttle pulley **(see illustration 13.3d)**. Thread the lower cable nut into the housing and the upper cable nut onto the cable, leaving them both loose. Assemble the housing onto the handlebar, making sure the pin locates in the hole, then fit the screws and tighten them **(see illustration)**. On CBF1000/A models feed the handlebar switch wiring back to the connector, locating it in any ties and guides and making sure it is correctly routed, and reconnect it **(see illustration 13.1)**. Align the cable elbows and tighten the nuts **(see illustration 13.3a)**.
9 Fit the opening cable into the rear of the bracket on the throttle bodies and lightly tighten the locknut **(see illustration 13.2b)**. Operate the throttle to check that it opens and closes freely.
10 Check and adjust the throttle cable freeplay (see Chapter 1). Turn the handlebars back-and-forth to make sure the cables don't cause the steering to bind.
11 Start the engine and check that the idle speed does not rise as the handlebars are turned. If it does, the throttle cables are routed incorrectly. Correct the problem before riding the motorcycle. On CBF1000/A models install the fairing (see Chapter 7).

14 Exhaust system

⚠️ *Warning: If the engine has been running the exhaust system will be very hot. Allow the system to cool before carrying out any work.*

> **HAYNES HINT** *Exhaust system clamp bolts tend to become corroded and seized. It is advisable to spray them with WD40 or a similar product before attempting to slacken them.*

Removal – CBF1000/A models

Silencers

1 Slacken the clamp bolt **(see illustration)**.
2 Unscrew the nut on the silencer mounting bolt **(see illustration)**. Support the silencer, then withdraw the bolt, noting the collar and washer, and ease the silencer out of the downpipe assembly **(see illustrations)**.
3 Check the condition of the sealing ring and replace it with a new one if it is damaged or deformed or no longer sealing correctly **(see**

14.1 Slacken the bolt (arrowed)

14.2a Unscrew the nut, withdraw the bolt . . .

14.2b . . . and remove the silencer

14.2c Note the collar fitted in the bush

illustration). If you do fit a new one, remove the clamp and expand the tangs on the end of the pipe slightly to make it easier to fit.
4 Check the condition of the nuts and bolts, washers, collars and rubbers and replace them with new ones if necessary.

Downpipe assembly

5 Remove the right-hand seat cowl (see Chapter 7).
6 Remove the silencers (see above).
7 Disconnect the oxygen sensor wiring connector **(see illustration 7.22a)**. Feed the wiring down to the sensor, noting its routing.
8 Unscrew the nut on the rear mounting bolt **(see illustration)**. Unscrew the nuts securing the downpipe flanges to the cylinder head **(see illustration 14.19b)**. Support the assembly, then withdraw the rear bolt, draw the flanges off the studs and manoeuvre the downpipe assembly off the head and remove it.
9 Remove the sealing ring from each port in the cylinder head and discard them as new ones must be used **(see illustration 14.20)**.
10 Check the condition of the rear mounting components and replace them with new ones if necessary.

Removal – CB1000R/RA models

Silencer

11 Slacken the clamp bolt securing the silencer to the middle chamber.
12 Unscrew the nut and remove the washer on the silencer rear mounting bolt **(see illustration)**. Unscrew the front mounting bolt and remove the washer **(see illustration)**. Support the silencer, then withdraw the rear bolt, noting the washer, and ease the silencer out of the middle chamber assembly. Note the collar in each mount and remove them for safekeeping if required **(see illustration)**.
13 Check the condition of the sealing ring and replace it with a new one if it is damaged or deformed or no longer sealing correctly **(see illustration)**. If you do fit a new one, remove the clamp and expand the tangs on the end of the pipe slightly to make it easier to fit.
14 If required detach the cover from the silencer by undoing the four screws, noting the collars **(see illustration)**.
15 Check the condition of the nuts and bolts, washers, collars and rubbers and replace them with new ones if necessary.

Downpipe assembly

16 Remove the silencer (see above).
17 Release the oxygen sensor wiring connector and disconnect it **(see illustration 7.22b)**. Feed the wiring down to the sensor, noting its routing.
18 Remove the shield from the left-hand side, noting the washers and collars on the screws **(see illustration)**.
19 Unscrew, but do not yet remove, the chamber mounting bolt **(see illustration)**.

14.3 Replace the sealing ring (arrowed) with a new one if necessary

14.8 Unscrew the nut (arrowed)

14.12a Unscrew the nut and remove the washer

14.12b Unscrew the bolt and remove the washer

14.12c Note the arrangement of the collars and rubber bushes

14.13 Dig the old sealing ring out and replace it with a new one if required

14.14 Undo the screws (arrowed) and remove the cover

14.18 Undo the screws (arrowed) and remove the shield

14.19a Unscrew the bolt (arrowed), but leave it in place as support

4•30 Engine management system

14.19b Unscrew the nuts (arrowed)

14.19c Carefully remove the downpipe assembly

14.20 Remove and discard the sealing rings

Unscrew the nuts securing the downpipe flanges to the cylinder head **(see illustration)**. Support the assembly, then withdraw the rear bolt, noting the washer, and draw the flanges off the studs and manoeuvre the downpipe assembly off the head and remove it **(see illustration)**.

20 Remove the sealing ring from each port in the cylinder head and discard them as new ones must be used **(see illustration)**.

21 Note the collar in the chamber mount and remove it for safekeeping if required **(see illustration)**. Check the condition of the nuts and bolt, washer, collar and rubbers and replace them with new ones if necessary.

22 If required detach the chamber from the downpipes by slackening the clamps and pulling them apart **(see illustrations)** – note which downpipe pair fits on which side.

23 Check the condition of the sealing rings and replace them with new ones if they are damaged or deformed or no longer sealing correctly **(see illustration)**. If you do fit new ones, remove the clamp and expand the tangs on the end of the pipe slightly to make them easier to fit.

Installation – all models

24 Installation is the reverse of removal, noting the following:
- Replace any damaged, deformed or deteriorated mounting rubbers with new ones. Replace any badly corroded collars, nuts bolts and washers with new ones. Make sure the collars are fitted in the rubbers.
- Check that the amount of protrusion of each stud from the cylinder head is 39 to 40 mm.
- Use a new sealing ring in each cylinder head port, and dab them with grease to stick them in place **(see illustration)**.
- Apply a smear of copper grease to all nuts and bolts to prevent them from seizing up. Fit and secure all mounts finger-tight before fully tightening them. On the downpipe assembly tighten the flange nuts before the mounting bolt. Tighten the nuts/bolts to the torque settings specified at the beginning of the Chapter for your model.
- Do not forget to reconnect the oxygen sensor wiring connector, and make sure the wiring is correctly routed and secured **(see illustration 7.22a or b)**.
- Run the engine and check the system for leaks.

15 Pulse secondary air (PAIR) system

General information

1 To reduce the amount of unburned hydrocarbons released in the exhaust gases, a pulse secondary air (PAIR) system is fitted. The system consists of the control valve (mounted under the fuel tank), the reed valves (fitted in the valve cover) and the hoses linking them. The control valve is actuated electronically by the ECM.

2 Under normal operating conditions the valve is open allowing filtered air to be drawn through the reed valves and cylinder head passages and into the exhaust ports. The air mixes with the exhaust gases, causing any unburned particles of the fuel in the mixture to be burnt in the exhaust port/pipes. This process changes a considerable amount of hydrocarbons and carbon monoxide into relatively harmless carbon dioxide and water. The reed valves in the valve cover are fitted to prevent the flow of exhaust gases back up the cylinder head passages and into the air filter housing.

Testing

3 Start the engine and warm it up normal temperature, then stop it.

4 Raise the fuel tank (see Section 2). Detach the PAIR hose from the air filter housing **(see illustration 3.4 or 3.19a)**. Check that the hose is clean – the presence or carbon deposits indicates a faulty system. Start the engine

14.21 Note the arrangement of the collars and rubber bushes

14.22 Slacken the clamp bolts and detach the pipes from the chamber

14.23 Replace the sealing rings (arrowed) with new ones if necessary

14.24 Fit a new sealing ring into each port

Engine management system 4•31

15.5 PAIR control valve test

15.9 Detach the hose (arrowed) from the reed valve housing on each side

again and open the throttle slightly, and check the air is being sucked into the detached hose. If not, stop the engine, then perform the following checks.

5 Disconnect the control valve wiring connector **(see illustration 3.17)**. Clean the end of the air filter housing hose. Manually check the operation of the system by blowing through the hose – air should flow through the control valve and reed valves **(see illustration)**. Apply battery voltage (12 volts) across the control valve terminals and repeat the check – no air should flow through the control valve. Disconnect the battery. If the valve does not behave as described check its resistance (Step 7).

6 Now suck on the air filter hose union; you should not be able to suck air back up the hose, indicating the reed valves are closing and sealing correctly. If you can suck air through, first identify which reed valve is faulty by blocking one hose, then the other. Having identified the faulty valve, remove it for cleaning, then test it again. Replace the valve with a new one if necessary.

7 Check the resistance of the control valve solenoid by connecting an ohmmeter between its connector terminals and compare the reading obtained to that given in the Specifications. Replace the valve with a new one if faulty.

Component renewal

Control valve

8 Remove the fuel tank (see Section 2). On CBF1000/A models remove the No. 1 and 4 cylinder ignition coil (see Section 18). On CB1000R/RA models remove the No. 2 and 3 cylinder ignition coil (see Section 18).

9 Detach the PAIR hoses from the reed valves **(see illustration)**. Detach the hose from the air filter housing **(see illustration 3.4 or 3.19a)**.

10 Disconnect the control valve wiring connector **(see illustration 3.17)**.

11 Displace the control valve from its mount and remove it along with the hoses, noting their routing **(see illustration)**. Detach the hoses from the valve if required, noting which fits where **(see illustration 3.5)**.

12 Installation is the reverse of removal.

Reed valves

13 Remove the fuel tank (see Section 2). Pull the No. 1 and 4 cylinder spark plug caps off the plugs, and move them and any other hoses and wiring aside as required for access **(see illustration 17.3)**.

14 Release the clamp and detach the air hose **(see illustration 15.9)**. Unscrew the bolts and remove the cover **(see illustration)**. Remove the reed valve and the base plate, noting which way around they fit **(see illustrations)**.

15 Installation is the reverse of removal. Make sure the reed valve components and housings are clean and free of carbon deposits, and that the base plates and valves seat correctly. Clean the threads of the cover bolts and apply fresh threadlock, and tighten the bolts to the torque setting specified at the beginning of the Chapter.

15.11 Slide the valve off its bracket and remove it with the hoses attached

15.14a Unscrew the bolts and remove the cover . . .

15.14b . . . then remove the reed valves . . .

15.14c . . . and the base plates

4•32 Engine management system

16 Catalytic converter(s)

General information

1 On CBF1000/A models there are two catalytic converters, and on CB1000R/RA models one, incorporated in the exhaust system to minimise the level of exhaust pollutants released into the atmosphere.
2 A catalytic converter consists of a canister containing a fine mesh impregnated with a catalyst material, over which the hot exhaust gases pass. The catalyst speeds up the oxidation of harmful carbon monoxide, unburned hydrocarbons and soot, effectively reducing the quantity of harmful products released into the atmosphere via the exhaust gases.
3 The catalytic converters are of the closed-loop type with exhaust gas oxygen content information being fed back to the engine control module (ECM) by the oxygen sensor.
4 The oxygen sensor contains a heating element which is controlled by the ECM. When the engine is cold, the ECM switches on the heating element which warms the exhaust gases as they pass over the sensor. This brings the catalytic converter quickly up to its normal operating temperature and decreases the level of exhaust pollutants emitted whilst the engine warms up. Once the engine is sufficiently warmed up, the ECM switches off the heating element.
5 Refer to Section 14 for exhaust system removal and installation, and Section 7 for oxygen sensor removal and installation information.

Precautions

6 A catalytic converter is a reliable and simple device which needs no maintenance in itself, but there are some facts of which an owner should be aware if the converter is to function properly for its full service life.
- DO NOT use leaded or lead replacement petrol (gasoline) – the additives will coat the precious metals, reducing their converting efficiency and will eventually destroy the catalytic converter.
- Always keep the ignition and fuel systems well-maintained in accordance with the manufacturer's schedule – if the fuel/air mixture is suspected of being incorrect have it checked on an exhaust gas analyser.
- If the engine develops a misfire, do not ride the bike at all (or at least as little as possible) until the fault is rectified.
- DO NOT use fuel or engine oil additives – these may contain substances harmful to the catalytic converter.
- DO NOT continue to use the bike if the engine burns oil to the extent of leaving a visible trail of blue smoke.
- Remember that the catalytic converter and oxygen sensor are FRAGILE – do not strike them with tools during servicing work.

17 Ignition system check

Warning: The energy levels in electronic systems can be very high. On no account should the ignition be switched on whilst the plugs or caps are being held. Shocks from the HT circuit can be most unpleasant. Secondly, it is vital that the engine is not turned over or run with any of the plug caps removed, and that the plugs are soundly earthed (grounded) when the system is checked for sparking. The ignition system components can be seriously damaged if the HT circuit becomes isolated.

1 As no means of adjustment is available, any failure of the system can be traced to failure of a system component or a simple wiring fault. Of the two possibilities, the latter is by far the most likely. In the event of failure, check the system in a logical fashion, as described below.
2 Raise the fuel tank (see Section 2).
3 Make sure the ignition is OFF. Working on one cylinder at a time, pull the cap off the spark plug **(see illustration)**. Connect the cap to a spare spark plug (preferably use a new plug). Earth the plug against the cylinder head – do not earth the plug against the valve cover itself. If necessary, hold the spark plug with an insulated tool.

Warning: Do not remove any of the spark plugs from the engine to perform this check – atomised fuel being pumped out of the open spark plug hole could ignite, causing severe injury! Make sure the plugs are securely held against the engine – if they are not earthed when the engine is turned over, the ECM could be damaged.

4 Having observed the above precautions, check that the kill switch is in the RUN position and the transmission is in neutral, then turn the ignition switch ON and turn the engine over on the starter motor. If the system is in good condition a regular, fat blue spark should be evident at the plug electrode. If the spark appears thin or yellowish, or is non-existent, further investigation is necessary. Turn the ignition OFF and repeat the check for each coil.
5 The ignition system must be able to produce a spark which is capable of jumping at least a 6 mm gap. Simple ignition spark gap testing tools are commercially available – follow the manufacturer's instructions **(see illustration)**.
6 If the test results are good the entire ignition system can be considered good. If the spark appears thin or yellowish, or is non-existent, further investigation is necessary.
7 Ignition faults can be divided into two categories, namely those where the ignition system has failed completely, and those which are due to a partial failure. The likely faults are listed below, starting with the most probable source of failure. Work through the list systematically, referring to the subsequent sections for full details of the necessary checks and tests. **Note:** *Before checking the following items ensure that the battery is fully charged and that all fuses are in good condition.*
- Loose, corroded or damaged wiring connections, broken or shorted wiring between any of the component parts of the ignition system.
- Loose spark plug cap connection, faulty spark plug cap or HT lead, faulty spark plug, dirty, worn or corroded plug electrodes.
- Faulty neutral, clutch or sidestand switch (see Chapter 8).
- Faulty ignition coil(s) (Section 18).
- Faulty ignition switch or engine kill switch (see Chapter 8).
- Faulty crankshaft position (CKP) sensor (Section 7) or damaged triggers on timing rotor (Chapter 2).
- Faulty engine stop relay (Section 7).
- Faulty electronic control module (Section 7).

8 If the above checks don't reveal the cause of the problem, have the ignition system tested by a Honda dealer.

17.3 Pull the cap off the spark plug

17.5 Typical ignition system spark gap testing tool

Engine management system 4•33

18.2a Ignition coil (arrowed) for cylinders 1 and 4 – CBF1000/A models

18.2b Ignition coil (arrowed) for cylinders 2 and 3 – CBF1000/A models

18.2c Ignition coil (arrowed) for cylinders 1 and 4 – CB1000R/RA models

18.2d Ignition coil (arrowed) for cylinders 2 and 3 – CB1000R/RA models

18 Ignition coils

Special tool: *Honda specify a peak voltage adapter (Honda pt. no. 07HGJ-0020100) plus an aftermarket digital multimeter having an impedance of 10 M-ohm/DCV minimum for the crankshaft position sensor test (see Step 7).*

Check

1 Disconnect the battery negative (–) lead (see Chapter 8).
2 Raise the fuel tank (see Section 2). There are two coils, one for cylinders 1 and 4, the other for cylinders 2 and 3 **(see illustrations)**.
3 Check each coil visually for loose or damaged connectors and terminals, cracks and other damage.
4 Disconnect the primary circuit wiring connectors from the coil **(see illustration)**. Pull the caps off the spark plugs **(see illustration 17.3)**.
5 To check the condition of the primary windings, set a multimeter to the ohms x 1 scale. Connect the meter probes to the primary terminals on the coil and measure the resistance **(see illustration)**. If the reading obtained is not as given in the Specifications, it is likely that the coil is defective.
6 To check the resistance of the secondary windings, set the meter to the K-ohm scale.

18.4 Disconnect the primary wiring connectors (arrowed)

18.5 To test the coil primary resistance, connect the multimeter leads to the primary wiring terminals

4•34 Engine management system

18.6a To test the coil secondary resistance, connect the multimeter probes to the spark plug sockets

18.6b Unscrew the cap from the lead . . .

18.6c . . . and the lead from the coil as required

18.6d Checking a spark plug cap resistance

18.11 Note the spacer fitted with each bolt

HAYNES HINT *Note if a fault exists in the ignition circuit for one pair of cylinders (e.g. 1 and 4), you can swap the coils over to check if the fault then appears on the other pair of cylinders (e.g. 2 and 3). If so, the coil is confirmed faulty.*

Removal and installation

8 Disconnect the battery negative (–) lead (see Chapter 8).
9 Raise the fuel tank (see Section 2).
10 Disconnect the primary circuit wiring connectors from the coil, making a note of which fits where (see illustration 18.4). Pull the caps off the spark plugs (see illustration 17.3).
11 Unscrew the coil mounting bolts and remove the coil, noting the spacers, and the collars in the grommets on the No. 2 and 3 cylinder coil on CBF1000/A models (see illustration).
12 If required, and except on the No. 2 and 3 cylinder coil on CBF1000/A models, unscrew the coil bracket bolts and remove the bracket from the frame – on CB1000R/RA models to remove the bracket on the left-hand side first release the wiring connector from its tab and the wiring loom clip from its post (see illustrations), and to remove the bracket from the right-hand side displace the PAIR valve (see illustration 15.11) and throttle cables, and disconnect the resistor wiring connector (see illustration), and note how the rear mount seats behind the thermostat housing bracket.

Connect the meter probes to the contacts in the spark plug caps and measure the resistance (see illustration). If the reading obtained is not as given in the Specifications, unscrew the plug caps and test the coil again, this time inserting the probes into the ends of the HT leads (see illustration). If the reading obtained is not as given in the Specifications (resistance with no caps) unscrew the leads from the coil and test the coil again, this time connecting the probes to the sockets in the coil (see illustration). If the reading obtained is not as given in the Specifications (resistance with no caps) it is likely the coil is defective. If the reading is good check the resistance of each plug cap, and if that is as specified replace the HT leads with new ones, otherwise replace the plug cap with new ones (see illustration).
7 If a peak voltage adapter is available (see **Special tool** note) the coil's primary peak voltage can be checked. Disconnect the plug caps from all four cylinders and earth spare plugs against the cylinder head as described in Section 17. If checking the coil for cylinders 1 and 4, connect the peak voltage adaptor positive probe to the yellow/blue wire primary terminal of the coil and connect the negative probe to earth; the primary wire should remain connected to its terminal. With the ignition ON, battery voltage should be shown on the meter. Crank the engine over on the stater motor and note the peak voltage registered on the meter – it should be above the minimum given in the Specifications at the beginning of this Chapter. Carry out the same test on the coil for cylinders 2 and 3, but connect the peak voltage adaptor's positive probe to the blue/yellow wire primary terminal.

18.12a Detach the connector from the tab on the bracket . . .

18.12b . . . and free the wiring loom clip

18.12c Disconnect the wiring connector (arrowed)

Engine management system 4•35

13 Installation is the reverse of removal, noting the following:
- On CB1000R/RA models the coil bracket bolts thread into rubber wellnuts fitted in holes in the frame, rather than threading directly into the frame itself. Each wellnut is held in its hole only by a rubber rim, and when fitting the bolt it is easy to push on the nut, at which point the rim gives way and the nut disappears inside the frame. If you are lucky it may drop down the back and fall out of the hole in the bottom of the frame, or lodge somewhere close to it so you can retrieve it. If it lodges high up you may be able to dislodge it using some wire. To prevent this happening make sure the mount in the housing is perfectly aligned with the nut before inserting the bolt, and push the mount against the rubber rim to help keep it in place. Insert the bolt carefully and make sure the threads have engaged before using a tool.
- On CBF1000/A models the coil for cylinders 1 and 4 goes on the frame and that for cylinders 2 and 3 goes on the fairing bracket **(see illustrations 18.2a and b)**.
- On CB1000R/RA models the coil for cylinders 1 and 4 goes on the right-hand side of the frame and that for cylinders 2 and 3 goes on the left **(see illustrations 18.2c and d)**.

19 Ignition timing

General information

1 Since no provision exists for adjusting the ignition timing and since no component is subject to mechanical wear, there is no need for regular checks; only if investigating a fault such as a loss of power or a misfire should the ignition timing be checked.
2 The ignition timing is checked dynamically (engine running) using a stroboscopic lamp. The inexpensive neon lamps should be adequate in theory, but in practice may produce a pulse of such low intensity that the timing mark remains indistinct. If possible, one of the more precise xenon tube lamps should be used, powered by an external source of the appropriate voltage.
Note: *Do not use the machine's own battery as an incorrect reading may result from stray impulses within the machine's electrical system.*

Check

3 Warm the engine up to normal operating temperature then stop it.
4 Unscrew the timing inspection cap from the crankcase cover **(see illustration)**. Discard the O-ring as a new one must be used.
5 The dynamic timing mark on the rotor which indicates the firing point at idle speed for the No. 1 cylinder is the line next to the F mark. The static timing mark with which this should align is a notch or pointer in the inspection hole rim.

> **HAYNES HiNT** *The timing marks can be highlighted with white paint to make them more visible under the stroboscope light.*

6 Connect the timing light to the No. 1 cylinder coil HT lead – raise the fuel tank to do this is if required, then lower it again (see Section 2).
7 Start the engine and aim the light at the static timing mark.
8 With the machine idling, the timing mark should align with the notch. Now increase engine speed above 2500 rpm. The dynamic timing mark should move anti-clockwise in relation to the static mark. This confirms the ignition is advancing.
9 As already stated, there is no means of adjustment of the ignition timing. If the ignition timing is incorrect, or suspected of being incorrect, one of the ignition system components is at fault, and the system must be tested as described in the preceding Sections of this Chapter.
10 When the check is complete, fit the timing inspection cap using a new O-ring, and smear it and the cap threads with grease. Tighten the cap to the torque setting specified at the beginning of the Chapter.

20 Immobiliser system

General information

1 An immobiliser system (known as HISS – Honda Ignition Security System) is fitted either as standard or as an option (depending on market) as an anti-theft device. The system will only allow the machine to be started if the correct registered key is used to turn the ignition ON. The system consists of a transponder which is part of the ignition key, a receiver which is fitted around the ignition switch, and the electronic control module (ECM).
2 When the ignition is switched ON, the ECM sends power through the receiver to the transponder. The transponder sends a coded signal back through the receiver to the ECM. If the signal sent by the transponder matches the signal stored in the ECM memory, the HISS immobiliser indicator light in the instrument cluster comes on for two seconds then goes out, and the ECM allows the engine to be started. If the key code signal is not recognised, or if there is a fault in the system, the indicator light stays on. If the light stays on, refer to the fault diagnosis and troubleshooting Sections below. Likewise if the light does not come on at all.
3 The ECM can store the codes for up to four registered keys. These keys should be kept separately (i.e. not on the same key-ring) as the proximity of another key to the one being used in the switch can lead to the signal from it being jammed, and the bike will not start. The key has a built in transponder which can be damaged if the key is dropped or knocked, gets too hot, is too close to a magnetic object, or is submerged in water for too long. If all the keys are lost, the ECM must be replaced with a new one, so always make sure you have at least one spare key. If a new key is obtained, it must be registered into the system before the bike can be started with the key.

Key registration procedure

With old ignition switch

Special tool: *The following procedures refer to the Honda special tools (pt. nos. 07XMZ-MBW0101 and 070MZ-MEC0100) which are wiring loom adapters to connect a battery into the loom side of the crankshaft position (CKP) sensor wiring connector.*

4 Obtain a new key from a Honda dealer, and have it cut to match the original key.
5 On CBF1000/A models remove the right-hand fairing side panel (see Chapter 7). On CB1000R/RA models remove the right-hand side cover (see Chapter 7). Disconnect the crankshaft position (CKP) sensor wiring connector **(see illustration 7.38a or b)**. Connect the special tools together at the connector, then connect the wiring connector end to the loom side of the CKP sensor connector, and connect the red clip of the tool to the battery positive (+) terminal and the green clip to the battery negative (–) terminal.
6 Turn the ignition switch ON using your original key. The immobiliser indicator light should come on and stay on – if it starts to flash after ten seconds, then there is a fault in the system, which will have gone into fault diagnosis, and the pattern of the flashes it emits should be matched with the fault code (see below). Now disconnect the red clip from the battery positive terminal and leave it disconnected for at least two seconds, then reconnect it. The indicator should now come on for two seconds, then begin to flash repeatedly four times. This indicates that the system is in registration mode. At this point the registrations of all keys except the one in the switch will have been cancelled, so if you have another spare apart from the new one you want to register, this will also have to be registered.
7 Turn the ignition OFF and remove the original key, placing it well away from the receiver.
8 Insert the new key into the switch and turn it ON. The indicator should now come on for four seconds, then begin to flash repeatedly

19.4 Unscrew the timing inspection cap

four times. This indicates that the system has registered the new key. Turn the ignition OFF and remove the key.

9 To register any other spare keys that will have been cancelled, repeat Step 8. Up to four keys can be registered.

10 On completion turn the ignition OFF, then remove the special tool and reconnect the crankshaft position (CKP) sensor wiring connector. Now turn the ignition ON using any of the registered keys to return the system to normal mode.

11 Check that all registered keys can start the motorcycle.

With a new ignition switch

12 Obtain a new switch and two (or more) new keys.

13 Remove the faulty switch (see Chapter 8), but retain the HISS receiver to fit with the new switch.

14 On CBF1000/A models remove the right-hand fairing side panel (see Chapter 7). On CB1000R/RA models remove the right-hand side cover (see Chapter 7). Disconnect the crankshaft position (CKP) sensor wiring connector **(see illustration 7.38a or b)**. Connect the special tools together at the connector, then connect the wiring connector end to the loom side of the CKP sensor connector, and connect the red clip of the tool to the battery positive (+) terminal and the green clip to the battery negative (–) terminal.

15 Place one of the original registered keys for the faulty switch next to the receiver.

16 Connect the new ignition switch to its connector in the wiring loom, but keep it away from the receiver. Turn the new switch ON with one of the new keys. The immobiliser indicator light should come on and stay on, which means the ECM recognises the old key that is next to the receiver – if it starts to flash after ten seconds, then there is a fault in the system, which will have gone into fault diagnosis, and the pattern of the flashes it emits should be matched with the fault code (see below). Now disconnect the red clip from the battery positive terminal and leave it disconnected for at least two seconds, then reconnect it. The indicator should now come on for two seconds, then begin to flash repeatedly four times. This indicates that the system is in registration mode. At this point the registrations of all keys except the one near the receiver will have been cancelled.

17 Turn the ignition OFF and remove the new key.

18 Install the new ignition switch, then fit the receiver onto it (see Chapter 8).

19 Insert the new key into the switch and turn it ON. The indicator should now come on for four seconds, then begin to flash repeatedly four times. This indicates that the system has registered the new key. If the indicator starts to flash after ten seconds, then there is a fault in the system, which will have gone into fault diagnosis, and the pattern of the flashes it emits should be matched with the fault code (see below). Turn the ignition OFF and disconnect the red clip of the special tool from the battery positive terminal.

20 Turn the ignition ON using the newly registered key. The indicator light should come on for two seconds, then go off.

21 Turn the ignition OFF and reconnect the red clip to the battery positive terminal.

22 Turn the ignition ON using the newly registered key. The indicator light should come on and stay on. Now disconnect the red clip from the battery positive terminal and leave it disconnected for at least two seconds, then reconnect it. The indicator should now come on for two seconds, then begin to flash repeatedly four times. This indicates that the system is in registration mode. At this point the registrations of all old keys (for the faulty switch) are cancelled.

23 Turn the ignition OFF and remove the key, placing it well away from the receiver.

24 Insert the second new unregistered key and turn the ignition ON. The indicator should now come on for four seconds, then begin to flash repeatedly four times. This indicates that the system has registered the second new key. Turn the ignition OFF and remove the key.

25 To register any other new spare keys, repeat Step 24. Up to four keys can be registered.

26 On completion turn the ignition OFF, then remove the special tool and reconnect the CKP sensor wiring connector. Now turn the ignition ON using any of the registered keys to return the system to normal mode.

27 Check that all newly registered keys can start the motorcycle.

With a new ECM (electronic control module)

28 Obtain a new ECM along with two new keys. Install the new ECM (see Section 7). Have the keys cut to match the original key for your ignition switch.

29 Insert a new key into the switch and turn it ON. The indicator should now come on for two seconds, then begin to flash repeatedly four times. This indicates that the system has registered the new key. If the indicator stays on for ten seconds then starts to flash, then there is a fault in the system, which will have gone into fault diagnosis, and the pattern of the flashes it emits should be matched with the fault code (see below).

30 Turn the ignition OFF and remove the key.

31 Insert the second new key and turn the ignition ON. The indicator should now come on for two seconds, then begin to flash repeatedly four times. This indicates that the system has registered the second new key.

32 Turn the ignition OFF and remove the key.

33 The new ECM will only register two new keys at this stage. If you have a third key to register, refer to Steps 4 to 10 to register it, noting that you will need the special tool mentioned therein.

34 Check that both newly registered keys can start the motorcycle.

Fault diagnosis

35 There are two fault diagnosis modes, one for faults which occur during normal use, and one for a fault that occurs when registering a new key. Make sure you refer to the correct table below when matching the fault code pattern.

36 If the indicator light has come on and stayed on during normal use, on CBF1000/A models remove the right-hand fairing side panel (see Chapter 7), and on CB1000R/RA models remove the right-hand side cover (see Chapter 7). Disconnect the crankshaft position (CKP) sensor wiring connector **(see illustration 7.38a or b)**. Connect the special tools together at the connector, then connect the wiring connector end to the loom side of the CKP sensor connector, and connect the red clip of the tool to the battery positive (+) terminal and the green clip to the battery negative (–) terminal.

37 Turn the ignition switch ON. The indicator light will come on for ten seconds, then start to flash. This means it has entered diagnostic mode, and the pattern of the flashes indicates the fault that has occurred. The pattern repeats continuously. Match the pattern with the fault codes below, making sure you refer to the relevant table. If the indicator stays on after ten seconds and does not flash, then there is no fault logged in the system.

If fault is indicated during normal use		
Flash pattern	Fault	Solution
Two short, one long, one short	Faulty ECM	Install new ECM
Two short, two long	Faulty receiver or wiring	Follow Troubleshooting procedure below
One long, three short	Signal jammed by other key	Place other key well away from receiver
One long, two short, one long	Signal jammed by other key	Place other key well away from receiver

If fault is indicated during key registration		
Flash pattern	Fault	Solution
One short, one long, one short, one long	Key already registered	Use a new or cancelled key
Two short, two long	Faulty receiver or wiring	Follow *Troubleshooting* procedure below
One short, one long, two short	Key already registered on old ECM	Use a new key

Troubleshooting procedure

Indicator light does not come on when ignition switched ON

38 Check the fuses (see Chapter 8).
39 If the fuses are good, make sure the engine is in neutral then turn the ignition ON and check whether the neutral light has come on.
40 If the light has not come on, on CBF1000/A models remove the fairing, and on CB1000R/RA models remove the instrument cowl (see Chapter 7). Pull back the rubber boot on the instrument cluster wiring connector. Using a voltmeter, connect the positive (+) probe to the black/brown wire terminal (connector still connected) and the negative (–) probe to the green (CBF1000/A models) or green/black (CB1000R/RA models) wire terminal in the connector. With the ignition ON there should be battery voltage. If voltage is present, the instrument cluster is faulty (see Chapter 8). If there is no voltage, check for continuity in the wiring, referring to the wiring diagrams at the end of Chapter 8. The green or green/black wire goes to earth (ground).
41 If the lights have come on, refer to Section 7 to access the ECM and disconnect the ECM grey wiring connector. Using a voltmeter, connect the positive (+) probe to the white/red wire terminal on the loom side of the ECM connector and the negative (–) probe to earth (ground). Turn the ignition ON – there should be battery voltage.
42 If there was no voltage, using a voltmeter, connect the positive (+) probe to the white/red wire terminal in the instrument cluster connector and the negative (–) probe to earth. Turn the ignition ON – there should be no voltage for two seconds, then there should be battery voltage. If there is no voltage after two seconds, check for continuity in the white/red wire, and also in the green or green/black wire to earth, referring to the wiring diagrams at the end of Chapter 8. If voltage is present, the instrument cluster is faulty (see Chapter 8).
43 If there is voltage in Step 41, using a voltmeter, connect the positive (+) probe to the black/white (ECM) wire terminal on the loom side of the ECM connector and the negative (–) probe to earth (ground). Turn the ignition ON – there should be battery voltage. If there is no voltage, check for continuity in the black/white wire. If voltage is present, check for continuity to earth (ground) in the green wire. If the wiring is good, check the ECM connector for loose, damaged or corroded terminals. If the connector is good, then the ECM could be faulty, and should be checked by a Honda dealer.

Indicator light stays on when ignition switched ON

44 Check that none of the other registered keys are close to the receiver. If they are, remove them and try the ignition again.
45 Turn the ignition ON with a spare key and check the indicator light, which should come on for two seconds, then go out. If it does, the first key is faulty. If it doesn't, perform the fault diagnosis procedure described above. If a fault code is displayed, use the appropriate table to determine the fault and the solution.
46 If no fault code is displayed, or the system does not go into fault diagnosis mode, refer to Section 7 to access the ECM and disconnect the ECM grey wiring connector. Using a voltmeter, connect the positive (+) probe to the white/red wire terminal on the loom side of the connector and the negative (–) probe to earth (ground). Turn the ignition ON – there should be battery voltage. If there is no voltage, check for continuity in the white/red wire between the ECM and the indicator unit.
47 If there is voltage, check for continuity in the yellow and white/yellow wires between the ECM and the crankshaft position (CKP) sensor, referring to the wiring diagrams at the end of Chapter 8. If there is no continuity, trace the fault and repair or replace the wiring as necessary. If there is continuity, the ECM could be faulty and should be taken to a Honda dealer for assessment.

Fault code indicated by flash pattern

48 If the 'two short, two long' flash pattern has been indicated during the fault diagnosis procedure, on CBF1000/A models remove the fairing (see Chapter 7), and on CB1000R/RA models remove the headlight (see Chapter 8). Trace the wiring from the receiver on the ignition switch and disconnect it at the 4-pin connector. Using a voltmeter, connect the positive (+) probe to the yellow/red wire terminal on the loom side of the receiver connector and the negative (–) probe to earth (ground). Turn the ignition ON – there should be approximately 5 volts present. If there is no voltage, check for continuity in the yellow/red wire between the ECM and the receiver, and repair or replace the wiring if there is no continuity.

20.52 HISS receiver screws (arrowed)

49 If there is 5 volts present, check for continuity to earth (ground) in the green/orange wire on the loom side of the connector, and repair or replace the wiring if there is no continuity.
50 If the wiring is good, using a voltmeter, connect the positive (+) probe to the pink wire terminal on the loom side of the receiver connector and the negative (–) probe to earth (ground). Turn the ignition ON – there should be approximately 5 volts present. If there is, the receiver is faulty.
51 If there is no voltage, check for continuity in the orange/blue and pink wires between the ECM and the receiver, and repair or replace the wiring if there is no continuity between the connectors, or if there is continuity in either to earth (ground). If the wiring is good, the receiver is faulty.

Replacement

52 To replace the receiver, on CBF1000/A models remove the fairing (see Chapter 7), and on CB1000R/RA models remove the headlight/sidelight/instrument cluster assembly (see Chapter 8). Trace the wiring from the receiver on the ignition switch and disconnect it at the 4-pin connector. Feed the wiring back to the receiver, freeing it from any ties and noting its routing. Undo the screws and remove the receiver, turning the handlebars as required for best access **(see illustration)**. If you can't easily access the screws, displace the top yoke (refer to Chapter 1, Section 14, following the relevant Steps).
53 To replace the ECM see Section 7.

Chapter 5
Frame and suspension

Contents

	Section number
Footrests, brake pedal and gearchange lever	3
Fork overhaul	8
Fork oil change	7
Fork removal and installation	6
Frame inspection and repair	2
General information	1
Handlebars and levers	5
Handlebar switches	see Chapter 8
Rear shock absorber	11
Rear suspension linkage (CBF models)	12

	Section number
Sidestand and centrestand	4
Stand lubrication	see Chapter 1
Sidestand switch	see Chapter 8
Steering head bearing check and adjustment	see Chapter 1
Steering head bearings	10
Steering stem	9
Suspension adjustment	14
Suspension check	see Chapter 1
Swingarm	13

Degrees of difficulty

Easy, suitable for novice with little experience	**Fairly easy,** suitable for beginner with some experience	**Fairly difficult,** suitable for competent DIY mechanic	**Difficult,** suitable for experienced DIY mechanic	**Very difficult,** suitable for expert DIY or professional

Specifications

Front forks

Fork oil type .... 10W fork oil (Honda Ultra Cushion 10W)
Fork oil capacity
   CBF1000/A models .... 437 ± 2.5 cc
   CB1000R model .... 511 ± 2.5 cc
   CB1000RA model .... 542 ± 2.5 cc
Fork oil level*
   CBF1000/A models .... 129 mm
   CB1000R model .... 91 mm
   CB1000RA model .... 67 mm
Fork spring free length (min)
   CBF1000/A models
     Standard .... 358.8 mm
     Service limit .... 352 mm
   CB1000R/RA models
     Standard .... 249.7 mm
     Service limit .... 244.7 mm
Fork tube runout limit .... 0.2 mm

*Oil level is measured from the top of the tube with the fork spring removed and the leg fully compressed.

Steering head bearings

Bearing pre-load (see text)
   CBF1000/A models .... 9.8 to 13.7 N (1.0 to 1.4 kgf; 2.2 to 3.1 lbf)
   CB1000R/RA models .... 9.8 to 12.5 N (1.0 to 1.3 kgf; 2.2 to 2.9 lbf)

5•2 Frame and suspension

Torque settings

Clutch master cylinder clamp bolts	12 Nm
Footrest bracket bolts	
CBF1000/A models	27 Nm
CB1000/RA models	37 Nm
Fork damper cartridge bolt	
CBF1000/A models	20 Nm
CB1000R/RA models	34 Nm
Fork top bolt	
CBF1000/A models	22 Nm
CB1000R/RA models	34 Nm
Fork clamp bolts	
Top yoke	22 Nm
Bottom yoke	
CBF1000/A models	39 Nm
CB1000R/RA models	27 Nm
Front brake master cylinder clamp bolts	12 Nm
Gearchange lever pivot bolt	27 Nm
Handlebar clamp bolts (CB1000R/RA models)	27 Nm
Shock absorber bolts/nuts	42 Nm
Sidestand pivot bolt	
CBF1000/A models	10 Nm
CB1000R/RA models	15 Nm
Sidestand pivot bolt nut – all models	39 Nm
Silencer mounting bolt/nut (CB1000R/RA models)	22 Nm
Steering head bearing adjuster nut	
CBF1000/A models	25 Nm
CB1000R/RA models	26 Nm
Steering stem nut	103 Nm
Suspension linkage bolts/nuts (CBF1000/A models)	42 Nm
Swingarm	
Pivot bolt nut	98 Nm
Pivot bracket bolt nuts	69 Nm

1 General information

All models have a mono-backbone frame, made from steel on CBF1000/A models and aluminium on CB1000R/RA models, which uses the engine as a stressed member.

On CBF1000/A models front suspension is by a pair of 41 mm oil-damped telescopic forks with cartridge dampers. The forks are not adjustable. At the rear, a box-section steel swingarm acts on a single shock absorber via a rising-rate linkage. The swingarm pivots through the frame. The shock absorber has adjustable spring pre-load.

On CB1000R/RA models front suspension is by a pair of 43 mm upside-down oil-damped telescopic forks with cartridge dampers. The forks have adjustable spring pre-load and both rebound and compression damping. At the rear, a single-sided aluminium swingarm acts on a single shock absorber. The swingarm pivots through the frame. The shock absorber has adjustable spring pre-load and rebound damping.

2 Frame inspection and repair

1 The frame should not require attention unless accident damage has occurred. In most cases, fitting a new frame is the only satisfactory remedy for such damage. A few frame specialists have the jigs and other equipment necessary for straightening frames to the required standard of accuracy, but even then there is no simple way of assessing to what extent the frame may have been over stressed.

2 After a high mileage, the frame should be examined closely for signs of cracking or splitting at the welded joints. Loose engine mounting bolts can cause ovaling or fracturing of the mounting points. Minor damage can often be repaired by specialised welding, depending on the extent and nature of the damage.

3 Remember that a frame that is out of alignment will cause handling problems. If, as the result of an accident, misalignment is suspected, it will be necessary to strip the machine completely so the frame can be thoroughly checked.

3 Footrests, brake pedal and gearchange lever

Footrests

Removal

1 On CBF1000/A models, to remove the rider's footrests remove the split pin and washer from the bottom of the footrest pivot pin, then withdraw the pivot pin and remove the footrest (see illustration). Note the fitting

3.1a Remove the split pin (arrowed) and washer, then draw the pivot pin out the top

Frame and suspension 5•3

3.1b Remove the split pin (arrowed) . . .

3.1c . . . then undo the screw (arrowed) and draw the pivot pin out the top

3.1d Unscrew the bolts (arrowed) to release the rubber

of the return spring. To remove the passenger footrests, remove the split pin from the bottom of the footrest pivot pin, then undo the pivot pin screw, withdraw the pin and remove the footrest **(see illustrations)**. Note the washer against the inner end of the rubber. If necessary you can replace the footrest rubbers with new ones – for the rider's footrests unscrew the bolts on the underside to release the rubber, and note the arrangement of the setting plates and cushion **(see illustration)**. The passenger footrest rubbers are a sliding fit on the peg, with the outer end locating around the plate.

2 On CB1000R/RA models, remove the split pin and washer from the bottom of the footrest pivot pin, then withdraw the pivot pin and remove the footrest **(see illustration)**. On the rider's footrests, note the fitting of the return spring. On the passenger footrests, note the fitting of the detent plate, ball and spring, and take care not to let the ball and spring ping away when removing the footrest.

Installation

3 Installation is the reverse of removal. Apply a small amount of grease to the pivot pin.

Brake pedal

Removal

4 On CB1000R/RA models remove the exhaust silencer (see Chapter 4).
5 Straighten the ends of the split pin and withdraw it from the master cylinder pushrod clevis pin **(see illustration)**. Withdraw the

3.2 Remove the split pin (arrowed) and washer, then draw the pivot pin out the top

clevis pin and detach the pushrod from the pedal.
6 Unhook the brake pedal return spring and the brake light switch spring from the pedal.
7 Release the circlip securing the brake pedal, then remove the washer. Slide the pedal off its pivot.

Installation

8 Installation is the reverse of removal, noting the following:
● Clean any old grease off the pedal and pivot, then apply fresh grease.
● Slide the pedal onto the pivot, followed by the washer. Make sure the circlip locates correctly in the groove, and use a new one if the old one deformed when removed **(see illustration 3.5)**. Connect the springs.
● Use a new split pin on the master cylinder pushrod clevis pin.

3.5 Remove the split pin (A) and clevis pin, unhook the springs (B), then release the circlip (C) and remove the washer and pedal

● Check the operation of the rear brake light switch (see Chapter 1).

Gearchange lever and linkage

Removal

9 Note the alignment of the existing punch marks between the gearchange linkage arm and shaft, or mark the alignment of the shaft with the slit in the linkage arm if they are not clear **(see illustration)**. Unscrew the linkage arm bolt and slide the arm off the shaft
10 On CBF1000/A models unscrew the linkage pivot bolt, noting the washer behind the pivot, then unscrew the lever pivot bolt, again noting the washer, and remove the lever and linkage assembly **(see illustrations)**.
11 On CB1000R/RA models unscrew the

3.9 Mark the alignment then unscrew the bolt and slide the arm off the shaft

3.10a Linkage pivot bolt (A), lever pivot bolt (B)

3.10b Note the washer fitted behind each pivot

5•4 Frame and suspension

gearchange lever pivot bolt, noting the washer behind the lever, and remove the lever and linkage assembly **(see illustration)**.

12 If you want to separate the lever from the linkage rod note how far the rod is threaded into the lever and arm as this determines the height of the lever relative to the footrest. Slacken the linkage rod locknuts, then unscrew the rod and separate it from the lever and the arm – the rod is reverse-threaded on one end and will simultaneously unscrew from both lever and arm when turned in the one direction.

Installation

13 Installation is the reverse of removal, noting the following:
- Clean off all old grease from the pivot components and apply fresh grease. Fit new pivot seals if necessary **(see illustration)**.
- Tighten the lever pivot bolt to the torque setting specified at the beginning of the Chapter.
- Align the slit in the linkage arm clamp with the mark made on the gearchange shaft.
- Adjust the gear lever height as required by screwing the linkage rod in or out of the lever and arm – to do this with the assembly in situ it is best to remove the oil filter (see Chapter 1) and sidestand assembly (see Section 4) to access the upper nut on the rod. Tighten the locknuts on completion.

3.11 Lever pivot bolt (arrowed)

4 Sidestand and centrestand

Sidestand

Removal

1 Support the bike on the centrestand on CBF1000A models, or using an auxiliary stand on all other models.
2 Carefully unhook and remove the stand springs **(see illustrations)**.
3 Unscrew the sidestand switch bolt and displace the switch, noting how it locates **(see illustrations)** – there is no need to disconnect its wiring connector or remove it completely, just let it hang from its wiring.
4 Unscrew the nut from the pivot bolt **(see illustrations)**. Unscrew the pivot bolt and remove the stand.

3.13 Fit a new seal on each side if required

Installation

5 Apply grease to the pivot bolt shank and tighten the bolt to the torque setting specified at the beginning of the Chapter. Fit the nut finger-tight, then counter-hold the bolt and tighten it to the specified torque **(see illustration 4.4a or b)**.
6 Fit the sidestand switch **(see illustration 4.3a or b)**.
7 Reconnect the springs and check that they hold the stand securely up when not in use – an accident is almost certain to occur if the stand extends while the machine is in motion **(see illustration 4.2a or b)**.
8 Check the operation of the stand and switch (see Chapter 1).

4.2a Stand springs (arrowed) – CBF1000/A

4.2b Stand springs (arrowed) – CB1000R/RA

4.3a Sidestand switch bolt (arrowed) – CBF1000/A

4.3b Sidestand switch bolt (arrowed) – CB1000R/RA

4.4a Sidestand pivot bolt nut (arrowed) – CBF1000/A

4.4b Sidestand pivot bolt nut (arrowed) – CB1000R/RA

Frame and suspension 5•5

4.10 Unhook the springs (arrowed) . . .

4.11 . . . then unscrew the bolt and withdraw the pivot

Centrestand (CBF1000A)

9 Remove the silencers (see Chapter 4).
10 Carefully unhook and remove the stand springs **(see illustration)**.
11 Unscrew the pivot holder bolt **(see illustration)**. Withdraw the pivot and remove the stand.
12 Installation is the reverse of removal. Apply grease to the pivot shaft.

5 Handlebars and levers

Note: *The handlebars can be displaced from the top yoke without detaching any of the assemblies from them – follow Step 9 only. Rest the assembly on some rag.*

Handlebar removal

1 As a precaution, remove the fuel tank (see Chapter 4) and any other painted or vulnerable components as required according to model – though not actually necessary, this will prevent the possibility of any damage in case a tool slips or you drop something.
2 On CB1000R/RA models remove the mirrors (see Chapter 7).
3 Undo the handlebar end-weight retaining screws and remove the weights from the ends of the handlebar **(see illustration)**.
4 Disconnect the wires from the brake light switch **(see illustration)**. Unscrew the two master cylinder assembly clamp bolts and position the assembly clear of the handlebar, making sure no strain is placed on the hydraulic hose **(see illustration)**. Keep the master cylinder reservoir upright to prevent possible fluid leakage.
5 Disconnect the wires from the clutch switch **(see illustration)**. Unscrew the two master cylinder assembly clamp bolts and position the assembly clear of the handlebar, making sure no strain is placed on the hydraulic hose **(see illustration)**. Keep the master cylinder reservoir upright to prevent possible fluid leakage.

5.3 Remove the handlebar end-weights

5.4a Disconnect the wiring connectors (arrowed)

5.4b Unscrew the brake master cylinder clamp bolts (arrowed) and displace the assembly

5.5a Disconnect the wiring connectors (arrowed)

5.5b Unscrew the clutch master cylinder clamp bolts (arrowed) and displace the assembly

5•6 Frame and suspension

5.6a Switch housing screws (arrowed) – CBF1000/A, right-hand switch

5.6b Switch housing screws (arrowed) – CBF1000/A, left-hand switch

5.6c Switch housing screws (arrowed) – CB1000R/A, right-hand switch

5.6d Switch housing screws (arrowed) – CB1000R/RA, left-hand switch

6 Unscrew the handlebar switch housing screws and detach the housings **(see illustrations)**. Free the cable-ties from the handlebars where fitted.

7 On CB1000R/RA models unscrew the two throttle pulley housing screws and detach the housing **(see illustration)**.

8 If required, slide the grip off the left-hand end – if it has been glued on, you will probably have to slit it with a knife to remove it, which means replacing it with a new one. On CBF1000/A models also slide the switch housing plate off.

9 Carefully prise the blanking caps out of the handlebar bolts **(see illustration)**. Unscrew the bolts, remove the handlebar clamp(s) and slide the handlebar out of the throttle pulley **(see illustration)**.

Handlebar holders (CBF1000/A models)

10 To remove the handlebar holders from the top yoke, first displace or remove the handlebars. Unscrew the nuts on the

5.7 Throttle pulley housing screws

5.9a Prise the blanking caps out then unscrew the bolts (arrowed) . . .

5.9b . . . and displace or remove the handlebars

Frame and suspension 5•7

5.10 Handlebar holder bolt nut (arrowed)

5.11 Inner weight retaining tab hole (arrowed)

5.12a Fit the clamps with the punch marks to the front

underside of the yoke and remove the holders **(see illustration)**. Note that the holders can be turned through 180° to move the handlebars slightly forwards or back (depending on their previous position) – there is a cut-away in the lower edge, which points to the rear for the standard position and to the front for the forward position.

Handlebar weights

11 If a new handlebar is being installed, you need to transfer the inner weights from the old bar to the new one – to do this, reinstall the end-weight and tighten its screw **(see illustration 5.3)**. Squirt some lubricant (such as WD40) into the inner weight retainer tab hole, then press down on the tab using a screwdriver, then twist and pull on the end-weight, drawing the inner weight assembly out **(see illustration)**. Remove the end-weight and discard the retainer as a new one should be used. Check the condition of the rubbers on the inner weight and fit new ones if they are damaged, deformed or deteriorated.

Installation

12 Installation is the reverse of removal, noting the following.
- To fit new grips onto the throttle twistgrip and left handlebar, apply a suitable glue (Pro Honda handgrip cement or equivalent) to each, making sure they are clean, then rotate the grip when in place to evenly distribute the glue. Allow the glue to fully dry before riding the bike.
- When fitting the right handlebar, smear some grease onto throttle twistgrip sliding surface. Slide the throttle pulley housing onto the handlebar before fitting the handlebar onto the yoke.
- On CBF1000/A models, if the handlebar holders are in the standard position (see Step 10), align the lower of the two punch marks on the back of the handlebar with the clamp/holder mating surfaces. If the handlebars are in the forward position, align the upper of the two punch marks on the back of the handlebar with the clamp/holder mating surfaces. Fit the handlebar clamps with the punch mark to the front, and tighten the front bolts first, then the rear **(see illustration 5.12a)**. Fit the caps into the bolts.

5.12b Align the clamp mating surfaces with the punch mark (arrowed)

- On CB1000R/RA models align the punch mark on the back of the handlebar with the clamp/holder mating surfaces **(see illustration 5.12b)**. Tighten the handlebar clamp bolts to the torque setting specified at the beginning of the Chapter, tightening the front bolts first, then the rear. Fit the caps into the bolts.
- When fitting the handlebar inner weights, locate the tab on the retainer in the hole in the handlebar.
- When fitting the handlebar end-weights, align the boss with the cut-out on the inner weight inside the handlebar **(see illustration 5.3)**.
- Make sure the front brake and clutch master cylinder clamps are installed with the UP mark facing up **(see illustrations 5.4b and 5.5b)**, and with the clamp mating surfaces aligned with the punch mark on the top of the handlebar. Tighten the master cylinder

5.12c Locate the pin (A) in the hole (B)

clamp bolts to the specified torque setting, tightening the top bolt first.
- Make sure the pin in the bottom half of each switch housing and the throttle pulley housing on CB1000R/RA models locates in its hole in the handlebar **(see illustration 5.12c)**. Do not forget to fit the plate with the left-hand housing on CBF1000/A models. Tighten the front housing screw first, then the rear. Secure the wiring with new cable-ties where removed.
- Do not forget to reconnect the front brake light switch and clutch switch wiring connectors **(see illustrations 5.4a and 5.5a)**.

Levers

13 Undo the lever pivot screw locknut, then undo the pivot screw and remove the lever – there is a bush in the clutch lever that could drop out, so take care not to lose it **(see illustrations)**.

5.13a Front brake lever locknut (A) and pivot screw (B)

5.13b Clutch lever locknut (A) and pivot screw (B)

5•8 Frame and suspension

6.4a Fork clamp bolt (A) and fork top bolt (B) – CBF1000/A

6.4b Fork clamp bolt (A) and fork top bolt (B) – CB1000R/RA

14 Installation is the reverse of removal. Apply silicone grease to all sliding surfaces and contact points. Apply a spray lubricant such as WD40, or a dry-film Teflon lubricant to the brake lever span adjuster mechanism. Fit the bush into the clutch lever, and locate the pushrod tip into its hole. Tighten the pivot screw lightly, then counter-hold it and tighten the nut.

6 Fork removal and installation

Removal

1 If the fork oil is being changed, or if the fork is to be disassembled, on CB1000R/RA models adjust spring pre-load and rebound damping to its minimum setting, noting the number of turns made so it can be reset the same (see Section 14).

2 Remove the front mudguard (see Chapter 7). On CBF1000/A models remove the fairing side panels (see Chapter 7). Note the routing of all cables, hoses and wiring around the forks. Measure or note the amount of protrusion (if any) of the fork inner tube above the top yoke.

3 Remove the front wheel (see Chapter 6). Tie the front brake calipers and hoses back so that they are out of the way.

4 Working on one fork at a time, slacken the fork clamp bolt in the top yoke (see illustrations).

5 If the fork oil is being changed, or if the fork is to be disassembled, slacken the fork top bolt (see illustration 6.4a or b).

6 Slacken the fork clamp bolt(s) in the bottom yoke, and remove the fork by twisting it and pulling it downwards (see illustrations).

HAYNES HiNT *If the fork legs are seized in the yokes, spray the area with penetrating oil and allow time for it to soak in before trying again.*

Installation

7 Remove all traces of corrosion from the fork tube and the yokes. Slide the fork up through the bottom yoke and into the top yoke, making sure all cables, hoses and wiring are routed on the correct side of the fork (see illustration 6.6c).

8 Set the amount of protrusion of the fork tube above the top yoke as noted on removal – Honda specify that the top of the fork tube (not the top bolt) should be flush with the upper surface of the yoke (see illustration 6.4a or b).

9 Tighten the fork clamp bolt(s) in the bottom yoke to the torque setting specified at the beginning of the Chapter (see illustration 6.6a or b).

10 If the fork oil was changed or if the fork has been dismantled, tighten the fork top bolt to the specified torque setting (see illustration 6.4a or b).

11 Now tighten the fork clamp bolt in the top yoke to the specified torque.

12 Install the front wheel (see Chapter 6) and the front mudguard (see Chapter 7).

13 Check the operation of the front forks and brakes before taking the machine out on the road.

14 On CB1000R/RA models reset the spring pre-load and rebound damping adjusters as noted or required (see Section 14).

7 Fork oil change

1 After a high mileage the fork oil will deteriorate and its damping and lubrication qualities will be impaired. Always change the oil in both fork legs.

2 Remove the fork – on CB1000R/RA models

6.6a Bottom yoke fork clamp bolt (arrowed) – CBF1000/A

6.6b Bottom yoke fork clamp bolts (arrowed) – CB1000R/RA

6.6c Draw the fork down and out of the yokes

Frame and suspension 5•9

7.3 Unscrew the top bolt...

7.4 ...then counter-hold the nut and thread the top bolt off the rod

7.5a Remove the spacer...

make sure you adjust the pre-load and rebound damping to its minimum (see Section 14), and on all models loosen the top bolt while the leg is still clamped in the bottom yoke (see Section 6).

CBF1000/A models

3 Unscrew the fork top bolt from the top of the inner tube **(see illustration)**. The bolt will remain on the damper rod, held by the locknut on its top.
4 Slide the inner tube down gently until it seats on the bottom. Hold the top bolt and push the spacer down against the spring to expose the locknut, and fit a spanner onto it. Counter-hold the locknut and unscrew the top bolt **(see illustration)**.
5 Remove the spacer, then hook the spacer seat and spring out of the tube **(see illustrations)**.
6 Invert the fork leg over a suitable container and pump the fork and damper rod several times to expel as much fork oil as possible **(see illustration 7.16)**. Support the fork upside down in the container for a while to allow as much oil as possible to drain, then pump the fork and rod again. If the fork oil contains metal particles inspect the fork bushes for wear (see Section 8). Wipe any excess oil off the spring and spacer.
7 Stand the fork upright. Slowly pour in the specified quantity of the specified grade of fork oil **(see illustration 7.17a)**. Now pump the fork and damper rod slowly at least ten times each to distribute the oil evenly and expel all air from the damper. Slide the inner tube down gently

7.5b ...the spring seat...

until it seats on the bottom. Measure the oil level from the top of the tube **(see illustration 7.17b)**. Add or subtract oil until it is at the level specified at the beginning of this Chapter.
8 Make sure the locknut is at the bottom of its threads on the damper rod. Pull the damper rod and inner tube out as far as possible, then fit the spring with the closer wound coils at the bottom **(see illustration 7.5c)**. Keeping the damper rod extended, fit the spacer seat and spacer **(see illustrations 7.5b and a)**.
9 Keeping the damper rod extended push down on the spacer to compress the spring and thread the top bolt onto the damper rod **(see illustration)**. Counter-hold the locknut using a spanner as before and tighten the top bolt securely against it **(see illustration 7.4)**.
10 If the top bolt O-ring is damaged or deteriorated fit a new one. Smear some fork oil onto the O-ring. Extend the inner tube and thread the top bolt into it, making sure it does not

7.5c ...and the spring

cross-thread, and tighten it as much as possible holding the inner tube by hand **(see illustration)**.
Note: *Tighten the top bolt to the specified torque setting when the fork has been installed in the bike and is held in the bottom yoke, but before the top yoke clamp bolt is tightened.*
11 Install the fork (see Section 6).

CB1000R/RA models

12 Unscrew the fork top bolt from the top of the outer tube **(see illustration)**. The bolt will remain on the damper rod, held by the locknut on its top.
13 Slide the outer tube down gently until it seats on the bottom. With the aid of an assistant, pull up on the fork top bolt and spacer seat, then press down on the spacer to compress the spring and expose the locknut on the bottom of the damping adjuster. **Note:** *Honda produces service tools (spacer holder Pt. No. 070MF-MBZC110 and*

7.9 Thread the top bolt onto the rod

7.10 Thread the top bolt into the fork tube

7.12 Thread the top bolt out of the tube

5•10 Frame and suspension

7.13a Spacer holding tool and slotted washer – home-made equivalent to the Honda tools

7.13b Push down on the holder and slip the washer under the nut

stopper plate Pt. No. 070MF-MBZC130) to do this. Alternatively, use the set-up shown, making sure the tool is wide enough to fit over the tube *(see illustration)*. Insert the stopper plate or slotted washer under the locknut and on top of the spacer, keeping the spacer seat above it *(see illustration)*. Carefully release the pressure on the spacer and allow the plate or slotted washer to rest against the underside of the locknut under spring pressure.

14 Counter-hold the pre-load adjuster and loosen the locknut, then thread the top bolt off the damper rod and draw the damping adjuster rod out *(see illustrations)*. **Note:** *The top bolt assembly should not be disassembled.* Remove the spacer seat.

15 Push down on the spacer and remove the plate or slotted washer, then carefully allow the spring to relax *(see illustration)*. Remove the spacer *(see illustration)*. Withdraw the spring from the tube, noting which way up it fits *(see illustration)*.

16 Invert the fork leg over a suitable container and pump the fork and damper rod several times to expel as much fork oil as possible *(see illustration)*. Support the fork upside down in the container for a while to allow as much oil as possible to drain, then pump the fork and rod again. If the fork oil contains metal particles inspect the fork bushes for wear (see Section 8). Wipe any excess oil off the spring and spacer.

17 Stand the fork upright. Slowly pour in the specified quantity of the specified grade of fork oil *(see illustration)*. Draw the outer tube fully up, then cover the top with your hand and slowly push it down. Remove your hand and draw it up, and repeat two or three times. Now pump the damper rod slowly at least ten times – this distributes the oil and expels all air from the damper. Slide the inner tube down gently until it seats on the bottom, and leave to stand for five minutes. Then measure the oil level from the top of the tube *(see illustration)*. Add or subtract oil until it is

7.14a Hold the pre-load adjuster and loosen the locknut . . .

7.14b . . . then unscrew the top bolt and draw the adjuster rod out, and remove the seat (arrowed)

7.15a Remove the slotted washer . . .

7.15b . . . the spacer . . .

7.15c . . . and the spring

7.16 Drain the oil as described

7.17a Fill the fork slowly to prevent air bubbles and overfilling

7.17b Measure the distance from the top of the tube to the oil

Frame and suspension 5•11

7.18a Make sure the tapered end is at the top

7.18b Tie some wire under the locknut . . .

7.18c . . . then fit the spacer

7.19a Push the spacer down and fit the washer under the nut

7.19b Set the locknut 13 mm from the top

at the level specified at the beginning of this Chapter.

18 To make it easier to re-fit the slotted washer later, thread the locknut up to the top of the damper rod. Pull the damper rod out as far as possible, then fit the spring with the tapered end at the top **(see illustration)**. Fit a piece of thin wire around the rod under the locknut to help keep it extended **(see illustration)**. Fit the spacer, sliding it down over the wire **(see illustration)**.

19 Keeping the damper rod extended push down on the spacer to compress the spring (see Step 13), then insert the stopper plate or slotted washer under the locknut **(see illustration)**. Remove the wire. Set the top of the locknut about 13 mm down from the top of its threads on the damper rod **(see illustration)**.

20 Fit the spacer seat, then insert the damping adjuster rod and thread the top bolt onto the damper rod **(see illustrations)**. Counter-hold the pre-load adjuster using a spanner as before and tighten the locknut securely against it **(see illustration 7.14a)**. Press down on the spacer to compress the spring and remove the plate or slotted washer, then carefully release the spring pressure **(see illustration 7.13b)**. Remove the holding tool.

21 If the top bolt O-ring is damaged or deteriorated fit a new one **(see illustration)**. Smear some fork oil onto the O-ring. Extend the outer tube and thread the top bolt into it, making sure it does not cross-thread, and tighten it as much as possible holding the inner tube by hand. **Note:** *Tighten the top bolt to the specified torque setting when the fork has been installed in the bike and is held in the bottom yoke, but before the top yoke clamp bolt is tightened.*

22 Make sure the rebound damping adjuster turns in three whole turns before seating – if it doesn't the position of the locknut on the damper rod must be adjusted, setting it slightly higher if the adjuster turns less than three turns, and lower if it turns more. Follow Steps 12 to 14, but do not thread the top bolt fully off the damper rod, then reset the locknut as required and tighten it, following Steps 20 and 21.

23 Install the fork (see Section 6). Set the spring pre-load and rebound damping adjusters as noted or required (see Section 14).

8 Fork overhaul

CBF1000/A models

Disassembly

1 Remove the fork – make sure you loosen the top bolt while the leg is still clamped in the bottom yoke (see Section 6). Always dismantle the fork legs separately to avoid interchanging parts and thus causing an accelerated rate of wear. Store all components in separate, clearly marked containers.

7.20a Fit the seat . . .

7.20b . . . and the top bolt assembly

7.21 Check the O-ring (arrowed), then thread the top bolt into the tube

5•12 Frame and suspension

8.2 Remove the protector, noting how it locates in the cut-out (arrowed)

8.3 Slacken the damper cartridge bolt

8.6a Withdraw the damper cartridge . . .

2 Remove the fork protector, noting how it locates **(see illustration)**.
3 Lay the fork flat on the bench with the caliper mounting lugs to the left. Remove the wheel axle clamp bolt. Hold the fork down and slacken the damper cartridge bolt in the base of the fork **(see illustration)**. If the damper cartridge rotates inside the fork whilst attempting to unscrew the bolt, compress the fork so that the spring exerts pressure on the cartridge body whilst the bolt is unscrewed. Alternatively, if available use an air wrench.
4 Refer to Section 7, Steps 3 to 6 and drain the oil from the fork.
5 Remove the damper cartridge bolt and its sealing washer from the bottom of the fork **(see illustration 8.24c)**. Discard the sealing washer as a new one must be used on reassembly.
6 Withdraw the damper cartridge from inside the fork tube **(see illustration)**. Remove the oil lock piece from the bottom of the damper **(see illustration)**. Pump the damper a few times over the oil drain tray to expel any residual oil.
7 Carefully prise out the dust seal from the top of the outer tube **(see illustration)**.
8 Carefully prise out the oil seal retaining clip, taking care not to scratch the surface of the inner tube **(see illustration)**.
9 To separate the inner and outer tubes it is necessary to displace the top bush and oil seal from the top of the outer tube. The bottom bush on the inner tube will not pass through the top bush, and this can be used to good effect. Grasp the inner tube in one hand and the outer tube in the other and compress them slightly, then pull them apart so that the bottom bush strikes the top bush **(see illustration)**. Repeat this operation until the top bush and seal are tapped out **(see illustration)**.

10 Slide the oil seal, the oil seal washer and top bush off the inner tube, noting which way up they fit **(see illustration 8.9b)**. Discard the oil seal and the dust seal as new ones must be used. Do not remove the bottom bush from the inner tube unless it is being replaced with a new one – to remove it carefully lever its ends apart using a screwdriver and slide it out of its recess **(see illustration)**.

Inspection

11 Clean all parts in solvent and blow them dry with compressed air, if available.
12 Check the fork inner tube for score marks, dents, pitting, scratches, flaking of its surface and excessive or abnormal wear. Fit a new tube if any are found. Check the inner tube for runout using V-blocks and a dial gauge. If the amount of runout exceeds the service limit specified, a new tube should be fitted.

8.6b . . . and remove the oil lock piece

8.7 Prise out the dust seal using a flat-bladed screwdriver

8.8 Prise out the retaining clip using a flat-bladed screwdriver

8.9a To separate the tubes pull them apart firmly several times . . .

8.9b . . . the slide-hammer effect will displace the oil seal, washer and top bush

8.10 Carefully lever the ends apart to expand it

Frame and suspension 5•13

8.15 Check the working surface (arrowed) of each bush for wear

8.16 Check the damper and rebound spring (arrowed)

⚠️ **Warning: If the inner tube is bent or exceeds the runout limit, it should not be straightened; replace it with a new one.**

13 Check the fork outer tube for cracks. Check the fork seal seat and housing for nicks, gouges and scratches. If damage is evident, leaks will occur. Also check the oil seal washer for damage or distortion and fit a new one if necessary.

14 Check the spring for cracks and other damage. Measure the spring free length and compare the measurement to the specifications at the beginning of the Chapter (see illustration 8.41). If it is defective or sagged below the service limit, replace the springs in both forks with new ones. Never renew only one spring.

15 Examine the working surfaces of the two bushes (i.e. the outer surface of the bottom bush and the inner surface of the top bush) (see illustration); if the grey Teflon outer surface has been worn away to reveal the copper inner surface over more than 75% of the surface area, or if the bushes are scored or badly scuffed, they must be replaced with new ones. Note that it is a good idea to replace the bushes with new ones as a matter of course as part of a fork overhaul.

16 Check the damper cartridge and rod, and the rebound spring fitted on it, for damage and wear (see illustration). Hold the body of the cartridge and pump the rod in and out. If any wear or damage is found, or if the rod does not move smoothly in the damper, a new damper cartridge must be fitted.

Reassembly

17 If necessary, fit a new bottom bush into its recess in the bottom of the inner tube (see illustration 8.10). Apply a smear of the specified clean fork oil to the bush. Slide the inner tube fully into the outer tube (see illustration).

18 Apply a smear of the specified clean fork oil to the inner surface of the top bush. Slide the bush down the inner tube and seat it in the top of the outer tube (see illustration). Slide the oil seal washer onto the bush (see illustration).

19 Support the fork upright. Using either the special service tools (Pt. Nos. 07947-KA50100 and 07947-KF00100) or a suitable drift, carefully drive the top bush fully into its recess – the oil seal washer prevents damaging the edges of the bush (see illustration). If using a drift, wrap tape around it to prevent scratching the inner tube. Make sure the bush enters the recess squarely. It is best to make sure that the inner tube is withdrawn as much as possible from the outer tube so that any accidental scratching is confined to the area that does not affect the oil seal.

20 Lift the washer to check the bush is seated fully and squarely in its recess in the outer tube, then wipe the recess clean and re-seat the washer (see illustration).

8.17 Slide the inner tube into the outer tube

8.18a Slide the top bush down and into the outer tube . . .

8.18b . . . then seat the washer on the bush . . .

8.19 . . . and drive the bush in and onto its seat

8.20 Make sure the bush (arrowed) has been fully driven in

5•14 Frame and suspension

8.21a Slide the seal down and into the outer tube . . .

8.21b . . . and drive it in and onto its seat

8.21c Make sure the retaining clip groove (arrowed) is fully exposed

21 Apply a smear of the clean fork oil to the lips of the new oil seal. Slide the seal onto the tube with its marked side facing up **(see illustration)**. Drive the seal into place as described in Step 19 until the retaining clip groove is visible **(see illustrations)**.
22 Fit the retaining clip, making sure it is correctly located in its groove **(see illustration)**.
23 Press the dust seal into the top of the outer tube **(see illustration)**.
24 Clean the threads of the damper cartridge bolt. Lay the fork flat on the bench with the caliper mounting lugs to the right. Fit the oil lock piece onto the bottom of the damper cartridge **(see illustration)**. Slide the cartridge fully into the fork tube **(see illustration)**. Fit a new sealing washer onto the cartridge bolt and apply a few drops of a suitable non-permanent thread locking compound **(see illustration)**. Fit the bolt into the bottom of the outer tube and thread it into the cartridge, tightening it to the torque setting specified at the beginning of the Chapter **(see illustration)**. If the damper cartridge rotates inside the tube as you tighten the bolt, wait until the fork is fully reassembled and tighten it then (the pressure of the spring on the cartridge will prevent it from turning).
25 Refer to Section 7, Steps 7 to 10 and fill the fork with oil and finish reassembly.
26 If the damper cartridge bolt requires tightening (see Step 24), place the fork upside down on the floor, using a rag to protect it, then have an assistant compress the fork so that maximum spring pressure is placed on the damper rod head while tightening the bolt to the specified torque setting.
27 Fit the axle clamp bolt. Fit the fork protector, aligning the tab with the groove **(see illustration 8.2)**.
28 Install the fork (see Section 6).

CB1000R/RA models

Disassembly

29 Remove the fork – make sure you adjust the pre-load and rebound damping to its minimum (see Section 14), and loosen the top bolt while the leg is still clamped in the bottom yoke (see Section 6). Always dismantle the fork legs separately to avoid interchanging parts and thus causing an accelerated rate of wear. Store all components in separate, clearly marked containers.
30 Lay the fork flat on the bench with the caliper mounting lugs to the left. Remove

8.22 Fit the retaining clip in its groove . . .

8.23 . . . then press the dust seal in

8.24a Fit the oil lock piece . . .

8.24b . . . then insert the damper cartridge

8.24c Fit a new sealing washer and apply threadlock . . .

8.24d . . . and tighten the bolt to the specified torque

Frame and suspension 5•15

8.30a Remove the axle clamp bolt

8.30b Slacken the damper cartridge bolt

the wheel axle clamp bolt **(see illustration)**. Hold the fork down and slacken the damper cartridge bolt in the base of the fork **(see illustration)**. If the damper cartridge rotates inside the fork whilst attempting to unscrew the bolt, compress the fork so that the spring exerts pressure on the cartridge body whilst the bolt is unscrewed. Alternatively, if available use an air wrench.

31 Refer to Section 7, Steps 12 to 16 and drain the oil from the fork.

32 Remove the damper cartridge bolt and its sealing washer from the bottom of the fork **(see illustration)**. Discard the sealing washer as a new one must be used on reassembly.

33 Withdraw the damper cartridge from inside the fork tube **(see illustration)**. Pump the damper a few times over the oil drain tray to expel any residual oil.

34 Carefully prise out the dust seal from the bottom of the outer tube **(see illustration)**.

35 Carefully prise out the oil seal retaining clip, taking care not to scratch the surface of the inner tube **(see illustration)**.

36 To separate the inner and outer tubes it is necessary to displace the bottom bush and oil seal from the bottom of the outer tube. The top bush on the inner tube will not pass through the bottom bush, and this can be used to good effect. Grasp the inner tube in one hand and the outer tube in the other and compress them slightly, then pull them apart so that the top bush strikes the bottom bush **(see illustration)**. Repeat this operation until the bottom bush and seal are tapped out **(see illustration)**.

37 To remove the bottom bush carefully lever its ends apart using a screwdriver and slide it

8.32 Remove the bolt . . .

8.33 . . . then withdraw the damper cartridge

8.34 Prise out the dust seal using a flat-bladed screwdriver

8.35 Prise out the retaining clip using a flat-bladed screwdriver

8.36a To separate the tubes pull them apart firmly several times . . .

8.36b . . . the slide-hammer effect will displace the oil seal, washer and top bush

5•16 Frame and suspension

8.37a Carefully lever the ends apart to expand it over the top bush

8.37b Slide the remaining components off

8.37c Only remove the top bush if you are replacing it with a new one

8.41 Measure the free length of the spring

8.42 Check the working surface (arrowed) of each bush for wear

8.43 Check the damper and oil lock valve (arrowed)

over the top bush **(see illustration)**. Slide the oil seal washer, the oil seal, the retaining ring and the dust seal over the top bush and off the inner tube, noting which way up they fit **(see illustration)**. Discard the oil seal and the dust seal as new ones must be used. Note that Honda specify to use a new top bush if it is removed from its recess – if required remove it by levering its ends apart until it clears its recess **(see illustration)**.

Inspection

38 Clean all parts in solvent and blow them dry with compressed air, if available.
39 Check the fork inner tube for score marks, dents, pitting, scratches, flaking of its surface and excessive or abnormal wear. Fit a new tube if any are found. Check the inner tube for runout using V-blocks and a dial gauge. If the amount of runout exceeds the service limit specified, a new tube should be fitted.

⚠️ *Warning: If the inner tube is bent or exceeds the runout limit, it should not be straightened; replace it with a new one.*

40 Check the fork outer tube for cracks. Check the fork seal seat and housing for nicks, gouges and scratches. If damage is evident, leaks will occur. Also check the oil seal washer for damage or distortion and fit a new one if necessary.
41 Check the spring for cracks and other damage. Measure the spring free length and compare the measurement to the specifications at the beginning of the Chapter

(see illustration). If it is defective or sagged below the service limit, replace the springs in both forks with new ones. Never renew only one spring.
42 Examine the working surfaces of the two bushes (i.e. the inner surface of the bottom bush and the outer surface of the top bush) **(see illustration)**; if the grey Teflon outer surface has been worn away to reveal the copper inner surface over more than 75% of the surface area, or if the bushes are scored or badly scuffed, they must be replaced with new ones. Note that it is a good idea to replace the bushes with new ones as a matter of course as part of a fork overhaul.
43 Check the damper cartridge and rod, and the oil lock valve fitted on it, for damage and wear **(see illustration)**. Hold the body of the

cartridge and pump the rod in and out. If any wear or damage is found, or if the rod does not move smoothly in the damper, a new damper must be installed.

Reassembly

44 Wrap some thin insulating tape over the edges of the recess for the top bush in the inner tube, or over the bush itself if not removed, to protect the seal lips **(see illustration)**. Smear some oil over the tape, and also over the oil seal lips. Slide the new dust seal, retaining clip, new oil seal, and oil seal washer onto the inner tube, making sure they are the correct way round **(see illustration)**. Remove the tape, then lubricate the inner surface of the bottom bush and

8.44a Use insulating tape to cover sharp edges . . .

8.44b . . . then slide the specified components over it

Frame and suspension 5•17

8.44c If the top bush is in place expand the ends of the bottom bush to fit over it

8.44d Check all components are correctly in place

8.45a Slide the inner tube into the outer tube

8.45b Slide the top bush down and into the outer tube, squeezing its ends together to fit it . . .

8.45c . . . and making sure it is fully seated

8.46 Use a drift to drive the bush in if necessary, using the washer as an interface

slide it on, over the top bush if in place **(see illustration)**. Make sure all components are correctly fitted **(see illustration)**. If removed fit the new top bush into its recess in the inner tube **(see illustration 8.37c)**. Apply a smear of the specified clean fork oil to the bushes.

45 Slide the inner tube fully into the outer tube **(see illustration)**. Support the fork upside down, and have an assistant hold the inner tube and the components on it up. Slide the bottom bush into the bottom of the outer tube, then squeeze the ends together using two suitable plastic or wooden tools to close the gap to allow the bush the drop in **(see illustrations)**.

46 If the bush is tight and does not want to go in slide the oil seal washer onto the bush **(see illustration 8.47)**. Using either the special service tool (Pt. No. 07YMD-MCF0100) or a suitable drift, carefully drive the bottom bush fully into its recess – the oil seal washer prevents damaging the edges of the bush **(see illustration)**. If using a drift, wrap tape around it to prevent scratching the inner tube. Make sure the bush enters the recess squarely. It is best to make sure that the inner tube is withdrawn as much as possible from the outer tube so that any accidental scratching is confined to the area that does not affect the oil seal. Lift the washer to check the bush is seated fully and squarely in its recess in the outer tube, then wipe the recess clean

47 Slide the oil seal washer onto the bush **(see illustration)**.

48 Slide the new oil seal down and into the outer tube **(see illustration)**. Push the seal

8.47 Fit the washer onto the bush

8.48a Slide the new seal down and into the outer tube

5•18 Frame and suspension

8.48b Cut the old seal in half . . .

8.48c . . . and use it to push the new seal in, or to protect it if driving it in . . .

8.48d . . . then use a small screwdriver to retrieve it

8.48e Make sure the retaining clip groove (arrowed) is fully exposed

8.49 Fit the retaining clip in its groove . . .

8.50 . . . then press the dust seal in

into place, driving it in if necessary as in Step 46, until the retaining clip groove is visible – to help push the seal in, or to avoid damaging it if driving it in, cut the old seal in half and use it as an interface between the drift and the new seal **(see illustrations)**.
49 Fit the retaining clip, making sure it is correctly located in its groove **(see illustration)**.
50 Press the dust seal into the top of the outer tube **(see illustration)**.
51 Clean the threads of the damper cartridge bolt. Lay the fork flat on the bench with the caliper mounting lugs to the right. Slide the damper cartridge fully into the fork tube **(see illustration)**. Fit a new sealing washer onto the cartridge bolt and apply a few drops of a suitable non-permanent thread locking compound **(see illustration)**. Fit the bolt into the bottom of the tube and thread it into the cartridge, tightening it to the torque setting specified at the beginning of the Chapter **(see illustration)**. If the cartridge rotates inside the tube as you tighten the bolt, wait until the fork is fully reassembled and tighten it then (the pressure of the spring on the cartridge will prevent it from turning).
52 Refer to Section 7, Steps 17 to 21 and fill the fork with oil and finish reassembly.
53 If the damper cartridge bolt requires tightening (see Step 51) place the fork upside down on the floor, using a rag to protect it, then have an assistant compress the fork so that maximum spring pressure is placed on the damper cartridge head while tightening the bolt to the specified torque setting.
54 Fit the axle clamp bolt **(see illustration 8.30a)**.

55 Install the fork (see Section 6). Set the spring pre-load and rebound damping adjusters as noted or required (see Section 14).

9 Steering stem

Special tool: Either the Honda special tool (Pt. No. 07916-3710101), equivalent peg spanner, or a suitably sized C-spanner is necessary for this procedure – see Step 8.

Removal

1 On CBF1000/A models remove the fairing (see Chapter 7). On CB1000R/RA models remove the headlight assembly (see Chapter 8).

8.51a Insert the damper cartridge

8.51b Fit a new sealing washer and apply threadlock . . .

8.51c . . . and tighten the bolt to the specified torque

Frame and suspension 5•19

9.4 Unscrew the brake hose guide bolt (arrowed) – CBF1000/A shown

9.5 Remove the cap from the nut

9.7 Unscrew the steering stem nut and lift the top yoke off

9.8a Bend down the lockwasher tabs . . .

9.8b . . . then unscrew the locknut . . .

9.8c . . . and remove the lockwasher

2 Displace the handlebars from the top yoke and rest them on some rag (see Section 5).
3 As a precaution, remove the fuel tank (see Chapter 4) – though not actually essential, this will prevent the possibility of damage should a tool slip.
4 Detach the front brake hose holder from the bottom yoke, and on models with ABS release the brake pipes from their mount **(see illustration)**. Take care not to strain or knock the brake hoses and pipes when removing the steering stem.
5 On CB1000R/RA models remove the cap from the steering stem nut **(see illustration)**.
6 Remove the front forks (see Section 6).
7 Unscrew the steering stem nut **(see illustration)**. Lift the top yoke up off the steering stem and support it clear, using a rag to protect the tank or other components. On CB1000R/RA models also displace the headlight bracket from the bottom yoke and support or tie the bracket/top yoke/handlebar assemblies and all the related wiring, cables and hoses to one side or fold it over the back and rest it on some rag on the frame.
8 Bend the lockwasher tabs out of the notches in the locknut **(see illustration)**. Unscrew the locknut using either your fingers (it shouldn't be tight) or a C-spanner located in one of the notches **(see illustration)**. Remove the lockwasher **(see illustration)**. Inspect the tabs for cracks or signs of fatigue. If there is any sign of damage, discard the lockwasher and use a new one; otherwise the old one can be re-used, but note that Honda recommend using a new one as a matter of course.
9 If the peg spanner or socket mentioned above is not available, make an alignment mark between the adjuster nut and the frame – this can serve as a rough guide for the tightness of the adjuster nut on installation. As you unscrew the nut count the number of turns.
10 Support the bottom yoke and unscrew the adjuster nut using a peg-spanner, socket or a C-spanner located in one of the notches **(see illustrations)**. Remove the bearing cover **(see illustration 9.14b)**. Gently lower the bottom yoke and steering stem out of the frame **(see illustration 9.14a)**.

9.10a Unscrew the nut using a peg spanner . . .

9.10b . . . or C-spanner

5•20 Frame and suspension

9.11a Remove the inner race . . .

9.11b . . . and upper bearing from the head . . .

9.11c . . . and the lower bearing from the stem

9.14a Fit the stem up through the head

9.14b Fit the cover . . .

9.14c . . . then thread the adjuster nut on

11 Remove the inner race and bearing from the top of the steering head **(see illustrations)**. Remove the bearing from the base of the steering stem **(see illustration)**.

12 Remove all traces of old grease from the bearings and races and check them for wear or damage as described in Section 10. **Note:** *Do not attempt to remove the races from the steering head or the steering stem unless they are to be replaced with new ones (see Section 10).*

Installation

13 Smear a liberal quantity of Urea based multi-purpose grease with EP2 rating onto the bearing races, and work some grease well into both the upper and lower bearings. Also smear the grease seal lip, using a new seal if necessary. Fit the lower bearing onto the steering stem **(see illustration 9.11c)**.

14 Fit the upper bearing and its inner race into the top of the steering head **(see illustrations 9.11b and a)**. Carefully lift the steering stem/ bottom yoke up through the steering head and support it there **(see illustration)**. Fit the bearing cover **(see illustration)**. Apply the oil to the adjuster nut threads and thread it onto the steering stem **(see illustration)**.

15 Using the Honda service tool (Pt. No. 07916-3710101) or a suitable peg spanner, which can be made by cutting castellations into an old socket **(see illustration 9.10a)**, tighten the adjuster nut to the torque setting specified at the beginning of the Chapter, then turn the steering from lock-to-lock five times, then reapply the specified torque setting to

the nut. Check that the steering stem is able to move smoothly (though it may feel a bit tight, but this is normal as the weight of the forks and wheel is not influencing the feel) from lock-to-lock following adjustment – note that it is best to check and if necessary reset the bearing adjustment as described in Chapter 1 after the forks and front wheel and all other components have been installed.

16 If the correct tools are not available, tighten the nut the number of turns recorded on removal using a C-spanner until the marks align **(see illustration 9.10b)**. Turn the steering from lock-to-lock five times, then slacken the nut, and tighten it again until the marks align. Install the forks and wheel, then refer to the procedure in Chapter 1 and check the feel of the bearings as described, and adjust if necessary.

Caution: Take great care not to apply

9.18 Bend the lockwasher tabs up into the notches in the lockwasher

excessive pressure because this will cause premature failure of the bearings.

17 With the bearings correctly adjusted, fit the lockwasher, using a new one if the tabs are weakened or cracked, onto the adjuster nut and fit the two short tabs into the notches in the adjuster nut **(see illustration 9.8c)**.

18 Fit the locknut and tighten it finger-tight **(see illustration 9.8b)**. Tighten the locknut further (but no more than 90°) until its notches align with the remaining lockwasher tabs, making sure the adjuster nut does not turn as well (though that is unlikely). Secure the locknut in position by bending up the long lock washer tabs into its notches **(see illustration)**.

19 On CB1000R/RA models seat the headlight bracket in the bottom yoke **(see illustration)**. On all models fit the top yoke onto the steering stem – on CB1000R/RA models

9.19a Make sure each rubber damper (arrowed) is in place, then seat the bracket in the bottom yoke . . .

Frame and suspension 5•21

9.19b ... and the top yoke on the bracket

9.19c Fit one of the forks to align the yokes

9.19d Tighten the stem nut to the specified torque

make sure the tops of the headlight bracket locate in the rubbers **(see illustration)**. Fit the steering stem nut and tighten it finger-tight **(see illustration 9.7)**. If not already fitted temporarily install one of the forks to align the top and bottom yokes, and secure it by tightening the bottom yoke clamp bolts only (see Section 6) **(see illustration)**. Now tighten the steering stem nut to the torque setting specified at the beginning of the Chapter **(see illustration)**. On CB1000R/RA models fit the cap into the nut **(see illustration 9.5)**.

20 Install the remaining components in a reverse of the removal procedure, referring to the relevant Sections or Chapters, and to the torque settings specified at the beginning of the Chapter.

21 Carry out a final check of the steering head bearing freeplay as described in Chapter 1, and if necessary re-adjust.

10.3 Check the outer races in the top and bottom of the steering head

10.4a Drive the bearing races out with a brass drift . . .

10 Steering head bearings

Inspection

1 Remove the steering stem (see Section 9).
2 Remove all traces of old grease from the bearings and races and check them for wear or damage.
3 The outer races in the top and bottom of the steering head should be polished and free from indentations **(see illustration)**. Inspect the bearing balls for signs of wear, damage or discoloration, and examine the ball retainer cage for signs of cracks or splits. If there are any signs of wear on any of the above components both upper and lower bearing assemblies must be renewed as a set. Only remove the outer races in the steering head and the lower bearing inner race on the steering stem if they need to be replaced with new ones – do not re-use them once they have been removed.

Replacement

4 The outer races are an interference fit in the steering head – tap them from position using a suitable drift located in the recesses provided in the steering head that expose the lip of the race **(see illustrations)**. Tap firmly and evenly between the recesses to ensure the race is driven out squarely. Curve the end of the drift slightly to improve access if necessary.
5 Press the new outer races into the head using

10.4b . . . locating it in the cut-outs (arrowed)

a drawbolt arrangement **(see illustration)**, or drive them in using a large diameter tubular drift. Ensure that the drawbolt washer or drift (as applicable) bears only on the outer edge of the race and does not contact the working surface. Alternatively, have the races installed by a Honda dealer equipped with the bearing race installation tools.

> **HAYNES HiNT** *Installation of new bearing outer races is made much easier if the races are left overnight in the freezer. This causes them to contract slightly making them a looser fit. Alternatively, use a freeze spray.*

6 Only remove the lower bearing inner race from the steering stem if a new one is being fitted. To remove the race, first thread the steering stem nut onto the top then position the yoke on its front for stability – the nut

10.5 Drawbolt arrangement for fitting steering stem bearing races

1 Long bolt or threaded bar
2 Thick washer
3 Guide for lower race

5•22 Frame and suspension

10.6a Remove the lower bearing race using a cold chisel . . .

10.6b . . . and/or screwdrivers . . .

10.6c . . . or using a puller if necessary

will protect the threads from the transmitted force of the impact of the chisel. Tap under the race using a cold chisel to displace it, and if required use two screwdrivers placed on opposite sides to work it free, using blocks of wood to improve leverage and protect the yoke **(see illustrations)**. If the race is firmly in place it will be necessary to use a puller **(see illustration)**. Take the steering stem to a Honda dealer if required.

7 Remove the dust seal from the bottom of the stem and replace it with a new one. Smear the new one with grease.

8 Fit the new lower race onto the steering stem. Drive the new race into position using a length of tubing with an internal diameter slightly larger than the steering stem **(see illustration)** – heating the race and cooling the steering stem will make installation easier, or use an hydraulic press if necessary.

9 Install the steering stem (see Section 9).

11 Rear shock absorber

Warning: *Do not attempt to disassemble the shock absorber in the home workshop. It is nitrogen-charged under high pressure. Improper disassembly could result in serious injury.*

Removal

1 On CBF1000A models support the motorcycle on the centrestand. On all other models support the motorcycle on an auxiliary stand so that no weight is transmitted through any part of the rear suspension – tie the front brake lever to the handlebar to ensure the bike can't roll forward. Position a support under the rear wheel or swingarm so that it does not drop when the shock absorber is removed, but also making sure that the weight of the machine is off the rear suspension so that the shock is not compressed.

2 On CBF1000/A models remove the seats and side covers. Undo the brake hose guide screws on the right-hand side of the swingarm **(see illustration)**.

3 On CB1000R/RA models remove the side covers (see Chapter 7) and the silencer (see Chapter 4). Unscrew the rider's left-hand footrest bracket bolts and remove the assembly, then remove the front drive chain guide **(see illustration)**. Release the wiring loom clip on the left side to access the top bolt **(see illustration)**. On RA models release the rear wheel sensor wire guide.

4 Unscrew the nut and withdraw the bolt securing the bottom of the shock absorber **(see illustrations)** – on CBF1000/A models lift

10.8 Drive the new inner race on using a suitable bearing driver or a length of pipe that bears only against the inner rim and not the bearing surface

11.2 Undo the hose guide screws (arrowed)

11.3a Remove the bracket to access the drive chain guide bolt

11.3b Detach the wiring clip from the frame

11.4a On CBF models unscrew the nut and withdraw the bolt

11.4b On CB-R models access the nut (arrowed) via the hole in the swingarm

Frame and suspension 5•23

11.5a On CBF models unscrew the nut (arrowed) . . .

11.5b . . . withdraw the bolt . . .

11.5c . . . and remove the shock absorber

11.5d On CB-R models unscrew the nut (arrowed) . . .

11.5e . . . withdraw the bolt . . .

11.5f . . . and remove the shock absorber

the brake hose off the swingarm and slip the tool under it to get on the bolt.

5 Unscrew the nut on the bolt securing the top of the shock absorber (see illustration). Support the shock and withdraw the bolt, then remove the shock absorber (see illustrations) – remove the support from under the wheel or swingarm to lower it for clearance if required.

Inspection

6 Check the shock absorber for obvious physical damage and oil leakage, and the spring for looseness, cracks or signs of fatigue.

7 Check the bush in the top of the shock absorber for wear or damage (see illustration).

8 Withdraw the spacer from the bottom mount (see illustration). Clean off old grease and dirt. Check the condition of the grease seals and bearing. If required lever out the grease seals (see illustration). Fit the spacer back in and check for play between it and the bearing. Refer to *Tools and Workshop Tips* (Section 5) in the Reference section for more information on bearings.

9 If the bearing is worn, drive it out of the bore using a suitable driver or socket or draw it out using a drawbolt (one can be made up as described in *Tools and Workshop Tips* in the Reference section) – do not re-use the bearing after removing it (see illustration). The new bearing should be pressed or drawn in, not driven in. When fitting the new bearing make sure it is central in the bore – the gap between the outer end and the rim of the bore should be 5.0 to 5.5 mm.

11.7 Check the bush (arrowed)

11.8a Withdraw the spacer and check the seals and bearing

11.8b If necessary lever the seals out using a screwdriver

11.9 Remove and install the bearing (arrowed) as described

5•24 Frame and suspension

11.10 You can fit the seals in using thumb pressure

11.12 Make sure the guide locates correctly

10 Press the new seals squarely into place **(see illustration)**. Fit the spacer **(see illustration 11.8a)**. Lubricate the bearing, spacer and new seals – Honda recommend a multi-purpose grease with EP2 rating for CBF models and Repsol MP2 grease for CB-R models. If the pre-load adjuster ring is hard to turn lubricate it with molybdenum paste.

11 Parts are not available for the shock absorber itself. If it is worn or damaged, it must be replaced with a new one. Before disposing of an old shock absorber, you should release the nitrogen gas from the top. To do this, make a drill point 35 mm below the middle of the top mount using a centre punch. Mount the shock in a vice. Drill a hole using a sharp 2 or 3 mm drill bit to release the gas – it is best to cover the shock and drill and avert your face to prevent the possibility of injury,

making sure the material used does not get caught in the chuck as it spins.

⚠ *Warning: Wear protective eyewear and be very careful when releasing the gas pressure – it is possible for fine debris particles to be released with it, and as the pressure is high these could damage your eyes if done carelessly.*

Installation

12 Installation is the reverse of removal, noting the following:
- Apply the recommended grease (see Step 10) to the shock absorber pivot points.
- On CB1000R/RA models install the shock absorber with the damping adjuster screw facing to the right.
- Tighten the nuts/bolts to the torque setting specified at the beginning of the Chapter.

- On CB1000R/RA models make sure the front chain guide locates correctly on its inner side **(see illustration)**. Tighten the footrest bracket bolts to the specified torque.

12 Rear suspension linkage (CBF models)

Removal

1 On CBF1000A models support the motorcycle on the centrestand. On CBF1000 models support the motorcycle on an auxiliary stand so that no weight is transmitted through any part of the rear suspension – tie the front brake lever to the handlebar to ensure the bike can't roll forward. Position a support under the rear wheel or swingarm so that it does not drop when the shock absorber is removed, but also making sure that the weight of the machine is off the rear suspension so that the shock is not compressed.

2 Remove the chainguard from the swingarm, noting how it locates **(see illustration)** – access to the front bolt is restricted by the left-hand footrest bracket (removing the bolt is not difficult, but getting it back in is tricky), so displace the bracket if required, supporting it to avoid straining the gearchange lever linkage, or alternatively displace the lever from the bracket first (see Section 3). Slacken the right-hand footrest bracket bolts enough to give sufficient clearance to withdraw the linkage arm-to-swingarm bolt **(see illustration)**.

3 Unscrew the nut and withdraw the bolt securing the bottom of the shock absorber to the linkage arm **(see illustration 11.4a)**.

4 Unscrew the nut and withdraw the bolt securing the linkage arm to the swingarm **(see illustration)**.

5 Unscrew the nut and withdraw bolt securing the linkage rod to the frame and remove the linkage assembly **(see illustration)**.

6 Unscrew the nut and withdraw the bolt securing the linkage arm to the linkage rod and separate them **(see illustration)**.

12.2a Unscrew the bolts (arrowed) and remove the chainguard

12.2b Slacken the footrest bracket bolts (arrowed)

12.4 Unscrew the nut and withdraw the bolt

12.5 Unscrew the nut, withdraw the bolt and remove the linkage assembly

12.6 Unscrew the nut, withdraw the bolt and separate the arm from the rod

Frame and suspension 5•25

12.7 Withdraw the sleeves

12.11 Lever the seals out

12.12 Remove and install the bearings as described

Inspection

7 Withdraw the sleeves from the linkage rod and arm **(see illustration)**.
8 Thoroughly clean all components, removing all traces of dirt, corrosion and grease.
9 Check the linkage rod and arm closely, looking for obvious signs of wear such as heavy scoring, or for damage such as cracks or distortion. Replace worn or damaged components with new ones as required.
10 Check the condition of the grease seals and bearings. Fit the sleeves back in and check for play between them and the bearings. Refer to *Tools and Workshop Tips* (Section 5) in the Reference section for more information on bearings. Inspect all components closely, looking for obvious signs of wear such as heavy scoring, or for damage such as cracks or distortion. Replace worn or damaged components with new ones as required.
11 If required lever out the grease seals using a seal hook or screwdriver **(see illustration)**. Discard them – new ones must be used.
12 Worn bearings can be driven or drawn out of their bores, but note that removal will destroy them; new bearings should be obtained before work commences **(see illustration)**. The new bearings should be pressed or drawn into their bores rather than driven into position. In the absence of a press, a suitable drawbolt tool can be made up as described in *Tools and Workshop Tips* in the Reference section. When fitting the new bearings make sure their marked side faces out and they are central in their bores, with a 5.3 to 5.7 mm gap between the outer end and the rim of the bore.
13 Lubricate the needle bearings, sleeves and seals with a multi-purpose grease with EP2 rating.
14 Press the new seals squarely into place, with the marked flat side facing out **(see illustration)**. Fit the sleeves **(see illustration 12.7)**.

Installation

15 Installation is the reverse of removal, noting the following:
- Apply molybdenum-disulphide grease to the pivot points.
- Make sure the UP mark on the linkage arm faces up.
- Tighten the suspension linkage bolt nuts and footrest bracket bolts to the torque settings specified at the beginning of the Chapter.

13 Swingarm

CBF1000/A models

Removal

1 On CBF1000A models support the bike on its centrestand. On CBF1000 models support the bike upright using an auxiliary stand or stands that will not interfere with swingarm removal. Make sure the bike is on level ground, and block the front wheel or tie the front brake on. Note the bike must not be supported through the rear suspension or under the pivot brackets. A hoist can be used to lift the rear of the bike off the ground if available. In the accompanying photos blocks of wood and axle stands are placed under the bottom of the frame as shown after removing the exhaust system (see Chapter 4). Work can be made easier by raising the machine to a suitable working height on an hydraulic ramp or a suitable platform. Make sure the motorcycle is secure and will not topple over (also see *Tools and Workshop Tips* in the Reference section).
2 If not already done, remove the silencers (see Chapter 4). Remove the rear wheel (see Chapter 6).
3 Remove the chainguard from the swingarm, noting how it locates **(see illustration 12.2a)** – access to the front bolt is restricted by the left-hand footrest bracket (removing the bolt is not difficult, but getting it back in is tricky), so displace the bracket if required, supporting it to avoid straining the gearchange lever linkage, or alternatively displace the lever from the bracket first (see Section 3). On the right-hand side unscrew the footrest bracket bottom bolt and slacken the top bolt **(see illustration 12.2b)** – this allows the bracket to be moved round for access to the swingarm pivot bracket bottom nut.
4 Unscrew the brake hose/pipe/ABS sensor wire (according to model) guide screws **(see illustration 11.2)**. Displace the brake caliper from the swingarm and tie the assembly up out of the way.
5 Unscrew the nut and withdraw the bolt securing the linkage arm to the swingarm **(see illustration 12.4)**.
6 Unscrew the nuts on the right-hand ends of the swingarm pivot bolt and pivot bracket bolts, counter-holding the bolt heads if necessary, and noting the washer with the swingarm bolt **(see illustration)**. Draw the left-hand pivot bracket out slightly.
7 Withdraw the swingarm pivot bolt and

12.14 Press the new seals in so they are flush

13.6 Unscrew the nuts (arrowed)

5•26 Frame and suspension

13.7 Withdraw the pivot bolt and remove the swingarm

13.10 Make sure the bosses locate correctly

13.12 Make sure the chain is correctly routed around the front

manoeuvre the swingarm back out of the frame **(see illustration)**.

8 Remove the chain slider from the swingarm if necessary, noting the collars that fit with the bolts. If it is badly worn or damaged, it should be replaced with a new one – look for the wear limit arrows on the front.

Inspection

9 See Steps 24 to 31, but lubricate the needle bearings, sleeves and seals with a multi-purpose grease with EP2 rating.

Installation

10 If removed, fit the chain slider, making sure it locates correctly over the lug at the front, and the mounting bosses fit in the holes **(see illustration)**.

11 Clean the swingarm pivot bolt and smear it with grease.

12 Offer up the swingarm, making sure the drive chain is looped over the front **(see illustration)**. Slide the pivot bolt through from the left-hand side **(see illustration 13.7)**. Push the pivot bracket in.

13 Fit the nuts onto the ends of the pivot bolt and bracket bolts, not forgetting the washer with the pivot bolt nut **(see illustration)**. Tighten the bracket bolt nuts to the torque setting specified at the beginning of the Chapter, counter-holding the bolt heads if necessary. Tighten the swingarm pivot bolt nut to the specified torque. Check the swingarm moves up and down smoothly and freely.

14 Install the remaining components in reverse order. Tighten the suspension linkage arm bolt/nut, footrest bracket bolts and gearchange lever pivot bolt to the specified torque settings.

15 Check and adjust the drive chain slack (see Chapter 1). Check the operation of the rear suspension and brake before taking the machine on the road.

CB1000R/RA models

Removal

16 Support the bike upright using an auxiliary stand or stands that will not interfere with swingarm removal. Make sure the bike is on level ground, and block the front wheel or tie the front brake on. Note the bike must not be supported through the rear suspension or under the pivot brackets. A hoist can be used to lift the rear of the bike off the ground if available. In the accompanying photographs blocks of wood and axle stands are placed under the bottom of the frame after removing the exhaust system (see Chapter 4). Work can be made easier by raising the machine to a suitable working height on an hydraulic ramp or a suitable platform. Make sure the motorcycle is secure and will not topple over (also see *Tools and Workshop Tips* in the Reference section).

17 Either remove the front sprocket, or split and remove the drive chain (see Chapter 6). Remove the rear wheel (see Chapter 6). Unscrew the brake hose/pipe/ABS sensor wire (according to model) bolts. Displace the caliper and tie it up out of the way (see Chapter 6).

18 If required remove the rear wheel bearing holder assembly (see Chapter 6).

19 Unscrew the rider's left-hand footrest bracket bolts and remove the assembly, then remove the front drive chain guide **(see illustration 11.3a)**. If required remove the chainguard.

20 Unscrew the nut and withdraw the bolt securing the bottom of the shock absorber **(see illustration 11.4b)**.

21 Unscrew the nuts on the right-hand ends of the swingarm pivot bolt and pivot bracket bolts, counter-holding the bolt heads if necessary, and noting the washers **(see illustration)**.

22 Withdraw the swingarm pivot bolt and manoeuvre the swingarm back out of the frame **(see illustrations)**.

23 Remove the chain slider from the swingarm if necessary, noting the collars that fit with the bolts. If it is badly worn or damaged, it should be replaced with a new one – there are some

13.13 Fit the washer with the swingarm bolt nut

13.21 Unscrew the nuts (arrowed)

13.22a Withdraw the pivot bolt and remove the swingarm . . .

13.22b . . . unhooking the chain from the sprocket if it wasn't split

Frame and suspension 5•27

13.23 Remove the caliper guide pin, noting the O-ring

13.24a Remove the sleeve from the left side ...

13.24b ... and the spacers from the right

wear limit arrows on the front. If required remove the rear drive chain guide. If required remove the brake caliper guide pin – discard its O-ring, and fit a new one **(see illustration)**.

Inspection

24 Withdraw the sleeve from the left-hand pivot and the spacers from the right-hand one **(see illustrations)**.
25 Thoroughly clean all pivot components, removing all traces of dirt, corrosion and grease.
26 Check the swingarm closely, looking for obvious signs of wear such as heavy scoring, or for damage such as cracks or distortion.
27 Check the condition of the grease seals and bearings – there are two ball bearings in the right-hand pivot and a needle bearing in the left. Check the ball bearings run smoothly. Fit the sleeve back in the needle bearing and check for play between them. Refer to *Tools and Workshop Tips* (Section 5) in the Reference section for more information on bearings. Inspect all components closely, looking for obvious signs of wear such as heavy scoring, or for damage such as cracks or distortion. Replace worn or damaged components with new ones as required.
28 If required lever out the grease seals using a seal hook or screwdriver **(see illustration)**. Discard them – new one must be used.
29 Worn bearings can be drifted or pressed out of their bores, but note that removal will destroy them – remove the circlip from the right-hand pivot before removing the ball bearings **(see illustration)**. New bearings should be obtained before work commences.

The new bearings should be pressed or drawn into their bores rather than driven into position. In the absence of a press, a suitable drawbolt tool can be made up as described in *Tools and Workshop Tips* in the Reference section. When fitting the new ball bearings pack them with grease and make sure their marked side faces out and that they are against the seat. Secure them with a new circlip. When fitting the needle bearing make sure the marked side faces out and there is a 5.0 to 6.0 mm gap between its outer end and the rim of the bore.
30 Lubricate the needle bearings, sleeves and seals with a molybdenum disulphide grease.
31 Press the new seals squarely into place, with the marked flat side facing out, and fitting the smaller seal to the inner side of the right-hand pivot **(see illustration)**. Fit the sleeve and spacers – on the right-hand pivot the short spacer fits to the inner side, the long to the outer **(see illustrations 11.24a and b)**.

Installation

32 If removed, fit the chain slider, making sure it locates correctly over the lug at the front, and the mounting bosses fit in the holes **(see illustration 13.10)**. Clean the threads of the bolts and apply some fresh thread locking compound. If removed fit the rear drive chain guide – again clean the threads of the bolts and apply some fresh thread locking compound. If removed fit the brake caliper guide pin using a new O-ring.
33 Clean the swingarm pivot bolt and smear it with grease.
34 Offer up the swingarm and have an assistant hold it in place. If not removed make sure the drive chain is looped over the driveshaft **(see illustration 13.22b)**. Slide the pivot bolt through from the left-hand side **(see illustration 13.22a)**.
35 Fit the washers and nuts onto the ends of the pivot bolt and bracket bolts **(see illustration)**. Tighten the pivot bolt nut to the torque setting specified at the beginning of the Chapter, counter-holding the bolt head if necessary. Tighten the pivot bracket bolt nuts to the specified torque. Check the swingarm moves up and down smoothly and freely.
36 Install the remaining components in reverse order. Tighten the shock absorber bolt/nut and footrest bracket bolts to the specified torque settings.
37 Check and adjust the drive chain slack (see Chapter 1). Check the operation of the rear suspension and brake before taking the machine on the road.

13.28 Lever the seals out

13.29 The ball bearings are secured by a circlip (arrowed)

13.31 Press the new seals in so they are flush

13.35 Fit the washer with the swingarm bolt nut

5•28 Frame and suspension

14.3 Turn the spring pre-load adjuster using the tool provided

14.5 Spring pre-load adjuster (arrowed)

14.6 Rebound damping adjuster (arrowed)

14 Suspension adjustment

CBF1000/A models

Front forks

1 The front forks are not adjustable.

Rear shock absorber

2 The shock absorber has adjustable spring pre-load.

3 Spring pre-load is adjusted using a suitable C-spanner (one is provided in the toolkit) to turn the spring seat on the bottom of the shock absorber **(see illustration)**. There are seven positions. Position 1 is the lowest setting for light loads, position 3 the standard, and position 7 the highest, for heavy loads. Align the setting required with the adjustment stopper.

CB1000R/RA models

Front forks

4 The front forks have adjustable spring pre-load and both rebound and compression damping. Always make sure both forks are set equally.

5 Spring pre-load is adjusted using a 19 mm spanner on the adjuster flats **(see illustration)** – a spanner should be provided in the toolkit. Turn the adjuster clockwise to increase pre-load and anti-clockwise to decrease it. To set the standard position, turn the adjuster fully anti-clockwise until it stops, then turn it clockwise 8 full turns.

6 Rebound damping is adjusted using a screwdriver in the slot in the top of the damper rod protruding from the pre-load adjuster **(see illustration)**. Turn it clockwise to increase damping and anti-clockwise to decrease it. To set the standard position, turn the adjuster fully clockwise until it stops, then turn it anti-clockwise 2 turns until the punch mark on the adjuster aligns with the index mark below the directional arrow.

7 Compression damping is adjusted using a screwdriver in the slot in the adjuster which is on the bottom of the fork **(see illustration)**. Turn it clockwise to increase damping and anti-clockwise to decrease it. To set the standard position, turn the adjuster fully clockwise until it stops, then turn it anti-clockwise 2 turns until the punch mark on the adjuster aligns with the index mark on the housing.

Rear shock absorber

8 The shock absorber has adjustable spring pre-load and rebound damping.

9 Spring pre-load is adjusted using a suitable C-spanner (one is provided in the toolkit) to turn the spring seat on the bottom of the shock absorber **(see illustration)**. There are ten positions. Position 1 is the lowest setting for light loads, position 3 the standard, and position 10 the highest, for heavy loads. Align the setting required with the adjustment stopper.

10 Rebound damping adjustment is made by turning the adjuster on the bottom of the shock absorber on the right-hand side using a flat-bladed screwdriver **(see illustration)**. To increase the damping, turn the adjuster clockwise. To decrease the damping, turn the adjuster anti-clockwise. To set the standard position, turn the adjuster clockwise until it stops, then turn it anti clockwise 1½ turns until the punch mark on the adjuster aligns with the index mark on the shock absorber.

14.7 Compression damping adjuster (arrowed)

14.9 Spring pre-load adjuster (arrowed)

14.10 Rebound damping adjuster (A) – access it via the hole (B) in the swingarm

Chapter 6
Brakes, wheels and final drive

Contents

	Section number
ABS components	14
ABS fault diagnosis	13
ABS operation	12
Brake fluid level check	see Pre-ride checks
Brake hoses and fittings	10
Brake light switches	see Chapter 8
Brake pad wear check	see Chapter 1
Brake system bleeding and fluid change	11
Brake system check	see Chapter 1
CBS components	15
Drive chain check, adjustment, cleaning and lubrication	see Chapter 1
Drive chain	22
Front brake calipers	3
Front brake discs	4
Front brake master cylinder	5
Front brake pads	2

	Section number
Front wheel	18
General information	1
Rear brake caliper	7
Rear brake disc	8
Rear brake master cylinder	9
Rear brake pads	6
Rear sprocket coupling/rubber dampers	24
Rear wheel	19
Sprockets	23
Tyres	21
Tyre pressure, tread depth and condition	see Pre-ride checks
Wheel alignment check	17
Wheel bearing check	see Chapter 1
Wheel bearings	20
Wheel check	see Chapter 1
Wheel inspection and repair	16

Degrees of difficulty

Easy, suitable for novice with little experience | **Fairly easy,** suitable for beginner with some experience | **Fairly difficult,** suitable for competent DIY mechanic | **Difficult,** suitable for experienced DIY mechanic | **Very difficult,** suitable for expert DIY or professional

Specifications

Brake fluid
Brake fluid type .... DOT 4

Front brake calipers

	New	Service limit
Caliper bore ID		
CBF1000	25.400 to 25.450 mm	25.460 mm
CBF1000A	22.650 to 22.700 mm	22.710 mm
CB1000R		
Upper bore	32.080 to 32.130 mm	32.140 mm
Lower bore	30.280 to 30.330 mm	30.340 mm
CB1000RA		
Right caliper		
Upper and lower bores	27.000 to 27.050 mm	27.062 mm
Centre bore	22.650 to 22.700 mm	22.712 mm
Left caliper		
Upper and lower bores	25.400 to 25.450 mm	25.460 mm
Centre bore	22.650 to 22.700 mm	22.712 mm
	New	**Service limit**
Caliper piston OD		
CBF1000	25.318 to 25.368 mm	25.310 mm
CBF1000A	22.585 to 22.618 mm	22.560 mm
CB1000R		
Upper piston	31.967 to 32.000 mm	31.957 mm
Lower piston	30.167 to 30.200 mm	30.157 mm
CB1000RA		
Right caliper		
Upper and lower pistons	26.935 to 26.968 mm	26.923 mm
Centre piston	22.585 to 22.618 mm	22.560 mm
Left caliper		
Upper and lower pistons	25.318 to 25.368 mm	25.310 mm
Centre piston	22.585 to 22.618 mm	22.560 mm

Front brake master cylinder

	New	Service limit
Front master cylinder bore ID		
CBF1000 and CBF1000A	12.700 to 12.743 mm	12.755 mm
CB1000R	19.050 to 19.093 mm	19.105 mm
CB1000RA	17.460 to 17.503 mm	17.515 mm
Front master cylinder piston OD	New	Service limit
CBF1000 and CBF1000A	12.657 to 12.684 mm	12.650 mm
CB1000R	19.018 to 19.043 mm	19.006 mm
CB1000RA	17.321 to 17.367 mm	17.309 mm

Front brake discs

Disc thickness
- Standard . . . . 4.5 mm
- Service limit . . . . 3.5 mm

Disc maximum runout . . . . 0.3 mm

Rear brake caliper

	New	Service limit
Rear caliper bore ID		
CBF1000	38.180 to 38.230 mm	38.240 mm
CBF1000A	25.400 to 25.450 mm	25.460 mm
CB1000R and CB1000RA	27.000 to 27.050 mm	27.062 mm
Rear caliper piston OD	New	Service limit
CBF1000	38.098 to 38.148 mm	38.09 mm
CBF1000A	25.318 to 25.368 mm	25.310 mm
CB1000R and CB1000RA	26.918 to 26.968 mm	26.910 mm

Rear brake master cylinder

	New	Service limit
Rear master cylinder bore ID		
CBF1000	14.000 to 14.043 mm	14.055 mm
CBF1000A	17.460 to 17.503 mm	17.515 mm
CB1000R	15.870 to 15.913 mm	15.925 mm
CB1000RA	17.460 to 17.503 mm	17.515 mm
Rear master cylinder piston OD	New	Service limit
CBF1000	13.957 to 13.984 mm	13.945 mm
CBF1000A	17.417 to 17.444 mm	17.405 mm
CB1000R	15.827 to 15.854 mm	15.815 mm
CB1000RA	17.321 to 17.367 mm	17.309 mm

Rear brake disc

Disc thickness

CBF1000
- Standard . . . . 5.0 mm
- Service limit . . . . 4.0 mm

CBF1000A
- Standard . . . . 6.0 mm
- Service limit . . . . 5.0 mm

CB1000R and CB1000RA
- Standard . . . . 5.0 mm
- Service limit . . . . 4.0 mm

Disc maximum runout . . . . 0.3 mm

ABS system

Wheel speed sensor air gap . . . . 0.2 to 1.2 mm

Wheels

Maximum wheel runout (front and rear)
- Axial (side-to-side) . . . . 2.0 mm
- Radial (out-of-round) . . . . 2.0 mm

Maximum axle runout (front and rear) . . . . 0.2 mm

Tyres

Tyre pressures . . . . see *Pre-ride* checks

Tyre sizes*

CBF1000/A
- Front 120/70-ZR17M/C (58W)
- Rear 160/60-ZR17M/C (69W)

CB1000R/RA
- Front 120/70-ZR17M/C (58W)
- Rear 180/55-ZR17M/C (73W)

Refer to the owners handbook or the tyre information label for approved tyre brands.

Final drive

Drive chain slack and lubricant	see Chapter 1
Drive chain type	
CBF1000/A	
DID	DID50VA8-120LE
RK	RK50HFOZ5-120LE
CB1000R/RA	
DID	DID50VA8-116YB
Joining link pin projection from side plate (unstaked)	
DID type chain	
CBF1000/A	1.15 to 1.55 mm
CB1000R/RA	1.30 to 1.50 mm
RK type chain	1.20 to 1.40 mm
Joining link staked ends diameter	
DID type chain	5.50 to 5.80 mm
RK type chain	5.30 to 5.70 mm
Sprocket sizes (No. of teeth)	
Front (engine) sprocket	16
Rear (wheel) sprocket	
CBF1000/A	43
CB1000R/RA	44

Torque settings

Brake caliper bleed valves	
Front calipers on CB1000R (radial calipers)	7 Nm
All other calipers	5.5 Nm
Brake disc bolts/nuts	
Front	20 Nm
Rear	
CBF1000/A	42 Nm
CB1000R/RA	34 Nm
Brake hose banjo bolts	34 Nm
Brake pipe nuts	
CBF1000A models	17 Nm
CB1000RA models	14 Nm
Delay valve bolts (CB1000RA)	12 Nm
Final drive housing nuts	44 Nm
Footrest bracket bolts	
CBF1000/A models	27 Nm
CB1000R/RA models	37 Nm
Front axle bolt	59 Nm
Front axle clamp bolts	22 Nm
Front brake caliper mounting bolts	
CBF1000/A, CB1000RA	30 Nm
CB1000R	45 Nm
Front brake master cylinder clamp bolts	12 Nm
Front brake pad retaining pin(s)	
CBF1000/A, CB1000RA	17 Nm
CB1000R	15 Nm
Front sprocket bolt	54 Nm
Front wheel pulse ring screws	7 Nm
Modulator mounting bolts (CBF1000A)	
Lower bolts	12 Nm
Side bolt	10 Nm
Proportional control valve bolt (CB1000RA)	12 Nm
Rear axle nut (CBF1000/A)	98 Nm
Rear brake caliper mounting bolts (CB1000R/RA)	30 Nm
Rear brake caliper mounting bolt/slider pin (CBF1000)	22 Nm
Rear brake pad retaining pin	17 Nm
Rear brake master cylinder mounting bolts	12 Nm
Rear sprocket nuts	
CBF1000/A	108 Nm
CB1000R/RA	64 Nm
Rear wheel nuts (CB1000R/RA)	108 Nm
Rear wheel pulse ring screws (CBF1000A)	7 Nm
Stub axle nut (CB1000R/RA)	201 Nm

6•4 Brakes, wheels and final drive

1 General information

All models covered in this manual are fitted with cast alloy wheels designed for tubeless tyres only. Both front and rear brakes are hydraulically operated disc brakes.

CBF1000 models have a conventional braking system with two twin piston sliding calipers acting on 296 mm discs at the front, and one single piston sliding caliper acting on a 240 mm disc at the rear.

CBF1000A models have a combined anti-lock braking system (CBS/ABS), with two triple piston sliding calipers acting on 296 mm discs at the front, and one triple piston sliding caliper acting on a 240 mm disc at the rear.

CB1000R models have a conventional braking system with two radial calipers with four opposed pistons acting on 310 mm discs at the front, and a twin piston sliding caliper acting on a 256 mm disc at the rear.

CB1000RA models have a combined anti-lock braking system (CBS/ABS), with two triple piston sliding calipers acting on 310 mm discs at the front, and a twin piston sliding caliper acting on a 256 mm disc at the rear.

CBS/ABS system

The CBS links the rear brake to part of the front, actuating the centre piston in the right-hand caliper via a proportional control valve, whenever the pedal is depressed. The ABS prevents a wheel locking up under heavy braking. A sensor on each wheel is linked to a modulator unit that determines if a wheel is about to lock up, and if so releases and pulses brake pressure via the modulator until there is no longer any danger of wheel lock.

Caution: Disc brake components rarely require disassembly. Do not disassemble components unless absolutely necessary. If an hydraulic brake hose is loosened or disconnected, the banjo union sealing washers must be replaced with new ones and the system must be bled upon reassembly. Do not use solvents on internal brake components. Solvents will cause the seals to swell and distort. Use only clean DOT 4 brake fluid for cleaning. Use care when working with brake fluid as it can injure your eyes and it will damage painted surfaces and plastic parts.

2 Front brake pads

Note: *Honda recommend using new caliper mounting bolts. This is because the bolts are pre-treated with a locking compound. If they are not available it is possible, however, to clean up the old bolts and reinstall them using a suitable non-permanent thread locking compound that is commercially available.*

Caution: Do not operate the brakes while the caliper is off the disc.

1 On CBF1000 models unscrew the pad retaining pin plug. Slacken the pad pin. Unscrew the caliper mounting bolts and slide the caliper assembly off the disc. Unscrew and remove the pad pin, then remove the pads, noting how they locate.

2 On CB1000R models slacken the pad retaining pins (see illustration). Unscrew the caliper mounting bolts and slide the caliper off the disc (see illustrations). Unscrew and remove the pad pins, then remove the pads from the bottom of the caliper (see illustrations). Remove the caliper locating dowels if loose.

2.2a Slacken the pad pins (arrowed)

2.2b Unscrew the bolts (arrowed) and slide the caliper off

2.2c Remove the pad pins . . .

2.2d . . . then remove the pads

Brakes, wheels and final drive 6•5

3 On CBF1000A and CB1000RA models slacken the pad retaining pin **(see illustration)**. Unscrew the caliper mounting bolts and slide the caliper assembly off the disc **(see illustration)**. Unscrew and remove the pad pin, then remove the pads, noting how they locate **(see illustrations)**.

4 On CBF1000, CBF1000A and CB1000RA models slide the caliper and bracket apart **(see illustration)**. Clean all old grease off the slider pins. Check the condition of the rubber boots and replace them with new ones if necessary.

5 Where fitted and if required remove the shim from the back of each pad, noting how it fits – note that new pads should come with new shims where applicable, but make sure they do, especially if fitting after-market pads, before discarding the old ones.

6 Inspect the surface of each pad for contamination and check that the friction material has not worn to or beyond its service limit (see Chapter 1, Section 3). If any pad is worn, fouled with oil or grease, or heavily scored or damaged, fit a complete set of new pads. Also check for even wear across the pad – uneven wear is indicative of a sticking or seized piston (see Steps 8 and 9). **Note:** *It is not possible to degrease the friction material; if the pads are contaminated in any way they must be replaced with new ones.*

7 If the pads are in good condition clean them carefully, using a fine wire brush which is completely free of oil and grease to remove all traces of road dirt and corrosion. Using a pointed instrument, dig out any embedded particles of foreign matter. If required, spray with a dedicated brake cleaner to remove any dust.

8 Remove the pad spring from the caliper if required, noting which way round it fits **(see illustration 2.12a or b)**. Clean around the exposed section of each piston to remove any dirt or debris that could cause the seals to be damaged. If new pads are being fitted, now push the pistons all the way back into the caliper to create room for them; if the old pads are still serviceable push the pistons in a little way. To push the pistons back use finger pressure or a piece of wood as leverage, or place the old pads back in the caliper and use a metal bar or a screwdriver inserted between them (but take care not to damage the friction surface if the pads are being re-used), or use grips and a piece of wood, with rag or card to protect the caliper body **(see illustration)**. Alternatively obtain a proper piston-pushing tool from a good tool supplier **(see illustration)**. It may be necessary to remove the master cylinder reservoir cover, plate and diaphragm and siphon out some fluid (see *Pre-ride checks*). If the pistons are difficult to push back, remove the bleed valve cap, then attach a length of clear hose to the bleed valve and place the open end in a suitable container, then open the valve and try again (see Section 11). Take great care not to draw any air into the system. If in doubt, bleed the brakes afterwards.

9 If any of the pistons appear seized, first block or hold the other pistons using wood or cable-ties, then apply the brake lever and check whether the piston in question moves at all. If it moves out but can't be pushed back in the chances are there is some hidden corrosion stopping it. If it doesn't move at all, or to fully clean and inspect the pistons, disassemble the caliper and overhaul it (see Section 3).

10 Remove all traces of corrosion from the pad pin(s) and check for wear and damage. Where fitted check the condition of the stopper ring on the pin and replace it with a

2.3a Slacken the pad pin (arrowed)

2.3b Unscrew the bolts (arrowed) and slide the caliper off

2.3c Remove the pad pin . . .

2.3d . . . then remove the pads

2.4 Slide the caliper and bracket apart. Clean and check the pins and the boots (arrowed)

2.8a Press the pistons in as described to make clearance for new pads

2.8b This is a commercially available piston pushing tool

6•6 Brakes, wheels and final drive

2.10 Check the condition of the stopper ring (arrowed)

2.12a Pad spring (arrowed) – CBF1000A and CB1000RA

2.12b Pad spring (arrowed) – CB1000R

new one if it is damaged or deformed **(see illustration)**.

11 Check the condition of the brake disc (see Section 4).

12 If the pad spring was removed fit it into the caliper, making sure it locates correctly **(see illustrations)**.

13 On CBF1000, CBF1000A and CB1000RA models make sure the pad guide on the bracket is correctly fitted **(see illustration)**. Make sure the slider pins are tight. Smear the slider pins and inside the rubber boots with silicone grease. Slide the caliper and bracket together, making sure each boot lip locates correctly in the groove in the pin **(see illustration 2.4)**.

14 Where fitted and if removed fit the shim onto the back of each pad, making sure it locates correctly.

15 Lightly smear the back of the pad backing material or shim and the edges of the backing material where it contacts the caliper body with copper-based grease, making sure that none gets on the friction material. Also smear the pad pin, but not the stopper ring on CBF1000A and CB1000RA models.

16 On CBF1000 models fit the pads into the caliper so the friction material on each pad faces the other, and seat the pads in the guide on the bracket. Press them up against the spring to align the holes, then insert the pad pin and tighten it finger-tight. Slide the caliper assembly onto the disc making sure the pads locate correctly on each side. Either fit the new caliper mounting bolts, or clean the threads of the original bolts and apply fresh thread locking compound, then tighten them to the torque setting specified at the beginning of the Chapter. Tighten the pad pin to the torque setting specified at the beginning of this Chapter. Fit the pad pin plug.

17 On CB1000R models fit the pads into the caliper so the friction material on each pad faces the other **(see illustration)**. Press them up against the spring to align the holes, then insert the pad pins and tighten them finger-tight **(see illustration)**. Make sure the caliper locating dowels are fitted. Slide the caliper onto the disc making sure the pads locate correctly on each side **(see illustration)**. Either fit the new caliper mounting bolts, or clean the threads of the original bolts and apply a suitable non-permanent thread locking compound, then tighten them to the torque setting specified at the beginning of the Chapter **(see illustration)**. Tighten the pad pins to the torque setting specified at the beginning of this Chapter **(see illustration 2.2a)**.

18 On CBF1000A and CB1000RA models apply a smear of silicone grease to the stopper ring on the pad pin **(see illustration 2.10)**. Fit the pads into the caliper so the friction material on each pad faces the other, and seat the pads in the guide on the bracket

2.13 Make sure the guide (arrowed) is clean and correctly fitted

2.17a Fit the pads . . .

2.17b . . . then insert the pins

2.17c Slide the caliper onto the disc . . .

2.17d . . . and fit the bolts

Brakes, wheels and final drive 6•7

(see illustration). Press them up against the spring to align the holes, then insert the pad pin and tighten it finger-tight (see illustration 2.3c). Slide the caliper assembly onto the disc making sure the pads locate correctly on each side (see illustration). Either fit the new caliper mounting bolts, or clean the threads of the original bolts and apply fresh thread locking compound, then tighten them to the torque setting specified at the beginning of the Chapter. Tighten the pad pin to the torque setting specified at the beginning of this Chapter (see illustration 2.3a).

19 Operate the brake lever until the pads contact the disc. On CBF1000A and CB1000RA models also operate the brake pedal until the centre piston in the right-hand caliper contacts the pads. Check the level of fluid in each reservoir and top-up if necessary (see Pre-ride checks).

20 Check the operation of the brakes before riding the motorcycle.

3 Front brake calipers

Warning: *If a caliper is in need of an overhaul it is best to drain all old brake fluid from the system, then fill with new fluid after the overhaul (see Section 11). Overhaul of the brake calipers must be done in a spotlessly clean work area to avoid contamination and possible failure of the brake hydraulic system components. Do not, under any circumstances, use petroleum-based solvents to clean brake parts. Use clean DOT 4 brake fluid, dedicated brake cleaner or denatured alcohol only, as described. To prevent damage from spilled brake fluid, always cover paintwork when working on the braking system.*

Removal

Note: *Honda recommend using new caliper mounting bolts. This is because the bolts are pre-treated with a locking compound. If they are not available it is possible, however, to clean up the old bolts and reinstall them using a suitable non-permanent thread locking compound that is commercially available.*

2.18a Fit the pads making sure the shaped ends locate correctly in the pad guide

Caution: Do not operate the brakes while the caliper is off the disc.

1 If you just want to displace the calipers for front wheel removal, displace the brake hose guide and where fitted the wheel sensor wire from the fork and mudguard as required according to model (see illustration). Unscrew the caliper mounting bolts and slide the caliper assembly off the disc (see illustrations 2.2b or 2.3b). Tie the front brake calipers and hoses back so that they are out of the way. On CB1000R models remove the caliper locating dowels if loose.

2 If the caliper is being completely removed or overhauled, unscrew the brake hose banjo bolt(s) and detach the banjo union(s), noting the alignment with the caliper (see illustrations). If the brake fluid has not been drained seal the banjo unions – a good way of doing this is to place a piece of rubber over each side of the union (rubber blanking caps

3.1 Release the brake hose(s) and wiring as required according to model

3.2b Brake hose banjo bolt (arrowed) – CB1000R models

2.18b Slide the caliper onto the disc and fit the bolts

have been used in the photo), and clamp them in place using a spring clamp. Discard the sealing washers – new ones must be used.

3 If the caliper is being overhauled, follow the procedure for your model in Section 2, Steps 1 to 4, and remove the brake pads – this involves removing the caliper from the disc, and where applicable sliding the caliper and bracket apart.

Overhaul

4 Clean the exterior of the caliper with denatured alcohol or brake system cleaner. Have some clean rag ready to catch any spilled brake fluid.

5 On CBF1000, CBF1000A and CB1000RA models place the caliper piston-side down and insert some rag or a piece of wood between the pistons and the inner side of the caliper (see illustration). On CB1000R models insert rag between the pistons.

3.2a Brake hose banjo bolts (arrowed) – right-hand caliper on ABS models

3.2c Seal each banjo union using pieces of rubber and a clamp

3.5 Use rag or a piece of wood to protect the pistons and caliper . . .

6•8 Brakes, wheels and final drive

3.6 ... then apply compressed air to force the pistons out

3.9a Remove the dust seal ...

3.9b ... and the piston seal

6 Apply compressed air gradually and progressively, starting with a fairly low pressure, to the fluid passage and allow the pistons to ease out of their bores **(see illustration)**. Make sure the pistons are displaced evenly, using pressure to block one while the other moves if necessary.

7 If a piston is stuck in its bore due to corrosion the caliper should be replaced with a new one. Do not try to remove a piston by levering it out or by using pliers or other grips.

8 Mark each piston and the caliper body to ensure that the pistons can be matched to their original bores on reassembly. Note that two sizes of piston are used in each caliper on CB1000R and RA models (see Specifications at the beginning of this Chapter).

9 Remove the dust seals and the piston seals from the piston bores using a plastic tool to avoid scratching the bores **(see illustrations)**.

Discard the seals as new ones must be fitted on reassembly.

10 Clean the pistons and bores with clean brake fluid. If compressed air is available, blow it through the fluid passages to ensure they are clear (make sure it is filtered and unlubricated).

Caution: Do not, under any circumstances, use a petroleum-based solvent to clean brake parts.

11 Inspect the caliper bores and pistons for signs of corrosion, nicks and burrs and loss of plating **(see illustration)**. If surface defects are present, the pistons and/or the caliper assembly must be replaced with new ones. If the necessary measuring equipment is available, compare the dimensions of the caliper bores and pistons to those specified at the beginning of this Chapter, and obtain new pistons or a new caliper if necessary. If one caliper is in poor condition, the other front caliper and the master cylinder should also be checked.

12 Lubricate the new piston seals with clean brake fluid and fit them into their grooves in the caliper bores **(see illustrations)**. Note that on CB1000R and RA models there are two sizes of bore in each caliper and care must therefore be taken to ensure that the correct size seals are fitted to the correct bores (see Specifications). The same applies when fitting the new dust seals and pistons.

13 Lubricate the new dust seals with silicone grease and fit them into their grooves in the caliper bores **(see illustrations)**.

14 Lubricate the pistons with clean brake fluid and fit them, closed-end first, into the caliper bores, taking care not to displace the seals **(see illustration)**. Using your thumbs, push the pistons all the way in, making sure they enter the bore squarely.

3.11 Check the surfaces of the pistons and bores

3.12a Lubricate the new piston seals with brake fluid ...

3.12b ... then fit them into their grooves

3.13a Lubricate the new dust seals with silicone grease ...

3.13b ... then fit them into their grooves

3.14 Fit the pistons and push them all the way in

Brakes, wheels and final drive 6•9

Installation

15 If the caliper was overhauled refer to Section 2 and if not already done clean and check the pads and pad spring. On CBF1000, CBF1000A and CB1000RA models also clean and check the caliper slider pins and rubber boots, and the pad guide, then join the caliper and bracket together. Fit the brake pads into the caliper and the caliper onto the disc following the procedure for your model in Section 2, Steps 12 to 19.

16 If the caliper was just displaced slide it onto the disc making sure the pads locate correctly on each side **(see illustrations 2.17a and b or 2.18)** – on CB1000R models make sure the caliper locating dowels are fitted. Either fit the new caliper mounting bolts, or clean the threads of the original bolts and apply fresh thread locking compound, then tighten them to the torque setting specified at the beginning of the Chapter.

17 If detached, connect the brake hose(s) to the caliper, using new sealing washers on each side of the banjo fitting(s) **(see illustration)**. Align the fittings as noted on removal. Tighten the banjo bolts to the specified torque setting.

18 Secure the brake hose/pipe/wiring on the front fork and mudguard as required according to model **(see illustration 3.1)**.

19 Refer to Section 11 and fill and/or bleed the system as required.

20 Operate the brake lever until the pads contact the disc. On CBF1000A and CB1000RA models also operate the brake pedal until the centre piston in the right-hand caliper contacts the pads. Check the level of fluid in each reservoir and top-up if necessary (see *Pre-ride checks*).

21 Check that there are no fluid leaks and test the operation of the brakes before riding the motorcycle.

4 Front brake discs

Inspection

1 Inspect the surface of the disc for score marks and other damage. Light scratches are normal after use and won't affect brake operation, but deep grooves and heavy score marks will reduce braking efficiency and accelerate pad wear. If a disc is badly grooved it must be replaced with a new one.

2 The disc must not be allowed to wear down to a thickness less than the service limit listed in this Chapter's Specifications. The minimum thickness is also stamped on the disc **(see illustration)**. Check the thickness of the disc in the middle of the pad contact area using a micrometer – do not measure across the rim of the disc with a ruler. Replace the disc with a new one if necessary.

3 To check if the disc is warped, position the bike on an auxiliary stand with the front wheel raised off the ground (on CBF1000A models use the bike's centrestand). Mount a dial gauge to the fork leg, with the gauge plunger touching the surface of the disc about 10 mm from its outer edge **(see illustration)**. Rotate the wheel and watch the gauge needle, comparing the reading with the limit listed in the Specifications at the beginning of this Chapter. If the runout is greater than the service limit, check the wheel bearings for play (see Chapter 1). If the bearings are worn, install new ones (see Section 20) and repeat this check. If the disc runout is still excessive, remove the disc (Steps 4 and 5) and check for corrosion where it seats on the hub and clean it up if necessary. You can also try moving the disc around the wheel one bolt hole at a time and after each movement rechecking for runout. In most cases a new disc will have to be fitted.

3.17 Use a new sealing washer on each side of the banjo union

Removal

Note: Honda recommend using new disc mounting bolts. This is because the bolts are pre-treated with a locking compound. If they are not available it is possible, however, to clean up the old bolts and reinstall them using a suitable non-permanent thread locking compound that is commercially available.

4 Remove the wheel (see Section 18). On models with ABS remove the pulse ring from the right-hand side of the wheel (see Section 14).

Caution: Don't lay the wheel down and allow it to rest on either disc – the disc could become warped. Set the wheel on wood blocks so the wheel rim supports the weight of the wheel.

5 If you are not replacing the disc with a new one, mark the relationship of the disc to the wheel, so it can be installed in the same position and on the same side as originally fitted. Unscrew the disc bolts, loosening them evenly and a little at a time in a criss-cross pattern to avoid distorting the disc, then remove the disc **(see illustration)**.

4.2 The minimum thickness (arrowed) is marked on the disc

Installation

6 Before installing the disc, make sure there is no dirt or corrosion where the disc seats on the hub. If the disc does not sit flat when it is bolted down, it will appear to be warped when checked or when the front brake is used.

7 Fit the disc on the wheel with its marked side facing out, aligning the previously applied matchmarks (if you're reinstalling the original disc), and making sure the arrow points in the direction of normal rotation.

8 Either fit the new bolts, or clean the threads of the original bolts and apply fresh thread locking compound, and tighten them evenly and a little at a time in a criss-cross pattern to the torque setting specified at the beginning of this Chapter. Clean the disc using acetone or brake system cleaner. If a new disc has been installed, remove any protective coating from its working surfaces and fit new brake pads.

9 On models with ABS fit the pulse ring onto the right-hand side of the wheel (see Section 14). Install the front wheel (see Section 18).

10 Operate the brake lever until the pads contact the disc. On CBF1000A and CB1000RA models also operate the brake pedal until the centre piston in the right-hand caliper contacts the pads. Check the level of fluid in each reservoir and top-up if necessary (see *Pre-ride checks*).

11 Check the operation of the brakes before riding the motorcycle.

4.3 Checking disc runout with a dial gauge

4.5 The disc is secured by six bolts

6•10 Brakes, wheels and final drive

5.1 Disconnect the brake light switch wires (A). Switch mounting screw (B)

5.2 Unscrew the bolts (arrowed) and remove the master cylinder and its clamp

5 Front brake master cylinder

⚠ **Warning:** *If the brake master cylinder is in need of an overhaul it is best to drain all old brake fluid from the system, then fill with new fluid after the overhaul (see Section 11). Overhaul must be done in a spotlessly clean work area to avoid contamination and possible failure of the brake hydraulic system components. Do not, under any circumstances, use petroleum-based solvents to clean brake parts. Use clean DOT 4 brake fluid, dedicated brake cleaner or denatured alcohol only, as described. To prevent damage from spilled brake fluid, always cover paintwork when working on the braking system.*

Removal

Note: *If the master cylinder is being overhauled (usually due to sticking or poor action, or fluid leaks) read through the entire procedure first and make sure that you have obtained all the new parts required, including some new DOT 4 brake fluid.*

1 Disconnect the brake light switch wiring connectors **(see illustrations)**. On CB1000R/RA models remove the mirror (see Chapter 7).
2 If the master cylinder is just being displaced unscrew the clamp bolts and remove the back of the clamp, noting how it fits, then cover the master cylinder and reservoir in rag and position it clear of the handlebar **(see illustration)**. Ensure no strain is placed on the hydraulic hose. Keep the reservoir upright to prevent air entering the system.
3 If the master cylinder is being overhauled, remove the brake lever (see Chapter 5).
4 If the brake fluid wasn't drained, on CBF1000/A models slacken the reservoir cover screws, and on CB1000R/RA models remove the reservoir cap clamp screw and clamp **(see illustrations)**.
5 Unscrew the brake hose banjo bolt and detach the banjo union, noting its alignment with the master cylinder **(see illustration)**. If the brake fluid has not been drained seal the banjo unions – a good way of doing this is to place a piece of rubber over each side of the union (rubber blanking caps work well), and

5.4a Slacken the cover screws . . .

5.4b . . . or remove the clamp

5.5 Brake hose banjo bolt (arrowed) – CB1000R shown

Brakes, wheels and final drive 6•11

5.9a Front brake master cylinder – CBF1000/A models

| 1 Rubber boot | 3 Seal | 5 Cup | 7 Brake light |
| 2 Circlip | 4 Piston | 6 Spring | switch |

5.9b Remove the boot from the end of the master cylinder piston . . .

5.9c . . . then depress the piston, remove the circlip, and draw out the piston and spring

clamp them in place using a spring clamp **(see illustration 3.2c)**. Discard the sealing washers – new ones must be used.

6 Unscrew the master cylinder clamp bolts and remove the back of the clamp, noting how it fits, then lift the master cylinder away from the handlebar **(see illustration 5.2)**.

7 Remove the reservoir cover or cap, the diaphragm plate and the diaphragm. If the brake fluid wasn't drained tip the fluid from the master cylinder and reservoir into a suitable container. Wipe any remaining fluid out of the reservoir with a clean rag.

8 If required, undo the screw securing the brake light switch to the bottom of the master cylinder and remove the switch **(see illustration 5.1)**.

Overhaul

9 On CBF1000/A models remove the rubber boot from the master cylinder **(see illustrations)**. Depress the piston and use circlip pliers to remove the circlip, then slide out the piston assembly and spring, noting how they fit **(see illustration)**. If they are difficult to remove, apply low pressure compressed air to the brake fluid outlet. Lay the parts out in the proper order to prevent confusion during reassembly.

10 On CB1000R/RA models remove the pushrod and the rubber boot from the master cylinder **(see illustrations)**. Depress the piston and use circlip pliers to remove the circlip, then slide out the piston assembly, the spring and the spring guide, noting how

5.10a Front brake master cylinder – CB1000R/RA models

1 Rubber boot	4 Seal	7 Spring	10 Reservoir
2 Pushrod	5 Piston	8 Spring guide	11 Reservoir O-rings
3 Circlip	6 Cup	9 Brake light switch	12 Bleed valve

6•12 Brakes, wheels and final drive

5.10b Remove the pushrod and boot from the end of the master cylinder piston . . .

5.10c . . . then depress the piston and remove the circlip . . .

5.10d . . . and draw out the piston . . .

5.10e . . . spring and guide

they fit **(see illustrations)**. If they are difficult to remove, apply low pressure compressed air to the brake fluid outlet. Lay the parts out in the proper order to prevent confusion during reassembly. Undo the screws inside the reservoir and pull it off. Discard the O-rings – new ones must be used.

11 Clean the master cylinder and reservoir with clean brake fluid. If compressed air is available, blow it through the fluid galleries to ensure they are clear (make sure the air is filtered and unlubricated).

Caution: Do not, under any circumstances, use a petroleum-based solvent to clean brake parts.

12 Check the master cylinder bore for corrosion, scratches, nicks and score marks. If the necessary measuring equipment is available, compare the dimensions of the piston and bore to those given in the Specifications at the beginning of this Chapter. If damage or wear is evident, the master cylinder must be replaced with a new one. If the master cylinder is in poor condition, then the calipers should be checked as well.

13 The dust boot, circlip, piston and its cup and seal, spring, and on CB1000R/RA models the spring guide, are all included in a master cylinder rebuild kit, and all other components are available individually. Use all of the new parts, regardless of the apparent condition of the old ones. Lubricate the master cylinder bore with new brake fluid. On CB1000R/RA models remove the pushrod from the boot as this does not come in the kit.

14 Smear the cup and seal with new brake fluid and if not already in place fit them into their grooves in the piston so their wider ends will fit into the master cylinder first **(see illustration)**.

5.14 Make sure the cup and seal are correctly installed – CB1000R shown

5.16 Feed the rim of the boot into the bore

15 On CBF1000/A models fit the spring wide end first into the master cylinder **(see illustration 5.9a)**. Lubricate the piston, cup and seal with clean brake fluid and slide it into the master cylinder and up against the spring. Make sure the lips on the cup and seal do not turn inside out. Push the piston in to compress the spring and fit the new circlip, making sure it locates in the groove **(see illustration 5.9c)**. Smear the outer end of the piston and the inside of the boot with silicone grease. Carefully push the wide rim of the boot onto its seat in the master cylinder and locate the narrow end lips in the groove in the piston **(see illustration 5.9b)**.

16 On CB1000R/RA models fit the spring guide into the end of the spring, then fit the spring guide and spring into the master cylinder **(see illustration 5.10e)**. Lubricate the piston, cup and seal with clean brake fluid and slide it into the master cylinder and up against the spring **(see illustration 5.10d)**. Make sure the lips on the cup and seal do not turn inside out. Push the piston in to compress the spring and fit the new circlip, making sure it locates in the groove **(see illustration 5.10c)**. Smear the inner end of the pushrod and inside the rubber boot with silicone grease. Fit the boot onto the pushrod so its narrow end lips locate in the groove **(see illustration 5.10b)**. Locate the inner end of the pushrod in the end of the piston and carefully push the wide rim of the boot onto its seat in the master cylinder **(see illustration)**. Fit new reservoir O-rings smeared with clean brake fluid. Clean the threads of the reservoir screws and apply some fresh threadlock, then fit the reservoir and tighten the screws.

17 Inspect the reservoir diaphragm and fit a new one it if it is damaged or deteriorated.

Installation

18 If removed, fit the brake light switch onto the bottom of the master cylinder, making sure the pin locates in the hole, and tighten the screw **(see illustration 5.1)**.

19 Attach the master cylinder to the handlebar, aligning the clamp joint with the punch mark on the top of the handlebar, then fit the back of the clamp with its UP mark facing up **(see illustration 5.2)**. Tighten the upper bolt to the torque setting specified at the beginning of this Chapter, followed by the lower bolt.

20 Connect the brake hose to the master cylinder, using new sealing washers on each side of the banjo fitting. Align the hose as noted on removal **(see illustration 5.5)**. Tighten the banjo bolt to the torque setting specified at the beginning of this Chapter.

21 Install the brake lever (see Chapter 5).

22 Connect the brake light switch wiring **(see illustration 5.1)**. On CB1000R/RA models install the mirror (see Chapter 7).

23 Refer to Section 11 and fill and/or bleed the system as required. Check that there are no fluid leaks and test the operation of the brakes before riding the motorcycle.

Brakes, wheels and final drive 6•13

6.1 Push the caliper against the disc to force the pistons in

6.4a Unscrew the pin (arrowed) . . .

6.4b . . . and remove the pads

6 Rear brake pads

Caution: Do not operate the brakes with the pads removed or the caliper off the disc.

1 Push the caliper against the disc, all the way across if new pads are being fitted so the pistons are pushed all the way back into the caliper to create room for them **(see illustration)**. It may be necessary to remove the master cylinder reservoir cover, plate and diaphragm and siphon out some fluid (see *Pre-ride checks*). If the pistons are difficult to push back, remove the bleed valve cap, then attach a length of clear hose to the bleed valve and place the open end in a suitable container, then open the valve and try again (see Section 11). Take great care not to draw any air into the system. If in doubt, bleed the brakes afterwards.

2 If the caliper is difficult to push in the chances are there is some hidden corrosion stopping it. If it doesn't move at all, or to fully clean and inspect the pistons, remove the caliper and overhaul it (see Section 7).

3 On CBF1000 models slacken the pad retaining pin. Unscrew the caliper rear mounting bolt/slider pin. Unscrew the retaining pin then pivot the back of the caliper up off the disc and remove the pads, noting how they fit.

4 On CBF1000A models unscrew and remove the pad pin, then draw the pads out **(see illustrations)**.

5 On CB1000R/RA models unscrew and remove the pad pin, then draw the pads out **(see illustrations)**.

6 Where fitted and if required remove the shim from the back of each pad, noting how it fits – note that new pads should come with new shims where applicable, but make sure they do, especially if fitting after-market pads, before discarding the old ones.

7 Inspect the surface of each pad for contamination and check that the friction material has not worn beyond its service limit (see Chapter 1, Section 3). If either pad is worn, is fouled with oil or grease, or heavily scored or damaged, fit a set of new pads. On CBF1000A and CB1000R/RA models check for even wear across the pad – uneven wear is indicative of a sticking or seized piston, in which case remove the caliper for further inspection (see Section 7). **Note:** *It is not possible to degrease the friction material; if the pads are contaminated in any way they must be replaced with new ones.*

8 If the pads are in good condition clean them carefully, using a fine wire brush which is completely free of oil and grease to remove all traces of road dirt and corrosion. Using a pointed instrument, dig out any embedded particles of foreign matter. If required, spray with a dedicated brake cleaner to remove any dust.

9 Remove all traces of corrosion from the pad pin and check it for wear and damage. Check the condition of the stopper ring on the pin and replace it with a new one if it is damaged or deformed **(see illustration 2.10)**.

10 Check the condition of the brake disc (see Section 8).

11 Where fitted and if removed fit the shim onto the back of each pad, making sure it locates correctly.

12 Lightly smear the back of the pad backing material or shim and the edges of the backing material where it contacts the caliper body with copper-based grease, making sure that none gets on the friction material. Also smear the pad pin, but not the stopper ring.

13 Apply a smear of silicone grease to the stopper ring on the pad pin **(see illustration 2.10)**.

14 On CBF1000 models fit the pads into the caliper so the friction material on each pad faces the other, then pivot the caliper down

6.5a Unscrew the pin (arrowed) . . .

6.5b . . . and remove the pads

6•14 Brakes, wheels and final drive

6.15a Slide the pads into the caliper . . .

6.15b . . . making sure they seat correctly against the guide . . .

6.15c . . . then press them up against the spring and insert the pin

6.16a Make sure the pads seat correctly against the guide . . .

6.16b . . . then press them up against the spring and insert the pin

and seat the pads in the guide on the bracket. Press the pads up against the spring to align the holes, then insert the pad pin and tighten it finger-tight. Fit the caliper rear mounting bolt/slider pin and tighten it to the torque setting specified at the beginning of this Chapter. Tighten the pad pin to the specified torque.

15 On CBF1000A models fit the pads into the caliper so the friction material on each pad faces the other, and seat the pads in the guide on the bracket (see illustrations). Press them up against the spring to align the holes, then insert the pad pin and tighten it to the torque setting specified at the beginning of this Chapter (see illustration).

16 On CB1000R/RA models fit the pads into the caliper so the friction material on each pad faces the other (see illustration 6.5b), and seat the pads in the guide on the bracket (see illustration). Press them up against the spring to align the holes, then insert the pad pin and tighten it to the torque setting specified at the beginning of this Chapter (see illustration).

17 Operate the brake pedal until the pads contact the disc. Check the level of fluid in each reservoir and top-up if necessary (see Pre-ride checks).

18 Check the operation of the brakes before riding the motorcycle.

7 Rear brake caliper

⚠️ Warning: *If the brake caliper is in need of an overhaul it is best to drain all old brake fluid from the* system, then fill with new fluid after the overhaul (see Section 11). Overhaul must be done in a spotlessly clean work area to avoid contamination and possible failure of the brake hydraulic system components. Do not, under any circumstances, use petroleum-based solvents to clean brake parts. Use clean DOT 4 brake fluid, dedicated brake cleaner or denatured alcohol only, as described. To prevent damage from spilled brake fluid, always cover paintwork when working on the braking system.

Removal

Note: *On CB1000R/RA models Honda recommend using new caliper mounting bolts. This is because the bolts are pre-treated with a locking compound. If they are not available it is possible, however, to clean up the old bolts and reinstall them using a suitable non-permanent thread locking compound that is commercially available.*

Caution: **Do not operate the brakes while the caliper is off the disc.**

1 If the caliper is being completely removed or overhauled, unscrew the brake hose banjo bolt and detach the banjo union, noting its alignment with the caliper (see illustrations). If the brake fluid has not been drained seal the banjo union – a good way of doing this is to place a piece of rubber over each side of the union (rubber blanking caps work well),

7.1a Brake hose banjo bolt (arrowed) – CBF1000A models

7.1b Brake hose banjo bolt (arrowed) – CB1000R models

Brakes, wheels and final drive 6•15

7.4 Slide the caliper and bracket apart

7.5a Unscrew the bolts (arrowed) and slide the caliper off the disc . . .

7.5b . . . then slide the caliper and bracket apart

and clamp them in place using a spring clamp (see illustration 3.2c). Discard the sealing washers – new ones must be used.

2 Remove the brake pads (see Section 6).

3 On CBF1000 models slide the caliper off the bracket. If you want to remove the caliper bracket remove the rear wheel (see Section 19), then displace the bracket from the swingarm, noting how it locates.

4 On CBF1000A models displace the wheel sensor from the caliper bracket (see Section 14). Remove the rear wheel (see Section 19). Slide the caliper and bracket apart **(see illustration)**.

5 On CB1000R/RA models remove the rear wheel (see Section 19). Unscrew the caliper mounting bolts and slide the caliper down off the disc **(see illustration)**. Slide the caliper and bracket apart **(see illustration)**.

6 Remove the pad spring from the caliper and the guide from the bracket if required **(see illustrations)**. Clean all old grease off the slider pins and rubber boots **(see illustration)**. Check the condition of the rubber boots and replace them with new ones if necessary. Note the sleeve in the caliper boot on CBF1000 models **(see illustration 7.17)**.

Overhaul

7 Clean the exterior of the caliper with denatured alcohol or brake system cleaner. Have some clean rag ready to catch any spilled brake fluid.

8 Place the caliper piston-side down and insert some rag or a piece of wood between the pistons and the inner side of the caliper **(see illustration 3.5)**. Apply compressed air gradually and progressively, starting with a fairly low pressure, to the fluid passage and allow the piston(s) to ease out of the bore(s), controlling with hand pressure on the caliper **(see illustration 3.6)**. On CBF1000A and CB1000R/RA models make sure the pistons are displaced evenly, using pressure to block one while the other(s) move(s) if necessary.

9 If a piston is stuck in its bore due to corrosion the caliper should be replaced with a new one. Do not try to remove a piston by levering it out or by using pliers or other grips.

10 On CBF1000A and CB1000R/RA models mark each piston and the caliper body to ensure that the pistons can be matched to their original bores on reassembly.

11 Remove the dust seal(s) and the piston seal(s) from the piston bore(s) using a plastic tool to avoid scratching the bores **(see illustrations 3.9a and b)**. Discard the seals as new ones must be fitted on reassembly.

12 Clean the piston(s) and bore(s) with clean brake fluid. If compressed air is available, blow it through the fluid passages to ensure they are clear (make sure it is filtered and unlubricated). **Caution: Do not, under any circumstances, use a petroleum-based solvent to clean brake parts.**

13 Inspect the caliper bore(s) and piston(s) for signs of corrosion, nicks and burrs and loss of plating **(see illustration 3.11)**. If surface defects are present, the piston(s) and/or the caliper assembly must be replaced with new ones. If the necessary measuring equipment is available, compare the dimensions of the caliper bore(s) and piston(s) to those specified at the beginning of this Chapter, and obtain new piston(s) or a new caliper if necessary. If the caliper is in poor condition, the master cylinder should also be checked.

7.6a Pad spring (arrowed) . . .

7.6b . . . and guide – CBF1000A

7.6c Pad spring (arrowed) . . .

7.6d . . . and guide – CB1000R

7.6e Clean and check the pins (A) and boots (B) – CB1000R shown

6•16 Brakes, wheels and final drive

7.17 Insert the sleeve inside the boot

7.20 Slide the caliper onto the disc and fit the bolts

14 Lubricate the new piston seal(s) with clean brake fluid and fit it/them into the groove(s) in the caliper bore(s) **(see illustrations 3.12a and b)**.
15 Lubricate the new dust seal(s) with silicone grease and fit it/them into the groove(s) in the caliper bore(s)**(see illustrations 3.13a and b)**.
16 Lubricate the piston(s) with clean brake fluid and fit it/them, closed-end first, into the caliper bore(s), taking care not to displace the seals **(see illustration 3.14)**. Using your thumbs, push the piston(s) all the way in, making sure it/they enter(s) the bore squarely.

Installation

17 If the pad spring was removed, make sure it is clean then fit it into the caliper, making sure it locates correctly **(see illustration 7.6a or c)**. Make sure the pad guide on the bracket is clean and correctly fitted **(see illustration 7.6b or d)**. Make sure the slider pins are tight **(see illustration 7.6e)**. Smear the slider pins and inside the rubber boots with silicone grease. On CBF1000 models make sure the sleeve is in the caliper boot **(see illustration)**.
18 On CBF1000 models, if removed locate the caliper bracket on the swingarm, then install the wheel (see Section 19). Slide the caliper onto the bracket.

19 On CBF1000A models slide the caliper and bracket together, making sure each boot lip locates correctly in the groove in the pin **(see illustration 7.4)**. Install the wheel (see Section 19). Fit the wheel sensor onto the caliper bracket (see Section 14).
20 On CB1000R/RA models slide the caliper and bracket together, making sure each boot lip locates correctly in the groove in the pin **(see illustration 7.5b)**. Slide the caliper onto the disc making sure the pads locate correctly on each side **(see illustration)**. Either fit the new caliper mounting bolts, or clean the threads of the original bolts and apply fresh thread locking compound, then tighten them to the torque setting specified at the beginning of the Chapter. Install the wheel (see Section 19).
21 If removed, connect the brake hose to the caliper, using new sealing washers on each side of the banjo fitting **(see illustration 3.17)**. Align the fitting as noted on removal **(see illustration 7.1a or b)**. Tighten the banjo bolt to the specified torque setting.
22 Install the brake pads (see Section 6).
23 Refer to Section 11 and fill and/or bleed the system as required. Check that there are no fluid leaks and test the operation of the brakes before riding the motorcycle.

8 Rear brake disc

Inspection

1 Refer to Section 4 of this Chapter, noting that the dial gauge should be attached to the swingarm.

Removal

Note: *On CBF1000/A models Honda recommend using new disc mounting bolts. This is because the bolts are pre-treated with a locking compound. It is possible, however, to clean up the old bolts and reinstall them using a suitable non-permanent thread locking compound that is commercially available.*
2 On CBF1000A models remove the rear wheel (see Section 19). Remove the pulse ring from the wheel (see Section 14).
3 On CB1000R/RA models remove the stub axle (see Section 19).
4 If you are not replacing the disc with a new one, mark the relationship of the disc to the wheel or stub axle so it can be installed in the same position. Unscrew the disc retaining bolts or nuts, loosening them evenly and a little at a time in a criss-cross pattern to avoid distorting the disc, then remove the disc, along with the pulse ring on CB1000RA models **(see illustrations)**.

Installation

5 Before installing the disc, make sure there is no dirt or corrosion where the disc seats on the hub. If the disc does not sit flat when it is bolted down, it will appear to be warped when checked or when the rear brake is used.
6 Fit the disc, and on CB1000RA models the pulse ring, on the wheel or stub axle with its marked side facing out, aligning the previously applied matchmarks (if you're reinstalling the original disc).
7 On CBF1000/A models either fit the new

8.4a Rear brake disc bolts (arrowed) – CBF1000A

8.4a Rear brake disc nuts (arrowed) – CB1000R/RA

Brakes, wheels and final drive 6•17

9.1a Reservoir bolt (arrowed) – CBF1000/A models

9.1b Reservoir bolt (arrowed) – CB1000R/RA models

bolts, or clean the threads of the original bolts and apply fresh thread locking compound. On all models tighten then bolts or nuts evenly and a little at a time in a criss-cross pattern to the torque setting specified at the beginning of this Chapter. Clean the disc using acetone or brake system cleaner. If a new disc has been installed, remove any protective coating from its working surfaces and fit new brake pads.

8 On CBF1000A models fit the pulse ring onto the wheel (see Section 14). Install the rear wheel (see Section 19).

9 On CB1000R/RA models install the stub axle (see Section 19).

10 Operate the brake pedal several times to bring the pads into contact with the disc. Check the operation of the brakes before riding the motorcycle.

9 Rear brake master cylinder

⚠️ **Warning:** *If the brake master cylinder is in need of an overhaul it is best to drain all old brake fluid from the system, then fill with new fluid after the overhaul (see Section 11). Overhaul must be done in a spotlessly clean work area to avoid contamination and possible failure of the brake hydraulic system components. Do not, under any circumstances, use petroleum-based solvents to clean brake parts. Use clean DOT 4 brake fluid, dedicated brake cleaner or denatured alcohol only, as described. To prevent damage from spilled brake fluid, always cover paintwork when working on the braking system.*

Removal

Note: *If the master cylinder is being overhauled (usually due to sticking or poor action, or fluid leaks) read through the entire procedure first and make sure that you have obtained all the new parts required, including some new DOT 4 brake fluid.*

1 Unscrew the reservoir bolt and displace the reservoir **(see illustrations)**.

2 Unscrew the brake hose banjo bolt and detach the banjo union, noting its alignment with the master cylinder **(see illustration)**. If the brake fluid has not been drained seal the banjo unions – a good way of doing this is to place a piece of rubber over each side of the union (rubber blanking caps work well), and clamp them in place using a spring clamp **(see illustration 3.2c)**. Discard the sealing washers – new ones must be used.

3 Straighten the ends of the split pin and withdraw it from the master cylinder pushrod clevis pin **(see illustration)** – on CB1000R/RA

9.2 Brake hose banjo bolt (arrowed)

9.4 Unscrew the bolts (arrowed) and remove the master cylinder

models if access is too restricted remove the silencer (see Chapter 4). Withdraw the clevis pin and detach the pushrod from the pedal.

4 Unscrew the master cylinder bolts and remove it along with the reservoir **(see illustration)**.

Overhaul

5 If the system wasn't drained undo the reservoir cap and tip the fluid out – on CB1000R/RA models first release the cap clamp. Release the clip securing the reservoir hose to the union on the master cylinder and detach the hose, being prepared to catch any residual fluid **(see illustration)**.

9.3 Remove the split pin (A) and withdraw the clevis pin (B)

9.5 Release the clip and pull the hose off its union

6•18 Brakes, wheels and final drive

9.6 Undo the screw and remove the union

9.8a Remove the rubber boot . . .

9.8b . . . then release the circlip . . .

9.8c . . . and remove the pushrod, piston and spring

9.10 Check the cylinder for damage and wear

9.12a Fit the seal onto the piston . . .

6 If required, undo the reservoir hose union screw and detach it from the master cylinder **(see illustration)**. Discard the O-ring as a new one must be used. Inspect the reservoir hose for cracks or splits and replace it with a new one if necessary.

7 If required (doing so will give extra clearance for your circlip pliers in the next step), note how far the clevis is threaded up the pushrod, then slacken its locknut and thread it off, followed by the locknut **(see illustration 9.16)**.

8 Dislodge the rubber dust boot from the base of the master cylinder and from around the pushrod, noting how it locates **(see illustration)**. Push the pushrod in and, using circlip pliers, remove the circlip from its groove in the master cylinder and slide out the pushrod, piston and spring on CBF1000 and CB1000R models, or the pushrod/piston assembly and spring on CBF1000A and CB1000RA models, noting how they fit **(see illustrations)**. Lay the parts out in order as you remove them to prevent confusion during reassembly.

9 Clean the master cylinder with clean brake fluid. If compressed air is available, blow it through the fluid galleries to ensure they are clear (make sure the air is filtered and unlubricated).

Caution: Do not, under any circumstances, use a petroleum-based solvent to clean brake parts.

10 Check the master cylinder bore for corrosion, scratches, nicks and score marks **(see illustration)**. If the necessary measuring equipment is available, compare the dimensions of the piston and bore to those given in the Specifications at the beginning of this Chapter. If damage or wear is evident, the master cylinder must be replaced with a new one. If the master cylinder is in poor condition, then the caliper should be checked as well.

11 The dust boot, circlip, piston, seal, cup and spring are all included in the master cylinder rebuild kit. Use all of the new parts, regardless of the apparent condition of the old ones. If the pushrod components are not assembled, assemble them according to the layout of the old one.

12 Smear the cup and seal with new brake fluid. If the seal is not already on the piston, fit it into its groove so the wider end will fit into the master cylinder first **(see illustrations)**. Fit the cup onto the narrow end of the spring, locating the peg in the hole **(see illustration)**. Lubricate the master cylinder bore with new brake fluid. Fit the new circlip onto the pushrod if not already in place.

13 Fit the spring wide-end first into the master cylinder and push the cup in, making sure its lips do not turn inside out **(see illustration)**.

14 On CBF1000 and CB1000R models lubricate the piston with clean brake fluid and

9.12b . . . as shown

9.12c Fit the cup onto the end of the spring, locating the peg in the hole

9.13 Fit the spring making sure the cup locates correctly in the bore . . .

Brakes, wheels and final drive 6•19

9.14a . . . then push the piston in

9.14b Position the circlip on the washer . . .

9.14c . . . then depress the pushrod and fit the circlip into the groove

9.14d Fit the new boot . . .

9.14e . . . then press it into the cylinder . . .

9.14f . . . and make sure it is correctly located around the pushrod

slide it into the master cylinder and up against the cup and spring **(see illustration)**. Make sure the lips on the seal do not turn inside out. Smear some silicone grease onto the rounded end of the pushrod and around the lips of the boot. Fit the new circlip onto the pushrod if not already in place **(see illustration)**. Push the piston in using the pushrod until the washer is beyond the circlip groove, then locate the circlip in the groove **(see illustration)**. Fit the rubber boot, making sure the lips are seated correctly in the master cylinder and around the pushrod **(see illustrations)**.

15 On CBF1000A and CB1000RA models lubricate the piston with clean brake fluid and slide the piston/pushrod assembly into the master cylinder and up against the cup and spring. Make sure the lips on the seal do not turn inside out. Fit the new circlip onto the pushrod if not already in place **(see illustration 9.14b)**. Push the piston in using the pushrod until the washer is beyond the circlip groove, then locate the circlip in the groove **(see illustration 9.14c)**. Fit the rubber boot, making sure the lips are seated correctly in the master cylinder and around the pushrod **(see illustrations 9.14d, e and f)**.

16 If not already in place thread the locknut and clevis onto the pushrod, setting them as noted on removal – Honda specify the distance between the centre of the clevis pin hole and the lower mounting bolt hole measured parallel to the pushrod should be 67.5 mm. Tighten the locknut securely against the clevis.

17 If removed fit a new fluid reservoir hose union O-ring smeared with brake fluid, then press the union into the master cylinder and secure it with the screw **(see illustrations)**.

18 Connect the hose to the union on the master cylinder and secure it with the clip **(see illustration)**. Check that the hose is secured with a clip at the reservoir end as well. If the clips have weakened, use new ones.

Installation

19 Locate the master cylinder on the footrest bracket and tighten the bolts to the torque setting specified at the beginning of this Chapter **(see illustration 9.4)**.

20 Fit the fluid reservoir onto the frame, on CBF1000/A models making sure the pin on the back locates in the hole **(see illustration 9.1a or b)**.

21 Align the brake hose as noted on removal and connect the hose to the master cylinder, using a new sealing washer on each side of the banjo fitting **(see illustration 9.2)**. Tighten the banjo bolt to the torque setting specified at the beginning of this Chapter.

22 Align the clevis with the brake pedal, then insert the pin and secure it with a new split pin

9.17a Fit a new O-ring . . .

9.17b . . . then press the union into place

9.18 Fit the reservoir hose onto its union

6•20 Brakes, wheels and final drive

(see illustration 9.3). Bend the ends of the pin round to lock it.

23 Refer to Section 11 and fill and/or bleed the system as required. Check that there are no fluid leaks and test the operation of the brakes before riding the motorcycle.

10 Brake hoses and fittings

Inspection

1 To fully inspect all the brake hoses and pipes on models with CBS/ABS remove the fuel tank (see Chapter 4).

2 Check brake hose condition according to the brake system check interval in the service schedule (see Chapter 1). Twist and flex the hoses while looking for cracks, bulges and seeping hydraulic fluid. Check extra carefully around the areas where the hoses connect with the banjo fittings, as these are common areas for hose failure.

3 On models with CBS/ABS also check the brake pipes, the hose and pipe joints, the proportional control valve, and the modulator, referring to the relevant Sections of this Chapter, for signs of fluid leakage and for any dents or cracks in the pipes.

4 Inspect the banjo fittings connected to the brake hoses and the pipe joints on CBS/ABS models. If the fittings are rusted, scratched or cracked, fit new ones.

Removal and installation

5 Drain all old brake fluid from the system (see Section 11).

6 The brake hoses have banjo fittings on each end. Cover the surrounding area with plenty of rags and unscrew the banjo bolt at each end of the hose, noting the alignment of the fitting with the master cylinder or brake caliper (see illustrations 3.2a and b, 5.5, 7.1a or b, and 9.2). Free the hose from any clips or guides and remove it, noting its routing. Discard the sealing washers. **Note:** *Do not operate the brake lever or pedal while a brake hose is disconnected.*

7 Position the new hose, making sure it isn't twisted or otherwise strained, and ensure that it is correctly routed through any clips or guides and is clear of all moving components.

8 Check that the fittings align correctly, then install the banjo bolts, using new sealing washers on both sides of the fittings (see illustration 3.2c). Tighten the banjo bolts to the torque setting specified at the beginning of this Chapter.

9 The brake pipes are held by nuts (see illustration 14.23a). There are no sealing washers. Unscrew the nuts and detach the pipes. Make sure the pipe is correctly positioned, fitted into any clips, and with any joint blocks secured, before tightening the nuts. If the correct tools are available tighten the nuts to the torque setting specified at the beginning of this Chapter for your model.

10 Refill the system with new DOT 4 brake fluid (see *Pre-ride checks*) and bleed the air from it (see Section 11).

11 Check the operation of the brakes before riding the motorcycle.

11 Brake system bleeding and fluid change

Special tool: *Honda recommend using a vacuum-type brake bleeding tool (see illustration 11.17). If bleeding the system using the conventional method does not work sufficiently well, it is advisable to obtain this tool and repeat the procedure detailed below, following the manufacturer's instructions for using the tool.*

1 Bleeding the brakes is simply the process of removing any air bubbles from the system. Bleeding is necessary whenever a brake hose or pipe joint is loosened or disconnected. Leaks in the system may also allow air to enter, but leaking brake fluid will reveal their presence and warn you of the need for repair.

2 To bleed the brakes, you will need some new DOT 4 brake fluid, a length of clear flexible hose, a small container partially filled with clean brake fluid, some rags, a spanner to fit the caliper bleed valve, and help from an assistant (see illustration). Bleeding kits that include the hose, a one-way valve and a container are available relatively cheaply from a good auto store, and simplify the task, with the one way valve negating the need of an assistant.

3 Cover painted components to prevent damage in the event that brake fluid is spilled. On CBF1000A and CB1000RA models remove the right-hand fairing side panel to access the proportional control valve bleed valve (see Chapter 7).

4 Refer to *Pre-Ride checks* and remove the reservoir cover or cap, diaphragm plate and diaphragm and slowly pump the brake lever or pedal a few times, until no air bubbles can be seen floating up from the holes in the bottom of the reservoir. Doing this bleeds the air from the master cylinder end of the line. Loosely refit the reservoir cover.

5 On CBF1000A and CB1000RA models bleed the front brake system using the upper bleed valve on the right-hand caliper (see illustration) (the left-hand caliper only has one bleed valve). When bleeding the rear brake system bleed the right-hand front caliper centre piston using the lower bleed valve first, then bleed the rear caliper, on CBF1000A models first using the rear bleed valve, then using the centre bleed valve (see illustration). Note that the rear brake pedal action may feel heavy – this is due to the proportional control valve and is normal, but make sure you push the pedal all the way down. On CB1000R/RA models there is also a bleed valve in the front master cylinder (see illustration) – Honda do not specify to use this during the standard bleeding procedure, but if the master cylinder has been overhauled and/or it is not possible to get a firm feeling at the lever after normal bleeding via the calipers use this valve to check there is no air trapped in the top of the master cylinder.

11.2 Set-up for bleeding the brakes

11.5a Upper and lower bleed valves (arrowed) – right-hand caliper on ABS models

11.5b Front and rear bleed valves (arrowed) – rear caliper on CBF1000A models

11.5c Front master cylinder bleed valve (arrowed) – CB1000R/RA models

11.6 Pull the rubber cap off the bleed valve

11.17 A vacuum-operated brake bleeding tool

12.5 ABS service check connector (arrowed) – CBF1000A shown

6 Pull the dust cap off the bleed valve (see illustration). If using a ring spanner fit it onto the valve. Attach one end of the hose to the bleed valve and, if not using a kit, submerge the other end in the clean brake fluid in the container (see illustration 11.2).

> **HAYNES HiNT** *To avoid damaging the bleed valve during the procedure, loosen it and then tighten it temporarily with a ring spanner before attaching the hose. With the hose attached, the valve can then be opened and closed either with an open-ended spanner, or by leaving the ring spanner located on the valve and fitting the hose above it.*

7 Do not allow the fluid level to drop below the lower mark during the bleeding process.
8 Carefully pump the brake lever or pedal three or four times and hold it in or down while opening the bleed valve. When the valve is opened, brake fluid will flow out of the valve into the clear tubing and the lever, pedal or pushrod will move in or down.
9 Tighten the bleed valve, then release the lever, pedal or pushrod gradually. Repeat the process until no air bubbles are visible in the brake fluid leaving the bleed valve and the lever, pedal or pushrod is firm when applied. On completion, disconnect the bleeding equipment, then tighten the bleed valve to the torque setting specified at the beginning of the chapter and fit the dust cap.
10 Top-up the reservoir, then install the diaphragm, diaphragm plate, and cover or cap (see *Pre-ride checks*). Wipe up any spilled brake fluid. Check the entire system for fluid leaks.
11 Check the operation of the brakes before riding the motorcycle.

> **HAYNES HiNT** *If it's not possible to produce a firm feel to the lever or pedal the fluid may be aerated. Let the brake fluid in the system stabilise for a few hours and then repeat the procedure when the tiny bubbles in the system have settled out.*

Fluid change

12 Changing the brake fluid is a similar process to bleeding the brakes and requires the same materials plus a suitable tool for siphoning the fluid out of the reservoirs. Also ensure that the container is large enough to take all the old fluid when it is flushed out of the system.
13 Follow Steps 3 and 6, then remove the reservoir cover or cap, diaphragm plate and diaphragm, and siphon the old fluid out of the reservoirs. Fill the reservoirs with new brake fluid, then follow the bleeding procedure until new fluid can be seen emerging from the bleed valves. Keep the reservoirs topped-up with new fluid or air may enter the system and greatly increase the length of the task.

> **HAYNES HiNT** *Old brake fluid is invariably much darker in colour than new fluid, making it easy to see when all old fluid has been expelled from the system.*

14 Disconnect the hose, then tighten the bleed valve to the specified torque setting and fit the dust cap.
15 Top-up the reservoir, then fit the diaphragm, diaphragm plate, and cover or cap (see *Pre-ride checks*). Wipe up any spilled brake fluid. Check the entire system for fluid leaks.
16 Check the operation of the brakes before riding the motorcycle.

Draining the system for overhaul

17 Draining the brake fluid is again a similar process to bleeding the brakes. The quickest and easiest way is to use a vacuum-type brake bleeding tool (see illustration) – follow the manufacturer's instructions. Otherwise follow the procedure described above for changing the fluid, but quite simply do not put any new fluid into the reservoir – the system fills itself with air instead.
18 To refill the system, again the quickest and easiest way is to use a vacuum-type brake bleeding tool, following the manufacturer's instructions, and making sure there is always enough fluid in the reservoir to prevent air being drawn in. Otherwise initially fill the reservoir, then follow the procedure described above for bleeding until fluid is pumped through the system and no more air comes out.

12 ABS operation

1 The ABS prevents the wheels from locking up under hard braking or on uneven road surfaces. A sensor on each wheel transmits information about the speed of rotation to the control unit in the ABS modulator; if the unit senses that a wheel is about to lock, it releases brake pressure to that wheel momentarily, preventing a skid.
2 The ABS is self-checking and is activated when the ignition switch is turned on – the ABS indicator light in the instrument cluster will come on and will remain on until road speed increases above 6 mph (10 kph) at which point, if the ABS is normal, the light will go off. **Note:** *If the ABS indicator light does not come on initially there is a fault in the system – see Section 13.*
3 If the indicator light remains on, or starts flashing while the machine is being ridden, there is a fault in the system and the ABS function will be switched off – the brakes will still function but in normal mode. If you turn the ignition OFF while the light is flashing, the fault code will not be displayed again if the ignition is switched on again, but will be stored in the system's memory.
4 The warning light emits long (1.3 second) and short (0.3 second) flashes to give out the fault code. A long flash is used to indicate the first digit of the double digit fault code. For example, two long (1.3 sec) flashes followed by three short (0.3 sec) flashes indicates the fault code number 23. If there is more than one fault code, there will be a 3.6 sec gap before the next code is revealed (the codes will be revealed in ascending numerical order). Once all codes have been revealed, the display will continuously run through the code(s) stored in its memory, revealing each one in turn with a short gap between them. The fault codes are shown in the table in Section 13.
5 To retrieve any stored fault codes, remove the seats, and on CBF1000A models the seat bracket (see Chapter 7) to gain access to the service check connector, which is a 3-pin blanked connector coming out of the wiring loom (see illustration). Ensure the ignition

6•22 Brakes, wheels and final drive

is switched OFF. Remove the blanking cap from the connector. Using a short jumper wire, connect between the brown/white and green/orange (CBF1000A) or green (CB1000RA) wire terminals in the connector. With the terminals connected, turn the ignition ON and observe the ABS warning light. If there are stored fault codes, the light will come on for 2 seconds, then go out for 3.6 seconds, then start to flash the fault code. If the light comes on and stays on without flashing after the 3.6 second gap no fault codes are stored. Do not apply the brake lever or pedal during code retrieval.

6 Turn the ignition switch OFF and remove the jumper wire when the code or codes have been recorded.

7 To check the ABS components see Section 14.

8 Once the fault has been corrected, erase the fault code(s) as follows. Follow Step 5 to connect the terminals in the service check connector. Hold the front brake lever on and turn the ignition switch on – the ABS light should come on for two seconds, then go out. When the light goes out immediately release the brake lever – the light should come on. When the light comes on immediately apply the brake lever – the light should go out. When the light goes out immediately release the brake lever. The code(s) should now be erased, in which case the light will flash twice, then come on and stay on.

9 Turn the ignition switch OFF and remove the jumper wire when the code or codes have been erased. Check that the ABS is operating normally (see Step 2).

10 If necessary, repeat the reset procedure.

Note: *The ABS indicator may diagnose a fault if tyre sizes other than those specified by Honda are fitted, if the tyre pressures are incorrect, if the machine has been run continuously over bumpy roads, if the front wheel comes off the ground whilst riding (wheelie) or if the machine is on an auxiliary stand with the engine running and the rear wheel turning.*

13 ABS fault diagnosis

1 If a fault is indicated in the ABS, first check that the battery is fully charged, then check the ABS fuses (see Chapter 8).

2 Unless specified otherwise, carry out all checks with the ignition switch OFF.

3 Refer to Chapter 8, Section 2, for general electrical fault finding procedures and equipment.

4 If after a thorough check, the source of a fault has not been identified, have the ABS tested by a Honda dealer.

Fault codes 11, 12, 21, 41 and 42

Note: *Before carrying out any of the checks, follow the procedure in Section 12 to reset the control unit memory, then activate the self-checking procedure. If the fault code is the result of unusual riding or conditions and the ABS is normal, the indicator light will go off. Otherwise perform the following checks.*

5 Measure the air gap between the front wheel speed sensor and the pulse ring with a feeler gauge, then compare the result with the Specification at the beginning of this Chapter **(see illustration)**. The gap is not adjustable – if it is outside the specification, check that the sensor and pulse ring fixings are tight, that the components are not damaged and that there is no dirt or anything else on the sensor tip or between the slots in the pulse ring. If any of the components are damaged they must be replaced with new ones.

6 Raise the fuel tank (see Chapter 4), and on

Fault codes	Faulty component or system	Possible causes
No code displayed	ABS light does not come on with ignition ABS light on all the time	Blown ABS main fuse Faulty wiring or wiring connector Faulty modulator Faulty ABS indicator light
11, 12, 21	Front wheel speed sensor circuit Front wheel speed sensor Front wheel pulse ring	Faulty wiring or wiring connector Faulty sensor Damaged pulse ring
13, 14, 23	Rear wheel speed sensor circuit Rear wheel speed sensor Rear wheel pulse ring	Faulty wiring or wiring connector Faulty sensor Damaged pulse ring
31, 32, 33, 34, 37 and 38	Modulator solenoid valve	Faulty modulator
41 and 42	Front wheel lock – riding conditions Front wheel speed sensor circuit Front wheel speed sensor Front wheel pulse ring	Faulty sensor Faulty wiring or wiring connector Damaged pulse ring
43	Rear wheel lock – riding conditions Rear wheel speed sensor circuit Rear wheel speed sensor Rear wheel pulse ring	Faulty wiring or wiring connector Faulty sensor Damaged pulse ring
51	Modulator motor lock	Faulty modulator
52	Modulator motor stuck OFF	Faulty modulator
53	Modulator motor stuck ON	Faulty modulator
54	Fail-safe relay circuit	ABS 30A fuse Faulty relay circuit Faulty modulator
61	Power supply voltage low	ABS 10A fuse Faulty wiring or wiring connector Faulty modulator
62	Power supply voltage high	ABS 10A fuse Faulty wiring or wiring connector Faulty modulator
71	Incorrect tyre size	Incorrect tyre
81	CPU in modulator control unit	Faulty modulator

Brakes, wheels and final drive 6•23

13.5 Measuring front wheel sensor air gap

13.6a Pull the security clip up . . .

13.6b . . . to release the connector

CBF1000A models remove the seat bracket (see Chapter 7). Disconnect the ABS modulator wiring connector **(see illustrations)**. Trace the wheel sensor wiring to the connector and disconnect it **(see illustration)**. Check for continuity first in the pink/black (CBF1000A) or yellow/black (CB1000RA) wire between the control unit wiring connector and the sensor wiring connector and then in the green/orange wire – there should be continuity in each wire. If not locate and repair the break.

7 If there is continuity in the wiring next check for continuity between each terminal in the sensor side of the sensor connector and earth (ground). If there is continuity in either of the wires the sensor is faulty and must be replaced with a new one.

8 If all the checks have failed to identify the fault, replace the wheel sensor with a known good one. Connect all wiring connectors then follow the procedure in Section 12 to reset the control unit memory, then activate the self-checking procedure. If the indicator light is no longer flashing, the original sensor was faulty. If the fault code reappears have the ABS modulator checked by a Honda dealer.

Fault codes 13, 14, 23 and 43

Note: *Before carrying out any of the checks, follow the procedure in Section 12 to reset the control unit memory, then activate the self-checking procedure. If the fault code is the result of unusual riding or conditions and the ABS is normal, the indicator light will go off. Otherwise perform the following checks.*

9 Measure the air gap between the rear wheel speed sensor and the pulse ring with a feeler gauge, then compare the result with the Specification at the beginning of this Chapter **(see illustration)**. The gap is not adjustable – if it is outside the specification, check that the sensor and pulse ring fixings are tight, that the components are not damaged and that there is no dirt or anything else on the sensor tip or between the slots in the pulse ring. If any of the components are damaged they must be replaced with new ones.

10 On CBF1000A models remove the seats, seat bracket and the right-hand seat cowl, and on CB1000RA models remove the seats and the right-hand seat rail cover (see Chapter 7). Disconnect the ABS modulator wiring connector **(see illustrations 13.6a and b)**. Trace the wheel sensor wiring to the connector and disconnect it **(see illustration)**. Check for continuity first in the pink/white wire between the control unit wiring connector and the sensor wiring connector and then in the green/red wire – there should be continuity in each wire. If not locate and repair the break.

11 If there is continuity in the wiring next check for continuity between each terminal in the sensor side of the sensor connector and earth (ground). If there is continuity in either of the wires the sensor is faulty and must be replaced with a new one.

12 If all the checks have failed to identify the fault, replace the wheel sensor with a known good one. Connect all wiring connectors then follow the procedure in Section 12 to reset the control unit memory, then activate the self-checking procedure. If the indicator light is no longer flashing, the original sensor was faulty. If the fault code reappears have the ABS modulator checked by a Honda dealer.

Fault codes 31, 32, 33, 34, 37 and 38

13 Erase the fault code (see Section 12). Start the engine and go for a short ride so the ABS system performs its self-diagnosis. If the ABS indicator light stays off, the fault was temporary.

14 If the ABS indicator light still flashes fault code 31, 32, 33, 34, 37 or 38 the ABS modulator is faulty.

Fault codes 51, 52 and 53

15 Check the ABS 30A motor fuse (see Chapter 8). If the fuse has blown, remove the seats, and on CBF1000A models the seat bracket (see Chapter 7). Disconnect the ABS modulator wiring connector **(see illustrations 13.6a and b)**. Check for continuity in the red wire terminal in the connector to earth. If there is continuity, repair the wire. If not replace the blown fuse with a new one. Connect all wiring connectors then follow the procedure in Section 12 to reset the control unit memory, then activate the self-checking procedure. If the fault code is no longer shown there was a temporary fault.

16 If the fuse has not blown, remove the seats, and on CBF1000A models the seat bracket (see Chapter 7). Disconnect the ABS modulator wiring connector **(see illustrations 13.6a and b)**. Check for battery voltage at the red wire terminal in the connector at all times (i.e. with the ignition

13.6c Front wheel sensor connector (arrowed) – CBF1000A

13.9 Measuring rear wheel sensor air gap

13.10 Rear wheel sensor connector (arrowed) – CBF1000A

on or off). If there is no voltage check the red wire from the connector to the fusebox for continuity, and if that is good check the red/green (CBF1000A) or red/blue (CB1000RA) wire for continuity to the battery, and repair the circuit as required.

17 If there is voltage erase the fault code (see Section 12). Start the engine and go for a short ride so the ABS system performs its self-diagnosis. If the ABS indicator light stays off, the fault was temporary.

18 If the ABS indicator light still flashes the same fault code, the ABS modulator is faulty.

Fault code 54

19 Check the ABS 30A fail safe relay fuse (see Chapter 8). If the fuse has blown, remove the seats, and on CBF1000A models the seat bracket (see Chapter 7). Disconnect the ABS modulator wiring connector **(see illustrations 13.6a and b)**. Check for continuity in the black wire terminal in the connector to earth. If there is continuity, repair the wire. If not replace the blown fuse with a new one. Connect all wiring connectors then follow the procedure in Section 12 to reset the control unit memory, then activate the self-checking procedure. If the fault code is no longer shown there was a temporary fault.

20 If the fuse has not blown, remove the seats, and on CBF1000A models the seat bracket (see Chapter 7). Disconnect the ABS modulator wiring connector **(see illustrations 13.6a and b)**. Check for battery voltage at the black wire terminal in the connector at all times (i.e. with the ignition on or off). If there is no voltage check the black wire from the connector to the fusebox for continuity, and if that is good check the red/green (CBF1000A) or red/blue (CB1000RA) wire for continuity to the battery, and repair the circuit as required.

21 If there is voltage erase the fault code (see Section 12). Start the engine and go for a short ride so the ABS system performs its self-diagnosis. If the ABS indicator light stays off, the fault was temporary.

22 If the ABS indicator light still flashes the same fault code, the ABS modulator is faulty.

Fault codes 61 and 62

23 Check the ABS 10A main fuse (see Chapter 8). If the fuse has blown, remove it. Remove the seats, and on CBF1000A models the seat bracket (see Chapter 7). Disconnect the ABS modulator wiring connector **(see illustrations 13.6a and b)**. Check for continuity in the red/brown wire terminal in the connector to earth. If there is continuity, repair the wire. If not replace the blown fuse with a new one. Connect all wiring connectors then follow the procedure in Section 12 to reset the control unit memory, then activate the self-checking procedure. If the fault code is no longer shown there was a temporary fault.

24 If the fuse has not blown, remove the seats, and on CBF1000A models the seat bracket (see Chapter 7). Disconnect the ABS modulator wiring connector **(see illustrations 13.6a and b)**. Check for battery voltage at the red/brown wire terminal in the connector with the ignition on. If there is no voltage check the red/brown wire from the connector to the fusebox for continuity, and if that is good check the red/black wire for continuity to the ignition switch, and repair the circuit as required.

25 If there is voltage erase the fault code (see Section 12). Start the engine and go for a short ride so the ABS system performs its self-diagnosis. If the ABS indicator light stays off, the fault was temporary.

26 If the ABS indicator light still flashes the same fault code, the ABS modulator is faulty.

Fault code 71

27 First check the tyre pressure (see *Pre-Ride Checks*). Next make sure the correct tyres are fitted, comparing the tyre size codes on the sidewall to the Specifications at the beginning of the Chapter. Also check the tyres and wheels for deformations. Correct any problems found.

28 Erase the fault code (see Section 12). Start the engine and go for a short ride so the ABS system performs its self-diagnosis. If the ABS indicator light stays off, the fault was temporary.

29 If the ABS indicator light still flashes the same fault code, the ABS modulator is faulty.

Fault code 81

30 Erase the fault code (see Section 12). Start the engine and go for a short ride so the ABS system performs its self-diagnosis. If the ABS indicator light stays off, the fault was temporary.

31 If the ABS indicator light still flashes the same fault code, the ABS modulator is faulty.

No fault code detected

32 If the ABS indicator light stays on the whole time, check the ABS 10A main fuse (see Chapter 8). If the fuse has blown, remove it. Remove the seats, and on CBF1000A models the seat bracket (see Chapter 7). Disconnect the ABS modulator wiring connector **(see illustrations 13.6a and b)**. Check for continuity in the red/brown wire terminal in the connector to earth. If there is continuity, repair the wire. If not replace the blown fuse with a new one. Connect all wiring connectors then follow the procedure in Section 12 to reset the control unit memory, then activate the self-checking procedure. If the fault code no longer shown there was a temporary fault.

33 If the fuse has not blown, remove the seats, and on CBF1000A models the seat bracket (see Chapter 7). Disconnect the ABS modulator wiring connector **(see illustrations 13.6a and b)**. Check for battery voltage at the red/brown wire terminal in the connector with the ignition on. If there is no voltage check the red/brown wire from the connector to the fusebox for continuity, and if that is good check the red/black wire for continuity to the ignition switch, and repair the circuit as required.

34 If there is voltage check for continuity in the brown/white wire terminal in the connector to earth. If there is continuity, repair the wire.

35 If there is no continuity, on CBF1000A remove the fairing, and on CB1000RA remove the instrument cowl (see Chapter 7). Using a suitable probe and jumper wire short the red/black wire in the instrument cluster wiring connector to earth with the connector still connected and the ignition ON. If the ABS indicator light stays on, the instrument cluster PCB is faulty (see Chapter 8).

36 If the ABS indicator light goes out check the red/black wire between the modulator and instrument cluster wiring connectors for continuity, and if there is none repair the wire.

37 If there is continuity short between the red/black and No. 1 green/orange wire terminals in the modulator connector using a jumper wire with the ignition on. If the ABS light goes out the modulator is faulty. If the light stays on check the green/orange wire for continuity to earth – if there is none repair the wire.

38 If the ABS indicator light does not come on with the ignition switch, check the instrument cluster power and earth wires (see Chapter 8).

39 If all is good, remove the seats, and on CBF1000A models the seat bracket (see Chapter 7). Disconnect the ABS modulator wiring connector **(see illustrations 13.6a and b)**. Turn the ignition on – if the light is on, the modulator is faulty.

40 If the light does not come on, on CBF1000A remove the fairing, and on CB1000RA remove the instrument cowl (see Chapter 7). Disconnect the instrument wiring connector. Check for continuity in the red/black wire in the instrument cluster wiring connector to earth. If there is, repair the wire. If there is no continuity the instrument cluster is faulty.

14 ABS components

Front wheel sensor

1 Raise the fuel tank (see Chapter 4). Trace the wheel sensor wiring to the connector and disconnect it **(see illustration 13.6c)**.

2 Release the sensor wiring from its guides and feed it down to the sensor, noting its routing. Unscrew the sensor bolts and wiring guide bolt and remove the sensor **(see illustration)**.

14.2 Front wheel sensor and wiring guide bolts (arrowed)

Brakes, wheels and final drive 6•25

3 Make sure the tip of the sensor, its mounting surfaces, and the pulse ring are clean. Fit the sensor and tighten the bolts. Feed the wiring up to the connector, routing and securing it as noted on removal.
4 Check the air gap (see Section 13, Step 5). Lower the fuel tank (see Chapter 4).

Front pulse ring

5 Remove the front wheel (see Section 18).
6 Undo the screws securing the ring and lift it off **(see illustration)**.
7 Ensure there is no dirt or corrosion where the ring seats on the hub – if the ring does not sit flat when it is installed the sensor air gap will be incorrect. Clean the threads of the bolts and apply a non-permanent thread locking compound (or alternatively use new bolts from Honda which come pre-treated) and tighten them to the torque setting specified at the beginning of the Chapter.
8 Install the front wheel (see Section 18). Check the speed sensor air gap (see Section 13, Step 5).

Rear wheel sensor

9 On CBF1000A models remove the right-hand seat cowl (see Chapter 7). On CB1000RA models remove the right-hand seat rail cover (see Chapter 7). Trace the wheel sensor wiring to the connector and disconnect it **(see illustration 13.10)**.
10 Release the sensor wiring from its guides and feed it down to the sensor, noting its routing. Unscrew the sensor bolts and remove the sensor **(see illustration)**.
11 Make sure the tip of the sensor, its mounting surfaces, and the pulse ring are clean. Fit the sensor and tighten the bolts. Feed the wiring up to the connector, routing and securing it as noted on removal.
12 Check the air gap (see Section 13, Step 9). Install the seat cowl or seat rail cover (see Chapter 7).

Rear pulse ring

CBF1000A

13 Remove the rear wheel (see Section 19).

14.6 Front pulse ring screws (arrowed)

14 Undo the screws securing the ring and lift it off **(see illustration)**.
15 Ensure there is no dirt or corrosion where the ring seats on the hub – if the ring does not sit flat when it is installed the sensor air gap will be incorrect. Clean the threads of the bolts and apply a non-permanent thread locking compound (or alternatively use new bolts from Honda which come pre-treated) and tighten them to the torque setting specified at the beginning of the Chapter.
16 Install the rear wheel (see Section 19). Check the sensor air gap (see Section 13, Step 9).

CB1000RA

17 Refer to Section 8 and follow the procedure to remove the rear brake disc – the pulse ring is secured by the same nuts. After unscrewing the nuts you can lift the pulse ring off the disc, leaving the disc on the stub axle. Refer to Step 15 on installation, and then check the sensor air gap (see Section 13, Step 9).

Modulator

Note: *Before the modulator can be removed from the bike, the brake fluid must be drained from both the front and rear brake systems (see Section 11).*

18 On CBF1000A models remove the seats,

14.10 Rear wheel sensor and wiring guide bolts (arrowed) – CBF1000A

seat bracket, side covers and rear mudguard (see Chapter 7).
19 On CB1000RA models remove the seats and seat rail covers (see Chapter 7), and the regulator/rectifier (see Chapter 8).
20 Drain the brake fluid (see Section 11).
21 Disconnect the modulator wiring connector **(see illustrations 13.6a and b)**.
22 Cover the area around the modulator with clean rag to prevent damage to paintwork in the event that brake fluid is spilled.
23 On CBF1000A models unscrew the five brake pipe nuts and detach the pipes **(see illustration)**. Unscrew the modulator mounting bolts and remove the modulator, taking care not to snag the brake pipes **(see illustration)**.

14.14 Rear pulse ring screws (arrowed)

14.23a Unscrew the nuts (A) and detach the pipes – CBF1000A shown. Side mounting bolt (B) ...

14.23b ... and lower mounting bolts

6•26 Brakes, wheels and final drive

24 On CB1000RA models unscrew the brake pipe nuts and detach the pipes. Unscrew the bolt securing the brake pipe joints to the right-hand side of the rear sub-frame. Unscrew the brake hose banjo bolt on the rear master cylinder (see illustration 9.2) – new sealing washers must be used. Unscrew the modulator bracket bolts and carefully lift the modulator and proportional control valve (PCV) assembly out, taking care not to snag the brake pipes. If required remove the PCV (see Section 15). If required detach the modulator from its bracket.
25 Installation is the reverse of removal, noting the following:
● Make sure the pipes are correctly connected. Smear the pipe nut threads with clean brake fluid, and if the correct tools are available tighten them to the torque setting specified at the beginning of the Chapter for your model.
● On CBF1000A models clean the threads of the lower mounting bolts and apply some fresh threadlock. Tighten the bolts to the specified torque settings.
● On CB1000RA models use new sealing washers on the rear master cylinder banjo union and tighten the bolt to the specified torque.
● Ensure the wiring connector is secure.
● Follow the procedure in Section 11 to refill and bleed the brake system. Check that there are no fluid leaks and test the operation of the brakes before riding the motorcycle.

15 CBS components

1 Neither the delay valve nor the proportional control valve can be dismantled for overhaul, and no component parts are available. If either valve fails, it must be replaced with a new one.

Proportional control valve

Removal – CBF1000A

2 Remove the right-hand seat cowl (see Chapter 7).
3 Unscrew the pipe joint nuts and detach the pipes from the valve (see illustration). If the brake fluid hasn't been drained plug the ends or wrap something tightly around them to minimise fluid loss and prevent dirt entering the system.
4 Unscrew the two bolts securing the valve, noting the wiring loom guide, and remove the valve.

Removal – CB1000RA

5 Remove the modulator (see Section 14).
6 Unscrew the pipe joint nuts and detach the pipes from the valve.
7 Unscrew the rear master cylinder hose banjo bolt – new sealing washers must be used.
8 Unscrew the bolt securing the valve.

15.3 Proportional control valve (arrowed)

Installation

9 Installation is the reverse of removal, noting the following:
● On CB1000RA models tighten the PCV mounting bolt to the torque setting specified at the beginning of the Chapter. Use new sealing washers on the rear master cylinder banjo union and tighten the bolt to the specified torque.
● Make sure the pipes are correctly connected. Smear the pipe nut threads with clean brake fluid, and if the correct tools are available tighten them to the torque setting specified at the beginning of the Chapter for your model.
● Refer to Section 11 and fill and/or bleed the system as required. Check that there are no fluid leaks and test the operation of the brakes before riding the motorcycle.

Delay valve (CB1000RA only)

Removal

10 Remove the fuel tank (see Chapter 4).
11 Unscrew the pipe joint nuts and detach the pipes from the valve. If the brake fluid hasn't been drained plug the ends or wrap something tightly around them to minimise fluid loss and prevent dirt entering the system.
12 Unscrew the bolts securing the valve.

Installation

13 Installation is the reverse of removal, noting the following:
● Tighten the valve mounting bolts to the torque setting specified at the beginning of the Chapter.
● Make sure the pipes are correctly connected. Smear the pipe nut threads with clean brake fluid, and if the correct tools are available tighten them to the specified torque setting.
● Refer to Section 11 and fill and/or bleed the system as required. Check that there are no fluid leaks and test the operation of the brakes before riding the motorcycle.

16 Wheel inspection and repair

1 In order to carry out a proper inspection of the wheels, support the bike on the centrestand on CBF1000A models, and on an auxiliary stand on all other models. Clean the wheels thoroughly to remove mud and dirt that may interfere with the inspection procedure or mask defects. Make a general check of the wheels (see Chapter 1) and tyres (see *Pre-ride checks*).
2 Inspect the wheels for cracks, flat spots on the rim and other damage. Look very closely for dents in the area where the tyre bead contacts the rim. Dents in this area may prevent complete sealing of the tyre against the rim, which leads to deflation of the tyre over a period of time. If damage is evident, or if runout in either direction is excessive, the wheel will have to be renewed. Never attempt to repair a damaged alloy wheel.
3 To check axial (side-to-side) runout of the wheel rim attach a dial gauge to the fork or the swingarm and position its tip against the side of the wheel rim. Spin the wheel slowly and check the amount of run-out, comparing it to the specification listed at the beginning of the Chapter (see illustration).
4 In order to accurately check radial (out of round) runout with the dial gauge, remove the wheel from the machine, and the tyre from the wheel. With the axle clamped in a vice and the dial gauge positioned on the top of the rim, the wheel can be rotated to check the runout (see illustration 16.3).
5 An easier, though slightly less accurate, method is to attach a stiff wire pointer to the fork or the swingarm and position the end a fraction of an inch from the wheel rim where the wheel and tyre join. If the wheel is true, the distance from the pointer to the rim will be constant as the wheel is rotated. **Note:** *If wheel runout is excessive, check the wheel bearings very carefully before renewing the wheel.*

16.3 Check the wheel for radial (out-of-round) runout (A) and axial (side-to-side) runout (B)

Brakes, wheels and final drive 6•27

17.5 Wheel alignment check using string

17 Wheel alignment check

1 Misalignment of the wheels due to a bent frame or forks can cause strange and possibly serious handling problems. If the frame or forks are at fault, repair by a frame specialist or renewal are the only options.
2 To check wheel alignment you will need an assistant, a length of string or a perfectly straight piece of wood and a ruler. A plumb bob or spirit level for checking that the wheels are vertical will also be required.
3 Support the bike on the centrestand on CBF1000A models, and on an auxiliary stand on all other models. Measure the width of both tyres at their widest points. Subtract the smaller measurement from the larger measurement, then divide the difference by two. The result is the amount of offset that should exist between the front and rear tyres on both sides of the machine.
4 If the string method is used, have your assistant hold one end of it about halfway between the floor and the rear axle, with the string touching the back edge of the rear tyre sidewall.
5 Run the other end of the string forward and pull it tight so that it is roughly parallel to the floor **(see illustration)**. Slowly bring the string into contact with the front edge of the rear tyre sidewall, then turn the front wheel until it is parallel with the string. Measure the distance from the front tyre sidewall to the string.

18.3 Slacken the axle clamp bolt (A), then unscrew the axle bolt (B)

6 Repeat the procedure on the other side of the motorcycle. The distance from the front tyre sidewall to the string should be equal on both sides.
7 As previously mentioned, a perfectly straight length of wood or metal bar may be substituted for the string **(see illustration)**.
8 If the distance between the string and tyre is greater on one side, or if the rear wheel appears to be out of alignment, have your machine checked by a Honda dealer or frame specialist.
9 If the front-to-back alignment is correct, the wheels still may be out of alignment vertically.
10 Using a plumb bob or spirit level, check the rear wheel to make sure it is vertical. To do this, hold the string of the plumb bob against the tyre upper sidewall and allow the weight to settle just off the floor. If the string touches both the upper and lower tyre sidewalls and is perfectly straight, the wheel is vertical. If it is not, adjust the stand until it is.
11 Once the rear wheel is vertical, check the front wheel in the same manner. If both wheels are not perfectly vertical, the frame and/or major suspension components are bent.

18 Front wheel

Removal

1 Position the motorcycle on the centrestand on CBF1000A models and on an auxiliary stand on all other models, and support it so that the front wheel is off the ground. If a jack is being placed under the engine place a piece of wood between the jack head and the sump to spread the load. Do not support the bike on the exhaust system. Always make sure the motorcycle is properly supported.
2 Displace the front brake calipers (see Section 3). Support the calipers with a cable-tie or a bungee cord so that no strain is placed on the hydraulic hoses. There is no need to disconnect the hoses from the calipers. **Note:** *Do not operate the front brake lever with the calipers removed.*
3 Slacken the axle clamp bolt on the bottom of the right-hand fork **(see illustration)**.

17.7 Wheel alignment check using a straight-edge

6•28 Brakes, wheels and final drive

18.5a Slacken the axle clamp bolt (arrowed) . . .

18.5b . . . then withdraw the axle and remove the wheel

18.6a Remove the long right-hand spacer . . .

18.6b . . . and the short left-hand spacer

4 Unscrew the axle bolt most of the way out of the right-hand end of the axle.

5 Slacken the axle clamp bolt on the bottom of the left-hand fork **(see illustration)**. Take the weight of the wheel, then push the axle through from the right using the axle bolt, then remove the bolt and withdraw the axle from the left – there is a hole in the end of the axle that can be used to hook a tool in to ease withdrawal if required **(see illustration)**. Carefully lower the wheel and draw it forwards.

6 Remove the long spacer from the right-hand side of the wheel and the short spacer from the left-hand side **(see illustrations)**. Clean all old grease off the spacers, axle and seals.

Caution: Don't lay the wheel down and allow it to rest on a disc – the disc could become warped. Set the wheel on wood blocks so the disc doesn't support the weight of the wheel.

7 Check the axle is straight by rolling it on a flat surface such as a piece of plate glass (first wipe off all old grease and remove any corrosion using steel wool). If the equipment is available, place the axle in V-blocks and measure the runout using a dial gauge. If the axle is bent or the runout exceeds the limit specified, replace it with a new one.

8 Check the condition of the grease seals and wheel bearings (see Section 20).

Installation

9 Apply a smear of grease to the inside of the wheel spacers, and also to the outside where they fit into the seals. Fit the long spacer into the right-hand side of the wheel and the short spacer into the left-hand side **(see illustration 18.6a and b)**. Each side of the wheel can be identified using the directional arrow (denoting the normal direction of wheel rotation) cast into one of the spokes or on the brake disc, or by the pulse ring fitted on the right-hand side on ABS models.

10 Manoeuvre the wheel into position between the forks. Apply a thin coat of grease to the axle.

11 Lift the wheel into place, making sure the spacers remain in position. Slide the axle all the way in from the left-hand side **(see illustration 18.5b)**.

12 Fit the axle bolt and tighten it to the torque setting specified at the beginning of the Chapter **(see illustrations)**. If the axle turns when tightening the bolt counter-hold it using a screwdriver through the holes in the left-hand end on CBF1000/A models, or a large hex key on CB1000R/RA models **(see illustration)**.

13 Tighten the axle clamp bolt on the bottom of the right-hand fork to the specified torque setting **(see illustration 18.3)**.

14 Lower the front wheel to the ground. Install the brake calipers (see Section 3, and the Note therein regarding the caliper mounting bolts).

15 Apply the brake lever and pedal a few times to bring the pads back into contact with the discs, then with the front brake applied pump the front forks a few times to settle all components in position, and in particular to align the left-hand fork on the axle. On CBF1000/A models there is an index line around the head of the axle which should align with the outer surface of the fork. On CB1000R/RA models the left-hand end of the axle should be flush with the outer surface of the fork.

16 Tighten the axle clamp bolt on the bottom of the left-hand fork to the specified torque **(see illustration 18.5a)**.

17 Clean the discs using brake system cleaner. Check for correct operation of the brakes before riding the motorcycle.

19 Rear wheel

CBF1000/A models

Removal

1 On CBF1000A models support the bike on its centrestand. On CBF1000 models position

18.12a Fit the axle bolt . . .

18.12b . . . and tighten it to the specified torque

18.12c Counter-hold the axle head using a hex bit on CB-R models

Brakes, wheels and final drive 6•29

19.2 Unscrew the axle nut and remove the washer and the plate (arrowed)

19.3a Withdraw the axle and lower the wheel

19.3b Remove the chain adjuster from each side

the motorcycle on an auxiliary stand so that the rear wheel is off the ground. Always make sure the motorcycle is properly supported. Create some slack in the chain (see Chapter 1).

2 Unscrew the axle nut and remove the washer and plate **(see illustration)**.

3 Take the weight of the wheel, then withdraw the axle from the left-hand side, bringing the plate with it, and lower the wheel to the ground **(see illustration)**. If the axle is difficult to withdraw, drive it out using a soft mallet to prevent damage to the threads. On CBF1000A models take care not to knock the head of the ABS wheel speed sensor. Remove the chain adjuster from each side of the swingarm **(see illustration)**.

4 Disengage the chain from the sprocket **(see illustration)**. Draw the wheel back until the caliper bracket is clear of its guide on the swingarm, then lift it out from between the swingarm and the wheel and support it clear **(see illustration)**. Remove the wheel. Fit the caliper bracket back onto the swingarm if required.

Caution: Do not lay the wheel down and allow it to rest on the disc or the sprocket – they could become warped. Set the wheel on wood blocks so the disc or the sprocket doesn't support the weight of the wheel. Do not operate the brakes with the wheel removed.

5 Remove the shouldered spacer from the left-hand side of the wheel and the plain spacer from the right-hand side **(see illustrations)**. Clean all old grease off the spacers, axle and seals.

6 Check the axle is straight by rolling it on a flat surface such as a piece of plate glass (if the axle is corroded, first remove the corrosion with steel wool). If the equipment is available, place the axle in V-blocks and check the runout using a dial gauge. If the axle is bent or the runout exceeds the limit specified at the beginning of the Chapter, replace it with a new one.

7 Check the condition of the grease seals and wheel bearings (see Section 20).

Installation

8 Apply a smear of grease to the inside of the wheel spacers, and also to the outside where they fit into the wheel. Fit the shouldered spacer into the left-hand side of the wheel and the plain spacer into the right-hand side **(see illustrations 19.5a and b)**. Apply a thin coat of grease to the axle. If the caliper bracket is located on the swingarm displace it and support it clear.

9 Manoeuvre the wheel into position between the ends of the swingarm, making sure the directional arrows on the disc, wheel and tyre are pointing in the normal direction of rotation. Slide the brake caliper bracket between the wheel and the swingarm **(see illustration 19.4b)** and locate it on its guide. On models with ABS take care not to knock the head of the wheel sensor. Engage the drive chain with the sprocket **(see illustration 19.4a)**.

10 Slide the chain adjusters into the swingarm **(see illustration 19.3b)**. Slide the plate onto the axle.

11 Lift the wheel into position and slide the axle in from the left **(see illustration 19.3a)**,

19.4a Slip the chain off the sprocket

19.4b Draw the wheel back and displace the caliper bracket when clear

making sure the spacers and caliper bracket remain correctly installed. Locate the bottom edge of the plate under the swingarm. Check that everything is correctly aligned. Fit the plate onto the right-hand end of the axle, then fit the washer and axle nut but leave it loose **(see illustration 19.2)**. Check and adjust the drive chain slack (see Chapter 1). On completion tighten the axle nut to the torque setting specified at the beginning of the Chapter.

12 Operate the brake pedal several times to bring the pads into contact with the disc. Check the operation of the rear brake carefully before riding the bike.

CB1000R/RA models

Wheel removal

13 Support the bike upright using an auxiliary stand so the rear wheel is off the ground.

19.5a Remove the shouldered left-hand spacer . . .

19.5b . . . and the plain right-hand spacer

6•30 Brakes, wheels and final drive

19.15 Unscrew the nuts (arrowed)...

19.16 ...and remove the wheel

14 Remove the silencer (see Chapter 4).
15 Place the transmission in gear then have an assistant apply the rear brake hard whilst you slacken the four wheel nuts **(see illustration)**.
16 Remove the wheel nuts then free the wheel from the stub axle and remove it from the bike **(see illustration)**.

Wheel installation

17 Fit the wheel to the stub axle and screw on the wheel nuts. Have an assistant apply the rear brake then tighten the wheel nuts evenly and progressively in a diagonal sequence to the specified torque.

18 Install the silencer (see Chapter 4).

Stub axle removal

19 Remove the rear wheel (see Steps 13 to 16).
20 Remove the air guide from the swingarm **(see illustration)**.
21 Remove the centre cap from the left-hand end of the stub axle. Unstake the nut using a hammer and a fine chisel or pin punch **(see illustration)**. Have an assistant apply the rear brake hard, and slacken the stub axle nut.
22 Fully slacken the drive chain (see Chapter 1). Slip the chain off the sprocket **(see illustration)**.

23 Unscrew the stub axle nut and remove the conical washer, noting which way around it is fitted, and the collar **(see illustrations)**. Slide the sprocket coupling assembly off the stub axle **(see illustration)**.
24 Unscrew the caliper bracket bolts then slide the caliper assembly off the disc and support it to avoid any strain on the hydraulic hose **(see illustration 7.5a)**. **Note:** *Honda recommend that new brake caliper bracket bolts should be used on installation (the bolts are supplied with their threads pre-coated with locking compound). If the old bolts are to be re-used, remove all original locking compound*

19.20 Unscrew the bolts (arrowed) and remove the air guide

19.21 Unstake the rim of the nut, then slacken it

19.22 Slip the chain off the sprocket

19.23a Unscrew the nut and remove the conical washer (arrowed)...

19.23b ...and the collar...

19.23c ...then draw the sprocket coupling off

Brakes, wheels and final drive 6•31

19.25 Draw the stub axle assembly out

19.31 Stake the rim of the nut into the groove

20.3 Lever out the bearing seals

from their threads and apply fresh compound before installing them.

25 Withdraw the stub axle and brake disc assembly from the bearing holder, taking care not to lose the spacer from the left (sprocket) side of the bearing holder **(see illustration)**. If the stub axle is damaged it must be replaced with a new one – if so, transfer the brake disc and pulse ring (CB1000RA models) to the new axle as described in Section 8.

26 Check the condition of the sprocket coupling grease seals and wheel bearings (see Section 20).

Stub axle installation

27 Apply a thin film of multi-purpose grease to the stub axle shaft then carefully slide the axle assembly into the bearing holder **(see illustration 19.25)**. Take care not to damage the right-hand bearing holder dust seal as the axle is fitted and make sure the spacer remains in position in the left dust seal. Clean off all excess grease using acetone or brake system cleaner.

28 Slide the caliper onto the disc making sure the pads locate correctly on each side **(see illustrations 7.20)**. Either fit the new caliper mounting bolts, or clean the threads of the original bolts and apply fresh thread locking compound, then tighten them to the torque setting specified at the beginning of the Chapter.

29 Slide the sprocket coupling assembly onto the stub axle and engage it with the axle splines **(see illustration 19.23c)**. Apply a smear of grease to the inside of the sprocket coupling collar, and also to the outside where

it fits into the seal. Fit the collar into the seal **(see illustration 19.23b)**.

30 Fit the conical washer with its marked side facing out **(see illustration 19.23a)**. Thread the nut onto the axle.

31 Have an assistant apply the rear brake hard and tighten the stub axle nut to the specified torque. Stake the rim of the axle nut into the groove in the stub axle using a hammer and punch, taking care not to damage the threads **(see illustration)**. Fit the centre cap.

32 Fit the drive chain around the sprocket **(see illustration 19.22)**.

33 Clean the threads of the air guide bolts and apply thread locking compound. Fit the guide and tighten the bolts **(see illustration 19.20)**.

34 Install the rear wheel.

35 Adjust the drive chain slack as described in Chapter 1 and check the operation of the rear brake before taking the machine on the road.

20 Wheel bearings

Note: *Always renew the wheel bearings in sets, never individually. Avoid using a high pressure cleaner on the wheel bearing area.*

Front wheel bearings

1 Remove the wheel (see Section 18). If required remove the discs (see Section 4) to prevent them being damaged or distorted during bearing removal – if you do leave them in place, take care to support the wheel on

wood blocks so that the wheel rim supports the weight of the wheel.

2 Inspect the seals and bearings – check that the bearing inner race turns smoothly and that the outer race is a tight fit in the hub (see *Tools and Workshop Tips* (Section 5) in the Reference Section). **Note:** *Do not remove the bearings unless they are going to be replaced with new ones.*

3 If new components are needed lever out the bearing seal from each side of the hub using a flat-bladed screwdriver or a seal hook **(see illustration)**. Take care not to damage the hub. Discard the seals as new ones must be fitted on reassembly.

4 Remove the bearings using an internal expanding puller with slide-hammer attachment, which can be obtained commercially – select the correct attachment and locate it behind the inner race of the bearing, then tighten the inner bolt to expand and lock the puller **(see illustration)**. Attach the slide-hammer, hold the wheel firmly down and jar the bearing out **(see illustration)**. Having removed the first bearing remove the spacer that fits between the bearings.

5 Turn the wheel over and remove the other bearing using the same procedure, or alternatively drive it out using a suitable drift inserted from the opposite side to the bearing.

6 Thoroughly clean the hub area of the wheel with a suitable solvent and inspect the bearing housing for scoring and wear.

7 Drive the new bearings into the hub using a bearing driver or suitable socket **(see illustration)**. Fit the right-hand bearing first,

20.4a Fit the attachment behind the bearing . . .

20.4b . . . then fit the slide-hammer and jar the bearing out

20.7 Using a socket to drive the bearing in

6•32 Brakes, wheels and final drive

20.9 Press the seal into place setting it flush with the rim

20.11 Lift the sprocket coupling off the wheel

20.14 Move the spacer aside then drive the bearing out using a drift

with its marked side facing outwards. Make sure that the driver or socket bears only on the outer race and the bearing fits squarely and all the way into its seat.

8 Turn the wheel over and fit the bearing spacer. Fit the second bearing in the same way as the first.

9 Fit the new seals into the hub using finger pressure or a socket that seats around the perimeter of the seal **(see illustration)**. Smear the seal lips with grease.

10 Install the brake discs if removed (see Section 4). Clean the discs using brake system cleaner, then install the wheel (see Section 18).

Rear wheel bearings

CBF1000/A models

11 Remove the wheel (see Section 19). If required remove the disc (see Section 8) to prevent it being damaged or distorted during bearing removal – if you do leave it in place, take care to support the wheel on wood blocks so that the wheel rim supports the weight of the wheel. Lift the sprocket coupling out of the hub **(see illustration)**.

12 Inspect the seals and bearings in both sides of the hub – check that the bearing inner race turns smoothly and that the outer race is a tight fit in the hub (see *Tools and Workshop Tips* (Section 5) in the Reference section). **Note:** *Do not remove the bearings unless they are going to be replaced with new ones.*

13 If new components are needed lever out the bearing seal from the right-hand side of the hub using a flat-bladed screwdriver or a seal hook **(see illustration 20.3)**. Take care not to damage the hub. Discard the seal as a new one should be fitted on reassembly.

14 Move the centre spacer to one side to expose the inner race of the bearing, then locate a drift on it and drive the bearing out **(see illustration)**. If you can't get sufficient purchase, remove the bearings using an internal expanding puller with slide-hammer attachment, which can be obtained commercially – select the correct attachment and locate it behind the inner race of the bearing, then tighten the inner bolt to expand and lock the puller **(see illustration 20.4a)**. Attach the slide-hammer, hold the wheel firmly down and jar the bearing out **(see illustration 20.4b)**. Having removed the first bearing remove the spacer which fits between the bearings.

15 Turn the wheel over and remove the other bearing using the same procedure.

16 Thoroughly clean the hub area of the wheel with a suitable solvent and inspect the bearing housing for scoring and wear.

17 Drive the new bearings into the hub using a bearing driver or suitable socket **(see illustration 20.7)**. Fit the right-hand bearing first, with its marked side facing outwards. Make sure that the driver or socket bears only on the outer race and the bearing fits squarely and all the way into its seat.

18 Turn the wheel over and fit the bearing spacer. Fit the second bearing in the same way as the first.

19 Fit the new seal into the left-hand side of the hub using finger pressure or a socket that seats around the perimeter of the seal **(see illustration 20.9)**. Smear the seal lips with grease.

20 Check the sprocket coupling/rubber dampers (see Section 24). Check the condition of the hub O-ring and clean it or replace it with a new one if necessary **(see illustration)**. Smear the O-ring with oil. Fit the sprocket coupling into the wheel **(see illustration 20.11)**. Clean the brake disc using acetone or brake system cleaner, then install the wheel (see Section 19).

CB1000R/RA models

21 Remove the stub axle assembly from the bearing holder (see Section 19).

22 On CB1000RA models unscrew the ABS wheel speed sensor bolts and displace the sensor.

23 Release the large circlip using a pair of circlip pliers, then remove the caliper mounting plate from the bearing holder **(see illustrations)**.

24 Fully slacken the clamp bolt and withdraw the bearing holder assembly from the

20.20 Fit a new O-ring if necessary

20.23a Release the circlip . . .

20.23b . . . and remove the plate

Brakes, wheels and final drive 6•33

20.24 Draw the bearing holder out of the swingarm

20.25 Remove the spacer

20.27 Lever the seal out from each side

swingarm **(see illustration)**. Note: *Do not remove the bearings from the holder unless they are to be replaced with new ones.*

25 Remove the spacer from the left (sprocket) side of the bearing holder **(see illustration)**. Inspect the holder closely, looking for obvious signs of wear such as heavy scoring, or for damage such as cracks or distortion.

26 Inspect the seals and bearings in both sides of the hub – check that the inner race of the ball bearing in the left-hand side turns smoothly and that the outer race is a tight fit in the hub (see *Tools and Workshop Tips* (Section 5) in the Reference section). Check the needle bearing is a tight fit in the hub and look for wear, damage and corrosion on the needles. Note: *Do not remove the bearings unless they are going to be replaced with new ones.*

27 If new components are needed lever out the bearing seal from each side of the holder using a flat-bladed screwdriver or a seal hook **(see illustration)**. Take care not to damage the hub. Discard the seals as new ones must be fitted on reassembly. Remove the ball bearing first.

28 To remove the ball bearing, prise out the bearing circlip from the holder – a new one should be used **(see illustration)**. Turn the bearing holder over and support it, then drive the bearing squarely out of position, using a hammer and suitable driver or socket inserted through the needle bearing.

29 To remove the needle bearing prise out the bearing circlip from the holder **(see illustration)** – a new one should be used. Turn the bearing holder over and support it, then press or drive the bearing out using a suitable drive or socket.

30 Thoroughly clean the bearing holder with a suitable solvent and inspect the bearing housings for scoring and wear.

31 The new needle bearing must be pressed or drawn into its bore rather than driven into position to prevent possible damage. In the absence of a press, a suitable drawbolt arrangement can be made up as described in *Tools and Workshop Tips* in the Reference section. Fit the bearing with its marked surface outwards. Make sure the bearing is firmly against its seat then secure it with a new circlip, making sure it locates in the

20.28 Remove the circlip then drive the ball bearing out from the opposite side

20.29 Remove the circlip (arrowed) before driving the needle bearing out from the opposite side

groove. Smear multi-purpose grease onto the bearing.

32 Locate the new ball bearing in its bore with its marked surface facing outwards. Tap it squarely into position using a driver or socket that bears only on the outer race **(see illustration)**. Make sure the bearing is firmly against its seat then secure it with a new circlip, making sure it locates in the groove.

33 Fit the new seals using finger pressure or a socket that seats around the perimeter of the seal **(see illustration)**. Smear the seal lips with molybdenum grease.

34 Remove all traces of corrosion from the outside of the bearing holder assembly and the inside of the swingarm bore.

35 Fit the spacer into the left (sprocket) side dust seal **(see illustration 20.25)**.

36 Fit the bearing holder into the swingarm

20.32 Use a socket to drive the bearing in

(see illustration 20.24). Locate the caliper mounting plate and secure it with the large circlip, making sure it is correctly seated in the groove **(see illustrations 20.23b and a)**.

37 On CB1000RA models install the ABS wheel speed sensor and tighten its bolts.

38 Install the stub axle assembly (see Section 19).

Sprocket coupling bearing

CBF1000/A models

39 Remove the wheel (see Section 19). Lift the sprocket coupling out of the hub **(see illustration 20.11)**.

40 Inspect the seal and bearing – check that the bearing inner races turn smoothly and that the outer race is a tight fit in the coupling (see *Tools and Workshop Tips (Section 5)* in the Reference Section). Note: *Do not remove the*

20.33 Fit the seals and press or tap them into place

20.41 Lever out the bearing seal

20.42 Drive the spacer out of the bearings from the outside

20.43 Drive the bearing out from the inside

bearing unless it is being replaced with a new one.

41 If new components are needed lever out the bearing seal using a flat-bladed screwdriver or a seal hook **(see illustration)**. Take care not to damage the rim of the coupling. Discard the seal – a new one must be fitted.

42 Remove the bearing spacer from inside the coupling – if it is tight place the coupling on the work surface, sprocket side up, and drive it out using a suitably sized socket **(see illustration)**.

43 Support the coupling on blocks of wood, sprocket side down, and drive the bearing out from the inside using a bearing driver or socket **(see illustration)**.

44 Thoroughly clean the coupling with a suitable solvent and inspect the bearing housing for scoring and wear.

45 Drive the new bearing onto the spacer, marked side facing up, until it seats on the rim using a socket that bears on the inner race of the bearing.

46 Drive the bearing and spacer as one squarely into the hub until the bearing seats using a driver or suitable socket on the outer race of the bearing (see *Tools and Workshop Tips*) **(see illustration)**.

47 Press the new seal into the coupling **(see illustration)**. Level the seal with the rim of the coupling with a small block of wood. Smear the seal lip with grease.

48 Check the sprocket coupling/rubber dampers (see Section 24). Check the condition of the hub O-ring and clean it or replace it with a new one if necessary **(see illustration 20.20)**. Smear the O-ring with oil. Fit the sprocket coupling into the wheel. Install the wheel (see Section 19).

CB1000R/RA models

49 Remove the rear sprocket coupling assembly from the stub axle (see Section 19, Steps 20, 21, 22 and 23) – there is no need to remove the rear wheel. Remove the driven flange, spacer and damper segments from it (see Section 24).

50 Inspect the seal and bearing – check that the bearing inner races turn smoothly and that the outer race is a tight fit in the coupling (see *Tools and Workshop Tips (Section 5)* in the Reference Section). **Note:** *Do not remove the bearing unless it is being replaced with a new one.*

51 If new components are needed lever out the bearing seal using a flat-bladed screwdriver or a seal hook **(see illustration)**. Take care not to damage the rim of the coupling. Discard the seal – a new one must be fitted.

52 Support the coupling on blocks of wood, sprocket side down, and drive the bearing out from the inside using a bearing driver or socket **(see illustration)**.

53 Thoroughly clean the coupling with a suitable solvent and inspect the bearing housing for scoring and wear.

54 Drive the new bearing squarely into the hub until it seats using a driver or suitable socket on the outer race of the bearing (see *Tools and Workshop Tips*) **(see illustration)**.

20.46 Drive the bearing in from the outside

20.47 Press the new seal into the hub

20.51 Lever out the bearing seal

20.52 Drive the bearing out from the inside

20.54 Drive the bearing in from the outside

Brakes, wheels and final drive 6•35

20.55 Press the new seal into the coupling

55 Press the new seal into the coupling **(see illustration)**. Level the seal with the rim of the coupling with a small block of wood. Smear the seal lip with grease.
56 Check, then assemble and install the sprocket coupling assembly (see Sections 24 and 19).

21 Tyres

General information

1 The wheels are designed to take tubeless tyres only. Tyre sizes are given in the Specifications at the beginning of this chapter.
2 Refer to the *Pre-ride checks* listed at the beginning of this manual for tyre maintenance.

Fitting new tyres

3 When selecting new tyres, refer to the tyre information in the Owner's Handbook. Ensure that front and rear tyre types are compatible, the correct size and correct speed rating; if necessary seek advice from a Honda dealer or tyre fitting specialist **(see illustration)**.
4 It is recommended that tyres are fitted by a motorcycle tyre specialist rather than attempted in the home workshop. This is particularly relevant in the case of tubeless tyres because the force required to break the seal between the wheel rim and tyre bead is substantial, and is usually beyond the capabilities of an individual working with normal tyre levers. Additionally, the specialist will be able to balance the wheels after tyre fitting.
5 Note that punctured tubeless tyres can in some cases be repaired. External repairs made using a repair kit should only ever be considered as a temporary measure to get you to a dealer for a new tyre, and riding at speed or with any extra load should be avoided. Internal repairs carried out by a motorcycle tyre fitting specialist are better. Make sure a wheel with a repaired tyre is balanced before it is fitted back on the bike. Honda advise that a repaired tyre should not be used at speeds above 50 mph (80 kmh) for the first 24 hours, and not above 80 mph (130 kmh) thereafter, and carrying heavy loads should be avoided.

21.3 Common tyre sidewall markings

6•36 Brakes, wheels and final drive

22.1 The master joining link is identified by the different pin ends (arrowed)

22.8 Measure joining link pin projection beyond sideplate

22 Drive chain

Note: *The original equipment drive chain fitted to these models has a staked-type master (joining) link which can be disassembled using either the Honda service tool, Pt. No. 07HMH-MR10103, or one of several commercially-available drive chain cutting/staking tools (but the cheap ones are best avoided). Such chains can be recognised by the master joining link side plate's identification marks (and usually its different colour), as well as by the staked ends of the link's two pins which look as if they have been deeply centre-punched, instead of peened over as with all the other pins.*

Removal

1 Support the motorcycle on the centrestand on CBF1000A models, and on an auxiliary stand so that the rear wheel is off the ground on all other models. Locate the joining link in a suitable position to work on by rotating the back wheel **(see illustration)**. Slacken the drive chain as described in Chapter 1.
2 If required, remove the chainguard(s).
3 Remove the front sprocket cover (see Section 23).
4 Split the chain at the joining link using the chain tool, following carefully the manufacturer's operating instructions (see also Section 8 in *Tools and Workshop Tips*

in the Reference Section). Remove the chain from the bike, noting its routing around the swingarm.

Cleaning

5 Refer to Chapter 1, Section 1, for details of routine cleaning with the chain installed on the sprockets.
6 If the chain is extremely dirty remove it from the motorcycle and soak it in paraffin (kerosene) for approximately five or six minutes, then clean it using a soft brush.
Caution: *Don't use gasoline (petrol), solvent or other cleaning fluids which might damage its internal sealing properties. Don't use high-pressure water. Remove the chain, wipe it off, then blow dry it with compressed air immediately. The entire process shouldn't take longer than ten minutes – if it does, the O-rings in the chain rollers could be damaged.*

Installation

⚠️ **Warning: NEVER install a drive chain which uses a clip-type master (split) link. Use ONLY the correct service tools to secure the staked-type of master link – if you do not have access to such tools, have the chain replaced by a Honda dealer.**
Note: *The specifications referred to in Steps 8 and 9 only apply to the drive chain types fitted as original equipment, i.e DID and RK.*

7 Route the drive chain around the sprockets, and through the swingarm on CB1000R/RA models, leaving the two ends mid-way between the sprockets along the bottom run.
8 Referring to Section 8 in *Tools and Workshop Tips* in the Reference Section, install the new joining link from the inside with the four O-rings correctly located between the link plate and side plate (install the new side plate with its identification marks facing out). Use the chain tool to press the side plate on, then measure the amount that the joining link pins project from the side plate and check they are within the measurements specified at the beginning of the Chapter **(see illustration)**. Stake the new link using the chain tool, following carefully the instructions of both the chain manufacturer and the tool manufacturer. DO NOT re-use old joining link components.
9 After staking, check the joining link and staking for any signs of cracking **(see illustration)**. If there is any evidence of cracking, the joining link, O-rings and side plate must be replaced. Measure the diameter of the staked ends in two directions and check that it is evenly staked and within the measurements specified at the beginning of the Chapter **(see illustration)**. Check that the link pivots freely.
10 Install the sprocket cover (see Section 23).
11 Install the chainguard(s) if removed.
12 On completion, adjust and lubricate the chain following the procedures described in Chapter 1.

23 Sprockets

Front sprocket cover removal and installation

1 Note the alignment of the existing punch marks between the gearchange linkage arm and shaft, or mark the alignment of the shaft with the slit in the linkage arm if they are not clear **(see illustration)**. Unscrew the linkage arm bolt and slide the arm off the shaft.

22.9a Check staking for any signs of cracking

22.9b Check the diameter of the staked pin ends

23.1 Note the alignment then unscrew the bolt and slide the arm off the shaft

Brakes, wheels and final drive 6•37

2 Displace the clutch release cylinder (see Chapter 2). There is no need to detach the hydraulic hose. Withdraw the pushrod **(see illustration)**.
3 Unscrew the bolts securing the front sprocket cover and remove the cover and the guide plate **(see illustrations)**. Remove the dowels if they are loose.
4 Fit the dowels if removed. Fit the guide plate onto the dowels, then fit the cover and tighten its bolts **(see illustrations 23.3c, b and a)**.
5 Slide the clutch pushrod in **(see illustration 23.2)**. Install the clutch release cylinder (see Chapter 2).
6 Slide the gearchange linkage arm onto the shaft, aligning the punch marks, or the slit in the clamp with your own mark, then tighten the pinch bolt **(see illustration 23.1)**.

Sprocket check

7 Check the wear pattern on both sprockets (see Chapter 1, Section 1). If the sprocket teeth are worn excessively, replace the chain and both sprockets as a set. Whenever the sprockets are inspected, the drive chain should be inspected also (see Chapter 1). Always renew the chain and sprockets as a set – worn sprockets can ruin a new drive chain and *vice versa*.
8 Adjust and lubricate the chain following the procedures described in Chapter 1.

Sprocket removal and installation

Front sprocket

9 Remove the front sprocket cover (see Steps 1 to 3).
10 Have an assistant apply the rear brake, then unscrew the sprocket bolt and remove the washer **(see illustration)**.
11 Fully slacken the drive chain as described in Chapter 1. On CBF1000/A models, if the rear sprocket is being removed as well, remove the rear wheel now to give full slack (see Section 19). On CB1000R/RA models, if the rear sprocket is being removed as well, do that now. Otherwise disengage the chain from the rear sprocket if required to provide more slack.

23.2 Withdraw the clutch pushrod

23.3b ...and remove the cover...

12 Slide the chain and sprocket off the shaft then slip the sprocket out of the chain **(see illustration)**.
13 Engage the new sprocket with the chain, making sure the marked side is facing out, and slide it on the shaft **(see illustration 23.12)**.
14 If removed, fit the rear sprocket now, and on CBF1000/A models install the wheel (see Section 19). If the chain was merely disengaged, fit it back onto the rear sprocket. Take up the slack in the chain.
15 Fit the sprocket bolt with its washer **(see illustration 23.10)**. Tighten the bolt to the torque setting specified at the beginning of the Chapter, holding the rear brake on to prevent the sprocket turning.
16 Fit the sprocket cover (see Steps 4 to 6). Adjust and lubricate the chain following the procedures described in Chapter 1.

23.3a Unscrew the bolts (arrowed)...

23.3c ...and the guide plate

Rear sprocket – CBF1000/A

17 Remove the rear wheel (see Section 19). Rest it sprocket side up on some blocks of wood.
18 Unscrew the nuts securing the sprocket to the hub assembly **(see illustration)**. Remove the sprocket, noting which way round it fits.
19 Fit the sprocket onto the hub with the marked side facing out. Fit the nuts and tighten them evenly and in a criss-cross sequence to the torque setting specified at the beginning of the Chapter.
20 Install the rear wheel (see Section 19).

Rear sprocket – CB1000R/RA

21 Remove the air guide from the swingarm **(see illustration 19.20)**.
22 Fully slacken the drive chain (see Chapter 1). Slip the chain off the sprocket **(see illustration 19.22)**.

23.10 Unscrew the bolt and remove the washer

23.12 Draw the sprocket off the shaft and disengage the chain

23.18 Unscrew the nuts (arrowed) and remove the sprocket – CBF

6•38 Brakes, wheels and final drive

23.23 Unscrew the nuts (arrowed) and remove the sprocket – CB-R

24.3 Check the rubber dampers as described

24.10a Ease the flange out of the hub using screwdrivers

23 Have an assistant apply the rear brake, then unscrew the nuts securing the sprocket and remove the washers (see illustration). Remove the sprocket noting which way round it fits.
24 Check the sprocket bolts and replace any which show signs of wear or damage with new ones. Make sure the flat edge of the bolt head seats along its corresponding flat on the hub.
25 Fit the sprocket onto the coupling with the marked side facing out. Fit the washers and nuts and tighten them to the specified torque, applying the rear brake as before.
26 Loop the chain around the sprocket. Fit the air guide (see illustration 19.20). Adjust and lubricate the chain following the procedures described in Chapter 1.

24 Rear sprocket coupling/ rubber dampers

CBF1000/A models

1 Remove the rear wheel (see Section 19). Check for play between the sprocket coupling and the wheel hub by turning the sprocket. Any play indicates worn rubber damper segments.
Caution: Do not lay the wheel down on the disc as it could become warped. Lay the wheel on wooden blocks so that the disc is off the ground.
2 Lift the sprocket coupling off the wheel leaving the rubber dampers in position (see illustration 20.11). Note the spacer inside the coupling – it should be a tight fit. Check the coupling for cracks or any obvious signs of damage.
3 Lift the rubber damper segments from the wheel and check them for cracks, hardening and general deterioration (see illustration). Replace them with a new set if necessary.
4 Check the condition of the hub O-ring and clean it or replace it with a new one if necessary (see illustration 20.20). Smear the O-ring with oil.
5 Checking and replacement procedures for the sprocket coupling bearing are in Section 20.
6 Installation is the reverse of removal. Make sure the spacer is correctly installed in the coupling. Align the coupling correctly with the rubber dampers and press it fully into the hub.
7 Install the rear wheel (see Section 19).

CB1000R/RA models

8 Remove the rear sprocket coupling assembly from the stub axle (see Section 19, Steps 20, 21, 22 and 23) – there is no need to remove the rear wheel.
9 Check for play between the driven flange and the wheel hub by turning the sprocket. Any play indicates worn rubber damper segments.
10 Ease out the driven flange from the rear of the coupling hub, leaving the rubber dampers in position inside (see illustration). Remove the spacer (see illustration). Remove the driven flange O-ring (see illustration) – a new one should be fitted.
11 Lift out the rubber damper segments and

24.10b Remove the spacer . . .

24.10c . . . and the O-ring

check them for cracks, hardening and general deterioration (see illustration). Replace the rubber dampers with a new set if necessary.
12 Inspect the coupling assembly components for signs of wear such as heavy scoring, or for damage such as cracks or distortion.
13 Checking and replacement procedures for the sprocket coupling bearing are in Section 20.
14 On reassembly, ensure the spacer is correctly fitted to the rear of the coupling bearing and all the damper segments are correctly installed (see illustration 24.10b).
15 Ensure the O-ring is correctly seated in the driven flange recess and lubricate it with a smear of molybdenum grease (see illustration 24.10c). Align the driven flange correctly with the rubber dampers and press it fully into the coupling (see illustration).
16 Install the sprocket coupling assembly (see Section 19).

24.11 Check the rubber dampers as described

24.15 Fit the flange into the rubbers, pressing it fully in

— # Chapter 7
Bodywork

Contents

	Section number		Section number
Body panels – CB1000R/RA	5	Mirrors	6
Fairing and body panels – CBF1000/A	4	Seats	3
General information	1	Trim clips	2

Degrees of difficulty

Easy, suitable for novice with little experience	Fairly easy, suitable for beginner with some experience	Fairly difficult, suitable for competent DIY mechanic	Difficult, suitable for experienced DIY mechanic	Very difficult, suitable for expert DIY or professional

Specifications

Torque settings
Front mudguard bolts.. 12 Nm
Mirror bolts (CBF1000/A)................................... 14 Nm
Passenger grab-rail bolts (CBF1000/A)............... 27 Nm

1 General information

This Chapter covers the procedures necessary to remove and install the bodywork. Since many service and repair operations on these motorcycles require the removal of the body panels, the procedures are grouped here and referred to from other Chapters.

In the case of damage to the bodywork, it is usually necessary to remove the broken component and replace it with a new (or used) one. Note that there are however some companies that specialise in 'plastic welding' and there are a number of bodywork repair kits now available for motorcycles.

When attempting to remove any body panel, first study it closely, noting any fasteners and associated fittings, to be sure of returning everything to its correct place on installation. Refer to Section 2 for more information on the types of trim clip used and how to release and refit them. In some cases the aid of an assistant will be required when removing panels, to help avoid the risk of damage to paintwork. Once the evident fasteners have been removed, try to withdraw the panel as described but DO NOT FORCE IT – if it will not release, check that all fasteners have been removed and try again.

When installing a body panel, first study it closely, noting any fasteners and associated fittings removed with it, to be sure of returning everything to its correct place. Check that all fasteners are in good condition, including the trim clips and damping/rubber mounts; replace any faulty fasteners with new ones before the panel is reassembled. Check also that all mounting brackets are straight and repair them or replace them with new ones if necessary before attempting to install the panel.

Tighten the fasteners securely, but be careful not to overtighten any of them or the panel may break (not always immediately) due to the uneven stress.

2 Trim clips

1 Three types of plastic trim clip may be used, so carefully note which fits where when removing the body panels.
2 The first and most widely used type has a centre pin which you push into the body of the

7•2 Bodywork

2.2a Push the centre pin (arrowed) . . .

2.2b . . . into the body to release the clip

2.2c Push the centre pin out before installing the clip, then push it in when installed to lock it

2.3 Pull the centre pin out to release the clip (A), and push it back in to lock it (B)

2.4a Undo the centre screw then pull the clip out

2.4b Fit the clip in the hole then push the centre in to lock it

clip to allow the clip to be drawn out of the panel **(see illustrations)**. To install the clip, first expand the pawls of the clip body and push the centre pin back out **(see illustration)**. Now fit the clip body into its hole, then push the centre pin in so that it is flush with the clip head. The clip should now be locked in place.

3 The second type has a protruding centre pin which you pull out of the body of the clip to allow the clip to be drawn out of the panel **(see illustration)**. To install the clip, fit the clip body into its hole, then push the centre pin in.

The clip should now be locked in place.

4 The third type of trim clip has a Phillips screw head. To release them unscrew the centre of the clip, then pull the body of the clip out of the panel **(see illustration)**. When installing them, insert it in the panel then push the centre fully into the body **(see illustration)**. As they are made of plastic, the threads easily become worn in which case the centres may not unscrew. If this happens, lever the centre out of the body using a small screwdriver and replace the trim clip with a new one.

3 Seats

Removal

Passenger seat

1 Unlock the seat using the ignition key, turning it clockwise **(see illustration)**. Draw the seat up and back to remove it, noting how the hooks at the front locate **(see illustrations)**.

3.1a On CBF1000/A models unlock the seat and lift it up . . .

3.1b . . . noting how the hooks locate under the catches (arrowed)

Bodywork 7•3

3.1c On CB1000R/RA models unlock the seat and lift it up, noting how the hooks (arrowed) locate

3.3a On CBF1000/A models unscrew the two bolts (arrowed) . . .

3.3b . . . and remove the seat, noting how the hook (arrowed) locates

3.3c On CB1000R/RA models unscrew the bolt . . .

3.3d . . . and remove the seat, noting how the hooks (arrowed) locate under the bars

Rider's seat

2 Remove the passenger seat.
3 Unscrew the bolt(s) securing the back of the seat and remove the collar(s) **(see illustrations)**. Draw the seat up and back, noting how the hook(s) at the front locate(s) **(see illustrations)**.

Rider's seat bracket – CBF1000/A models

4 Remove the rider's seat.
5 Before removing the bracket note its position – there are three heights it can be set at, determined by which bolt holes are used.

6 Unscrew the bolts and remove the bracket **(see illustrations)**.

Installation

7 Installation is the reverse of removal, noting the following:
● To adjust the height of the rider's seat on

3.6a Unscrew the bolts (arrowed) . . .

3.6b . . . and remove the bracket

7•4 Bodywork

4.1 Unscrew the bolt (arrowed) . . .

4.2 . . . then release the peg from the grommet

4.4 Pull the cover off

CBF models re-position the bracket as required by changing which mounting holes are used for the bolts – there are three positions **(see illustration 3.6b)**.
- Make sure the hook(s) on each seat locate(s) correctly.
- Push down on the back of the passenger seat to engage the latch.

4 Fairing and body panels – CBF1000/A

Side covers

1 Unscrew the bolt **(see illustration)**.
2 Carefully pull the top of the cover away from the tank to free the peg from the grommet, then draw the cover forwards from under the rider's seat **(see illustration)**.
3 Installation is the reverse of removal. Make sure the grommet is in good condition and correctly seated. Smear the grommet with oil. Make sure the peg locates fully in the grommet.

Windshield

4 Carefully pull the windshield screw covers off **(see illustration)**.
5 Undo the screws, noting the spacers, and lift the windshield off, noting which mounting holes were used **(see illustrations)** – there are two different positions for height adjustment.
6 Installation is the reverse of removal. Set the windshield at the desired height.

Fairing inner trim panels

7 Release the trim clip on the inner side (see Section 2) **(see illustration)**.
8 Release the panel from the fairing and fairing side panel by lowering it **(see illustration)**.
9 Installation is the reverse of removal.

Instrument cover

Removal

10 Unscrew the bolt joining the fairing side panel to the upper edge of the instrument cover **(see illustration 4.17c)**.
11 Remove the fairing inner trim panels.
12 Remove the windshield.
13 Undo the screws at the front and release the tabs from the fairing **(see illustration)**.
14 Carefully pull the panel up to free the

4.5a Undo the screws (arrowed) . . .

4.5b . . . and remove the windshield . . .

4.5c . . . noting the shaped spacers with the screws and how they locate

4.7 Release the trim clip (arrowed) . . .

4.8 . . . and remove the panel, noting how the tab (arrowed) locates

4.13 Undo the screws (arrowed) and release the cover from the fairing . . .

Bodywork 7•5

4.14 ... then lift it to release the peg (arrowed) from the grommet

4.16 Release the trim clip (arrowed)

4.17a Unscrew the inner bolt (arrowed), noting the collar ...

4.17b ... the rear bolt (arrowed) ...

4.17c ... and the top bolt (arrowed)

centre peg from the grommet in the instrument cluster **(see illustration)**.

Installation

15 Installation is the reverse of removal.

Fairing side panels

Removal

16 Release the trim clip on the underside (see Section 2) **(see illustration)**.
17 Unscrew the three bolts, noting the collar with the front one **(see illustrations)**.
18 Release the peg from the grommet and the tabs from the fairing, then disconnect the turn signal wiring connector and remove the panel **(see illustrations)**.

Installation

19 Installation is the reverse of removal.

Fairing

Removal

20 Remove the fairing side panels.
21 Remove the instrument cover.
22 Remove the mirrors (see Section 6).
23 Carefully lift each side up off the mirror mounting bosses and draw the fairing forwards, noting how the pegs locate in the

4.18a Release the peg (arrowed) ...

4.18b ... and the tabs ...

4.18c ... then disconnect the wiring connector and remove the panel

7•6 Bodywork

4.23a Lift the fairing sides off the mirror mount pegs . . .

4.23b . . . then draw it forwards . . .

4.23c . . . and disconnect the wiring connector

4.25 Remove the rubber shroud if required

4.26a Make sure the dampers (arrowed) are in place on each side

grommets in the stay, then disconnect the headlight wiring connector and remove the fairing **(see illustrations)**.
24 If required remove the headlight assembly from the fairing (see Chapter 8).
25 If required remove the rubber shroud from the instrument cluster **(see illustration)**.

Installation

26 Installation is the reverse of removal. Make sure the rubber shroud is correctly located over the mirror mounts on the fairing stay **(see illustration 4.25)**. Make sure the rubber dampers for the windshield screws are in place **(see illustration)**. Make sure the fairing pegs locate correctly in the grommets on the stay **(see illustration)**.

Seat cowl

Removal

27 Remove the seat(s) (see Section 3) – if you only want to remove the rear section of the cowl, only remove the passenger seat, but if you are removing either or both side sections remove both seats.
28 Carefully prise the blanking caps out of the grab-rail bolt heads **(see illustration)**. Unscrew the bolts and remove the grab-rails **(see illustration)**.
29 Unscrew the two bolts and remove the rear section of the seat cowl **(see illustrations)**.
30 To remove either of the side sections release the trim clip (see Section 2) and undo the two

4.26b The pegs locate in the grommets (arrowed)

4.28a Remove the blanking caps . . .

4.28b . . . then unscrew the bolts and remove the rails

4.29a Unscrew the bolts (arrowed) . . .

4.29b . . . and remove the rear section

Bodywork 7•7

4.30a Release the trim clip (A) and unscrew the bolts (B) . . .

4.30b . . . then release the rear tab and remove the cowl

bolts on each side, noting the collar with the rear bolt **(see illustration)**. Release the tab at the rear and remove the cowl **(see illustration)**.

Installation

31 Installation is the reverse of removal. Make sure the rear tab on each side section locates correctly. The upper rims of the grommets for the rear section must be above the surface of the cowl, so the cowl is seated in the grommet recess – use a small screwdriver to do this **(see illustration)**. Tighten the grab-rail bolts to the torque setting specified at the beginning of the Chapter.

Front mudguard

32 Unscrew the rear bolt on each side and release the brake hose(s) and wheel sensor wiring as required according to model **(see illustrations)**.
33 Unscrew the front bolt on each side, then carefully draw the mudguard forwards and remove it.
34 Installation is the reverse of removal. Tighten the bolts to the torque setting specified at the beginning of the Chapter.

5 Body panels – CB1000R/RA

4.31 Ease the grommet rims up over the surface of the cowl

4.32a Mudguard bolt and hose arrangement – left side

4.32b Mudguard bolt and hose arrangement – right side, ABS model

5.1 Release the trim clips (arrowed) and remove the grille

Protection grille

1 Release trim clips (see Section 2) and remove the grille **(see illustration)**.
2 Installation is the reverse of removal.

Side covers

Removal

3 Remove the seats (see Section 3).
4 Unscrew the bolt **(see illustration)** – note how the tab locates in the groove in the seat rail cover.
5 To remove the right-hand cover carefully pull the rear of the cover away to free the peg from the grommet **(see illustration)**, then lower the

5.4 Unscrew the bolt (A), noting the tab (B)

5.5 Pull the peg from the grommet and release the tabs

7•8 Bodywork

5.6a Free the bottom tab . . .

5.6b . . . and the top tab

5.10a Release the tab from the grommet . . .

5.10b . . . and the hook from the seat cowl

5.12 Unscrew the two bolts (arrowed) on each side

5.13 Release the guide and the peg from the grommet on each side

cover to release the tab from the tank **(see illustration 5.6b)** and remove the cover.
6 To remove the left-hand cover pull the bottom of the cover away to free the tab from the grommet, then lower the cover to release the tab from the tank and remove the cover **(see illustrations)**.

Installation

7 Installation is the reverse of removal. Make sure the grommets are in good condition and correctly seated. Smear the grommet with oil. Make sure the peg and tabs locate fully in the grommets.

Seat rail covers

Removal

8 Remove the seats (see Section 3).
9 Unscrew the side cover bolt **(see illustration 5.4)**.

10 Lift the rear of the side cover to release the tab from the groove in the seat rail cover, then pull the bottom of the seat rail cover away to free the tab from the grommet, and release the hook from the seat cowl **(see illustrations)**.

Installation

11 Installation is the reverse of removal. Make sure the grommets are in good condition and correctly seated. Smear the grommet with oil. Make sure the peg locates fully in the grommet.

Radiator shroud

Removal

12 Unscrew the four bolts and remove the washers **(see illustration)**.
13 Carefully pull each side away from the tank to free the guide and the peg from the grommet **(see illustration)**.

14 Release the front grille from the radiator top and bottom, then draw the shroud forwards **(see illustration)**.
15 Remove the collars for the bolts for safekeeping.
16 If required detach each side section from the centre grill.

Installation

17 Installation is the reverse of removal. Make sure the grommets are in good condition and correctly seated. Smear the grommet with oil. Make sure the collars are fitted. Make sure each peg locates fully in its grommet. Make sure the reserve tank hose is correctly routed.

Instrument cowl

18 Release the trim clips (see Section 2) **(see illustration)**. Release the tabs from the headlight and remove the cowl **(see illustration)**.

5.14 Release the grille from the radiator and remove the shroud

5.18a Release the trim clips (arrowed) . . .

5.18b . . . then release the tabs and remove the cowl

Bodywork 7•9

5.21 Undo the screws (arrowed)

5.22a Release the grommets . . .

5.22b . . . the tabs . . .

5.22c . . . the hooks . . .

5.22d . . . and the tab

5.24 Unscrew the nuts (arrowed)

19 Installation is the reverse of removal.

Seat cowl

Removal

20 Remove the seats (see Section 3).
21 Undo the three screws **(see illustration)**.
22 Release the grommets at the front from the pegs on the frame, then release the tabs along each underside, draw the cowl back to release the slots on each underside from the hooks, and the tab from the tail light **(see illustrations)**.

Installation

23 Installation is the reverse of removal. Make sure the tabs and hooks locate correctly.

Front mudguard

Removal

24 Unscrew the nut on each side and release the brake hose(s) and wheel sensor wiring as required according to model **(see illustration)**.
25 Unscrew the bolts on each side, noting the washers with the front bolts, then carefully draw the mudguard forwards and remove it, taking care not to scratch it on the brake hose guides, and noting how the wheel sensor guide locates in the grommet on ABS models **(see illustrations)**.
26 Remove the collars from the bolts for safekeeping.

Installation

27 Installation is the reverse of removal. Make sure the collars are fitted. Tighten the bolts to the torque setting specified at the beginning of the Chapter.

5.25a Unscrew the bolts (arrowed) on each side . . .

5.25b . . . and remove the mudguard

6.1 Unscrew the bolts and remove the mirrors

6.3 Pull the boot up, then slacken the locknut (A) and thread the mirror out of the base nut (B)

6 Mirrors

CBF1000/A

1 Unscrew the bolts and remove the mirrors **(see illustration)**.

2 Installation is the reverse of removal. Tighten the bolts to the torque setting specified at the beginning of the Chapter.

CB1000R/RA

3 Pull the rubber boot up off the base of the mirror stem **(see illustration)**.
4 Slacken the top nut, then unscrew the mirror from the base nut, turning it clockwise. If required unscrew the base nut.
5 Installation is the reverse of removal.
6 To adjust the position of the mirror stem slacken the locknut, adjust the mirror, then tighten the locknut.

Chapter 8
Electrical system

Contents

	Section number
Alternator	29
Battery charging	4
Battery removal and maintenance	3
Brake light switches	14
Brake/tail/licence plate light bulbs	9
Charging system testing	28
Clutch switch	22
Diode block	23
Electrical system fault finding	2
Fuses	5
General information	1
Handlebar switches	19
Headlight	8
Headlight and sidelight bulbs	7
Horn	24
Ignition switch	18

	Section number
Ignition system components	see Chapter 4
Instrument check and replacement	16
Instrument removal and installation	15
Lighting system check	6
Neutral switch	20
Oil pressure switch	17
Regulator/rectifier	30
Sidestand switch	21
Starter motor overhaul	27
Starter motor removal and installation	26
Starter relay	25
Tail light	10
Turn signal assemblies	13
Turn signal bulbs	12
Turn signal circuit check	11
Vehicle speed sensor	16

Degrees of difficulty

Easy, suitable for novice with little experience
Fairly easy, suitable for beginner with some experience
Fairly difficult, suitable for competent DIY mechanic
Difficult, suitable for experienced DIY mechanic
Very difficult, suitable for expert DIY or professional

Specifications

Battery
Capacity ... 12 V, 8.6 Ah
Voltage
  Fully-charged ... 13.0 to 13.2 V
  Discharged ... below 12.3 V
Charging rate
  Normal ... 0.9 A for 5 to 10 hrs
  Quick ... 4.5 A for 1 hr

Charging system
Alternator stator coil resistance ... 0.1 to 1.0 ohms
Output
  CBF1000/A models ... 344 W @ 5000 rpm
  CB1000R/RA models ... 350 W @ 5000 rpm
Regulated voltage ... 15.5 V @ 5000 rpm
Current leakage ... 2 mA (max)

8•2 Electrical system

Starter motor
Brush length
- Standard . . . . 12.0 to 13.0 mm
- Service limit (min) . . . . 6.5 mm

Fuses
See Wiring Diagrams at the end of this Chapter for fuse identification
CBF1000
- Main 30A
- Others . . . . 20A x 3, 10A x 3

CBF1000A
- Main 30A
- Others . . . . 30A x 2, 20A x 3, 10A x 4

CB1000R
- Main 30A
- Others . . . . 20A x 2, 10A x 5

CB1000RA
- Main 30A
- Others . . . . 30A x 2, 20A x 2, 10A x 6

Bulbs
CBF1000/A
- Headlights
  - High beam . . . . 55 W
  - Low beam . . . . 55 W
- Sidelight . . . . 5 W x 2
- Brake/tail light . . . . 21/5 W
- License plate light . . . . 5 W
- Turn signal lights . . . . 21 W x 4
- Instrument and warning lights . . . . LED

CB1000R/RA
- Headlight . . . . 60/55 W
- Sidelight . . . . LED
- Brake/tail light . . . . LED
- License plate light . . . . 5 W
- Turn signal lights . . . . 21 W x 4
- Instrument and warning lights . . . . LED

Torque settings
- Alternator rotor bolt . . . . 103 Nm
- Alternator stator bolts . . . . 12 Nm
- Footrest bracket bolts
  - CBF1000/A models . . . . 27 Nm
  - CB1000R/RA models . . . . 37 Nm
- Ignition switch bolts . . . . 25 Nm
- Neutral switch . . . . 12 Nm
- Oil pressure switch . . . . 12 Nm
- Sidestand switch bolt . . . . 10 Nm

1 General information

All models have a 12 volt electrical system charged by a three-phase alternator with a separate regulator/rectifier.

The regulator maintains the charging system output within the specified range to prevent overcharging, and the rectifier converts the ac (alternating current) output of the alternator to dc (direct current) to power the lights and other components and to charge the battery. The alternator rotor is mounted on the left-hand end of the crankshaft.

The starter motor is mounted on the top of the crankcase behind the cylinders. The starting system includes the motor, the battery, the relay and the various wires and switches. Some of the switches are part of a starter interlock system which prevents the engine from being started if the sidestand is down and the engine is in gear. The engine can be started with the sidestand up when it is in gear as long as the clutch lever is pulled in. The system will also cut the engine should the sidestand extend while the engine is running and in gear – see Chapter 1 for further information and checks on the system.

Note: *Keep in mind that electrical parts, once purchased, often cannot be returned. To avoid unnecessary expense, make very sure the faulty component has been positively identified before buying a replacement part.*

2 Electrical system fault finding

1 A typical electrical circuit consists of an electrical component, the switches, relays, etc, related to that component and the wiring and connectors that link the component to the battery and the frame.

2 Before tackling any troublesome electrical circuit, first study the wiring diagram thoroughly to get a complete picture of what makes up that individual circuit. Trouble spots, for instance, can often be narrowed down by noting if other components related to that circuit are operating properly or not. If

Electrical system 8•3

2.2 Common earth point (arrowed) on CBF models – raise the fuel tank to check it

2.4a A digital multimeter can be used for all electrical tests

2.4b A battery-powered continuity tester

several components or circuits fail at one time, chances are the fault lies either in the fuse or in a common earth (ground) connection, as several circuits are often routed through the same fuse and earth (ground) connections **(see illustration)**.

3 Electrical problems often stem from simple causes, such as loose or corroded connections or a blown fuse. Prior to any electrical fault finding, always visually check the condition of the fuse, wires and connections in the problem circuit. Intermittent failures can be especially frustrating, since you can't always duplicate the failure when it's convenient to test. In such situations, a good practice is to clean all connections in the affected circuit, whether or not they appear to be good – where possible use a dedicated electrical cleaning spray along with sandpaper, wire wool or other abrasive material to remove corrosion, and a dedicated electrical protection spray to prevent further problems. All of the connections and wires should also be wiggled to check for looseness which can cause intermittent failure.

4 If you don't have a multimeter it is highly advisable to obtain one – they are not expensive and will enable a full range of electrical tests to be made **(see illustration)**. Go for a modern digital one with LCD display as they are easier to use. A continuity tester and/or test light are useful for certain electrical checks as an alternative, though are limited in their usefulness compared to a multimeter **(see illustrations)**.

Continuity checks

5 The term continuity describes the uninterrupted flow of electricity through an electrical circuit. Continuity can be checked with a multimeter set either to its continuity function (a beep is emitted when continuity is found), or to the resistance (ohms / Ω) function, or with a dedicated continuity tester. Both instruments are powered by an internal battery, therefore the checks are made with the ignition OFF. As a safety precaution, always disconnect the battery negative (-) lead before making continuity checks, particularly if ignition switch checks are being made.

6 If using a multimeter, select the continuity function if it has one, or the resistance (ohms) function. Touch the meter probes together and check that a beep is emitted or the meter reads zero, which indicates continuity. If there is no continuity there will be no beep or the meter will show infinite resistance. After using the meter, always switch it OFF to conserve its battery.

7 A continuity tester can be used in the same way – its light should come on or it should beep to indicate continuity in the switch ON position, but should be off or silent in the OFF position.

8 Note that the polarity of the test probes doesn't matter for continuity checks, although care should be taken to follow specific test procedures if a diode or solid-state component is being checked.

Switch continuity checks

9 If a switch is at fault, trace its wiring to the wiring connectors. Separate the connectors and inspect them for security and condition. A build-up of dirt or corrosion here will most likely be the cause of the problem – clean up and apply a water dispersant such as WD40, or alternatively use a dedicated contact cleaner and protection spray.

10 If using a multimeter, select the continuity function if it has one, or the resistance (ohms) function, and connect its probes to the terminals in the connector **(see illustration)**. Simple ON/OFF type switches, such as brake light switches, only have two wires whereas combination switches, like the handlebar switches, have many wires. Study the wiring diagram to ensure that you are connecting to the correct pair of wires. Continuity should be indicated with the switch ON and no continuity with it OFF.

Wiring continuity checks

11 Many electrical faults are caused by damaged wiring, often due to incorrect routing or chaffing on frame components. Loose, wet or corroded wire connectors can also be the cause of electrical problems.

12 A continuity check can be made on a single length of wire by disconnecting it at each end and connecting the meter or continuity tester probes to each end of the wire **(see illustration)**. Continuity (low or no

2.4c A simple test light is useful for voltage tests

2.10 Continuity should be indicated across switch terminals when lever is operated

2.12 Wiring continuity check. Connect the meter probes across each end of the same wire

8•4 Electrical system

2.15 Voltage check. Connect the meter positive probe to the component and the negative probe to earth

2.23 A selection of insulated jumper wires

resistance – 0 ohms) should be indicated if the wire is good. If no continuity (high resistance) is shown, suspect a broken wire.

13 To check for continuity to earth in any earth wire connect one probe of your meter or tester to the earth wire terminal in the connector and the other to the frame, engine, or battery earth (-) terminal. Continuity (low or no resistance – 0 ohms) should be indicated if the wire is good. If no continuity (high resistance) is shown, suspect a broken wire or corroded or loose earth point (see below).

Voltage checks

14 A voltage check can determine whether power is reaching a component. Use a multimeter set to the dc voltage scale, or a test light. The test light is the cheaper component, but the meter has the advantage of being able to give a voltage reading.

15 Connect the meter or test light in parallel, i.e. across the load **(see illustration)**.

16 First identify the relevant wiring circuit by referring to the wiring diagram at the end of this manual. If other electrical components share the same power supply (i.e. are fed from the same fuse), take note whether they are working correctly – this is useful information in deciding where to start checking the circuit.

17 If using a meter, check first that the meter leads are plugged into the correct terminals on the meter (red to positive (+), black to negative (-). Set the meter to the dc volts function, where necessary at a range suitable for the battery voltage – 0 to 20 vdc. Connect the meter red probe (+) to the power supply wire and the black probe to a good metal earth (ground) on the bike's frame or directly to the battery negative terminal. Battery voltage should be shown on the meter with the ignition switch, and if necessary any other relevant switch, ON.

18 If using a test light, connect its positive (+) probe to the power supply terminal and its negative (-) probe to a good earth (ground) on the bike's frame. With the switch, and if necessary any other relevant switch, ON, the test light should illuminate.

19 If no voltage is indicated, work back towards the fuse continuing to check for voltage. When you reach a point where there is voltage, you know the problem lies between that point and your last check point.

Earth (ground) checks

20 Earth connections are made either directly to the engine or frame via the mounting of the component, or by a separate wire into the earth circuit of the wiring harness. Alternatively a short earth wire is sometimes run from the component directly to the bike's frame.

21 Corrosion is a common cause of a poor earth connection, as is a loose earth terminal fastener.

22 If total or multiple component failure is experienced, check the security of the main earth lead from the negative (-) terminal of the battery, the earth lead bolted to the engine, and the main earth point(s) on the frame. If corroded, dismantle the connection and clean all surfaces back to bare metal. Remake the connection and prevent further corrosion from forming by smearing battery terminal grease over the connection.

23 To check the earth of a component, use an insulated jumper wire to temporarily bypass its earth connection **(see illustration)** – connect one end of the jumper wire to the earth terminal or metal body of the component and the other end to the bike's frame. If the circuit works with the jumper wire installed, the earth circuit is faulty.

24 To check an earth wire first check for corroded or loose connections, then check the wiring for continuity (Step 13) between each connector in the circuit in turn, and then to its earth point, to locate the break.

3 Battery removal and maintenance

Caution: Be extremely careful when handling or working around the battery. The electrolyte is very caustic and an explosive gas (hydrogen) is given off when the battery is charging.

Removal and installation

CBF1000/A models

1 Make sure the ignition is switched OFF.

2 Remove the right-hand side cover (see Chapter 7).

3 Unscrew the negative (–) terminal bolt first and disconnect the lead from the battery **(see illustration)**. Lift up the red insulating cover to access the positive (+) terminal, then unscrew the bolt and disconnect the lead.

4 On models with ABS displace the ABS fusebox holder **(see illustration)**.

3.3 Disconnect the negative lead (A) first then disconnect the positive lead (B)

3.4 Displace the fusebox holder and release the wiring (arrowed)

Electrical system 8•5

3.5a Unscrew the bolts (arrowed) and remove the battery holder . . .

3.5b . . . then remove the battery

3.9 Disconnect the negative lead first then disconnect the positive lead (arrowed)

5 Unscrew the battery holder bolts and remove the holder **(see illustration)**. Draw the battery out **(see illustration)**.
6 Installation is the reverse of removal. Clean the battery terminals and lead ends with a wire brush, emery paper or steel wool. Reconnect the leads, connecting the positive (+) terminal first.

> **HAYNES HINT** *Battery corrosion can be kept to a minimum by applying a layer of battery terminal grease or petroleum jelly (Vaseline) to the terminals after the leads have been connected. DO NOT use a mineral based grease.*

CB1000R/RA models

7 Make sure the ignition is switched OFF.
8 Remove the seats.
9 Unscrew the negative (–) terminal bolt first and disconnect the lead from the battery **(see illustration)**. Lift up the red insulating cover to access the positive (+) terminal, then unscrew the bolt and disconnect the lead.
10 Release the retaining strap then lift the battery out **(see illustrations)**.
11 Installation is the reverse of removal. Clean the battery terminals and lead ends with a wire brush, emery paper or steel wool. Reconnect the leads, connecting the positive (+) terminal first.

Inspection and maintenance

12 The battery on all models is of the maintenance free (sealed) type, therefore requiring no regular maintenance. However, the following checks should still be performed.
Note: *Do not attempt to remove the battery caps to check the electrolyte level or battery specific gravity. Removal will damage the caps, resulting in electrolyte leakage and battery damage.*
13 Check the state of charge by measuring the voltage at the battery terminals **(see illustration)**. Connect the voltmeter positive (+) probe to the battery positive (+) terminal, and the negative (–) probe to the battery negative (–) terminal. When fully-charged there should be 13.0 to 13.2 volts present. If the voltage falls below 12.3 volts remove the battery (see above), and recharge it as described below in Section 4.
14 Check the battery terminals and leads are tight and free of corrosion. If corrosion is evident, clean the terminals as described above, then protect them from further corrosion (see **Haynes Hint**).
15 Keep the battery case clean to prevent current leakage, which can discharge the battery over a period of time (especially when it sits unused). Wash the outside of the case with a solution of baking soda and water. Rinse the battery thoroughly, then dry it.
16 Look for cracks in the case and replace the battery with a new one if any are found. If acid has been spilled on the frame or battery box, neutralise it with a baking soda and water solution, dry it thoroughly, then touch up any damaged paint.
17 If the motorcycle sits unused for long periods of time, disconnect the leads from the battery terminals, negative (–) terminal first. Refer to Section 4 and charge the battery once every month to six weeks.

4 Battery charging

Caution: Be extremely careful when handling or working around the battery. The electrolyte is very caustic and an explosive gas (hydrogen) is given off when the battery is charging.

1 Remove the battery (see Section 3). Connect the charger to the battery, making sure that the positive (+) lead on the charger is connected to the positive (+) terminal on the battery, and the negative (–) lead is connected to the negative (–) terminal.
2 Honda recommend that the battery is charged at the normal rate specified at the beginning of the Chapter. A higher 'quick charge' rate that can be used if absolutely necessary is also specified, but note that exceeding this could cause the battery to overheat, buckling the plates and rendering

3.10a Release the strap . . .

3.10b . . . and remove the battery

3.13 Checking battery voltage

8•6 Electrical system

4.2 Battery connected to a charger

5.2a Disconnect the wiring connector . . .

5.2b . . . to access the main fuse (A). Spare fuse (B) is in the bottom of the relay holder

5.3a Fusebox (arrowed)

it useless. If a normal domestic charger is used check that after a possible initial peak, the charge rate falls to a safe level **(see illustration)**. If the battery becomes hot during charging **stop**. Further charging will cause damage. Note that there are many bike-specific chargers available from good suppliers that are designed for the maintenance and recovery of motorcycle batteries, in particular catering for the requirements of heavily discharged MF batteries. They are not expensive, and are a worthwhile investment, especially if the bike is not used over winter. Follow the manufacturer's instructions.

3 If the recharged battery discharges rapidly if left disconnected it is likely that an internal short caused by physical damage or sulphation has occurred. A new battery will be required. A sound item will tend to lose its charge at about 1% per day.

4 Install the battery (see Section 3).

5 If the motorcycle sits unused for long periods of time, charge the battery once every month to six weeks and leave it disconnected.

5 Fuses

1 The electrical system as a whole is protected by the main fuse, and individual circuits are protected by other fuses of different ratings.

CBF1000/A models

2 The main fuse is integral with the starter relay – to access it remove the battery (see Section 3). Disconnect the wiring connector – the fuse is under it **(see illustration)**. A spare main fuse is housed in the bottom of the relay holder **(see illustration)**.

3 On CBF1000 models all other fuses are housed in the fuse box, located under the passenger seat **(see illustration)** – remove the seat for access (see Chapter 7). Lift the cover to reveal the box – the location, identity and rating of each fuse is marked on the box lid **(see illustration)**. Unclip the lid to access the fuses **(see illustration)**. A spare fuse of each rating is provided.

4 On CBF1000A models the 30A ABS fuses and the fuel injection system/ignition fuse

5.3b Lift the cover and check the label for fuse identity . . .

5.3c . . . then unclip the lid to access the fuses

Electrical system 8•7

5.4 ABS and FI/ignition fuses

5.5a Remove the relay cover...

5.5b ...to access the main fuse (A). FI/IGN fuse (B)

are on the outside of the battery holder **(see illustration)** – remove the right-hand side cover for access (see Chapter 7). Unclip the fuse holder lid to access the fuse(s). All other fuses are housed in the fuse box, located under the passenger seat **(see illustration 5.3a)** – remove the seat for access (see Chapter 7). Lift the cover to reveal the box – the location, identity and rating of each fuse is marked on the box lid **(see illustration 5.3b)**. Unclip the lid to access the fuses **(see illustration 5.3c)**. A spare fuse of each rating is provided.

CB1000R/RA models

5 The main fuse and fuel injection system/ignition fuse are integral with the starter relay – to access it remove the seats (see Chapter 7). Remove the relay cover to access the fuses **(see illustrations)**. A spare fuse of each rating is housed in the fuse box (Step 6).

6 All other fuses are housed in the fuse box **(see illustration)** – to access it remove the seats (see Chapter 7). Unclip the lid to access the fuses – the location, identity and rating of each fuse is marked on the box lid. A spare fuse of each rating is provided.

All models

7 The fuses can be removed and checked visually – use the tool provided in the toolkit, your fingers, or a suitable pair of pliers **(see illustration)**. A blown fuse is easily identified by a break in the element **(see illustration)**, but if there is any doubt check the fuse for continuity (see Section 2). Each fuse is clearly marked with its rating and must only

5.6a Fuse box (arrowed)...

5.6b ...unclip the lid to access the fuses

be replaced by a fuse of the correct rating. If a spare fuse is used, always replace it with a new one so that a spare of each rating is carried on the bike at all times.

⚠ **Warning: Never put in a fuse of a higher rating or bridge the terminals with any other substitute, however temporary it may be. Serious damage may be done to the circuit, or a fire may start.**

8 If the new fuse blows immediately check the wiring circuit very carefully for evidence of a short-circuit. Look for bare wires and chafed, melted or burned insulation.

9 Occasionally a fuse will blow or cause an open-circuit for no obvious reason. Corrosion of the fuse ends and fusebox terminals may occur and cause poor fuse contact. If this happens, remove the corrosion with a wire brush or emery paper, then spray the fuse end and terminals with electrical contact cleaner.

5.7a Pull the fuse out

5.7b A blown fuse can be identified by a break in its element

6 Lighting system check

Note: *Refer to electrical system fault finding in Section 2 and to the wiring diagram for your model at the end of this Chapter.*

1 If a light fails first check the bulb (see relevant Section), and the bulb terminals in the holder. If none of the lights work, check the battery (see Section 3). Low battery voltage indicates either a faulty battery or a defective charging system. Refer to Section 3 for battery checks and Section 28 for charging system tests. Also, check the fuses (Section 5) – if there is more than one problem at the same time, it is likely to be a fault relating to a multi-function component, such as one of the fuses governing more than one circuit, or the ignition switch. When checking for a blown filament in a bulb, it is advisable to back up a visual check with a continuity test of the filament as it is not always apparent that a bulb has blown.

Headlight

CBF1000/A models

2 CBF1000/A models have two single filament bulbs – the left-hand bulb works on LO beam and both bulbs work on HI beam. If one headlight beam fails to work, first check the bulb (see Section 7). If both headlight beams fail to work, first check the fuse (see Section 5), and then the bulbs (see Section 7). If

8•8 Electrical system

6.3a Displace the turn signal relay . . .

6.3b . . . then displace the relay box

6.3c Release the blue connector . . .

6.3d . . . then pull the relay off it

6.3e Relay test set-up

they are good, the problem lies in the wiring or connectors, the HI beam relay or the dimmer switch. Refer to Section 19 for the switch testing procedures, and also to the wiring diagrams at the end of this Chapter.

3 If the HI beam does not work and the relay is suspected of being faulty, remove the right-hand seat cowl (see Chapter 7). The relay is in the relay box. Displace the turn signal relay, then displace the relay box **(see illustrations)**. Release the retainers for the blue connector and draw the connector out **(see illustration)**. Pull the relay off its connector and test it as follows **(see illustrations)**: set a multimeter to the ohms x 1 scale and connect it across the relay's A and B terminals. There should be no continuity (infinite resistance). Using a fully-charged 12 volt battery and two insulated jumper wires, connect the positive (+) terminal of the battery to the C terminal on the relay, and the negative (–) terminal to the D terminal. At this point the relay should be heard to click and the meter read 0 ohms (continuity). If this is the case the relay is good. If the relay does not click when battery voltage is applied and indicates no continuity (infinite resistance) across its terminals, it is faulty and must be replaced with a new one.

4 If the relay is good, check there is battery voltage at the black/red wire terminal on the relay wiring connector with the ignition ON. If there is no voltage, check the wiring between the relay wiring connector and the ignition switch, via the fusebox. If voltage is present, check all wires between the relay connector, the headlight connector and the dimmer switch for continuity, and check there is continuity to earth (ground) in the green wire from the headlight connector. Repair or renew the wiring or connectors as necessary.

5 If the LO beam does not work, check for battery voltage at the blue/white wire terminal on the headlight wiring connector with the ignition ON **(see illustration 7.3)**. If voltage is present, check for continuity to earth (ground) in the green wire from the wiring connector. If no voltage is present check the blue/white wire from the connector to the starter button and the dimmer switch, and then check the switches themselves, and then the wiring between them and the fuse box. Repair or renew the wiring or connectors as necessary.

CB1000R/RA models

6 CB1000R/RA models have one twin filament bulb. If both headlight beams fail to work, check the fuse (see Section 5). If either the LO beam or the HI beam fails to work check the bulb (see Section 7). If all seems good, the problem lies in the wiring or connectors, or the dimmer switch. Refer to Section 19 for the switch testing procedures.

7 If the HI beam does not work, check for battery voltage at the blue wire terminal on the headlight wiring connector with the ignition ON **(see illustration 7.15b)**. If voltage is present, check for continuity to earth (ground) in the green wire from the wiring connector. Repair or renew the wiring or connectors as necessary.

8 If the LO beam does not work, check for battery voltage at the white wire terminal on the headlight wiring connector with the ignition ON **(see illustration 7.15b)**. If voltage is present, check for continuity to earth (ground) in the green wire from the wiring connector. Repair or renew the wiring or connectors as necessary.

Tail light

CBF1000/A models

9 If the tail light fails to work, check the bulb (see Section 9). If it is good, check there is battery voltage at the black/brown wire terminal in the bulb holder with the ignition switch ON. If voltage is present, check there is continuity to earth (ground) in the green wire from the wiring connector. If no voltage is indicated, check the wiring and connectors between the tail light and the fusebox.

CB1000R/RA models

10 If the tail light fails to work, refer to Section 10 and disconnect the tail light wiring connector, and check for battery voltage at the black/brown wire terminal on the loom side of the connector with the ignition switch ON. If voltage is present, check for continuity to earth (ground) in the green wire from the wiring connector. If no voltage is indicated, check the wiring and connectors between the tail light and the fuse box. Refer to the wiring diagrams at the end of this Chapter.

11 If the power, wiring and connectors are good, or if only one or some of the tail light LEDs have failed leaving others working, then the tail light unit is faulty and must be replaced with a new one – individual LEDs are not available.

Brake light

CBF1000/A models

12 If the brake light fails to work, check the bulb (see Section 9). If it is good, check there is battery voltage at the green/yellow wire terminal in the bulb holder with the ignition ON, and first with the front brake lever on, then with the rear brake pedal on. If voltage is present with one brake on but not the other, then the switch or its wiring is faulty. If voltage is present in both cases, check there is continuity to earth (ground) in the green wire from the wiring connector. If no voltage is indicated, check the wiring and connectors between the brake light and the brake switches, and the fusebox, then check the brake light switches themselves. Refer to Section 14 for the switch testing procedures.

CB1000R/RA models

13 If the brake light fails to work, refer to Section 10 and disconnect the tail light wiring connector, and check for battery voltage at the green/yellow wire terminal on the loom side of the connector, first with the front brake lever on, then with the rear brake pedal on. If voltage is present with one brake on but not the other, then the switch or its wiring is faulty. If voltage is present in both cases, check for continuity to earth (ground) in the green wire from the wiring connector. If no voltage is indicated, check the wiring and connectors between the brake light and the brake switches, and the fuse box, then check the switches themselves. Refer to Section 14 for the switch testing procedures.

14 If the power, wiring and connectors are good, or if only one or some of the brake light LEDs have failed leaving others working, then the tail light unit is faulty and must be replaced with a new one – individual LEDs are not available.

Sidelight

CBF1000/A models

15 If one sidelight fails to work, check the bulb (see Section 7); if both sidelights fail check there is battery voltage at the black/brown wire terminal on the loom side of the headlight wiring connector with the ignition switch ON. If voltage is present, check there is continuity to earth (ground) in the green wire from the wiring connector. If no voltage is indicated, check the wiring and connectors between the tail light and the fusebox.

CB1000R/RA models

16 If the sidelight fails to work, check there is battery voltage at the black/brown wire terminal on the loom side of the headlight wiring connector with the ignition switch ON. If voltage is present, check there is continuity to earth (ground) in the green wire from the wiring connector. If no voltage is indicated, check the wiring and connectors between the tail light and the fusebox. If all the wiring is good the LED is faulty – replace the sidelight unit with a new one (see Section 7).

Licence plate light

17 If the light fails to work, check the bulb (see Section 9). If the bulb is good, check there is battery voltage at the black/brown wire terminal on the loom side of the wiring connector with the ignition switch ON. If voltage is present, check there is continuity to earth (ground) in the green wire from the wiring connector. If no voltage is indicated, check the wiring and connectors between the tail light and the fusebox.

Turn signals

18 See Section 11.

Instrument and warning lights

19 See Section 16.

7 Headlight and sidelight bulbs

Note: *The headlight bulbs are of the quartz-halogen type. Do not touch the bulb glass as skin acids will shorten the bulb's service life. If the bulb is accidentally touched, it should be wiped carefully when cold with a rag soaked in methylated spirit and dried before fitting. Always use a paper towel or dry cloth when handling new bulbs to prevent injury if the bulb should break and to increase bulb life.*

CBF1000/A models

Headlights

1 Remove the relevant fairing side panel (see Chapter 7).
2 Remove the rubber dust cover, noting how it fits **(see illustration)**.
3 Disconnect the wiring connector from the bulb in question **(see illustration)**.
4 Release the bulb retaining clip, noting how it fits, then remove the bulb **(see illustrations)**.
5 Fit the new bulb into the headlight bearing in mind the information in the **Note** above. Make sure the bulb locates correctly and secure it in position with the retaining clip **(see illustrations 7.4b and a)**.
6 Connect the wiring connector **(see illustrations 7.3)**.
7 Fit the dust cover, locating the tab in the cut-out **(see illustration 7.2)**.
8 Check the operation of the headlight.

Sidelights

9 Remove the relevant fairing side panel (see Chapter 7).

7.2 Dislodge the cover . . .

7.3 . . . then disconnect the wiring connector

7.4a Release the clip . . .

7.4b . . . and remove the bulb

8•10 Electrical system

7.10 Pull the bulbholder out . . .

7.11 . . . then pull the bulb out of the holder

7.14 Unscrew the bolt (arrowed) on each side and remove the collar

10 Carefully pull the bulbholder out of the headlight **(see illustration)**.
11 Carefully pull the bulb out of the holder **(see illustration)**.
12 Fit the new bulb in the bulbholder, then fit the bulbholder into the headlight – make sure the rubber seal is in good condition and correctly seated.
13 Check the operation of the sidelight.

CB1000R/RA models

Headlight

14 Unscrew the bolt and remove the collar on each side **(see illustration)**. Lay some rag or a towel on the front mudguard.
15 Slightly raise the headlight to free the grommets from their locating pegs, then draw it forwards and disconnect the wiring connector **(see illustrations)**.
16 If required lay the headlight on the front mudguard, making sure it is secure.
17 Remove the rubber dust cover, noting how it fits **(see illustration)**.
18 Release the bulbholder by turning it anti-clockwise, then remove the bulb **(see illustrations)**.
19 Fit the new bulb into the headlight bearing in mind the information in the **Note** above. Make sure the bulb locates correctly, and secure it in position with the holder, turning it clockwise to lock it **(see illustrations 7.18b and a)**.
20 Fit the dust cover with the TOP mark at the top **(see illustration 7.17)**.
21 Connect the wiring connector **(see illustration 7.15b)**.
22 Fit the headlight onto its bracket, locating the grommets over the pegs **(see illustration)**. Fit the bolts with their collars **(see illustration 7.14)**.
23 Check the operation of the headlight.

Sidelight

24 Remove the headlight, then remove the lower cover from it (see Section 8).
25 Undo the sidelight unit screws, then release the tab from the holder and remove the sidelight LED unit.
26 If required release the holder from the lower cover.
27 Fit the new unit into the lower cover in reverse order.
28 Check the operation of the sidelight.

7.15a Displace the headlight unit as described . . .

7.15b . . . and disconnect the wiring connector

7.17 Remove the dust cover

7.18a Release the clip . . .

7.18b . . . and remove the bulb

7.22 Seat the grommet over the peg (arrowed) on each side

Electrical system 8•11

8.2 Undo the screws (arrowed) and remove the headlight from the fairing

8.6a Disconnect the sidelight and turn signal wiring connectors ...

8 Headlight

CBF1000/A models

1 Remove the fairing (see Chapter 7).
2 Undo the screws securing the headlight assembly to the fairing, noting the washers and wiring clamp, and lift it out **(see illustration)**.
3 If required remove the headlight and sidelight bulbs (see Section 7).
4 Installation is the reverse of removal. Check the operation of the headlights and sidelights. Check the headlight aim (see Chapter 1).

CB1000R/RA models

5 Remove the instrument cowl (see Chapter 7).
6 Disconnect the sidelight, turn signal and instrument cluster wiring connectors **(see illustrations)**.
7 Unscrew the bolt and remove the collar on each side **(see illustration 7.14)**. Slightly raise the headlight to free the grommets from their locating pegs, then draw it forwards and disconnect the headlight wiring connector **(see illustrations 7.15a and b)**. Free the wiring from the guide and remove the headlight/

8.6b ... and the instrument wiring connector

sidelight/instrument cluster assembly **(see illustration)**.
8 Remove the instrument cluster (see Section 15).
9 Undo the lower cover screws, then carefully release it from the headlight and side covers and draw the sidelight wiring through **(see illustrations)**.
10 Undo the side cover screws and remove the covers with the turn signals.
11 If required remove the headlight bulb (see Section 7).
12 Installation is the reverse of removal. Check the operation of the headlight and sidelight. Check the headlight aim (see Chapter 1).

8.7 Free the wiring from the guide (arrowed)

9 Brake/tail/licence plate light bulbs

Note: *It is a good idea to use a paper towel or dry cloth when handling bulbs to prevent injury if it breaks, and to increase bulb life.*

Brake/tail light

CBF1000/A models

1 Undo the screws and remove the lens **(see illustration)**.

8.9a Undo the screws (arrowed) ...

8.9b ... and remove the lower cover, drawing the wiring through

9.1 Undo the screws and remove the lens

8•12 Electrical system

9.2 Push the bulb in and turn it anti-clockwise to release it

10.2a Undo the screws and bolts (arrowed) . . .

10.2b . . . and displace the tail light

2 Carefully push the bulb in and turn it anti-clockwise to release it **(see illustration)**.
3 Check the socket terminals for corrosion and clean them if necessary.
4 Line up the pins of the new bulb with the slots in the socket, then push the bulb in and turn it clockwise until it locks into place. Fit the lens – do not overtighten the screws as the lens and threads are easily damaged.

CB1000R/RA models

5 The tail light contains LEDs rather than a conventional bulb. If one or more of the LEDs within the brake or tail light unit has failed, replace the entire tail light assembly with a new one – individual LEDs are not available (see Section 10).

Licence plate light

6 Undo the screws and remove the lens.
7 Carefully pull the bulb out.
8 Check the socket terminals for corrosion and clean them if necessary.
9 Fit the new bulb, then fit the lens – do not overtighten the screws as the lens and threads are easily damaged.

10 Tail light

CBF1000/A models

1 Remove the rear section of the seat cowl (see Chapter 7).
2 Undo the screws and bolts securing the tail light and draw it back off the bike **(see illustration)**. Displace the bulbholder covers **(see illustration)**. Make a note of which wire connects where, then disconnect the wiring connectors from the bulbholders **(see illustration)**.
3 Remove the lenses and bulbs as required – all components are available separately.
4 Installation is the reverse of removal. Check the operation of the tail and brake lights and turn signals.

CB1000R/RA models

5 Remove the seat cowl (see Chapter 7).
6 Undo the screw on the underside of the licence plate/turn signal holder, then release the cover tabs. Disconnect the tail light, turn signal and licence plate light wiring connectors.
7 Unscrew the bolts securing the licence plate/turn signal holder assembly and remove it.
8 Undo the screw and bolts securing the tail light and remove it, noting the collars with the bolts.
9 Installation is the reverse of removal. Check the operation of the tail and brake lights, turn signals and licence plate light.

11 Turn signal circuit check

1 Most turn signal problems are the result of a burned out bulb or corroded socket. This is especially true when the turn signals function properly in one direction, but fail to flash in the other direction. If this is the case, first check the bulbs, the sockets and the wiring connectors (see Section 12). If all the turn signals fail to work, check the fuses (see Section 5), and then the relay (see Steps 2 to 4). If they are good, the problem lies in the wiring or connectors, or the switch. Refer to Section 19 for the switch testing procedures, and also to the wiring diagrams at the end of this Chapter.
2 To check the relay, on CBF1000/A models remove the right-hand seat cowl, and on CB1000R/RA models remove the seats (see Chapter 7).
3 Displace the relay and disconnect the wiring connector **(see illustrations)**. Check for battery voltage at the red/green wire terminal on the loom side of the connector with the ignition ON. If no voltage is present, check the red/green wire from the relay to the fusebox for continuity. Refer to electrical system fault finding in Section 2 and to the wiring diagrams at the end of this Chapter. If voltage was present check the green wire for continuity to earth, and repair or renew the wiring or connectors as required.
4 If voltage was present, short between the white/green and grey wire terminals on the loom side of the connector using a jumper wire. Turn the ignition ON and operate the turn signal switch. If the lights come on, the relay is faulty and must be replaced with a new one.
5 If the lights do not come on, check the grey wire for continuity to the left-hand switch housing and the white/green wire for continuity

10.2c Remove the covers and disconnect the wires, noting which fits where

11.3a Turn signal relay (arrowed) – CBF1000/A models

11.3b Turn signal relay (arrowed) – CB1000R/RA models

Electrical system 8•13

12.2 Release the bulbholder...

12.3 ...then remove the bulb from it

12.7 Undo the screw and remove the lens

to the fuse box, and repair or renew the wiring or connectors as required.

6 If all is good so far, or if the lights came on one side but not the other, check the wiring between the left-hand switch housing and the turn signals themselves. Repair or renew the wiring or connectors as necessary.

12 Turn signal bulbs

Note: *It is a good idea to use a paper towel or dry cloth when handling bulbs to prevent injury if the bulb should break and to increase bulb life.*

CBF1000/A models

Front turn signals

1 Remove the relevant fairing side panel (see Chapter 7).
2 Turn the bulbholder anti-clockwise to release it **(see illustration)**.
3 Carefully push the bulb in and turn it anti-clockwise to release it **(see illustration)**. Check the socket terminals for corrosion and clean them if necessary.
4 Line up the pins of the new bulb with the slots in the socket, then push the bulb in and turn it clockwise until it locks into place. Fit the bulbholder and turn it clockwise.
5 Install the fairing side panel.

12.8 Push the bulb in and turn it anti-clockwise to release it

Rear turn signals

6 Undo the tail/brake light lens screws and remove the lens **(see illustration 9.1)**.
7 Undo the turn signal lens screw and remove the lens **(see illustration)**.
8 Carefully push the bulb in and turn it anti-clockwise to release it **(see illustration)**. Check the socket terminals for corrosion and clean them if necessary.
9 Line up the pins of the new bulb with the slots in the socket, then push the bulb in and turn it clockwise until it locks into place.
10 Fit the lenses – do not overtighten the screws as the lens and threads are easily damaged.

CB1000R/RA models

11 Undo the screw securing the lens and

12.11 Undo the screw and remove the lens

detach it from the housing, noting how it fits **(see illustration)**. Remove the rubber seal if it is loose, and discard it if it is damaged, deformed or deteriorated.
12 Push the bulb in and twist it anti-clockwise to release it **(see illustration)**. Check the socket terminals for corrosion and clean them if necessary.
13 Line up the pins of the new bulb with the slots in the socket, then push the bulb in and turn it clockwise until it locks into place.
14 Fit a new rubber seal if required, and make sure it is properly seated and does not get pinched. Fit the lens onto the housing, locating the tab in the cutout in the housing, and install the screw **(see illustration)**. Do not overtighten the screw as it is easy to strip the threads or crack the lens.

12.12 Push the bulb in and turn it anti-clockwise to release it

12.14 Make sure the tab (arrowed) locates correctly

8•14 Electrical system

13 Turn signal assemblies

CBF1000/A models

Front turn signals

1 Remove the relevant fairing side panel (see Chapter 7).
2 Undo the screws and remove the turn signal, noting the routing of the wire **(see illustration)**.
3 Installation is the reverse of removal. Check the operation of the turn signal.

Rear turn signals

4 See Section 10.

CB1000R/RA models

Front turn signals

5 Remove the headlight/instrument assembly (see Section 8, Steps 5 to 7).
6 Unscrew the nut, remove the plate and remove the turn signal, taking care as you draw the wire through **(see illustration)**.
7 Installation is the reverse of removal. Check the operation of the turn signal.

Rear turn signals

8 Undo the screw on the underside of the licence plate/turn signal holder, then release the cover tabs. Disconnect the turn signal wiring connector.
9 Undo the screws securing the licence plate/turn signal holder and remove it.

13.2 Front turn signal screws (arrowed)

13.6 Unscrew the nut (arrowed)

10 Unscrew the nut, remove the plate and remove the turn signal, taking care as you draw the wire through.
11 Installation is the reverse of removal. Check the operation of the turn signal.

14 Brake light switches

Circuit check

Note: *Refer to electrical system fault finding in Section 2 and to the wiring diagram for your model at the end of this Chapter.*

1 Before checking the switches, and if not already done, check the brake light circuit (see Section 6).

2 The front brake light switch is mounted on the underside of the brake master cylinder. Disconnect the wiring connectors from the switch **(see illustrations)**. Using a continuity tester, connect the probes to the terminals of the switch. With the brake lever at rest, there should be no continuity. With the brake lever applied, there should be continuity. If the switch does not behave as described, replace it with a new one.

3 The rear brake light switch is mounted on the inside of the rider's right-hand footrest bracket. On CB1000R/RA models remove the seats (see Chapter 7). On CBF1000/A models if required release the switch wiring from its tie. Disconnect the wiring connector **(see illustrations)**. Using a continuity tester, connect the probes to the terminals on the switch side of the wiring connector. With the brake pedal at rest, there should be no continuity. With the brake pedal applied, there should be continuity. If the switch does not behave as described, replace it with a new one, although check first that the spring has not broken and the switch is adjusted correctly (see Chapter 1).

4 If the switches are good, check for voltage at the white/green wire on the loom side of the connector, in each case with the ignition switch ON – there should be battery voltage. If there's no voltage present, check the wiring between the connector and the fuse box (see the wiring diagrams at the end of this Chapter). If voltage is present, check the other wire for continuity to the brake light, referring to the relevant wiring diagram. Repair or renew the wiring as necessary.

Switch replacement

Front brake lever switch

5 The switch is mounted on the underside of the brake master cylinder. Disconnect the wiring connectors from the switch **(see illustration 14.2a or b)**.
6 Undo the single screw securing the switch to the master cylinder and remove the switch.
7 Installation is the reverse of removal. Make sure the peg on the switch is correctly located in its hole before tightening the screw. The switch isn't adjustable.

14.2a Front brake switch wiring connectors (A) and mounting screw (B) – CBF1000/A

14.2b Front brake switch wiring connectors (A) and mounting screw (B) – CB1000R/RA

14.3a Rear brake switch wiring connector (arrowed) – CBF1000/A

14.3b Rear brake switch wiring connector – CB1000R/RA

Electrical system 8•15

14.9 Detach the spring (A) and remove the switch (B) as described

15.2 Pull the boot back and disconnect the wiring connectors

15.3 Unscrew the bolts (arrowed) and remove the instrument cluster – CBF1000/A

15.5 Unscrew the bolts (arrowed) and remove the instrument cluster – CB1000R/RA

Rear brake pedal switch

8 The rear brake light switch is mounted on the inside of the rider's right-hand footrest bracket. On CB1000R/RA models remove the seats (see Chapter 7). Disconnect the wiring connector **(see illustration 14.3a or b)**. Feed the wiring down to the switch, noting its routing and releasing it from any ties.

9 Detach the end of the switch spring from the brake pedal **(see illustration)**. Thread the switch out of its adjuster nut, then pull the nut out of the bracket. For improved access, detach the footrest bracket from the frame (see Chapter 5).

10 Installation is the reverse of removal, noting the following:
- Tighten the footrest bracket bolts to the torque setting specified at the beginning of the Chapter.
- Make sure the brake light is activated just before the rear brake pedal takes effect. If adjustment is necessary, refer to Chapter 1, Section 3.

15 Instrument removal and installation

Removal

CBF1000/A models

1 Remove the fairing and the rubber shroud (see Chapter 7).
2 Disconnect the instrument cluster wiring connector **(see illustration)**.
3 Unscrew the bolts and remove the instrument cluster **(see illustration)**. Note the collars in the grommets.

CB1000R/RA models

4 Remove the headlight/sidelight/instrument cluster assembly (see Section 8).
5 Unscrew the bolts and remove the instrument cluster **(see illustration)**. Note the collars in the grommets.

Installation

6 Installation is the reverse of removal. On CBF1000/A models check the rubber grommets and replace them with new ones if necessary, and make sure the collars are fitted **(see illustration)**.

15.6 Check the grommets and make sure the collars are fitted

16 Instrument check and replacement

Check

Note: *Refer to electrical system fault finding in Section 2 and to the wiring diagram for your model at the end of this Chapter.*

Instrument cluster power check

1 If none of the instruments or displays are working, first check the lighting fuse (see Section 5).

2 If the fuse is good, on CBF1000/A models remove the fairing and the rubber shroud, and on CB1000R/RA models remove the instrument cowl (see Chapter 7). Pull the rubber cover off the instrument cluster wiring connector and check for loose or broken connections **(see illustration 15.2 or 8.6b)**.

3 To check the power input wire, check for battery voltage between the black/brown wire terminal and a good earth (ground) with the ignition switch ON. There should be battery voltage. If there is no voltage, refer to the wiring diagrams and check the wire between the instrument cluster and the fusebox for loose or broken connections or a damaged wire.

4 To check the back-up power wire, check for battery voltage between the red/green wire terminal on the wiring loom side of the connector and a good earth (ground) with the ignition switch OFF. There should be battery voltage. If there is no voltage, refer to the wiring diagrams and check the red/green wire between the instrument cluster and the fusebox for loose or broken connections or a damaged wire, then check the red wire from the fusebox to the main fuse and battery.

5 If there is voltage, and to check the earth (ground) wire, check for continuity between the green wire terminal on CBF1000/A models and the green/black wire terminal on CB1000R/RA models, and earth (ground). If there is no continuity, check the circuit for loose or broken connections or a damaged wire and repair as necessary.

6 If all power input and earth wires are good, but there is no display or instrument function, then the printed circuit board (PCB) is faulty. Disassemble the instrument cluster and replace the PCB with a new one (see the relevant Steps below for your model).

Speedometer and vehicle speed sensor

7 On CBF1000/A models remove the fairing and the rubber shroud, and on CB1000R/RA models remove the instrument cowl (see Chapter 7). Pull the rubber cover off the instrument cluster wiring connector and check for loose or broken connections **(see illustration 15.2 or 8.6b)**.

8 If the wiring is good, disconnect the instrument wiring connector. Place the bike on the centrestand on CBF1000A models, and on an auxiliary stand on all other models so the rear wheel is off the ground. Connect a voltmeter between the pink/green (+) and green/black (-) wire terminals on CBF1000/A models, and between the pink/blue (+) and green/black (-) wire terminals on CB1000R/RA models in the connector – make sure the probes make good contact when inserted into the connector. With the ignition switch ON, have an assistant turn the rear wheel by hand and check that a fluctuating voltage reading between 0 and 5 volts is obtained. If the correct reading is obtained the printed circuit board (PCB) is faulty. Disassemble the instrument cluster and replace the PCB with a new one (see the relevant Steps below for your model). If no reading is obtained, check for continuity in the pink/green or pink/blue wire to the speed sensor wiring connector, which is behind the starter motor, and in the green/black wire to earth. To access the wiring connector remove the air filter housing/throttle body assembly (see Chapter 4).

9 If the wiring is good, remove the air filter housing/throttle body assembly (see Chapter 4). Disconnect the speed sensor 3-pin black wiring connector **(see illustration 16.30)**. Check the connector for loose terminals. With the ignition switch ON, check for battery voltage between the yellow/red (+) and green/black (-) wire terminals on CBF1000/A models, and between the white/black (+) and green/black (-) wire terminals on CB1000R/RA models on the wiring loom side of the connector. If there is no voltage refer to the wiring diagrams and check the wires for continuity to the fuse box and earth respectively and repair any loose or broken connection or damaged wire.

10 If a reading is obtained, repeat the check in Step 9, but connect the meter between the pink and green wire terminals on the sensor side of the wiring connector, with the connector connected and the ignition on. If no fluctuating voltage is obtained, the speed sensor is faulty and must be replaced with a new one (see Steps 29 to 32).

Tachometer

11 On CB1000R/RA models when the ignition is switched on the tachometer display segments should all come on sequentially from zero to maximum, then go out in the same order.

12 If the tachometer does not work, on CBF1000/A models remove the fairing and the rubber shroud, and on CB1000R/RA models remove the instrument cowl (see Chapter 7). Pull the rubber cover off the instrument cluster wiring connector and check for loose or broken connections **(see illustration 15.2 or 8.6b)**.

13 If the wiring is good, check the tachometer input peak voltage using the peak voltage adapter (Pt. No. 07HGJ-0020100) with an aftermarket digital multimeter having an impedance of 10 M-ohm/DCV minimum, for this test. Connect the positive (+) lead of the voltmeter and peak voltage adapter arrangement to the yellow/green wire terminal on the loom side of the instrument wiring connector and the negative (–) lead to a good earth (ground). Start the engine and measure the tachometer input peak voltage, which should be at least 10.5 volts. If the peak voltage is normal, check the instrument cluster earth wire (see Step 5). If it is good then the tachometer is faulty. Disassemble the instrument cluster and replace the PCB with a new one (see the relevant Steps below for your model).

14 If there is no reading, on CBF1000/A models remove the right-hand seat cowl, and on CB1000R/RA models remove the right-hand side cover (see Chapter 7), and check there is continuity in the yellow/green wire to the ECM wiring connector. If there is no continuity there is a break in the wire or faulty connector. Refer to the wiring diagrams and trace and rectify the fault. If the wiring is good the ECM could be faulty (see Chapter 4).

All other functions

15 If none of the functions are working, check the instrument cluster power input (see above) and earth wires. If all is good, disassemble the instrument cluster (see below) and check for any obvious internal fault. If none is apparent replace the PCB with a new one.

16 If an individual function is not working, refer to Chapter 3 for the coolant temperature and warning display, Chapter 4 for the low fuel warning, FI and HISS lights, Chapter 6 for the ABS light, Section 6 for the HI beam light, Section 17 for the oil pressure switch, Section 20 for the neutral switch. If the particular component and its circuit are good replace the faulty component with a new one – on CBF1000/A models the fuel gauge and FI/HISS/ABS display units are available separately from the main PCB, while on CB1000R/RA models the entire display is one PCB.

Instrument and warning lights

17 All instrument and warning lights are LEDs, which are part of the instrument cluster printed circuit board and are not available individually. If one of the LEDs fails disassemble the instrument cluster and replace the PCB or indicator board with a new one (see below).

Instrument disassembly and replacement

CBF1000/A models

18 Remove the instrument cluster (see Section 15).

19 Undo the screws on the front and lift

Electrical system 8•17

16.19a Undo the screws (arrowed) . . .

16.19b . . . and remove the cover . . .

16.19c . . . and the plate

the front cover and reflecting plate off **(see illustrations)**.
20 To remove the main instrument PCB undo the relevant screws on the back **(see illustration)**. Turn the instrument cluster over and disconnect the fuel gauge and FI/HISS/ABS display wiring connectors **(see illustrations)**. Undo the two main PCB screws and lift the PCB out, noting how it locates **(see illustration)**.
21 To remove the fuel gauge undo the relevant screws on the back **(see illustration 16.20a)**. Turn the instrument cluster over and disconnect the fuel gauge wiring connector and remove the gauge **(see illustration 16.20b)**.
22 To remove the FI/HISS/ABS display undo the relevant screws on the back **(see illustration 16.20a)**. Turn the instrument cluster over and disconnect the FI/HISS/ABS display wiring connector and remove the display **(see illustration 16.20c)**.
23 Installation is the reverse of removal. Do not over-tighten the screws. Make sure the wiring connectors are secure.

CB1000R/RA models

24 Remove the instrument cluster (see Section 15).
25 Undo the screws on the back and remove the rear cover, then remove the PCB from the front cover **(see illustrations)**.

16.20a Fuel gauge screws (A), FI/HISS/ABS display screws (B), all others secure the main PCB

16.20b Fuel gauge wiring connector (arrowed)

16.20c FI/HISS/ABS display wiring connector (arrowed)

16.20d Undo the screws (arrowed) and remove the PCB

16.25a Undo the screws (arrowed) . . .

16.25b . . . and remove the rear cover . . .

16.25c . . . and the front cover

8•18 Electrical system

26 Remove the button rods and lift the reflecting plate off **(see illustrations)**.
27 If required undo the indicator lens screws and detach the lens from the PCB.
28 Installation is the reverse of removal. Do not over-tighten the screws.

Vehicle speed sensor

29 The speed sensor is mounted behind the starter motor. To access it remove the air filter housing/throttle body assembly (see Chapter 4).
30 Disconnect the wiring connector **(see illustration)**.
31 Unscrew the bolt and remove the sensor. Check the condition of its O-ring and replace it with a new one if it is damaged or there is evidence of leakage around it. While the sensor is removed plug the orifice with clean rag.
32 Installation is the reverse of removal, using a new O-ring if necessary.

17 Oil pressure switch

Check

Note: *Refer to electrical system fault finding in Section 2 and to the wiring diagram for your model at the end of this Chapter.*

1 The oil pressure warning light should come on when the ignition switch is turned ON and go out a few seconds after the engine is started. If the oil pressure warning light does not go out or comes on whilst the engine is running, stop the engine immediately and carry out an oil level check (see *Pre-ride checks*), and if the level is correct, an oil pressure check (see Chapter 2).
2 If the oil pressure warning light does not come on when the ignition is turned ON, but all other instrument functions work, pull the

16.26a Remove the button rods . . .

rubber cover off the oil pressure switch (located in the right-hand side of the crankcase just ahead of the oil level inspection window), and undo the screw securing the wiring connector **(see illustration)**. With the ignition switched ON, earth (ground) the wire on the crankcase and check that the warning light comes on. If the light comes on, the switch is defective and must be replaced with a new one.
3 If the light still does not come on, check for voltage at the wire terminal with the ignition ON. If there is no voltage present, on CBF1000/A models remove the fairing, and on CB1000R/RA models remove the instrument cowl (see Chapter 7). Pull the rubber cover off the instrument cluster wiring connector and check for loose or broken connections **(see illustration 15.2 or 8.6b)**. Check there is continuity in the wire between the switch and the instrument cluster connector. Repair the wiring if necessary. If the wiring is all good and the switch is good the instrument PCB could be faulty (see Section 16).
4 If the warning light does not go out when the engine is started or comes on whilst the engine is running, yet the oil pressure is satisfactory, detach the wire from the oil pressure switch (see above). With the wire detached and the ignition switched ON the light should be out.

16.26b . . . and the reflecting plate

If it is illuminated, the wire between the switch and instrument cluster is earthed (grounded) at some point. If the wiring is good, the switch must be assumed faulty and replaced with a new one.

Removal

5 The oil pressure switch is screwed into the right-hand side of the crankcase just ahead of the oil level inspection window. Put the bike on its sidestand.
6 Pull the rubber cover off the switch, then undo the screw securing the wiring connector **(see illustration 17.2)**.
7 Unscrew and remove the switch.

Installation

8 Apply a suitable sealant to the upper portion of the switch threads near the switch body, leaving the bottom 3 to 4 mm of thread clean. Thread the switch into the crankcase and tighten it to the torque setting specified at the beginning of the Chapter.
9 Attach the wiring connector and secure it with the screw, then fit the rubber cover **(see illustration 17.2)**.
10 Run the engine and check that the switch operates correctly and without leakage.

16.30 Vehicle speed sensor wiring connector (A) and mounting bolt (B)

17.2 Pull back the rubber cover then undo the terminal screw (arrowed) and detach the wire

Electrical system 8•19

18.2a Ignition switch wiring connector (arrowed) – CBF1000/A

18.2b Ignition switch wiring connector (arrowed) – CB1000R/RA

18 Ignition switch

Warning: To prevent the risk of short circuits, disconnect the battery negative (–) lead before making any ignition switch checks.

Check

Note: *Refer to electrical system fault finding in Section 2 and to the wiring diagram for your model at the end of this Chapter.*

1 The switch can be checked for continuity using an ohmmeter or a continuity test light. Always disconnect the battery negative (–) lead, which will prevent the possibility of a short circuit, before making the checks (see Section 3).
2 To access the connector, on CBF1000/A models remove the fairing and the rubber shroud (see Chapter 7). On CB1000R/RA models remove the headlight/sidelight/instrument cluster assembly (see Section 8). Trace the wiring from the switch and disconnect it at the connector **(see illustrations)**.
3 Using an ohmmeter or a continuity tester, check the continuity of the connector terminal pairs (see the wiring diagrams at the end of this Chapter). Continuity should exist between the terminals connected by a solid line on the diagram when the switch is in the indicated position.
4 If the switch fails any of the tests, replace it with a new one.

Removal

5 On CBF1000/A models remove the fairing and the rubber shroud (see Chapter 7). On CB1000R/RA models remove the headlight/sidelight/instrument cluster assembly (see Section 8). Disconnect the battery negative (–) lead (see Section 3).
6 Trace the wiring from the switch and disconnect it at the connector **(see illustration 18.2a or b)**. Feed the wiring back to the switch, freeing it from any clips and ties and noting its routing.
7 Undo the screws securing the HISS immobiliser receiver around the ignition switch and displace it, noting how it fits **(see illustration)**.
8 One-way security bolts (which can be done up but not undone using conventional tools) are fitted **(see illustration)** – drive the heads around using a cold chisel. If you can't move the bolts displace the top yoke for improved access (refer to Chapter 1, Section 14, following the relevant Steps).
9 If required separate the contact plate from the bottom of the switch – it is available separately from the main body of the switch.

Installation

10 Installation is the reverse of removal. Tighten the ignition switch bolts to the torque setting specified at the beginning of the Chapter, using new ones if necessary. Make sure the wiring connector is correctly routed and securely connected.

18.7 Undo the screws (arrowed) and displace the receiver

18.8 Ignition switch one-way security bolt (arrowed)

8•20 Electrical system

19.3a Right-hand switch wiring connectors (A), left-hand switch wiring connectors (B) – CBF1000/A

19.3b Right-hand switch wiring connectors (A), left-hand switch wiring connectors (B) – CB1000R/RA

19 Handlebar switches

Check

Note: *Refer to electrical system fault finding in Section 2 and to the wiring diagram for your model at the end of this Chapter.*

1 Generally speaking, the switches are reliable and trouble-free. Most troubles, when they do occur, are caused by dirty or corroded contacts, but wear and breakage of internal parts is a possibility that should not be overlooked. If breakage does occur, the entire switch and related wiring harness will have to be replaced with a new one, as individual parts are not available.
2 The switches can be checked for continuity using an ohmmeter or a continuity test light. Always disconnect the battery negative (–) lead, which will prevent the possibility of a short circuit, before making the checks (see Section 3).
3 To access the connectors, on CBF1000/A models remove the fairing and the rubber shroud (see Chapter 7). On CB1000R/RA models remove the headlight/sidelight/

19.8 Switch housing screws (arrowed)

instrument cluster assembly (see Section 8). Trace the wiring from the switch and disconnect it at the connector(s) **(see illustrations)**.
4 Check for continuity between the terminals of the switch connector with the switch in the various positions (i.e. switch off – no continuity, switch on – continuity) – see the wiring diagram for your model at the end of this Chapter. Continuity should exist between the terminals connected by a solid line on the diagram when the switch is in the indicated position.
5 If the continuity check indicates a problem exists, displace the switch housing (Step 8 or 9), and spray the switch contacts with electrical contact cleaner (there is no need to remove the switch completely). If they are accessible, the contacts can be scraped clean with a knife or polished with crocus cloth. If switch components are damaged or broken, it will be obvious when the switch is disassembled.

Removal and installation

6 To access the connectors, on CBF1000/A models remove the fairing and the rubber shroud (see Chapter 7). On CB1000R/RA models remove the headlight/sidelight/instrument cluster assembly (see Section 8). Trace the wiring from the switch and disconnect it at the connector(s) **(see illustration 19.3a or b)**. Feed the wiring back to the switch, freeing it from any clips and ties and noting its routing.
7 If removing the right-hand switch disconnect the wires from the brake light switch **(see illustration 14.2a or b)**. If removing the left-hand switch disconnect the wires from the clutch switch **(see illustration 22.2)**.
8 To remove the left-hand switch housing, and the right-hand switch housing on CB1000R/RA models, undo the screws and free the switch from the handlebar by separating the halves **(see illustration)**.
9 To remove the right-hand switch on

CBF1000/A models housing refer to Chapter 4 and detach the throttle cables.
10 Installation is the reverse of removal. Make sure the locating pin in the switch housing locates in the hole in the handlebar.

20 Neutral switch

Check

Note: *Refer to electrical system fault finding in Section 2 and to the wiring diagram for your model at the end of this Chapter.*

1 The neutral switch is located in the back of the engine. The neutral light should come whenever the ignition switch is ON and the transmission is in neutral. The switch is part of the starter interlock safety circuit which prevents or stops the engine running if the transmission is in gear whilst the sidestand is down, and prevents the engine from starting if the transmission is in gear unless the sidestand is up and the clutch is pulled in.
2 If the light does not come on when it should, but all other instrument functions work, trace the wiring connector. On CBF1000/A models raise the fuel tank (see Chapter 4) for access and on CB1000R/RA models remove the left-hand side cover (see Chapter 7). Disconnect the engine sub-harness wiring connector – it is an 8-pin grey connector on CBF1000/A models, and a 6-pin black connector on CB1000R/RA models, with the wires from the neutral switch, oil pressure switch, speed sensor, and on CBF models the IAT sensor.
3 Check for continuity between the light green wire terminal in the switch side of the connector and the crankcase. With the transmission in neutral, there should be continuity. With the transmission in gear, there should be no continuity. If not, then first check the wiring connector is secure on the switch itself and

Electrical system 8•21

there is continuity in the wire between the switch and the connector, and if that is good remove the switch (see below) and check whether the plunger is bent or damaged, or just stuck **(see illustration)**. Replace the switch with a new one if necessary.

4 If the switch and its wire are good check for continuity in the light green wire from the loom side of the connector to the diode block in the fuse box. Next check the other components (clutch switch, sidestand switch, diode block) in the starter safety circuit, and check the wiring between them for continuity, and the connectors for loose or broken connections.

Removal and installation

5 The switch is located in the back of the engine. Remove the engine from the frame (see Chapter 2).
6 Pull the rubber boot off the switch, then unscrew the nut and detach the wiring connector.
7 Clean the area around the switch, then unscrew it from the crankcase **(see illustration)**. Discard the sealing washer as a new one should be used.
8 Install the switch using a new washer and tighten it to the torque setting specified at the beginning of the Chapter.
9 Connect the wiring connector and check the operation of the neutral light.

21 Sidestand switch

Check

Note: *Refer to electrical system fault finding in Section 2 and to the wiring diagram for your model at the end of this Chapter.*

1 The sidestand switch is mounted on the stand pivot. The switch is part of the starter interlock safety circuit which prevents or stops the engine running if the transmission is in gear whilst the sidestand is down, and prevents the engine from starting if the transmission is in gear unless the sidestand is up and the clutch is pulled in.
2 On CBF1000/A models remove the left-hand seat cowl (see Chapter 7). On CB1000R/RA models remove the left-hand side cover (see Chapter 7), then undo the air intake duct cover screws and remove the cover **(see illustration)**. Trace the wiring from the switch and disconnect at the connector **(see illustrations)**.
3 Check the operation of the switch using an ohmmeter or continuity test light. Connect the meter between the terminals on the switch side of the connector. With the sidestand up there should be continuity (zero resistance) between the terminals, and with the stand down there should be no continuity (infinite resistance).
4 If the switch does not perform as expected, it is faulty and must be replaced with a new one.
5 If the switch is good, check the other components (clutch switch, neutral switch, diode block) in the starter safety circuit, and check the wiring between them for continuity, and the connectors for loose or broken connections.

Removal

6 The sidestand switch is mounted on the stand pivot. On CBF1000/A models remove the left-hand side cover and seat cowl (see Chapter 7). On CB1000R/RA models remove the left-hand side cover (see Chapter 7), then undo the air intake duct cover screws and remove the cover **(see illustration 21.2a)**. Trace the wiring from the switch and disconnect at the connector **(see illustration 21.2b or c)**. Feed the wiring back to the switch, freeing it from any clips and ties and noting its routing.
7 Unscrew the switch bolt and remove the switch from the stand, noting how it fits **(see illustrations)**. Honda specify that the switch

20.3 Make sure the plunger moves in and out smoothly and freely

20.7 Unscrew and remove the switch

21.2a Undo the screws and remove the cover

21.2b Sidestand switch wiring connector (arrowed) – CBF1000/A

21.2c Sidestand switch wiring connector (arrowed) – CB1000R/RA

21.7a Sidestand switch bolt (arrowed) – CBF1000/A

21.7b Sidestand switch bolt (arrowed) – CB1000R/RA

8•22 Electrical system

22.2 Clutch switch wiring connectors (A) and mounting screw (B)

23.2a The diode block (arrowed) – CBF1000/A

23.2b The diode block (arrowed) – CB1000R/RA

bolt be replaced with a new one every time it is disturbed – the new bolt has a locking compound already applied to its threads. However there is nothing to stop you cleaning up the threads on the old bolt and applying a suitable non-permanent thread locking compound on installation.

Installation

8 Fit the new switch onto the sidestand, making sure the pin locates in the hole, and the lug on the stand bracket locates into the cut-out in the switch body. Secure the switch with a new or cleaned and threadlocked bolt and tighten it to the torque setting specified at the beginning of the Chapter **(see illustration 21.7a or b)**.
9 Feed the wiring up to its connector, making sure it is correctly routed and secured by any clips.
10 Reconnect the wiring connector and check the operation of the sidestand switch.

22 Clutch switch

Check

Note: Refer to electrical system fault finding in Section 2 and to the wiring diagram for your model at the end of this Chapter.

1 The clutch switch is mounted on the front of the master cylinder. The switch is part of the starter interlock safety circuit which prevents or stops the engine running if the transmission is in gear whilst the sidestand is down, and prevents the engine from starting if the transmission is in gear unless the sidestand is up and the clutch lever is pulled in. The switch isn't adjustable.
2 To check the switch, disconnect the wiring connectors from it **(see illustration)**. Connect the probes of an ohmmeter or a continuity tester to the two switch terminals. With the clutch lever pulled in, continuity should be indicated. With the clutch lever out, no continuity (infinite resistance) should be indicated.
3 If the switch is good, check the other components (sidestand switch, neutral switch,

diode block) in the starter safety circuit, and check the wiring between them for continuity, and the connectors for loose or broken connections.

Removal and installation

4 The clutch switch is mounted on the front of the master cylinder.
5 Disconnect the wiring connectors from the switch **(see illustration 22.2)**.
6 Undo the single screw securing the switch and remove it, noting how it fits.
7 Installation is the reverse of removal. Make sure the switch is correctly located before tightening its screw.

23 Diode block

Note: Refer to electrical system fault finding in Section 2 and to the wiring diagram for your model at the end of this Chapter.

1 The diode block plugs into a connector in the fusebox, which is located under the passenger seat on CBF1000/A models and under the rider's seat on CB1000R/RA models. The diode block contains two diodes which are part of the starter interlock safety circuit that prevents or stops the engine running if the transmission is in gear whilst the sidestand is down, and prevents the engine from starting if the transmission is in gear unless the sidestand is up and the clutch lever is pulled in.

23.3 Test the diode as described

2 Remove the seat(s) (see Chapter 7), then open the fuse box lid **(see illustrations 5.3a, b and c or 5.6a and b)**. Pull the diode block out of its socket **(see illustrations)**.
3 Using an ohmmeter or continuity tester, connect the positive (+) probe to one of the outer terminals of the diode block and the negative (–) probe to the middle terminal of the block **(see illustration)**. The diode being tested should show continuity. Now reverse the probes. The diode should show no continuity. Repeat the tests between the other outer terminal and the middle terminal. The same results should be achieved. If it doesn't behave as stated, replace the diode block with a new one.
4 If the diode block is good, push it back into its socket, then check the other components (sidestand switch, neutral switch, clutch switch) in the starter safety circuit, and check the wiring between them for continuity, and the connectors for loose or broken connections.

24 Horn

Check

1 The horn is mounted below the radiator on the right-hand side. If it doesn't work first check the fuse (see Section 5).
2 Disconnect the wiring connectors from the horn **(see illustrations)**. Check them for loose wires. Using two jumper wires, apply voltage

24.2a Horn wiring connectors (A) and mounting bolt (B) – CBF1000/A

Electrical system 8•23

24.2b Horn wiring connectors (A) and mounting bolt (B) – CB1000R/RA

25.2 Lift the rubber cover to access the starter motor lead terminal (A) and battery lead terminal (B)

from a fully-charged 12V battery directly to the terminals on the horn. If the horn doesn't sound, replace it with a new one.

3 If the horn sounds, check for voltage at the black wire connector with the ignition ON and the horn switch (button) pressed (if both wires are black make sure there is voltage at one of them). If voltage is present, check the green or other black wire for continuity to earth. Refer to electrical system fault finding in Section 2 and to the wiring diagrams at the end of this Chapter.

4 If no voltage was present, check the black wire for continuity between the horn and the switch in the left-hand switch gear. Next, with the ignition switch ON, check that there is voltage at the black/brown (CBF1000/A models) or white/green (CB1000R/RA models) wire to the horn switch. If there is, check the switch contacts in the switch housing (see Section 19).

5 If there isn't voltage at the black/brown (CBF1000/A models) or white/green (CB1000R/RA models) wire, check the wire from the switch to the fuse box.

Replacement

6 The horn is mounted below the radiator on the right-hand side.
7 Unplug the wiring connectors from the horn **(see illustration 24.2a or b)**. Unscrew the bolt securing the horn.
8 Fit the horn and tighten the bolt. Connect the wiring to the horn. Check that it works.

25 Starter relay

Check

1 If the starter circuit is faulty, first check the fuse (see Section 5).
2 On CBF1000/A models remove the battery (see Section 3) to access the relay. Lift the rubber terminal cover and unscrew the bolt securing the starter motor lead, identified by the letter M (the other lead, marked B, is the battery lead) **(see illustration)**; position the lead away from the relay. Install and connect the battery.

3 On CB1000R/RA models remove the seats to access the relay (see Chapter 7), then remove the relay cover **(see illustration)**. Make sure the transmission is in neutral. Unscrew the bolt securing the starter motor lead, identified by the letter M (the other lead, marked B, is the battery lead) **(see illustration)**; be careful not to touch the battery lead with the tool while unscrewing the starter motor lead, and then position the lead away from the relay.

4 With the ignition switch ON, the engine kill switch in the RUN position, and the transmission in neutral, press the starter switch. The relay should be heard to click.

5 If the relay doesn't click, switch off the ignition and remove the relay as described below; test it as follows:

25.3a Lift the cover . . .

25.3b . . . to access the starter motor lead terminal (A) and battery lead terminal (B)

8•24 Electrical system

25.13a On CBF1000/A models disconnect the wiring connector . . .

25.13b . . . then unscrew the lead bolts (A) and pull the relay off its mount (B)

6 Set a multimeter to the ohms x 1 scale and connect it across the relay's starter motor and battery lead terminals. There should be no continuity. Using a fully-charged 12 volt battery and two insulated jumper wires, connect the positive (+) terminal of the battery to the yellow/red wire terminal of the relay, and the negative (–) terminal to the green/red wire terminal of the relay. At this point the relay should be heard to click and the multimeter read 0 ohms (continuity). If this is the case the relay is proved good. If the relay does not click when battery voltage is applied and indicates no continuity (infinite resistance) across its terminals, it is faulty and must be replaced with a new one.

7 If the relay is good, check for continuity in the main lead from the battery to the relay. Also check that the terminals and connectors at each end of the lead are tight and corrosion-free.

8 Next check for battery voltage at the yellow/red wire terminal on the relay wiring connector with the ignition ON, the kill switch in the RUN position and the starter button pressed. If there is no voltage, check the wiring between the relay wiring connector and the starter button.

9 If voltage is present, check that there is continuity to earth in the green/red wire with the transmission in neutral (note that there will be a very slight resistance due to the diodes in the starter interlock circuit. If not check the wiring and connectors between the relay, the fusebox and the neutral switch, then if that is good check the switch itself and the diode block.

10 Now shift the transmission into gear, raise the sidestand and pull the clutch lever in and check for continuity to earth again. If there is no continuity, check the clutch switch and sidestand switch as described in the relevant sections of this Chapter. If all components are good, check the wiring between the various components (see the wiring diagrams at the end of this Chapter).

Replacement

11 To access the relay on CBF1000/A models remove the battery (see Section 3). On CB1000R/RA models remove the seats (see Chapter 7), then remove the relay cover **(see illustration 25.3a)**.

12 On CB1000R/RA models disconnect the battery terminals, remembering to disconnect the negative (–) terminal first.

13 Disconnect the relay wiring connector **(see illustrations)**. Unscrew the bolts securing the starter motor and battery leads to the relay and detach the leads. If the relay is being replaced with a new one fit the main fuse, and on CB1000R/RA models the FI/IGN fuse, into the new relay **(see illustration 5.2b or 5.5b)**. If you are fitting a new rubber sleeve on CBF1000/A models remove the spare main fuse from its pocket and fit it into the new sleeve.

14 Installation is the reverse of removal. Connect the lead from the battery to the terminal marked B and the lead from the starter motor to the terminal marked M, and make sure the terminal bolts are securely tightened **(see illustration 25.2 or 25.3b)**.

25.13c On CB1000R/RA models disconnect the wiring connector and unscrew the lead bolts (arrowed) . . .

25.13d . . . then pull the relay off its mount

Electrical system 8•25

26.2 Pull back the terminal cover then unscrew the nut (arrowed) and detach the lead

26.3 Unscrew the two bolts (arrowed), noting the earth lead

Do not forget to fit the main fuse, and on CB1000R/RA models the FI/IGN fuse, into the relay, and on CBF1000/A models the spare into the rubber sleeve, if removed **(see illustration 5.2b or 5.5b)**. Connect the negative (–) lead last when reconnecting the battery.

26 Starter motor removal and installation

Removal

1 The starter motor is mounted on the crankcase behind the starter motor. Disconnect the battery negative (–) lead. Remove the air filter housing/throttle body assembly (see Chapter 4).
2 Peel back the rubber terminal cover on the starter motor **(see illustration)**. Unscrew the nut and detach the lead.
3 Unscrew the two bolts securing the starter motor to the crankcase, noting the earth lead **(see illustration)**. Slide the starter motor out, using a screwdriver as leverage if required.
4 Remove the O-ring on the end of the starter motor and discard it as a new one must be used **(see illustration 26.5)**.

Installation

5 Fit a new O-ring onto the end of the starter motor, making sure it is seated in its groove **(see illustration)**. Apply a smear of engine oil to the O-ring.
6 Manoeuvre the motor into position and slide it into the crankcase, meshing starter motor teeth with those of the starter idle/reduction gear. Fit the mounting bolts, not forgetting to secure the earth lead with the rear bolt, and tighten them **(see illustration 26.3)**.
7 Connect the starter lead to the motor and secure it with the nut **(see illustration 26.2)**. Fit the rubber cover over the terminal.
8 Install the air filter housing/throttle body assembly (see Chapter 4).

27 Starter motor overhaul

Check

1 Remove the starter motor (see Section 26). Cover the body in some rag and clamp the motor in a soft-jawed vice – do not overtighten it.
2 Using a fully-charged 12 volt battery and two insulated jumper wires, connect the positive (+) terminal of the battery to the protruding terminal on the starter motor, and the negative (–) terminal to one of the motor's mounting lugs. At this point the starter motor should spin. If this is the case the motor is proved good, though it is worth disassembling it and checking it if you suspect it of not working properly under load. If the motor does not spin, disassemble it for inspection.

Disassembly

3 Remove the starter motor (see Section 26).
4 Note any alignment marks between the main housing and the front and rear covers, or make your own if they aren't clear **(see illustration)**.

26.5 Fit a new O-ring and lubricate it

27.4 Note the alignment marks between the housing and the covers

8•26 Electrical system

27.5a Unscrew and remove the two bolts (arrowed) . . .

27.5b . . . then remove the front cover and sealing ring (arrowed)

5 Unscrew the two long bolts, noting the O-rings, then remove the front cover from the motor along with its sealing ring **(see illustrations)**. Discard the sealing ring as a new one must be used. Remove the tabbed washer from the cover and slide the insulating washer and shim(s) from the front end of the armature, noting the number of shims and their correct fitted order **(see illustrations)**.

6 Remove the rear cover from the motor along with its sealing ring **(see illustration)**. Discard the sealing ring as a new one must be used. Remove the shim(s) from the rear end of the armature noting how many **(see illustration 27.21a)**.

7 Withdraw the armature from the main housing – it will be held in by the attraction of the magnets.

8 At this stage check for continuity between the terminal bolt and the brush on the insulated base – there should be continuity (zero resistance) **(see illustration)**. Check for continuity between the terminal bolt and the cover – there should be no continuity (infinite resistance) **(see illustration)**. Also check for continuity between the uninsulated brush and the brushplate – there should be continuity (zero resistance). If there is no continuity when there should be or *vice versa*, identify the faulty component and replace it with a new one.

9 Noting the correct fitted location of each component, unscrew the nut from the terminal bolt and remove the plain washer, the one large and two small insulating washers **(see**

27.5c Remove the tabbed washer . . .

27.5d . . . and the insulating washer and shim(s)

27.6 Remove the rear cover and its sealing ring (arrowed)

27.8a Check for continuity between the terminal and its brush . . .

Electrical system 8•27

27.8b ... and between the terminal and the cover

27.9a Unscrew the nut (arrowed) and remove the plain washer and the large and small insulating washers

illustration). Remove the brushplate assembly and terminal bolt from the main housing, noting how it locates **(see illustration)**. Remove the O-ring and the insulator from the bolt **(see illustration)**.

10 Move each brush spring end aside and slide the brushes out **(see illustration)**.

Inspection

11 The parts of the starter motor that are most likely to require attention are the brushes. Measure the length of each brush and compare the results to the length listed in this Chapter's Specifications **(see illustration)**. If either of the brushes are worn beyond the service limit, fit a new brush and brushplate assembly. If the brushes are not worn excessively, nor cracked, chipped, or otherwise damaged, they may be reused.

12 Inspect the commutator bars on the armature for scoring, scratches and discoloration. The commutator can be cleaned and polished with crocus cloth, but do not use sandpaper or emery paper. After cleaning, wipe away any residue with a cloth soaked in electrical system cleaner or denatured alcohol.

13 Using an ohmmeter or a continuity test light, check for continuity between the commutator bars **(see illustration)**. Continuity should exist between each bar and all of the others. Also, check for continuity between the commutator bars and the armature shaft **(see illustration)**. There should be no continuity (infinite resistance) between the commutator and the shaft. If the checks indicate otherwise, the armature is defective and a new starter motor bust be obtained – the armature is not available separately.

27.9b Remove the brushplate assembly ...

27.9c ... then remove the O-ring and the insulator

27.10 Move the brush springs aside and slide the brushes out

27.11 Measure the length of each brush

27.13a There should be continuity between the bars ...

27.13b ... and no continuity between the bars and the shaft

8•28 Electrical system

27.15a Check the bearing and seal in the front cover . . .

27.15b . . . and the bush in the rear cover

27.18 Fit the brushes into their housings and locate the spring ends

27.19a Fit the insulator onto the bolt . . .

27.19b . . . fit the brushplate into the rear cover . . .

27.19c . . . locating the tab in the groove (arrowed)

14 Check the front end of the armature shaft for worn, cracked, chipped and broken teeth. If the shaft is damaged or worn, a new starter motor bust be obtained – the armature is not available separately.

15 Inspect the front and rear covers for signs of cracks or wear. Check the oil seal and the needle bearing in the front cover and the bush in the rear cover for wear and damage – the seal, bearing, bush and covers are not listed as being available separately so if necessary a new starter motor must be fitted **(see illustrations)**.

16 Inspect the magnets in the main housing and the housing itself for cracks.

17 Inspect the insulating washers, O-ring, and sealing rings for signs of damage, deformation and deterioration and replace them with new ones if necessary.

Reassembly

18 Slide the brushes back into position in their housings and locate the brush spring ends onto the outer ends of the brushes **(see illustration)**.

19 Fit the insulator onto the terminal bolt **(see illustration)**. Insert the terminal bolt through its hole in the rear cover then fit the brushplate into the cover, making sure its tab is correctly located in the groove in the cover **(see illustration)**. Fit the O-ring down over the bolt and press it into place between the bolt and the cover **(see illustrations)**. Slide the small insulating washers onto the terminal bolt, followed by the large insulating washer and the plain washer **(see illustration 27.9a)**. Fit the nut onto the terminal bolt and tighten it.

20 At this stage check again for continuity between the terminal bolt and the brush on the insulated base – there should be continuity (zero resistance) **(see illustration 27.8a)**. Check for continuity between the terminal bolt and the cover – there should be no continuity (infinite resistance) **(see illustration 27.8b)**. Also check for continuity between the uninsulated brush and the brushplate – there should be continuity (zero resistance). If there is no continuity when there should be or *vice versa*, identify the faulty component and replace it with a new one.

21 Fit the shim(s) onto the rear of the armature shaft **(see illustration)**. Apply a smear of grease to the end of the shaft. Insert the armature into the brushplate at an angle so that the brushes locate against the commutator, then straighten the armature, pushing the brushes back into their housings against the springs, and slide it into the rear

27.19d Fit the O-ring over the bolt . . .

27.19e . . . then slide it down and press it into place

27.21a Fit the shim(s) onto the shaft . . .

Electrical system 8•29

27.21b ... then fit the armature into the rear cover making sure the brushes locate correctly onto the commutator

27.22a Fit a new sealing ring onto the rear of the housing ...

27.22b ... then fit the housing onto the armature ...

27.22c ... locating the cut-out (A) over the tab (B)

cover so that the shaft end locates in its bush **(see illustration)**.
22 Fit the sealing ring onto the rear of the main housing **(see illustration)**. Grasp both the armature and the rear cover in one hand and hold them together – this will prevent the armature being drawn out by the magnets in the housing. Note however that you should take care not to let the housing be drawn forcibly onto the armature by the magnets. Carefully allow the housing to be drawn onto the armature, making sure the end with the cut-out faces the rear cover and aligns with the brushplate outer tab **(see illustrations)** – aligning the marks between the cover and housing (Step 4) will help.
23 Apply a smear of grease to the front cover oil seal lip. Fit the tabbed washer into the cover so that its teeth are correctly located between the cover ribs **(see illustration 27.5c)**.

24 Fit the sealing ring onto the front of the housing **(see illustration)**. Slide the shim(s) onto the front end of the armature shaft then fit the insulating washer **(see illustration 27.5d)**. Slide the front cover into position, aligning the marks made on removal **(see illustration 27.5b)**.
25 Check the marks made on removal are correctly aligned then fit the long bolts, not forgetting the O-rings (using new ones if necessary) and tighten them **(see illustration)**.
26 Install the starter motor (see Section 26).

28 Charging system testing

1 If the performance of the charging system is suspect, the system as a whole should be checked first, followed by testing of the individual components. **Note:** *Before beginning the checks, make sure the battery is fully charged and that all system connections are clean and tight.*
2 Checking the output of the charging system and the performance of the various components within the charging system requires the use of a multimeter (with voltage, current, resistance checking facilities).
3 When making the checks, follow the procedures carefully to prevent incorrect connections or short circuits resulting in irreparable damage to electrical system components.

Output test

4 On CBF1000/A models remove the right-hand side cover (see Chapter 7). On CB1000R/RA models remove the seats (see Chapter 7). Start the engine and warm it up.
5 To check the regulated (DC) voltage output, allow the engine to idle with the headlight main beam (HI) turned ON. Connect a multimeter set to the 0-20 volts DC scale across the terminals of the battery with the positive (+) meter probe to battery positive (+) terminal and the negative (-) meter probe to battery negative (-) terminal (see Section 3) **(see illustration)**.
6 Slowly increase the engine speed to 5000 rpm and note the reading obtained. Compare the result with the Specification at the beginning of this Chapter. If the regulated voltage output is outside the specification, check the alternator and the regulator/rectifier (see Sections 29 and 30).

HAYNES HINT *Clues to a faulty regulator are constantly blowing bulbs, with brightness varying considerably with engine speed, and battery overheating.*

Leakage test

Caution: *Always connect an ammeter in series, never in parallel with the battery, otherwise it will be damaged. Do not turn the ignition ON or operate the starter motor when the ammeter is connected – a sudden surge in current will blow the meter's fuse.*
7 Ensure the ignition is OFF. On CBF1000/A models remove the right-hand side cover (see

27.24 Fit a new sealing ring onto the front of the housing

27.25 Fit the long bolts with their O-rings

28.5 Checking the charging rate – connect the meter as shown

8•30 Electrical system

Chapter 7). On CB1000R/RA models remove the seats (see Chapter 7). Disconnect the battery negative (-) lead (see Section 3).

8 Set the multimeter to the Amps function and connect its negative (-) probe to the battery negative (-) terminal, and positive (+) probe to the disconnected negative (-) lead **(see illustration)**. Always set the meter to a high amps range initially and then bring it down to the mA (milli Amps) range; if there is a high current flow in the circuit it may blow the meter's fuse.

9 Battery current leakage should not exceed the maximum limit (see Specifications). If a higher leakage rate is shown there is a short circuit in the wiring, although if an after-market immobiliser or alarm is fitted, its current draw should be taken into account. Disconnect the meter and reconnect the battery negative (-) lead.

10 If leakage is indicated, refer to Wiring Diagrams at the end of this Chapter to systematically disconnect individual electrical components and repeat the test until the source is identified.

29 Alternator

Check

1 On CBF1000/A models remove the left-hand seat cowl (see Chapter 7). On CB1000R/RA models remove the seats and the left hand side cover (see Chapter 7).

2 Disconnect the 3-pin alternator wiring connector with the three yellow wires **(see illustrations)**. Check the connector terminals for corrosion and security.

3 Using a multimeter set to the ohms x 1 (ohmmeter) scale measure the resistance between each of the yellow wires on the alternator side of the connector, taking a total of three readings, then check for continuity between each terminal and ground (earth). If the stator coil windings are in good condition the three readings should be within the range shown in the Specifications at the start of this Chapter, and there should be no continuity (infinite resistance) between any of the terminals and ground (earth). If not, the alternator stator coil assembly is at fault and should be replaced with a new one. **Note:** *Before condemning the stator coils, check the fault is not due to damaged wiring between the connector and the coils.*

Removal

4 On CBF1000/A models remove the left-hand seat cowl and side cover (see Chapter 7). On CB1000R/RA models remove the seats and left-hand side cover (see Chapter 7), then undo the air intake duct cover screws and remove the cover.

5 On CBF1000A models put the bike on its centrestand. On all other models, if you have an auxiliary stand place the bike on it so that it is level – this minimises oil loss. If you do not have an auxiliary stand it is best to drain the oil. Alternatively place a container under the engine to catch the oil that will come out when the alternator cover is removed.

6 Disconnect the 3-pin alternator wiring connector with the three yellow wires **(see illustration 29.2a or b)**. Feed the wiring down to the alternator cover, releasing it from any ties and noting its routing.

7 Working in a criss-cross pattern, evenly slacken the alternator cover bolts **(see illustration)**. Draw the cover off the engine, noting that it will be restrained by the force of the rotor magnets, and be prepared to catch any residual oil. Remove the dowels from either the cover or the crankcase if they are loose.

8 To remove the rotor bolt it is necessary to stop the rotor from turning using either a commercially available rotor strap, or by counter-holding the flats on the rotor boss using a suitable, preferably offset, spanner **(see illustration)**. Unscrew the bolt, noting the washer.

28.8 Checking the charging system leakage rate – connect the meter as shown

29.2a Alternator wiring connector – CBF1000/A models

29.2b Alternator wiring connector – CB1000R/RA models

29.7 Alternator cover bolts (arrowed)

29.8 Using a spanner to hold the rotor while unscrewing the bolt

Electrical system 8•31

29.9a Thread the puller into the rotor . . .

29.9b . . . then hold the rotor and turn the puller, using a bar for leverage

29.10 Unscrew the stator bolts (A) and the wiring clamp bolt (B) and free the grommet (C)

29.11 Apply sealant to the grommet

9 To remove the rotor from the shaft it is necessary to use a rotor puller. Thread the rotor puller into the centre of the rotor and turn it until the rotor is displaced from the shaft, holding the rotor to prevent the engine turning **(see illustrations)**.

10 To remove the stator from the cover, unscrew its bolts, and the bolt securing the wiring clamp, then remove the assembly, noting how the rubber wiring grommet fits **(see illustration)**.

Installation

11 Fit the stator into the cover, aligning the rubber wiring grommet with the groove **(see illustration 29.10)**. Install the bolts and tighten them to the torque setting specified at the beginning of the Chapter. Apply a suitable sealant to the wiring grommet, then press it into the cut-out in the cover **(see illustration)**. Secure the wiring with its clamp and tighten the bolt.

12 Clean the tapered end of the crankshaft and the corresponding mating surface on the inside of the rotor with a suitable solvent.

13 Make sure that no metal objects have attached themselves to the magnet on the inside of the rotor. Slide the rotor onto the shaft **(see illustration)**.

14 Apply some clean oil to the rotor bolt threads, the underside of the head, and the washer **(see illustration)**. Fit the bolt with its washer and tighten it to the torque setting

29.13 Slide the rotor onto the shaft

29.14a Lubricate the bolt then install it with its washer . . .

8•32 Electrical system

29.14b . . . and tighten it to the specified torque

29.15a Apply sealant to the mating surface

29.15b Make sure the dowels (arrowed) are in place . . .

29.15c . . . then fit the cover

specified at the beginning of the Chapter, using the method employed on removal to prevent the rotor from turning **(see illustration)**.

15 Apply a smear of suitable sealant to the mating surface of the alternator cover **(see illustration)**. Fit the dowels into the cover or crankcase if removed **(see illustration)**. Fit the alternator cover, noting that the rotor magnets will forcibly draw the cover/stator on, making sure the dowels locate **(see illustration)**. Tighten the cover bolts evenly in a criss-cross sequence.

16 Reconnect the wiring at the connector, making sure it is correctly routed and secured **(see illustration 29.2a or b)**.

17 Fill the engine with oil, or top it up to the correct level, as required according to your removal method (see Chapter 1). Install the body parts (see Chapter 7).

30 Regulator/rectifier

Check

1 On CBF1000/A models remove the left-hand seat cowl (see Chapter 7). On CB1000R/RA models remove the seats (see Chapter 7).

2 Disconnect the regulator/rectifier wiring connectors **(see illustration 30.9 or 30.14)**. Check the connector terminals for corrosion and security.

3 Set the multimeter to the 0 to 20 dc volts setting. Connect the meter positive (+) probe to the red wire terminal on the loom side of the connector and the negative (–) probe to a suitable ground (earth) and check for voltage. Full battery voltage should be present at all times.

4 Switch the multimeter to the resistance (ohms) scale. Check for continuity between the green wire terminal on the loom side of the connector and ground (earth). There should be continuity to earth.

5 Set the multimeter to the ohms x 1 (ohmmeter) scale and measure the resistance between each of the yellow wires on the alternator side of the connector, taking a total of three readings, then check for continuity between each terminal and ground (earth). The three readings should be within the range shown in the Specifications for the alternator stator coil at the start of this Chapter, and there should be no continuity (infinite resistance) between any of the terminals and ground (earth).

6 If the above checks do not provide the expected results check the wiring and connectors between the battery, regulator/rectifier and alternator for shorts, breaks, and loose or corroded terminals (see the wiring diagrams at the end of this chapter).

Electrical system 8•33

30.9 Regulator/rectifier wiring connectors (A) and its mounting bolts (B) – CBF1000/A models

30.14 Regulator/rectifier wiring connectors (arrowed) – CB1000R/RA models

7 If the wiring checks out, the regulator/rectifier unit is probably faulty. Honda provide no test data for the unit itself. Take it to a Honda dealer for confirmation of its condition before replacing it with a new one.

> **HAYNES HiNT** *Clues to a faulty regulator are constantly blowing bulbs, with brightness varying considerably with engine speed, and battery overheating.*

Removal and installation

CBF1000/A models

8 Remove the left-hand seat cowl (see Chapter 7).
9 Disconnect the regulator/rectifier wiring connectors **(see illustration)**.
10 Unscrew the two bolts securing the regulator/rectifier bracket to the frame, noting the washers, and remove it, noting the collars fitted from the back.
11 If required unscrew the nuts, withdraw the bolts and detach the regulator/rectifier from the bracket.
12 Installation is the reverse of removal.

CB1000R/RA models

13 Remove the seats (see Chapter 7).
14 Release the wiring tie and disconnect the regulator/rectifier wiring connectors **(see illustration)**.
15 Unscrew the two bolts on each side securing the regulator/rectifier bracket to the frame **(see illustration)**. On ABS models unscrew the PCV bolt.
16 Unscrew the nuts, withdraw the bolts and

30.15 Unscrew the two bolts (arrowed) on each side and remove the regulator/rectifier with its bracket

detach the regulator/rectifier from the bracket, noting the washers and collars.
17 Installation is the reverse of removal.

8•34 Wiring diagrams

CBF1000

Wiring diagrams 8•35

CBF1000

8•36 Wiring diagrams

CBF1000A

Wiring diagrams 8•37

8•38 Wiring diagrams

CB1000R

Wiring diagrams 8•39

CB1000R

8•40 Wiring diagrams

Instruments — pins 1 3 4 5 6 7 10 11 13 14 15 16 17 18 20

Engine stop switch
Starter switch
Ignition switch (ON / OFF / LOCK)
Rear brake light switch
Engine stop relay
Lean angle sensor
Immobiliser
Fuel level sensor
Fuel pump
Fuel cut-off relay

Front brake light switch
Turn signal relay

Front right turn signal
Headlight
Sidelight
Front left turn signal

Cooling fan relay
Horn
Horn switch
Passing switch
Clutch switch
Diode block

Dimmer switch (HI / LO)
Turn signal switch (R / N / L)
Hazard warning switch (OFF / ON)

Fuse box:
- A 10A Headlight, passing light
- B 10A Lighting
- C 10A Turn signal, brake light, horn
- D 10A Starter, bank angle sensor
- E 20A Fan motor
- F 10A ABS main
- G 10A Turn signal relay, clock, odometer
- H 30A ABS fail safe relay
- I 30A ABS motor

Engine cooling fan

Neutral switch
Oil pressure switch
Vehicle speed sensor

H47358

CB1000RA

Wiring diagrams 8•41

CB1000RA

Notes

Reference REF•1

Reference

Tools and Workshop Tips — REF•2
- Building up a tool kit and equipping your workshop
- Using tools
- Understanding bearing, seal, fastener and chain sizes and markings
- Repair techniques

Security — REF•20
- Locks and chains
- U-locks
- Disc locks
- Alarms and immobilisers
- Security marking systems
- Tips on how to prevent bike theft

Lubricants and fluids — REF•23
- Engine oils
- Transmission (gear) oils
- Coolant/anti-freeze
- Fork oils and suspension fluids
- Brake/clutch fluids
- Spray lubes, degreasers and solvents

Conversion Factors — REF•26
- Formulae for conversion of the metric (SI) units used throughout the manual into Imperial measures

34 Nm × 0.738 = 25 lbf ft

MOT Test Checks — REF•27
- A guide to the UK MOT test
- Which items are tested
- How to prepare your motorcycle for the test and perform a pre-test check

Storage — REF•32
- How to prepare your motorcycle for going into storage and protect essential systems
- How to get the motorcycle back on the road

Fault Finding — REF•35
- Common faults and their likely causes

Technical Terms Explained — REF•44
- Component names, technical terms and common abbreviations explained

Index — REF•48

REF•2 Tools and Workshop Tips

Buying tools

A toolkit is a fundamental requirement for servicing and repairing a motorcycle. Although there will be an initial expense in building up enough tools for servicing, this will soon be offset by the savings made by doing the job yourself. As experience and confidence grow, additional tools can be added to enable the repair and overhaul of the motorcycle. Many of the specialist tools are expensive and not often used so it may be preferable to hire them, or for a group of friends or motorcycle club to join in the purchase.

As a rule, it is better to buy more expensive, good quality tools. Cheaper tools are likely to wear out faster and need to be renewed more often, nullifying the original saving.

> **Warning:** To avoid the risk of a poor quality tool breaking in use, causing injury or damage to the component being worked on, always aim to purchase tools which meet the relevant national safety standards.

The following lists of tools do not represent the manufacturer's service tools, but serve as a guide to help the owner decide which tools are needed for this level of work. In addition, items such as an electric drill, hacksaw, files, soldering iron and a workbench equipped with a vice, may be needed. Although not classed as tools, a selection of bolts, screws, nuts, washers and pieces of tubing always come in useful.

For more information about tools, refer to the Haynes *Motorcycle Workshop Practice Techbook* (Bk. No. 3470).

Manufacturer's service tools

Inevitably certain tasks require the use of a service tool. Where possible an alternative tool or method of approach is recommended, but sometimes there is no option if personal injury or damage to the component is to be avoided. Where required, service tools are referred to in the relevant procedure.

Service tools can usually only be purchased from a motorcycle dealer and are identified by a part number. Some of the commonly-used tools, such as rotor pullers, are available in aftermarket form from mail-order motorcycle tool and accessory suppliers.

Maintenance and minor repair tools

1. Set of flat-bladed screwdrivers
2. Set of Phillips head screwdrivers
3. Combination open-end and ring spanners
4. Socket set (3/8 inch or 1/2 inch drive)
5. Set of Allen keys or bits
6. Set of Torx keys or bits
7. Pliers, cutters and self-locking grips (Mole grips)
8. Adjustable spanners
9. C-spanners
10. Tread depth gauge and tyre pressure gauge
11. Cable oiler clamp
12. Feeler gauges
13. Spark plug gap measuring tool
14. Spark plug spanner or deep plug sockets
15. Wire brush and emery paper
16. Calibrated syringe, measuring vessel and funnel
17. Oil filter adapters
18. Oil drainer can or tray
19. Pump type oil can
20. Grease gun
21. Straight-edge and steel rule
22. Continuity tester
23. Battery charger
24. Hydrometer (for battery specific gravity check)
25. Anti-freeze tester (for liquid-cooled engines)

Tools and Workshop Tips REF•3

Repair and overhaul tools

1. Torque wrench (small and mid-ranges)
2. Conventional, plastic or soft-faced hammers
3. Impact driver set
4. Vernier gauge
5. Circlip pliers (internal and external, or combination)
6. Set of cold chisels and punches
7. Selection of pullers
8. Breaker bars
9. Chain breaking/riveting tool set
10. Wire stripper and crimper tool
11. Multimeter (measures amps, volts and ohms)
12. Stroboscope (for dynamic timing checks)
13. Hose clamp (wingnut type shown)
14. Clutch holding tool
15. One-man brake/clutch bleeder kit

Specialist tools

1. Micrometers (external type)
2. Telescoping gauges
3. Dial gauge
4. Cylinder compression gauge
5. Vacuum gauges (left) or manometer (right)
6. Oil pressure gauge
7. Plastigauge kit
8. Valve spring compressor (4-stroke engines)
9. Piston pin drawbolt tool
10. Piston ring removal and installation tool
11. Piston ring clamp
12. Cylinder bore hone (stone type shown)
13. Stud extractor
14. Screw extractor set
15. Bearing driver set

REF•4 Tools and Workshop Tips

1 Workshop equipment and facilities

The workbench

● Work is made much easier by raising the bike up on a ramp - components are much more accessible if raised to waist level. The hydraulic or pneumatic types seen in the dealer's workshop are a sound investment if you undertake a lot of repairs or overhauls **(see illustration 1.1)**.

1.1 Hydraulic motorcycle ramp

● If raised off ground level, the bike must be supported on the ramp to avoid it falling. Most ramps incorporate a front wheel locating clamp which can be adjusted to suit different diameter wheels. When tightening the clamp, take care not to mark the wheel rim or damage the tyre - use wood blocks on each side to prevent this.
● Secure the bike to the ramp using tie-downs **(see illustration 1.2)**. If the bike has only a sidestand, and hence leans at a dangerous angle when raised, support the bike on an auxiliary stand.

1.2 Tie-downs are used around the passenger footrests to secure the bike

● Auxiliary (paddock) stands are widely available from mail order companies or motorcycle dealers and attach either to the wheel axle or swingarm pivot **(see illustration 1.3)**. If the motorcycle has a centrestand, you can support it under the crankcase to prevent it toppling whilst either wheel is removed **(see illustration 1.4)**.

1.3 This auxiliary stand attaches to the swingarm pivot

1.4 Always use a block of wood between the engine and jack head when supporting the engine in this way

Fumes and fire

● Refer to the Safety first! page at the beginning of the manual for full details. Make sure your workshop is equipped with a fire extinguisher suitable for fuel-related fires (Class B fire - flammable liquids) - it is not sufficient to have a water-filled extinguisher.
● Always ensure adequate ventilation is available. Unless an exhaust gas extraction system is available for use, ensure that the engine is run outside of the workshop.
● If working on the fuel system, make sure the workshop is ventilated to avoid a build-up of fumes. This applies equally to fume build-up when charging a battery. Do not smoke or allow anyone else to smoke in the workshop.

Fluids

● If you need to drain fuel from the tank, store it in an approved container marked as suitable for the storage of petrol (gasoline) **(see illustration 1.5)**. Do not store fuel in glass jars or bottles.

1.5 Use an approved can only for storing petrol (gasoline)

● Use proprietary engine degreasers or solvents which have a high flash-point, such as paraffin (kerosene), for cleaning off oil, grease and dirt - never use petrol (gasoline) for cleaning. Wear rubber gloves when handling solvent and engine degreaser. The fumes from certain solvents can be dangerous - always work in a well-ventilated area.

Dust, eye and hand protection

● Protect your lungs from inhalation of dust particles by wearing a filtering mask over the nose and mouth. Many frictional materials still contain asbestos which is dangerous to your health. Protect your eyes from spouts of liquid and sprung components by wearing a pair of protective goggles **(see illustration 1.6)**.

1.6 A fire extinguisher, goggles, mask and protective gloves should be at hand in the workshop

● Protect your hands from contact with solvents, fuel and oils by wearing rubber gloves. Alternatively apply a barrier cream to your hands before starting work. If handling hot components or fluids, wear suitable gloves to protect your hands from scalding and burns.

What to do with old fluids

● Old cleaning solvent, fuel, coolant and oils should not be poured down domestic drains or onto the ground. Package the fluid up in old oil containers, label it accordingly, and take it to a garage or disposal facility. Contact your local authority for location of such sites or ring the oil care hotline.

Note: It is illegal and anti-social to dump oil down the drain. To find the location of your local oil recycling bank in the UK, call 08708 506 506 or visit www.oilbankline.org.uk

In the USA, note that any oil supplier must accept used oil for recycling.

Tools and Workshop Tips REF•5

2 Fasteners - screws, bolts and nuts

Fastener types and applications

Bolts and screws

- Fastener head types are either of hexagonal, Torx or splined design, with internal and external versions of each type **(see illustrations 2.1 and 2.2)**; splined head fasteners are not in common use on motorcycles. The conventional slotted or Phillips head design is used for certain screws. Bolt or screw length is always measured from the underside of the head to the end of the item **(see illustration 2.11)**.

2.1 Internal hexagon/Allen (A), Torx (B) and splined (C) fasteners, with corresponding bits

2.2 External Torx (A), splined (B) and hexagon (C) fasteners, with corresponding sockets

- Certain fasteners on the motorcycle have a tensile marking on their heads, the higher the marking the stronger the fastener. High tensile fasteners generally carry a 10 or higher marking. Never replace a high tensile fastener with one of a lower tensile strength.

Washers (see illustration 2.3)

- Plain washers are used between a fastener head and a component to prevent damage to the component or to spread the load when torque is applied. Plain washers can also be used as spacers or shims in certain assemblies. Copper or aluminium plain washers are often used as sealing washers on drain plugs.

2.3 Plain washer (A), penny washer (B), spring washer (C) and serrated washer (D)

- The split-ring spring washer works by applying axial tension between the fastener head and component. If flattened, it is fatigued and must be renewed. If a plain (flat) washer is used on the fastener, position the spring washer between the fastener and the plain washer.
- Serrated star type washers dig into the fastener and component faces, preventing loosening. They are often used on electrical earth (ground) connections to the frame.
- Cone type washers (sometimes called Belleville) are conical and when tightened apply axial tension between the fastener head and component. They must be installed with the dished side against the component and often carry an OUTSIDE marking on their outer face. If flattened, they are fatigued and must be renewed.
- Tab washers are used to lock plain nuts or bolts on a shaft. A portion of the tab washer is bent up hard against one flat of the nut or bolt to prevent it loosening. Due to the tab washer being deformed in use, a new tab washer should be used every time it is disturbed.
- Wave washers are used to take up endfloat on a shaft. They provide light springing and prevent excessive side-to-side play of a component. Can be found on rocker arm shafts.

Nuts and split pins

- Conventional plain nuts are usually six-sided **(see illustration 2.4)**. They are sized by thread diameter and pitch. High tensile nuts carry a number on one end to denote their tensile strength.

2.4 Plain nut (A), shouldered locknut (B), nylon insert nut (C) and castellated nut (D)

- Self-locking nuts either have a nylon insert, or two spring metal tabs, or a shoulder which is staked into a groove in the shaft - their advantage over conventional plain nuts is a resistance to loosening due to vibration. The nylon insert type can be used a number of times, but must be renewed when the friction of the nylon insert is reduced, ie when the nut spins freely on the shaft. The spring tab type can be reused unless the tabs are damaged. The shouldered type must be renewed every time it is disturbed.
- Split pins (cotter pins) are used to lock a castellated nut to a shaft or to prevent slackening of a plain nut. Common applications are wheel axles and brake torque arms. Because the split pin arms are deformed to lock around the nut a new split pin must always be used on installation - always fit the correct size split pin which will fit snugly in the shaft hole. Make sure the split pin arms are correctly located around the nut **(see illustrations 2.5 and 2.6)**.

2.5 Bend split pin (cotter pin) arms as shown (arrows) to secure a castellated nut

2.6 Bend split pin (cotter pin) arms as shown to secure a plain nut

> **Caution: If the castellated nut slots do not align with the shaft hole after tightening to the torque setting, tighten the nut until the next slot aligns with the hole - never slacken the nut to align its slot.**

- R-pins (shaped like the letter R), or slip pins as they are sometimes called, are sprung and can be reused if they are otherwise in good condition. Always install R-pins with their closed end facing forwards **(see illustration 2.7)**.

REF•6 Tools and Workshop Tips

2.7 Correct fitting of R-pin. Arrow indicates forward direction

Circlips (see illustration 2.8)

● Circlips (sometimes called snap-rings) are used to retain components on a shaft or in a housing and have corresponding external or internal ears to permit removal. Parallel-sided (machined) circlips can be installed either way round in their groove, whereas stamped circlips (which have a chamfered edge on one face) must be installed with the chamfer facing away from the direction of thrust load **(see illustration 2.9)**.

2.8 External stamped circlip (A), internal stamped circlip (B), machined circlip (C) and wire circlip (D)

● Always use circlip pliers to remove and install circlips; expand or compress them just enough to remove them. After installation, rotate the circlip in its groove to ensure it is securely seated. If installing a circlip on a splined shaft, always align its opening with a shaft channel to ensure the circlip ends are well supported and unlikely to catch **(see illustration 2.10)**.

2.9 Correct fitting of a stamped circlip

2.10 Align circlip opening with shaft channel

● Circlips can wear due to the thrust of components and become loose in their grooves, with the subsequent danger of becoming dislodged in operation. For this reason, renewal is advised every time a circlip is disturbed.

● Wire circlips are commonly used as piston pin retaining clips. If a removal tang is provided, long-nosed pliers can be used to dislodge them, otherwise careful use of a small flat-bladed screwdriver is necessary. Wire circlips should be renewed every time they are disturbed.

Thread diameter and pitch

● Diameter of a male thread (screw, bolt or stud) is the outside diameter of the threaded portion **(see illustration 2.11)**. Most motorcycle manufacturers use the ISO (International Standards Organisation) metric system expressed in millimetres, eg M6 refers to a 6 mm diameter thread. Sizing is the same for nuts, except that the thread diameter is measured across the valleys of the nut.

● Pitch is the distance between the peaks of the thread **(see illustration 2.11)**. It is expressed in millimetres, thus a common bolt size may be expressed as 6.0 x 1.0 mm (6 mm thread diameter and 1 mm pitch). Generally pitch increases in proportion to thread diameter, although there are always exceptions.

● Thread diameter and pitch are related for conventional fastener applications and the accompanying table can be used as a guide. Additionally, the AF (Across Flats), spanner or socket size dimension of the bolt or nut **(see illustration 2.11)** is linked to thread and pitch specification. Thread pitch can be measured with a thread gauge **(see illustration 2.12)**.

2.11 Fastener length (L), thread diameter (D), thread pitch (P) and head size (AF)

2.12 Using a thread gauge to measure pitch

AF size	Thread diameter x pitch (mm)
8 mm	M5 x 0.8
8 mm	M6 x 1.0
10 mm	M6 x 1.0
12 mm	M8 x 1.25
14 mm	M10 x 1.25
17 mm	M12 x 1.25

● The threads of most fasteners are of the right-hand type, ie they are turned clockwise to tighten and anti-clockwise to loosen. The reverse situation applies to left-hand thread fasteners, which are turned anti-clockwise to tighten and clockwise to loosen. Left-hand threads are used where rotation of a component might loosen a conventional right-hand thread fastener.

Seized fasteners

● Corrosion of external fasteners due to water or reaction between two dissimilar metals can occur over a period of time. It will build up sooner in wet conditions or in countries where salt is used on the roads during the winter. If a fastener is severely corroded it is likely that normal methods of removal will fail and result in its head being ruined. When you attempt removal, the fastener thread should be heard to crack free and unscrew easily - if it doesn't, stop there before damaging something.

● A smart tap on the head of the fastener will often succeed in breaking free corrosion which has occurred in the threads **(see illustration 2.13)**.

● An aerosol penetrating fluid (such as WD-40) applied the night beforehand may work its way down into the thread and ease removal. Depending on the location, you may be able to make up a Plasticine well around the fastener head and fill it with penetrating fluid.

2.13 A sharp tap on the head of a fastener will often break free a corroded thread

Tools and Workshop Tips REF•7

- If you are working on an engine internal component, corrosion will most likely not be a problem due to the well lubricated environment. However, components can be very tight and an impact driver is a useful tool in freeing them (see illustration 2.14).

2.14 Using an impact driver to free a fastener

- Where corrosion has occurred between dissimilar metals (eg steel and aluminium alloy), the application of heat to the fastener head will create a disproportionate expansion rate between the two metals and break the seizure caused by the corrosion. Whether heat can be applied depends on the location of the fastener - any surrounding components likely to be damaged must first be removed (see illustration 2.15). Heat can be applied using a paint stripper heat gun or clothes iron, or by immersing the component in boiling water - wear protective gloves to prevent scalding or burns to the hands.

2.15 Using heat to free a seized fastener

- As a last resort, it is possible to use a hammer and cold chisel to work the fastener head unscrewed (see illustration 2.16). This will damage the fastener, but more importantly extreme care must be taken not to damage the surrounding component.

> **Caution:** Remember that the component being secured is generally of more value than the bolt, nut or screw - when the fastener is freed, do not unscrew it with force, instead work the fastener back and forth when resistance is felt to prevent thread damage.

2.16 Using a hammer and chisel to free a seized fastener

Broken fasteners and damaged heads

- If the shank of a broken bolt or screw is accessible you can grip it with self-locking grips. The knurled wheel type stud extractor tool or self-gripping stud puller tool is particularly useful for removing the long studs which screw into the cylinder mouth surface of the crankcase or bolts and screws from which the head has broken off (see illustration 2.17). Studs can also be removed by locking two nuts together on the threaded end of the stud and using a spanner on the lower nut (see illustration 2.18).

2.17 Using a stud extractor tool to remove a broken crankcase stud

2.18 Two nuts can be locked together to unscrew a stud from a component

- A bolt or screw which has broken off below or level with the casing must be extracted using a screw extractor set. Centre punch the fastener to centralise the drill bit, then drill a hole in the fastener (see illustration 2.19). Select a drill bit which is approximately half to three-quarters the diameter of the fastener and drill to a depth which will accommodate the extractor. Use the largest size extractor possible, but avoid leaving too small a wall thickness otherwise the extractor will merely force the fastener walls outwards wedging it in the casing thread.

- If a spiral type extractor is used, thread it anti-clockwise into the fastener. As it is screwed in, it will grip the fastener and unscrew it from the casing (see illustration 2.20).

2.19 When using a screw extractor, first drill a hole in the fastener . . .

2.20 . . . then thread the extractor anti-clockwise into the fastener

- If a taper type extractor is used, tap it into the fastener so that it is firmly wedged in place. Unscrew the extractor (anti-clockwise) to draw the fastener out.

> ⚠ **Warning:** Stud extractors are very hard and may break off in the fastener if care is not taken - ask an engineer about spark erosion if this happens.

- Alternatively, the broken bolt/screw can be drilled out and the hole retapped for an oversize bolt/screw or a diamond-section thread insert. It is essential that the drilling is carried out squarely and to the correct depth, otherwise the casing may be ruined - if in doubt, entrust the work to an engineer.

- Bolts and nuts with rounded corners cause the correct size spanner or socket to slip when force is applied. Of the types of spanner/socket available always use a six-point type rather than an eight or twelve-point type - better grip

REF•8 Tools and Workshop Tips

2.21 Comparison of surface drive ring spanner (left) with 12-point type (right)

is obtained. Surface drive spanners grip the middle of the hex flats, rather than the corners, and are thus good in cases of damaged heads **(see illustration 2.21)**.

- Slotted-head or Phillips-head screws are often damaged by the use of the wrong size screwdriver. Allen-head and Torx-head screws are much less likely to sustain damage. If enough of the screw head is exposed you can use a hacksaw to cut a slot in its head and then use a conventional flat-bladed screwdriver to remove it. Alternatively use a hammer and cold chisel to tap the head of the fastener around to slacken it. Always replace damaged fasteners with new ones, preferably Torx or Allen-head type.

HAYNES HiNT

A dab of valve grinding compound between the screw head and screwdriver tip will often give a good grip.

Thread repair

- Threads (particularly those in aluminium alloy components) can be damaged by overtightening, being assembled with dirt in the threads, or from a component working loose and vibrating. Eventually the thread will fail completely, and it will be impossible to tighten the fastener.
- If a thread is damaged or clogged with old locking compound it can be renovated with a thread repair tool (thread chaser) **(see illustrations 2.22 and 2.23)**; special thread

2.22 A thread repair tool being used to correct an internal thread

2.23 A thread repair tool being used to correct an external thread

chasers are available for spark plug hole threads. The tool will not cut a new thread, but clean and true the original thread. Make sure that you use the correct diameter and pitch tool. Similarly, external threads can be cleaned up with a die or a thread restorer file **(see illustration 2.24)**.

2.24 Using a thread restorer file

- It is possible to drill out the old thread and retap the component to the next thread size. This will work where there is enough surrounding material and a new bolt or screw can be obtained. Sometimes, however, this is not possible - such as where the bolt/screw passes through another component which must also be suitably modified, also in cases where a spark plug or oil drain plug cannot be obtained in a larger diameter thread size.
- The diamond-section thread insert (often known by its popular trade name of Heli-Coil) is a simple and effective method of renewing the thread and retaining the original size. A kit can be purchased which contains the tap, insert and installing tool **(see illustration 2.25)**. Drill out the damaged thread with the size drill specified **(see illustration 2.26)**. Carefully retap the thread **(see illustration 2.27)**. Install the

2.25 Obtain a thread insert kit to suit the thread diameter and pitch required

2.26 To install a thread insert, first drill out the original thread . . .

2.27 . . . tap a new thread . . .

2.28 . . . fit insert on the installing tool . . .

2.29 . . . and thread into the component . . .

2.30 . . . break off the tang when complete

insert on the installing tool and thread it slowly into place using a light downward pressure **(see illustrations 2.28 and 2.29)**. When positioned between a 1/4 and 1/2 turn below the surface withdraw the installing tool and use the break-off tool to press down on the tang, breaking it off **(see illustration 2.30)**.

- There are epoxy thread repair kits on the market which can rebuild stripped internal threads, although this repair should not be used on high load-bearing components.

Tools and Workshop Tips

Thread locking and sealing compounds

- Locking compounds are used in locations where the fastener is prone to loosening due to vibration or on important safety-related items which might cause loss of control of the motorcycle if they fail. It is also used where important fasteners cannot be secured by other means such as lockwashers or split pins.
- Before applying locking compound, make sure that the threads (internal and external) are clean and dry with all old compound removed. Select a compound to suit the component being secured - a non-permanent general locking and sealing type is suitable for most applications, but a high strength type is needed for permanent fixing of studs in castings. Apply a drop or two of the compound to the first few threads of the fastener, then thread it into place and tighten to the specified torque. Do not apply excessive thread locking compound otherwise the thread may be damaged on subsequent removal.
- Certain fasteners are impregnated with a dry film type coating of locking compound on their threads. Always renew this type of fastener if disturbed.
- Anti-seize compounds, such as copper-based greases, can be applied to protect threads from seizure due to extreme heat and corrosion. A common instance is spark plug threads and exhaust system fasteners.

3 Measuring tools and gauges

Feeler gauges

- Feeler gauges (or blades) are used for measuring small gaps and clearances (see illustration 3.1). They can also be used to measure endfloat (sideplay) of a component on a shaft where access is not possible with a dial gauge.
- Feeler gauge sets should be treated with care and not bent or damaged. They are etched with their size on one face. Keep them clean and very lightly oiled to prevent corrosion build-up.

3.1 Feeler gauges are used for measuring small gaps and clearances - thickness is marked on one face of gauge

- When measuring a clearance, select a gauge which is a light sliding fit between the two components. You may need to use two gauges together to measure the clearance accurately.

Micrometers

- A micrometer is a precision tool capable of measuring to 0.01 or 0.001 of a millimetre. It should always be stored in its case and not in the general toolbox. It must be kept clean and never dropped, otherwise its frame or measuring anvils could be distorted resulting in inaccurate readings.
- External micrometers are used for measuring outside diameters of components and have many more applications than internal micrometers. Micrometers are available in different size ranges, eg 0 to 25 mm, 25 to 50 mm, and upwards in 25 mm steps; some large micrometers have interchangeable anvils to allow a range of measurements to be taken. Generally the largest precision measurement you are likely to take on a motorcycle is the piston diameter.
- Internal micrometers (or bore micrometers) are used for measuring inside diameters, such as valve guides and cylinder bores. Telescoping gauges and small hole gauges are used in conjunction with an external micrometer, whereas the more expensive internal micrometers have their own measuring device.

External micrometer

Note: *The conventional analogue type instrument is described. Although much easier to read, digital micrometers are considerably more expensive.*

- Always check the calibration of the micrometer before use. With the anvils closed (0 to 25 mm type) or set over a test gauge (for

3.2 Check micrometer calibration before use

the larger types) the scale should read zero (see illustration 3.2); make sure that the anvils (and test piece) are clean first. Any discrepancy can be adjusted by referring to the instructions supplied with the tool. Remember that the micrometer is a precision measuring tool - don't force the anvils closed, use the ratchet (4) on the end of the micrometer to close it. In this way, a measured force is always applied.
- To use, first make sure that the item being measured is clean. Place the anvil of the micrometer (1) against the item and use the thimble (2) to bring the spindle (3) lightly into contact with the other side of the item (see illustration 3.3). Don't tighten the thimble down because this will damage the micrometer - instead use the ratchet (4) on the end of the micrometer. The ratchet mechanism applies a measured force preventing damage to the instrument.
- The micrometer is read by referring to the linear scale on the sleeve and the annular scale on the thimble. Read off the sleeve first to obtain the base measurement, then add the fine measurement from the thimble to obtain the overall reading. The linear scale on the sleeve represents the measuring range of the micrometer (eg 0 to 25 mm). The annular scale

3.3 Micrometer component parts

| 1 Anvil | 3 Spindle | 5 Frame |
| 2 Thimble | 4 Ratchet | 6 Locking lever |

Tools and Workshop Tips

on the thimble will be in graduations of 0.01 mm (or as marked on the frame) - one full revolution of the thimble will move 0.5 mm on the linear scale. Take the reading where the datum line on the sleeve intersects the thimble's scale. Always position the eye directly above the scale otherwise an inaccurate reading will result.

In the example shown the item measures 2.95 mm (see illustration 3.4):

Linear scale	2.00 mm
Linear scale	0.50 mm
Annular scale	0.45 mm
Total figure	**2.95 mm**

3.5 Micrometer reading of 46.99 mm on linear and annular scales . . .

3.7 Expand the telescoping gauge in the bore, lock its position . . .

3.4 Micrometer reading of 2.95 mm

3.6 . . . and 0.004 mm on vernier scale

3.8 . . . then measure the gauge with a micrometer

Most micrometers have a locking lever (6) on the frame to hold the setting in place, allowing the item to be removed from the micrometer.
● Some micrometers have a vernier scale on their sleeve, providing an even finer measurement to be taken, in 0.001 increments of a millimetre. Take the sleeve and thimble measurement as described above, then check which graduation on the vernier scale aligns with that of the annular scale on the thimble **Note:** *The eye must be perpendicular to the scale when taking the vernier reading - if necessary rotate the body of the micrometer to ensure this.* Multiply the vernier scale figure by 0.001 and add it to the base and fine measurement figures.

In the example shown the item measures 46.994 mm (see illustrations 3.5 and 3.6):

Linear scale (base)	46.000 mm
Linear scale (base)	00.500 mm
Annular scale (fine)	00.490 mm
Vernier scale	00.004 mm
Total figure	**46.994 mm**

Internal micrometer

● Internal micrometers are available for measuring bore diameters, but are expensive and unlikely to be available for home use. It is suggested that a set of telescoping gauges and small hole gauges, both of which must be used with an external micrometer, will suffice for taking internal measurements on a motorcycle.
● Telescoping gauges can be used to measure internal diameters of components. Select a gauge with the correct size range, make sure its ends are clean and insert it into the bore. Expand the gauge, then lock its position and withdraw it from the bore **(see illustration 3.7)**. Measure across the gauge ends with a micrometer **(see illustration 3.8)**.
● Very small diameter bores (such as valve guides) are measured with a small hole gauge. Once adjusted to a slip-fit inside the component, its position is locked and the gauge withdrawn for measurement with a micrometer **(see illustrations 3.9 and 3.10)**.

Vernier caliper

Note: *The conventional linear and dial gauge type instruments are described. Digital types are easier to read, but are far more expensive.*
● The vernier caliper does not provide the precision of a micrometer, but is versatile in being able to measure internal and external diameters. Some types also incorporate a depth gauge. It is ideal for measuring clutch plate friction material and spring free lengths.
● To use the conventional linear scale vernier, slacken off the vernier clamp screws (1) and set its jaws over (2), or inside (3), the item to be measured **(see illustration 3.11)**. Slide the jaw into contact, using the thumbwheel (4) for fine movement of the sliding scale (5) then tighten the clamp screws (1). Read off the main scale (6) where the zero on the sliding scale (5) intersects it, taking the whole number to the left of the zero; this provides the base measurement. View along the sliding scale and select the division which

3.9 Expand the small hole gauge in the bore, lock its position . . .

3.10 . . . then measure the gauge with a micrometer

lines up exactly with any of the divisions on the main scale, noting that the divisions usually represents 0.02 of a millimetre. Add this fine measurement to the base measurement to obtain the total reading.

Tools and Workshop Tips REF•11

Plastigauge

● Plastigauge is a plastic material which can be compressed between two surfaces to measure the oil clearance between them. The width of the compressed Plastigauge is measured against a calibrated scale to determine the clearance.

● Common uses of Plastigauge are for measuring the clearance between crankshaft journal and main bearing inserts, between crankshaft journal and big-end bearing inserts, and between camshaft and bearing surfaces. The following example describes big-end oil clearance measurement.

● Handle the Plastigauge material carefully to prevent distortion. Using a sharp knife, cut a length which corresponds with the width of the bearing being measured and place it carefully across the journal so that it is parallel with the shaft (see illustration 3.15). Carefully install both bearing shells and the connecting rod. Without rotating the rod on the journal tighten its bolts or nuts (as applicable) to the specified torque. The connecting rod and bearings are then disassembled and the crushed Plastigauge examined.

3.11 Vernier component parts (linear gauge)

1 Clamp screws
2 External jaws
3 Internal jaws
4 Thumbwheel
5 Sliding scale
6 Main scale
7 Depth gauge

In the example shown the item measures 55.92 mm (see illustration 3.12):

Base measurement	55.00 mm
Fine measurement	00.92 mm
Total figure	**55.92 mm**

● Some vernier calipers are equipped with a dial gauge for fine measurement. Before use, check that the jaws are clean, then close them fully and check that the dial gauge reads zero. If necessary adjust the gauge ring accordingly. Slacken the vernier clamp screw (1) and set its jaws over (2), or inside (3), the item to be measured (see illustration 3.13). Slide the jaws into contact, using the thumbwheel (4) for fine movement. Read off the main scale (5) where the edge of the sliding scale (6) intersects it, taking the whole number to the left of the zero; this provides the base measurement. Read off the needle position on the dial gauge (7) scale to provide the fine measurement; each division represents 0.05 of a millimetre. Add this fine measurement to the base measurement to obtain the total reading.

In the example shown the item measures 55.95 mm (see illustration 3.14):

Base measurement	55.00 mm
Fine measurement	00.95 mm
Total figure	**55.95 mm**

3.12 Vernier gauge reading of 55.92 mm

3.13 Vernier component parts (dial gauge)

1 Clamp screw
2 External jaws
3 Internal jaws
4 Thumbwheel
5 Main scale
6 Sliding scale
7 Dial gauge

3.14 Vernier gauge reading of 55.95 mm

3.15 Plastigauge placed across shaft journal

● Using the scale provided in the Plastigauge kit, measure the width of the material to determine the oil clearance (see illustration 3.16). Always remove all traces of Plastigauge after use using your fingernails.

Caution: Arriving at the correct clearance demands that the assembly is torqued correctly, according to the settings and sequence (where applicable) provided by the motorcycle manufacturer.

3.16 Measuring the width of the crushed Plastigauge

REF•12 Tools and Workshop Tips

Dial gauge or DTI (Dial Test Indicator)

- A dial gauge can be used to accurately measure small amounts of movement. Typical uses are measuring shaft runout or shaft endfloat (sideplay) and setting piston position for ignition timing on two-strokes. A dial gauge set usually comes with a range of different probes and adapters and mounting equipment.
- The gauge needle must point to zero when at rest. Rotate the ring around its periphery to zero the gauge.
- Check that the gauge is capable of reading the extent of movement in the work. Most gauges have a small dial set in the face which records whole millimetres of movement as well as the fine scale around the face periphery which is calibrated in 0.01 mm divisions. Read off the small dial first to obtain the base measurement, then add the measurement from the fine scale to obtain the total reading.

In the example shown the gauge reads 1.48 mm (see illustration 3.17):

Base measurement	1.00 mm
Fine measurement	0.48 mm
Total figure	**1.48 mm**

3.17 Dial gauge reading of 1.48 mm

- If measuring shaft runout, the shaft must be supported in vee-blocks and the gauge mounted on a stand perpendicular to the shaft. Rest the tip of the gauge against the centre of the shaft and rotate the shaft slowly whilst watching the gauge reading (see illustration 3.18). Take several measurements along the length of the shaft and record the maximum gauge reading as the amount of runout in the shaft. Note: *The reading obtained will be total runout at that point - some manufacturers specify that the runout figure is halved to compare with their specified runout limit.*
- Endfloat (sideplay) measurement requires that the gauge is mounted securely to the surrounding component with its probe touching the end of the shaft. Using hand pressure, push and pull on the shaft noting the maximum endfloat recorded on the gauge (see illustration 3.19).

3.18 Using a dial gauge to measure shaft runout

3.19 Using a dial gauge to measure shaft endfloat

- A dial gauge with suitable adapters can be used to determine piston position BTDC on two-stroke engines for the purposes of ignition timing. The gauge, adapter and suitable length probe are installed in the place of the spark plug and the gauge zeroed at TDC. If the piston position is specified as 1.14 mm BTDC, rotate the engine back to 2.00 mm BTDC, then slowly forwards to 1.14 mm BTDC.

Cylinder compression gauges

- A compression gauge is used for measuring cylinder compression. Either the rubber-cone type or the threaded adapter type can be used. The latter is preferred to ensure a perfect seal against the cylinder head. A 0 to 300 psi (0 to 20 Bar) type gauge (for petrol/gasoline engines) will be suitable for motorcycles.
- The spark plug is removed and the gauge either held hard against the cylinder head (cone type) or the gauge adapter screwed into the cylinder head (threaded type) (see illustration 3.20). Cylinder compression is measured with the engine turning over, but not running - carry out the compression test as described in *Fault Finding Equipment*. The gauge will hold the reading until manually released.

3.20 Using a rubber-cone type cylinder compression gauge

Oil pressure gauge

- An oil pressure gauge is used for measuring engine oil pressure. Most gauges come with a set of adapters to fit the thread of the take-off point (see illustration 3.21). If the take-off point specified by the motorcycle manufacturer is an external oil pipe union, make sure that the specified replacement union is used to prevent oil starvation.

3.21 Oil pressure gauge and take-off point adapter (arrow)

- Oil pressure is measured with the engine running (at a specific rpm) and often the manufacturer will specify pressure limits for a cold and hot engine.

Straight-edge and surface plate

- If checking the gasket face of a component for warpage, place a steel rule or precision straight-edge across the gasket face and measure any gap between the straight-edge and component with feeler gauges (see illustration 3.22). Check diagonally across the component and between mounting holes (see illustration 3.23).

3.22 Use a straight-edge and feeler gauges to check for warpage

3.23 Check for warpage in these directions

Tools and Workshop Tips REF•13

4 Torque and leverage

What is torque?

● Torque describes the twisting force about a shaft. The amount of torque applied is determined by the distance from the centre of the shaft to the end of the lever and the amount of force being applied to the end of the lever; distance multiplied by force equals torque.

● The manufacturer applies a measured torque to a bolt or nut to ensure that it will not slacken in use and to hold two components securely together without movement in the joint. The actual torque setting depends on the thread size, bolt or nut material and the composition of the components being held.

● Too little torque may cause the fastener to loosen due to vibration, whereas too much torque will distort the joint faces of the component or cause the fastener to shear off. Always stick to the specified torque setting.

Using a torque wrench

● Check the calibration of the torque wrench and make sure it has a suitable range for the job. Torque wrenches are available in Nm (Newton-metres), kgf m (kilograms-force metre), lbf ft (pounds-feet), lbf in (inch-pounds). Do not confuse lbf ft with lbf in.

● Adjust the tool to the desired torque on the scale (see illustration 4.1). If your torque wrench is not calibrated in the units specified, carefully convert the figure (see Conversion Factors). A manufacturer sometimes gives a torque setting as a range (8 to 10 Nm) rather than a single figure - in this case set the tool midway between the two settings. The same torque may be expressed as 9 Nm ± 1 Nm. Some torque wrenches have a method of locking the setting so that it isn't inadvertently altered during use.

● Install the bolts/nuts in their correct location and secure them lightly. Their threads must be clean and free of any old locking compound. Unless specified the threads and flange should be dry - oiled threads are necessary in certain circumstances and the manufacturer will take this into account in the specified torque figure. Similarly, the manufacturer may also specify the application of thread-locking compound.

● Tighten the fasteners in the specified sequence until the torque wrench clicks, indicating that the torque setting has been reached. Apply the torque again to double-check the setting. Where different thread diameter fasteners secure the component, as a rule tighten the larger diameter ones first.

● When the torque wrench has been finished with, release the lock (where applicable) and fully back off its setting to zero - do not leave the torque wrench tensioned. Also, do not use a torque wrench for slackening a fastener.

Angle-tightening

● Manufacturers often specify a figure in degrees for final tightening of a fastener. This usually follows tightening to a specific torque setting.

● A degree disc can be set and attached to the socket (see illustration 4.2) or a protractor can be used to mark the angle of movement on the bolt/nut head and the surrounding casting (see illustration 4.3).

4.2 Angle tightening can be accomplished with a torque-angle gauge . . .

4.3 . . . or by marking the angle on the surrounding component

4.1 Set the torque wrench index mark to the setting required, in this case 12 Nm

Loosening sequences

● Where more than one bolt/nut secures a component, loosen each fastener evenly a little at a time. In this way, not all the stress of the joint is held by one fastener and the components are not likely to distort.

● If a tightening sequence is provided, work in the REVERSE of this, but if not, work from the outside in, in a criss-cross sequence (see illustration 4.4).

4.4 When slackening, work from the outside inwards

Tightening sequences

● If a component is held by more than one fastener it is important that the retaining bolts/nuts are tightened evenly to prevent uneven stress build-up and distortion of sealing faces. This is especially important on high-compression joints such as the cylinder head.

● A sequence is usually provided by the manufacturer, either in a diagram or actually marked in the casting. If not, always start in the centre and work outwards in a criss-cross pattern (see illustration 4.5). Start off by securing all bolts/nuts finger-tight, then set the torque wrench and tighten each fastener by a small amount in sequence until the final torque is reached. By following this practice,

4.5 When tightening, work from the inside outwards

REF•14 Tools and Workshop Tips

the joint will be held evenly and will not be distorted. Important joints, such as the cylinder head and big-end fasteners often have two- or three-stage torque settings.

Applying leverage

● Use tools at the correct angle. Position a socket wrench or spanner on the bolt/nut so that you pull it towards you when loosening. If this can't be done, push the spanner without curling your fingers around it **(see illustration 4.6)** - the spanner may slip or the fastener loosen suddenly, resulting in your fingers being crushed against a component.

4.6 If you can't pull on the spanner to loosen a fastener, push with your hand open

● Additional leverage is gained by extending the length of the lever. The best way to do this is to use a breaker bar instead of the regular length tool, or to slip a length of tubing over the end of the spanner or socket wrench.
● If additional leverage will not work, the fastener head is either damaged or firmly corroded in place (see *Fasteners*).

5 Bearings

Bearing removal and installation

Drivers and sockets

● Before removing a bearing, always inspect the casing to see which way it must be driven out - some casings will have retaining plates or a cast step. Also check for any identifying markings on the bearing and if installed to a certain depth, measure this at this stage. Some roller bearings are sealed on one side - take note of the original fitted position.
● Bearings can be driven out of a casing using a bearing driver tool (with the correct size head) or a socket of the correct diameter. Select the driver head or socket so that it contacts the outer race of the bearing, not the balls/rollers or inner race. Always support the casing around the bearing housing with wood blocks, otherwise there is a risk of fracture. The bearing is driven out with a few blows on the driver or socket from a heavy mallet. Unless access is severely restricted (as with wheel bearings), a pin-punch is not recommended unless it is moved around the bearing to keep it square in its housing.

● The same equipment can be used to install bearings. Make sure the bearing housing is supported on wood blocks and line up the bearing in its housing. Fit the bearing as noted on removal - generally they are installed with their marked side facing outwards. Tap the bearing squarely into its housing using a driver or socket which bears only on the bearing's outer race - contact with the bearing balls/rollers or inner race will destroy it **(see illustrations 5.1 and 5.2)**.
● Check that the bearing inner race and balls/rollers rotate freely.

5.1 Using a bearing driver against the bearing's outer race

5.2 Using a large socket against the bearing's outer race

Pullers and slide-hammers

● Where a bearing is pressed on a shaft a puller will be required to extract it **(see illustration 5.3)**. Make sure that the puller clamp or legs fit securely behind the bearing and are unlikely to slip out. If pulling a bearing

5.3 This bearing puller clamps behind the bearing and pressure is applied to the shaft end to draw the bearing off

off a gear shaft for example, you may have to locate the puller behind a gear pinion if there is no access to the race and draw the gear pinion off the shaft as well **(see illustration 5.4)**.

> **Caution:** Ensure that the puller's centre bolt locates securely against the end of the shaft and will not slip when pressure is applied. Also ensure that puller does not damage the shaft end.

5.4 Where no access is available to the rear of the bearing, it is sometimes possible to draw off the adjacent component

● Operate the puller so that its centre bolt exerts pressure on the shaft end and draws the bearing off the shaft.
● When installing the bearing on the shaft, tap only on the bearing's inner race - contact with the balls/rollers or outer race with destroy the bearing. Use a socket or length of tubing as a drift which fits over the shaft end **(see illustration 5.5)**.

5.5 When installing a bearing on a shaft use a piece of tubing which bears only on the bearing's inner race

● Where a bearing locates in a blind hole in a casing, it cannot be driven or pulled out as described above. A slide-hammer with knife-edged bearing puller attachment will be required. The puller attachment passes through the bearing and when tightened expands to fit firmly behind the bearing **(see illustration 5.6)**. By operating the slide-hammer part of the tool the bearing is jarred out of its housing **(see illustration 5.7)**.
● It is possible, if the bearing is of reasonable weight, for it to drop out of its housing if the casing is heated as described opposite. If this

Tools and Workshop Tips REF•15

5.6 Expand the bearing puller so that it locks behind the bearing . . .

5.7 . . . attach the slide hammer to the bearing puller

method is attempted, first prepare a work surface which will enable the casing to be tapped face down to help dislodge the bearing - a wood surface is ideal since it will not damage the casing's gasket surface. Wearing protective gloves, tap the heated casing several times against the work surface to dislodge the bearing under its own weight **(see illustration 5.8)**.

5.8 Tapping a casing face down on wood blocks can often dislodge a bearing

● Bearings can be installed in blind holes using the driver or socket method described above.

Drawbolts

● Where a bearing or bush is set in the eye of a component, such as a suspension linkage arm or connecting rod small-end, removal by drift may damage the component. Furthermore, a rubber bushing in a shock absorber eye cannot successfully be driven out of position. If access is available to a engineering press, the task is straightforward. If not, a drawbolt can be fabricated to extract the bearing or bush.

5.9 Drawbolt component parts assembled on a suspension arm

1 Bolt or length of threaded bar
2 Nuts
3 Washer (external diameter greater than tubing internal diameter)
4 Tubing (internal diameter sufficient to accommodate bearing)
5 Suspension arm with bearing
6 Tubing (external diameter slightly smaller than bearing)
7 Washer (external diameter slightly smaller than bearing)

5.10 Drawing the bearing out of the suspension arm

● To extract the bearing/bush you will need a long bolt with nut (or piece of threaded bar with two nuts), a piece of tubing which has an internal diameter larger than the bearing/bush, another piece of tubing which has an external diameter slightly smaller than the bearing/bush, and a selection of washers **(see illustrations 5.9 and 5.10)**. Note that the pieces of tubing must be of the same length, or longer, than the bearing/bush.
● The same kit (without the pieces of tubing) can be used to draw the new bearing/bush back into place **(see illustration 5.11)**.

5.11 Installing a new bearing (1) in the suspension arm

Temperature change

● If the bearing's outer race is a tight fit in the casing, the aluminium casing can be heated to release its grip on the bearing. Aluminium will expand at a greater rate than the steel bearing outer race. There are several ways to do this, but avoid any localised extreme heat (such as a blow torch) - aluminium alloy has a low melting point.
● Approved methods of heating a casing are using a domestic oven (heated to 100°C) or immersing the casing in boiling water **(see illustration 5.12)**. Low temperature range localised heat sources such as a paint stripper heat gun or clothes iron can also be used **(see illustration 5.13)**. Alternatively, soak a rag in boiling water, wring it out and wrap it around the bearing housing.

> ⚠ **Warning: All of these methods require care in use to prevent scalding and burns to the hands. Wear protective gloves when handling hot components.**

5.12 A casing can be immersed in a sink of boiling water to aid bearing removal

5.13 Using a localised heat source to aid bearing removal

● If heating the whole casing note that plastic components, such as the neutral switch, may suffer - remove them beforehand.
● After heating, remove the bearing as described above. You may find that the expansion is sufficient for the bearing to fall out of the casing under its own weight or with a light tap on the driver or socket.
● If necessary, the casing can be heated to aid bearing installation, and this is sometimes the recommended procedure if the motorcycle manufacturer has designed the housing and bearing fit with this intention.

REF•16 Tools and Workshop Tips

- Installation of bearings can be eased by placing them in a freezer the night before installation. The steel bearing will contract slightly, allowing easy insertion in its housing. This is often useful when installing steering head outer races in the frame.

Bearing types and markings

- Plain shell bearings, ball bearings, needle roller bearings and tapered roller bearings will all be found on motorcycles (see illustrations 5.14 and 5.15). The ball and roller types are usually caged between an inner and outer race, but uncaged variations may be found.

5.14 Shell bearings are either plain or grooved. They are usually identified by colour code (arrow)

5.15 Tapered roller bearing (A), needle roller bearing (B) and ball journal bearing (C)

- Shell bearings (often called inserts) are usually found at the crankshaft main and connecting rod big-end where they are good at coping with high loads. They are made of a phosphor-bronze material and are impregnated with self-lubricating properties.
- Ball bearings and needle roller bearings consist of a steel inner and outer race with the balls or rollers between the races. They require constant lubrication by oil or grease and are good at coping with axial loads. Taper roller bearings consist of rollers set in a tapered cage set on the inner race; the outer race is separate. They are good at coping with axial loads and prevent movement along the shaft - a typical application is in the steering head.
- Bearing manufacturers produce bearings to ISO size standards and stamp one face of the bearing to indicate its internal and external diameter, load capacity and type (see illustration 5.16).
- Metal bushes are usually of phosphor-bronze material. Rubber bushes are used in suspension mounting eyes. Fibre bushes have also been used in suspension pivots.

5.16 Typical bearing marking

Bearing fault finding

- If a bearing outer race has spun in its housing, the housing material will be damaged. You can use a bearing locking compound to bond the outer race in place if damage is not too severe.
- Shell bearings will fail due to damage of their working surface, as a result of lack of lubrication, corrosion or abrasive particles in the oil (see illustration 5.17). Small particles of dirt in the oil may embed in the bearing material whereas larger particles will score the bearing and shaft journal. If a number of short journeys are made, insufficient heat will be generated to drive off condensation which has built up on the bearings.

5.17 Typical bearing failures

- Ball and roller bearings will fail due to lack of lubrication or damage to the balls or rollers. Tapered-roller bearings can be damaged by overloading them. Unless the bearing is sealed on both sides, wash it in paraffin (kerosene) to remove all old grease then allow it to dry. Make a visual inspection looking to dented balls or rollers, damaged cages and worn or pitted races (see illustration 5.18).
- A ball bearing can be checked for wear by listening to it when spun. Apply a film of light oil to the bearing and hold it close to the ear - hold the outer race with one hand and spin the inner race with the other hand (see illustration 5.19). The bearing should be almost silent when spun; if it grates or rattles it is worn.

5.18 Example of ball journal bearing with damaged balls and cages

5.19 Hold outer race and listen to inner race when spun

6 Oil seals

Oil seal removal and installation

- Oil seals should be renewed every time a component is dismantled. This is because the seal lips will become set to the sealing surface and will not necessarily reseal.
- Oil seals can be prised out of position using a large flat-bladed screwdriver (see illustration 6.1). In the case of crankcase seals, check first that the seal is not lipped on the inside, preventing its removal with the crankcases joined.

6.1 Prise out oil seals with a large flat-bladed screwdriver

- New seals are usually installed with their marked face (containing the seal reference code) outwards and the spring side towards the fluid being retained. In certain cases, such as a two-stroke engine crankshaft seal, a double lipped seal may be used due to there being fluid or gas on each side of the joint.

Tools and Workshop Tips REF•17

- Use a bearing driver or socket which bears only on the outer hard edge of the seal to install it in the casing - tapping on the inner edge will damage the sealing lip.

Oil seal types and markings

- Oil seals are usually of the single-lipped type. Double-lipped seals are found where a liquid or gas is on both sides of the joint.
- Oil seals can harden and lose their sealing ability if the motorcycle has been in storage for a long period - renewal is the only solution.
- Oil seal manufacturers also conform to the ISO markings for seal size - these are moulded into the outer face of the seal **(see illustration 6.2)**.

6.2 These oil seal markings indicate inside diameter, outside diameter and seal thickness

7 Gaskets and sealants

Types of gasket and sealant

- Gaskets are used to seal the mating surfaces between components and keep lubricants, fluids, vacuum or pressure contained within the assembly. Aluminium gaskets are sometimes found at the cylinder joints, but most gaskets are paper-based. If the mating surfaces of the components being joined are undamaged the gasket can be installed dry, although a dab of sealant or grease will be useful to hold it in place during assembly.
- RTV (Room Temperature Vulcanising) silicone rubber sealants cure when exposed to moisture in the atmosphere. These sealants are good at filling pits or irregular gasket faces, but will tend to be forced out of the joint under very high torque. They can be used to replace a paper gasket, but first make sure that the width of the paper gasket is not essential to the shimming of internal components. RTV sealants should not be used on components containing petrol (gasoline).
- Non-hardening, semi-hardening and hard setting liquid gasket compounds can be used with a gasket or between a metal-to-metal joint. Select the sealant to suit the application: universal non-hardening sealant can be used on virtually all joints; semi-hardening on joint faces which are rough or damaged; hard setting sealant on joints which require a permanent bond and are subjected to high temperature and pressure. **Note:** *Check first if the paper gasket has a bead of sealant impregnated in its surface before applying additional sealant.*
- When choosing a sealant, make sure it is suitable for the application, particularly if being applied in a high-temperature area or in the vicinity of fuel. Certain manufacturers produce sealants in either clear, silver or black colours to match the finish of the engine. This has a particular application on motorcycles where much of the engine is exposed.
- Do not over-apply sealant. That which is squeezed out on the outside of the joint can be wiped off, whereas an excess of sealant on the inside can break off and clog oilways.

Breaking a sealed joint

- Age, heat, pressure and the use of hard setting sealant can cause two components to stick together so tightly that they are difficult to separate using finger pressure alone. Do not resort to using levers unless there is a pry point provided for this purpose **(see illustration 7.1)** or else the gasket surfaces will be damaged.
- Use a soft-faced hammer **(see illustration 7.2)** or a wood block and conventional hammer to strike the component near the mating surface. Avoid hammering against cast extremities since they may break off. If this method fails, try using a wood wedge between the two components.

Caution: If the joint will not separate, double-check that you have removed all the fasteners.

7.1 If a pry point is provided, apply gently pressure with a flat-bladed screwdriver

7.2 Tap around the joint with a soft-faced mallet if necessary - don't strike cooling fins

Removal of old gasket and sealant

- Paper gaskets will most likely come away complete, leaving only a few traces stuck on the sealing faces of the components. It is imperative that all traces are removed to ensure correct sealing of the new gasket.
- Very carefully scrape all traces of gasket away making sure that the sealing surfaces are not gouged or scored by the scraper **(see illustrations 7.3, 7.4 and 7.5)**. Stubborn deposits can be removed by spraying with an aerosol gasket remover. Final preparation of

> **HAYNES HiNT**
>
> *Most components have one or two hollow locating dowels between the two gasket faces. If a dowel cannot be removed, do not resort to gripping it with pliers - it will almost certainly be distorted. Install a close-fitting socket or Phillips screwdriver into the dowel and then grip the outer edge of the dowel to free it.*

7.3 Paper gaskets can be scraped off with a gasket scraper tool . . .

7.4 . . . a knife blade . . .

7.5 . . . or a household scraper

REF•18 Tools and Workshop Tips

7.6 Fine abrasive paper is wrapped around a flat file to clean up the gasket face

7.7 A kitchen scourer can be used on stubborn deposits

8.1 Tighten the chain breaker to push the pin out of the link . . .

8.2 . . . withdraw the pin, remove the tool . . .

8.3 . . . and separate the chain link

8.4 Insert the new soft link, with O-rings, through the chain ends . . .

8.5 . . . install the O-rings over the pin ends . . .

8.6 . . . followed by the sideplate

8.7 Push the sideplate into position using a clamp

the gasket surface can be made with very fine abrasive paper or a plastic kitchen scourer **(see illustrations 7.6 and 7.7)**.

● Old sealant can be scraped or peeled off components, depending on the type originally used. Note that gasket removal compounds are available to avoid scraping the components clean; make sure the gasket remover suits the type of sealant used.

8 Chains

Breaking and joining final drive chains

● Drive chains for all but small bikes are continuous and do not have a clip-type connecting link. The chain must be broken using a chain breaker tool and the new chain securely riveted together using a new soft rivet-type link. Never use a clip-type connecting link instead of a rivet-type link, except in an emergency. Various chain breaking and riveting tools are available, either as separate tools or combined as illustrated in the accompanying photographs - read the instructions supplied with the tool carefully.

> ⚠ **Warning:** The need to rivet the new link pins correctly cannot be overstressed - loss of control of the motorcycle is very likely to result if the chain breaks in use.

● Rotate the chain and look for the soft link. The soft link pins look like they have been deeply centre-punched instead of peened over like all the other pins **(see illustration 8.9)** and its sideplate may be a different colour. Position the soft link midway between the sprockets and assemble the chain breaker tool over one of the soft link pins **(see illustration 8.1)**. Operate the tool to push the pin out through the chain **(see illustration 8.2)**. On an O-ring chain, remove the O-rings **(see illustration 8.3)**. Carry out the same procedure on the other soft link pin.

> **Caution: Certain soft link pins (particularly on the larger chains) may require their ends to be filed or ground off before they can be pressed out using the tool.**

● Check that you have the correct size and strength (standard or heavy duty) new soft link - do not reuse the old link. Look for the size marking on the chain sideplates **(see illustration 8.10)**.

● Position the chain ends so that they are engaged over the rear sprocket. On an O-ring chain, install a new O-ring over each pin of the link and insert the link through the two chain ends **(see illustration 8.4)**. Install a new O-ring over the end of each pin, followed by the sideplate (with the chain manufacturer's marking facing outwards) **(see illustrations 8.5 and 8.6)**. On an unsealed chain, insert the link through the two chain ends, then install the sideplate with the chain manufacturer's marking facing outwards.

● Note that it may not be possible to install the sideplate using finger pressure alone. If using a joining tool, assemble it so that the plates of the tool clamp the link and press the sideplate over the pins **(see illustration 8.7)**. Otherwise, use two small sockets placed over

Tools and Workshop Tips REF•19

8.8 Assemble the chain riveting tool over one pin at a time and tighten it fully

8.9 Pin end correctly riveted (A), pin end unriveted (B)

the rivet ends and two pieces of the wood between a G-clamp. Operate the clamp to press the sideplate over the pins.
• Assemble the joining tool over one pin (following the maker's instructions) and tighten the tool down to spread the pin end securely **(see illustrations 8.8 and 8.9)**. Do the same on the other pin.

> **Warning: Check that the pin ends are secure and that there is no danger of the sideplate coming loose. If the pin ends are cracked the soft link must be renewed.**

Final drive chain sizing

• Chains are sized using a three digit number, followed by a suffix to denote the chain type **(see illustration 8.10)**. Chain type is either standard or heavy duty (thicker sideplates), and also unsealed or O-ring/X-ring type.
• The first digit of the number relates to the pitch of the chain, ie the distance from the centre of one pin to the centre of the next pin **(see illustration 8.11)**. Pitch is expressed in eighths of an inch, as follows:

8.10 Typical chain size and type marking

8.11 Chain dimensions

Sizes commencing with a 4 (eg 428) have a pitch of 1/2 inch (12.7 mm)

Sizes commencing with a 5 (eg 520) have a pitch of 5/8 inch (15.9 mm)

Sizes commencing with a 6 (eg 630) have a pitch of 3/4 inch (19.1 mm)

• The second and third digits of the chain size relate to the width of the rollers, again in imperial units, eg the 525 shown has 5/16 inch (7.94 mm) rollers **(see illustration 8.11)**.

9 Hoses

Clamping to prevent flow

• Small-bore flexible hoses can be clamped to prevent fluid flow whilst a component is worked on. Whichever method is used, ensure that the hose material is not permanently distorted or damaged by the clamp.
a) A brake hose clamp available from auto accessory shops **(see illustration 9.1)**.
b) A wingnut type hose clamp **(see illustration 9.2)**.
c) Two sockets placed each side of the hose and held with straight-jawed self-locking grips **(see illustration 9.3)**.
d) Thick card each side of the hose held between straight-jawed self-locking grips **(see illustration 9.4)**.

9.1 Hoses can be clamped with an automotive brake hose clamp . . .

9.2 . . . a wingnut type hose clamp . . .

9.3 . . . two sockets and a pair of self-locking grips . . .

9.4 . . . or thick card and self-locking grips

Freeing and fitting hoses

• Always make sure the hose clamp is moved well clear of the hose end. Grip the hose with your hand and rotate it whilst pulling it off the union. If the hose has hardened due to age and will not move, slit it with a sharp knife and peel its ends off the union **(see illustration 9.5)**.
• Resist the temptation to use grease or soap on the unions to aid installation; although it helps the hose slip over the union it will equally aid the escape of fluid from the joint. It is preferable to soften the hose ends in hot water and wet the inside surface of the hose with water or a fluid which will evaporate.

9.5 Cutting a coolant hose free with a sharp knife

REF•20 Security

Introduction

In less time than it takes to read this introduction, a thief could steal your motorcycle. Returning only to find your bike has gone is one of the worst feelings in the world. Even if the motorcycle is insured against theft, once you've got over the initial shock, you will have the inconvenience of dealing with the police and your insurance company.

The motorcycle is an easy target for the professional thief and the joyrider alike and the official figures on motorcycle theft make for depressing reading; on average a motorcycle is stolen every 16 minutes in the UK!

Motorcycle thefts fall into two categories, those stolen 'to order' and those taken by opportunists. The thief stealing to order will be on the look out for a specific make and model and will go to extraordinary lengths to obtain that motorcycle. The opportunist thief on the other hand will look for easy targets which can be stolen with the minimum of effort and risk.

Whilst it is never going to be possible to make your machine 100% secure, it is estimated that around half of all stolen motorcycles are taken by opportunist thieves. Remember that the opportunist thief is always on the look out for the easy option: if there are two similar motorcycles parked side-by-side, they will target the one with the lowest level of security. By taking a few precautions, you can reduce the chances of your motorcycle being stolen.

Security equipment

There are many specialised motorcycle security devices available and the following text summarises their applications and their good and bad points.

Once you have decided on the type of security equipment which best suits your needs, we recommended that you read one of the many equipment tests regularly carried out by the motorcycle press. These tests compare the products from all the major manufacturers and give impartial ratings on their effectiveness, value-for-money and ease of use.

No one item of security equipment can provide complete protection. It is highly recommended that two or more of the items described below are combined to increase the security of your motorcycle (a lock and chain plus an alarm system is just about ideal). The more security measures fitted to the bike, the less likely it is to be stolen.

Lock and chain

Pros: *Very flexible to use; can be used to secure the motorcycle to almost any immovable object. On some locks and chains, the lock can be used on its own as a disc lock (see below).*

Cons: *Can be very heavy and awkward to carry on the motorcycle, although some types will be supplied with a carry bag which can be strapped to the pillion seat.*

● Heavy-duty chains and locks are an excellent security measure **(see illustration 1)**. Whenever the motorcycle is parked, use the lock and chain to secure the machine to a solid, immovable object such as a post or railings. This will prevent the machine from being ridden away or being lifted into the back of a van.

● When fitting the chain, always ensure the chain is routed around the motorcycle frame or swingarm **(see illustrations 2 and 3)**. Never merely pass the chain around one of the wheel rims; a thief may unbolt the wheel and lift the rest of the machine into a van, leaving you with just the wheel! Try to avoid having excess chain free, thus making it difficult to use cutting tools, and keep the chain and lock off the ground to prevent thieves attacking it with a cold chisel. Position the lock so that its lock barrel is facing downwards; this will make it harder for the thief to attack the lock mechanism.

1 Ensure the lock and chain you buy is of good quality and long enough to shackle your bike to a solid object

2 Pass the chain through the bike's frame, rather than just through a wheel . . .

3 . . . and loop it around a solid object

Security REF•21

U-locks

Pros: *Highly effective deterrent which can be used to secure the bike to a post or railings. Most U-locks come with a carrier which allows the lock to be easily carried on the bike.*

Cons: *Not as flexible to use as a lock and chain.*

● These are solid locks which are similar in use to a lock and chain. U-locks are lighter than a lock and chain but not so flexible to use. The length and shape of the lock shackle limit the objects to which the bike can be secured **(see illustration 4)**.

Disc locks

Pros: *Small, light and very easy to carry; most can be stored underneath the seat.*

Cons: *Does not prevent the motorcycle being lifted into a van. Can be very embarrassing if you forget to remove the lock before attempting to ride off!*

● Disc locks are designed to be attached to the front brake disc. The lock passes through one of the holes in the disc and prevents the wheel rotating by jamming against the fork/brake caliper **(see illustration 5)**. Some are equipped with an alarm siren which sounds if the disc lock is moved; this not only acts as a theft deterrent but also as a handy reminder if you try to move the bike with the lock still fitted.

● Combining the disc lock with a length of cable which can be looped around a post or railings provides an additional measure of security **(see illustration 6)**.

Alarms and immobilisers

Pros: *Once installed it is completely hassle-free to use. If the system is 'Thatcham' or 'Sold Secure-approved', insurance companies may give you a discount.*

Cons: *Can be expensive to buy and complex to install. No system will prevent the motorcycle from being lifted into a van and taken away.*

● Electronic alarms and immobilisers are available to suit a variety of budgets. There are three different types of system available: pure alarms, pure immobilisers, and the more expensive systems which are combined alarm/immobilisers **(see illustration 7)**.

● An alarm system is designed to emit an audible warning if the motorcycle is being tampered with.

● An immobiliser prevents the motorcycle being started and ridden away by disabling its electrical systems.

● When purchasing an alarm/immobiliser system, check the cost of installing the system unless you are able to do it yourself. If the motorcycle is not used regularly, another consideration is the current drain of the system. All alarm/immobiliser systems are powered by the motorcycle's battery; purchasing a system with a very low current drain could prevent the battery losing its charge whilst the motorcycle is not being used.

4 U-locks can be used to secure the bike to a solid object – ensure you purchase one which is long enough

5 A typical disc lock attached through one of the holes in the disc

6 A disc lock combined with a security cable provides additional protection

7 A typical alarm/immobiliser system

REF•22 Security

Indelible markings can be applied to most areas of the bike – always apply the manufacturer's sticker to warn off thieves

Chemically-etched code numbers can be applied to main body panels . . .

. . . again, always ensure that the kit manufacturer's sticker is applied in a prominent position

Security marking kits

Pros: Very cheap and effective deterrent. Many insurance companies will give you a discount on your insurance premium if a recognised security marking kit is used on your motorcycle.

Cons: Does not prevent the motorcycle being stolen by joyriders.

● There are many different types of security marking kits available. The idea is to mark as many parts of the motorcycle as possible with a unique security number **(see illustrations 8, 9 and 10)**. A form will be included with the kit to register your personal details and those of the motorcycle with the kit manufacturer. This register is made available to the police to help them trace the rightful owner of any motorcycle or components which they recover should all other forms of identification have been removed. Always apply the warning stickers provided with the kit to deter thieves.

Ground anchors, wheel clamps and security posts

Pros: An excellent form of security which will deter all but the most determined of thieves.

Cons: Awkward to install and can be expensive.

● Whilst the motorcycle is at home, it is a good idea to attach it securely to the floor or a solid wall, even if it is kept in a securely locked garage. Various types of ground anchors, security posts and wheel clamps are available for this purpose **(see illustration 11)**. These security devices are either bolted to a solid concrete or brick structure or can be cemented into the ground.

Permanent ground anchors provide an excellent level of security when the bike is at home

Security at home

A high percentage of motorcycle thefts are from the owner's home. Here are some things to consider whenever your motorcycle is at home:

✔ Where possible, always keep the motorcycle in a securely locked garage. Never rely solely on the standard lock on the garage door, these are usual hopelessly inadequate. Fit an additional locking mechanism to the door and consider having the garage alarmed. A security light, activated by a movement sensor, is also a good investment.

✔ Always secure the motorcycle to the ground or a wall, even if it is inside a securely locked garage.

✔ Do not regularly leave the motorcycle outside your home, try to keep it out of sight wherever possible. If a garage is not available, fit a motorcycle cover over the bike to disguise its true identity.

✔ It is not uncommon for thieves to follow a motorcyclist home to find out where the bike is kept. They will then return at a later date. Be aware of this whenever you are returning home on your motorcycle. If you suspect you are being followed, do not return home, instead ride to a garage or shop and stop as a precaution.

✔ When selling a motorcycle, do not provide your home address or the location where the bike is normally kept. Arrange to meet the buyer at a location away from your home. Thieves have been known to pose as potential buyers to find out where motorcycles are kept and then return later to steal them.

Security away from the home

As well as fitting security equipment to your motorcycle here are a few general rules to follow whenever you park your motorcycle.

✔ Park in a busy, public place.
✔ Use car parks which incorporate security features, such as CCTV.

✔ At night, park in a well-lit area, preferably directly underneath a street light.
✔ Engage the steering lock.
✔ Secure the motorcycle to a solid, immovable object such as a post or railings with an additional lock. If this is not possible, secure the bike to a friend's motorcycle. Some public parking places provide security loops for motorcycles.

✔ Never leave your helmet or luggage attached to the motorcycle. Take them with you at all times.

Lubricants and fluids

A wide range of lubricants, fluids and cleaning agents is available for motor-cycles. This is a guide as to what is available, its applications and properties.

Four-stroke engine oil

● Engine oil is without doubt the most important component of any four-stroke engine. Modern motorcycle engines place a lot of demands on their oil and choosing the right type is essential. Using an unsuitable oil will lead to an increased rate of engine wear and could result in serious engine damage. Before purchasing oil, always check the recommended oil specification given by the manufacturer. The manufacturer will state a recommended 'type or classification' and also a specific 'viscosity' range for engine oil.

● The oil 'type or classification' is identified by its API (American Petroleum Institute) rating. The API rating will be in the form of two letters, e.g. SG. The S identifies the oil as being suitable for use in a petrol (gasoline) engine (S stands for spark ignition) and the second letter, ranging from A to J, identifies the oil's performance rating. The later this letter, the higher the specification of the oil; for example API SG oil exceeds the requirements of API SF oil. **Note:** *On some oils there may also be a second rating consisting of another two letters, the first letter being C, e.g. API SF/CD. This rating indicates the oil is also suitable for use in a diesel engines (the C stands for compression ignition) and is thus of no relevance for motorcycle use.*

● The 'viscosity' of the oil is identified by its SAE (Society of Automotive Engineers) rating. All modern engines require multigrade oils and the SAE rating will consist of two numbers, the first followed by a W, e.g. 10W/40. The first number indicates the viscosity rating of the oil at low temperatures (W stands for winter – tested at –20ºC) and the second number represents the viscosity of the oil at high temperatures (tested at 100ºC). The lower the number, the thinner the oil. For example an oil with an SAE 10W/40 rating will give better cold starting and running than an SAE 15W/40 oil.

● As well as ensuring the 'type' and 'viscosity' of the oil match the recommendations, another consideration to make when buying engine oil is whether to purchase a standard mineral-based oil, a semi-synthetic oil (also known as a synthetic blend or synthetic-based oil) or a fully-synthetic oil. Although all oils will have a similar rating and viscosity, their cost will vary considerably; mineral-based oils are the cheapest, the fully-synthetic oils the most expensive with the semi-synthetic oils falling somewhere in-between. This decision is very much up to the owner, but it should be noted that modern synthetic oils have far better lubricating and cleaning qualities than traditional mineral-based oils and tend to retain these properties for far longer. Bearing in mind the operating conditions inside a modern, high-revving motorcycle engine it is highly recommended that a fully synthetic oil is used. The extra expense at each service could save you money in the long term by preventing premature engine wear.

● As a final note always ensure that the oil is specifically designed for use in motorcycle engines. Engine oils designed primarily for use in car engines sometimes contain additives or friction modifiers which could cause clutch slip on a motorcycle fitted with a wet-clutch.

Two-stroke engine oil

● Modern two-stroke engines, with their high power outputs, place high demands on their oil. If engine seizure is to be avoided it is essential that a high-quality oil is used. Two-stroke oils differ hugely from four-stroke oils. The oil lubricates only the crankshaft and piston(s) (the transmission has its own lubricating oil) and is used on a total-loss basis where it is burnt completely during the combustion process.

● The Japanese have recently introduced a classification system for two-stroke oils, the JASO rating. This rating is in the form of two letters, either FA, FB or FC – FA is the lowest classification and FC the highest. Ensure the oil being used meets or exceeds the recommended rating specified by the manufacturer.

● As well as ensuring the oil rating matches the recommendation, another consideration to make when buying engine oil is whether to purchase a standard mineral-based oil, a semi-synthetic oil (also known as a synthetic blend or synthetic-based oil) or a fully-synthetic oil. The cost of each type of oil varies considerably; mineral-based oils are the cheapest, the fully-synthetic oils the most expensive with the semi-synthetic oils falling somewhere in-between. This decision is very much up to the owner, but it should be noted that modern synthetic oils have far better lubricating properties and burn cleaner than traditional mineral-based oils. It is therefore recommended that a fully synthetic oil is used. The extra expense could save you money in the long term by preventing premature engine wear, engine performance will be improved, carbon deposits and exhaust smoke will be reduced.

Lubricants and fluids

- Always ensure that the oil is specifically designed for use in an injector system. Many high quality two-stroke oils are designed for competition use and need to be pre-mixed with fuel. These oils are of a much higher viscosity and are not designed to flow through the injector pumps used on road-going two-stroke motorcycles.

Transmission (gear) oil

- On a two-stroke engine, the transmission and clutch are lubricated by their own separate oil bath which must be changed in accordance with the Maintenance Schedule.
- Although the engine and transmission units of most four-strokes use a common lubrication supply, there are some exceptions where the engine and gearbox have separate oil reservoirs and a dry clutch is used.
- Motorcycle manufacturers will either recommend a monograde transmission oil or a four-stroke multigrade engine oil to lubricate the transmission.
- Transmission oils, or gear oils as they are often called, are designed specifically for use in transmission systems. The viscosity of these oils is represented by an SAE number, but the scale of measurement applied is different to that used to grade engine oils. As a rough guide a SAE90 gear oil will be of the same viscosity as an SAE50 engine oil.

Shaft drive oil

- On models equipped with shaft final drive, the shaft drive gears are will have their own oil supply. The manufacturer will state a recommended 'type or classification' and also a specific 'viscosity' range in the same manner as for four-stroke engine oil.
- Gear oil classification is given by the number which follows the API GL (GL standing for gear lubricant) rating, the higher the number, the higher the specification of the oil, e.g. API GL5 oil is a higher specification than API GL4 oil. Ensure the oil meets or exceeds the classification specified and is of the correct viscosity. The viscosity of gear oils is also represented by an SAE number but the scale of measurement used is different to that used to grade engine oils. As a rough guide an SAE90 gear oil will be of the same viscosity as an SAE50 engine oil.
- If the use of an EP (Extreme Pressure) gear oil is specified, ensure the oil purchased is suitable.

Fork oil and suspension fluid

- Conventional telescopic front forks are hydraulic and require fork oil to work. To ensure the forks function correctly, the fork oil must be changed in accordance with the Maintenance Schedule.
- Fork oil is available in a variety of viscosities, identified by their SAE rating; fork oil ratings vary from light (SAE 5) to heavy (SAE 30). When purchasing fork oil, ensure the viscosity rating matches that specified by the manufacturer.
- Some lubricant manufacturers also produce a range of high-quality suspension fluids which are very similar to fork oil but are designed mainly for competition use. These fluids may have a different viscosity rating system which is not to be confused with the SAE rating of normal fork oil. Refer to the manufacturer's instructions if in any doubt.

Brake and clutch fluid

- All disc brake systems and some clutch systems are hydraulically operated. To ensure correct operation, the hydraulic fluid must be changed in accordance with the Maintenance Schedule.
- Brake and clutch fluid is classified by its DOT rating with most motorcycle manufacturers specifying DOT 3 or 4 fluid. Both fluid types are glycol-based and can be mixed together without adverse effect; DOT 4 fluid exceeds the requirements of DOT 3 fluid. Although it is safe to use DOT 4 fluid in a system designed for use with DOT 3 fluid, never use DOT 3 fluid in a system which specifies the use of DOT 4 as this will adversely affect the system's performance. The type required for the system will be marked on the fluid reservoir cap.
- Some manufacturers also produce a DOT 5 hydraulic fluid. DOT 5 hydraulic fluid is silicone-based and is not compatible with the glycol-based DOT 3 and 4 fluids. Never mix DOT 5 fluid with DOT 3 or 4 fluid as this will seriously affect the performance of the hydraulic system.

Coolant/antifreeze

- When purchasing coolant/antifreeze, always ensure it is suitable for use in an aluminium engine and contains corrosion inhibitors to prevent possible blockages of the internal coolant passages of the system. As a general rule, most coolants are designed to be used neat and should not be diluted whereas antifreeze can be mixed with distilled water to provide a coolant solution of the required strength. Refer to the manufacturer's instructions on the bottle.
- Ensure the coolant is changed in accordance with the Maintenance Schedule.

Chain lube

- Chain lube is an aerosol-type spray lubricant specifically designed for use on motorcycle final drive chains. Chain lube has two functions, to minimise friction between the final drive chain and sprockets and to prevent corrosion of the chain. Regular use of a good-quality chain lube will extend the life of the drive chain and sprockets and thus maximise the power being transmitted from the transmission to the rear wheel.
- When using chain lube, always allow some time for the solvents in the lube to evaporate before riding the motorcycle. This will minimise the amount of lube which will

Lubricants and fluids REF•25

'fling' off from the chain when the motorcycle is used. If the motorcycle is equipped with an 'O-ring' chain, ensure the chain lube is labelled as being suitable for use on 'O-ring' chains.

Degreasers and solvents

● There are many different types of solvents and degreasers available to remove the grime and grease which accumulate around the motorcycle during normal use. Degreasers and solvents are usually available as an aerosol-type spray or as a liquid which you apply with a brush. Always closely follow the manufacturer's instructions and wear eye protection during use. Be aware that many solvents are flammable and may give off noxious fumes; take adequate precautions when using them (see Safety First!).

● For general cleaning, use one of the many solvents or degreasers available from most motorcycle accessory shops. These solvents are usually applied then left for a certain time before being washed off with water.

Brake cleaner is a solvent specifically designed to remove all traces of oil, grease and dust from braking system components. Brake cleaner is designed to evaporate quickly and leaves behind no residue.

Carburettor cleaner is an aerosol-type solvent specifically designed to clear carburettor blockages and break down the hard deposits and gum often found inside carburettors during overhaul.

Contact cleaner is an aerosol-type solvent designed for cleaning electrical components. The cleaner will remove all traces of oil and dirt from components such as switch contacts or fouled spark plugs and then dry, leaving behind no residue.

Gasket remover is an aerosol-type solvent designed for removing stubborn gaskets from engine components during overhaul. Gasket remover will minimise the amount of scraping required to remove the gasket and therefore reduce the risk of damage to the mating surface.

Spray lubricants

● Aerosol-based spray lubricants are widely available and are excellent for lubricating lever pivots and exposed cables and switches. Try to use a lubricant which is of the dry-film type as the fluid evaporates, leaving behind a dry-film of lubricant. Lubricants which leave behind an oily residue will attract dust and dirt which will increase the rate of wear of the cable/lever.

● Most lubricants also act as a moisture dispersant and a penetrating fluid. This means they can also be used to 'dry out' electrical components such as wiring connectors or switches as well as helping to free seized fasteners.

Greases

● Grease is used to lubricate many of the pivot-points. A good-quality multi-purpose grease is suitable for most applications but some manufacturers will specify the use of specialist greases for use on components such as swingarm and suspension linkage bushes. These specialist greases can be purchased from most motorcycle (or car) accessory shops; commonly specified types include molybdenum disulphide grease, lithium-based grease, graphite-based grease, silicone-based grease and high-temperature copper-based grease.

Gasket sealing compounds

● Gasket sealing compounds can be used in conjunction with gaskets, to improve their sealing capabilities, or on their own to seal metal-to-metal joints. Depending on their type, sealing compounds either set hard or stay relatively soft and pliable.

● When purchasing a gasket sealing compound, ensure that it is designed specifically for use on an internal combustion engine. General multi-purpose sealants available from DIY stores may appear visibly similar but they are not designed to withstand the extreme heat or contact with fuel and oil encountered when used on an engine (see 'Tools and Workshop Tips' for further information).

Thread locking compound

● Thread locking compounds are used to secure certain threaded fasteners in position to prevent them from loosening due to vibration. Thread locking compounds can be purchased from most motorcycle (and car) accessory shops. Ensure the threads of the both components are completely clean and dry before sparingly applying the locking compound (see 'Tools and Workshop Tips' for further information).

Fuel additives

● Fuel additives which protect and clean the fuel system components are widely available. These additives are designed to remove all traces of deposits that build up on the carburettors/injectors and prevent wear, helping the fuel system to operate more efficiently. If a fuel additive is being used, check that it is suitable for use with your motorcycle, especially if your motorcycle is equipped with a catalytic converter.

● Octane boosters are also available. These additives are designed to improve the performance of highly-tuned engines being run on normal pump-fuel and are of no real use on standard motorcycles.

Conversion factors

Length (distance)
Inches (in)	x 25.4	= Millimetres (mm)	x 0.0394	= Inches (in)
Feet (ft)	x 0.305	= Metres (m)	x 3.281	= Feet (ft)
Miles	x 1.609	= Kilometres (km)	x 0.621	= Miles

Volume (capacity)
Cubic inches (cu in; in^3)	x 16.387	= Cubic centimetres (cc; cm^3)	x 0.061	= Cubic inches (cu in; in^3)
Imperial pints (Imp pt)	x 0.568	= Litres (l)	x 1.76	= Imperial pints (Imp pt)
Imperial quarts (Imp qt)	x 1.137	= Litres (l)	x 0.88	= Imperial quarts (Imp qt)
Imperial quarts (Imp qt)	x 1.201	= US quarts (US qt)	x 0.833	= Imperial quarts (Imp qt)
US quarts (US qt)	x 0.946	= Litres (l)	x 1.057	= US quarts (US qt)
Imperial gallons (Imp gal)	x 4.546	= Litres (l)	x 0.22	= Imperial gallons (Imp gal)
Imperial gallons (Imp gal)	x 1.201	= US gallons (US gal)	x 0.833	= Imperial gallons (Imp gal)
US gallons (US gal)	x 3.785	= Litres (l)	x 0.264	= US gallons (US gal)

Mass (weight)
Ounces (oz)	x 28.35	= Grams (g)	x 0.035	= Ounces (oz)
Pounds (lb)	x 0.454	= Kilograms (kg)	x 2.205	= Pounds (lb)

Force
Ounces-force (ozf; oz)	x 0.278	= Newtons (N)	x 3.6	= Ounces-force (ozf; oz)
Pounds-force (lbf; lb)	x 4.448	= Newtons (N)	x 0.225	= Pounds-force (lbf; lb)
Newtons (N)	x 0.1	= Kilograms-force (kgf; kg)	x 9.81	= Newtons (N)

Pressure
Pounds-force per square inch (psi; lbf/in^2; lb/in^2)	x 0.070	= Kilograms-force per square centimetre (kgf/cm^2; kg/cm^2)	x 14.223	= Pounds-force per square inch (psi; lbf/in^2; lb/in^2)
Pounds-force per square inch (psi; lbf/in^2; lb/in^2)	x 0.068	= Atmospheres (atm)	x 14.696	= Pounds-force per square inch (psi; lbf/in^2; lb/in^2)
Pounds-force per square inch (psi; lbf/in^2; lb/in^2)	x 0.069	= Bars	x 14.5	= Pounds-force per square inch (psi; lbf/in^2; lb/in^2)
Pounds-force per square inch (psi; lbf/in^2; lb/in^2)	x 6.895	= Kilopascals (kPa)	x 0.145	= Pounds-force per square inch (psi; lbf/in^2; lb/in^2)
Kilopascals (kPa)	x 0.01	= Kilograms-force per square centimetre (kgf/cm^2; kg/cm^2)	x 98.1	= Kilopascals (kPa)
Millibar (mbar)	x 100	= Pascals (Pa)	x 0.01	= Millibar (mbar)
Millibar (mbar)	x 0.0145	= Pounds-force per square inch (psi; lbf/in^2; lb/in^2)	x 68.947	= Millibar (mbar)
Millibar (mbar)	x 0.75	= Millimetres of mercury (mmHg)	x 1.333	= Millibar (mbar)
Millibar (mbar)	x 0.401	= Inches of water (inH$_2$O)	x 2.491	= Millibar (mbar)
Millimetres of mercury (mmHg)	x 0.535	= Inches of water (inH$_2$O)	x 1.868	= Millimetres of mercury (mmHg)
Inches of water (inH$_2$O)	x 0.036	= Pounds-force per square inch (psi; lbf/in^2; lb/in^2)	x 27.68	= Inches of water (inH$_2$O)

Torque (moment of force)
Pounds-force inches (lbf in; lb in)	x 1.152	= Kilograms-force centimetre (kgf cm; kg cm)	x 0.868	= Pounds-force inches (lbf in; lb in)
Pounds-force inches (lbf in; lb in)	x 0.113	= Newton metres (Nm)	x 8.85	= Pounds-force inches (lbf in; lb in)
Pounds-force inches (lbf in; lb in)	x 0.083	= Pounds-force feet (lbf ft; lb ft)	x 12	= Pounds-force inches (lbf in; lb in)
Pounds-force feet (lbf ft; lb ft)	x 0.138	= Kilograms-force metres (kgf m; kg m)	x 7.233	= Pounds-force feet (lbf ft; lb ft)
Pounds-force feet (lbf ft; lb ft)	x 1.356	= Newton metres (Nm)	x 0.738	= Pounds-force feet (lbf ft; lb ft)
Newton metres (Nm)	x 0.102	= Kilograms-force metres (kgf m; kg m)	x 9.804	= Newton metres (Nm)

Power
Horsepower (hp)	x 745.7	= Watts (W)	x 0.0013	= Horsepower (hp)

Velocity (speed)
Miles per hour (miles/hr; mph)	x 1.609	= Kilometres per hour (km/hr; kph)	x 0.621	= Miles per hour (miles/hr; mph)

Fuel consumption*
Miles per gallon (mpg)	x 0.354	= Kilometres per litre (km/l)	x 2.825	= Miles per gallon (mpg)

Temperature

Degrees Fahrenheit = (°C x 1.8) + 32   Degrees Celsius (Degrees Centigrade; °C) = (°F - 32) x 0.56

It is common practice to convert from miles per gallon (mpg) to litres/100 kilometres (l/100km), where mpg x l/100 km = 282

MOT Test Checks REF•27

About the MOT Test

In the UK, all vehicles more than three years old are subject to an annual test to ensure that they meet minimum safety requirements. A current test certificate must be issued before a machine can be used on public roads, and is required before a road fund licence can be issued. Riding without a current test certificate will also invalidate your insurance.

For most owners, the MOT test is an annual cause for anxiety, and this is largely due to owners not being sure what needs to be checked prior to submitting the motorcycle for testing. The simple answer is that a fully roadworthy motorcycle will have no difficulty in passing the test.

This is a guide to getting your motorcycle through the MOT test. Obviously it will not be possible to examine the motorcycle to the same standard as the professional MOT tester, particularly in view of the equipment required for some of the checks. However, working through the following procedures will enable you to identify any problem areas before submitting the motorcycle for the test.

It has only been possible to summarise the test requirements here, based on the regulations in force at the time of printing. Test standards are becoming increasingly stringent, although there are some exemptions for older vehicles. More information about the MOT test can be obtained from the TSO publications, *How Safe is your Motorcycle* and *The MOT Inspection Manual for Motorcycle Testing*.

Many of the checks require that one of the wheels is raised off the ground. If the motorcycle doesn't have a centre stand, note that an auxiliary stand will be required. Additionally, the help of an assistant may prove useful.

Certain exceptions apply to machines under 50 cc, machines without a lighting system, and Classic bikes - if in doubt about any of the requirements listed below seek confirmation from an MOT tester prior to submitting the motorcycle for the test.

Check that the frame number is clearly visible.

Electrical System

Lights, turn signals, horn and reflector

✔ With the ignition on, check the operation of the following electrical components. **Note:** *The electrical components on certain small-capacity machines are powered by the generator, requiring that the engine is run for this check.*

   a) *Headlight and tail light. Check that both illuminate in the low and high beam switch positions.*
   b) *Position lights. Check that the front position (or sidelight) and tail light illuminate in this switch position.*
   c) *Turn signals. Check that all flash at the correct rate, and that the warning light(s) function correctly. Check that the turn signal switch works correctly.*
   d) *Hazard warning system (where fitted). Check that all four turn signals flash in this switch position.*
   e) *Brake stop light. Check that the light comes on when the front and rear brakes are independently applied. Models first used on or after 1st April 1986 must have a brake light switch on each brake.*
   f) *Horn. Check that the sound is continuous and of reasonable volume.*

✔ Check that there is a red reflector on the rear of the machine, either mounted separately or as part of the tail light lens.

✔ Check the condition of the headlight, tail light and turn signal lenses.

Headlight beam height

✔ The MOT tester will perform a headlight beam height check using specialised beam setting equipment **(see illustration 1)**. This equipment will not be available to the home mechanic, but if you suspect that the headlight is incorrectly set or may have been maladjusted in the past, you can perform a rough test as follows.

✔ Position the bike in a straight line facing a brick wall. The bike must be off its stand, upright and with a rider seated. Measure the height from the ground to the centre of the headlight and mark a horizontal line on the wall at this height. Position the motorcycle 3.8 metres from the wall and draw a vertical line up the wall central to the centreline of the motorcycle. Switch to dipped beam and check that the beam pattern falls slightly lower than the horizontal line and to the left of the vertical line **(see illustration 2)**.

Headlight beam height checking equipment

Home workshop beam alignment check

REF•28 MOT Test Checks

Exhaust System and Final Drive

Exhaust

✔ Check that the exhaust mountings are secure and that the system does not foul any of the rear suspension components.
✔ Start the motorcycle. When the revs are increased, check that the exhaust is neither holed nor leaking from any of its joints. On a linked system, check that the collector box is not leaking due to corrosion.
✔ Note that the exhaust decibel level ("loudness" of the exhaust) is assessed at the discretion of the tester. If the motorcycle was first used on or after 1st January 1985 the silencer must carry the BSAU 193 stamp, or a marking relating to its make and model, or be of OE (original equipment) manufacture. If the silencer is marked NOT FOR ROAD USE, RACING USE ONLY or similar, it will fail the MOT.

Final drive

✔ On chain or belt drive machines, check that the chain/belt is in good condition and does not have excessive slack. Also check that the sprocket is securely mounted on the rear wheel hub. Check that the chain/belt guard is in place.
✔ On shaft drive bikes, check for oil leaking from the drive unit and fouling the rear tyre.

Steering and Suspension

Steering

✔ With the front wheel raised off the ground, rotate the steering from lock to lock. The handlebar or switches must not contact the fuel tank or be close enough to trap the rider's hand. Problems can be caused by damaged lock stops on the lower yoke and frame, or by the fitting of non-standard handlebars.
✔ When performing the lock to lock check, also ensure that the steering moves freely without drag or notchiness. Steering movement can be impaired by poorly routed cables, or by overtight head bearings or worn bearings. The tester will perform a check of the steering head bearing lower race by mounting the front wheel on a surface plate, then performing a lock to lock check with the weight of the machine on the lower bearing (see illustration 3).
✔ Grasp the fork sliders (lower legs) and attempt to push and pull on the forks (see illustration 4). Any play in the steering head bearings will be felt. Note that in extreme cases, wear of the front fork bushes can be misinterpreted for head bearing play.
✔ Check that the handlebars are securely mounted.
✔ Check that the handlebar grip rubbers are secure. They should by bonded to the bar left end and to the throttle cable pulley on the right end.

Front wheel mounted on a surface plate for steering head bearing lower race check

Front suspension

✔ With the motorcycle off the stand, hold the front brake on and pump the front forks up and down (see illustration 5). Check that they are adequately damped.

Checking the steering head bearings for freeplay

Hold the front brake on and pump the front forks up and down to check operation

MOT Test Checks REF•29

Inspect the area around the fork dust seal for oil leakage (arrow)

Bounce the rear of the motorcycle to check rear suspension operation

Checking for rear suspension linkage play

✔ Inspect the area above and around the front fork oil seals **(see illustration 6)**. There should be no sign of oil on the fork tube (stanchion) nor leaking down the slider (lower leg). On models so equipped, check that there is no oil leaking from the anti-dive units.

✔ On models with swingarm front suspension, check that there is no freeplay in the linkage when moved from side to side.

Rear suspension

✔ With the motorcycle off the stand and an assistant supporting the motorcycle by its handlebars, bounce the rear suspension **(see illustration 7)**. Check that the suspension components do not foul on any of the cycle parts and check that the shock absorber(s) provide adequate damping.

✔ Visually inspect the shock absorber(s) and check that there is no sign of oil leakage from its damper. This is somewhat restricted on certain single shock models due to the location of the shock absorber.

✔ With the rear wheel raised off the ground, grasp the wheel at the highest point and attempt to pull it up **(see illustration 8)**. Any play in the swingarm pivot or suspension linkage bearings will be felt as movement. **Note:** *Do not confuse play with actual suspension movement.* Failure to lubricate suspension linkage bearings can lead to bearing failure **(see illustration 9)**.

✔ With the rear wheel raised off the ground, grasp the swingarm ends and attempt to move the swingarm from side to side and forwards and backwards - any play indicates wear of the swingarm pivot bearings **(see illustration 10)**.

Worn suspension linkage pivots (arrows) are usually the cause of play in the rear suspension

Grasp the swingarm at the ends to check for play in its pivot bearings

REF•30 MOT Test Checks

Brake pad wear can usually be viewed without removing the caliper. Most pads have wear indicator grooves (1) and some also have indicator tangs (2)

On drum brakes, check the angle of the operating lever with the brake fully applied. Most drum brakes have a wear indicator pointer and scale.

Brakes, Wheels and Tyres

Brakes

✔ With the wheel raised off the ground, apply the brake then free it off, and check that the wheel is about to revolve freely without brake drag.

✔ On disc brakes, examine the disc itself. Check that it is securely mounted and not cracked.

✔ On disc brakes, view the pad material through the caliper mouth and check that the pads are not worn down beyond the limit **(see illustration 11)**.

✔ On drum brakes, check that when the brake is applied the angle between the operating lever and cable or rod is not too great **(see illustration 12)**. Check also that the operating lever doesn't foul any other components.

✔ On disc brakes, examine the flexible hoses from top to bottom. Have an assistant hold the brake on so that the fluid in the hose is under pressure, and check that there is no sign of fluid leakage, bulges or cracking. If there are any metal brake pipes or unions, check that these are free from corrosion and damage. Where a brake-linked anti-dive system is fitted, check the hoses to the anti-dive in a similar manner.

✔ Check that the rear brake torque arm is secure and that its fasteners are secured by self-locking nuts or castellated nuts with split-pins or R-pins **(see illustration 13)**.

✔ On models with ABS, check that the self-check warning light in the instrument panel works.

✔ The MOT tester will perform a test of the motorcycle's braking efficiency based on a calculation of rider and motorcycle weight. Although this cannot be carried out at home, you can at least ensure that the braking systems are properly maintained. For hydraulic disc brakes, check the fluid level, lever/pedal feel (bleed of air if its spongy) and pad material. For drum brakes, check adjustment, cable or rod operation and shoe lining thickness.

Wheels and tyres

✔ Check the wheel condition. Cast wheels should be free from cracks and if of the built-up design, all fasteners should be secure. Spoked wheels should be checked for broken, corroded, loose or bent spokes.

✔ With the wheel raised off the ground, spin the wheel and visually check that the tyre and wheel run true. Check that the tyre does not foul the suspension or mudguards.

✔ With the wheel raised off the ground, grasp the wheel and attempt to move it about the axle (spindle) **(see illustration 14)**. Any play felt here indicates wheel bearing failure.

Brake torque arm must be properly secured at both ends

Check for wheel bearing play by trying to move the wheel about the axle (spindle)

MOT Test Checks REF•31

Checking the tyre tread depth

Tyre direction of rotation arrow can be found on tyre sidewall

Castellated type wheel axle (spindle) nut must be secured by a split pin or R-pin

Two straightedges are used to check wheel alignment

✔ Check the tyre tread depth, tread condition and sidewall condition **(see illustration 15)**.
✔ Check the tyre type. Front and rear tyre types must be compatible and be suitable for road use. Tyres marked NOT FOR ROAD USE, COMPETITION USE ONLY or similar, will fail the MOT.
✔ If the tyre sidewall carries a direction of rotation arrow, this must be pointing in the direction of normal wheel rotation **(see illustration 16)**.
✔ Check that the wheel axle (spindle) nuts (where applicable) are properly secured. A self-locking nut or castellated nut with a split-pin or R-pin can be used **(see illustration 17)**.
✔ Wheel alignment is checked with the motorcycle off the stand and a rider seated. With the front wheel pointing straight ahead, two perfectly straight lengths of metal or wood and placed against the sidewalls of both tyres **(see illustration 18)**. The gap each side of the front tyre must be equidistant on both sides. Incorrect wheel alignment may be due to a cocked rear wheel (often as the result of poor chain adjustment) or in extreme cases, a bent frame.

General checks and condition

✔ Check the security of all major fasteners, bodypanels, seat, fairings (where fitted) and mudguards.
✔ Check that the rider and pillion footrests, handlebar levers and brake pedal are securely mounted.
✔ Check for corrosion on the frame or any load-bearing components. If severe, this may affect the structure, particularly under stress.

Sidecars

A motorcycle fitted with a sidecar requires additional checks relating to the stability of the machine and security of attachment and swivel joints, plus specific wheel alignment (toe-in) requirements. Additionally, tyre and lighting requirements differ from conventional motorcycle use. Owners are advised to check MOT test requirements with an official test centre.

REF•32 Storage

Preparing for storage

Before you start

If repairs or an overhaul is needed, see that this is carried out now rather than left until you want to ride the bike again.

Give the bike a good wash and scrub all dirt from its underside. Make sure the bike dries completely before preparing for storage.

Engine

● Remove the spark plug(s) and lubricate the cylinder bores with approximately a teaspoon of motor oil using a spout-type oil can **(see illustration 1)**. Reinstall the spark plug(s). Crank the engine over a couple of times to coat the piston rings and bores with oil. If the bike has a kickstart, use this to turn the engine over. If not, flick the kill switch to the OFF position and crank the engine over on the starter **(see illustration 2)**. If the nature on the ignition system prevents the starter operating with the kill switch in the OFF position, remove the spark plugs and fit them back in their caps; ensure that the plugs are earthed (grounded) against the cylinder head when the starter is operated **(see illustration 3)**.

⚠️ **Warning: It is important that the plugs are earthed (grounded) away from the spark plug holes otherwise there is a risk of atomised fuel from the cylinders igniting.**

> **HAYNES HiNT** *On a single cylinder four-stroke engine, you can seal the combustion chamber completely by positioning the piston at TDC on the compression stroke.*

● Drain the carburettor(s) otherwise there is a risk of jets becoming blocked by gum deposits from the fuel **(see illustration 4)**.

● If the bike is going into long-term storage, consider adding a fuel stabiliser to the fuel in the tank. If the tank is drained completely, corrosion of its internal surfaces may occur if left unprotected for a long period. The tank can be treated with a rust preventative especially for this purpose. Alternatively, remove the tank and pour half a litre of motor oil into it, install the filler cap and shake the tank to coat its internals with oil before draining off the excess. The same effect can also be achieved by spraying WD40 or a similar water-dispersant around the inside of the tank via its flexible nozzle.

● Make sure the cooling system contains the correct mix of antifreeze. Antifreeze also contains important corrosion inhibitors.

● The air intakes and exhaust can be sealed off by covering or plugging the openings. Ensure that you do not seal in any condensation; run the engine until it is hot,

1 Squirt a drop of motor oil into each cylinder

2 Flick the kill switch to OFF . . .

3 . . . and ensure that the metal bodies of the plugs (arrows) are earthed against the cylinder head

4 Connect a hose to the carburettor float chamber drain stub (arrow) and unscrew the drain screw

Storage   REF•33

Exhausts can be sealed off with a plastic bag

Disconnect the negative lead (A) first, followed by the positive lead (B)

Use a suitable battery charger - this kit also assess battery condition

then switch off and allow to cool. Tape a piece of thick plastic over the silencer end(s) **(see illustration 5)**. Note that some advocate pouring a tablespoon of motor oil into the silencer(s) before sealing them off.

Battery

● Remove it from the bike - in extreme cases of cold the battery may freeze and crack its case **(see illustration 6)**.

● Check the electrolyte level and top up if necessary (conventional refillable batteries). Clean the terminals.
● Store the battery off the motorcycle and away from any sources of fire. Position a wooden block under the battery if it is to sit on the ground.
● Give the battery a trickle charge for a few hours every month **(see illustration 7)**.

Tyres

● Place the bike on its centrestand or an auxiliary stand which will support the motorcycle in an upright position. Position wood blocks under the tyres to keep them off the ground and to provide insulation from damp. If the bike is being put into long-term storage, ideally both tyres should be off the ground; not only will this protect the tyres, but will also ensure that no load is placed on the steering head or wheel bearings.
● Deflate each tyre by 5 to 10 psi, no more or the beads may unseat from the rim, making subsequent inflation difficult on tubeless tyres.

Pivots and controls

● Lubricate all lever, pedal, stand and footrest pivot points. If grease nipples are fitted to the rear suspension components, apply lubricant to the pivots.
● Lubricate all control cables.

Cycle components

● Apply a wax protectant to all painted and plastic components. Wipe off any excess, but don't polish to a shine. Where fitted, clean the screen with soap and water.
● Coat metal parts with Vaseline (petroleum jelly). When applying this to the fork tubes, do not compress the forks otherwise the seals will rot from contact with the Vaseline.
● Apply a vinyl cleaner to the seat.

Storage conditions

● Aim to store the bike in a shed or garage which does not leak and is free from damp.
● Drape an old blanket or bedspread over the bike to protect it from dust and direct contact with sunlight (which will fade paint). This also hides the bike from prying eyes. Beware of tight-fitting plastic covers which may allow condensation to form and settle on the bike.

Getting back on the road

Engine and transmission

● Change the oil and replace the oil filter. If this was done prior to storage, check that the oil hasn't emulsified - a thick whitish substance which occurs through condensation.
● Remove the spark plugs. Using a spout-type oil can, squirt a few drops of oil into the cylinder(s). This will provide initial lubrication as the piston rings and bores comes back into contact. Service the spark plugs, or fit new ones, and install them in the engine.

● Check that the clutch isn't stuck on. The plates can stick together if left standing for some time, preventing clutch operation. Engage a gear and try rocking the bike back and forth with the clutch lever held against the handlebar. If this doesn't work on cable-operated clutches, hold the clutch lever back against the handlebar with a strong elastic band or cable tie for a couple of hours **(see illustration 8)**.
● If the air intakes or silencer end(s) were blocked off, remove the bung or cover used.
● If the fuel tank was coated with a rust

Hold clutch lever back against the handlebar with elastic bands or a cable tie

Storage

preventative, oil or a stabiliser added to the fuel, drain and flush the tank and dispose of the fuel sensibly. If no action was taken with the fuel tank prior to storage, it is advised that the old fuel is disposed of since it will go off over a period of time. Refill the fuel tank with fresh fuel.

Frame and running gear

● Oil all pivot points and cables.
● Check the tyre pressures. They will definitely need inflating if pressures were reduced for storage.
● Lubricate the final drive chain (where applicable).
● Remove any protective coating applied to the fork tubes (stanchions) since this may well destroy the fork seals. If the fork tubes weren't protected and have picked up rust spots, remove them with very fine abrasive paper and refinish with metal polish.
● Check that both brakes operate correctly. Apply each brake hard and check that it's not possible to move the motorcycle forwards, then check that the brake frees off again once released. Brake caliper pistons can stick due to corrosion around the piston head, or on the sliding caliper types, due to corrosion of the slider pins. If the brake doesn't free after repeated operation, take the caliper off for examination. Similarly drum brakes can stick due to a seized operating cam, cable or rod linkage.
● If the motorcycle has been in long-term storage, renew the brake fluid and clutch fluid (where applicable).
● Depending on where the bike has been stored, the wiring, cables and hoses may have been nibbled by rodents. Make a visual check and investigate disturbed wiring loom tape.

Battery

● If the battery has been previously removal and given top up charges it can simply be reconnected. Remember to connect the positive cable first and the negative cable last.
● On conventional refillable batteries, if the battery has not received any attention, remove it from the motorcycle and check its electrolyte level. Top up if necessary then charge the battery. If the battery fails to hold a charge and a visual checks show heavy white sulphation of the plates, the battery is probably defective and must be renewed. This is particularly likely if the battery is old. Confirm battery condition with a specific gravity check.
● On sealed (MF) batteries, if the battery has not received any attention, remove it from the motorcycle and charge it according to the information on the battery case - if the battery fails to hold a charge it must be renewed.

Starting procedure

● If a kickstart is fitted, turn the engine over a couple of times with the ignition OFF to distribute oil around the engine. If no kickstart is fitted, flick the engine kill switch OFF and the ignition ON and crank the engine over a couple of times to work oil around the upper cylinder components. If the nature of the ignition system is such that the starter won't work with the kill switch OFF, remove the spark plugs, fit them back into their caps and earth (ground) their bodies on the cylinder head. Reinstall the spark plugs afterwards.
● Switch the kill switch to RUN, operate the choke and start the engine. If the engine won't start don't continue cranking the engine - not only will this flatten the battery, but the starter motor will overheat. Switch the ignition off and try again later. If the engine refuses to start, go through the fault finding procedures in this manual. **Note:** *If the bike has been in storage for a long time, old fuel or a carburettor blockage may be the problem. Gum deposits in carburettors can block jets - if a carburettor cleaner doesn't prove successful the carburettors must be dismantled for cleaning.*
● Once the engine has started, check that the lights, turn signals and horn work properly.
● Treat the bike gently for the first ride and check all fluid levels on completion. Settle the bike back into the maintenance schedule.

Fault Finding REF•35

This Section provides an easy reference-guide to the more common faults that are likely to afflict your machine. Obviously, the opportunities are almost limitless for faults to occur as a result of obscure failures, and to try and cover all eventualities would require a book. Indeed, a number have been written on the subject.

Successful troubleshooting is not a mysterious 'black art' but the application of a bit of knowledge combined with a systematic and logical approach to the problem. Approach any troubleshooting by first accurately identifying the symptom and then checking through the list of possible causes, starting with the simplest or most obvious and progressing in stages to the most complex.

Take nothing for granted, but above all apply liberal quantities of common sense.

The main symptom of a fault is given in the text as a major heading below which are listed the various systems or areas which may contain the fault. Details of each possible cause for a fault and the remedial action to be taken are given, in brief, in the paragraphs below each heading. Further information should be sought in the relevant Chapter.

1 Engine doesn't start or is difficult to start
- [ ] Starter motor doesn't rotate
- [ ] Starter motor rotates but engine does not turn over
- [ ] Starter works but engine won't turn over (seized)
- [ ] No fuel flow
- [ ] Engine flooded
- [ ] No spark or weak spark
- [ ] Compression low
- [ ] Stalls after starting
- [ ] Rough idle

2 Poor running at low speed
- [ ] Spark weak
- [ ] Fuel/air mixture incorrect
- [ ] Compression low
- [ ] Poor acceleration

3 Poor running or no power at high speed
- [ ] Firing incorrect
- [ ] Fuel/air mixture incorrect
- [ ] Compression low
- [ ] Knocking or pinking
- [ ] Miscellaneous causes

4 Overheating
- [ ] Engine overheats
- [ ] Firing incorrect
- [ ] Fuel/air mixture incorrect
- [ ] Compression too high
- [ ] Engine load excessive
- [ ] Lubrication inadequate
- [ ] Miscellaneous causes

5 Clutch problems
- [ ] Clutch slipping
- [ ] Clutch not disengaging completely

6 Gearchanging problems
- [ ] Doesn't go into gear, or lever doesn't return
- [ ] Jumps out of gear
- [ ] Overselects

7 Abnormal engine noise
- [ ] Knocking or pinking
- [ ] Piston slap or rattling
- [ ] Valve noise
- [ ] Other noise

8 Abnormal driveline noise
- [ ] Clutch noise
- [ ] Transmission noise
- [ ] Final drive noise

9 Abnormal frame and suspension noise
- [ ] Front end noise
- [ ] Shock absorber noise
- [ ] Brake noise

10 Oil pressure warning light comes on
- [ ] Engine lubrication system
- [ ] Electrical system

11 Excessive exhaust smoke
- [ ] White smoke
- [ ] Black smoke
- [ ] Brown smoke

12 Poor handling or stability
- [ ] Handlebar hard to turn
- [ ] Handlebar shakes or vibrates excessively
- [ ] Handlebar pulls to one side
- [ ] Poor shock absorbing qualities

13 Braking problems
- [ ] Brakes are spongy, don't hold
- [ ] Brake lever or pedal pulsates
- [ ] Brakes drag

14 Electrical problems
- [ ] Battery dead or weak
- [ ] Battery overcharged

REF•36 Fault Finding

1 Engine doesn't start or is difficult to start

Starter motor doesn't rotate
- [ ] Engine kill switch OFF.
- [ ] Fuse blown. Check main fuse and FI fuses (Chapter 8).
- [ ] Battery voltage low. Check and recharge battery (Chapter 8).
- [ ] Starter motor defective. Make sure the wiring to the starter is secure. Make sure the starter relay clicks when the start button is pushed. If the relay clicks, then the fault is in the wiring or motor (Chapter 8).
- [ ] Starter switch not contacting. The contacts could be wet, corroded or dirty. Disassemble and clean the switch (Chapter 8).
- [ ] Wiring open or shorted. Check all wiring connections and harnesses to make sure that they are dry, tight and not corroded. Also check for broken or frayed wires that can cause a short to ground (earth) (see *Wiring diagrams*, Chapter 8).
- [ ] Ignition switch defective. Check the switch and replace with a new one if it is defective (Chapter 8).
- [ ] Engine kill switch defective. Check for wet, dirty or corroded contacts. Clean or replace the switch with a new one as necessary (Chapter 8).
- [ ] Faulty neutral switch, sidestand switch or clutch switch. Check the wiring to each switch and the switch itself (Chapter 8).
- [ ] Faulty diode (Chapter 8).
- [ ] Fuel injection system shutdown due to system fault (Chapter 4).

Starter motor rotates but engine does not turn over
- [ ] Starter clutch defective. Inspect and repair or replace with a new one (Chapter 2).
- [ ] Damaged idler or starter gears. Inspect and replace the damaged parts (Chapter 2).

Starter works but engine won't turn over (seized)
- [ ] Seized engine caused by one or more internally damaged components. Failure due to wear, abuse or lack of lubrication. Damage can include seized valves, followers, camshafts, pistons, crankshaft, connecting rod bearings, or transmission gears or bearings. Refer to Chapter 2 for engine disassembly.

No fuel flow
- [ ] No fuel in tank.
- [ ] Fuel tank breather hose obstructed.
- [ ] Faulty fuel cut-off relay. Check the relay (Chapter 4).
- [ ] Fuel pump faulty or blocked (Chapter 4).
- [ ] Fuel hose clogged. Remove the fuel hose and carefully blow through it.
- [ ] Fuel rail or injector clogged. For all of the injectors to be clogged, either a very bad batch of fuel with an unusual additive has been used, or some other foreign material has entered the tank. In some cases, if a machine has been unused for several months, the fuel turns to a varnish-like liquid which can cause an injector needle to stick to its seat. Drain the tank and fuel system (Chapter 4).

Engine flooded
- [ ] Injector needle valve worn or stuck open causing excess fuel to be admitted to the throttle body. In this case, the injectors should be renewed.
- [ ] Starting technique incorrect. Under normal circumstances (i.e. if all the components of the fuel injection system are good) the machine should start with the throttle closed.

No spark or weak spark
- [ ] Ignition switch OFF.
- [ ] Engine kill switch turned to the OFF position.
- [ ] Ignition or kill switch shorted. This is usually caused by water, corrosion, damage or excessive wear. The switches can be disassembled and cleaned with electrical contact cleaner. If cleaning does not help, replace the switches (Chapter 8).
- [ ] Battery voltage low. Check and recharge the battery as necessary (Chapter 8).
- [ ] Spark plug caps not making good contact. Make sure that the caps fit snugly over the plug ends.
- [ ] Spark plugs dirty, defective or worn out. Locate reason for fouled plugs using spark plug condition chart on the inside back cover and follow the plug maintenance procedures (Chapter 1).
- [ ] Incorrect spark plugs. Wrong type or heat range. Check and install correct plugs (Chapter 1).
- [ ] Ignition coil or spark plug cap defective. Test and renew if necessary (Chapter 4).
- [ ] Fuel injection system shutdown due to system fault (Chapter 4).
- [ ] Crankshaft position (CKP) sensor defective (Chapter 4).
- [ ] Faulty engine stop relay or lean angle sensor (Chapter 4).
- [ ] Engine control module (ECM) defective (Chapter 4).
- [ ] Wiring shorted or broken between:
    a) Ignition switch and engine kill switch (or blown fuse)
    b) ECM and engine kill switch
    c) ECM and ignition coils
    d) ECM and CKP sensor
- [ ] Make sure that all wiring connections are clean, dry and tight. Look for chafed and broken wires (Chapters 4 and 8).

Compression low
- [ ] Spark plugs loose. Remove the plugs and inspect their threads. Reinstall and tighten securely (Chapter 1).
- [ ] Cylinder head not sufficiently tightened down. If the cylinder head is suspected of being loose, then there's a chance that the gasket or head is damaged if the problem has persisted for any length of time. The head bolts should be tightened to the proper torque and in the correct sequence (Chapter 2).
- [ ] Improper valve clearance. This means that the valve is not closing completely and compression pressure is leaking past the valve. Check and adjust the valve clearances (Chapter 1).
- [ ] Cylinder and/or piston worn. Excessive wear will cause compression pressure to leak past the rings. This is usually accompanied by worn rings as well. A top-end overhaul is necessary (Chapter 2).
- [ ] Piston rings worn, weak, broken, or sticking. Broken or sticking piston rings usually indicate a lubrication or fuelling problem that causes excess carbon deposits to form on the pistons and rings. Top-end overhaul is necessary (Chapter 2).
- [ ] Piston ring-to-groove clearance excessive. This is caused by excessive wear of the piston ring lands. Piston renewal is necessary (Chapter 2).
- [ ] Cylinder head gasket damaged. If a head is allowed to become loose, or if excessive carbon build-up on the piston crown and combustion chamber causes extremely high compression, the head gasket may leak. Retorquing the head is not always sufficient to restore the seal, so a new gasket is necessary (Chapter 2).
- [ ] Cylinder head warped. This is caused by overheating or improperly tightened head bolts. Machine shop resurfacing or head renewal is necessary (Chapter 2).
- [ ] Valve spring broken or weak. Caused by component failure or wear; the springs must be renewed (Chapter 2).
- [ ] Valve not seating properly. This is caused by a bent valve (from over-revving or improper valve adjustment), burned valve or seat (improper fuelling) or an accumulation of carbon deposits on the seat. The valves must be cleaned and/or renewed and the seats serviced (Chapter 2).

Fault Finding REF•37

1 Engine doesn't start or is difficult to start (continued)

Stalls after starting
- ☐ Engine idle speed incorrect. Faulty idle speed control system (Chapter 4).
- ☐ Ignition malfunction (Chapter 4).
- ☐ Fuel injection system malfunction (Chapter 4).
- ☐ Fuel contaminated. The fuel can be contaminated with either dirt or water, or can change chemically if the machine has been unused for several months. Drain the tank and fuel system (Chapter 4).
- ☐ Intake air leak. Check for loose throttle body-to-intake manifold connections or a loose or damaged PAIR vacuum hose (Chapter 4).

Rough idle
- ☐ Idle speed incorrect (Chapter 4).
- ☐ Ignition fault (Chapter 4).
- ☐ Fuel injection system malfunction (Chapter 4).
- ☐ Fuel contaminated. The fuel can be contaminated with either dirt or water, or can change chemically if the machine has been unused for several months. Drain the tank and the fuel system (Chapter 4).
- ☐ Intake air leak. Check for loose throttle body-to-intake manifold connections or a loose or damaged PAIR vacuum hose (Chapter 4).
- ☐ Air filter clogged. Clean the air filter element or replace it with a new one (Chapter 1).

2 Poor running at low speeds

Spark weak
- ☐ Battery voltage low. Check and recharge battery (Chapter 8).
- ☐ Spark plug caps not making good contact. Make sure that the caps fit snugly over the plug ends.
- ☐ Spark plugs dirty, defective or worn out. Locate reason for fouled plugs using spark plug condition chart on the inside back cover and follow the plug maintenance procedures (Chapter 1).
- ☐ Incorrect spark plugs. Wrong type or heat range. Check and install correct plugs (Chapter 1).
- ☐ Ignition coil or spark plug cap defective. Test and renew if necessary (Chapter 4).

Fuel/air mixture incorrect
- ☐ Fuel tank breather hose obstructed.
- ☐ Fuel pump faulty or blocked (Chapter 4).
- ☐ Fuel hose clogged. Remove the fuel hose and carefully blow through it.
- ☐ Fuel rail or injector clogged. For all of the injectors to be clogged, either a very bad batch of fuel with an unusual additive has been used, or some other foreign material has entered the tank. In some cases, if a machine has been unused for several months, the fuel turns to a varnish-like liquid which can cause an injector needle to stick to its seat. Drain the tank and fuel system (Chapter 4).
- ☐ Intake air leak. Check for loose throttle body-to-intake duct connections, or loose or damaged vacuum hoses (Chapter 4).
- ☐ Air filter clogged. Clean the air filter element or replace it with a new one (Chapter 1).

Compression low
- ☐ Spark plugs loose. Remove the plugs and inspect their threads. Reinstall and tighten securely (Chapter 1).
- ☐ Cylinder head not sufficiently tightened down. If the cylinder head is suspected of being loose, then there's a chance that the gasket or head is damaged if the problem has persisted for any length of time. The head bolts should be tightened to the proper torque and in the correct sequence (Chapter 2).
- ☐ Improper valve clearance. This means that the valve is not closing completely and compression pressure is leaking past the valve. Check and adjust the valve clearances (Chapter 1).
- ☐ Cylinder and/or piston worn. Excessive wear will cause compression pressure to leak past the rings. This is usually accompanied by worn rings as well. A top-end overhaul is necessary (Chapter 2).
- ☐ Piston rings worn, weak, broken, or sticking. Broken or sticking piston rings usually indicate a lubrication or fuelling problem that causes excess carbon deposits to form on the pistons and rings. Top-end overhaul is necessary (Chapter 2).
- ☐ Piston ring-to-groove clearance excessive. This is caused by excessive wear of the piston ring lands. Piston renewal is necessary (Chapter 2).
- ☐ Cylinder head gasket damaged. If the head is allowed to become loose, or if excessive carbon build-up on the piston crown and combustion chamber causes extremely high compression, the head gasket may leak. Retorquing the head is not always sufficient to restore the seal, so a new gasket is necessary (Chapter 2).
- ☐ Cylinder head warped. This is caused by overheating or improperly tightened head bolts. Machine shop resurfacing or head renewal is necessary (Chapter 2).
- ☐ Valve spring broken or weak. Caused by component failure or wear; the springs must be renewed (Chapter 2).
- ☐ Valve not seating properly. This is caused by a bent valve (from over-revving or improper valve adjustment), burned valve or seat (improper fuelling) or an accumulation of carbon deposits on the seat (from fuelling or lubrication problems). The valves must be cleaned and/or renewed and the seats serviced (Chapter 2).

Poor acceleration
- ☐ Timing not advancing. The crankshaft position sensor (CKP) or the engine control module (ECM) may be defective (Chapter 4). If so, they must be renewed.
- ☐ Engine oil viscosity too high. Using a heavier oil than that recommended in Chapter 1 can damage the oil pump or lubrication system and cause drag on the engine.
- ☐ Brakes dragging. Usually caused by debris which has entered the brake caliper piston seals, or from a warped disc or bent axle (Chapter 6).

Fault Finding

3 Poor running or no power at high speed

Firing incorrect

- ☐ Spark plug caps not making good contact. Make sure that the caps fit snugly over the plug ends and that the wiring is secure.
- ☐ Spark plugs dirty, defective or worn out. Locate reason for fouled plugs using spark plug condition chart on the inside back cover and follow the plug maintenance procedures (Chapter 1).
- ☐ Incorrect spark plugs. Wrong type or heat range. Check and install correct plugs (Chapter 1).
- ☐ Ignition coil or spark plug cap defective. Test and renew if necessary (Chapter 4).
- ☐ Faulty ECM (engine control module) (Chapter 4).

Fuel/air mixture incorrect

- ☐ Fuel tank breather hose obstructed.
- ☐ Fuel pump faulty or blocked (Chapter 4).
- ☐ Fuel hose clogged. Remove the fuel hose and carefully blow through it.
- ☐ Fuel rail or injector clogged. For all of the injectors to be clogged, either a very bad batch of fuel with an unusual additive has been used, or some other foreign material has entered the tank. In some cases, if a machine has been unused for several months, the fuel turns to a varnish-like liquid which can cause an injector needle to stick to its seat. Drain the tank and fuel system (Chapter 4).
- ☐ Intake air leak. Check for loose throttle body-to-intake duct connections, or loose or damaged vacuum hoses (Chapter 4).
- ☐ Air filter clogged. Clean the air filter element or replace it with a new one (Chapter 1).

Compression low

- ☐ Spark plugs loose. Remove the plugs and inspect their threads. Reinstall and tighten securely (Chapter 1).
- ☐ Cylinder head not sufficiently tightened down. If the cylinder head is suspected of being loose, then there's a chance that the gasket or head is damaged if the problem has persisted for any length of time. The head bolts should be tightened to the proper torque and in the correct sequence (Chapter 2).
- ☐ Improper valve clearance. This means that the valve is not closing completely and compression pressure is leaking past the valve. Check and adjust the valve clearances (Chapter 1).
- ☐ Cylinder and/or piston worn. Excessive wear will cause compression pressure to leak past the rings. This is usually accompanied by worn rings as well. A top-end overhaul is necessary (Chapter 2).
- ☐ Piston rings worn, weak, broken, or sticking. Broken or sticking piston rings usually indicate a lubrication or fuelling problem that causes excess carbon deposits to form on the pistons and rings. Top-end overhaul is necessary (Chapter 2).
- ☐ Piston ring-to-groove clearance excessive. This is caused by excessive wear of the piston ring lands. Piston renewal is necessary (Chapter 2).
- ☐ Cylinder head gasket damaged. If a head is allowed to become loose, or if excessive carbon build-up on the piston crown and combustion chamber causes extremely high compression, the head gasket may leak. Retorquing the head is not always sufficient to restore the seal, so a new gasket is necessary (Chapter 2).
- ☐ Cylinder head warped. This is caused by overheating or improperly tightened head bolts. Machine shop resurfacing or head renewal is necessary (Chapter 2).
- ☐ Valve spring broken or weak. Caused by component failure or wear; the springs must be replaced with new ones (Chapter 2).
- ☐ Valve not seating properly. This is caused by a bent valve (from over-revving or improper valve adjustment), burned valve or seat (improper fuelling) or an accumulation of carbon deposits on the seat (from fuelling or lubrication problems). The valves must be cleaned and/or renewed and the seats serviced (Chapter 2).

Knocking or pinking

- ☐ Carbon build-up in combustion chamber. Use of a fuel additive that will dissolve the adhesive bonding the carbon particles to the piston crown and chamber is the easiest way to remove the build-up. Otherwise, the cylinder head will have to be removed and decarbonised (Chapter 2).
- ☐ Incorrect or poor quality fuel. Old or improper grades of fuel can cause detonation. This causes the piston to rattle, thus the knocking or pinking sound. Drain old fuel and always use the recommended fuel grade.
- ☐ Spark plug heat range incorrect. Uncontrolled detonation indicates the plug heat range is too hot. The plug in effect becomes a glow plug, raising cylinder temperatures. Install the proper heat range plug (Chapter 1).
- ☐ Improper air/fuel mixture. This will cause the cylinders to run hot, which leads to detonation. A blockage in the fuel system or an air leak can cause this imbalance (Chapter 4).

Miscellaneous causes

- ☐ Throttle valve doesn't open fully. Adjust the throttle twistgrip freeplay (Chapter 1).
- ☐ Clutch slipping due loose or worn clutch components (Chapter 2).
- ☐ Timing not advancing. The crankshaft position sensor (CKP) or the engine control module (ECM) may be defective (Chapter 4). If so, they must be replaced with new ones.
- ☐ Engine oil viscosity too high. Using a heavier oil than the one recommended in Chapter 1 can damage the oil pump or lubrication system and cause drag on the engine.
- ☐ Brakes dragging. Usually caused by debris which has entered the brake caliper piston seals, or from a warped disc or bent axle (Chapter 6).

Fault Finding REF•39

4 Overheating

Engine overheats
- [ ] Coolant level low. Check the level and add coolant (see *Pre-ride checks*).
- [ ] Leak in cooling system. Check cooling system hoses and radiator for leaks and other damage. Repair or renew parts as necessary (Chapter 3).
- [ ] Faulty thermostat. Check and renew as described in Chapter 3.
- [ ] Faulty radiator cap. Remove the cap and have it pressure tested.
- [ ] Coolant passages clogged. Have the entire system drained and flushed, then refill with fresh coolant.
- [ ] Water pump defective. Remove the pump and check the components (Chapter 3).
- [ ] Clogged or damaged radiator fins (Chapter 3).
- [ ] Faulty cooling fan, relay or ECT sensor (Chapter 3).

Firing incorrect
- [ ] Wrongly connected ignition coil wiring or plug leads.
- [ ] Spark plugs dirty, defective or worn out. Locate reason for fouled plugs using spark plug condition chart on the inside back cover and follow the plug maintenance procedures (Chapter 1).
- [ ] Incorrect spark plugs. Wrong type or heat range. Check and install correct plugs (Chapter 1).
- [ ] Ignition coil or spark plug cap defective. Test and replace with a new one if necessary (Chapter 4).
- [ ] Faulty ECM (engine control module) (Chapter 4).

Fuel/air mixture incorrect
- [ ] Fuel tank breather hose obstructed.
- [ ] Fuel pump faulty or blocked (Chapter 4).
- [ ] Fuel hose clogged. Remove the fuel hose and carefully blow through it.
- [ ] Fuel rail or injector clogged. For all of the injectors to be clogged, either a very bad batch of fuel with an unusual additive has been used, or some other foreign material has entered the tank. In some cases, if a machine has been unused for several months, the fuel turns to a varnish-like liquid which can cause an injector needle to stick to its seat. Drain the tank and fuel system (Chapter 4).
- [ ] Intake air leak. Check for loose throttle body-to-intake duct connections, or loose or damaged vacuum hoses (Chapter 4).
- [ ] Air filter clogged. Clean the air filter element or replace it with a new one (Chapter 1).

Compression too high
- [ ] Carbon build-up in combustion chamber. Use of a fuel additive that will dissolve the adhesive bonding the carbon particles to the piston crown and chamber is the easiest way to remove the build-up. Otherwise, the cylinder head will have to be removed and decarbonised (Chapter 2).
- [ ] Improperly machined head surface or installation of incorrect gasket during engine assembly.

Engine load excessive
- [ ] Clutch slipping due to loose or worn clutch components (Chapter 2).
- [ ] Engine oil level too high. Too much oil will cause pressurisation of the crankcase and inefficient engine operation. Check Specifications and drain to proper level (Chapter 1 and *Pre-ride checks*).
- [ ] Engine oil viscosity too high. Using a heavier oil than the one recommended in Chapter 1 can damage the oil pump or lubrication system as well as cause drag on the engine.
- [ ] Brakes dragging. Usually caused by debris which has entered the brake caliper piston seals, or from a warped disc or bent axle (Chapter 6).

Lubrication inadequate
- [ ] Engine oil level too low. Friction caused by intermittent lack of lubrication or from oil that is overworked can cause overheating. The oil provides a definite cooling function in the engine. Check the oil level (see *Pre-ride checks*).
- [ ] Low engine oil pressure. Check the pressure (Chapter 2).
- [ ] Blocked oil filter or oil cooler (Chapters 1 and 2).
- [ ] Poor quality engine oil or incorrect viscosity or type. Oil is rated not only according to viscosity but also according to type. Some oils are not rated high enough for use in this engine. Check the Specifications section and change to the correct oil (Chapter 1).

Miscellaneous causes
- [ ] Modification to exhaust system. Most aftermarket exhaust systems cause the engine to run leaner, which make them run hotter. When installing an accessory exhaust system, always check with the manufacturer/supplier as to whether the ECM requires re-mapping.

5 Clutch problems

Clutch slipping
- [ ] Clutch plates worn or warped. Overhaul the clutch assembly (Chapter 2).
- [ ] Clutch springs broken or weak. Old or heat-damaged (from slipping clutch) springs should be renewed (Chapter 2).
- [ ] Faulty clutch release mechanism. Check the pushrod and release cylinder components (Chapter 2).
- [ ] Clutch centre or housing unevenly worn. This causes improper engagement of the plates. Replace the damaged or worn parts (Chapter 2).

Clutch not disengaging completely
- [ ] Clutch fluid level low (see *Pre-ride checks*).
- [ ] Clutch master cylinder seals or release cylinder seals worn (Chapter 2).
- [ ] Clutch plates warped or damaged. This will cause clutch drag, which in turn will cause the machine to creep. Overhaul the clutch assembly (Chapter 2).
- [ ] Clutch springs fatigued or broken. Check and renew the springs (Chapter 2).
- [ ] Engine oil deteriorated. Old, thin oil will not provide proper lubrication for the plates, causing the clutch to drag. Renew the oil and filter (Chapter 1).
- [ ] Engine oil viscosity too high. Using a heavier oil than recommended in Chapter 1 can cause the plates to stick together. Change to the correct weight oil.
- [ ] Clutch housing guide seized on the transmission input shaft. Lack of lubrication, severe wear or damage can cause the bearing to seize. Overhaul of the clutch, and perhaps transmission, may be necessary to repair the damage (Chapter 2).
- [ ] Loose clutch centre nut. Causes housing and centre misalignment putting a drag on the engine. Engagement adjustment continually varies. Overhaul the clutch assembly (Chapter 2).

REF•40 Fault Finding

6 Gearchanging problems

Doesn't go into gear or lever doesn't return
- [ ] Clutch not disengaging (above).
- [ ] Gearchange mechanism stopper arm spring weak or broken, or arm roller broken or worn. Replace the spring or arm with a new one (Chapter 2).
- [ ] Selector fork(s) bent, worn or seized. Overhaul the transmission (Chapter 2).
- [ ] Gear(s) stuck on shaft. Most often caused by a lack of lubrication or excessive wear in transmission bearings and bushes. Overhaul the transmission (Chapter 2).
- [ ] Selector drum binding. Caused by lubrication failure or excessive wear. Replace the drum and/or its bearing with a new one (Chapter 2).
- [ ] Gearchange mechanism return spring weak or broken (Chapter 2).
- [ ] Gearchange linkage arm broken. Splines stripped out of arm or shaft, caused by a loose linkage arm pinch bolt or from dropping the machine (Chapter 2).

Jumps out of gear
- [ ] Selector fork(s) worn (Chapter 2).
- [ ] Selector fork groove(s) in selector drum worn (Chapter 2).
- [ ] Gear pinion dogs or dog slots worn or damaged. The gear pinions should be inspected and renewed. No attempt should be made to repair the worn parts.

Overselects
- [ ] Gearchange mechanism stopper arm spring weak or broken, or arm roller broken or worn. Renew the spring or arm (Chapter 2).
- [ ] Gearchange mechanism return spring weak or broken (Chapter 2).

7 Abnormal engine noise

Knocking or pinking
- [ ] Carbon build-up in combustion chamber. Use of a fuel additive that will dissolve the adhesive bonding the carbon particles to the piston crown and chamber is the easiest way to remove the build-up. Otherwise, the cylinder head will have to be removed and decarbonised (Chapter 2).
- [ ] Incorrect or poor quality fuel. Old or improper grades of fuel can cause detonation. This causes the pistons to rattle, thus the knocking or pinking sound. Drain old fuel and always use the recommended fuel grade.
- [ ] Spark plug heat range incorrect. Uncontrolled detonation indicates the plug heat range is too hot. The plug in effect becomes a glow plug, raising cylinder temperatures. Install the proper heat range plug (Chapter 1).
- [ ] Improper air/fuel mixture. This will cause the cylinders to run hot, which leads to detonation. A blockage in the fuel system or an air leak can cause this imbalance (Chapter 4).

Piston slap or rattling
- [ ] Cylinder-to-piston clearance excessive. Cylinder and/or piston worn, usually accompanied by worn rings as well. A top-end overhaul is necessary (Chapter 2).
- [ ] Piston ring(s) worn, broken or sticking. Overhaul the top-end (Chapter 2).
- [ ] Piston pin, piston pin bore or connecting rod small-end worn from high mileage or seized due to lack of lubrication (Chapter 2).
- [ ] Piston seizure damage. Usually from lack of lubrication or overheating. Replace the pistons and upper crankcase, as necessary (Chapter 2).
- [ ] Connecting rod big-end clearance excessive. Caused by excessive wear or lack of lubrication. Replace worn parts.
- [ ] Connecting rod bent. Caused by over-revving, trying to start a badly flooded engine or from ingesting a foreign object into the combustion chamber. Replace the damaged parts (Chapter 2).

Valve noise
- [ ] Incorrect valve clearances – check and adjust (Chapter 1).
- [ ] Valve spring broken or weak. Check and replace weak valve springs with new ones (Chapter 2).
- [ ] Camshaft or camshaft journals in the cylinder head worn or damaged. Lubrication failure at high rpm is usually the cause of damage due to insufficient oil or failure to change the oil at the recommended intervals. Since there are no replaceable bearings in the head, the head itself will have to be replaced with a new one (Chapter 2).

Other noise
- [ ] Cylinder head gasket leaking. Check around the joint for blowing with the engine running.
- [ ] Exhaust pipe leaking at cylinder head connection. Caused by incorrect fit of pipe(s), loose exhaust flange or damaged gasket. All exhaust system fasteners should be tightened evenly and carefully to avoid leaks (Chapter 4).
- [ ] Crankshaft runout excessive. Caused by a bent crankshaft (from over-revving) or damage from an upper cylinder component failure. Can also be attributed to dropping the machine on either of the crankshaft ends.
- [ ] Engine mounting bolts loose – ensure all the bolts are tightened to the specified torque settings (Chapter 2).
- [ ] Crankshaft bearings worn (Chapter 2).
- [ ] Cam chain rattle, due to worn chain or defective tensioner. Also worn chain tensioner/guide blades (Chapter 2).
- [ ] Gear whine or clatter from the front of the engine. Too little or too much backlash between the balancer shaft gear and its drive gear on the crankshaft. Carry out the dynamic backlash adjustment procedure (Chapter 2).

Fault Finding

8 Abnormal driveline noise

Clutch noise
- [ ] Clutch housing/friction plate clearance excessive (Chapter 2).
- [ ] Wear between the clutch housing splines and input shaft splines (Chapter 2).
- [ ] Worn release bearing (Chapter 2).

Transmission noise
- [ ] Bearings worn. Also includes the possibility that the shafts are worn. Overhaul the transmission (Chapter 2).
- [ ] Gears worn or chipped (Chapter 2).
- [ ] Metal chips jammed in gear teeth. Probably pieces from a broken clutch, gear or selector mechanism that were picked up by the gears. This will cause early bearing failure (Chapter 2).
- [ ] Engine oil level too low. Causes a howl from transmission. Also affects engine power and clutch operation (see *Pre-ride checks*).

Final drive noise
- [ ] Chain not adjusted properly (Chapter 1).
- [ ] Front or rear sprocket loose. Tighten fasteners (Chapter 6).
- [ ] Sprockets and/or chain worn. Fit new sprockets and chain (Chapter 6).
- [ ] Rear sprocket warped. Fit a new sprocket (Chapter 6).
- [ ] Rubber dampers worn in sprocket coupling (Chapter 6).

9 Abnormal frame and suspension noise

Front end noise
- [ ] Low fluid level or improper viscosity oil in forks. This can sound like spurting and is usually accompanied by irregular fork action (Chapter 5).
- [ ] Spring weak or broken. Makes a clicking or scraping sound. Fork oil, when drained, will have a lot of metal particles in it (Chapter 5).
- [ ] Steering head bearings loose or damaged. Clicks when braking. Check and adjust or replace with new ones as necessary (Chapters 1 and 5).
- [ ] Fork yoke clamp bolts loose – ensure all the bolts are tightened to the specified torque (Chapter 6).
- [ ] Forks bent. Good possibility if machine has been dropped. Replace the inner and outer tubes with new ones as required (Chapter 5).
- [ ] Front axle or axle pinch bolts loose. Tighten them to the specified torque (Chapter 6).
- [ ] Loose or worn wheel bearings. Check and replace with new ones as needed (Chapters 1 and 6).

Shock absorber noise
- [ ] Fluid level incorrect. Indicates a leak caused by defective seal. Shock will be covered with oil. Replace shock with a new one or seek advice on repair from a suspension specialist (Chapter 5).
- [ ] Defective shock absorber with internal damage. This is in the body of the shock and can't be remedied. The shock must be replaced with a new one or rebuilt (Chapter 5).
- [ ] Bent or damaged shock body. Replace the shock with a new one (Chapter 5).
- [ ] Loose or worn suspension linkage components (CBF1000/A models). Check and replace with new ones as necessary (Chapter 5).

Brake noise
- [ ] Squeal caused by pad shim not installed or positioned correctly (where fitted) (Chapter 6).
- [ ] Squeal caused by dust on brake pads. Usually found in combination with glazed pads. Clean using brake cleaning solvent (Chapter 6).
- [ ] Pads glazed. Caused by excessive heat from prolonged hard use or from contamination. DO NOT use sandpaper, emery cloth, carborundum cloth or any other abrasive to roughen the pad surfaces as abrasives will stay in the pad material and damage the disc. A very fine flat file can be used, but new pads is the best remedy (Chapter 6).
- [ ] Contamination of brake pads. Oil or brake fluid can cause the brake pads to chatter or squeal. Fit new pads. Identify the cause of the contamination, especially check the caliper piston seals for leaking fluid. Clean disc thoroughly with brake system cleaner (Chapter 6).
- [ ] Disc warped. Can cause a chattering, clicking or intermittent squeal. Usually accompanied by a pulsating lever and uneven braking. Replace the disc with new one (Chapter 6).
- [ ] Loose or worn wheel bearings. Check and replace with new ones as needed (Chapters 1 and 6).

10 Oil pressure warning light comes on

Engine lubrication system
- [ ] Engine oil level low. Inspect for leak or other problem causing low oil level and add recommended oil (see *Pre-ride checks*).
- [ ] Engine oil pump defective, blocked oil strainer gauze or failed pressure relief valve. Carry out an oil pressure check (Chapter 2).
- [m] Engine oil viscosity too low. Very old, thin oil or an improper weight of oil used in the engine. Change to correct oil (Chapter 1).
- [ ] Camshaft or crankshaft journals worn. Excessive wear causing drop in oil pressure. Abnormal wear could be caused by oil starvation at high rpm from low oil level or improper weight or type of oil (Chapter 1).

Electrical system
- [ ] Oil pressure switch defective. Check the switch according to the procedure in Chapter 8. Replace it with a new one it if it is defective.
- [ ] Oil pressure warning LED defective. Check for pinched, shorted, disconnected or damaged wiring (Chapter 8).

Fault Finding

11 Excessive exhaust smoke

White smoke
- ☐ Piston rings worn or broken, causing oil from the crankcase to be pulled past the piston into the combustion chamber. Replace the rings with new ones (Chapter 2).
- ☐ Cylinders worn or scored. Caused by overheating or oil starvation. Rebore cylinders (Chapter 2).
- ☐ Valve stem oil seal damaged or worn. Replace the oil seals with new ones (Chapter 2).
- ☐ Valve guide worn. Perform a complete valve job (Chapter 2).
- ☐ Engine oil level too high, which causes the oil to be forced past the rings. Drain oil to the proper level (see *Pre-ride checks*).
- ☐ Head gasket broken between oil return and cylinder. Causes oil to be pulled into the combustion chamber. Replace the head gasket with a new ones and check the head for warpage (Chapter 2).
- ☐ Abnormal crankcase pressurisation which forces oil past the rings, usually caused by a clogged breather.

Black smoke
- ☐ Air filter clogged. Clean the air filter element or replace it with a new one (Chapter 1).
- ☐ Fuel injection system malfunction (Chapter 4).

Brown smoke
- ☐ Air filter poorly sealed or not installed (Chapter 1).
- ☐ Fuel injection system malfunction (Chapter 4).

12 Poor handling or stability

Handlebar hard to turn
- ☐ Steering head bearing adjuster nut too tight. Check adjustment as described in Chapter 1.
- ☐ Bearings damaged. Roughness can be felt as the bars are turned from side-to-side. Replace the bearings with new ones (Chapter 5).
- ☐ Races dented or worn. Denting results from wear in only one position (e.g., straight ahead), from a collision or hitting a pothole or from dropping the machine. Replace the bearings with new ones (Chapter 5).
- ☐ Steering stem lubrication inadequate. Causes are grease getting hard from age or being washed out by high pressure car washes. Disassemble steering head and repack bearings (Chapter 5).
- ☐ Steering stem bent. Caused by a collision, hitting a pothole or by dropping the machine. Replace damaged part. Don't try to straighten the steering stem (Chapter 5).
- ☐ Front tyre air pressure too low (see *Pre-ride checks*).

Handlebar shakes or vibrates excessively
- ☐ Tyres worn or out of balance (Chapter 6).
- ☐ Swingarm bearings worn. Replace the bearings with new ones (Chapter 5).
- ☐ Wheel rim(s) warped or damaged. Inspect wheels for runout (Chapter 6).
- ☐ Wheel bearings worn. Worn front or rear wheel bearings can cause poor tracking. Worn front bearings will cause wobble (Chapters 1 and 6).
- ☐ Fork yoke clamp bolts or handlebar clamp bolts loose. Tighten them to the specified torque (Chapter 5).
- ☐ Engine mounting bolts loose. Will cause excessive vibration with increased engine rpm – ensure all the bolts are tightened to the specified torque settings (Chapter 2).

Machine pulls to one side
- ☐ Frame bent. Definitely suspect this if the machine has been dropped. May or may not be accompanied by cracking near the steering head, swingarm mountings or engine mountings. Replace the frame with a new one (Chapter 5).
- ☐ Wheels out of alignment. Caused by poor chain adjustment, improper location of axle spacers or from bent steering stem or frame (Chapters 1 and 5).
- ☐ Forks bent. Disassemble the forks and replace the damaged parts (Chapter 5).
- ☐ Swingarm bent or twisted. Replace the arm with a new one (Chapter 5).
- ☐ Fork oil level uneven. Check and add or drain as necessary (Chapter 5).

Poor shock absorbing qualities
- ☐ Too hard:
  - a) Suspension settings incorrect.
  - b) Fork oil level excessive (Chapter 5).
  - c) Fork oil viscosity too high. Use a lighter oil (see the Specifications in Chapter 5).
  - d) Fork tube bent. Causes a harsh, sticking feeling (Chapter 5).
  - e) Fork internal damage (Chapter 5).
  - f) Shock shaft or body bent or damaged (Chapter 5).
  - g) Shock internal damage.
  - h) Tyre pressure too high (see *Pre-ride checks*).
- ☐ Too soft:
  - a) Suspension settings incorrect.
  - b) Fork oil level too low (Chapter 5).
  - c) Fork oil viscosity too light (Chapter 5).
  - d) Fork springs weak or broken (Chapter 5).
  - e) Fork or shock oil leaking (Chapter 5).
  - f) Shock internal damage (Chapter 5).

Fault Finding

13 Braking problems

Brakes are spongy, don't hold
- [ ] Low brake fluid level (see *Pre-ride checks*).
- [ ] Air in hydraulic system. Caused by inattention to master cylinder fluid level or by leakage. Locate problem and bleed brakes (Chapter 6).
- [ ] Pad or disc worn (Chapters 1 and 6).
- [ ] Contaminated pads. Caused by contamination with oil, grease, brake fluid, etc. Fit new pads. Identify the cause of the contamination, especially check the caliper piston seals for leaking fluid. Clean disc thoroughly with brake system cleaner (Chapter 6).
- [ ] Brake fluid deteriorated. Fluid is old or contaminated. Drain system, replenish with new fluid and bleed the system (Chapter 6).
- [ ] Master cylinder internal seals worn or damaged causing fluid to bypass (Chapter 6).
- [ ] Master cylinder bore scratched by foreign material or broken spring. Fit a new master cylinder (Chapter 6).
- [ ] Disc warped. Replace disc with new one (Chapter 6).
- [ ] ABS system faulty (Chapter 6).

Brake lever or pedal pulsates
- [ ] Disc warped. Replace disc with new one (Chapter 6).
- [ ] Axle bent. Replace axle with new one (Chapter 6).
- [ ] Brake caliper bolts loose – tighten the bolts to the specified torque (Chapter 6).
- [ ] Wheel warped or otherwise damaged (Chapter 6).
- [ ] Wheel bearings damaged or worn (Chapters 1 and 6).
- [ ] ABS system faulty (Chapter 6).

Brakes drag
- [ ] Master cylinder piston seized. Caused by wear or damage to piston or cylinder bore (Chapter 6).
- [ ] Lever balky or stuck. Check pivot and lubricate (Chapter 6).
- [ ] Brake caliper piston seized in bore. Caused by corrosion or ingestion of dirt past deteriorated seal (Chapter 6).
- [ ] Brake pad damaged. Pad material separated from backing plate. Usually caused by faulty manufacturing process or from contact with chemicals. Fit new pads (Chapter 6).
- [ ] Pads improperly installed (Chapter 6).
- [ ] Brake caliper incorrectly installed (Chapter 6).
- [ ] ABS system faulty (Chapter 6).

14 Electrical problems

Battery dead or weak
- [ ] Battery faulty. Caused by sulphated plates which are shorted through sedimentation. Confirm with battery condition check (Chapter 8).
- [ ] Broken battery terminal making only occasional contact.
- [ ] Battery leads making poor contact (Chapter 8).
- [ ] Load excessive. Caused by addition of high wattage lights or other electrical accessories.
- [ ] Ignition switch defective. Switch either grounds (earths) internally or fails to shut off system. Renew the switch (Chapter 8).
- [ ] Regulator/rectifier defective (Chapter 8).
- [ ] Alternator stator coil open or shorted (Chapter 8).
- [ ] Charging system fault. Check for excessive current leakage (Chapter 8).
- [ ] Wiring faulty. Wiring grounded (earthed) or connections loose in ignition, charging or lighting circuits (Chapter 8).

Battery overcharged
- [ ] Regulator/rectifier defective. Overcharging is noticed when battery gets excessively warm (Chapter 8).
- [ ] Battery faulty. Confirm with battery condition check (Chapter 8).
- [ ] Battery amperage too low, wrong type or size of battery. Install manufacturer's specified amp-hour battery to handle charging load (Chapter 8).

Technical Terms Explained

A

ABS (Anti-lock braking system) A system, usually electronically controlled, that senses incipient wheel lockup during braking and relieves hydraulic pressure at wheel which is about to skid.
Aftermarket Components suitable for the motorcycle, but not produced by the motorcycle manufacturer.
Allen key A hexagonal wrench which fits into a recessed hexagonal hole.
Alternating current (ac) Current produced by an alternator. Requires converting to direct current by a rectifier for charging purposes.
Alternator Converts mechanical energy from the engine into electrical energy to charge the battery and power the electrical system.
Ampere (amp) A unit of measurement for the flow of electrical current. Current = Volts ÷ Ohms.
Ampere-hour (Ah) Measure of battery capacity.
Angle-tightening A torque expressed in degrees. Often follows a conventional tightening torque for cylinder head or main bearing fasteners **(see illustration)**.

Angle-tightening cylinder head bolts

Antifreeze A substance (usually ethylene glycol) mixed with water, and added to the cooling system, to prevent freezing of the coolant in winter. Antifreeze also contains chemicals to inhibit corrosion and the formation of rust and other deposits that would tend to clog the radiator and coolant passages and reduce cooling efficiency.
Anti-dive System attached to the fork lower leg (slider) to prevent fork dive when braking hard.
Anti-seize compound A coating that reduces the risk of seizing on fasteners that are subjected to high temperatures, such as exhaust clamp bolts and nuts.
API American Petroleum Institute. A quality standard for 4-stroke motor oils.
Asbestos A natural fibrous mineral with great heat resistance, commonly used in the composition of brake friction materials. Asbestos is a health hazard and the dust created by brake systems should never be inhaled or ingested.
ATF Automatic Transmission Fluid. Often used in front forks.
ATU Automatic Timing Unit. Mechanical device for advancing the ignition timing on early engines.
ATV All Terrain Vehicle. Often called a Quad.
Axial play Side-to-side movement.
Axle A shaft on which a wheel revolves. Also known as a spindle.

B

Backlash The amount of movement between meshed components when one component is held still. Usually applies to gear teeth.
Ball bearing A bearing consisting of a hardened inner and outer race with hardened steel balls between the two races.
Bearings Used between two working surfaces to prevent wear of the components and a build-up of heat. Four types of bearing are commonly used on motorcycles: plain shell bearings, ball bearings, tapered roller bearings and needle roller bearings.
Bevel gears Used to turn the drive through 90°. Typical applications are shaft final drive and camshaft drive **(see illustration)**.

Bevel gears are used to turn the drive through 90°

BHP Brake Horsepower. The British measurement for engine power output. Power output is now usually expressed in kilowatts (kW).
Bias-belted tyre Similar construction to radial tyre, but with outer belt running at an angle to the wheel rim.
Big-end bearing The bearing in the end of the connecting rod that's attached to the crankshaft.
Bleeding The process of removing air from an hydraulic system via a bleed nipple or bleed screw.
Bottom-end A description of an engine's crankcase components and all components contained there-in.
BTDC Before Top Dead Centre in terms of piston position. Ignition timing is often expressed in terms of degrees or millimetres BTDC.
Bush A cylindrical metal or rubber component used between two moving parts.
Burr Rough edge left on a component after machining or as a result of excessive wear.

C

Cam chain The chain which takes drive from the crankshaft to the camshaft(s).
Canister The main component in an evaporative emission control system (California market only); contains activated charcoal granules to trap vapours from the fuel system rather than allowing them to vent to the atmosphere.
Castellated Resembling the parapets along the top of a castle wall. For example, a castellated wheel axle or spindle nut.
Catalytic converter A device in the exhaust system of some machines which converts certain pollutants in the exhaust gases into less harmful substances.
Charging system Description of the components which charge the battery, ie the alternator, rectifer and regulator.
Circlip A ring-shaped clip used to prevent endwise movement of cylindrical parts and shafts. An internal circlip is installed in a groove in a housing; an external circlip fits into a groove on the outside of a cylindrical piece such as a shaft. Also known as a snap-ring.
Clearance The amount of space between two parts. For example, between a piston and a cylinder, between a bearing and a journal, etc.
Coil spring A spiral of elastic steel found in various sizes throughout a vehicle, for example as a springing medium in the suspension and in the valve train.
Compression Reduction in volume, and increase in pressure and temperature, of a gas, caused by squeezing it into a smaller space.
Compression damping Controls the speed the suspension compresses when hitting a bump.
Compression ratio The relationship between cylinder volume when the piston is at top dead centre and cylinder volume when the piston is at bottom dead centre.
Continuity The uninterrupted path in the flow of electricity. Little or no measurable resistance.
Continuity tester Self-powered bleeper or test light which indicates continuity.
Cp Candlepower. Bulb rating commonly found on US motorcycles.
Crossply tyre Tyre plies arranged in a criss-cross pattern. Usually four or six plies used, hence 4PR or 6PR in tyre size codes.
Cush drive Rubber damper segments fitted between the rear wheel and final drive sprocket to absorb transmission shocks **(see illustration)**.

Cush drive rubbers dampen out transmission shocks

D

Degree disc Calibrated disc for measuring piston position. Expressed in degrees.
Dial gauge Clock-type gauge with adapters for measuring runout and piston position. Expressed in mm or inches.
Diaphragm The rubber membrane in a master cylinder or carburettor which seals the upper chamber.
Diaphragm spring A single sprung plate often used in clutches.
Direct current (dc) Current produced by a dc generator.

Technical Terms Explained REF•45

Decarbonisation The process of removing carbon deposits - typically from the combustion chamber, valves and exhaust port/system.
Detonation Destructive and damaging explosion of fuel/air mixture in combustion chamber instead of controlled burning.
Diode An electrical valve which only allows current to flow in one direction. Commonly used in rectifiers and starter interlock systems.
Disc valve (or rotary valve) A induction system used on some two-stroke engines.
Double-overhead camshaft (DOHC) An engine that uses two overhead camshafts, one for the intake valves and one for the exhaust valves.
Drivebelt A toothed belt used to transmit drive to the rear wheel on some motorcycles. A drivebelt has also been used to drive the camshafts. Drivebelts are usually made of Kevlar.
Driveshaft Any shaft used to transmit motion. Commonly used when referring to the final driveshaft on shaft drive motorcycles.

E

Earth return The return path of an electrical circuit, utilising the motorcycle's frame.
ECU (Electronic Control Unit) A computer which controls (for instance) an ignition system, or an anti-lock braking system.
EGO Exhaust Gas Oxygen sensor. Sometimes called a Lambda sensor.
Electrolyte The fluid in a lead-acid battery.
EMS (Engine Management System) A computer controlled system which manages the fuel injection and the ignition systems in an integrated fashion.
Endfloat The amount of lengthways movement between two parts. As applied to a crankshaft, the distance that the crankshaft can move side-to-side in the crankcase.
Endless chain A chain having no joining link. Common use for cam chains and final drive chains.
EP (Extreme Pressure) Oil type used in locations where high loads are applied, such as between gear teeth.
Evaporative emission control system Describes a charcoal filled canister which stores fuel vapours from the tank rather than allowing them to vent to the atmosphere. Usually only fitted to California models and referred to as an EVAP system.
Expansion chamber Section of two-stroke engine exhaust system so designed to improve engine efficiency and boost power.

F

Feeler blade or gauge A thin strip or blade of hardened steel, ground to an exact thickness, used to check or measure clearances between parts.
Final drive Description of the drive from the transmission to the rear wheel. Usually by chain or shaft, but sometimes by belt.
Firing order The order in which the engine cylinders fire, or deliver their power strokes, beginning with the number one cylinder.
Flooding Term used to describe a high fuel level in the carburettor float chambers, leading to fuel overflow. Also refers to excess fuel in the combustion chamber due to incorrect starting technique.

Free length The no-load state of a component when measured. Clutch, valve and fork spring lengths are measured at rest, without any preload.
Freeplay The amount of travel before any action takes place. The looseness in a linkage, or an assembly of parts, between the initial application of force and actual movement. For example, the distance the rear brake pedal moves before the rear brake is actuated.
Fuel injection The fuel/air mixture is metered electronically and directed into the engine intake ports (indirect injection) or into the cylinders (direct injection). Sensors supply information on engine speed and conditions.
Fuel/air mixture The charge of fuel and air going into the engine. See **Stoichiometric ratio**.
Fuse An electrical device which protects a circuit against accidental overload. The typical fuse contains a soft piece of metal which is calibrated to melt at a predetermined current flow (expressed as amps) and break the circuit.

G

Gap The distance the spark must travel in jumping from the centre electrode to the side electrode in a spark plug. Also refers to the distance between the ignition rotor and the pickup coil in an electronic ignition system.
Gasket Any thin, soft material - usually cork, cardboard, asbestos or soft metal - installed between two metal surfaces to ensure a good seal. For instance, the cylinder head gasket seals the joint between the block and the cylinder head.
Gauge An instrument panel display used to monitor engine conditions. A gauge with a movable pointer on a dial or a fixed scale is an analogue gauge. A gauge with a numerical readout is called a digital gauge.
Gear ratios The drive ratio of a pair of gears in a gearbox, calculated on their number of teeth.
Glaze-busting see **Honing**
Grinding Process for renovating the valve face and valve seat contact area in the cylinder head.
Gudgeon pin The shaft which connects the connecting rod small-end with the piston. Often called a piston pin or wrist pin.

H

Helical gears Gear teeth are slightly curved and produce less gear noise that straight-cut gears. Often used for primary drives.

Installing a Helicoil thread insert in a cylinder head

Helicoil A thread insert repair system. Commonly used as a repair for stripped spark plug threads **(see illustration)**.
Honing A process used to break down the glaze on a cylinder bore (also called glaze-busting). Can also be carried out to roughen a rebored cylinder to aid ring bedding-in.
HT (High Tension) Description of the electrical circuit from the secondary winding of the ignition coil to the spark plug.
Hydraulic A liquid filled system used to transmit pressure from one component to another. Common uses on motorcycles are brakes and clutches.
Hydrometer An instrument for measuring the specific gravity of a lead-acid battery.
Hygroscopic Water absorbing. In motorcycle applications, braking efficiency will be reduced if DOT 3 or 4 hydraulic fluid absorbs water from the air - care must be taken to keep new brake fluid in tightly sealed containers.

I

lbf ft Pounds-force feet. An imperial unit of torque. Sometimes written as ft-lbs.
lbf in Pound-force inch. An imperial unit of torque, applied to components where a very low torque is required. Sometimes written as in-lbs.
IC Abbreviation for Integrated Circuit.
Ignition advance Means of increasing the timing of the spark at higher engine speeds. Done by mechanical means (ATU) on early engines or electronically by the ignition control unit on later engines.
Ignition timing The moment at which the spark plug fires, expressed in the number of crankshaft degrees before the piston reaches the top of its stroke, or in the number of millimetres before the piston reaches the top of its stroke.
Infinity (∞) Description of an open-circuit electrical state, where no continuity exists.
Inverted forks (upside down forks) The sliders or lower legs are held in the yokes and the fork tubes or stanchions are connected to the wheel axle (spindle). Less unsprung weight and stiffer construction than conventional forks.

J

JASO Quality standard for 2-stroke oils.
Joule The unit of electrical energy.
Journal The bearing surface of a shaft.

K

Kickstart Mechanical means of turning the engine over for starting purposes. Only usually fitted to mopeds, small capacity motorcycles and off-road motorcycles.
Kill switch Handebar-mounted switch for emergency ignition cut-out. Cuts the ignition circuit on all models, and additionally prevent starter motor operation on others.
km Symbol for kilometre.
kmh Abbreviation for kilometres per hour.

L

Lambda (λ) sensor A sensor fitted in the exhaust system to measure the exhaust gas oxygen content (excess air factor).

Technical Terms Explained

Lapping see **Grinding**.
LCD Abbreviation for Liquid Crystal Display.
LED Abbreviation for Light Emitting Diode.
Liner A steel cylinder liner inserted in a aluminium alloy cylinder block.
Locknut A nut used to lock an adjustment nut, or other threaded component, in place.
Lockstops The lugs on the lower triple clamp (yoke) which abut those on the frame, preventing handlebar-to-fuel tank contact.
Lockwasher A form of washer designed to prevent an attaching nut from working loose.
LT Low Tension Description of the electrical circuit from the power supply to the primary winding of the ignition coil.

M

Main bearings The bearings between the crankshaft and crankcase.
Maintenance-free (MF) battery A sealed battery which cannot be topped up.
Manometer Mercury-filled calibrated tubes used to measure intake tract vacuum. Used to synchronise carburettors on multi-cylinder engines.
Micrometer A precision measuring instrument that measures component outside diameters **(see illustration)**.

Tappet shims are measured with a micrometer

MON (Motor Octane Number) A measure of a fuel's resistance to knock.
Monograde oil An oil with a single viscosity, eg SAE80W.
Monoshock A single suspension unit linking the swingarm or suspension linkage to the frame.
mph Abbreviation for miles per hour.
Multigrade oil Having a wide viscosity range (eg 10W40). The W stands for Winter, thus the viscosity ranges from SAE10 when cold to SAE40 when hot.
Multimeter An electrical test instrument with the capability to measure voltage, current and resistance. Some meters also incorporate a continuity tester and buzzer.

N

Needle roller bearing Inner race of caged needle rollers and hardened outer race. Examples of uncaged needle rollers can be found on some engines. Commonly used in rear suspension applications and in two-stroke engines.
Nm Newton metres.
NOx Oxides of Nitrogen. A common toxic pollutant emitted by petrol engines at higher temperatures.

O

Octane The measure of a fuel's resistance to knock.
OE (Original Equipment) Relates to components fitted to a motorcycle as standard or replacement parts supplied by the motorcycle manufacturer.
Ohm The unit of electrical resistance. Ohms = Volts ÷ Current.
Ohmmeter An instrument for measuring electrical resistance.
Oil cooler System for diverting engine oil outside of the engine to a radiator for cooling purposes.
Oil injection A system of two-stroke engine lubrication where oil is pump-fed to the engine in accordance with throttle position.
Open-circuit An electrical condition where there is a break in the flow of electricity - no continuity (high resistance).
O-ring A type of sealing ring made of a special rubber-like material; in use, the O-ring is compressed into a groove to provide the sealing action.
Oversize (OS) Term used for piston and ring size options fitted to a rebored cylinder.
Overhead cam (sohc) engine An engine with single camshaft located on top of the cylinder head.
Overhead valve (ohv) engine An engine with the valves located in the cylinder head, but with the camshaft located in the engine block or crankcase.
Oxygen sensor A device installed in the exhaust system which senses the oxygen content in the exhaust and converts this information into an electric current. Also called a Lambda sensor.

P

Plastigauge A thin strip of plastic thread, available in different sizes, used for measuring clearances. For example, a strip of Plastigauge is laid across a bearing journal. The parts are assembled and dismantled; the width of the crushed strip indicates the clearance between journal and bearing.
Polarity Either negative or positive earth (ground), determined by which battery lead is connected to the frame (earth return). Modern motorcycles are usually negative earth.
Pre-ignition A situation where the fuel/air mixture ignites before the spark plug fires. Often due to a hot spot in the combustion chamber caused by carbon build-up. Engine has a tendency to 'run-on'.
Pre-load (suspension) The amount a spring is compressed when in the unloaded state. Preload can be applied by gas, spacer or mechanical adjuster.
Premix The method of engine lubrication on older two-stroke engines. Engine oil is mixed with the petrol in the fuel tank in a specific ratio. The fuel/oil mix is sometimes referred to as "petroil".
Primary drive Description of the drive from the crankshaft to the clutch. Usually by gear or chain.
PS Pfedestärke - a German interpretation of BHP.
PSI Pounds-force per square inch. Imperial measurement of tyre pressure and cylinder pressure measurement.
PTFE Polytetrafluroethylene. A low friction substance.
Pulse secondary air injection system A process of promoting the burning of excess fuel present in the exhaust gases by routing fresh air into the exhaust ports.

Q

Quartz halogen bulb Tungsten filament surrounded by a halogen gas. Typically used for the headlight **(see illustration)**.

Quartz halogen headlight bulb construction

R

Rack-and-pinion A pinion gear on the end of a shaft that mates with a rack (think of a geared wheel opened up and laid flat). Sometimes used in clutch operating systems.
Radial play Up and down movement about a shaft.
Radial ply tyres Tyre plies run across the tyre (from bead to bead) and around the circumference of the tyre. Less resistant to tread distortion than other tyre types.
Radiator A liquid-to-air heat transfer device designed to reduce the temperature of the coolant in a liquid cooled engine.
Rake A feature of steering geometry - the angle of the steering head in relation to the vertical **(see illustration)**.

Steering geometry

Technical Terms Explained REF•47

Rebore Providing a new working surface to the cylinder bore by boring out the old surface. Necessitates the use of oversize piston and rings.
Rebound damping A means of controlling the oscillation of a suspension unit spring after it has been compressed. Resists the spring's natural tendency to bounce back after being compressed.
Rectifier Device for converting the ac output of an alternator into dc for battery charging.
Reed valve An induction system commonly used on two-stroke engines.
Regulator Device for maintaining the charging voltage from the generator or alternator within a specified range.
Relay A electrical device used to switch heavy current on and off by using a low current auxiliary circuit.
Resistance Measured in ohms. An electrical component's ability to pass electrical current.
RON (Research Octane Number) A measure of a fuel's resistance to knock.
rpm revolutions per minute.
Runout The amount of wobble (in-and-out movement) of a wheel or shaft as it's rotated. The amount a shaft rotates 'out-of-true'. The out-of-round condition of a rotating part.

S

SAE (Society of Automotive Engineers) A standard for the viscosity of a fluid.
Sealant A liquid or paste used to prevent leakage at a joint. Sometimes used in conjunction with a gasket.
Service limit Term for the point where a component is no longer useable and must be renewed.
Shaft drive A method of transmitting drive from the transmission to the rear wheel.
Shell bearings Plain bearings consisting of two shell halves. Most often used as big-end and main bearings in a four-stroke engine. Often called bearing inserts.
Shim Thin spacer, commonly used to adjust the clearance or relative positions between two parts. For example, shims inserted into or under tappets or followers to control valve clearances. Clearance is adjusted by changing the thickness of the shim.
Short-circuit An electrical condition where current shorts to earth (ground) bypassing the circuit components.
Skimming Process to correct warpage or repair a damaged surface, eg on brake discs or drums.
Slide-hammer A special puller that screws into or hooks onto a component such as a shaft or bearing; a heavy sliding handle on the shaft bottoms against the end of the shaft to knock the component free.
Small-end bearing The bearing in the upper end of the connecting rod at its joint with the gudgeon pin.
Spalling Damage to camshaft lobes or bearing journals shown as pitting of the working surface.
Specific gravity (SG) The state of charge of the electrolyte in a lead-acid battery. A measure of the electrolyte's density compared with water.
Straight-cut gears Common type gear used on gearbox shafts and for oil pump and water pump drives.
Stanchion The inner sliding part of the front forks, held by the yokes. Often called a fork tube.
Stoichiometric ratio The optimum chemical air/fuel ratio for a petrol engine, said to be 14.7 parts of air to 1 part of fuel.
Sulphuric acid The liquid (electrolyte) used in a lead-acid battery. Poisonous and extremely corrosive.
Surface grinding (lapping) Process to correct a warped gasket face, commonly used on cylinder heads.

T

Tapered-roller bearing Tapered inner race of caged needle rollers and separate tapered outer race. Examples of taper roller bearings can be found on steering heads.
Tappet A cylindrical component which transmits motion from the cam to the valve stem, either directly or via a pushrod and rocker arm. Also called a cam follower.
TCS Traction Control System. An electronically-controlled system which senses wheel spin and reduces engine speed accordingly.
TDC Top Dead Centre denotes that the piston is at its highest point in the cylinder.
Thread-locking compound Solution applied to fastener threads to prevent slackening. Select type to suit application.
Thrust washer A washer positioned between two moving components on a shaft. For example, between gear pinions on gearshaft.
Timing chain See **Cam Chain**.
Timing light Stroboscopic lamp for carrying out ignition timing checks with the engine running.
Top-end A description of an engine's cylinder block, head and valve gear components.
Torque Turning or twisting force about a shaft.
Torque setting A prescribed tightness specified by the motorcycle manufacturer to ensure that the bolt or nut is secured correctly. Undertightening can result in the bolt or nut coming loose or a surface not being sealed. Overtightening can result in stripped threads, distortion or damage to the component being retained.
Torx key A six-point wrench.
Tracer A stripe of a second colour applied to a wire insulator to distinguish that wire from another one with the same colour insulator. For example, Br/W is often used to denote a brown insulator with a white tracer.
Trail A feature of steering geometry. Distance from the steering head axis to the tyre's central contact point.
Triple clamps The cast components which extend from the steering head and support the fork stanchions or tubes. Often called fork yokes.
Turbocharger A centrifugal device, driven by exhaust gases, that pressurises the intake air. Normally used to increase the power output from a given engine displacement.
TWI Abbreviation for Tyre Wear Indicator. Indicates the location of the tread depth indicator bars on tyres.

U

Universal joint or U-joint (UJ) A double-pivoted connection for transmitting power from a driving to a driven shaft through an angle. Typically found in shaft drive assemblies.
Unsprung weight Anything not supported by the bike's suspension (ie the wheel, tyres, brakes, final drive and bottom (moving) part of the suspension).

V

Vacuum gauges Clock-type gauges for measuring intake tract vacuum. Used for carburettor synchronisation on multi-cylinder engines.
Valve A device through which the flow of liquid, gas or vacuum may be stopped, started or regulated by a moveable part that opens, shuts or partially obstructs one or more ports or passageways. The intake and exhaust valves in the cylinder head are of the poppet type.
Valve clearance The clearance between the valve tip (the end of the valve stem) and the rocker arm or tappet/follower. The valve clearance is measured when the valve is closed. The correct clearance is important - if too small the valve won't close fully and will burn out, whereas if too large noisy operation will result.
Valve lift The amount a valve is lifted off its seat by the camshaft lobe.
Valve timing The exact setting for the opening and closing of the valves in relation to piston position.
Vernier caliper A precision measuring instrument that measures inside and outside dimensions. Not quite as accurate as a micrometer, but more convenient.
VIN Vehicle Identification Number. Term for the bike's engine and frame numbers.
Viscosity The thickness of a liquid or its resistance to flow.
Volt A unit for expressing electrical "pressure" in a circuit. Volts = current x ohms.

W

Water pump A mechanically-driven device for moving coolant around the engine.
Watt A unit for expressing electrical power. Watts = volts x current.
Wear limit see **Service limit**
Wet liner A liquid-cooled engine design where the pistons run in liners which are directly surrounded by coolant **(see illustration)**.

Wet liner arrangement

Wheelbase Distance from the centre of the front wheel to the centre of the rear wheel.
Wiring harness or loom Describes the electrical wires running the length of the motorcycle and enclosed in tape or plastic sheathing. Wiring coming off the main harness is usually referred to as a sub harness.
Woodruff key A key of semi-circular or square section used to locate a gear to a shaft. Often used to locate the alternator rotor on the crankshaft.
Wrist pin Another name for gudgeon or piston pin.

REF•48 Index

A

ABS (Anti-lock Braking System) – 6•2, 6•4, 6•21, 6•22, 6•24
Acknowledgements – 0•8
Air filter – 1•29
Air filter housing – 4•6
Air intake system – 4•20
Alternator – 8•30

B

Balancer shaft – 2•64
Battery – 1•32, 8•1, 8•4, 8•5
Bodypanels (CB1000R/RA) – 7•7
Bodywork – 7•1 *et seq*
Brake
 ABS – 6•4, 6•21, 6•22, 6•24
 CBS – 6•4, 6•26
 bleeding and fluid change – 6•20
 caliper – 6•7, 6•14
 disc – 6•9, 6•16
 fluid level checks – 0•12
 hoses and fittings – 6•20
 lever – 5•7
 master cylinders – 6•2, 6•10, 6•17
 pads – 1•11, 6•4, 6•13
 pedal – 5•3
 specifications – 6•1
 system check – 1•12

Brake light
 bulb (CBF) – 8•11
 circuit check – 8•8
 switches – 1•12, 8•14
Bulb
 brake/tail light (CBF) – 8•11
 headlight – 8•9
 licence plate light – 8•12
 sidelight – 8•9
 turn signal – 8•13
 wattages – 8•2

C

Cables (throttle) – 1•14, 1•29, 4•26
Caliper (brake) – 6•1, 6•2, 6•7, 6•14
Cam chain, tensioner blade and front guide – 2•19
Cam chain tensioner – 2•14
Camshafts and followers – 2•2, 2•15
Catalytic converter – 4•32
CBS (Combined Braking System) – 6•4, 6•26
Centrestand (CBF1000A) – 1•23, 5•5
Chain (drive)
 check and adjustment – 1•8
 cleaning and lubrication – 1•9
 lubricant – 1•2
 specifications – 6•2
Charging system – 8•1, 8•29
CKP (Crankshaft Position) sensor – 4•18

Clutch
 bleeding – 2•34
 check – 1•13
 fluid level check – 0•14
 lever – 5•7
 master cylinder – 2•31
 overhaul – 2•26
 release cylinder – 2•33
 release mechanism – 2•31
 specifications – 2•3
 switch – 8•22
Coils (ignition) – 4•2, 4•33
Connecting rods – 2•4, 2•56, 2•58
Coolant – 1•2
 change – 1•21
 level check – 0•11
 reservoir – 3•8
Cooling system – 3•1 *et seq*
 check – 1•20
 coolant reservoir – 3•8
 hoses, pipes and unions – 3•9
 fan and fan relay – 3•2
 radiator – 3•6
 temperature display and ECT sensor – 3•4
 thermostat and housing – 3•5
 water pump – 3•7
Conversion factors – REF•26
Crankcase breather – 1•11
Crankcases – 2•50, 2•54
Crankshaft – 2•4, 2•56
Cylinder bores – 2•4, 2•55
Cylinder compression check – 2•7
Cylinder head – 2•2, 2•20, 2•21

Index REF•49

D

Dimensions (model) – 0•17
Diode block – 8•22
Disc (brake) – 6•2, 6•9, 6•16
Drive chain – 6•36
  check and adjustment – 1•8
  cleaning and lubrication – 1•9
  lubricant – 1•2
  specifications – 6•2

E

ECM (Engine Control Module) – 4•19
ECT (Engine Coolant Temperature) sensor – 3•1, 3•4, 4•15
Electrical system – 8•1 *et seq*
  alternator – 8•30
  battery – 1•32, 8•4, 8•5
  brake light switches – 1•12, 8•14
  clutch switch – 8•22
  diode block – 8•22
  fault finding – 8•2
  fuses – 8•6
  handlebar switches – 8•20
  headlight – 8•9, 8•11
  horn – 8•22
  ignition switch – 8•19
  instruments – 8•15, 8•16
  lighting system check – 8•7
  neutral switch – 8•20
  oil pressure switch – 8•18
  regulator/rectifier – 8•32
  sidestand switch – 8•21
  specifications – 8•1
  starter motor – 8•23, 8•25
  tail light – 8•11, 8•12
  turn signals – 8•12, 8•13, 8•14
  wiring diagrams – 8•34
Engine
  balancer shaft – 2•64
  cam chain, tensioner blade and front guide – 2•19
  cam chain tensioner – 2•14
  camshafts and followers – 2•15
  compression check – 2•7
  connecting rods – 2•56, 2•58
  crankcase breather – 1•11
  crankcases – 2•50, 2•54
  crankshaft – 2•56
  cylinder bores – 2•55
  cylinder head – 2•20, 2•21
  oil change and filter – 1•17
  oil cooler – 2•13
  oil level check – 0•14
  oil pressure check – 2•7
  oil pump – 2•49
  oil sump, oil strainer and pressure relief valve – 2•47
  overhaul – 2•12
  piston rings – 2•62
  pistons – 2•61
  removal and installation – 2•8
  running-in – 2•66
  specifications – 0•18, 1•2, 2•1
  starter clutch and gears – 2•25
  valve clearances – 1•2, 1•30
  valve cover – 2•13
Engine management system – 4•1 *et seq*
Engine number – 0•9
Engine stop relay – 4•18
Exhaust system – 4•28

F

Fairing and body panels (CBF) – 7•4
Fan and fan relay – 3•2
Fault finding – REF•35 *et seq*
  ABS – 6•22
  electrical system – 8•2
  fuel injection – 4•13
Filter
  air – 1•29
  fuel – 4•23
  oil – 1•17
Firing order – 4•1
Footrests – 5•2
Frame – 5•2
Frame number – 0•9
Front brake
  calipers – 6•1, 6•7
  discs – 6•9
  master cylinder – 6•2, 6•10
  pads – 1•11, 6•4,
Front forks
  adjustment – 5•28
  check – 1•23
  oil change – 1•25, 5•8
  overhaul – 5•11
  removal – 5•8
  specifications – 5•1
Front mudguard
  CB1000R/RA – 7•9
  CBF1000/A – 7•4
Front wheel – 6•27
  ABS pulse ring – 6•25
  ABS sensor – 6•24
Fuel cut-off relay – 4•19
Fuel grade – 4•1
Fuel injection
  components – 4•14
  description – 4•13
  fault diagnosis – 4•13
  specifications – 4•2
Fuel gauge and level sensor – 4•2, 4•25, 8•16
Fuel system
  air filter housing and throttle bodies – 4•6
  check – 1•14
  fuel rails and injectors – 4•11
  pressure check – 4•23
  pump – 4•23
  tank – 4•1, 4•3
Fuses – 8•2, 8•6

G

Gearbox
  cassette removal – 2•37
  shaft and bearing removal – 2•38
  shaft overhaul – 2•40
  specifications – 2•5
Gearchange lever and linkage – 5•3
Gearchange mechanism – 2•35
Grille (CB1000R/RA) – 7•7

H

Handlebar holders – 5•6
Handlebar levers – 5•7
Handlebar switches – 8•20
Handlebar weights – 5•7
Handlebars – 5•5
Headlight – 8•11
  aim – 1•22
  bulbs – 8•9
  circuit check – 8•7
  relay – 8•8
Horn – 8•22

I

IAT (Intake Air Temperature) sensor – 4•16
Idle speed control system – 4•22
Ignition switch – 8•19
Ignition system
  check – 4•32
  coils – 4•2, 4•33
  spark plugs – 1•15
  timing – 4•35
Immobiliser – 4•35
Injectors (fuel) – 4•11
Instrument cover (CBF) – 7•4
Instrument cowl (CB-R) – 7•8
Instruments – 8•15, 8•16
Introduction – 0•5

L

Lean angle sensor – 4•17
Legal and safety checks – 0•16
Licence plate light
  bulb – 8•12
  circuit check – 8•9
Lubricants – 1•2, REF•23
Lubrication
  throttle cables – 1•29
  pivot points – 1•28

M

Maintenance schedule – 1•3
MAP (Manifold Absolute Pressure) sensor – 4•14
Master cylinder
  clutch – 2•31
  front brake – 6•10
  rear brake – 6•17
Mirrors – 7•10
Model development – 0•17
Modulator (ABS) – 6•25
MOT test checks – REF•27
Mudguard (front)
  CB1000R/RA – 7•9
  CBF1000/A – 7•7

Index

N

Neutral switch – 8•20

O

Oil (engine) – 1•2
    level check – 0•14
    oil change and filter – 1•17
Oil (front forks) – 5•1, 5•8
Oil cooler – 2•13
Oil pressure check – 2•7
Oil pressure switch – 8•18
Oil pump – 2•3, 2•49
Oil sump, oil strainer and pressure relief valve – 2•47
Oxygen sensor – 4•16

P

PAIR (pulse secondary air) system – 1•22, 4•2, 4•30
Pedal (brake) – 1•13, 5•3
Piston rings – 2•5, 2•62
Pistons – 2•4, 2•61
Pre-ride checks – 0•11 et seq
Pressure check
    cylinder compression – 2•7
    engine oil – 2•7
    fuel – 4•23
    tyre – 0•16
Pressure relief valve (oil) – 2•47
Pressure switch (oil) – 8•18
Pump
    fuel – 4•23
    oil – 2•49
    water – 3•7

R

Radiator – 3•1, 3•6
Radiator shroud (CB1000R/RA) – 7•8
Rear brake
    caliper – 6•2, 6•14
    disc – 6•16
    master cylinder – 6•2, 6•17
    pads – 1•11, 6•13
Rear shock absorber – 5•22, 5•28
Rear suspension
    checks – 1•24
    linkage (CBF) – 5•24

Rear wheel – 6•28
    ABS sensor and pulse ring – 6•25
Regulator/rectifier – 8•32
Relays
    engine stop – 4•18
    fan – 3•3
    fuel cut-off – 4•19
    headlight – 8•8
    starter motor – 8•23
    turn signal – 8•12
Release cylinder (clutch) – 2•33

S

Safety checks – 0•10, 0•16
Seat – 7•2
Seat cowl
    CB1000R/RA – 7•9
    CBF1000/A – 7•6
Seat rail covers (CB-R) – 7•8
Security – REF•20
Selector drum and forks – 2•4
Side covers
    CB1000R/RA – 7•7
    CBF1000/A – 7•4
Sidelight
    bulb/LED – 8•9
    circuit check – 8•9
Sidestand – 1•23, 5•4
Sidestand switch – 8•21
Spark plugs – 1•15
Speed sensor – 8•18
Speedometer – 8•16
Sprocket coupling (rear)
    bearing – 6•33
    rubber dampers – 6•38
Sprockets – 6•36
    wear check – 1•10, 6•37
Starter clutch – 2•2, 2•25
Starter interlock circuit – 1•23
Starter motor – 8•2, 8•25
Starter relay – 8•23
Steering head bearings – 5•21
    freeplay check and adjustment – 1•25
    specifications – 5•1
Steering stem – 5•18
Storage – REF•32
Swingarm – 5•25
Suspension
    adjustment – 5•28
    check – 1•23
    front forks – 5•8, 5•11
    rear linkage (CBF) – 5•24
    rear shock – 5•22
    swingarm – 5•25

T

Tachometer – 8•16
Tail light
    bulb – 8•11
    circuit check – 8•8
Tank (fuel) – 4•1, 4•3
Temperature display – 3•4, 8•16
Thermostat – 3•1, 3•5
Throttle bodies – 4•6
Throttle cables – 1•14, 1•29, 4•25
Tools and workshop tips – REF•2 et seq
Torque settings – 1•2, 2•6, 3•1, 4•2, 5•2, 6•3, 8•2
TP (Throttle Position) sensor – 4•15
Transmission
    cassette removal – 2•37
    shaft and bearing removal – 2•38
    shaft overhaul – 2•40
    specifications – 2•5
Trim clips – 7•1
Turn signal – 8•14
    bulb – 8•2, 8•13
    circuit check and relay – 8•12
Tyre – 6•35
    checks – 1•28
    pressure and tread depth – 0•16
    sizes – 6•2

V

Valve clearances – 1•2, 1•30
Valve cover – 2•13
Valves – 2•2, 2•21
Vehicle speed sensor – 8•18
VIN – 0•9

W

Water pump – 3•7
Weight (model) – 0•17
Windshield (CBF) – 7•4
Wiring diagrams – 8•34 et seq
Wheel – 6•27, 6•28
    alignment – 6•27
    bearings – 1•28, 6•31
    checks – 1•28
    inspection and repair – 6•26
    specifications – 6•2

Haynes Motorcycle Manuals – The Complete List

Title	Book No
APRILIA RS50 (99 - 06) & RS125 (93 - 06)	4298
Aprilia RSV1000 Mille (98 - 03)	♦ 4255
Aprilia SR50	4755
BMW 2-valve Twins (70 - 96)	♦ 0249
BMW F650	♦ 4761
BMW K100 & 75 2-valve Models (83 - 96)	♦ 1373
BMW R850, 1100 & 1150 4-valve Twins (93 - 04)	♦ 3466
BMW R1200 (04 - 06)	♦ 4598
BSA Bantam (48 - 71)	0117
BSA Unit Singles (58 - 72)	0127
BSA Pre-unit Singles (54 - 61)	0326
BSA A7 & A10 Twins (47 - 62)	0121
BSA A50 & A65 Twins (62 - 73)	0155
Chinese Scooters	4768
DUCATI 600, 620, 750 and 900 2-valve V-Twins (91 - 05)	♦ 3290
Ducati MK III & Desmo Singles (69 - 76)	◊ 0445
Ducati 748, 916 & 996 4-valve V-Twins (94 - 01)	♦ 3756
GILERA Runner, DNA, Ice & SKP/Stalker (97 - 07)	4163
HARLEY-DAVIDSON Sportsters (70 - 08)	♦ 2534
Harley-Davidson Shovelhead and Evolution Big Twins (70 - 99)	♦ 2536
Harley-Davidson Twin Cam 88 (99 - 03)	♦ 2478
HONDA NB, ND, NP & NS50 Melody (81 - 85)	◊ 0622
Honda NE/NB50 Vision & SA50 Vision Met-in (85 - 95)	◊ 1278
Honda MB, MBX, MT & MTX50 (80 - 93)	0731
Honda C50, C70 & C90 (67 - 03)	0324
Honda XR80/100R & CRF80/100F (85 - 04)	2218
Honda XL/XR 80, 100, 125, 185 & 200 2-valve Models (78 - 87)	0566
Honda H100 & H100S Singles (80 - 92)	0734
Honda CB/CD125T & CM125C Twins (77 - 88)	◊ 0571
Honda CG125 (76 - 07)	◊ 0433
Honda NS125 (86 - 93)	◊ 3056
Honda CBR125R (04 - 07)	4620
Honda MBX/MTX125 & MTX200 (83 - 93)	◊ 1132
Honda CD/CM185 200T & CM250C 2-valve Twins (77 - 85)	0572
Honda XL/XR 250 & 500 (78 - 84)	0567
Honda XR250L, XR250R & XR400R (86 - 03)	2219
Honda CB250 & CB400N Super Dreams (78 - 84)	◊ 0540
Honda CR Motocross Bikes (86 - 01)	2222
Honda CRF250 & CRF450 (02 - 06)	2630
Honda CBR400RR Fours (88 - 99)	◊ ♦ 3552
Honda VFR400 (NC30) & RVF400 (NC35) V-Fours (89 - 98)	◊ ♦ 3496
Honda CB500 (93 - 02) & CBF500 03 - 08	◊ 3753
Honda CB400 & CB550 Fours (73 - 77)	0262
Honda CX/GL500 & 650 V-Twins (78 - 86)	0442
Honda CBX550 Four (82 - 86)	◊ 0940
Honda XL600R & XR600R (83 - 08)	♦ 2183
Honda XL600/650V Transalp & XRV750 Africa Twin (87 to 07)	♦ 3919
Honda CBR600F1 & 1000F Fours (87 - 96)	♦ 1730
Honda CBR600F2 & F3 Fours (91 - 98)	♦ 2070
Honda CBR600F4 (99 - 06)	♦ 3911
Honda CB600F Hornet & CBF600 (98 - 06)	◊ ♦ 3915
Honda CBR600RR (03 - 06)	♦ 4590
Honda CB650 sohc Fours (78 - 84)	0665
Honda NTV600 Revere, NTV650 and NT650V Deauville (88 - 05)	◊ ♦ 3243
Honda Shadow VT600 & 750 (USA) (88 - 03)	2312
Honda CB750 sohc Four (69 - 79)	0131
Honda V45/65 Sabre & Magna (82 - 88)	0820
Honda VFR750 & 700 V-Fours (86 - 97)	♦ 2101
Honda VFR800 V-Fours (97 - 01)	♦ 3703
Honda VFR800 V-Tec V-Fours (02 - 05)	♦ 4196
Honda CB750 & CB900 dohc Fours (78 - 84)	0535
Honda VTR1000 (FireStorm, Super Hawk) & XL1000V (Varadero) (97 - 08)	♦ 3744
Honda CBR900RR FireBlade (92 - 99)	♦ 2161
Honda CBR900RR FireBlade (00 - 03)	♦ 4060
Honda CBR1000RR Fireblade (04 - 07)	♦ 4604
Honda CBR1100XX Super Blackbird (97 - 07)	♦ 3901
Honda ST1100 Pan European V-Fours (90 - 02)	♦ 3384
Honda Shadow VT1100 (USA) (85 - 98)	2313
Honda GL1000 Gold Wing (75 - 79)	0309

Title	Book No
Honda GL1100 Gold Wing (79 - 81)	0669
Honda Gold Wing 1200 (USA) (84 - 87)	2199
Honda Gold Wing 1500 (USA) (88 - 00)	2225
KAWASAKI AE/AR 50 & 80 (81 - 95)	1007
Kawasaki KC, KE & KH100 (75 - 99)	1371
Kawasaki KMX125 & 200 (86 - 02)	◊ 3046
Kawasaki 250, 350 & 400 Triples (72 - 79)	0134
Kawasaki 400 & 440 Twins (74 - 81)	0281
Kawasaki 400, 500 & 550 Fours (79 - 91)	0910
Kawasaki EN450 & 500 Twins (Ltd/Vulcan) (85 - 07)	2053
Kawasaki EX500 (GPZ500S) & ER500 (ER-5) (87 - 08)	♦ 2052
Kawasaki ZX600 (ZZ-R600 & Ninja ZX-6) (90 - 06)	♦ 2146
Kawasaki ZX-6R Ninja Fours (95 - 02)	♦ 3541
Kawasaki ZX-6R (03 - 06)	♦ 4742
Kawasaki ZX600 (GPZ600R, GPX600R, Ninja 600R & RX) & ZX750 (GPX750R, Ninja 750R)	♦ 1780
Kawasaki 650 Four (76 - 78)	0373
Kawasaki Vulcan 700/750 & 800 (85 - 04)	♦ 2457
Kawasaki 750 Air-cooled Fours (80 - 91)	0574
Kawasaki ZR550 & 750 Zephyr Fours (90 - 97)	♦ 3382
Kawasaki Z750 & Z1000 (03 - 08)	♦ 4762
Kawasaki ZX750 (Ninja ZX-7 & ZXR750) Fours (89 - 96)	♦ 2054
Kawasaki Ninja ZX-7R & ZX-9R (94 - 04)	♦ 3721
Kawasaki 900 & 1000 Fours (73 - 77)	0222
Kawasaki ZX900, 1000 & 1100 Liquid-cooled Fours (83 - 97)	♦ 1681
KTM EXC Enduro & SX Motocross (00 - 07)	♦ 4629
MOTO GUZZI 750, 850 & 1000 V-Twins (74 - 78)	0339
MZ ETZ Models (81 - 95)	◊ 1680
NORTON 500, 600, 650 & 750 Twins (57 - 70)	0187
Norton Commando (68 - 77)	0125
PEUGEOT Speedfight, Trekker & Vivacity Scooters (96 - 08)	◊ 3920
PIAGGIO (Vespa) Scooters (91 - 06)	◊ 3492
SUZUKI GT, ZR & TS50 (77 - 90)	0799
Suzuki TS50X (84 - 00)	◊ 1599
Suzuki 100, 125, 185 & 250 Air-cooled Trail bikes (79 - 89)	0797
Suzuki GP100 & 125 Singles (78 - 93)	◊ 0576
Suzuki GS, GN, GZ & DR125 Singles (82 - 05)	◊ 0888
Suzuki GSX-R600/750 (06 - 09)	♦ 4790
Suzuki 250 & 350 Twins (68 - 78)	0120
Suzuki GT250X7, GT200X5 & SB200 Twins (78 - 83)	◊ 0469
Suzuki GS/GSX250, 400 & 450 Twins (79 - 85)	0736
Suzuki GS500 Twin (89 - 06)	♦ 3238
Suzuki GS550 (77 - 82) & GS750 Fours (76 - 79)	0363
Suzuki GS/GSX550 4-valve Fours (83 - 88)	1133
Suzuki SV650 & SV650S (99 - 08)	♦ 3912
Suzuki GSX-R600 & 750 (96 - 00)	♦ 3553
Suzuki GSX-R600 (01 - 03), GSX-R750 (00 - 03) & GSX-R1000 (01 - 02)	♦ 3986
Suzuki GSX-R600/750 (04 - 05) & GSX-R1000 (03 - 06)	♦ 4382
Suzuki GSF600, 650 & 1200 Bandit Fours (95 - 06)	♦ 3367
Suzuki Intruder, Marauder, Volusia & Boulevard (85 - 06)	♦ 2618
Suzuki GS850 Fours (78 - 88)	0536
Suzuki GS1000 Four (77 - 79)	0484
Suzuki GSX-R750, GSX-R1100 (85 - 92), GSX600F, GSX750F, GSX1100F (Katana) Fours	♦ 2055
Suzuki GSX600/750F & GSX750 (98 - 02)	♦ 3987
Suzuki GS/GSX1000, 1100 and 1150 4-valve Fours (79 - 88)	◊ 0737
Suzuki TL1000S/R & DL1000 V-Strom (97 - 04)	♦ 4083
Suzuki GSF650/1250 (05 - 09)	♦ 4798
Suzuki GSX1300R Hayabusa (99 - 04)	♦ 4184
Suzuki GSX1400 (02 - 07)	♦ 4758
TRIUMPH Tiger Cub & Terrier (52 - 68)	0414
Triumph 350 & 500 Unit Twins (58 - 73)	0137
Triumph Pre-Unit Twins (47 - 62)	0251
Triumph 650 & 750 2-valve Unit Twins (63 - 83)	0122
Triumph Trident & BSA Rocket 3 (69 - 75)	0136
Triumph Bonneville (01 - 07)	4364
Triumph Daytona, Speed Triple, Sprint & Tiger (97 - 05)	♦ 3755
Triumph Triples and Fours (carburettor engines) (91 - 04)	♦ 2162
VESPA P/PX125, 150 & 200 Scooters (78 - 06)	0707
Vespa Scooters (59 - 78)	0126
YAMAHA DT50 & 80 Trail Bikes (78 - 95)	◊ 0800
Yamaha T50 & 80 Townmate (83 - 95)	◊ 1247

Title	Book No
Yamaha YB100 Singles (73 - 91)	◊ 0474
Yamaha RS/RXS100 & 125 Singles (74 - 95)	0331
Yamaha RD & DT125LC (82 - 95)	◊ 0887
Yamaha TZR125 (87 - 93) & DT125R (88 - 07)	◊ 1655
Yamaha TY50, 80, 125 & 175 (74 - 84)	◊ 0464
Yamaha XT & SR125 (82 - 03)	◊ 1021
Yamaha YBR125	4797
Yamaha Trail Bikes (81 - 00)	2350
Yamaha 2-stroke Motocross Bikes 1986 - 2006	2662
Yamaha YZ & WR 4-stroke Motocross Bikes (98 - 08)	2689
Yamaha 250 & 350 Twins (70 - 79)	0040
Yamaha XS250, 360 & 400 sohc Twins (75 - 84)	0378
Yamaha RD250 & 350LC Twins (80 - 82)	0803
Yamaha RD350 YPVS Twins (83 - 95)	1158
Yamaha RD400 Twin (75 - 79)	0333
Yamaha XT, TT & SR500 Singles (75 - 83)	0342
Yamaha XZ550 Vision V-Twins (82 - 85)	0821
Yamaha FJ, FZ, XJ & YX600 Radian (84 - 92)	2100
Yamaha XJ600S (Diversion, Seca II) & XJ600N Fours (92 - 03)	♦ 2145
Yamaha YZF600R Thundercat & FZS600 Fazer (96 - 03)	♦ 3702
Yamaha FZ-6 Fazer (04 - 07)	♦ 4751
Yamaha YZF-R6 (99 - 02)	♦ 3900
Yamaha YZF-R6 (03 - 05)	♦ 4601
Yamaha 650 Twins (70 - 83)	0341
Yamaha XJ650 & 750 Fours (80 - 84)	0738
Yamaha XS750 & 850 Triples (76 - 85)	0340
Yamaha TDM850, TRX850 & XTZ750 (89 - 99)	◊ ♦ 3540
Yamaha YZF750R & YZF1000R Thunderace (93 - 00)	♦ 3720
Yamaha FZR600, 750 & 1000 Fours (87 - 96)	♦ 2056
Yamaha XV (Virago) V-Twins (81 - 03)	♦ 0802
Yamaha XVS650 & 1100 Drag Star/V-Star (97 - 05)	♦ 4195
Yamaha XJ900F Fours (83 - 94)	♦ 3239
Yamaha XJ900S Diversion (94 - 01)	♦ 3739
Yamaha YZF-R1 (98 - 03)	♦ 3754
Yamaha YZF-R1 (04 - 06)	♦ 4605
Yamaha FZS1000 Fazer (01 - 05)	♦ 4287
Yamaha FJ1100 & 1200 Fours (84 - 96)	♦ 2057
Yamaha XJR1200 & 1300 (95 - 06)	♦ 3981
Yamaha V-Max (85 - 03)	♦ 4072
ATVs	
Honda ATC70, 90, 110, 185 & 200 (71 - 85)	0565
Honda Rancher, Recon & TRX250EX ATVs	2553
Honda TRX300 Shaft Drive ATVs (88 - 00)	2125
Honda Foreman (95 - 07)	2465
Honda TRX300EX, TRX400EX & TRX450R/ER ATVs (93 - 06)	2318
Kawasaki Bayou 220/250/300 & Prairie 300 ATVs (86 - 03)	2351
Polaris ATVs (85 - 97)	2302
Polaris ATVs (98 - 06)	2508
Yamaha YFS200 Blaster ATV (88 - 06)	2317
Yamaha YFB250 Timberwolf ATVs (92 - 00)	2217
Yamaha YFM350 & YFM400 (ER and Big Bear) ATVs (87 - 03)	2126
Yamaha Banshee and Warrior ATVs (87 - 03)	2314
Yamaha Kodiak and Grizzly ATVs (93 - 05)	2567
ATV Basics	10450
TECHBOOK SERIES	
Twist and Go (automatic transmission) Scooters Service and Repair Manual	4082
Motorcycle Basics TechBook (2nd Edition)	3515
Motorcycle Electrical TechBook (3rd Edition)	3471
Motorcycle Fuel Systems TechBook	3514
Motorcycle Maintenance TechBook	4071
Motorcycle Modifying	4272
Motorcycle Workshop Practice TechBook (2nd Edition)	3470

◊ = not available in the USA   ♦ = Superbike

The manuals on this page are available through good motorcycle dealers and accessory shops.
In case of difficulty, contact: **Haynes Publishing**
(UK) +44 1963 442030   (USA) +1 805 498 6703
(SV) +46 18 124016
(Australia/New Zealand) +61 3 9763 8100

MCL24.08/09

Haynes Manuals – The Complete UK Car List

Title	Book No.
ALFA ROMEO Alfasud/Sprint (74 - 88) up to F *	0292
Alfa Romeo Alfetta (73 - 87) up to E *	0531
AUDI 80, 90 & Coupe Petrol (79 - Nov 88) up to F	0605
Audi 80, 90 & Coupe Petrol (Oct 86 - 90) D to H	1491
Audi 100 & 200 Petrol (Oct 82 - 90) up to H	0907
Audi 100 & A6 Petrol & Diesel (May 91 - May 97) H to P	3504
Audi A3 Petrol & Diesel (96 - May 03) P to 03	4253
Audi A4 Petrol & Diesel (95 - 00) M to X	3575
Audi A4 Petrol & Diesel (01 - 04) X to 54	4609
AUSTIN A35 & A40 (56 - 67) up to F *	0118
Austin/MG/Rover Maestro 1.3 & 1.6 Petrol (83 - 95) up to M	0922
Austin/MG Metro (80 - May 90) up to G	0718
Austin/Rover Montego 1.3 & 1.6 Petrol (84 - 94) A to L	1066
Austin/MG/Rover Montego 2.0 Petrol (84 - 95) A to M	1067
Mini (59 - 69) up to H *	0527
Mini (69 - 01) up to X	0646
Austin/Rover 2.0 litre Diesel Engine (86 - 93) C to L	1857
Austin Healey 100/6 & 3000 (56 - 68) up to G *	0049
BEDFORD CF Petrol (69 - 87) up to E	0163
Bedford/Vauxhall Rascal & Suzuki Supercarry (86 - Oct 94) C to M	3015
BMW 316, 320 & 320i (4-cyl) (75 - Feb 83) up to Y *	0276
BMW 320, 320i, 323i & 325i (6-cyl) (Oct 77 - Sept 87) up to E	0815
BMW 3- & 5-Series Petrol (81 - 91) up to J	1948
BMW 3-Series Petrol (Apr 91 - 99) H to V	3210
BMW 3-Series Petrol (Sept 98 - 03) S to 53	4067
BMW 520i & 525e (Oct 81 - June 88) up to E	1560
BMW 525, 528 & 528i (73 - Sept 81) up to X *	0632
BMW 5-Series 6-cyl Petrol (April 96 - Aug 03) N to 03	4151
BMW 1500, 1502, 1600, 1602, 2000 & 2002 (59 - 77) up to S *	0240
CHRYSLER PT Cruiser Petrol (00 - 03) W to 53	4058
CITROËN 2CV, Ami & Dyane (67 - 90) up to H	0196
Citroën AX Petrol & Diesel (87 - 97) D to P	3014
Citroën Berlingo & Peugeot Partner Petrol & Diesel (96 - 05) P to 55	4281
Citroën BX Petrol (83 - 94) A to L	0908
Citroën C15 Van Petrol & Diesel (89 - Oct 98) F to S	3509
Citroën C3 Petrol & Diesel (02 - 05) 51 to 05	4197
Citroen C5 Petrol & Diesel (01-08) Y to 08	4745
Citroën CX Petrol (75 - 88) up to F	0528
Citroën Saxo Petrol & Diesel (96 - 04) N to 54	3506
Citroën Visa Petrol (79 - 88) up to F	0620
Citroën Xantia Petrol & Diesel (93 - 01) K to Y	3082
Citroën XM Petrol & Diesel (89 - 00) G to X	3451
Citroën Xsara Petrol & Diesel (97 - Sept 00) R to W	3751
Citroën Xsara Picasso Petrol & Diesel (00 - 02) W to 52	3944
Citroen Xsara Picasso (03-08)	4784
Citroën ZX Diesel (91 - 98) J to S	1922
Citroën ZX Petrol (91 - 98) H to S	1881
Citroën 1.7 & 1.9 litre Diesel Engine (84 - 96) A to N	1379
FIAT 126 (73 - 87) up to E *	0305
Fiat 500 (57 - 73) up to M *	0090
Fiat Bravo & Brava Petrol (95 - 00) N to W	3572
Fiat Cinquecento (93 - 98) K to R	3501
Fiat Panda (81 - 95) up to M	0793
Fiat Punto Petrol & Diesel (94 - Oct 99) L to V	3251
Fiat Punto Petrol (Oct 99 - July 03) V to 03	4066
Fiat Punto Petrol (03-07) 03 to 07	4746
Fiat Regata Petrol (84 - 88) A to F	1167
Fiat Tipo Petrol (88 - 91) E to J	1625
Fiat Uno Petrol (83 - 95) up to M	0923
Fiat X1/9 (74 - 89) up to G *	0273
FORD Anglia (59 - 68) up to G *	0001

Title	Book No.
Ford Capri II (& III) 1.6 & 2.0 (74 - 87) up to E *	0283
Ford Capri II (& III) 2.8 & 3.0 V6 (74 - 87) up to E	1309
Ford Cortina Mk I & Corsair 1500 ('62 - '66) up to D*	0214
Ford Cortina Mk III 1300 & 1600 (70 - 76) up to P *	0070
Ford Escort Mk I 1100 & 1300 (68 - 74) up to N *	0171
Ford Escort Mk I Mexico, RS 1600 & RS 2000 (70 - 74) up to N *	0139
Ford Escort Mk II Mexico, RS 1800 & RS 2000 (75 - 80) up to W *	0735
Ford Escort (75 - Aug 80) up to V *	0280
Ford Escort Petrol (Sept 80 - Sept 90) up to H	0686
Ford Escort & Orion Petrol (Sept 90 - 00) H to X	1737
Ford Escort & Orion Diesel (Sept 90 - 00) H to X	4081
Ford Fiesta (76 - Aug 83) up to Y	0334
Ford Fiesta Petrol (Aug 83 - Feb 89) A to F	1030
Ford Fiesta Petrol (Feb 89 - Oct 95) F to N	1595
Ford Fiesta Petrol & Diesel (Oct 95 - Mar 02) N to 02	3397
Ford Fiesta Petrol & Diesel (Apr 02 - 07) 02 to 57	4170
Ford Focus Petrol & Diesel (98 - 01) S to Y	3759
Ford Focus Petrol & Diesel (Oct 01 - 05) 51 to 05	4167
Ford Galaxy Petrol & Diesel (95 - Aug 00) M to W	3984
Ford Granada Petrol (Sept 77 - Feb 85) up to B *	0481
Ford Granada & Scorpio Petrol (Mar 85 - 94) B to M	1245
Ford Ka (96 - 02) P to 52	3570
Ford Mondeo Petrol (93 - Sept 00) K to X	1923
Ford Mondeo Petrol & Diesel (Oct 00 - Jul 03) X to 03	3990
Ford Mondeo Petrol & Diesel (July 03 - 07) 03 to 56	4619
Ford Mondeo Diesel (93 - 96) L to N	3465
Ford Orion Petrol (83 - Sept 90) up to H	1009
Ford Sierra 4-cyl Petrol (82 - 93) up to K	0903
Ford Sierra V6 Petrol (82 - 91) up to J	0904
Ford Transit Petrol (Mk 2) (78 - Jan 86) up to C	0719
Ford Transit Petrol (Mk 3) (Feb 86 - 89) C to G	1468
Ford Transit Diesel (Feb 86 - 99) C to T	3019
Ford Transit Diesel (00-06)	4775
Ford 1.6 & 1.8 litre Diesel Engine (84 - 96) A to N	1172
Ford 2.1, 2.3 & 2.5 litre Diesel Engine (77 - 90) up to H	1606
FREIGHT ROVER Sherpa Petrol (74 - 87) up to E	0463
HILLMAN Avenger (70 - 82) up to Y	0037
Hillman Imp (63 - 76) up to R *	0022
HONDA Civic (Feb 84 - Oct 87) A to E	1226
Honda Civic (Nov 91 - 96) J to N	3199
Honda Civic Petrol (Mar 95 - 00) M to X	4050
Honda Civic Petrol & Diesel (01 - 05) X to 55	4611
Honda CR-V Petrol & Diesel (01-06)	4747
Honda Jazz (01 - Feb 08) 51 - 57	4735
HYUNDAI Pony (85 - 94) C to M	3398
JAGUAR E Type (61 - 72) up to L *	0140
Jaguar MkI & II, 240 & 340 (55 - 69) up to H *	0098
Jaguar XJ6, XJ & Sovereign; Daimler Sovereign (68 - Oct 86) up to D	0242
Jaguar XJ6 & Sovereign (Oct 86 - Sept 94) D to M	3261
Jaguar XJ12, XJS & Sovereign; Daimler Double Six (72 - 88) up to F	0478
JEEP Cherokee Petrol (93 - 96) K to N	1943
LADA 1200, 1300, 1500 & 1600 (74 - 91) up to J	0413
Lada Samara (87 - 91) D to J	1610
LAND ROVER 90, 110 & Defender Diesel (83 - 07) up to 56	3017
Land Rover Discovery Petrol & Diesel (89 - 98) G to S	3016
Land Rover Discovery Diesel (Nov 98 - Jul 04) S to 04	4606
Land Rover Freelander Petrol & Diesel (97 - Sept 03) R to 53	3929
Land Rover Freelander Petrol & Diesel (Oct 03 - Oct 06) 53 to 56	4623

Title	Book No.
Land Rover Series IIA & III Diesel (58 - 85) up to C	0529
Land Rover Series II, IIA & III 4-cyl Petrol (58 - 85) up to C	0314
MAZDA 323 (Mar 81 - Oct 89) up to G	1608
Mazda 323 (Oct 89 - 98) G to R	3455
Mazda 626 (May 83 - Sept 87) up to E	0929
Mazda B1600, B1800 & B2000 Pick-up Petrol (72 - 88) up to F	0267
Mazda RX-7 (79 - 85) up to C *	0460
MERCEDES-BENZ 190, 190E & 190D Petrol & Diesel (83 - 93) A to L	3450
Mercedes-Benz 200D, 240D, 240TD, 300D & 300TD 123 Series Diesel (Oct 76 - 85)	1114
Mercedes-Benz 250 & 280 (68 - 72) up to L *	0346
Mercedes-Benz 250 & 280 123 Series Petrol (Oct 76 - 84) up to B *	0677
Mercedes-Benz 124 Series Petrol & Diesel (85 - Aug 93) C to K	3253
Mercedes-Benz A-Class Petrol & Diesel (98-04) S to 54	4748
Mercedes-Benz C-Class Petrol & Diesel (93 - Aug 00) L to W	3511
Mercedes-Benz C-Class (00-06)	4780
MGA (55 - 62) *	0475
MGB (62 - 80) up to W	0111
MG Midget & Austin-Healey Sprite (58 - 80) up to W *	0265
MINI Petrol (July 01 - 05) Y to 05	4273
MITSUBISHI Shogun & L200 Pick-Ups Petrol (83 - 94) up to M	1944
MORRIS Ital 1.3 (80 - 84) up to B	0705
Morris Minor 1000 (56 - 71) up to K	0024
NISSAN Almera Petrol (95 - Feb 00) N to V	4053
Nissan Almera & Tino Petrol (Feb 00 - 07) V to 56	4612
Nissan Bluebird (May 84 - Mar 86) A to C	1223
Nissan Bluebird Petrol (Mar 86 - 90) C to H	1473
Nissan Cherry (Sept 82 - 86) up to D	1031
Nissan Micra (83 - Jan 93) up to K	0931
Nissan Micra (93 - 02) K to 52	3254
Nissan Micra Petrol (03-07) 52 to 57	4734
Nissan Primera Petrol (90 - Aug 99) H to T	1851
Nissan Stanza (82 - 86) up to D	0824
Nissan Sunny Petrol (May 82 - Oct 86) up to D	0895
Nissan Sunny Petrol (Oct 86 - Mar 91) D to H	1378
Nissan Sunny Petrol (Apr 91 - 95) H to N	3219
OPEL Ascona & Manta (B Series) (Sept 75 - 88) up to F *	0316
Opel Ascona Petrol (81 - 88)	3215
Opel Astra Petrol (Oct 91 - Feb 98)	3156
Opel Corsa Petrol (83 - Mar 93)	3160
Opel Corsa Petrol (Mar 93 - 97)	3159
Opel Kadett Petrol (Nov 79 - Oct 84) up to B	0634
Opel Kadett Petrol (Oct 84 - Oct 91)	3196
Opel Omega & Senator Petrol (Nov 86 - 94)	3157
Opel Rekord Petrol (Feb 78 - Oct 86) up to D	0543
Opel Vectra Petrol (Oct 88 - Oct 95)	3158
PEUGEOT 106 Petrol & Diesel (91 - 04) J to 53	1882
Peugeot 205 Petrol (83 - 97) A to P	0932
Peugeot 206 Petrol & Diesel (98 - 01) S to X	3757
Peugeot 206 Petrol & Diesel (02 - 06) 51 to 06	4613
Peugeot 306 Petrol & Diesel (93 - 02) K to 02	3073
Peugeot 307 Petrol & Diesel (01 - 04) Y to 54	4147
Peugeot 309 Petrol (86 - 93) C to K	1266
Peugeot 405 Petrol (88 - 97) E to P	1559
Peugeot 405 Diesel (88 - 97) E to P	3198
Peugeot 406 Petrol & Diesel (96 - Mar 99) N to T	3394
Peugeot 406 Petrol & Diesel (Mar 99 - 02) T to 52	3982

* Classic reprint

Title	Book No.
Peugeot 505 Petrol (79 - 89) up to G	0762
Peugeot 1.7/1.8 & 1.9 litre Diesel Engine (82 - 96) up to N	0950
Peugeot 2.0, 2.1, 2.3 & 2.5 litre Diesel Engines (74 - 90) up to H	1607
PORSCHE 911 (65 - 85) up to C	0264
Porsche 924 & 924 Turbo (76 - 85) up to C	0397
PROTON (89 - 97) F to P	3255
RANGE ROVER V8 Petrol (70 - Oct 92) up to K	0606
RELIANT Robin & Kitten (73 - 83) up to A *	0436
RENAULT 4 (61 - 86) up to D *	0072
Renault 5 Petrol (Feb 85 - 96) B to N	1219
Renault 9 & 11 Petrol (82 - 89) up to F	0822
Renault 18 Petrol (79 - 86) up to D	0598
Renault 19 Petrol (89 - 96) F to N	1646
Renault 19 Diesel (89 - 96) F to N	1946
Renault 21 Petrol (86 - 94) C to M	1397
Renault 25 Petrol & Diesel (84 - 92) B to K	1228
Renault Clio Petrol (91 - May 98) H to R	1853
Renault Clio Diesel (91 - June 96) H to N	3031
Renault Clio Petrol & Diesel (May 98 - May 01) R to Y	3906
Renault Clio Petrol & Diesel (June '01 - '05) Y to 55	4168
Renault Espace Petrol & Diesel (85 - 96) C to N	3197
Renault Laguna Petrol & Diesel (94 - 00) L to W	3252
Renault Laguna Petrol & Diesel (Feb 01 - Feb 05) X to 54	4283
Renault Mégane & Scénic Petrol & Diesel (96 - 99) N to T	3395
Renault Mégane & Scénic Petrol & Diesel (Apr 99 - 02) T to 52	3916
Renault Megane Petrol & Diesel (Oct 02 - 05) 52 to 55	4284
Renault Scenic Petrol & Diesel (Sept 03 - 06) 53 to 06	4297
ROVER 213 & 216 (84 - 89) A to G	1116
Rover 214 & 414 Petrol (89 - 96) G to N	1689
Rover 216 & 416 Petrol (89 - 96) G to N	1830
Rover 211, 214, 216, 218 & 220 Petrol & Diesel (Dec 95 - 99) N to V	3399
Rover 25 & MG ZR Petrol & Diesel (Oct 99 - 04) V to 54	4145
Rover 414, 416 & 420 Petrol & Diesel (May 95 - 98) M to R	3453
Rover 45 / MG ZS Petrol & Diesel (99 - 05) V to 55	4384
Rover 618, 620 & 623 Petrol (93 - 97) K to P	3257
Rover 75 / MG ZT Petrol & Diesel (99 - 06) S to 06	4292
Rover 820, 825 & 827 Petrol (86 - 95) D to N	1380
Rover 3500 (76 - 87) up to E *	0365
Rover Metro, 111 & 114 Petrol (May 90 - 98) G to S	1711
SAAB 95 & 96 (66 - 76) up to R *	0198
Saab 90, 99 & 900 (79 - Oct 93) up to L	0765
Saab 900 (Oct 93 - 98) L to R	3512
Saab 9000 (4-cyl) (85 - 98) C to S	1686
Saab 9-3 Petrol & Diesel (98 - Aug 02) R to 02	4614
Saab 9-3 Petrol & Diesel (02-07) 52 to 57	4749
Saab 9-5 4-cyl Petrol (97 - 04) R to 54	4156
SEAT Ibiza & Cordoba Petrol & Diesel (Oct 93 - Oct 99) L to V	3571
Seat Ibiza & Malaga Petrol (85 - 92) B to K	1609
SKODA Estelle (77 - 89) up to G	0604
Skoda Fabia Petrol & Diesel (00 - 06) W to 06	4376
Skoda Favorit (89 - 96) F to N	1801
Skoda Felicia Petrol & Diesel (95 - 01) M to X	3505
Skoda Octavia Petrol & Diesel (98 - Apr 04) R to 04	4285
SUBARU 1600 & 1800 (Nov 79 - 90) up to H *	0995

Title	Book No.
SUNBEAM Alpine, Rapier & H120 (67 - 74) up to N *	0051
SUZUKI SJ Series, Samurai & Vitara (4-cyl) Petrol (82 - 97) up to P	1942
Suzuki Supercarry & Bedford/Vauxhall Rascal (86 - Oct 94) C to M	3015
TALBOT Alpine, Solara, Minx & Rapier (75 - 86) up to D	0337
Talbot Horizon Petrol (78 - 86) up to D	0473
Talbot Samba (82 - 86) up to D	0823
TOYOTA Avensis Petrol (98 - Jan 03) R to 52	4264
Toyota Carina E Petrol (May 92 - 97) J to P	3256
Toyota Corolla (80 - 85) up to C	0683
Toyota Corolla (Sept 83 - Sept 87) A to E	1024
Toyota Corolla (Sept 87 - Aug 92) E to K	1683
Toyota Corolla Petrol (Aug 92 - 97) K to P	3259
Toyota Corolla Petrol (July 97 - Feb 02) P to 51	4286
Toyota Hi-Ace & Hi-Lux Petrol (69 - Oct 83) up to A	0304
Toyota RAV4 Petrol & Diesel (94-06) L to 55	4750
Toyota Yaris Petrol (99 - 05) T to 05	4265
TRIUMPH GT6 & Vitesse (62 - 74) up to N *	0112
Triumph Herald (59 - 71) up to K *	0010
Triumph Spitfire (62 - 81) up to X	0113
Triumph Stag (70 - 78) up to T *	0441
Triumph TR2, TR3, TR3A, TR4 & TR4A (52 - 67) up to F *	0028
Triumph TR5 & 6 (67 - 75) up to P *	0031
Triumph TR7 (75 - 82) up to Y *	0322
VAUXHALL Astra Petrol (80 - Oct 84) up to B	0635
Vauxhall Astra & Belmont Petrol (Oct 84 - Oct 91) B to J	1136
Vauxhall Astra Petrol (Oct 91 - Feb 98) J to R	1832
Vauxhall/Opel Astra & Zafira Petrol (Feb 98 - Apr 04) R to 04	3758
Vauxhall/Opel Astra & Zafira Diesel (Feb 98 - Apr 04) R to 04	3797
Vauxhall/Opel Astra Petrol (04 - 08)	4732
Vauxhall/Opel Astra Diesel (04 - 08)	4733
Vauxhall/Opel Calibra (90 - 98) G to S	3502
Vauxhall Carlton Petrol (Oct 78 - Oct 86) up to D	0480
Vauxhall Carlton & Senator Petrol (Nov 86 - 94) D to L	1469
Vauxhall Cavalier Petrol (81 - Oct 88) up to F	0812
Vauxhall Cavalier Petrol (Oct 88 - 95) F to N	1570
Vauxhall Chevette (75 - 84) up to B	0285
Vauxhall/Opel Corsa Diesel (Mar 93 - Oct 00) K to X	4087
Vauxhall Corsa Petrol (Mar 93 - 97) K to R	1985
Vauxhall/Opel Corsa Petrol (Apr 97 - Oct 00) P to X	3921
Vauxhall/Opel Corsa Petrol & Diesel (Oct 00 - Sept 03) X to 53	4079
Vauxhall/Opel Corsa Petrol & Diesel (Oct 03 - Aug 06) 53 to 06	4617
Vauxhall/Opel Frontera Petrol & Diesel (91 - Sept 98) J to S	3454
Vauxhall Nova Petrol (83 - 93) up to K	0909
Vauxhall/Opel Omega Petrol (94 - 99) L to T	3510
Vauxhall/Opel Vectra Petrol & Diesel (95 - Feb 99) N to S	3396
Vauxhall/Opel Vectra Petrol & Diesel (Mar 99 - May 02) T to 02	3930
Vauxhall/Opel Vectra Petrol & Diesel (June 02 - Sept 05) 02 to 55	4618
Vauxhall/Opel 1.5, 1.6 & 1.7 litre Diesel Engine (82 - 96) up to N	1222
VW 411 & 412 (68 - 75) up to P *	0091
VW Beetle 1200 (54 - 77) up to S	0036
VW Beetle 1300 & 1500 (65 - 75) up to P	0039

Title	Book No.
VW 1302 & 1302S (70 - 72) up to L *	0110
VW Beetle 1303, 1303S & GT (72 - 75) up to P	0159
VW Beetle Petrol & Diesel (Apr 99 - 07) T to 57	3798
VW Golf & Jetta Mk 1 Petrol 1.1 & 1.3 (74 - 84) up to A	0716
VW Golf, Jetta & Scirocco Mk 1 Petrol 1.5, 1.6 & 1.8 (74 - 84) up to A	0726
VW Golf & Jetta Mk 1 Diesel (78 - 84) up to A	0451
VW Golf & Jetta Mk 2 Petrol (Mar 84 - Feb 92) A to J	1081
VW Golf & Vento Petrol & Diesel (Feb 92 - Mar 98) J to R	3097
VW Golf & Bora Petrol & Diesel (April 98 - 00) R to X	3727
VW Golf & Bora 4-cyl Petrol & Diesel (01 - 03) X to 53	4169
VW Golf & Jetta Petrol & Diesel (04 - 07) 53 to 07	4610
VW LT Petrol Vans & Light Trucks (76 - 87) up to E	0637
VW Passat & Santana Petrol (Sept 81 - May 88) up to E	0814
VW Passat 4-cyl Petrol & Diesel (May 88 - 96) E to P	3498
VW Passat 4-cyl Petrol & Diesel (Dec 96 - Nov 00) P to X	3917
VW Passat Petrol & Diesel (Dec 00 - May 05) X to 05	4279
VW Polo & Derby (76 - Jan 82) up to X	0335
VW Polo (82 - Oct 90) up to H	0813
VW Polo Petrol (Nov 90 - Aug 94) H to L	3245
VW Polo Hatchback Petrol & Diesel (94 - 99) M to S	3500
VW Polo Hatchback Petrol & Diesel (00 - Jan 02) V to 51	4150
VW Polo Petrol & Diesel (02 - May 05) 51 to 05	4608
VW Scirocco (82 - 90) up to H *	1224
VW Transporter 1600 (68 - 79) up to V	0082
VW Transporter 1700, 1800 & 2000 (72 - 79) up to V *	0226
VW Transporter (air-cooled) Petrol (79 - 82) up to Y *	0638
VW Transporter (water-cooled) Petrol (82 - 90) up to H	3452
VW Type 3 (63 - 73) up to M *	0084
VOLVO 120 & 130 Series (& P1800) (61 - 73) up to M *	0203
Volvo 142, 144 & 145 (66 - 74) up to N *	0129
Volvo 240 Series Petrol (74 - 93) up to K	0270
Volvo 262, 264 & 260/265 (75 - 85) up to C *	0400
Volvo 340, 343, 345 & 360 (76 - 91) up to J	0715
Volvo 440, 460 & 480 Petrol (87 - 97) D to P	1691
Volvo 740 & 760 Petrol (82 - 91) up to J	1258
Volvo 850 Petrol (92 - 96) J to P	3260
Volvo 940 petrol (90 - 98) H to R	3249
Volvo S40 & V40 Petrol (96 - Mar 04) N to 04	3569
Volvo S40 & V50 Petrol & Diesel (Mar 04 - Jun 07) 04 to 07	4731
Volvo S60 Petrol & Diesel (01-08)	4793
Volvo S70, V70 & C70 Petrol (96 - 99) P to V	3573
Volvo V70 / S80 Petrol & Diesel (98 - 05) S to 55	4263

DIY MANUAL SERIES

Title	Book No.
The Haynes Air Conditioning Manual	4192
The Haynes Car Electrical Systems Manual	4251
The Haynes Manual on Bodywork	4198
The Haynes Manual on Brakes	4178
The Haynes Manual on Carburettors	4177
The Haynes Manual on Diesel Engines	4174
The Haynes Manual on Engine Management	4199
The Haynes Manual on Fault Codes	4175
The Haynes Manual on Practical Electrical Systems	4267
The Haynes Manual on Small Engines	4250
The Haynes Manual on Welding	4176

* Classic reprint

All the products featured on this page are available through most motor accessory shops, cycle shops and book stores. Our policy of continuous updating and development means that titles are being constantly added to the range. For up-to-date information on our complete list of titles, please telephone: (UK) +44 1963 442030 • (USA) +1 805 498 6703 • (Sweden) +46 18 124016 • (Australia) +61 3 9763 8100

Preserving Our Motoring Heritage

The Model J Duesenberg Derham Tourster. Only eight of these magnificent cars were ever built – this is the only example to be found outside the United States of America

Almost every car you've ever loved, loathed or desired is gathered under one roof at the Haynes Motor Museum. Over 300 immaculately presented cars and motorbikes represent every aspect of our motoring heritage, from elegant reminders of bygone days, such as the superb Model J Duesenberg to curiosities like the bug-eyed BMW Isetta. There are also many old friends and flames. Perhaps you remember the 1959 Ford Popular that you did your courting in? The magnificent 'Red Collection' is a spectacle of classic sports cars including AC, Alfa Romeo, Austin Healey, Ferrari, Lamborghini, Maserati, MG, Riley, Porsche and Triumph.

A Perfect Day Out

Each and every vehicle at the Haynes Motor Museum has played its part in the history and culture of Motoring. Today, they make a wonderful spectacle and a great day out for all the family. Bring the kids, bring Mum and Dad, but above all bring your camera to capture those golden memories for ever. You will also find an impressive array of motoring memorabilia, a comfortable 70 seat video cinema and one of the most extensive transport book shops in Britain. The Pit Stop Cafe serves everything from a cup of tea to wholesome, home-made meals or, if you prefer, you can enjoy the large picnic area nestled in the beautiful rural surroundings of Somerset.

John Haynes O.B.E., Founder and Chairman of the museum at the wheel of a Haynes Light 12.

The 1936 490cc sohc-engined International Norton – well known for its racing success

The Museum is situated on the A359 Yeovil to Frome road at Sparkford, just off the A303 in Somerset. It is about 40 miles south of Bristol, and 25 minutes drive from the M5 intersection at Taunton.
Open 9.30am - 5.30pm (10.00am - 4.00pm Winter) 7 days a week, *except Christmas Day, Boxing Day and New Years Day*
Special rates available for schools, coach parties and outings Charitable Trust No. 292048